THE HANDBOOK OF EMPLOYEE BENEFITS

DESIGN, FUNDING, AND ADMINISTRATION

THE HANDBOOK OF EMPLOYEE BENEFITS

DESIGN, FUNDING, AND ADMINISTRATION

Third Edition

VOLUME I

Edited by Jerry S. Rosenbloom

BUSINESS ONE IRWIN
Homewood, IL 60430

This publication is designed to provide accurate and authoritative information in regard to the subject matter covered. It is sold with the understanding that neither the author nor the publisher is engaged in rendering legal, accounting, or other professional service. If legal advice or other expert assistance is required, the services of a competent professional person should be sought.

From a Declaration of Principles jointly adopted by a Committee of the American Bar Association and a Committee of Publishers.

Sponsoring editor: Amy Hollands
Project editor: Jane Lightell
Production manager: Ann Cassady
Designer: Heidi J. Baughman
Compositor: Carlisle Communications, Ltd.
Typeface: 11/13 Times Roman
Printer: R. R. Donnelley & Sons Company

Library of Congress Cataloging-in-Publication Data

Rosenbloom, Jerry S.
The handbook of employee benefits : design, funding, and administration / Jerry S. Rosenbloom.—3rd ed.
p. cm.
Includes index.
ISBN Vol. 1, 1-55623-483-X Vol. 2, 1-55623-884-3 (Hardback)
Vol. 1, 1-55623-503-8 Vol. 2, 1-55623-886-X (Paperback)
1-55623-887-8 (2 volume set, paperback)
1. Employee fringe benefits—United States. 2. Employee fringe benefits—Law and legislation—United States. 3. Employee fringe benefits—Taxation—Law and legislation—Unites States. I. Title.
HD4928.N62U6353 1992
331.25'5'0973—dc20 91–40776

Printed in the United States of America

1 2 3 4 5 6 7 8 9 0 DOC 9 8 7 6 5 4 3 2

PREFACE

Much has taken place in the employee benefits field since the publication of the second edition of *The Handbook of Employee Benefits* in 1988. Dramatic changes have been caused by major new pieces of legislation, and many new employee benefit concepts have been developed and implemented. Moreover, the last several years have witnessed an ever-increasing emphasis on cost containment in all forms of employee benefits. This third edition of *The Handbook* recognizes these fundamental changes with revisions of many of the chapters in the second edition and the addition of chapters covering new and emerging areas in employee benefits. These changes emphasize the basic premise that employee benefits can no longer be considered "fringe benefits" but must be regarded as an integral and extremely important component of an individual's financial security. The most recent U.S. Chamber of Commerce study on employee benefits indicates that, on average, employee benefits account for nearly 40 percent of a worker's total compensation. In light of the ever-increasing importance of benefit plans, those dealing with them must be well versed in the objectives, design, costing, funding, implementation, and administration of such plans.

While *The Handbook of Employee Benefits* is intended for students in the benefits field and for professionals as a handy reference, it can serve as a valuable tool for anyone with an interest in the field in general or in a specific employee benefit topic. *The Handbook* can be used as a reference work for benefit professionals or as a textbook for college courses, professional education, and company training programs. Each chapter of *The Handbook* stands alone and is complete in itself. While this produces some overlap in certain areas, in many cases it eliminates the need to refer to other chapters and provides important reinforcement of difficult concepts.

The chapters of *The Handbook* are structured into 13 parts, each covering a major component of the employee benefit planning process. These are: Part One, The Environment of Employee Benefit Plans; Part Two, Social Insurance Programs; Part Three, Death Benefits; Part Four, Medical and Other Health Benefits; Part Five, Disability Income Plans; Part Six, Other Welfare Benefit Plans; Part Seven, Flexible Benefit Plans; Part Eight, Retirement and Capital Accumulation Plans; Part Nine, Accounting, Funding, and Taxation of Employee Benefit Plans; Part Ten, Employee Benefit Plan Administration; Part Eleven, Employee Benefit Plan Communication; Part Twelve, Employee Benefit Plans for Small Business; and Part Thirteen, Employee Benefit Plan Issues.

The Handbook consists of 63 chapters written by distinguished experts—academics, actuaries, attorneys, consultants, and other benefit professionals—covering all areas of the employee benefits field. Their practical experience and breadth of knowledge provide insightful coverage of the employee benefits mechanism, and the examples presented throughout *The Handbook* illustrate the concepts presented.

The chapters that remain from the second edition have been updated to incorporate legislative and other changes in the field, and several of the chapters from the second edition have been expanded to include related topics such as eldercare. The coverage of certain subjects has been amplified with additional chapters on disability income, flexible benefits, and communication. New chapters have been added on: Risk Concepts and Employee Benefit Planning; Workers' Compensation; Fundamentals of Unemployment Compensation Programs; Health Maintenance Organizations; Preferred Provider Organizations; Managed Care; Long-term Care; Family Leave Programs; Payments for Nonproduction Time, Time Not Worked and Miscellaneous Benefits; Cash Balance Plans; Retirement Plans for Not-for-Profit Organizations; Section 457 Deferred Compensation Plans; Accounting and Financial Reporting for Health and Welfare Plans; Federal Taxation Environment for Welfare Benefit Plans; ERISA Fiduciary Liability Issues and Multiemployer Plans.

In such a massive project, many people provided invaluable assistance, and it would be impossible to mention them all here. Thanks must be extended, however, to the authors of the individual chapters for the outstanding coverage of their subject areas in a comprehensive and readable manner. Special thanks are due to Mr. Everett T. Allen, Jr., a long-time friend who read the entire manuscript and made many constructive comments and suggestions. I would like to thank Dr. Davis

W. Gregg, the former president of The American College, for his encouragement over the years to undertake such a project. Appreciation also must go to my most able assistant Diana Krigelman, who spent many hours on all aspects of the manuscript and handled her duties in her usual totally professional manner.

In a work of this magnitude, it is almost inevitable that some mistakes may have escaped the eyes of the many readers of the manuscript. For these oversights I accept full responsibility and ask the reader's indulgence.

Jerry S. Rosenbloom

CONTRIBUTORS

Bradley J. Allen, Partner, Coopers & Lybrand

Everett T. Allen, Jr., Vice President and Principal, Towers, Perrin, Forster & Crosby, Retired

Mark S. Allen, Consultant, Hewitt Associates

Dwight K. Bartlett III, Visiting Executive Professor, Wharton School, University of Pennsylvania

Burton T. Beam, Jr., CLU, CPCU, Associate Professor of Insurance, The American College

John M. Bernard, Esq., Partner, Ballard Spahr, Andrews & Ingersoll

Melvin W. Borleis, CEBS, Managing Director, William M. Mercer, Incorporated

Sarah H. Bourne, Consultant, Hewitt Associates

Lawrence T. Brennan, FSA, Partner, Kwasha Lipton

Henry Bright, FSA, Vice President, The Wyatt Company

Gregory K. Brown, Esq., Attorney, Keck, Mahin & Cate

Eugene B. Burroughs, CFA, Senior Advisor, The Prudential Asset Management Company, Inc.

Mary A. Carroll, CPCU, CEBS, ARM, Benefits Consultant

Joseph Casey, University of Central Florida

Alan P. Cleveland, Esq., Partner, Sheehan, Phinney, Bass & Green

William M. Cobourn, Jr., Manager, Coopers & Lybrand

Dennis Coleman, Esq., Partner, Kwasha Lipton

Ann Costello, Ph.D., Associate Professor of Insurance, School of Business and Public Administration, University of Hartford

William E. Decker, Partner, Coopers & Lybrand

Douglas R. Divelbiss, Senior Manager, National Office, Ernst & Young

Donald J. Doudna, Ph.D., CLU, CPCU, Director of Insurance Education, State of Iowa, and Executive Vice President, Bryton Management Corporation

Cynthia J. Drinkwater, J.D., Director of Research, International Foundation of Employee Benefit Plans

James C. Fee, Associate Professor of Accountancy, College of Commerce and Finance, Villanova University

Edmund W. Fitzpatrick, Ph.D, CFP, Vice President and Professor of Financial Planning, The American College

Anthony J. Gajda, Principal, William M. Mercer, Incorporated

Susan Garrahan, Market Research Analyst, Merck & Company, Inc.

Sharon S. Graham, D.B.A., CFA, Assistant Professor of Finance, University of Central Florida

Linda Grosso, Director, Pensions-Communications Services, Metropolitan Life Insurance Company

Donald S. Grubbs, Jr., J.D., FSA, President, Grubbs and Company, Incorporated

Charles P. Hall, Jr., Ph.D., Professor of Health, Administration, Insurance and Risk, Department of Risk Management and Insurance, Temple University

G. Victor Hallman III, Ph.D., J.D., CPCU, CLU, Lecturer in Financial and Estate Planning, Wharton School, University of Pennsylvania

Carlton Harker, FSA, EA, CLU, President, ACS Group, a North Carolina Actuarial/Benefit Consulting/TPA

Waldo L. Hayes, Director, LTD Products/Markets, EB Disability Development, UNUM Life Insurance Company

Charles E. Hughes, D.B.A., CLU, CPCU, Associate Professor of Insurance, The American College

Ronald L. Huling, Principal, Williams, Thacher & Rand

David R. Klock, Ph.D., CLU, Professor of Insurance, University of Central Florida

Harry V. Lamon, Jr., Esq., Partner, Hurt, Richardson, Garner, Todd & Cadenhead

Robert T. LeClair, Ph.D., Associate Professor, Finance-Marketing Department, College of Commerce and Finance, Villanova University

Howard Lichtenstein, Executive Vice President, Mutual of America Life Insurance Company

Claude C. Lilly III, Ph.D., CLU, CPCU, Professor of Risk Management and Insurance, Florida State University

Zelda Lipton, Vice President of Marketing, Blue Cross/Blue Shield of Maryland

Ernest L. Martin, Ph.D., FLMI, Director, Examinations Department, Life Office Management Association (LOMA)

Thomas Martinez, Assistant Professor, Villanova University

Harry McBrierty, Vice President, The Wyatt Company

Dan M. McGill, Ph.D., Professor Emeritus, Insurance and Risk Management Department, Wharton School, University of Pennsylvania

Alfred F. Meyer, President, Delaware Valley HMO

Ronald J. Murray, Director, Accounting, Auditing and SEC Consulting, Coopers & Lybrand

Robert J. Myers, L.L.D., FSA, Professor Emeritus, Temple University, Chief Actuary, Social Security Administration, 1947–70; Deputy Commissioner, Social Security Administration, 1981–82; and Executive Director, National Commission on Social Security Reform, 1982–83

Robert V. Nally, J.D., CLU, Associate Professor, Villanova University

Richard Ostuw, FSA, Vice President, Towers, Perrin, Forster & Crosby, Inc.

Bruce A. Palmer, Ph.D., CLU, Professor of Risk Management and Insurance, Georgia State University

Phillip D. Pierce, Assistant Vice President, Aetna Life Insurance Company

William H. Rabel, Ph.D., FLMI, CLU, Senior Vice President, Life Management Institute, Life Office Management Association (LOMA)

George E. Rejda, Ph.D., CLU, V.J. Skutt Distinguished Professor of Insurance, University of Nebraska

Jerry S. Rosenbloom, Ph.D., CLU, CPCU, Chairman and Frederick H. Ecker Professor of Life Insurance, Department of Insurance and Risk Management, and Academic Director, Certified Employee Benefit Specialist (CEBS) Program, The Wharton School, University of Pennsylvania

Daniel J. Ryterband, Associate, Legal and Research Services, A. Foster Higgins & Co., Inc.

Dallas L. Salisbury, President, Employee Benefit Research Institute

Bernard E. Schaeffer, Senior Vice President, Research Group, Hay/Huggins Company, Inc.

Clifford J. Schoner, Esq., Associate Tax Counsel, Sun Company, Incorporated

Kathleen Hunter Sloan, Ph.D., Associate Professor and Chairman, Department of Public Administration, Barney School of Business and Public Administration, University of Hartford

Robert W. Smiley, Jr., L.L.B., Chairman and Chief Executive Officer, Benefit Capital, Incorporated

Gary K. Stone, Ph.D., Vice President-Academics, The American College

Garry N. Teesdale, Vice President, Hay Group

Richard L. Tewksbury, Jr., Vice President, Vice President and Director, Consulting and Marketing Services, Miller, Mason & Dickenson

Richard H. Towers, Director, National Office, Ernst & Young

Jack L. VanDerhei, Ph.D., CEBS, Associate Professor, Department of Risk Management and Insurance, Temple University

Bernard L. Webb, CPCU, FCAS, MAAA, Professor, Georgia State University

Joel Wells, Esq., Attorney

William G. Williams, Director, Health Care Relations, Provident Mutual Insurance Company of Philadelphia, Retired

Jack D. Worrall, Ph.D., Professor of Economics, Rutgers University

Eugene J. Ziurys, Jr., Product Manager, Managed Care and Employee Benefit Operations, Marketing and Product Development, The Travelers Companies

CONTENTS

VOLUME I

CONTENTS

VOLUME II

PART 13 EMPLOYEE BENEFIT PLAN ISSUES 453

PART 1

THE ENVIRONMENT OF EMPLOYEE BENEFIT PLANS

Employee benefits constitute a major part of almost every individual's financial and economic security. Such benefits have gone from being considered ''fringe'' benefits to the point where they constitute approximately 40 percent of an employee's compensation, and the plans under which they are provided are a major concern of employers.

Individuals responsible for the design, pricing, selling and administration of employee benefits carry a broad range of responsibilities, and the role of the benefits professional has changed rapidly and radically in the past two decades. During that period the number of employee benefits has virtually exploded with expansion occurring in many of the more traditional benefits and the addition of totally new forms of benefits.

Part One of *The Handbook* is concerned with the environment in which employee benefit plans are designed and operated, and Chapter 1 considers many important design issues. Chapter 2 extends the discussion of employee benefit plan design concepts by looking at the functional approach to employee benefit planning which provides a framework for various strategies for considering benefits on a risk-by-risk basis and as a part of total compensation. The third chapter in this part considers some of the risk and insurance concepts inherent in many approaches to employee benefit planning and provides a background for many of the concepts discussed throughout *The Handbook*.

The final chapter in Part One is a brief overview of the regulatory environment surrounding employee benefit plans. Later chapters cover in greater detail the extremely important regulatory issues that are so much a part of employee benefit planning.

CHAPTER 1

THE ENVIRONMENT OF EMPLOYEE BENEFIT PLANS

Jerry S. Rosenbloom

Employee benefits are an extremely important part of almost everyone's financial security. Once considered to be "fringe" benefits because of their relatively small magnitude, today there is no way that employee benefits can be considered as fringe anything. Employee benefits account for almost 40 percent of an individual's total compensation. In many firms, an even higher percentage can apply. To ensure that both employers and employees utilize employee benefit plans in the most effective manner requires a thorough knowledge of all aspects of employee benefit plan design, funding, and administration including benefit communications. This chapter gives the necessary background for the rest of the volume by outlining what employee benefits are, the reasons for their growth, what they are intended to achieve from both the employer and employee perspective, and what makes such plans work.

EMPLOYEE BENEFITS DEFINED

Broad View of Employee Benefits

There are many definitions of employee benefits, ranging from broad to narrow interpretations. In the broad view, employee benefits are virtually any form of compensation other than direct wages paid to employees.[1] For

[1]Jerry S. Rosenbloom and G. Victor Hallman, *Employee Benefit Planning*, 3rd ed. (Englewood Cliffs, N.J.: Prentice-Hall, 1991), pp. 2–3.

example, in the annual U.S. Chamber of Commerce survey of employee benefits, such benefits are defined broadly to include the following:[2]

1. Employer's share of legally required payments.
2. Employer's share of retirement and savings plan payments.
3. Employer's share of life insurance and death benefits.
4. Employer's share of medical and medically related benefit payments.
5. Payments for nonproduction time while on the job (e.g., paid rest periods, lunch periods, wash-up time, travel time, etc.).
6. Payments for time not worked (e.g., paid sick leave, paid vacations, and holidays).
7. Miscellaneous benefit payments (including employee discounts, meals, educational expenditures, child care, and other).

Table 1–1 on pages 6 and 7 illustrates the preceding breakdown of employee benefits for all companies as well as a breakdown by manufacturing and nonmanufacturing companies. As the table indicates, employee benefits are intertwined with almost every facet of an individual's economic and financial security.

A More Limited View of Employee Benefits

The broad view of employee benefits encompasses both legally mandated benefits such as Social Security and other governmental programs and private plans, while the narrow view can be summarized as "any type of plan sponsored or initiated unilaterally or jointly by employers and employees in providing benefits that stem from the employment relationship that are not underwritten or paid directly by government."[3]

This narrow definition of employee benefits will be the one primarily used in the *Handbook*. That does not mean in any way, however, that legally required benefits are unimportant. Quite the contrary, these benefits are extremely important and must be considered in employee benefit plan design and in integrating private employee benefit plans with

---

[2]Chamber of Commerce of the United States, *Employee Benefits 1990* (Washington, D.C., 1990).

[3]Martha Remey Yohalem, "Employee Benefit Plans—1975," *Social Security Bulletin* 40, no.11 (November 1977), p. 19.

the benefits provided by governmental bodies. This interrelationship is stressed throughout the book. In addition to benefits provided through government bodies and those provided through the employment relationship, benefits provided by an individual for his or her own welfare also are described when appropriate. This so-called tripod of economic security or three-legged stool underlies the foundation of individual and family financial security.

REASONS FOR THE GROWTH OF EMPLOYEE BENEFIT PLANS

The reasons behind the evolution of employee benefit plans from fringes to a major component of financial security today are numerous. They arise from external forces as well as the desire of employers and employees to achieve certain goals and objectives.

Business Reasons

A multitude of business reasons explain why employee benefit plans were established and why they have expanded greatly. Employers want to attract and hold capable employees. Having employee benefit plans in place serves this objective. Also, in many cases an employer's competition has certain benefit plans and therefore it is necessary to have equal or better plans to retain current employees. Moreover, employers hope that corporate efficiency, productivity, and improved employee morale will be fostered by good benefit plans. Concern for employees' welfare and social objectives also encouraged the providing of benefits.

Collective Bargaining

Labor unions, through the collective bargaining process, have had a major impact on the growth of employee benefit plans. The Labor Management Relations Act (LMRA) which is administered by the National Labor Relations Board (NLRB) requires good-faith collective bargaining over wages, hours and other terms and conditions of employment. A notable event occurred in 1948 when the NLRB ruled that the meaning of the term *wages* includes a pension plan, and this position was upheld in the landmark case of *Inland Steel Co.* v. *National Labor*

TABLE 1–1
Employee Benefits, by Type of Benefit: All Employees 1989

Type of Benefit	*Total, All Companies*	*Total, All Manufacturing*	*Total, All Nonmanufacturing*
Total employee benefits as percent of payroll	37.6%	37.0%	37.9%
1. Legally required payments (employer's share only)	8.7	8.7	8.7
a. Old-Age, Survivors, Disability, and Health Insurance (FICA taxes) and Railroad Retirement Tax	6.9	6.8	7.0
b. Unemployment Compensation	0.7	0.7	0.6
c. Workers' Compensation (including estimated cost of self-insured)	1.1	1.2	1.0
d. State sickness benefits insurance	0.0	0.0	0.0
2. Retirement and Savings Plan Payments (employer's share only)	5.1	4.1	5.6
a. Defined benefit pension plan contributions	1.9	0.8	2.5
b. Defined contribution plan payments	1.0	1.1	1.0
c. Profit sharing	0.8	1.0	0.7
d. Pension plan premiums (net) under insurance and annuity contracts (insured and trusteed)	0.5	0.1	0.7
e. Administration and other costs	0.6	0.7	0.5
3. Life Insurance and Death Benefits (employer's share only)	0.5	0.6	0.5
4. Medical and Medically Related Benefit Payments (employer's share only)	9.3	9.7	9.1
a. Hospital, surgical, medical, and major medical insurance premiums (net)	7.0	7.3	6.9
b. Retiree (payments for retired employees) hospital, surgical, medical, and major medical insurance premiums (net)	0.9	1.0	0.8

TABLE 1–1 (*concluded*)

c. Short-term disability, sickness or accident insurance (company plan or insured plan)	0.3	0.3	0.3
d. Long-term disability or wage continuation (insured, self-administered, or trust)	0.2	0.1	0.2
e. Dental insurance premiums	0.6	0.7	0.6
f. Other (vision care, physical and mental fitness, benefits for former employees	0.3	0.3	0.4
5. Paid Rest Periods, Coffee Breaks, Lunch Periods, Wash-Up Time, Travel Time, Clothes-Change Time, Get Ready Time, etc.	2.3	2.0	2.4
6. Payments for Time Not Worked	10.8	10.9	10.7
a. Payments for or in lieu of vacations	5.6	5.6	5.6
b. Payments for or in lieu of holidays	3.4	3.6	3.4
c. Sick leave pay	1.3	1.2	1.4
d. Parental leave (maternity and paternity leave payments)	0.0	0.0	0.0
e. Other	0.4	0.5	0.3
7. Miscellaneous Benefit Payments	0.9	1.1	0.9
a. Discounts on goods and services purchased from company by employees	0.2	0.1	0.3
b. Employee meals furnished by company	0.1	0.1	0.1
c. Employee education expenditures	0.2	0.2	0.2
d. Child Care	0.0	0.0	0.0
e. Other	0.5	0.7	0.3
Total employee benefits as cents per payroll hour.	555.9	535.8	555.9
Total employee benefits as dollars per year per employee	11,527.0	12,707.0	11,003.0

Source: Chamber of Commerce of the United States, *Employee Benefits 1990* (Washington, D.C., 1990), p. 6.

Relations Board in the same year. Shortly thereafter, in 1949, the good-faith bargaining requirements were held to include a group health and accident plan (*W. W. Cross & Co.* v. *National Labor Relations Board*). As a result of these two decisions it was clearly established that the LMRA provisions applied to both retirement and welfare benefit plans, and their subsequent growth has been substantial.

The LMRA, or Taft-Hartley Act, as it commonly is known, also has played other significant roles with respect to the development of employee benefit plans. It, along with the Internal Revenue Code (IRC), established the distinction between retirement benefits and welfare benefits. Additionally, the statute sets forth the basic regulatory framework under which both of these major categories of benefits are to be jointly administered within the collective bargaining process. As such it is the legislative basis on which jointly trusteed benefit plans are founded.

Favorable Tax Legislation

Over the years the tax laws have favored employee benefit plans. Such preferential tax legislation has greatly encouraged the development of employee benefit plans as well as helping to shape their design since many plans seek to maximize the tax treatment or tax consequences of various employee benefit plans. The main tax benefits of employee benefit plans are as follows: (1) most contributions to employee benefit plans by employers are deductible as long as they are reasonable business expenses; (2) contributions from employers within certain limits on behalf of employees are generally not considered income to employees; and (3) on certain types of retirement and capital accumulation plans, assets set aside to fund such plans accumulate tax-free until distributed. Some additional tax benefits may be available when such distributions are made. All in all, favorable tax legislation has had great impact on the development and expansion of employee benefit plans.

Efficiency of the Employee Benefits Approach

The bringing together after the industrial revolution of employees and employers in cities and in business firms made it possible for the employee benefits concept to flourish by covering many employees under one contract or plan instead of each employee having to go out and purchase an individual contract. The simplicity and convenience of providing coverage to people through their place of employment made sense from many standpoints. Employee benefit providers and suppliers, such as insurance companies, banks, and various types of health organizations, all found the marketing of such benefits through the employer to be a cost-effective and administratively efficient channel of distribution.

Other Factors

Many other factors have contributed to the growth of employee benefit plans. One such factor was the imposition during World War II and the Korean conflict of limitations on the size of wage increases granted during these periods. While wages were frozen, employee benefits were not. As a result, compensation of employees could effectively be increased by provision of larger benefits. The result was a major expansion of employee benefits during these two periods.

Some have argued that various legislative action over the years has encouraged employee benefit plans not only through providing favorable tax treatment but by the government's "moral suasion" that if such benefit plans were not established voluntarily by employers and employees, additional governmental programs might result. Allowing employee benefits to be integrated with governmental benefits also has enhanced the private employee benefit approach by taking into consideration benefits provided by governmental plans in benefit plan design.

Development of the group approach to certain employee benefits has also helped expand the employee benefit mechanism. The techniques inherent in the group selection process made possible the providing of benefits that previously could only be provided on an individual basis, with coverage often determined by medical selection.

GROUP TECHNIQUE

In many types of insurance programs such as group life insurance and group health insurance, the group technique enables these coverages to be written as employee benefit plans.[4] Unlike individual insurance, group

---

[4]See Chapter 8 for an additional discussion of the "group mechanism" to providing employee benefits.

insurance is based on a view of the group rather than the individual as a unit. Usually, individual insurance eligibility requirements are not required for group insurance written under an employee benefit plan.[5] The concepts that make the group technique work are all designed to prevent "adverse selection"—that is, to reduce the possibility that less healthy individuals may join a group or be a larger percentage of a group than anticipated because of the availability of insurance or other benefits.

Characteristics of the group technique of providing employee benefits include some or all of the following:[6]

1. *Only certain groups eligible* While most groups qualify, this requirement is intended to make sure that the obtaining of insurance is incidental to the group seeking coverage. Thus, a group should not be formed solely for the purpose of obtaining insurance.

2. *Steady flow of lives through the group* The theory behind this concept is that younger individuals should come into the group while older individuals leave the group thus maintaining a fairly constant mortality or morbidity ratio in the group. If the group doesn't maintain this "flow through the group" and the average age of the group increases substantially, costs could increase dramatically.

3. *Minimum number of persons in the group* A minimum number of persons, typically ten, must be in the group to be eligible for group benefits. However, this requirement has been liberalized to the point where two or three individuals in a group may obtain coverage. This minimum-number provision is designed to prevent unhealthy lives from being a major part of the group and to spread the expenses of the benefits plan over a larger number of individuals.[7]

4. *A minimum portion of the group must participate* Typically in group life and health insurance plans if the plan is noncontributory (that is, solely paid for by the employer), 100 percent of eligible employees must be covered. If the plan is contributory (both employer and employee share the cost), 75 percent of the employees must participate. The rationale for this provision is also to reduce adverse selection and spread the expense of administration.[8]

---

[5]A discussion of the insurance technique and how and why it works is presented in Chapter 3.

[6]See Rosenbloom and Hallman, *Employee Benefit Planning*, pp. 15–20

[7]*Ibid.*, p. 17

[8]*Ibid.*, p. 17

5. *Eligibility requirements* Frequently eligibility requirements are imposed under group plans for the purpose, once again, of preventing adverse selection. Such provision can include only full-time employees who are actively at work on the date the benefits become effective. A waiting or eligibility period may be used for certain benefits. Also, if employees don't join when eligible and want to enroll at a later date, some form of medical information may be required.

6. *Maximum limits for any one person* In certain cases, maximum limits on the amount of life or health benefits may be imposed to prevent the possibility of excessive amounts of coverage on any particular unhealthy individual.

7. *Automatic determination of benefits* To prevent unhealthy lives in a group from obtaining an extremely large amount of a particular benefit or benefits, coverage is determined for all individuals in the group on an automatic basis. This basis may be determined by an employee's salary, service, or position, may be a flat amount for all employees, or may be a combination of these factors.

8. *A central and efficient administrative agency* To keep expenses to a minimum and to handle the mechanics of the benefit plan, a central and efficient administrative agency is necessary for the successful operation of an employee benefit plan. An employer is an almost ideal unit because he or she maintains the payroll and other employee information needed in meeting appropriate tax and recordkeeping requirements.[9]

Over the years many of the requirements just described have been liberalized as providers of employee benefits have gained experience in handling group employee benefits, and because of the competitive environment. Nevertheless, the basic group selection technique is important in understanding why employee benefits can work on a group basis and how any problems that exist might be corrected.

OVERALL EMPLOYEE BENEFIT CONCERNS

Because employee benefits, as noted previously, provide such an important dimension of financial security in our society, some overall questions need to be asked to evaluate any existing or newly created employee

---

[9]*Ibid.*

benefit plan. While future chapters in this *Handbook* analyze benefit design, costing, funding, administration, and communication issues, some principles permeate all these areas and need brief mention early in this text.[10]

Employer and Employee Objectives

The design of any employee benefit plan must start with the objectives of the benefits plan from the standpoint of both employer and employee.

What Benefits Should Be Provided?

There should be clearly stated reasons or objectives for the type of benefits to be provided. Benefits provided both under governmental programs and by the individual employees also should be considered.

Who Should Be Covered by the Benefit Plans?

Should only full-time employees be covered? What about retirees or dependents? What about survivors of deceased employees? These and a host of similar questions must be carefully thought through. Of course, some of these issues depend on regulatory and legislative rules and regulations.

Should Employees Have Benefit Options?

This is becoming more and more of a crucial question under employee benefit plans. With the growth of flexible or cafeteria benefit plans, employee choice is on the increase. Even in nonflexible benefit plan situations, should limited choices be given?

How Should Benefit Plans Be Financed?

Several important questions need to be answered in determining the approach to funding employee benefit plans. Should financing be entirely

---

[10]Some of the ideas presented here are based on Rosenbloom and Hallman, *Employee Benefit Planning*, 3rd ed., Chapter 23. For a more detailed analysis, consult this publication.

provided by the employer (a noncontributory approach) or on some shared basis by the employer and employee (contributory approach)? If on a contributory basis, what percentage should each bear?

What funding method should be used? A wide range of possibilities exists, from a total insurance program to total self-funding with many options in between. Even when one of these options is selected, still further questions remain concerning the specific funding instrument to be used.

How Should the Benefit Plan Be Administered?

Should the firm itself administer the plan? Should an insurance carrier or other benefit plan provider do the administration? Should some outside organization such as a third-party administrator (TPA) do this work? Once the decision is made, the specific entity must be selected.

How Should the Benefit Plan Be Communicated?

The best employee benefit plan in existence may not achieve any of its desired objectives if it is improperly communicated to all affected parties. The communication of employee benefit plans has become increasingly important in recent years with increased reporting and disclosure requirements. Effective communication of what benefit plans will and won't do is essential if employees are to rely on such plans to provide part of their financial security at all stages of their lives.

Future of Employee Benefits

With the spate of recent legislation restricting certain aspects of employee benefit plans, and the specter of a large and growing federal deficit, some benefit experts believe there may be still greater employee benefit cutbacks in the future. While certain new limitations and restrictions may be imposed, employee benefit plans are woven into the fabric of our society in such a way that the basic character or importance of such plans will not be changed. With pressures to contain costs ever increasing, greater efficiencies in the benefits approach, more tailoring to individual needs in the growth of flexible benefits or cafeteria compensation plans, and other refinements will drive the employee benefits mechanism. While it seems certain that employee benefits will not grow as rapidly as they have in the past, their place is secure and will continue to demand people who are knowledgeable about all aspects of the design, funding, administration, and communication of employee benefits in order to make such plans more effective while helping to provide for the economic security of society at large.

CHAPTER 2

FUNCTIONAL APPROACH TO EMPLOYEE BENEFITS

G. Victor Hallman III

This chapter deals with the functional approach toward analyzing an existing employee benefit program and evaluating the need for new employee benefits. The functional approach can be defined as an organized system for classifying and analyzing the risks and needs of active employees, their dependents, and various other categories of persons into logical categories of exposures to loss and employee needs. These exposures and needs may include medical expenses, losses resulting from death, losses caused by short- and long-term disabilities, retirement income needs, capital accumulation needs, needs arising out of short- and long-term unemployment, custodial care (long-term care) needs, and other employee needs.

TEST

THE FUNCTIONAL APPROACH IN CONCEPT

As indicated above, the functional approach essentially is the application of a systematic method of analysis to an employer's total employee benefits program. It analyzes the employer's employee benefits program as a coordinated whole in terms of its ability to meet various employees' (and others') needs and to manage loss exposures within the employer's overall compensation goals and cost parameters. This approach can be useful in overall employee benefit plan design, in evaluating proposals for new or revised benefits, for evaluation of cost-saving proposals, and in effective communication of an employer's total benefits program to its employees.

The functional approach to employee benefits is not really a new concept. In 1967, George C. Foust outlined the functional approach in the American Management Association book *The Total Approach to Employee Benefits*.[1] Similarly, Robert M. McCaffery in his 1972 work *Managing the Employee Benefits Program* stated:

> The "package" or total approach to employee benefits is simply the purposeful management of an integrated program. Rather than continually reacting to current fads, outside pressures, and salesmen's pitches, the contemporary businessman relies on fundamental principles of management in developing, organizing, directing, and evaluating systems of employee benefits for his organization.[2]

The functional approach represents such systematic management of the employee benefits function.

NEED FOR THE FUNCTIONAL APPROACH

The functional approach is needed in planning, designing, and administering employee benefits for several reasons.

First, in most instances, employee benefits are a very significant element of the total compensation of employees. They have become an important part of the work rewards provided by employers to their employees. Therefore, it is important to employees, and hence their employers, that this increasingly important element of compensation be planned and organized to be effective as possible in meeting employee needs.

Second, employee benefits currently represent a large item of labor cost for employers. Depending on the industry, the particular employer, and how employee benefits are defined, benefits may range from less than 18 percent to over 65 percent of an employer's payroll. Therefore, effective planning and hence avoidance of waste in providing benefits can be an important cost-control measure for employers.

Third, in the past, employee benefits often were adopted by employers on a piecemeal basis without being coordinated with existing benefit

---

[1]George C. Foust, Jr., "The Total Approach Concept," in *The Total Approach to Employee Benefits*, ed., Arthur J. Deric (New York: American Management Association, 1967), chap. 1.

[2]Robert M. McCaffery, *Managing the Employee Benefits Program* (New York: American Management Association, 1972), p. 17. There also is a revised (1983) edition of this pioneering book.

programs. Thus, some benefit plans just "grew like Topsy." For this reason, it usually is fruitful to apply the functional approach in reviewing existing employee benefit plans to determine where overlapping benefits may exist and costs can be saved, and where gaps in benefits may exist and new benefits or revised benefits may be in order.

Fourth, because new benefits and coverages, changes in the tax laws, changes in the regulatory environment, and other developments in employee benefit planning have come about so rapidly in recent years, it is important to have a systematic approach to planning benefits to keep them current, competitive, and in compliance with regulatory requirements.

Finally, a given employee benefit or program, such as a pension plan, often provides benefits relating to several separate employee needs or loss exposures. Therefore, an employer's benefit plan needs to be analyzed according to the functional approach so its various benefit programs can be integrated properly with each other.

CONSISTENCY WITH AN EMPLOYER'S TOTAL COMPENSATION PHILOSOPHY

In designing the total compensation package, an employer should seek to balance the various elements of its compensation system, including basic cash wages and salary, current incentive compensation (current cash bonuses and company stock plans), and so-called employee benefits, to help meet the needs and desires of the employees on the one hand and the employer's basic compensation philosophy and objectives on the other. Thus, it is clear that the functional approach to planning and designing an employee benefit plan must remain consistent with the employer's total compensation philosophy. A particular employer, therefore, may not cover a certain employee desire for benefits, or may cover it in a rather spartan manner, not because the desire is not recognized but because the employer's total compensation philosophy calls for a relatively low level of employee benefits or, perhaps, benefits oriented in a different direction.

Employers may adopt different business policies regarding the general compensation of their employees. For example, many employers want to compensate their employees at a level about in line with that generally prevailing in their industry or community, or both. They do not wish to be much above or below average compensation levels. The employee benefit programs of such employers also frequently follow this general philosophy. Other employers may follow a high-compensation philosophy (including employee benefits) with the goal of attempting to attract higher levels of management, technical, and general employee talent. This may be particularly true in industries where the need for a highly skilled work force is great. On the other hand, there may be employers that follow a low-compensation policy, feeling that, for them, the resultant lower payroll costs more than outweigh the resulting higher employee turnover and lower skill level of their work force. An employer with this kind of philosophy also may want to adopt more modest employee benefit programs.

Type of industry and employer characteristics also will have an impact on an employer's total compensation philosophy and on the design of its employee benefit plan. Figure 2–1 is a grid presented by one employee benefit consulting firm showing the relationship between type of organization, working climate, and compensation mix.

Thus, a larger well-established employer in a mature industry, a financial institution, or a nonprofit organization may take a relatively liberal approach toward meeting the benefits needs and desires of its

FIGURE 2–1
Organizational Style and Compensation Mix

		Reward Management Components			
		Cash		***Noncash***	
Type of Organization	***Working Climate***	***Base Salary***	***Short-Term Incentives***	***Level***	***Characteristics***
Mature Industrial	Balanced	Medium	Medium	Medium	Balanced
Developing Industrial	Growth, Creativity	Medium	High	Low	Short-Term-Oriented
Conservative Financial	Security	Low	Low	High	Long-Term, Security-Oriented
Nonprofit	Societal Impact, Personal Fulfillment	Low	None	Low to Medium	Long-Term, Security-Oriented
Sales	Growth, Freedom to Act	Low	High	Low	Short-Term-Oriented

Source: Hay-Huggins, member of the Hay Group.

employees. But developing industrial firms and other growth companies, which may have considerable current needs for capital, may seek to rely more heavily on short-term-oriented incentive types of compensation. Further, industries that are highly competitive, subject to cyclical fluctuations, or perhaps in a currently depressed state, may not be willing to add to their relatively fixed labor costs by adopting or liberalizing employee benefits, even if there may be a functional need for them. In fact, such firms may seek to cut back on their employee benefit commitments when possible. However, even in these situations firms should attempt to allocate their available compensation dollars in as consistent and logical a manner as possible to meet the needs and goals of their employees as well as their own corporate compensation objectives. In fact, the functional approach may be even more appropriate in such cases because their resources for compensating employees are relatively scarce.

Another area of employer philosophy that affects the functional approach and how it is actually applied is whether the employer tends to follow a compensation/service-oriented benefit philosophy or a benefit- or needs-oriented philosophy. Employers having a compensation/service-oriented philosophy tend to relate employee benefits primarily to compensation or service, or both, in designing their employee benefit plans. Thus, the level of benefits would tend to be tied in with compensation level, and eligibility for benefits may be conditioned directly or indirectly on salary level. For example, separate benefits plans may be provided for salaried and for hourly rated employees with more generous benefits being made available to the former group. Further, some types of benefits may be available only to certain higher-paid employees or executives. In addition, such employers tend to emphasize service with the employer in determining benefit levels and eligibility for benefits. The theory of this approach is that employee benefits generally should be aimed to reward the longer-service employees who have shown a commitment to the employer. The benefit- or needs-oriented philosophy, on the other hand, tends to focus primarily on the needs of employees and their dependents rather than on compensation and service.

In practice, the design of employee benefit plans tends to be a compromise between these two philosophies. On one side, certain kinds of employee benefits, such as medical expense benefits, tend to be primarily benefit- or needs-oriented. On the other side, benefits like group life insurance and pensions customarily are compensation-oriented, at least for nonunion employees. Thus, this distinction in philosophy really is one of degree. However, the extent to which eligibility for benefits, participation requirements, and levels of employee benefits reflect compensation or service, or both, may affect the extent to which the needs of employees or certain categories of employees will be met by an employee benefit plan.

APPLICATION OF THE FUNCTIONAL APPROACH

While the functional approach to planning employee benefits has been actively discussed since the early 1960s, no clearly developed procedure or technique exists for the application of this approach to individual benefit plans. However, based on the underlying concept and the way it is applied in practice, the following are the logical steps in applying the functional approach to employee benefit plan design, revision, or review. For convenience of presentation, these steps can be listed as follows:

1. Classify employee (and dependent) needs or objectives in logical functional categories.
2. Classify the categories of persons (e.g., employees, some former employees, and dependents) the employer may want to protect, at least to some extent, through its employee benefit plan.
3. Analyze the benefits presently available under the plan in terms of the functional categories of needs or objectives and in terms of the categories of persons the employer may want to benefit.
4. Determine any gaps in benefits or overlapping benefits, or both, provided from *all* sources under the employer's employee benefit plan and from other benefit plans in terms of the functional categories of needs and the persons to be protected.
5. Consider recommendations for changes in the employer's present employee benefit plan to meet any gaps in benefits and to correct any overlapping benefits, including possible use of the flexible benefits (cafeteria plan) approach.
6. Estimate the costs or savings from each of the recommendations made in step 5.
7. Evaluate alternative methods of financing or securing the benefits recommended above, as well as the employee benefit plan's existing benefits.

8. Consider other cost-saving techniques in connection with the recommended benefits or existing benefits (i.e., plan possible cost-containment strategies).
9. Decide upon the appropriate benefits, methods of financing, and sources of benefits as a result of the preceding analysis.
10. Implement the changes.
11. Communicate benefit changes to employees.
12. Periodically reevaluate the employee benefit plan.

Each of these steps is considered in greater detail below. Naturally, it must be recognized in applying this process to a particular employee benefit plan that some of these steps may be combined with others and some will be taken implicitly. However, each step represents a logical decision point or consideration in the design or revision of an employee benefit plan.

Classify Employee and Dependent Needs in Functional Categories

The needs and exposures to loss of employees, their dependents, and certain others can be classified in a variety of ways, some being more complete than others. The following classification appears to cover most of the commonly accepted needs and exposures to loss that may be covered under an employee benefit plan:

1. Medical expenses incurred by active employees, by their dependents, by retired (or certain otherwise terminated or suspended) former employees, and by their dependents.
2. Losses due to employees' disability (short-term and long-term).
3. Losses resulting from active employees' deaths, from their dependents' deaths, and from the deaths of retired (or certain otherwise terminated or suspended) former employees.
4. Retirement needs of employees and their dependents.
5. Capital accumulation needs or goals (short-term and long-term).
6. Needs arising from unemployment or from temporary termination or suspension of employment.
7. Needs for financial counseling, retirement counseling, and other counseling services.
8. Losses resulting from property and liability exposures, needs for legal services, and the like.

9. Needs for dependent care assistance (e.g., child-care services).
10. Needs for educational assistance for employees themselves or for employees' dependents, or for both.
11. Other employee benefit needs (such as custodial care expenses of employees or their dependents or of retired employees or their dependents).

Naturally, a given functional analysis often does not encompass all these needs or loss exposures. The above classification is intended to be more exhaustive than frequently is included in a functional analysis. However, the history of employee benefit planning, particularly since the end of World War II, has been one of continually expanding the areas of employees' (and others') needs for which the employer is providing benefits of various kinds. It seems likely, therefore, that additional categories of needs and loss exposures will be added to the above list from time to time. Also, some of those needs and exposures mentioned only incidentally may become more important in the future.

Figure 2–2 on pages 24 through 26 provides an illustration of the functional approach to employee benefit planning, using the employee benefit plan of a large corporation and the functional categories used by that corporation. Note that the employee needs and exposures to loss are shown on the left-hand margin of the grid while the components of this corporation's employee benefit plan are shown across the top of the grid. This arrangement shows how each benefit plan applies to each of these employee needs or loss exposures. Any gaps or duplications in coverage (or need for further information) can be seen more easily through this systematic process of analysis.

Classify by Categories the Persons the Employer May Want to Protect

This step basically involves the issues of who should be protected by an employee benefit plan, for what benefits, for what time period, and under what conditions. These issues have become increasingly important in employee benefit planning as the scope of employee benefit plans has increased not only in terms of the benefits provided but also in terms of continuing to protect employees once the formal employment relationship has ended and of protecting dependents of employees in a variety of circumstances. It is a logical part of the functional approach since the needs and loss exposures of employees imply consideration not only of the kinds of benefits to be provided but also of the persons to be protected and when they will be protected. Thus, in designing its employee benefit plan the employer also should consider how the various functional categories of needs and goals will be met for different categories of persons under a variety of circumstances.

In this type of analysis, the following are among the categories of persons whom the employer may want to consider protecting under its employee benefit plan—under at least some circumstances and for at least some benefits:

1. Active full-time employees.
2. Dependents of active full-time employees.
3. Retired former employees.
4. Dependents of retired former employees.
5. Disabled employees and their dependents.
6. Surviving dependents of deceased employees.
7. Terminated employees and their dependents.
8. Employees (and their dependents) who are temporarily separated from the employer's service, such as during layoffs, leaves of absence, military duty, strikes, and so forth.
9. Other than full-time active employees (e.g., part-time employees, directors, and so forth).

The employer basically must decide how far it wants to extend its employee benefit program, and for what kinds of benefits, to persons who may not be active full-time employees. This represents a significant issue in employee benefit planning both in terms of adequacy of employee protection and of the cost implications for the employer. Some extensions of benefits, such as provision of medical expense benefits to retirees and perhaps their dependents (retiree medical benefits) and continuation of group term life insurance (normally in reduced amounts) on retirees' lives, can be quite expensive. The importance of this issue has been further heightened for employers by the adoption by the Financial Accounting Standards Board (FASB) of Financial Accounting Standard (FAS) 106—*Employers' Accounting for Postretirement Benefits other than Pensions*. FAS 106, which generally is effective for employers' fiscal years beginning after December 15, 1992, generally will require employers to recognize during the covered employees' period of service

FIGURE 2–2
Illustration of Functional Approach to Employee Benefit Planning

Employee Needs or Exposures to Loss	*Health Care Plan*	*Basic Salary Continuation Plan*	*Extended Salary Continuation Plan*	*Long Term Disability Plan*	*Basic Life Insurance Plan*
Medical expenses	Choice among 3 base plans; a major medical plan supplements selected base plan. Dental, hearing, and vision care also covered				
Disability losses	Coverage continues while employee receives disability benefits under company plans	Full salary for up to 30 days of absence each year for illness or injury	After the basic allowance is exhausted, employee's full salary less offsetting benefits is maintained up to a maximum of 25 months depending on length of service	After extended plan ends, 75% of base monthly pay less offsetting benefits for up to 25 months; then, a voluntary payroll deduction LTD benefit of 50% of salary	Coverage continues while employee receives disability benefits under company plans
In case of death	Dependent coverage continues for 4 months plus an additional period depending upon employee service, at the employer's expense. Thereafter, the plan meets COBRA requirements	Coverage terminates	Coverage terminates	Coverage terminates	Provides beneficiary with a benefit of $3,000
Retirement	Major medical plan continues for life during retirement after age 65 at the employer's expense	Coverage terminates	Coverage terminates	Coverage terminates	$3,000 coverage continues after retirement for as long as employee lives
Capital accumulation					
Dependent care assistance					

FIGURE 2–2 (*continued*)

	Primary Life Insurance Plan	*Travel Accident Plan*	*Savings Plan*	*Employees' Stock Purchase Plan*
	Coverage continues while employee receives disability benefits under company plans	Pays a benefit of up to 3 times employee's annual base pay if disability involves an accidental dismemberment while traveling on company business	Contributions are discontinued when long-term disability benefits begin. Participation may continue unless employee becomes permanently and totally disabled or until formal retirement. Withdrawals are permitted	Employee receiving disability benefits may suspend any payments being made to the plan for a period not to exceed 6 months or a specified date in the offering
	Provides beneficiary with a benefit of 3 times employee's current annual base pay (offset by pension plan's preretirement survivor benefit). Employee also has the option to purchase additional life insurance at favorable group rates, up to 3 times current base pay	Pays beneficiary a lump–sum benefit of 3 times employee's annual base pay if death is the result of an accident while traveling on company business	Beneficiary receives the amount credited to employee's account	Payment is made of any amount being accumulated during a "purchase period" with interest
	Continues after retirement with the amount and duration of coverage depending on the option employee chooses	Coverage terminates	Employee may receive the balance in the plan account upon retirement	Stock purchased under plan available at and before retirement; retirees not eligible for future offerings
			Employees may contribute up to 16% of pay or $7,000 (indexed) before-tax per year. Employer matches 50% of contributions, up to 6% of pay. 4 investment options. Withdrawals permitted on termination of employment or in service in special cases. Plan loans available subject to tax law requirements.	Employees can purchase company stock in amounts based on salary at 85% of stock price at either the beginning or the end of any purchase period; payment in installments

FIGURE 2–2 *(concluded)*

Pension Plan	*Social Security*	*Workers' Compensation*	*Supplemental Workers' Compensation*	*Flexible Spending Accounts (FSAs)*
		Pays if illness or injury is job-related under the workers' compensation laws		Allows employees to set aside before-tax up to $3,000 per year for tax-eligible health care expenses
Participation continues while employee receives company disability benefits; service credits accumulate until end of extended disability period or up to 3 months	Pays after 5 months of continuous total disability when approved by Social Security	Pays if disability is job-related under the workers' compensation laws	Increases disability income if employee receives workers' compensation benefits	
Active employees: preretirement survivors benefit for vested employees' spouses if employees die before retirement; no cost to employee; coordinated with primary life insurance plan. Retired employees: retiree may elect pension option to provide benefits to beneficiary upon retiree's death, subject to QJSA rules	Pays a lump-sum death benefit and monthly survivor income to spouse and children	Pays if death is job-related under the workers' compensation laws	Coverage terminates	
Defined benefit plan integrated with Social Security pays regular benefit at 65, with alternatives for early retirement before age 65.	Pays unreduced retirement benefits at full-benefit retirement age (currently age 65) or reduced benefits as early as age 62. In addition, health care expenses may be covered under Medicare	Coverage terminates in accordance with the workers' compensation laws	Coverage terminates	
				Allows employees to set aside before-tax up to $5,000/yr. for tax-eligible child or other dependent care

the accrued benefit cost of these postretirement benefits (the net periodic postretirement benefit cost) as a current business expense and to recognize the liabilities for and any plan assets funding these benefits for balance-sheet purposes. This will replace the past practice of generally accounting for these benefits on a pay-as-you-go basis. It is expected that this change in accounting standards for these postretirement benefits will have a significant impact on the earnings and net worth of many employers with such plans.

The extent to which employers may want to extend coverage of their benefit plans to one or more of these categories of persons varies with employer philosophy, cost constraints, funding and accounting considerations, union negotiations, and employee benefit practices in the particular industry and geographic area involved. Such extensions also vary considerably among the different kinds of benefits. For example, medical expense benefits may be extended to active employees, various categories of dependents of active employees, retired former employees, dependents of retired former employees, surviving spouses and other dependents of retired former employees, disabled employees, dependents of disabled employees, and surviving dependents of deceased active employees. Further, medical expense coverage may be provided, and indeed may be required to be provided under the Consolidated Omnibus Budget Reconciliation Act of 1985, as amended (COBRA), for terminated employees, dependents of terminated employees, dependents of active employees who no longer meet the definition of an eligible dependent under the regular employee benefit plan, dependents of deceased employees, and in certain other situations. Group term life insurance, however, may be provided to active full-time employees, disabled employees who meet the definition of disability under the plan, and retired employees in reduced amounts. Also, some plans provide dependents group life insurance to eligible dependents of active employees. At the other extreme, cash disability income benefits normally are provided only to active full-time employees.

Another factor to consider in this analysis is to what extent and on what contribution basis certain employee benefits will be provided or continued to various categories of persons. Benefits may be provided or continued without contribution by the employee or covered person in full or in a reduced amount. Or, the benefits could be provided or continued with contribution to the cost by the employee or covered person in full or on a reduced basis. Finally, benefits may be provided or continued to covered persons on an elective basis at the covered person's own cost.

Analyze Benefits Presently Available

The next step in the functional approach is to analyze the benefits, terms of coverage, and plan participation by employees in terms of how well the existing or proposed employee benefit plan meets employee needs and desires in the various functional categories for those classes of persons the employer wants to protect or benefit. This step involves measuring the employee benefit plan against the objectives and coverage criteria set up for it under the functional approach just outlined.

Types of Benefits

A common application of the functional approach to employee benefit planning is to outline the different types of benefits under an employee benefit plan that apply to each of the functional categories of employee needs and goals. This may be done in the form of a grid as shown in Figure 2–2. In that figure, for example, employee needs and exposures to loss are shown on the left-hand margin of the grid while the components of the corporation's employee benefit plan are shown across the top of the grid.

Levels of Benefits

In a similar fashion, the levels of benefits under the various components of the employee benefit plan can be determined or shown, or both, for each of the functional categories of needs or goals.

To supplement this analysis, it may be helpful to use benefit illustrations to determine or illustrate the levels of benefits that would be provided under the various components of the employee benefit plan or proposed plan in the event of certain contingencies and using certain assumptions. For example, it might be assumed an employee with certain earnings and using certain salary projections will retire at age 65 with 30 years of service with the employer. This employee's total retirement income then may be estimated from various components of the employer's employee benefit plan as well as from Social Security as of the assumed retirement date. This can be expressed as a percentage of the employee's estimated final pay, which often is referred to as the employee's retirement income "replacement ratio." The employee benefits used in such an analysis may include only the employer's pension plan and Social Security; but it would be more logical to include all potential sources of retirement income available through the employee benefit plan, such as a pension plan, profit-sharing plan, thrift or savings plan, supplemental executive retirement plans, and perhaps other kinds of plans or benefits intended primarily to provide capital accumulation or stock-purchase benefits. Naturally, assumptions must be made for a variety of factors if all these sources of retirement income are considered. Also, different assumptions as to employee earnings, year of retirement, final pay, years of service, and so forth may be used to test the adequacy of retirement income for employees under different conditions.

The same kind of analysis can be made for disability benefits from all sources under the employee benefit plan. When the analysis is made of disability benefits, it may be found that excessive benefits will be paid under certain conditions and for certain durations of disability, while inadequate benefits will be paid under other conditions. Thus, better coordination of disability benefits may be called for in making recommendations for changes in the plan. This approach also may prove fruitful for other employee loss exposures, such as death, medical expenses at various levels and under various conditions, long-term care (custodial care), and so forth. Finally, the adequacy of benefit levels can be tested for different categories of persons the employer may want to protect.

Another interesting kind of analysis in terms of benefit levels is to estimate the potential for capital accumulation available to employees under the various components of an employee benefit plan designed primarily for this purpose. These may include, for example, profit-sharing plans, thrift or savings plans, stock-purchase plans, stock options, employee stock ownership plans (ESOPs), and so forth. Employees often are pleasantly surprised to learn how much capital can be accumulated under such plans over a period even using relatively conservative investment assumptions.

In evaluating levels of benefits and benefit adequacy, consideration also may be given to optional benefits that may be available to employees under the employee benefit plan. Such options may involve the opportunity for employees to purchase coverage or additional levels of coverage beyond a basic level of benefits. Through such optional benefits, the employer in effect is giving employees the opportunity at a given cost to themselves to make their total benefits more adequate in certain specific areas. As an example, the life insurance plan shown in Figure 2–2 allows eligible employees to purchase additional life insurance at favorable group rates up to three times their base pay over and above the employer provided benefit of three times annual base pay (subject to certain individual underwriting requirements). Of course, an employer may extend the idea of optional benefits or employee choice-making even further by adopting a flexible benefits (cafeteria compensation) program as part of its employee benefit plan. This idea is discussed again in this chapter with regard to "Flexibility Available to Employees."

Probationary Periods

In assessing how well an existing employee benefit plan meets the needs and loss exposures of employees and certain other individuals, it also is helpful to analyze the probationary periods required for the various types of benefits contained in the plan. Such probationary periods, or the length of service otherwise eligible employees must have with the employer before they become eligible to participate in the various types of benefits, will have an effect on the plan's protection for employees, their dependents, and possibly others. The longer the probationary period required, the greater is the exposure of employees and others to a loss not covered by the plan. But, many employers believe only employees with certain minimum periods of service, and hence demonstrable connection with the employer, should be eligible for at least certain types of benefits.

Probationary periods by their nature create gaps in coverage for newly hired or newly eligible employees and their dependents. Thus, probationary periods should be analyzed as part of the functional approach to determine whether the resulting gaps in coverage are appropriate and consistent with the employer's objectives and the employees' needs.

It seems desirable that the use of probationary periods in an employee benefit plan should be based on a reasonably consistent employer philosophy. One possible philosophy in this regard is to divide employee benefits into "protection-oriented" benefits and "accumulation-oriented" benefits. *Protection-oriented* benefits would consist of medical expense benefits, life insurance benefits, short- and long-term disability benefits, and so forth. These benefits protect employees and their dependents against serious loss exposures which, if they were to occur, could spell immediate financial disaster for the employees or their dependents, or both. For such benefits, where the need/protection orientation is great, there might be no probationary period, or a relatively short probationary period. The rationale for this would be that the need for immediate coverage would overcome the traditional reasons for using probationary periods or longer probationary periods. *Accumulation-oriented* benefits, such as pension plans, profit-sharing plans, thrift plans, stock-bonus plans, stock-purchase plans, and so forth, could involve relatively long probationary periods if desired by the employer. The theory might be that these kinds of benefits should be a reward for relatively long service with the employer. Also, an employee who stays with the employer would have a relatively long time in which to accumulate such benefits, and thus longer probationary periods would not really place the employee at any serious disadvantage or risk.

Eligibility Requirements

Requirements for eligibility for benefits, including definitions of covered persons, obviously affect those who may benefit from or be protected by various employee benefits. In this area, for example, the employer and union—or unions—with whom the employer negotiates should consider such issues as

1. Which dependents of active employees (and perhaps dependents of retired former employees, disabled employees, and deceased employees—see 2, 3, 4, and 5 below) should or must be covered for medical expense benefits?

2. Should retirees (and perhaps their spouses and other dependents) continue to be covered and, if so, for what benefits?

3. Should survivors of deceased active employees continue to be covered and, if so, for what benefits and for how long?

4. Should survivors of retired former employees continue to be covered and, if so, for what benefits?

5. Should employees or former employees on disability (and perhaps their dependents) continue to be covered and, if so, for what benefits, how long, and under what conditions?

6. Should coverage be extended to employees during layoffs, leaves of absence, strikes, and other temporary interruptions of employment and, if so, for what benefits, how long, and under what conditions?

7. Should coverage be limited only to full-time employees (or employees meeting ERISA requirements) or should coverage or some coverage be extended to part-time employees as well?

8. What coverage should or must be continued or made available to persons after termination of their employment with the employer (or for the dependents of such persons) and on what basis?

The resolution of some of these issues depends in part on statutory or other legal requirements, insurance company underwriting rules, collective bargaining agreements, and similar factors. However, the philosophy or rationale of the employer and union concerning the employee benefit program will have a substantial impact on how some of these coverage and eligibility issues are resolved. At the heart of many of these issues is the basic question of how far an employer (or union) should feel obligated to go, either legally or morally—or possibly can afford to go—in meeting the various needs and loss exposures of its employees, their dependents, and persons who once were employees or dependents of employees but who now have various other relationships or no relationship with the employer.

Employee Contribution Requirements

If certain employee benefits under an employer's employee benefit plan are contributory (i.e., the employees or possibly their dependents must contribute to the cost of the benefit), this will have an impact on employee participation and hence on how well the plan meets the needs of the employee group as a whole. This really represents a trade-off: between the financing and other advantages of a contributory plan—and the loss of employee participation in the plan, which results from requiring employee contributions, assuming employee participation in the contributory plan is voluntary. Thus, an employer, and union if the plan is negotiated, may have to decide whether a particular employee benefit will be noncontributory or contributory, and, if it is to be contributory, how much the employees will have to contribute toward the cost of the plan. Further, if the plan is contributory, the employer (and union) will have to decide whether participation will be voluntary or mandatory as a condition of employment. Making a contributory plan mandatory solves the employee participation problem, but it may create serious employee relations problems. Therefore, most employers do not have mandatory contributory plans.

In the context of this cost/employee participation trade-off, one approach that can help planners strike an agreeable balance is to rank employee benefits in terms of the relative degree to which the employer feels that all employees and their dependents should be protected, and hence those benefits for which the plan should aim for 100 percent participation, compared with benefits for which such a high level of participation is not deemed essential. This same kind of analysis also might be helpful in determining the level of employee contribution if it is decided to have the plan be contributory. Another factor bearing on this decision is whether other benefits in the employer's overall plan also may be available to meet the same functional need. For example, employee benefit plans frequently contain a number of kinds of benefits intended to help provide retirement income for employees. Still another factor to consider is the extent to which employees or their dependents, or both, may have similar benefits available to them elsewhere. Those employees or dependents who have an alternative source of similar benefits may opt not to participate if the plan is made contributory, thereby helping to avoid duplication of benefits. An example of this is the availability of multiple plans of medical expense benefits when both a husband and wife are employed outside the home.

There is a tendency toward providing employees with alternative benefits or levels of benefits, with varying degrees of employee contributions (if any) required. In any event, as part of its benefit planning system, it will be helpful for an employer to make a benefit-by-benefit analysis, within the context of its overall benefit and compensation philosophy, to evaluate the desirability of any employee (and possibly dependent) contributions to the cost of the various employee benefits or levels of benefits.

Of course, to the extent that voluntary salary reduction (normally before-tax) is part of a flexible benefits (cafeteria compensation) plan, the covered employees themselves really are making the decision as to the level of their contributions (through salary reduction) to pay for the benefits they select within the scope of the plan. To this degree, the decision making regarding contributions into these plans is at least partly shifted to the covered employees, depending on the benefit options they select.

Flexibility Available to Employees

The degree to which employees have flexibility in making such choices as whether they will participate in a given employee benefit; the amounts of additional coverage they may wish to purchase; the opportunity to select from among two or more alternative plans of benefits; and even the opportunity to structure their own benefit program, as under a flexible benefits (cafeteria compensation) approach, clearly has an impact on the extent to which employees may tailor an employee benefit plan to meet their own needs and goals within the functional categories described previously. In fact, it may be argued that the more flexibility employees have, the more likely it is that the benefit program they select will meet their individual needs and goals. It thus can be argued, on the one hand, that flexibility in employee benefit plan design should facilitate the goals of the functional approach to employee benefit planning. On the other hand, it also can be argued that allowing too much employee flexibility in choosing types and amounts of employee benefits may work against the functional approach, because employees may misperceive or not understand their and their families' needs and hence leave some important needs uncovered. This concern often is addressed in employee benefit planning by limiting the choices of employees or by specifying a core of benefits that are not subject to employee choice.

A distinct trend exists toward giving employees more flexibility in the structuring of their own employee benefits. As discussed above, this trend probably buttresses the functional approach, in that it may be presumed that rational employees will opt for those benefits and benefit amounts that will best meet their individual needs and goals.

Actual Employee Participation in Benefit Plans

It was noted above that under the functional approach an employer may analyze the types of benefits provided to employees and their dependents according to the various functional categories. The employer also may estimate or project benefit levels for the benefits in the different categories under certain assumptions and given certain contingencies or events. However, these analyses and estimates of benefits and benefit levels may not completely show how well certain employee benefits actually reach a given employee group. Therefore, an employer also may want to calculate the actual participation ratios of its employees and their dependents for given employee benefit plans. These ratios can be calculated in terms of the employees (and their dependents) actually participating in the plan as a ratio of total full-time employees, as a ratio of total eligible employees, or as both.

A given employee benefit plan may have many good features, and may even be quite liberal in some respects; but if the ratio of employee participation is low, the particular benefit may not be meeting the employer's objectives in terms of its total compensation system.

Of course, if a given employee benefit is noncontributory, and if its eligibility requirements are reasonably liberal, all the eligible employees will be covered and, probably, a reasonably high percentage of total employees also will be covered. However, when employee benefit plans are contributory, or are optional benefits under a flexible benefits plan, and/or eligibility requirements are tighter, the participation ratios may drop significantly. When this is the case, an employer may wish to evaluate the reason(s) for the low participation and what steps, if any, it might take to increase participation in the particular plan or plans.

Determine Gaps in Benefits and Any Overlapping Benefits

From the preceding steps, it is possible to analyze more effectively any gaps in the employer's present employee benefit plan. These gaps may exist in terms of the benefits available from all sources in the plan to meet the various functional categories of employee needs, in terms of the projected levels of benefits for those needs, in terms of the coverage of the various categories of persons the employer may want to protect, and finally in terms of the actual participation of employees in the various components of the employee benefit plan. In a similar fashion, the employer will want to determine any overlapping benefits that presently may be provided from all sources in its employee benefit plan to meet certain categories of needs.

Consider Recommendations for Changes in Present Plan

As a result of the functional approach described here, the employer may consider various recommendations or alternative recommendations for changes in its present employee benefit plan to eliminate gaps in benefits or persons covered and to avoid any overlap in benefits. Part of this step may also involve consideration of adopting or modifying an existing flexible benefits (cafeteria compensation) plan to meet employee needs. Essentially, this step involves the consideration of alternatives, which is implicit in any decision-making system.

Estimate Costs (or Savings) for Each Recommendation

The cost or savings estimate is an important step before any recommendations for improvements, reductions, or changes in an employee benefit plan can be adopted. These estimates are based upon certain assumptions and may be expressed in terms of ranges of possible cost (or savings) results. An employer normally will have certain overall cost constraints on its employee benefit planning. Therefore, recommended improvements or changes in the plan may have to be assigned certain priorities in terms of which ones the employer can afford to adopt.

Evaluate Alternative Methods of Financing Benefits

This step involves the evaluation of how the recommended changes in benefits for the present plan or existing benefits in the present plan, or both, should be financed or secured. While this may not strictly involve the functional analysis of benefits in relation to needs, it is an essential step in analyzing any employee benefit plan.

Consider Other Cost-Saving or Cost-Containment Techniques

At this point, the employer also should consider other cost-saving techniques concerning its employee benefits. These may involve changes in benefit plan design, elimination or reduction of certain benefits, adoption or modification of a flexible benefits (cafeteria compensation) approach, use of alternative methods of financing certain benefits, changes in insurers or servicing organizations, changes in investment policies or advisors, the decision to self-fund or retain certain benefits as opposed to seeking insurance coverage, and other similar techniques. Again, while consideration of such techniques may not be directly involved in the functional analysis of an employee benefit plan, it is a logical step in the planning process once such a functional analysis is begun.

Decide on Appropriate Benefits and Financing Methods

Once the preceding analysis is complete, the employer or union is in a position to decide on the particular benefit recommendations it wants to adopt or bargain for. The employer also may decide on appropriate financing methods. This is essentially the selection of the best alternative or alternatives in the decision-making process.

Implement Any Changes

This step involves the implementation of the changes or recommendations decided on above. It is the implementation phase of the decision-making process.

Communicate Benefit Changes to Employees

The effective communication of employee benefits and changes in such benefits is a vital element in the overall success of any employee benefit plan. It often is a neglected element. An employer may go to a great deal of time, trouble, and expense in making improvements in its employee benefit plan, but all this effort and cost may not be as effective as it could be in terms of good employee relations and meeting the employer's personnel policies if the improvements are not effectively communicated to the employees.

Many employers communicate periodically to employees the current overall status and value of their employee benefits. This frequently is done annually. Such a communication concerning the status and total value of an employee's benefits may be accomplished at least in part by using categories of benefits similar to those classified in the functional approach described above. See Part 11 (Employee Benefit Plan Communication) of the *Handbook* for a more detailed discussion of communications.

Periodically Reevaluate the Plan

Employee benefit planning is a task that is never complete. Concepts of employee needs, the benefits available to meet those needs, and how those benefits should be made available to employees, are constantly changing. Therefore, the employee benefit plan must be constantly reevaluated and updated.

CHAPTER 3

RISK CONCEPTS AND EMPLOYEE BENEFIT PLANNING

Gary K. Stone

RISK AND EMPLOYEE BENEFITS

Definition of Risk

The concept of risk is fundamental in any discussion of employee benefit planning. For our purposes risk will mean *uncertainty* with respect to possible *loss*. In other words, it is the inability to determine a future loss and to figure out how expensive it will be should the loss take place. For example, individuals have very little ability to know when they will die, become ill or unemployed, or if they will reach old age. All the typical potential losses associated with employee benefits are ''risks'' from the standpoint of the individual. *Loss* is meant to convey any decrease in value suffered. A hospital bill associated with an illness could result in a loss because it would cause a decrease in the value of assets held by a person.

Peril and Hazard Distinguished from Risk

The concept of risk is different from the concepts of peril and hazard, but the three do have an interrelationship. Peril and hazard are primarily insurance terms, used particularly in property and liability insurance but also in life and health insurance. They also have considerable application in employee benefit planning.

A peril is defined as the cause of some occasion of personal or property loss, destruction, or damage. Common perils involving property are fires, floods, earthquakes, thefts, and burglaries. These same perils also can cause personal harm. Other perils that cause personal losses are illnesses, bodily injuries, and death. A number of insurance policies are identified by the perils covered. Life insurance and health policies, obviously, are an exception. Actually they originally were called death insurance policies and accident and sickness policies, but their names were changed for euphemistic and marketing reasons.

A hazard is a condition that either increases the probability that a peril will occur or that tends to increase the loss when a peril has struck. The three basic types of hazards are designated as physical hazards, moral hazards, and morale hazards.

Physical hazards are physical conditions that fit within the definition of hazard. In the workplace there can be numerous physical hazards—for example, the presence of flammable materials and absence of fire extinguishing equipment, machines without appropriate safety devices, and faulty heating and air conditioning units.

Dishonest, unethical, and immoral people are moral hazards. Unfortunately, some employees qualify as moral hazards. The category includes those who steal from the employer, purposely damage firm property, file fraudulent medical claims, abuse sick leave and personal time off, or file false overtime and expense statements.

Morale hazards exist when people act with carelessness or indifference. Some individuals appear to be accident- or disaster-prone and, as such, are morale hazards. On the other hand, specific morale hazards include the failure to lock rooms, vaults, or areas from which valuable items are stolen; forgetting to notify the employer of faulty materials that ultimately cause personal injuries to a handler; or ignoring the fact that a number of employees all experience the same symptoms of physical discomfort, which ultimately can be traced to a job-related cause.

Types of Risk

Risk can be classified into many categories depending upon the use of the term. For the purposes of this chapter, a simple classification is used. Risk is divided into two types or classes, (1) pure risk and (2) speculative risk.

Pure risk is risk in which only two alternatives are possible: (1) Either the risk will *not* happen (no financial loss); or (2) It *will* happen, and a financial loss takes place. Nothing positive can result from a pure risk. An example is illness. The best thing that can happen is that a person does not become ill. If a person does become ill, a negative result takes place. Many examples of pure risk are available. The risks of loss from fire, auto accidents, illness, unemployment, disability, theft of property, and earthquake all would be pure risks. Many of the risks covered by employee benefits fall into this classification. Pure risks for the most part can be insured.

Speculative risk inserts another possibility not existing in pure risk. The additional alternative is the possibility of a gain. Speculative risks then would have three potential outcomes: (1) a loss, (2) no loss, and (3) a gain. Examples of speculative risk would be the purchase of a share of common stock, acquiring a new business venture, or gambling. The emphasis of this chapter is on pure risk rather than speculative risk.

Pure Risk

Pure risk can be subclassified depending upon the type of financial loss. The three classifications of pure risk are

1. Personal risk.
2. Property risk.
3. Legal liability risk.

The most important classification of pure risk from an employee benefit standpoint is personal risk. Personal risks are losses that have a direct impact on an individual's life or health. Many risks involving employee benefit plans fall into the category of personal risk. Death, illness, accidents, unemployment, and old age would all be considered to be personal losses. This type of risk can be measured with some degree of accuracy. It is difficult to be precise, but by estimating potential lost income from a particular risk and the medical and other costs associated with it, one can approximate the potential loss. With that information one can estimate needed protection and seek insurance or whatever other risk-handling measure is appropriate.

Property risks are the uncertainty (possible loss) that decreases the value of one's real or personal property. Fire, flood, earthquake, wind, theft, and automobile collisions all are examples of types of property risks. The home, furniture, cars, and jewelry would be the types of property subject to possible loss. Legal liability risk is a loss resulting from negligent actions of a person that result in injury to another person. It stems from lawsuits by the injured party seeking damages from the negligent party. Common sources of legal liability would be negligent behavior associated with automobiles, one's home or business, the sale of products, or professional misconduct (malpractice). A serious difficulty connected with liability risk is that it has an unlimited potential loss. The dollar impact of this risk is a function of the seriousness of the negligence and the status of the parties involved. Malpractice awards against physicians or arising from automobile accidents are examples in which potential losses can run into the millions of dollars.

As previously noted, employee benefit plans deal substantially with personal risks. The magnitude of life insurance, medical expense, disability income, retirement, and other personal risk-oriented benefit plans reflect this. However, property and liability risk coverage also can be found in a number of plans. For example, homeowner's insurance, automobile insurance, and group legal services and financial planning services all are examples of property and liability risk coverages available through employee benefit plans. Nevertheless, there is a considerably greater emphasis on personal risk coverages, and there are important factors that explain why benefit plans are less likely to include various property and liability coverages.

Methods of Handling Risk

There are several methods of handling risk. Although the main focus of this chapter is on the use of some type of insurance method to handle the risks associated with benefit plans, it should be recognized that other alternatives are available and are used. The primary risk-handling alternatives are

1. Avoidance.
2. Control.
3. Retention.
4. Transfer.
5. Insurance.

Avoidance

Avoidance is a perfect device for handling risk. It means one does not acquire the risk to begin with and hence would not be subject to the risk.

For example, if a person does not want the risk associated with driving automobiles, he or she won't drive a car. The problem with avoidance is that many times one cannot help but have the risk (the nondriver as a pedestrian or passenger still is exposed to the risk of other persons' driving), or one does not want to avoid it. For risks covered by employee benefits, it is almost impossible to use the avoidance technique. How does one avoid the risk of death or illness? The point is that one is unable to avoid some risks. Attention, then, must be focused on the other alternatives.

Control

Control is a mechanism by which one attempts either to prevent or reduce the probability of a loss taking place, or to reduce the severity of the loss after it has taken place. Many examples of control devices exist. Smoke detectors, fire-resistant building materials, seat belts, air bags, and crash-resistant bumpers on autos, nonsmoking office buildings, physical examinations, and proper diets would be considered control devices.

Employee benefit plans can use control in conjunction with other risk-handling techniques such as insurance. Any procedure used to reduce or prevent accidents, illnesses, or premature death would help in lowering the cost of most benefit plans. It is not unusual for employers to adopt accident-prevention programs, wellness programs, a smoke-free environment at work, and other programs with the intent of lowering workers' compensation and other employee benefit costs.

Retention

Retention means that the risk is assumed and paid for by the person suffering the loss. Assumption or retention can be used with losses that are small in terms of their financial impact on a person or company. The cost of insurance or some other risk-handling device could be higher than paying for such a loss when it happens, and some losses can be handled more efficiently simply by paying for them as they occur. For example, assume you have an old automobile worth $600. Collision insurance with a typical deductible of $250 would give you only a $350 recovery upon a total loss. In other words, the cost of the insurance plus the deductible could be higher than the value of the loss. In such cases, it may be more economical to retain the risk than to insure it. One has to be careful with retention in that it should be used only with the types of loss that will not cause a financial disaster. Retaining or assuming risks with high severity potential can result in financial catastrophe. It should not be assumed that because a loss is unlikely to happen (low probability), it could or should be retained. The crucial factor is the financial result (severity) if it does take place. A fire that destroys one's home is unlikely, but it is devastating if it happens.

Retention can be a useful tool in handling employee benefit plans. An employer (insured) might decide to retain the first $1,000 of employee medical costs, by purchasing an insurance plan with a $1,000 deductible. Another use of retention can be found in the administration of benefit plans. Employers can take over many of the administrative duties of the insurance company. Payroll deduction, claims administration, answering questions of plan members, and filing of forms sometimes can be done more efficiently by the insured than the insurance company, and by carrying out these functions itself, an employer may be able to lower its direct dollar outlay. However, this form of retention should be examined carefully before being adopted, as the administrative burden and other negative factors may outweigh any potential savings.

Transfer

Transfer is a concept in which one switches or shifts the financial burden of risk to another party. Two forms of transfer usually are recognized. They are (1) insurance, which is covered in the next section of this chapter, and (2) noninsurance transfers, which can take place in many different forms. For example, a landlord may require new tenants to pay extra money up front as a security deposit for potential damage to the premises. This would be a form of transfer. The landlord would be transferring his or her possible loss to the tenant. Another example involves travel agents. A client may want to travel to the Middle East during a time of potential military conflict. The travel agent suggests avoiding the area. The client insists upon taking the trip, but the travel agent has the client sign a form waiving legal claims against the travel agent for dissatisfaction with a trip that the travel agent has recommended against. The hope is that if a lawsuit develops, the travel agent can assert that the traveler took the responsibility for the burden of any loss upon himself.

Employee benefit plans use transfer extensively but it usually is in the form of insurance contracts. Noninsurance transfers typically do not lend themselves as risk-handling mechanisms in benefit plans.

Insurance

Insurance is a common method of financing employee benefits. The definition of insurance varies slightly depending upon the source. However, for purposes of this chapter, insurance generally may be defined as

> A device for reducing risk by combining a sufficient number of exposure units to make their individual losses collectively predictable. The predictable loss is then shared by or distributed proportionately among all units in combination.[1]

This definition includes two elements essential for insurance. They are (1) reducing of risk (uncertainty with respect to possible loss) and (2) sharing of the loss by the members of the combination. From the standpoint of an employee benefit plan, insurance would be a mechanism in which the insured (employer/employee) would pay money (premiums) into a fund (insurance company). Upon the occurrence of a loss, reimbursement would be provided to the person suffering the loss. Thus, the risk has been reduced or eliminated for the insured, and all the individuals who paid into the fund share the resulting loss.

Insurance is but one method by which an employee benefit plan may be financed. Large benefit plans may rely on insurance, self-funding and various combinations of the two. However, many small- to medium-size firms rely almost exclusively on the insurance mechanism.

Before continuing with the discussion of insurance, it is important to clarify the difference between insurance and gambling. Since both insurance and gambling have a relationship to risk, they sometimes are viewed erroneously as essentially the same. However, there are several important features of insurance that distinguish it from gambling. First, insurance is a mechanism for *handling an existing risk*, whereas gambling *creates* a risk where one did not previously exist. Insurance may be purchased to deal with the risk of illness; however, the outcome of a sports event is financially meaningless to the typical fan until he or she bets on the final score. Second, the risk created by gambling is a speculative risk, whereas insurance deals with pure risks. Third, gambling involves a gain for one party, the winner, at the expense of another, the loser, whereas insurance is based on a mutual sharing of any losses

---

[1]Robert I. Mehr, *Fundamentals of Insurance*, 2nd ed. (Homewood, Ill.: Richard D. Irwin, Inc., 1986), p. 38.

that occur. Fourth, the loser in a gambling transaction remains in that negative situation, whereas an insured who suffers a loss is financially restored in whole or in part to his or her original situation. Obviously the insurance-gambling discussion is more appropriate to individual, rather than group insurance, but the comparison also has some applicability to the group mechanism.

Additionally, the use of insurance to make the victims of losses whole reflects the principle of indemnification on which insurance is structured. An insured is indemnified if a covered loss occurs. That is, he or she is placed somewhat in the same situation that existed prior to the loss, e.g., by reimbursement for damaged property or medical bills, disability income, and the like.

Summary of Risk-Handling Alternatives

It is possible to use a number of alternatives in the design of employee benefit plans. One or more of the alternatives in some combination is common. The one alternative that is mutually exclusive of the others is avoidance. If you avoid the risk, you are not subjected to potential losses, so that no need exists for insurance, loss control, or any other risk-handling technique. The remaining alternatives, however, could be used in combination.

Assume a typical medical benefit plan for a firm's employees. The firm might purchase a medical insurance plan with a deductible of $500 per year per covered member. The plan is insured, and so transfer has been used. In addition, someone must pay the $500 deductible, so there is retention or assumption of part of the risk. Further, assume that the firm is interested in keeping the cost of medical benefits down. It may initiate a number of control devices such as a smoke-free work environment and an accident-prevention program to aid the effort. Thus, a number of the risk-handling alternatives are used together.

What factors should be considered in deciding upon the "best-"method of handling the risk of a particular benefit plan? In general, one should consider the most economical from a financial standpoint, but with proper consideration given to employee welfare. What is being suggested is that there is nothing wrong with opting for the lowest-cost alternative as long as proper consideration is given to the nonfinancial aspects of the employees' welfare. Failing to put a guard on a machine to prevent injury is generally unacceptable even if it might cost less to let the accident take place. Firms must consider employee welfare in evaluating the alternatives for handling risk.

INSURANCE AND INSURABLE RISK

Insurance is one of the most popular methods of funding employee benefit plans, but, as explained in later chapters of the *Handbook*, many other options exist. The advantages and disadvantages of using insurance in the design of a benefit plan are discussed in the next section.

Advantages of Insurance

A number of reasons account for why insurance can be used effectively in an employee benefit plan. One advantage is the known premium (cost); it is set in advance by the insurance company. The employer may have better control over its budget with a known premium because any high shock losses would be the problem of the insurance company and not the insured. Having an outside administrator also can be an advantage to the employer. The employer does not have to get involved in disputes involving employees over coverage of the plan, because these would be handled by the insurance company. Employees may prefer insurance to some other form of funding in order to obtain the financial backing of an outside financial institution. This, of course, depends upon the financial strength of the insurance company selected, and care should go into this choice. Insurance companies often are leaders in the area of loss control, and may well help in the design and implementation of systems designed to control costs for the employer. A final advantage is that it may be more economical for an employer to use insurance than other alternatives. The insurance company may be more efficient and able to do the job at a lower total cost than another method.

Disadvantages of Insurance

Insurance is not always the preferred method of funding employee benefit plans. A number of costs are involved that must be considered. Insurance companies charge administrative expenses that are added to the premium (or loaded) to compensate for their overhead expenses. Home office costs, licensing costs, commissions, taxes, loss-adjustment expenses, and the like all must go into the loading. One must realize that the premium covers not only direct losses but the insurance company's overhead as well. The amount may vary from a small percent of the premium (e.g., 2–5 percent) to potentially a very high amount (25 percent or more) depending on the type of contract involved. Another potential disadvantage is that employer satisfaction is directly affected by the claims and problem-solving abilities of the insurer. Slow payment or restrictive claim practices can have an adverse affect on employees.

Whether something is an advantage or disadvantage often depends upon the specific insurance company involved. It is important to use care in the selection of an insurer. Checking out the insurer with other clients and carefully analyzing the carrier's financial stability are critical elements in the selection process.

Characteristics of an Insurable Risk

It often is said that anything can be insured if one is willing to pay the premium required. Insurance companies, however, normally will insure a risk only if it meets certain standards. These standards or prerequisites are needed for an insurer to manage the company in a sound financial manner. Without suitable risks, an insurance company can find itself in serious financial trouble. An insurance company is subject to the same problems as any other business—inadequate capitalization, a weak investment portfolio, poor management—that can create financial problems. Insurance companies have the additional problem of insuring risks that could result in catastrophic losses.

The following is a list of the characteristics of a risk that are desired in order for it to be considered an "insurable risk":

1. There should be a large number of homogeneous risks (exposure units).
2. The loss should be verifiable and measurable.
3. The loss should not be catastrophic in nature.
4. The chance of loss should be subject to calculation.
5. The premium should be reasonable or economically feasible.
6. The loss should be accidental from the standpoint of the insured.

It should be noted that this list is what is considered ideal from the standpoint of the insurance company. Most risks are not perfect in all aspects, and insurance companies have to weigh all aspects of a risk to determine if overall it meets the criteria of an insurable risk.

Large Number of Homogeneous Risks

The insurance company must be able to calculate the number of losses it will incur from the total number of risks it insures. Assume that a life insurance company has just been formed and it is to insure its first two people. Each wants $100,000 of life insurance. The company needs to know what the chance of dying for each of the two people would be in order to calculate a premium. Without this information, the company will have no idea of whether these people will live or die during the policy period. Should both die during this period, $200,000 would be needed for the claims. If neither dies, the company would need nothing for the claims. The conclusion one reaches is that the premium should be somewhere between 0 and $200,000. This information is not very helpful, and the insurance company could not insure the risk. What is needed is a large number of similar risks so that statistics can be developed to determine an accurate probability of loss for each risk being evaluated. Insurance is based on the *law of the large numbers,* which means that the greater the number of exposures, the more closely the actual results will approach the probable results that are expected from an infinite member of exposures. For example, life insurance companies have accumulated information over the years that enable them to develop mortality tables that reflect the expected mortality for a given type of risk. They are able to do this because of the large number of lives that have been insured over the years. Medical, dental, disability, and life risks all require large numbers of cases to determine proper premium rates.

Employee benefit plans may or may not have the numbers needed to determine loss expectations accurately. This would depend upon the specific plan. Those plans with large numbers of homogeneous risks can be experience rated. This means the premiums will be calculated with the data from the plan experience itself. Smaller plans would not have an adequate number of risks, and other alternatives would be needed. For example, small plans can be combined with other small plans to get creditable statistics, or insurance companies might ignore small-plan statistics and rely on loss statistics developed independently of the plan.

Verifiable and Measurable Losses

It is important that an insurance company be able to verify a loss and to determine the financial loss involved. Certain risks pose no problem in determining if a loss has taken place. Examples would be fire and windstorm losses with a home or a collision loss with one's auto. Furthermore, the financial value of these losses can be determined accurately by the use of appraisals and other forms of valuation. Other risks are harder to evaluate. An example is a claim for theft of money from a home. Did the theft take place? Did the person have any money at home to be stolen? With risks that are difficult to evaluate, the insurance company has to take other precautions to protect itself from false and inflated claims.

Employee benefits are subject to the same types of problems. Death claims and retirement benefit claims probably would be the easiest in which to determine whether a loss has taken place or not. Once a death claim is verified, the amount of loss is normally the face value of the insurance contract. Few problems result from death claims. The same would be true of retirement benefits. Assuming the age of the retiree can be verified, then the benefit promised by the plan will be paid. The other extreme might be disability income claims. In some situations, an insurer might be uncertain whether a valid claim exists or not. Some disability losses, such as back injuries, are very difficult to determine. Is the insured actually disabled or not? Still other employee benefit losses may fall between these two extremes. Medical and dental losses might fall into this category. When an employee benefit loss is difficult to verify or measure, the insurer may attempt to overcome the problem through one or more of several methods. Policy provisions are helpful in such situations. Benefit maximums, waiting periods, pre-existing conditions clauses, alternate medical verification, required second opinion on certain surgical procedures, and hospital stay monitoring are a few of the provisions which help in these situations.

Loss Should Not be Catastrophic in Nature

A serious problem occurs when a large percentage of the risks insured can be lost from the same event. Assume a fire insurance company insured all of its risks in one geographical location. A serious fire could result in catastrophic losses to the company. This did happen in the early history of fire insurance. Fires in London, Chicago, Baltimore, and San Francisco resulted in insurance company bankruptcies and loss of confidence in the industry. It became obvious that a geographic spread of the risks insured was essential because a concentration of losses from one event could seriously impair or even bankrupt a company. Cases exist in which it is almost impossible to obtain a spread of the risks. In such cases, insurance becomes difficult or impossible to obtain. Flood and unemployment losses would be examples. Unemployment can cover wide geographic areas, and a geographic spread would not help prevent a catastrophic loss. The same could be true for flood losses. The federal or state government might insure this type of risk, but it wouldbe necessary for it to subsidize the premium rates to make them affordable.

Employee benefits are seldom subject to problems relating to inability to get a geographic spread of the risk. Benefit plans often insure life risks, hospital and dental risks, and disability income losses. For the most part, these type of risks are not subject to catastrophic loss due to geographic location, but examples can be imagined in which catastrophic losses might exist. The possibility of a plant explosion or a poison gas leak causing a large number of deaths or medical losses, or a concentration of certain diseases because of the exposure to certain elements that are indigenous to a specific employee group theoretically exist. Usually, however, this is not an important consideration in underwriting typical benefit plans. Policy limitations, reinsurance, and restrictions on groups insured all can be used to minimize the problem to the extent it exists.

Premium Subject to Calculation

For an insurance company to be able to calculate a premium that is reasonable to the insured and that represents the losses of a particular risk, certain information is essential. Both the frequency of losses and the severity of the losses must be available to determine the loss portion of the premium. This often is referred to as the ''pure premium'' portion of the premium. Essential to the pure premium calculation would be a large number of homogeneous exposure units as previously discussed. If an employer is large enough, the plan losses alone could be used to determine the pure premium portion. The meaning of ''large'' depends upon the type of risk involved. At least several hundred employees probably would be needed for full reliance upon the data.

Premium Should Be Reasonable or Economical

For an employee benefit plan to be acceptable to an employer and to employees, the plan must have a premium that is considered reasonable relative to the risk being insured; that is, the insured must be able to pay the premium. An insurance company's expenses not related to the losses covered by the pure premium must be added to that premium to obtain the total premium. The expense portion may be referred to as the "loading" associated with the risk. The "pure premium" plus the "loading" would make up the total premium to be paid by the plan. Employees who pay a part or all of the premium (participating plan) will not participate if they can obtain a lower premium in an individual insurance plan or if they can be insured through a spouse's plan at a lower cost, and the employer will be unable or unwilling to pay the premium if the rate is not reasonable.

Why would a premium be noncompetitive? This could happen for any number of reasons. For example, a plan could be populated by a high number of older employees. The resulting rate may mean that the younger employees can find lower-cost insurance outside of the plan. The younger employees are unwilling to subsidize the rates for the older employees. Also, the employer may not want to pay the needed premiums. Other reasons for noncompetitive plans could be poor loss experience from a high number of sick and disabled in a plan, or a plan having specific benefits that have resulted in high loss payout. For example, a plan may provide unlimited benefits for drug- or alcohol-related sickness or mental disorders, and the plan member makeup may have resulted in heavy payout for these problems. The bottom line is that the resulting loss experience has made the plan noncompetitive. It is not unusual for an employee group initially to pay a rate that is considered reasonable only to have the plan premiums become unreasonable over time. Failure to keep the average age of the members in the plan low or a higher incidence of illness could be the reason.

The employer must keep track of the factors contributing to premium increases. Inflation related to medical benefits has in recent years resulted in plan costs increasing beyond the regular cost-of-living index. Constant review of benefits, benefit levels, employees covered by the plan and competitive rates for alternative plans must take place. It has become common for plans to move away from "first dollar" medical benefits and to incorporate deductibles, waiting periods, and other cost saving features. Also, it is not uncommon for plans to limit or eliminate coverage for drug abuse and mental disorders. An obvious factor to review is the cost of alternative plans. Would it be financially sound to use an alternative insurance plan or an alternative method of delivering the benefits, such as a health maintenance organization (HMO) or a preferred provider organization (PPO)?

The Losses Should Be Accidental from the Standpoint of the Insured

This problem can be serious in some forms of insurance, such as property and liability coverage, but is of less importance in the life and health areas of employee benefits. The insurance company does not want to pay for a loss if it is intentionally caused by the insured. It is obvious that payment should not be made if one intentionally destroys his or her home by arson or purposely wrecks an automobile.

An employee could intentionally cause a personal loss, but it would mean causing harm to himself or herself. For example, suicide or attempted suicide could result in death or medical claims. This type of problem can be reduced or eliminated by policy provisions restricting benefits in some manner if it is felt necessary. Determining whether a loss is accidental normally is not a problem in life, medical, and disability claims.

Insurable Risk Summary

Insurance companies consider providing insurance to employee benefit plans if they meet the minimum standards of an insurable risk. Benefit plans in general fit the minimum standards as set forth above. Such plans would include life insurance, medical and dental insurance, disability income, and retirement programs. Policy provisions, benefit restrictions, and reinsurance can be used to help alleviate problems to the extent they exist. Life insurance probably is the best example of a plan that meets all the desirable standards of an insurable risk. Disability income, although normally insurable, creates more of a problem from an insurability standpoint. Although not a common employee benefit, excess unemployment insurance would be a benefit that borders on being uninsurable.

Handling Adverse Selection

Adverse selection is the phenomenon in the insurance mechanism whereby individuals who have higher-than-average potentially insurable risks "select against" the insurer. That is, those with the greater probabilities of loss, and who therefore need insurance more than the average insured, attempt to obtain the coverage. For example, people who need hospitalization or surgical coverage seek to purchase medical insurance, those who own property subject to possible loss by fire or flood obtain insurance, and individuals who own valuable jewelry or objects of art purchase appropriate coverages. This tendency can result in a disproportionate number of insureds who experience losses that are greater than those anticipated. Thus the actual losses can be greater than the expected losses. Because adverse selection is of concern to insurers for both individual and group contracts, certain safeguards are used in each case to prevent it from happening.

Under a block of individual insurance contracts, the desirable situation for an insurance company is to have a spread of risks throughout a range of acceptable insureds. The so-called spread ideally will include some risks that are higher and some that are lower than the average risk within the range. Insurers attempt to control adverse selection by the use of sophisticated underwriting methods used to select and classify applicants for insurance and by supportive policy provisions such as preexisting-conditions clauses in medical expense policies, suicide clauses in life insurance policies, and the exclusion of certain types of losses under homeowners policies.

The management of adverse selection under group insurance contracts necessarily is different from the approach used in individual insurance. Group insurance is based on the group as a unit, and, typically, individual insurance eligibility requirements are not used for the group insurance underwriting used in employee benefit plans. As an alternative, the group technique itself is used to control the problem of adverse selection. The characteristics of the group technique are covered in Chapter 1 of the *Handbook* in the discussion of the factors that have contributed to the development of employee benefits, and again in Chapter 8 in the context of its application to group life insurance contracts.

Self-Funding/Self-Insurance

Self-funding, or self-insurance, is a common method of providing financing for employee benefit plans. Essentially this means that the organization is retaining the risk. It is important to realize, however, that many of the activities performed by the insurance company under an insured plan still have to be done. The identical problems associated with insurable risks for an insurance company exist for the firm that is self-funding or self-insuring. Therefore, the characteristics of an ideally insurable risk would be just as important for those firms that use self-funding as they are for an insurance company. The mechanism used for funding is not directly related to the question of whether a risk is a good one to include in the benefit plan. One should realize that only large firms with many employees would be able to meet all the characteristics of the ideally insurable risk. It is not uncommon to find that firms that say they self-fund or self-insure have, in fact, some arrangement with an insurance company or companies to insure part or all of a particular benefit. Many firms use insurance to provide backup coverage for catastrophic losses or coverage for losses the firm feels cannot be self-funded. The self-funded or self-insured plan has most of the characteristics found in the definition of insurance and has many of the same problems.

SUMMARY

Risk may be defined as uncertainty with respect to future loss or decrease in financial value. A common manner of classification of risk is into either pure or speculative risk. The difference between the two types is that speculative risk has the possibility of gain associated with it as well as loss. Pure risk on the other hand involves only the possibility of loss. Insurance is designed to handle pure risk but not speculative risk. Most employee benefit plans involve pure risk, so it is not uncommon to find these plans funded with insurance.

Pure risk can be classified as property, liability, or personal risk. Personal risk was the focus of this chapter and would include any loss suffered directly to a person, such as death, disability, illness, unemployment, or old age. Many risk-handling methods are used to solve the problems connected with the uncertainty of risk. Avoidance, retention, control, noninsurance transfer, and insurance are typical methods. Employee benefit plans often use a combination of methods such as control, retention, and insurance.

Insurance is a mechanism by which one's risk (uncertainty) can be handled by transferring the risk to a third party called the insurance company. Although insurance is a popular risk handling device, it is not appropriate for all risks. Insurance companies desire that the risk have certain characteristics. The risk must have a large number of similar exposure units, the loss should be able to be verified and measured, the risk should not be subject to catastrophic loss, the premium should be able to be calculated, the premium should be reasonable, and the loss should be accidental from the standpoint of the insured. Fortunately, most employee benefit plans cover insurable risks, and so insurance is a feasible solution. Life risks are very good from a desirable-risk standpoint, with unemployment being poor as an insurable risk for private insurance companies.

The functional approach to planning employee benefits (Chapter 2) considers the factors discussed in this chapter. Risk alternatives, characteristics of insurable risks, and types of risk all are important concepts in developing an employee benefit plan, and failure to consider these factors could result in eventual failure of the plan itself.

CHAPTER 4

REGULATORY ENVIRONMENT OF EMPLOYEE BENEFIT PLANS

Dallas L. Salisbury

The regulatory environment of employee benefit plans has changed dramatically over the past 50 years. Major legislation was passed in 1942, 1958, and 1974, with a continuous flow of legislation, regulations, and rulings from then until the recent passage of the 1991 federal budget. The combined effect of these laws and rules has been to make the administration of employee benefit plans increasingly complex.

This chapter briefly reviews the regulatory environment for private pension and welfare plans; insurance programs; federal, state, and local government pension plans; and disability programs. It is intended to heighten awareness of the complexity of the regulatory environment.

The chapter is not intended to provide legal guidance or to be a guide to compliance. Many of the issues touched upon here are explained more fully in subsequent *Handbook* chapters, and there are several ''loose-leaf'' services available that should be consulted to keep abreast of the constant changes taking place.

PRIVATE PENSION AND WELFARE PLANS

Pre-ERISA

Before the enactment of the Employee Retirement Income Security Act (ERISA) on Labor Day 1974, only three principal statutes governed private pension plans: the Internal Revenue Code (IRC), the Federal Welfare and Pension Plans Disclosure Act of 1958 (WPPDA), and the Taft-Hartley Act, more formally known as the Labor Management Relations Act of 1947. The latter regulated collectively bargained multiemployer pension plans.

Amendments to the Internal Revenue Code enacted in 1942 established standards for the design and operation of pension plans. The principal purposes were to prevent plans from discriminating or disproportionately benefiting one group of employees over another and to prevent plans from taking excessive or unjustified tax deductions. Until 1974, the Internal Revenue Service was not concerned with the actuarial soundness of plans.

The Federal Welfare and Pension Plans Disclosure Act of 1958 was enacted to protect plan assets against fraudulent behavior by the plan administrator. The act mandated that, upon request, participants concerned with plan malpractice would be provided with information concerning the plan. If misuse or fraud were suspected, it was up to the participant to bring charges against the administrator. A significant amendment to the WPPDA was enacted in 1962. That amendment authorized the Department of Justice to bring appropriate legal action to protect plan participants' interests and authorized the Department of Labor to interpret and enforce the Act. For the first time, the burden of plan asset protection was placed upon the government rather than the individual participants.

Employee Retirement Income Security Act of 1974 (ERISA)

The shift to government protection of participants' rights enacted in 1962 would carry through to ERISA. It reflected a concern for workers, which was confirmed by President John Kennedy in 1962 with appointment of the Committee on Corporate Pension Funds and Other Retirement and Welfare Programs. That committee issued its report in 1965, concluding that private pension plans should continue as a major element in the nation's total retirement security program. The report advocated many changes in the breadth of private plan regulation.

The report received widespread attention and led to the introduction of a number of legislative proposals. Congress concluded that most plans were operated for the benefit of participants on a sound basis, but some were not. To solve this problem, Congress enacted ERISA. ERISA governs every aspect of private pension and welfare plans and requires employers who sponsor plans to operate them in compliance with ERISA standards.

TITLE I: PROTECTION OF EMPLOYEE BENEFIT RIGHTS

Title I of ERISA placed primary jurisdiction over reporting, disclosure, and fiduciary matters in the Department of Labor. The Department of the Treasury is given primary jurisdiction over participation, vesting, and funding. During the first years of ERISA, this ''dual-jurisdiction'' led to a number of problems, which were addressed in 1979 by Reorganization Plan Number 4, discussed in a later part of this chapter. As a result of reorganizations and administrative experience under ERISA, many requirements have been adjusted, resulting in a reduction of regulatory burdens.

Reporting and Disclosure

Plan sponsors are required to provide plan participants with summary plan descriptions and benefit statements. They also are provided access to plan financial information. Documents provided to participants are to be written in ''plain English'' so they can be easily understood.

Plan sponsors file an annual financial report (Form 5500 series) with the IRS, which is made available to other agencies. In addition, plan sponsors must file amendments when modifications to the plan are made. Taken together, these provisions seek to assure that the government has accurate information on employer-sponsored plans.

Fiduciary Requirements

Plan sponsors are subject to an ERISA fiduciary standard mandating the plan be operated solely for the benefit of plan participants. The fiduciary standard, or ''prudent man standard,'' requires the plan fiduciary perform duties solely in the interest of plan participants with the care a prudent person acting under like circumstances would use. This means any person who exercises discretion in the management and maintenance of the plan or in the investment of the plan assets must do so in the interest of the plan participants and beneficiaries, in accordance with the plan documents, and in a manner that minimizes the risk of loss to the participant. The standard applies to plan sponsors, trustees, and cofiduciaries, and to investment advisers with discretionary authority over the purchase and sale of plan securities. Underlying the standard are prohibitions against business or investment transactions between the plan and fiduciaries or interested parties. Upon violation of the prohibitions, the fiduciary may be held personally liable to the plan for any misuse, fraud, or mismanagement. Exemptions can be applied for when parties feel that actions are not to the detriment of the plan and its participants and should be allowed. Both the IRS and the Department of Labor are responsible for enforcing the fiduciary standards. The Department of Labor may file charges on behalf of the participants if the fiduciary has breached or violated the standards imposed by ERISA. The IRS may fine the employer and revoke the plan's favorable tax treatment. Both civil and criminal actions may arise for violations.

TITLE II: MINIMUM STANDARDS

Title II of ERISA contains minimum standards for participation, vesting, and funding of benefits, which must be satisfied for qualification of a plan. It also contains amendments to the IRC that increase the scope of federal regulation over certain pension plans, whether tax qualified or not.

Participation

Although ERISA (as amended) does not require every employer to set up an employer pension or welfare benefit plan, it does impose requirements on those who do. For those employers sponsoring plans, the age of employee eligibility cannot be higher than 21. A maximum of one year of service and 1,000 hours of work also may be required for eligibility.

Vesting

Upon satisfying the participation requirements, further conditions must be met for the participant to become entitled to receive a benefit—that is, to have a vested right to the benefits. There are two alternative vesting requirements contained in ERISA (as amended).

- Full vesting after five years of service, with no vesting before the five-year requirement is met.
- Graduated vesting from the time the participant completes three years of service (full vesting after seven years).

Benefits

Under ERISA, benefits generally must be earned in a uniform manner while the participant is employed. This does not affect the levels of benefits provided by the plan, only the rate at which the benefits are earned.

Funding

The minimum funding standards attempt to ensure that plans will have sufficient assets to pay benefits. Those employers with plans subject to the standards must establish and maintain a funding standard account. The sponsor must annually contribute the normal cost—the annual cost of future pension benefits and administrative expenses—plus amounts necessary to amortize in equal installments unfunded past service liabilities and any experience losses less experience gains. The presence of these standards has changed the environment for pension plans, creating greater need for long-range planning.

Tax-Qualified Plans

Requirements for tax qualification of plans has not materially changed since 1942. Meeting these requirements allows the employer to deduct contributions from income and makes investment earnings on plan assets exempt from current taxation.

The structure of tax-qualified plans is determined by ERISA requirements. The terms of the plan must be set forth in a written document. Copies of the plan and related documents must be made available to participants. In addition, a summary of the plan must be made available. The plan sponsor must have created the plan with the intent of permanency.

The provisions of the pension plans also are dictated by the requirements of the IRC:

- As referred to above, the plan must meet minimum participation, vesting, and funding standards, and plan assets must be legally segregated from other assets of the sponsor.
- The plan must not benefit only a limited number of favored employees but must benefit employees in general in such a way as to be deemed nondiscriminatory by the IRS. This status must extend to contributions and benefits such that officers, shareholders, or highly compensated employees are not favored when the plan is viewed in its entirety.
- The pension plan must provide definitely determinable benefits.

Overall, the IRC implementing regulations and rulings have had the goal of fostering accrual and preservation of benefits for present and potential plan participants and beneficiaries.

The requirements for a tax-qualified profit-sharing plan are somewhat different in that the plan must cover all employees and the benefit is not determinable.

Fulfillment of all tax qualification requirements entitles the employer to a current deduction from gross income for contributions to the plan. The participating employee recognizes no taxable income until the funds are distributed in the form of benefits or are distributed as a lump-sum distribution. When the distribution is made upon termination of service, taxes become due unless, in the case of a lump-sum distribution, the funds are rolled over into another plan.

Employees may voluntarily be allowed, or in some cases required, to make contributions to qualified plans. The employee's required contributions are limited to the maximum amount provided in the plan and no tax deduction is allowed.

Nonqualified Plans

Nonqualified employee benefit plans have not been designed to satisfy the IRC requirements and may either be funded or nonfunded. Under the funded plan, the employer agrees to make contributions to the plan for the benefit of the employee. Under an unfunded plan, the employer promises to provide a benefit to the participant at some future time. Most funded plans must satisfy ERISA, while unfunded plans must only meet ERISA's reporting and disclosure provisions.

TITLE IV: PLAN TERMINATION INSURANCE

Title IV of ERISA established the Pension Benefit Guaranty Corporation (PBGC), a governmental body that insures payment of plan benefits under certain circumstances.

Most defined benefit pension plans (those that provide a fixed monthly benefit at retirement) are required to participate in the program and pay premiums to the PBGC.

There are certain restrictions and limitations on the amount of benefits insured, and the amount is adjusted annually to reflect the increasing average wages of the American work force. The limit applies to all plans under which a participant is covered so that it is not possible to spread coverage under several plans to increase the guaranteed benefit. To be fully insured, the benefit must have been vested before the plan terminated and the benefit level must have been in effect for 60 months or else benefits are proportionately reduced. Further, the guarantee applies only to benefits earned while the plan is eligible for favorable tax treatment.

In an effort to protect against employers establishing plans without intending to continue them, ERISA introduced the concept of contingent employer liability in the event of plan termination for single-employer plans and for multiemployer plans in the event of employer withdrawal or insolvency. Additional complex requirements that apply to multiemployer plans also were established by Congress in 1980.

The PBGC has served to change substantially the environment in which plans operate. For present sponsors, and for those thinking of establishing new defined benefit plans, Title IV should be carefully reviewed so that its implications are fully understood.

LEGISLATION 1980–1990

The 1980s saw a series of legislative measures with common themes enacted into law. The laws included the Economic Recovery Tax Act of 1981 (ERTA), the Tax Equity and Fiscal Responsibility Act of 1982 (TEFRA), the Retirement Equity Act of 1984 (REA), the Deficit Reduction Act of 1984 (DEFRA), the Consolidated Budget and Reconciliation Act of 1985 (COBRA), the Tax Reform Act of 1986 (TRA '86), the Omnibus Reconciliation Act of 1987 (OBRA '87), the Omnibus Budget

Reconciliation Act of 1989 (OBRA '89), and the Budget Act of 1990. The themes included the following:

- Employee benefit tax incentives should be limited to those benefits that offer a clear social purpose and provide protection against some risk.
- Coverage and nondiscrimination rules should be designed to ensure that low- and middle-income employees actually benefit from plans.
- Benefits provided to the highly compensated on a tax-favored basis should be restricted to those provided to other employees (in the case of most health and welfare plans) and by both dollar and percentage limits (in the case of retirement programs), and those with a top-heavy work force must pay a minimum benefit to all participants.
- Tax deductions for programs that are not subject to coverage and nondiscrimination rules, such as individual retirement accounts (IRAs), should not be available to high-income taxpayers with pension coverage.
- Defined benefit and defined contribution programs should have a common primary purpose of delivering income at or near normal retirement ages and should not serve the purpose of short-term savings or an overriding purpose of encouraging early retirement.
- Defined benefit and defined contribution plans should always be a supplement to Social Security, and there should be absolute limits on the total amount of tax-favored retirement income that can be received from tax-favored plans.
- Defined benefit and defined contribution benefit values should be treated as common property, and survivor benefits should generally be available, decisions on benefit forms being common decisions.

COBRA established rules to ensure that individuals and their dependents would have access to continued group health insurance upon job termination and certain other qualifying events, and Congress can be expected to expand this concept to one of assured access for all Americans.

OBRA of 1987 significantly tightened funding standards for defined benefit plans, further restricted plan terminations, and moved the PBGC to a much higher and variable premium. Legislation consistent with the themes just noted will continue to be considered and enacted with emphasis on the larger theme that employers should be responsible for keeping promises once made *regardless of the financial implications for the business.*

In 1989 the Congress again consolidated employee benefits changes into the budget, restricting tax incentives for ESOPs, reforming the method of physician payment in the Medicare program, expanding COBRA protections, and repealing the 1988 Medicare Catastrophic Coverage Act and Section 89 (nondiscrimination tests for welfare plans) of TRA '86.

The year 1990 saw the enactment of child care legislation, expansion of Medicaid, further restrictions on asset reversions, allowance for some pension asset transfers for retiree medical expenses, ADEA amendments to expand protections in early retirement programs, and passage of the American with Disabilities Act.

ADDITIONAL REGULATORY AGENCIES

Labor Laws

A number of laws, from both statutory and case law, give the Department of Labor authority to monitor and regulate employee benefit plans.

Among them is the National Labor Relations Act, which promotes collective bargaining between employers and employees' representatives. The Taft-Hartley Act contains specific provisions similar to ERISA and the IRC relating to plan structure and content. The landmark case of *Inland Steel Company* v. *the National Labor Relations Board* prohibits an employer from refusing to bargain with employees upon a properly presented demand to bargain regarding employee benefit plans.

Equal Employment Opportunity Commission (EEOC)

The EEOC's interest in employee benefit plans stems from various acts that prohibit discriminatory plan practices. The Civil Rights Act of 1964, Title VII, is interpreted by the EEOC as defining discrimination between men and women with regard to fringe benefits as an unlawful employment practice. The Equal Pay Act of 1963 makes employer discrimination between the sexes in the payment of wages for equal work unlawful. Benefits under employee benefit plans are a form of wages and must be free from discrimination, held one EEOC decision. The Age Discrimination in Employment Act of 1967 and its 1975 and 1979 amendments clearly prohibit discrimination on the basis of age. The so-called Betts changes enacted in 1990 and relating to early retirement programs make clear the significant role of the EEOC in regulating retirement plans.

Securities and Exchange Commission (SEC)

Under the Securities Act of 1933, information concerning securities publicly offered and sold in interstate commerce or through the mails is required to be disclosed to the SEC. At first blush, the act does not seem to apply to employee benefit plans. However, a security is defined by the act as including participation in any profit-sharing agreement. The Securities Act of 1934 affects the administration of plans by imposing disclosure and registration requirements and antifraud provisions. The SEC has not actively enforced requirements, but the scope of legal SEC jurisdiction has been debated and litigated.

The Investment Company Act of 1940 regulates reporting and disclosure, structure, content, and administration of investment companies. A pension benefit plan could be subject to this act if it fits the definition of an investment company. An investment company, as defined by the act, is one engaged in the business of holding, trading, investing, or owning securities.

The SEC expanded its interest in pension plan proxy voting and corporate governance in the late 1980s, and this interest is likely to expand further in the 1990s.

Other Acts and Agencies

The Small Business Administration (SBA) receives complaints from small businesses regarding the relationship of small business to agencies of the federal government.

Banking laws also apply. The National Bank Act permits national banks to act as trustees in a fiduciary capacity in which state banks or trust companies are permitted to act under the laws of the state where the national bank is located. This affects private employee benefit plans because banks act as fiduciaries. The Federal Reserve Act and the Federal

Reserve System can affect pension and welfare plans, since plans may either be borrowers or lenders. Because there is regulation of interest payable on deposits in banks that are members of the Federal Reserve System, IRA and Keogh plans are affected in terms of possible rates of return. The Federal Deposit Insurance Act also affects these plans if they are not covered by the PBGC since funds held by an insured bank, in its capacity as fiduciary, will be insured up to $100,000 per participant. (Financial system reform proposals of the Bush Administration could reduce the level of insurance.)

The Commerce Department is concerned with ERISA's impact on the health of the economy. The Department of Health and Human Services (HHS) tries to keep track of individuals with deferred vested benefit plans and administers Social Security and other public programs that have a substantial impact on private plan design.

THE REGULATION OF INSURANCE

Both the individual state governments and the federal government regulate insurance. The states regulate rates, financial examination, formation of the company, qualification of officers, licensing, and taxing. The federal government provides for regulation as noted above in addition to the activity of the Federal Insurance Administrator, the Interstate Commerce Commission, and the Federal Trade Commission.

A growing concern exists over which level of government is the most appropriate for the regulation of insurance. It is felt by many that there should be greater federal involvement. Advocates of federal regulation argue that state regulation lacks uniformity and that multiple state regulation is more costly than federal regulation, that the state insurance commissioners are unqualified, and that the states cannot effectively regulate interstate companies. Those who favor state regulation feel the states are more responsive to local conditions and needs, that state regulation encourages innovation and experimentation, and that the decentralization of power is advantageous.

At present there exists an ongoing disagreement between the states and the federal government over the extent of preemption of state laws by ERISA. The federal government believes it could move toward greater regulation without legal difficulty. This is based upon the federal ability to regulate interstate commerce, to provide for the general welfare, and to tax. Section 514(a) of ERISA states that it shall supersede any and all state laws insofar as they may now or later relate to any employee benefit plan. The preemption does not apply to any state law that regulates insurance. But a question remains: To what extent does ERISA preempt laws enacted under the insurance codes of the states, when such laws are designed specifically to apply to the insurance-type functions of employee benefit plans?

The Department of Labor advocated a broad interpretation of Section 514, which would preempt most state statutes even if the laws deal with areas not explicitly covered by ERISA, such as the content of health benefit plans. The federal courts have not been so consistent in their interpretation of the statute. In one case, *Fleck* v. *Spannaus,* the court decided ERISA does not preempt causes of action occurring before January 1, 1975. But in another case, *Azzaro* v. *Harnett,* the court held that Congress intended absolute preemption in the field of employee benefits. Even the insurance exception found in section 514 is subject to limitations: ''No employee benefit plan shall be deemed to be an insurance company or engaged in the business of insurance for the purpose of any law of any state purporting to regulate an insurance company.''

In general, the courts, including the Supreme Court, have tended to preempt state regulation that relates to employee pension and retirement plans. This stems from the broad-based protections incorporated in ERISA for pension plan participants. The courts are less inclined to preempt state laws that apply to employee health and insurance plans. ERISA has had a more limited application to welfare plans and a more narrow view of the preemptive effect in the health and welfare plan area. When health insurance benefits are mandated in traditional insurance contracts, rather than through comprehensive health care legislation, claims of federal preemption will not hold. However, when an employer's prepaid health care plan satisfies the ERISA definition, state regulation is preempted.

Where the line eventually will be drawn between state and federal regulation of health and welfare plans is very uncertain. The debate will most likely center on the degree to which arrangements have insurance versus noninsurance characteristics, with states arguing that even stop-loss coverage makes the underlying plan ''insured,'' thus subject to state regulation. The courts will continue to be heavily involved.

Finally, the ongoing debate over national health policy will assure legislative consideration of where the state-federal regulatory line should be drawn.

FEDERAL, STATE, AND LOCAL GOVERNMENT PENSION PLANS

Public plans represent a substantial level of retirement income promises for federal, state, and local employees. Benefit levels promised in public plans exceed those of the private sector. Public plans exist free of federal regulatory controls like those imposed by ERISA. For practical purposes there is only a limited "regulatory environment."

Public employee pension programs are receiving a considerable amount of attention today because of the sharp increases in current appropriations necessary to support retirement programs, the increased activism of public plans in the realm of corporate governance, and the greater frequency of public pension purchases of public debt to "bail out" deficits. Federal regulation of private plans has given rise to a Congressional commitment to the study of public plans and to an assessment of whether a public plan version of ERISA should be enacted.

Research has revealed that large cities with their own pension plans are likely to provide some of the most generous benefits available in the public sector. Public employees generally have more liberal early retirement provisions in their pension plans than private employees, and public plans usually include a provision for automatic increases in retirees' benefits when the cost of living increases.

State and local plans are viewed by many as being substantially underfunded. Actuarial, financial, auditing, and disclosure requirements are viewed as deficient. Many charge that fiduciary standards are seriously breached. Other characteristics of public plans have led to criticisms, including the following:

- Their retirement benefits replace a substantial percentage of final pay after only 20 to 25 years of service.
- Their normal retirement ages are set well ahead of the end of productive working lifetimes.
- They are generous in granting a high proportion of early disability retirements in "high risk" professions (police, firemen, and the like), rather than retaining the work force in less hazardous positions.

Substantial concern also is generated because some federal, state, and local employees currently are not covered by the Social Security program. Because of noninclusion, or lack of integration when both programs are involved, there is a belief that public employees obtain "windfall" benefits or unnecessarily large benefits, or both. For example, a recent government study indicated that income replacement ratios for public employees serving 30 years at average wages received more than 100 percent of salary in 53 percent of all cases, and 125 percent of salary in more than 10 percent of all cases.

These and other issues have led to the development of state commissions to advise state legislators on pension issues. The threat of an impending federal intervention (in the form of PERISA—the Public Employee Retirement Income Security Act) has stimulated efforts in many states to monitor state and local pension funds more closely and to improve reporting and disclosure practices.

DISABILITY PROGRAMS

In 1975, cash disability payments equaled 25 percent of all cash payments to retirees, survivors, and the disabled. Disability programs resemble pension programs in that their purposes are similar (both, generally, are intended to maintain the income of workers and their dependents or survivors when they are unable to work), program finances are intertwined, and disability programs are sometimes used to substitute for retirement programs.

Disability program trends indicate that cash disability programs have grown rapidly and that the federal role in disability programs has increased. Analyses indicate workers of all ages are being awarded disability benefits more frequently than in previous years. Per capita benefits generally have grown more rapidly than earnings and the difference in growth rates has been larger since 1970.

Social factors also add to the increase in disability payouts. Society is doing more to support the disabled. More and more people identify themselves as disabled. It is indicated that disability programs may be repeating the welfare crisis of the 1960s, the dramatic increase in beneficiaries largely representing a growing percentage of eligible persons claiming benefits.

Social Security Disability Benefits

To qualify for Social Security disability benefits, the wage earner must be unable to engage in any substantial activity by reason of medically determined physical or mental impairment that can be expected to result in death or to last for a continuous period. Total disability exists if the claimant's disability equals or exceeds the standards as established and is documented by a medical report using the language required by the regulations. The Social Security Act considers age, education, and previous work experience when applying the disability standard. The wage earner also must meet special earnings requirements to be covered. The wage earner must have performed 20 quarters of employment in the 40 quarters immediately prior to the alleged onset of disability. The benefit payout begins on the sixth month of disability.

CONCLUSION

The regulatory environment of employee benefit programs is far-reaching and complex. It involves all levels of government in at least some areas, and numerous different agencies at each level, all with the purpose of protecting the potential recipient and adding security to the benefit promise.

The degree to which the environment is refined is constantly changing. There has been no rest from discussion of new legislative proposals or new regulatory initiatives. Some proposals aim at reducing regulation, others at increasing it. Frequently the short-term effect is the same: creation of uncertainty, which inhibits the growth and development of employee benefit programs.

The challenge for the practitioner is to understand the environment, to understand how it affects particular situations, and to affect it when the opportunity arises.

PART 2

SOCIAL INSURANCE PROGRAMS

Part Two covers the fundamentals of several social insurance programs which provide a basic layer of protection against various exposures. Chapter 5 discusses Social Security and Medicare, Chapter 6 explores Workers' Compensation programs and Chapter 7 examines Unemployment Compensation systems. It is essential to understand these social insurance programs because their coordination with private benefit programs is vital to sound employee benefit planning.

CHAPTER 5

SOCIAL SECURITY AND MEDICARE

Robert J. Myers

Economic security for retired workers, disabled workers, and survivors of deceased workers in the United States is, in the vast majority of cases, provided through the multiple means of Social Security, private pensions, and individual savings. This is sometimes referred to as a "three-legged stool" or the three pillars of economic-security protection. It can also be seen as a layered arrangement, with Social Security providing the floor of protection, private sector activities building on top of it, and public assistance programs, such as Supplemental Security Income (SSI), providing a net of protection for those whose total retirement income does not attain certain levels or meet minimum subsistence needs.

Although some people may view the Social Security program as one that should provide complete protection, over the years it generally has been agreed that it should only be the foundation of protection.

As described elsewhere in this book, private pension plans have, to a significant extent, been developed to supplement Social Security. This is done in a number of ways, both directly and indirectly. The net result, however, is a broad network of retirement protection.

This chapter discusses in detail the retirement, disability, and survivor provisions of the Social Security program, not only their historical development and present structure but also a summary of the financial crises of the late 1970s and early 1980s (and what was done to solve them) and possible future changes. Following this, the Medicare program is described. Also, descriptions of the two public assistance programs (Supplemental Security Income and Medicaid) that supplement Old-Age, Survivors and Disability Insurance (OASDI) and Medicare are given.

The term *Social Security* is used here with the meaning generally accepted in the United States, namely, the cash benefits provisions of the OASDI program. International usage of the term *social security* is much broader than this and includes all other types of programs protecting individuals against the economic risks of a modern industrial system, such as unemployment, short-term sickness, work-connected accidents and diseases, and medical care costs.

OLD-AGE, SURVIVORS, AND DISABILITY INSURANCE PROGRAM

Persons Covered Under OASDI

OASDI coverage—for both taxes and earnings credits toward benefit rights—currently applies to somewhat more than 90 percent of the total work force of the United States. About half of those not covered have protection through a special employee retirement system, while the remaining half are either very low-paid intermittent workers or unpaid family workers.

The vast majority of persons covered under OASDI are so affected on a mandatory, or compulsory, basis. Several categories, however, have optional or semioptional coverage. It is important to note that OASDI coverage applies not only to employees, both salaried and wage earner, but also to self-employed persons. Some individuals who are essentially employees are nonetheless classified as self-employed for the sake of convenience in applying coverage.

Compulsory coverage is applicable to all employees in commerce and industry (interpreting these classifications very broadly) except railroad workers, who are covered under a separate program, the Railroad Retirement system. However, financial and other coordinating provisions exist between these two programs, so that, in reality, railroad workers are covered under OASDI. Members of the armed forces are covered compulsorily, as are federal civilian employees hired after 1983. Compulsory coverage also applies to lay employees of churches (with certain minor exceptions), to employees of nonprofit charitable and educational institutions, to employees of state and local governments that do not have retirement systems (first effective after July 1, 1991; before then, coverage was elective, on a group basis, by the employing entity), and to

American citizens who work abroad for American corporations. Self-employed persons of all types (except ministers) also are covered compulsorily unless their earnings are minimal (i.e., less than $400 a year); beginning in 1990, covered self-employment is taken as 92.35 percent of the self-employment net income (such figure being 100 percent minus the OASDI–Hospital Insurance tax rate applicable to employees).

From a geographical standpoint, OASDI applies not only in the 50 states and the District of Columbia but also in all outlying areas (American Samoa, Guam, the Northern Mariana Islands, Puerto Rico, and the Virgin Islands).

Elective coverage applies to a number of categories. Employees of state and local governments who are under a retirement system can have coverage at the option of the employing entity, and only when the current employees vote in favor of coverage. Similar provisions are available for American employees of foreign subsidiaries of American corporations, the latter having the right to opt for coverage. Once that coverage has been elected by a state or local government, it cannot be terminated. Approximately 75 percent of state and local government employees are now covered as a result of this election basis.

Because of the principle of separation of church and state, ministers are covered on the self-employed basis, regardless of their actual status. Furthermore, they have the right to opt out of the system within a limited time after ordination on grounds of religious principles or conscience. Americans employed in the United States by a foreign government or by an international organization are covered compulsorily on the self-employed basis.

Historical Development of Retirement Provisions

When what is now the OASDI program was developed in 1934–35, it was confined entirely to retirement benefits plus lump-sum refund payments to represent the difference, if any, between employee taxes paid, plus an allowance for interest, and retirement benefits received. It was not until the 1939 Act that auxiliary (or dependents) and survivors benefits were added, and not until the 1956 Act that disability benefits were made available. The likely reason that only retirement benefits were instituted initially is that such type of protection was the most familiar to the general public, especially in light of the relatively few private pension plans then in existence.

The "normal retirement age" (NRA) was originally established at 65. This figure was selected in a purely empirical manner; it was a middle figure between two perceived extremes. Age 70 seemed too high, because of the common belief that relatively so few people reached that age, while 60 seemed too low, because of the large costs that would be involved if that age had been selected. Many of the existing private pension plans at that time had a retirement age of 65, although some in the railroad industry used age 70. Furthermore, labor-force participation data showed that a relatively high proportion of workers continued in employment after age 60. A widely cited, but erroneous, explanation of why age 65 was selected is that Bismarck chose this age when he established the German national pension program in the 1880s; the age used originally in Germany actually was 70. The 1983 Act provided for the NRA to increase from age 65 to age 67 in a deferred, gradual manner. Specifically, the NRA is 65 for those attaining this age before 2003 and first becomes 67 for those attaining this age in 2027.

The original program applied only to workers in commerce and industry. It was not until the 1950s that coverage was extended to additional categories of workers. Now, almost all are covered, including the self-employed.

The initial legislation passed by the House of Representatives did not require eligible persons to retire at age 65 or over in order to receive benefits, although it was recognized that inclusion of a retirement requirement would be essential in the final legislation. The Senate inserted a requirement of a general nature that benefits would be payable only upon retirement, and this was included in the final legislation. Over the years, this retirement test, or work clause, has been the subject of much controversy, and it has been considerably liberalized and made more flexible over the years.

Beginning in the 1950s, pressure developed to provide early-retirement benefits, first for spouses and then for insured workers. The minimum early-retirement age was set at 62, again a pragmatic political compromise rather than a number based on any completely logical reason. The three-year differential, however, did represent the approximate average difference in age between men and their wives, but of course, as with any averages, the difference actually is larger in many cases. The benefit amounts are reduced when claimed before the NRA is reached, and are increased, although currently to not as great an extent, when retirement is delayed beyond the NRA. As the NRA increases beyond age 65, the reduction for claiming benefits at age 62 becomes larger.

Eligibility Conditions for Retirement Benefits

To be eligible for OASDI retirement benefits, individuals must have a certain amount of covered employment. In general, these conditions were designed to be relatively easy to meet in the early years of operation, thus bringing the program into effectiveness quickly. Eligibility for retirement benefits—termed *fully insured status*—depends upon having a certain number of ''quarters of coverage'' (QC), varying with the year of birth or, expressed in another manner, depending on the year of an individual's attainment of age 62.

Before 1978, a QC was defined simply as a calendar quarter during which the individual was paid $50 or more in wages from covered employment; the self-employed ordinarily received four QCs for each year of coverage at $400 or more of earnings. Beginning in 1978, the number of QCs acquired for each year depends upon the total earnings in the year. For 1978, each full unit of $250 of earnings produced a QC, up to a maximum of four QCs for the year. In subsequent years the requirement has increased, and it will continue to increase in the future, in accordance with changes in the general wage level; for 1992, it is $570.

The number of QCs required for fully insured status is determined from the number of years in the period beginning in 1951, or with the year of attainment of age 22, if later, and the year before the year of attainment of age 62, with a minimum requirement of six QCs. As a result, an individual who attained age 62 before 1958 needed only six QCs to be fully insured. A person attaining age 62 in 1990 has a requirement of 39 QCs, while a person attaining age 65 in 1990 needs 36 QCs. The maximum number of QCs that will ever be required for fully insured status is 40, applicable to persons attaining age 62 after 1990. It is important to note that, although the requirement for the number of QCs is determined from 1951, or from year of attainment of age 22, and before attainment of age 62, the QCs to meet the requirement can be obtained at any time (e.g., before 1951, before age 22, and after age 61).

Beneficiary Categories for Retirement Benefits

Insured workers can receive unreduced retirement benefits in the amount of the Primary Insurance Amount (or PIA), the derivation of which will be discussed next, beginning at the NRA, or actuarially reduced benefits beginning at earlier ages, down to age 62. For retirement at age 62 currently (and until 1999), the benefit is 80 percent of the PIA. As the NRA increases beyond 65, the reduction will become larger (eventually being 30 percent).

Retired workers also can receive supplementary payments for spouses and eligible children. The spouse receives a benefit at the rate of 50 percent of the PIA if claim is first made at the NRA or over, and at a reduced rate if claimed at ages down to 62 (currently, a 25 percent reduction at age 62—i.e., to 37.5 percent of the PIA); as the NRA increases beyond 65, the reduction for age 62 will be larger, eventually being 35 percent. However, if a child under age 16 (or a child aged 16 or over who was disabled before age 22) is present, the spouse receives benefits regardless of age, in an unreduced amount. Divorced spouses, when the marriage had lasted at least 10 years, are eligible for benefits under the same conditions as undivorced spouses.

Children under age 18 (and children aged 18 or over and disabled before age 22, plus children attending high school full-time at age 18) also are eligible for benefits, at a rate of 50 percent of the PIA; prior to legislation in 1981, post-secondary-school students aged 18–21 were eligible for benefits, and spouses with children in their care could receive benefits as long as a child under age 18 was present. Grandchildren and great-grandchildren can qualify as "children" if they are dependent on the grandparent *and* if both parents of the child are disabled or deceased.

An overall maximum on total family benefits is applicable, as is discussed later. If a person is eligible for more than one type of benefit (e.g., both as a worker and as a spouse), in essence only the largest benefit is payable.

Computation and Indexing Procedures for Retirement Benefits

As indicated in the previous section, OASDI benefits are based on the PIA. The method of computing the PIA is quite complicated, especially because several different methods are available. The only method dealt with here in any detail is the one generally applicable to people who reach age 65 after 1981.

Persons who attained age 65 before 1982 use a method based on the average monthly wage (AMW). This is based essentially on a career average, involving the consideration of all earnings back through 1951. To take into account the general inflation in earnings that has occurred in the last three decades, automatic-adjustment procedures are involved in the benefit computations. However, these turned out to be faulty, because they did not—and would not in the future—produce stable benefit results (as to the relationships of initial benefits to final earnings). Accordingly, in the 1977 amendments, a new procedure applicable to those attaining age 62 after 1978 was adopted, but the old procedure was retained for earlier attainments of age 62. The result has been to give unusually and inequitably large benefits to those who attained age 62 before 1979 who worked well beyond age 62, as against similar people who attained age 62 after 1978, thus creating a "notch" situation.

Persons who attain age 62 in 1979–83 can use an alternative method somewhat similar to the AMW method (but with certain restrictions) if this produces a larger PIA than the new, permanent method. In actual practice, however, this modified-AMW method generally produces more favorable results only for persons attaining age 62 in 1979–81 and not continuing in employment after that age.

Still another method is available for all individuals who have earnings before 1951. In the vast majority of such cases, however, the new-start methods based on earnings after 1950 produce more favorable results.

The first step in the ongoing permanent method of computing the PIA applicable to persons attaining age 65 in 1982 or after is to calculate the Average Indexed Monthly Earnings (AIME). The AIME is a career-average earnings formula, but it is determined in such a manner as to closely approximate a final average formula. In a national social insurance plan, it would be inadvisable to use solely an average of the last few years of employment, because that could involve serious manipulation through the cooperation of both the employee and the employer, whereas in a private pension plan, the employer has a close financial interest not to do so. Furthermore, as described later, OASDI benefit computation is not proportionate to years of coverage or proportion of worklife in covered employment, as is the case for private pension plans generally.

The first step in computing the AIME is to determine the number of years over which it must be computed. On the whole, the number depends solely on the year in which the individual attains age 62. The general rule is that the computation period equals the number of years beginning with 1951, or with the year of attaining age 22, if later, up through the year before attainment of age 62, minus the so-called five dropout years. The latter is provided so that the very lowest five years of earnings can be eliminated. Also, years of high earnings in or after the year of attaining age 62 can be substituted for earlier, lower years.

As an example, persons attaining age 62 in 1990 have a computation period of 34 years (the 39 years in 1951–89, minus 5). The maximum period will be 35 years for those attaining age 62 after 1990. For the infrequent case of an individual who had qualified for OASDI disability benefits and who recovered from the disability, the number of computation years for the AIME for retirement benefits is reduced by the number of full years after age 21 and before age 62 during any part of which the person was under a disability.

The AIME is not computed from the actual covered earnings, but rather after indexing them, to make them more current as compared with the wage level at the time of retirement. Specifically, covered earnings for each year before attainment of age 60 are indexed to that age, while all subsequent covered earnings are used in their actual amount. No earnings before 1951 can be utilized, but all earnings subsequently, either before age 22 or after age 61, are considered.

The indexing of the earnings record is accomplished by multiplying the actual earnings of each year before the year that age 60 was attained by the increase in earnings from the particular year to the age-60 year. For example, for persons attaining age 62 in 1990 (i.e., age 60 in 1988), any earnings in 1951 would be converted to indexed earnings by multiplying them by 6.90709, which is the ratio of the nationwide average wage in 1988 to that in 1951. Similarly, the multiplying factor for 1952 earnings is 6.50251, and so on. Once the earnings record for each year in the past has been indexed, the earnings for the number of years required to be averaged are selected to include the highest ones possible; if there are not sufficient years with earnings, then zeroes must be used. Then, the AIME is obtained by dividing the total indexed earnings for such years by 12 times such number of years.

Now, having obtained the AIME, the PIA is computed from a benefit formula. There is a different formula for each annual cohort of persons attaining age 62. For example, for those who reached age 62 in 1979, the formula was 90 percent of the first $180 of AIME, plus 32 percent of the next $905 of AIME, plus 15 percent of the AIME in excess of $1,085. For the 1980 cohort, the corresponding dollar bands are $194, $977, and $1,171, while those for the 1992 cohort are $387, $1,946, and $2,333. These bands are adjusted automatically according to changes in nationwide average wages.

A different method of computing the PIA for retirement benefits (and also for disability benefits, but not for survivor benefits) is applicable for certain persons who receive pensions based in whole or in part on earnings from employment not covered by OASDI or Railroad Retirement (in the past or in the future, and in other countries as well as in the United States). This is done to eliminate the windfall benefits (due to the weighted nature of the benefit formula) that would otherwise arise. Excluded from this provision are the following categories: (1) persons who attain age 62 before 1986; (2) persons who were *eligible* for such pension before 1986; (3) disabled-worker beneficiaries who became disabled before 1986 (and were entitled to such benefits in at least one month in the year before attaining age 62); (4) persons who have at least 30 years of coverage (as defined hereafter); (5) persons who were employed by the federal government on January 1, 1984, and were then brought into coverage by the 1983 Amendments; and (6) persons who were employed on January 1, 1984, by a nonprofit organization that was not covered on December 31, 1983, and had not been so covered at any time in the past.

Under this method of computation of the PIA, ultimately the percentage factor applicable to the lowest band of earnings will be 40 percent, instead of 90 percent. As a transitional measure, those who become first eligible for OASDI benefits in 1986 have an 80 percent factor, while it is 70 percent for the 1987 cohort, 60 percent for the 1988 cohort, and 50 percent for the 1989 cohort.

For persons who have 21–29 "years of coverage" (as defined hereafter), an alternative phase-in procedure is used (if it produces a larger PIA). The percentage factor applicable to the lowest band of earnings in the PIA formula is 80 percent for 29 years of coverage, 70 percent for 28 years, 60 percent for 27 years, and 50 percent for 26 years.

In any event, under any of the foregoing procedures, the PIA as computed in the regular manner will never be reduced by more than 50 percent of the pension based on noncovered employment (or the pro rata portion thereof based on noncovered employment after 1956 if it is based on both covered and noncovered employment).

Prior to legislation in 1981, if the PIA benefit formula produced a smaller amount than $122 in the initial benefit computation, then this amount was nonetheless payable. However, for persons first becoming eligible after 1981, no such minimum is applicable.

A special minimum applies to the PIA for individuals who have a long period of covered work, but with low earnings. As of December

1991, this minimum is approximately $23.90 times the "years of coverage" in excess of 10, but not in excess of 30; thus, for 30 or more years of coverage, the minimum benefit is $478.20. Before 1991, a "year of coverage" is defined as a year in which earnings are at least 25 percent of the maximum taxable earnings base, while after 1990, a factor of 15 percent is used; for 1979 and after, this base is taken to be what would have prevailed if the ad hoc increases in the base provided by the 1977 act had not been applicable, and, instead, the automatic increases had occurred. Thus, for this purpose, the 1992 base is taken as $41,400, instead of the actual one of $55,500.

The resulting PIAs then are increased for any automatic adjustments applicable because of annual increases in the consumer price index (CPI)—or, when the balance of the OASDI Trust Funds is relatively low, by the annual increase in nationwide wages if this is less than the CPI rise—that occur in or after the year of attaining age 62, even though actual retirement is much later. These automatic adjustments are made for benefits for each December. Such CPI increases in the recent past have been 9.9 percent for 1979, 14.3 percent for 1980, 11.2 percent for 1981, 7.4 percent for 1982, 3.5 percent for 1983 and 1984, 3.1 percent for 1985, 1.3 percent for 1986, 4.2 percent for 1879, 4.0 percent for 1988, 4.7 percent for 1989, 5.4 percent for 1990, and 3.7 percent for 1991.

The resulting PIA then is reduced, in the manner described previously, for those who first claim benefits before the NRA. Conversely, retired workers who do not receive benefits for any months after they attain the NRA, essentially because of the earnings test, which will be described later, receive increases that are termed *delayed-retirement credits* (DRC). Such credits for those who attained age 65 in 1982–89 are at the rate of 3 percent per year of delay (actually 0.25 percent per month) for the period between ages 65 and 70. For those who attained age 65 before 1982, the DRC is at a rate of only 1 percent per year. For those who attain the NRA after 1989, such credit is gradually increased from 3.5 percent for the 1990–91 cases and 4 percent for the 1992–93 cases until it is 8 percent for those attaining the NRA (then 66) in 2009. The DRC applies only to the worker's benefit and not to that for spouses or children (but it does apply to any subsequent widow(er)'s benefits).

A Maximum Family Benefit (MFB) is applicable when there are more than two beneficiaries receiving benefits on the same earnings record (i.e., the retired worker and two or more auxiliary beneficiaries). Not considered within the limit established by the MFB are the additional benefits arising from delayed-retirement credits and the benefits payable to divorced spouses. The MFB is determined prior to any reductions made because of claiming benefits before the NRA, but after the effect of the earnings test as it applies to any auxiliary beneficiary (e.g., if the spouse has high earnings, any potential benefit payable to her or him would not be considered for purposes of the MFB of the other spouse).

The MFB is determined from the PIA by a complex formula. This formula varies for each annual cohort of persons attaining age 62. The resulting MFB is adjusted for increases in the CPI in the future (in the same manner as is the PIA). For the 1992 cohort, the MFB formula is 150 percent of the first $495 of PIA, plus 272 percent of the next $219 of PIA, plus 134 percent of the next $217 of PIA, plus 175 percent of PIA in excess of $931. For future cohorts, the dollar figures are changed according to changes in nationwide average wages. The result of this formula is to produce MFBs that are 150 percent of the PIA for the lowest PIAs, with this proportion rising to a peak of 188 percent for middle-range PIAs, and then falling off to 175 percent—and leveling there—for higher PIAs.

Earnings Test and Other Restrictions on Retirement Benefits

From the inception of the OASDI program, there has been some form of restriction on the payment of benefits to persons who have substantial earnings from employment. This provision is referred to as the "retirement earnings test." It does not apply to nonearned income, such as from investments or pensions. The general underlying principle of this test is that retirement benefits should be paid only to persons who are substantially retired.

The basic feature of the earnings test is that an annual exempt amount applies, so that full benefits are paid if earnings, including those from both covered and noncovered employment, are not in excess thereof. Then, for persons under the NRA (which is age 65 until 2003), for each $2 of excess earnings, $1 in benefits is withheld; the reduction is on a "$1 for $3" basis for those at and above the NRA in 1990 and after. For persons aged 65–69 (at any time in the year), the annual exempt amount is $10,200 for 1992, with the amounts for persons at and above the NRA for subsequent years being automatically determined by the increases in nationwide wages. Beginning with the month of attainment of age 70, the test no longer applies. For persons under age 65, the exempt amount is $7,440 in 1992, with automatic adjustment thereafter.

An alternative test applies for the initial year of retirement, or claim, if it results in more benefits being payable. Under this, full benefits are payable for all months in which the individual did not have substantial services in self-employment and had wages of 1/12 of the annual exempt amount or less. This provision properly takes care of the situation where an individual fully retires during a year, but had sizable earnings in the first part of the year, and thus would have most or all of the benefits withheld if only the annual test had been applicable.

Earnings of the ''retired'' worker affect, under the earnings test, the total family benefits payable. However, if an auxiliary beneficiary (spouse or child) has earnings, and these are sizable enough to affect the earnings test, any reduction in benefits is applicable only to such individual's benefits.

If an individual receives a pension from service under a government-employee pension plan under which the members were not covered under OASDI on the last day of her or his employment, the OASDI spouse benefit is reduced by two thirds of the amount of such pension. This provision, however, is not applicable to women—or to men who are dependent on their wives—who become eligible for such a pension before December 1982, while for December 1982 thorough June 1983, the provision applies only to those (both men and women) who cannot prove dependency on their spouse. This general provision results in the same treatment as occurs when both spouses have OASDI benefits based on their own earnings records; and then each receives such benefit, plus the excess, if any, of the spouse's benefit arising from the other spouse's earnings over the benefit based on their own earnings, rather than the full amount of the spouse's benefit.

Historical Development of Disability Provisions

It was not until the 1956 Act that monthly disability benefits were added to the OASDI program, although the ''disability freeze'' provision (in essence, a waiver-of-premium provision), described later, was added in the 1952 Act.[1] It may well be said that long-term disability is merely premature old-age retirement.

---

[1] Actually, it was so written in the 1952 legislation as to be inoperative, but then was reenacted in 1954 to be on a permanent, ongoing basis.

The monthly disability benefits initially were available only at age 50 and over, that is, deferred to that age for those disabled earlier, with no auxiliary benefits for the spouse and dependent children. These limitations were quickly removed, by the 1958 and 1960 acts.

Eligibility Conditions for Disability Benefits

To be eligible for disability benefits, individuals must be both fully insured and disability insured.[2] Disability-insured status requires 20 QCs earned in the 40-quarter period ending with the quarter of disability, except that persons disabled before age 31 also can qualify if they have QCs in half of the quarters after age 21.[3] The definition of disability is relatively strict. The disability must be so severe that the individual is unable to engage in any substantial gainful activity, and the impairment must be a medically determinable physical or mental condition that is expected to continue for at least 12 months or to result in prior death. Benefits are first payable after completion of six full calendar months of disability.

Beneficiary Categories for Disability Benefits

In addition to the disabled worker, dependents in the same categories that apply to old-age retirement benefits can receive monthly benefits.

Benefit Computation Procedures for Disability Benefits

In all cases, the benefits are based on the Primary Insurance Amount (PIA), computed in the same manner as retirement benefits, except that fewer dropout years than five are allowed in the computation of the Averaged Indexed Monthly Earnings (AIME) for persons disabled before age 47. The disabled worker receives a benefit equal to 100 percent of the PIA, and the auxiliary beneficiaries each receive 50 percent of the PIA, subject to the Maximum Family Benefit.

An overall maximum on total family benefits is applicable, which is lower than that for survivor and retirement benefits—namely, no more than the smaller of (1) 150 percent of the PIA or (2) 85 percent of AIME (but not less than the PIA).

---

[2] Blind persons need be only fully insured.

[3] For those disabled before age 24, the requirement is six QCs in the last 12 quarters.

Eligibility Test for Disability Benefits and Other Restrictions on Benefits

The earnings or retirement test applies to the auxiliary beneficiaries of disabled workers, but *not* to the disabled worker beneficiary. However, the earnings of one beneficiary (e.g., the spouse of the disabled worker) do not affect the benefits of the other beneficiaries in the family (e.g., the disabled worker or the children). The test does not apply to disabled worker beneficiaries, because any earnings are considered in connection with whether recovery has occurred, except those during trial work periods (which earnings may possibly lead to removal from the benefit roll later).

OASDI disability benefits are coordinated with disability benefits payable under other governmental programs (including programs of state and local governments), except for needs-tested ones, benefits payable by the Veterans Administration, and government employee plans coordinated with OASDI. The most important of such coordinations is with Workers' Compensation (WC) programs, whose benefits are taken into account in determining the amount of the OASDI disability benefit (except in a few states that provide for their WC benefits to be reduced when OASDI disability benefits are payable—possible only for states that did this before February 19, 1981). The total of the OASDI disability benefit (including any auxiliary benefits payable) and the other disability benefit recognized cannot exceed 80 percent of "average current earnings" (generally based on the highest year of earnings in covered employment in the last six years, but indexed for changes in wage levels following the worker's disablement).

Disability Freeze

In the event that a disability beneficiary recovers, the so-called disability-freeze provision applies. Under this, the period of disability is "blanked out" in the computation of insured status and benefit amounts for subsequent retirement, disability, and survivor benefits.

Historical Development of Survivor Provisions

When what is now the OASDI program was developed in 1934–35, it was confined entirely to retirement benefits (plus lump-sum refund payments to represent the difference, if any, between employee taxes paid, plus an allowance for interest, and retirement benefits received). It was not until the 1939 Act that monthly survivor benefits were added with respect to deaths of both active workers and retirees, in lieu of the refund benefit.

The term "widow" is used here to include also widowers. Until 1983, the latter did not receive OASDI benefits on the same basis as widows, either being required to prove dependence on the deceased female worker or not being eligible at all. Now, because of legislative changes and court decisions, complete equality of treatment by sex prevails for OASDI survivor benefits.

The minimum eligibility age for aged widows was initially established at age 65. This figure was selected in a purely empirical manner, because it was a round figure (see the earlier discussion about retirement benefits as to why this was selected as the minimum retirement age).

Beginning in the 1950s, pressure developed to provide early-retirement benefits, first for widows and spouses and then for insured workers themselves. The minimum early-retirement age was set at 62, again a pragmatic political compromise, rather than a completely logical choice and was later lowered to 60 for widows. The three-year differential, however, did represent about the average difference in age between men and their wives (but, of course, as with any averages, in many cases the actual difference is larger). The benefit amounts were not reduced for widows when they claimed before age 65 under the original amendatory legislation, but this is no longer the case.

Eligibility Conditions for Survivor Benefits

To be eligible for OASDI survivor benefits, individuals must have either *fully insured status* or *currently insured status*. The latter requires only 6 QCs earned in the 13-quarter period ending with the quarter of death.

Survivor Beneficiary Categories

Two general categories of survivors of insured workers can receive monthly benefits. Aged survivors are widows aged 60 or over (or at ages 50–59 if disabled) and dependent parents aged 62 or over. Young survivors are children under age 18 (or at any age if disabled before age 22), children aged 18 who are full-time students in elementary or secondary educational institutions (i.e., defined just the same as in the case of retirement and disability beneficiaries), and the widowed parent of such children who are under age 16 or disabled. In addition, a death benefit of $255 is payable to widows or, in the absence of a widow, to children eligible for immediate monthly benefits.

The disabled widow receives a benefit at the rate of 71.5 percent of the deceased worker's PIA if claim is first made at ages 50–59. The benefit rate for other widows grades up from 71.5 percent of the PIA if claimed at age 60 to 100 percent if claimed at the Normal Retirement Age, which is age 65 for those attaining age 60 before 2000, grading up to 67 for those attaining age 60 in 2022 and after. Any Delayed-Retirement Credits which the deceased worker had earned also are applicable to the widow's benefit. Widows, regardless of age, caring for an eligible child (under age 16 or disabled) have a benefit of 75 percent of the PIA. Divorced spouses, when the marriage lasted at least 10 years, are eligible for benefits under the same conditions as undivorced spouses.

The benefit rate for eligible children is 75 percent of the PIA. The benefit rate for dependent parents is 82.5 percent of the PIA, unless two parents are eligible, in which case it is 75 percent for each one.

The same overall maximum on total family benefits is applicable as is the case for retirement benefits. If a person is eligible for more than one type of benefit, e.g., both as a worker and as a surviving spouse, in essence only the largest benefit is payable.

Benefit Computation Procedures for Survivor Benefits

In all cases, the monthly survivor benefits are based on the PIA, and then are adjusted to reflect the Maximum Family Benefit, both of which are computed in essentially the same manner as is the case for retirement benefits.[4]

Eligibility Test for Survivor Benefits and Other Restrictions

Marriage (or remarriage) of the survivor beneficiary generally terminates benefit rights. The only exceptions are remarriage of widows after age 60

---

[4] For individuals who die before age 62, the computation is made as though the individual had attained age 62 in the year of death. In addition, for deferred widow's benefits, an alternative computation based on indexing the deceased's earnings record up to the earlier of age 60 of the worker or age 60 of the widow is used if this produces a more favorable result.

(or after age 50 for disabled widows) and marriage to another OASDI beneficiary (other than one who is under age 18).

From the inception of the OASDI program, there has been some form of restriction on the payment of benefits to persons who have substantial earnings from employment, the earnings or retirement test. The same test applies to survivor beneficiaries as to retirement benefits. However, the earnings of one beneficiary (e.g., the widowed mother) do not affect the benefits of the other beneficiaries in the family (e.g., the orphaned children).

If a widow receives a pension from service under a government-employee pension plan under which the members were not covered under OASDI on the last day of her employment, the OASDI widow's benefit is reduced by two thirds of the amount of such pension. This provision, however, is not applicable to women (or men who were dependent on their wives) who became eligible for such a pension before December 1982 or to individuals who became first so eligible from December 1982 through June 1983 and who were dependent on their spouses.

Financing Provisions of OASDI Program

From its inception until the 1983 Act, the OASDI program has been financed entirely by payroll taxes (and interest earnings on the assets of the trust funds), with only minor exceptions, such as the special benefits at a subminimum level for certain persons without insured status who attained age 72 before 1972. Thus, on a permanent ongoing basis, no payments from general revenues were available to the OASDI system; the contributions for covered federal civilian employees and members of the armed forces are properly considered as "employer" taxes.

The 1983 Act introduced two instances of general-revenues financing of the OASDI program. As a one-time matter, the tax rate in 1984 was increased to what had been previously scheduled for 1985 (i.e., for both the employer and employee, from 5.4 percent to 5.7 percent), but the increase for employees was, in essence, rescinded, and the General Fund of the Treasury made up the difference to the OASDI Trust Funds. On an ongoing basis, the General Fund passes on to the trust funds the proceeds of the income taxation of OASDI benefits (first effective for 1984), and, in fact, does so somewhat in advance of actual receipt of such moneys.

The payroll taxes for the retirement and survivors benefits go into the OASI Trust Fund, while those for the disability benefits go into the DI

Trust Fund, and all benefit payments and administrative expenses for these provisions are paid therefrom. The balances in the trust fund are invested in federal government obligations of various types, with interest rates at the current market values. The federal government does not guarantee the payments of benefits. If the trust fund were to be depleted, it could not obtain grants, or even loans, from the general treasury. However, a temporary provision (effective only in 1982) permitted the OASI Trust Fund to borrow, repayable with interest, from the DI and HI Trust Fund. A total of $17.5 billion was borrowed ($12.4 billion from HI). The last of such loans were repaid in 1986.

Payroll taxes are levied on earnings up to only a certain annual limit, which is termed the *earnings base*. This base is applicable to the earnings of an individual from each employer in the year, but the person can obtain a refund (on the income tax form) for all employee taxes paid in excess of those on the earnings base. The self-employed pay taxes on their self-employment income on no more than the excess of the earnings base over any wages which they may have had.

Since 1975, the earnings base has been determined by the automatic-adjustment procedure, on the basis of increases in the nationwide average wage. However, for 1979–81, ad hoc increases of a higher amount were legislated; the 1981 base was established at $29,700. The 1982 and subsequent bases were determined under the automatic-adjustment provision. The 1991 base was $53,400, while that for 1992 is $55,500.

The payroll tax rate is a combined one for Old-Age and Survivors Insurance (OASI), Disability Insurance (DI), and Hospital Insurance (HI), but it is allocated among the three trust funds. The employer and employee rates are equal. The self-employed pay the combined employer-employee rate. In 1984–89, they had an allowance for the reduction in income taxes if half of the OASDI-HI tax were to be considered as a business expense (as it is for incorporated employers); such allowance was a uniform reduction in the tax rate—2.7 percentage points in 1984, 2.2 percentage points in 1985, and 2.0 percentage points in 1986–89. After 1989, the direct procedure of considering half of the OASDI-HI taxes as a deduction from income is done. Also, until 1991, the earnings base was the same for OASDI and HI, but in 1991, the base for HI was raised to $125,000, and it is $130,200 in 1992.

The employer and employee rates were 1 percent each in 1937–49, but have gradually increased over the years, until being 7.15 percent in 1986–87 (the latter subdivided 5.2 percent for OASI, 0.5 percent for DI, and 1.45 percent for HI). These rates increased to 7.51 percent in 1988, and then to 7.65 percent in 1990 (and after), the latter being subdivided 5.6 percent for OASI, 0.6 percent for DI, and 1.45 percent for HI.

Past Financing Crises of OASDI Program

In the mid-1970s, the OASI and DI Trust Funds were projected to have serious financing problems over both the long range and the short range. The short-range problem was thought to be remedied by the 1977 Act, which raised taxes (both the rates and the earnings bases). At the same time, the long-range problem was partially solved by phased-in significant benefit reductions, by lowering the general benefit level, by freezing the minimum benefit, and by the ''spouse government pension'' offset, although an estimated deficit situation was still present for the period beginning after about 30 years.

The short-range problem was not really solved. The actuarial cost estimates assumed that earnings would rise at a somewhat more rapid rate than prices in the short range, but the reverse occurred—and to a significant extent—in 1979–81. Because increases in tax income depend on earnings and because increases in benefit outgo depend on prices, the financial result for the OASI Trust Fund was catastrophic. It would have been exhausted in late 1982 if not for legislation enacted in 1981. The DI Trust Fund did not have this problem, because the disability experience, which had worsened significantly in 1970–76, turned around and became relatively favorable—more than offsetting the unfavorable economic experience.

The 1981 Act significantly reduced benefit outgo in the short range by the following actions:

1. The regular minimum benefit (an initial PIA of $122) was eliminated for all new eligibles after 1981, except for certain covered members of religious orders under a vow of poverty.
2. Child school attendance benefits at ages 18–21 were eliminated by a gradual phase-out, except for high school students aged 18.
3. Mother's and father's benefits with respect to nondisabled children terminate when the youngest child is aged 16 (formerly 18).
4. Lump-sum death payments were eliminated, except when a surviving spouse who was living with the deceased worker is present, or when a spouse or child is eligible for immediate monthly benefits.

5. Sick pay in the first six months of illness is considered to be covered wages.
6. Lowering of the exempt age under the earnings test to age 70 in 1982 was delayed until 1983.
7. The Workers' Compensation offset against disability benefits was extended to several other types of governmental disability benefits.
8. Interfund borrowing among the OASI, DI, and HI Trust Funds was permitted, but only until December 31, 1982, and then no more than sufficient to allow payments of OASI benefits through June 1983.

Further action beyond the 1981 Amendments was essential to restore both the short-range and long-range solvency of the OASDI program. Because of the difficult political situation, President Reagan established the National Commission on Social Security Reform—a bipartisan group whose members were appointed both by President Reagan and the Congressional leadership—to study the problem and make recommendations for its solution. Such recommendations were adopted almost in their entirety in the 1983 Act.

This legislation made the following significant changes in the OASDI program (as well as some in the HI program):

1. OASDI and HI Coverage Provisions
   a. OASDI-HI coverage of new federal employees and current political appointees, elected officials, and judges. (HI coverage of all federal civilian employees was effective in 1983 under previous law.)
   b. Coverage of all nonprofit employees.
   c. State and local employees once covered are prohibited from withdrawing.
   d. Employee contributions to cash-or-deferred arrangements (Sec. 401[k]) and under nonqualified deferred-compensation plans when no substantial risk of forfeiture is present are covered.
2. OASDI Benefit Provisions
   a. Cost-of-living adjustments are deferred for six months (i.e., will always be in checks for December payable in early January).
   b. The indexing of benefits in payment status is changed from being based only on the CPI to the lower of CPI or wage increases when the trust funds are relatively low.

c. Gradual increases will be made in the normal retirement age from the present 65, beginning with those attaining age 62 in 2000—so that it will be 66 for those attaining such age in 2009–20, then rising to 67 for those attaining such age in 2027 and after. Age 62 is retained as the early-retirement age, but with appropriate, larger actuarial reductions.
d. Gradual increases will be made in the credit for postponing claiming (or not receiving) benefits beyond the normal retirement age from 3 percent per year for persons attaining age 65 in 1982–89 to 8 percent for persons attaining normal retirement age in 2009 and after.
e. The retirement earnings test for persons at the normal retirement age up to age 70 is liberalized, beginning in 1990, by changing the "$1 for $2" reduction in benefits for earnings above the annual exempt amount to a "$1 for $3" basis.
f. Several minor changes are made to liberalize benefits that primarily affect women (e.g., indexing deferred widow(er)'s benefits by whichever is more favorable, prices or wages, and increasing the benefit rate for disabled widow(er)s aged 50–59 from 50–71.5 percent depending on age at entitlement to a uniform 71.5 percent.)
g. The situation as to windfall benefits for retired and disabled workers who have pensions from noncovered employment and OASDI benefits based on a short period of covered employment is alleviated.
h. The offset of government employee pensions based on employment not covered by OASDI against OASDI spouse and widow(er) benefits is reduced from a full offset to a two-thirds offset.
i. Restrictions are placed on the payment of benefits to prisoners receiving retirement and survivor benefits (previous law related essentially to disability beneficiaries).
j. Restrictions are placed on the payment of benefits to aliens residing abroad who have, in general, not had at least five years of residence in the United States.

3. Revenue Provisions, OASDI and HI
   a. OASDI tax rate scheduled for 1985 was moved to 1984 for employers, but not employees. Trust funds receive, from general revenues, additional amount of taxes as if employee rate had been increased.

   b. Self-employed pay the combined OASDI-HI employer-employee rate, minus (for 1984–89) a credit (in lieu of a business expense deduction for such taxes). The trust funds receive, from general revenues, the additional amount of taxes as if the full employer-employee rate had been paid.
   c. About 72 percent of the OASDI tax rate increase scheduled for 1990 was moved forward to 1988.
   d. Part of OASDI benefits (but not more than 50 percent) will be subject to income tax for persons with high incomes, with the proceeds going into the OASDI Trust Funds.
   e. A lump-sum transfer of general revenues will be made to meet the cost of certain gratuitous military-service wage credits (which, under previous law, would have been paid for in future years).
   f. Interfund borrowing (which, under previous law, was permitted only in 1982) was allowed in 1983–87, with specific repayment provisions (before 1990 at the latest) and with prohibitions against borrowing from a fund that is relatively low.
   g. Operations of OASDI and HI Trust Funds will be removed from Unified Budget after FY 1992 (subsequent legislation moved this up to 1986 for OASDI).
   h. Two public members will be added to the Boards of Trustees.
4. HI Reimbursement Provisions
   a. A new method of reimbursement of providers of services will be gradually phased in. This will be done on the basis of uniform amounts (but varying as among nine geographical areas and as between rural and urban facilities) for each of 467 Diagnosis Related Groups.
   b. No change is made in the minimum eligibility age for HI benefits for the aged (i.e., it remains at 65).
5. SMI Provisions
   a. The enrollee premium rate is changed to a calendar-year basis (to correspond with the OASDI COLAs). The rate for July 1982 through June 1983 was to continue through December 1983.
   b. No change is made in the minimum eligibility age for SMI benefits for the aged (i.e., it remains at 65).

Possible Future OASDI Developments

Advisory groups have, over the years, advocated so-called universal coverage. Following the 1983 Amendments, relatively little remains to be done in this area, except perhaps to cover compulsorily all new hires in state and local government employment (as was done in the federal area).

The minimum retirement age at which unreduced benefits are payable was increased from the present 65 to age 67, phased in over a period of years, by the 1983 Act. This was done in recognition of the significant increase in life expectancy that has occurred in the last 40 years, as well as the likely future increases. If life expectancy increases even more rapidly than currently projected, a further increase in such age would reduce the higher long-range future cost of the program resulting from such increase.

The earnings test has always been subject to criticism by many persons, who argue that it is a disincentive to continued employment and that "the benefits have been bought and paid for, and therefore should be available at age 65." The 1983 Act, by increasing ultimately (beginning with those who attain age 66 in 2009) the size of the delayed retirement credits (to 8 percent per year) to approximately the actuarial-equivalent level, virtually eliminated the earnings test insofar as the cost aspects thereof are concerned. In other words, when the DRC is at an 8 percent level, the individual receives benefits for delayed retirement having approximately the same value as if benefits were paid without regard to the earnings test, beginning at the Normal Retirement Age. Some persons have advocated that the DRC should be at the 8 percent rate as soon as possible.

As to disability benefits, the definition might be tightened, such as by using "medical only" factors (and not vocational ones). Conversely, the definition could be liberalized so as to be on an occupational basis at age 50 and over. Also, the five-month waiting period could be shortened.

The general benefit level was significantly increased in 1969–72 (by about 23 percent in real terms), but financial problems caused this increase to be partially reversed in subsequent legislation (1974 and 1977). Nonetheless, there will be efforts by many persons to reverse the situation and expand the benefit level.

Over the years, the composition of the OASDI benefit structure—between individual-equity aspects and social-adequacy ones—tended to shift more toward social adequacy. The 1981 Amendments, however, moved in the other direction (e.g., by phasing out student benefits and the minimum-benefit provision). There may well be efforts in the future to inject more social adequacy into the program—or, conversely, more individual equity.

It frequently has been advocated that people should be allowed to opt out of the OASDI system and provide their own economic security through private-sector mechanisms, using both their own taxes and those of their employer. Although this approach has certain appealing aspects, it has some significant drawbacks. First, it is not possible to duplicate to any close extent the various features of OASDI, most notably the automatic adjustment of benefits for increases in the CPI.

Second, because the low-cost individuals (young, high-earnings ones) would be the most likely to opt out, there is the question of where the resulting financing shortfalls of the OASDI program would come from. Those who make such proposals (or even the more extreme ones, which involve terminating OASDI for all except those currently covered who are near retirement age) do not answer this question. The only source of financing would be from general revenues, and this means more general taxes, which would be paid to a considerable extent by those who have opted out.

Many have argued that part of the cost of OASDI should be met from general revenues. At times, an indirect manner of implementing such a funding method has been advocated, such as by moving part of the HI tax rate to OASDI and then partially financing HI from general revenues. The difficulty with this procedure is that no general-revenues moneys are available; the General Fund of the Treasury has large deficits. In turn, this would mean either that additional taxes of other types would have to be raised or that the budget deficit would become larger, and inflation would be fueled. Those opposed to general-revenues financing of OASDI, and of HI as well, believe that the financing, instead, should be entirely from direct, visible payroll taxes. Nonetheless, it is likely that pressure for general-revenues financing of OASDI will continue.

According to the latest intermediate-cost estimate for present law, the OASDI Trust Funds will have large annual excesses of income over outgo for the next three decades. As a result, mammoth fund balances will accumulate—amounting to somewhat over $8 trillion in 2025. Under current budgetary procedures, such annual excesses are considered as meeting the budget-deficit targets, and thus they hide the extent of titanic general-budget deficits. Further, the presence of such large fund balances could well encourage over-liberalization of the OASDI program now—e.g., by raising benefit levels or by postponing the scheduled increases in the NRA beginning in about a decade.

To prevent these undesirable results from occurring, Senator Daniel Patrick Moynihan proposed that the financing basis of the OASDI program should be returned to a pay-as-you-go basis. This would be done by an immediate reduction in the contribution rates and the introduction of a graded schedule of increases in the contribution rates, beginning in about 20 years. This proposal produced a vast amount of discussion (and also education of the public). Such a proposal will undoubtedly continue to be raised, although it has strong opposition from those who are concerned with the general-budget deficits and seek to hide them through "counting Social Security surpluses."

SUPPLEMENTAL SECURITY INCOME PROGRAM (SSI)

The SSI program replaced the federal/state public assistance programs of aid to the aged, blind, and disabled, except in Guam, Puerto Rico, and the Virgin Islands. Persons must be at least age 65 or be blind or disabled to qualify for the SSI payments.

The basic payment amount, before reduction for other income, for 1992 is $422 per month for one recipient and 50 percent more for an eligible couple. An automatic-adjustment provision closely paralleling that used under OASDI is applicable.

A number of "income disregards" are present. The most important is the disregard of $20 of income per month per family from such sources as OASDI, other pensions, earnings, and investments. The first $65 per month of earned income is disregarded, plus 50 percent of the remainder.

SSI has certain resource exemptions. In order to receive SSI, for 1992, resources cannot exceed $2,000 for an individual and $3,000 for a couple. However, in the calculation of resources, certain items are excluded—the home, household goods and personal effects (depending on value), an automobile with value of $4,500 or less, burial plots, and property needed for self-support—if these are found to be reasonable. Also, if life insurance policies have a face amount of $1,500 or less for an individual, their cash values are not counted as assets.

Some states pay supplements to SSI.

In addition to SSI, a public assistance program provides payments for widowed mothers (and fathers) with children. This is on a state-by state basis, with part of the cost borne by the federal government.

MEDICARE PROGRAM

Health (or medical care) benefits for active and retired workers and their dependents in the United States is, in the vast majority of cases, provided through the multiple means of the Medicare portion of Social Security for persons aged 65 and over and for long-term disabled persons, private employer-sponsored plans, and individual savings. As mentioned earlier, this is sometimes referred to as a "three-legged stool" or the three pillars of economic security protection. Another view of the situation for persons aged 65 and over and for long-term disabled persons is of Medicare providing the floor of protection for certain categories, or, in other cases, providing the basic protection, with public assistance programs, such as Medicaid, providing a safety net of protection for those whose income is not sufficient to purchase the needed medical care not provided through some form of prepaid insurance.

Private health benefit plans supplement Medicare to some extent. In other instances—essentially for active workers and their families—health benefit protection is provided by the private sector. The net result, however, is a broad network of health benefit protection.

Historical Development of Provisions

Beginning in the early 1950s, efforts were made to provide medical care benefits (primarily for hospitalization) for beneficiaries under the OASDI program. In 1965, such efforts succeeded, and the resulting program is called Medicare.

Initially, Medicare applied only to persons age 65 and over. In 1972, disabled Social Security beneficiaries who had been on the benefit rolls for at least two years were made eligible, as were virtually all persons in the country who have end-stage renal disease (i.e., chronic kidney disease). Since 1972, relatively few changes in coverage or benefit provisions have been made. In 1988, legislation that provided catastrophic-coverage benefits, to be financed largely through a surtax on the income tax of eligible beneficiaries, was enacted. However, as a result of massive protests from those who would be required to pay the surtax, these provisions were repealed in 1989.

Medicare is really two separate programs. One part, Hospital Insurance (HI),[5] is financed primarily from payroll taxes on workers covered under OASDI, including those under the Railroad Retirement system. Beginning in 1983, all civilian employees of the federal government were

---

[5] Sometimes referred to as Part A. Supplementary Medical Insurance is Part B.

covered under HI, even though, in general, not covered by OASDI. Also, beginning in April 1986, all newly hired state and local government employees are covered compulsorily (and, at the election of the governmental entity, all employees in service on March 31, 1986, who were not covered under OASDI can be covered for HI). The other part, Supplementary Medical Insurance (SMI), is on an individual voluntary basis and is financed partially by enrollee premiums, with the remainder, currently slightly more than 75 percent, coming from general revenues.

Persons Protected by HI

All individuals age 65 and over who are eligible for monthly benefits under OASDI or the Railroad Retirement program also are eligible for HI benefits (as are federal employees and state and local employees who have sufficient earnings credit from their special HI coverage). Persons are "eligible" for OASDI benefits if they could receive them when the person on whose earnings record they are eligible is deceased or receiving disability or retirement benefits, or could be receiving retirement benefits except for having had substantial earnings. Thus, the HI eligibles include not only insured workers, but also spouses, disabled children (in the rare cases where they are at least age 65), and survivors, such as widowed spouses and dependent parents. As a specific illustration, HI protection is available for an insured worker and spouse, both at least age 65, even though the worker has such high earnings that OASDI cash benefits are not currently payable.

In addition, HI eligibility is available for disabled beneficiaries who have been on the benefit roll for at least two years (beyond a 5-month waiting period). Such disabled eligibles include not only insured workers, but also disabled child beneficiaries aged 18 and over but disabled before age 22, and disabled widowed spouses, aged 50–64.

Further, persons under age 65 with end-stage renal disease (ESRD) who require dialysis or renal transplant are eligible for HI benefits if they meet one of a number of requirements. Such requirements for ESRD benefits include being fully or currently insured, being a spouse or a dependent child of an insured worker or of a monthly beneficiary, or being a monthly beneficiary.

Individuals aged 65 and over who are not eligible for HI as a result of their own or some other person's earnings can elect coverage, and then must make premium payments, whereas OASDI eligibles do not. The standard monthly premium rate is $192 for 1992.

Benefits Provided under HI

The principal benefit provided by the HI program is for hospital services. The full cost for all such services, other than luxury items, is paid by HI during a so-called spell of illness, after an initial deductible has been paid and with daily coinsurance for all hospital days after the 60th one, but with an upper limit on the number of days covered. A spell of illness is a period beginning with the first day of hospitalization and ending when the individual has been out of both hospitals and skilled nursing facilities for 60 consecutive days. The initial deductible is $652 for 1992. The daily coinsurance is $163 for the 61st to 90th days of hospitalization. A nonrenewable lifetime reserve of 60 days is available after the regular 90 days have been used; these lifetime reserve days are subject to daily coinsurance of $326 for 1992. The deductible and coinsurance amounts are adjusted automatically each year after 1992 to reflect past changes in hospital costs.

Benefits also are available for care provided in skilled nursing facilities, following at least three days of hospitalization. Such care is provided only when it is for convalescent or recuperative care, and not for custodial care. The first 20 days of such care in a spell of illness are provided without cost to the individual. The next 80 days, however, are subject to a daily coinsurance payment, which is $81.50 in 1992, and it will be adjusted automatically in the future in the same manner as the hospital cost-sharing amounts. No benefits are available after 100 days of care in a skilled nursing facility for a particular spell of illness.

In addition, an unlimited number of home health service benefits are provided by HI without any payment being required from the beneficiary. Also, hospice care for terminally ill persons is covered if all Medicare benefits other than physician services are waived; certain cost restrictions and coinsurance requirements apply with respect to prescription drugs.

HI benefit protection is provided only within the United States, with the exception of certain emergency services available when in or near Canada. Not covered by HI are those cases where services are performed in a Veterans Administration hospital or where the person is eligible for medical services under a workers' compensation program. Furthermore, Medicare is the secondary payor in cases when (a) medical care is payable under any liability policy, especially automobile ones; (b) during the first 18 months of treatment for ESRD cases when private group health insurance provides coverage; (c) for persons aged 65 and over (employees and spouses) who are under employer-sponsored group health insurance plans (which is required for all plans of employers with at least 20 employees) unless the employee opts out of it; and (d) for disability beneficiaries under the plan of an employer with at least 100 employees when the beneficiary is either an "active individual" or a family member of an employee.

Financing of HI

With the exception of the small group of persons who voluntarily elect coverage, the HI program is financed by payroll taxes on workers in employment covered by OASDI. This payroll tax rate is combined with that for OASDI. The HI tax rate is the same for employers and employees; self-employed persons pay the combined employer-employee tax rate, but have an offset to allow for the effect of business expenses on income taxes as described earlier in connection with OASDI taxes). Such HI tax rate for employees is 1.45 percent in 1990 and all future years. The maximum taxable earnings base for HI was the same as that for OASDI for all years before 1991, but was then raised to $125,000 (versus $53,400 for OASDI) and to $130,200 in 1992 (versus $55,500 for OASDI). It should be noted that long-range actuarial cost estimates indicate that this rate will not provide adequate financing after about 2000 (or perhaps even sooner).

The vast majority of persons who attained age 65 before 1968, and who were not eligible for HI benefit protection on the basis of an earnings record, were nonetheless given full eligibility for benefits without any charge. The cost for this closed blanketed-in group is met from general revenues rather than from HI payroll taxes.

The HI Trust Fund receives the income of the program from the various sources and makes the required disbursements for benefits and administrative expenses. The assets are invested and earn interest in the same manner as the OASDI Trust Funds.

Although the federal government is responsible for the administration of the HI program, the actual dealing with the various medical facilities is through fiscal intermediaries, such as Blue Cross and insurance companies, which are reimbursed for their expenses on a cost basis. Beginning in 1988, reimbursement for inpatient hospital services is based on uniform sums for each type of case for about 475 diagnosis-related groups.

Persons Protected under Supplementary Medical Insurance

Individuals aged 65 or over can elect SMI coverage on an individual basis regardless of whether they have OASDI insured status. In addition, disabled OASDI beneficiaries eligible for HI and persons with ESRD eligible under HI can elect SMI coverage. In general, coverage election must be made at about the time of initial eligibility, that is, attainment of age 65 or at the end of the disability-benefit waiting period. Subsequent election during general enrollment periods is possible but with higher premium rates being applicable. Similarly, individuals can terminate coverage and cease premium payment of their own volition.

Benefits Provided under SMI

The principal SMI benefit is partial reimbursement for the cost of physician services, although other medical services, such as diagnostic tests, ambulance services, prosthetic devices, physical therapy, medical equipment, and drugs not self-administerable, are covered. Not covered are out-of-hospital drugs, most dental services, most chiropractic services, routine physical and eye examinations, eyeglasses and hearing aids, and services outside of the United States, except those in connection with HI services that are covered in Canada. Just as for HI, there are limits on SMI coverage in Workers' Compensation cases, medical care under liability policies, private group health insurance applicable to ESRD, and employer-sponsored group health insurance for employees and their spouses.

SMI pays 80 percent of "recognized" charges, under a complicated determination basis that usually produces a lower charge than the reasonable and prevailing one, after the individual has paid a calendar-year deductible of $100 for 1991 and after (increased from $75 in 1982–90). Special limits apply on out-of-hospital mental health care costs and on the services of independent physical and occupational therapists. The cost-sharing payments ($100 deductible and 20 percent coinsurance) are waived for certain services—e.g., home health services, pneumococcal vaccine, and certain clinical diagnostic laboratory tests.

Financing of SMI

The standard monthly premium rate was $29.90 for 1991. The premium is higher for those who fail to enroll as early as they possibly can, with an increase of 10 percent for each full 12 months of delay. The premium is deducted from the OASDI benefits of persons currently receiving them, or is paid by direct submittal in other cases.

The remainder of the cost of the program is met by general revenues. In the aggregate, persons aged 65 and over pay only about 25 percent of the cost, while for disabled persons such proportion is only about 20 percent. As a result, enrollment in SMI is very attractive, and about 95 percent of those eligible to do so actually enroll.

The enrollee premium rate is changed every year, effective for January. In practice, the rate of increase in the premium rate is determined, in fact, by the percentage rise in the level of OASDI cash benefits in the previous year under the automatic adjustment provisions, and in part by the percentage rises in the per capita cost of the program. However, for the premium years 1984–90, the premium rate was set at 25 percent of the cost for persons aged 65 or over. The premium rates for 1992–95 have been established by legislation, being $31.80, $36.60, $41.10, and $46.10, respectively for each year.

The SMI Trust Fund was established to receive the enrollee premiums and the payments from general revenues. From this fund are paid the benefits and the accompanying administrative expenses. Although the program is under the general supervision of the federal government, most of the administration is accomplished through ''carriers'', such as Blue Shield or insurance companies, on an actual cost basis for their administrative expenses.

Possible Future Development of Medicare

Over the years, numerous proposals have been made to modify the Medicare program. Some of these would expand it significantly, while others would curtail it to some extent.

Among the proposals that would expand the program are those to establish some type of national health insurance program, having very comprehensive coverage of medical services applicable to the entire population. Somewhat less broadly, other proposals would extend Medicare coverage to additional categories of OASDI beneficiaries beyond old-age beneficiaries aged 65 and over and disabled beneficiaries on the roll for at least two years—such as to early-retirement cases at ages 62–64 and to all disability beneficiaries.

In another direction, liberalizing proposals have been made to add further services, such as out-of-hospital drugs, physical examinations, and dental services. Still other proposals have been made in the direction of reducing the extent of cost-sharing on the part of the beneficiary by lowering or eliminating the deductible and coinsurance provisions and by eliminating the duration-of-stay limits on HI benefit eligibility.

Proposals have been made to reduce the cost of the Medicare program by increasing the cost-sharing payments made by the beneficiary. For example, the cost-sharing in the first 60 days of hospitalization could be changed from a one-time payment of the initial deductible to some type of daily coinsurance that would foster the incentive to shorten hospital stays. Another proposal is to adjust automatically, from year to year, the SMI annual deductible, which, unlike the HI cost-sharing payments, is a fixed amount, although it has been increased by ad hoc changes from the initial $50 in 1966 to $75 in 1982 and to $100 in 1991.

A major risk for persons aged 65 and over that is not covered by Medicare is the cost of long-term custodial nursing-home care and homemaker services for disabled or frail persons. Although many persons recognize the serious nature of this problem, it is currently being met only on a means-test basis by the Medicaid program. Some people believe that the problem should be met on an ''insurance'' basis under a new Part C of Medicare, but others think that it is not an ''insurable'' risk and must be handled on a means-test basis (possibly liberalized somewhat).

Proposals have also been made recently to cover compulsorily under HI all state and local government employees (and not merely new hires after March 1986)—as has been done for federal employees.

As to financing aspects, proposals have been made to eliminate the enrollee premiums under SMI and to replace them by complete financing from general revenues or by partial financing from payroll taxes, while at the same time reducing the HI tax rates and making up for this by partial general revenue financing of HI. It also has been proposed that the HI program should be financed partially, or even completely, by general revenues.

Proposals concerning the reimbursement of physicians under SMI have been made to discourage or prevent them from charging the beneficiaries more than the allowable charges. In 1989, legislation was enacted that would eventually restrict such charges so that they could not be more than 15 percent higher than 95 percent of the recognized charges applicable to physicians who take assignment (as well as requiring the physician to submit the bill to the Medicare carrier in all instances). Similarly, various proposals have been made—and some have been enacted—to lower the cost of the HI program as far as reimbursement of hospitals and skilled nursing facilities is concerned, although this would have no effect on the Medicare beneficiary directly.

MEDICAID

Over the years, the cost of medical care for recipients of public assistance and for other low-income persons has been met in a variety of ways. Some years ago, these provisions were rather haphazard, and the medical care costs were met by inclusion with the public assistance payments. In 1960, a separate public assistance program in this area was enacted—namely, Medical Assistance for the Aged (MAA), which applied to persons aged 65 and over, both those receiving Old-Age Assistance and other persons not having sufficient resources to meet large medical expenses.

Then in 1965, the MAA program and the federal matching for medical vendor payments for public assistance categories other than MAA were combined into the Medicaid program. This new program covered not only public assistance recipients, but also persons of similar demographic characteristics who were medically indigent.

The Medicaid program is operated by the several states, with significant federal financing being available. Some states cover only public assistance recipients.

Medicaid programs are required to furnish certain services, to receive federal financial participation. These services include those for physicians, hospitals (both inpatient and outpatient), laboratory and X-ray tests, home health visits, and nursing home care. Most other medical services, such as drugs, dental care, and eyeglasses, can be included at the option of the state, and then federal matching will be made available. Also, as a result of legislation enacted in 1988, states must pay the SMI premiums and the HI and SMI cost-sharing payments for persons who are eligible for Medicare and who have incomes below the poverty level and have resources of no more than twice the standard under the Supplemental Security Income program. Thus, the states have the advantage of the relatively large general-revenues financing in that program.

The federal government pays a proportion of the total cost of the Medicaid expenditures for medical care that varies inversely with the average per capita income of the state. This proportion is 55 percent for a state with the same average per capita income as the nation as a whole. States with above-average income have a lower matching proportion, but never less than 50 percent. Conversely, states with below-average income have a higher federal matching percentage, which can be as much as 83 percent. The federal government also pays part of the administrative costs of the Medicaid programs; generally, this is 50 percent, although for certain types of expenses which are expected to control costs, the federal percentage is higher.

CHAPTER 6

WORKERS' COMPENSATION INSURANCE

John D. Worrall

The United States has several social "insurance" programs: the massive Social Security Program (discussed in Chapter 5 of the *Handbook)* that includes Old Age, Survivors, and Disability Insurance (OASDI); the Temporary Disability Insurance Program (TDI), which is available in five jurisdictions and provides benefits for up to six months for nonwork-related illnesses or injuries; the Unemployment Insurance (UI) program; and Workers' Compensation Insurance (WC). Workers' compensation, a no-fault insurance program that provides both indemnity (cash) and medical benefits for injuries arising "out of and in the course of employment," is the oldest of these programs. The workers' compensation program was paying cash benefits 25 years before the advent of unemployment insurance and 40 years before the Social Security Disability Insurance (SSDI) program. The first state workers' compensation laws to pass constitutional muster were enacted by nine states in 1911. Most of the remaining states passed workers' compensation acts by 1920.

The regulation of workers' compensation insurance has been left to the states, and there has been much controversy over state, rather than federal, administration of the program. This controversy continues to date, with some parties pushing for more federal involvement in all aspects of the program. Although the individual state workers' compensation laws have some features in common, the benefit levels, program structure, offset provisions, and self-insurance requirements (where permitted) differ greatly from state to state. Because the state workers' compensation laws are so complex, legal, actuarial, and underwriting advice should be sought from attorneys, Fellows of the Casualty Actuarial Society, and licensed agents and brokers, respectively. This chapter is an introduction to the topic of workers' compensation insurance and should not be construed as professional advice. The differences in benefit levels and utilization, method of administration, propensity to litigate, industrial structure, and injury frequency and severity are among the major factors resulting in the differences in workers' compensation insurance costs among states. Workers with the same injury in two different states can receive very different cash benefits. However, in virtually every state, they would receive nearly unlimited medical coverage. Workers' compensation is part of a larger disability income system designed to provide income maintenance or income support. Some of the programs in the disability income system are based on labor-force attachment. For example, a person who suffers an injury "in and out of the course of employment" may be eligible for cash benefits designed to maintain his or her income (workers' compensation). Benefits provided through other programs in the disability income system, such as veterans' benefits, are based on other statuses and affiliations, and some of the programs designed to provide income support, such as public assistance, are entitlement programs. Each of the programs in the disability income system gives rise to questions of program efficiency and the adequacy and equity of benefits.

Because workers' compensation laws vary dramatically by state, a careful reading of each state's statute is essential. Similarly, there is a large body of case law on workers' compensation. A cottage industry has arisen to follow changes in legislative and case law. The National Council on Compensation Insurance (NCCI), the largest workers' compensation rating organization in the United States, maintains a staff that does in-depth analyses of the laws of each state in which it is licensed. The U.S. Chamber of Commerce publishes an annual *Analysis of Workers' Compensation Laws* that provides valuable information on each state's program. The state legislatures set the coverage conditions and benefit provisions, but the workers' compensation program is financed through the private sector. The state insurance departments regulate workers' compensation prices, which vary by state and by the nature of the business being insured, but the workers' compensation insurance business is competitive, with approximately six hundred insurers competing for it.

Workers' compensation insurance is a mandatory, "no fault" program in 47 of the 50 states. In exchange for giving up their right to sue under the workers' compensation laws, employees are expected to get swift and certain payment of medical and cash benefits for injuries or occupational diseases regardless of fault. In exchange for giving up their right to contest claims, employers are protected against the risk of negligence suits for occupational injury or disease brought by their employees. The state workers' compensation laws were intended to eliminate or minimize the litigation that characterized work place injury before their adoption. Unfortunately, litigation rates remain high in a number of states. Although workers' compensation insurance is elective in three states, virtually all employers elect coverage in those three states. Employers who fail to elect coverage expose themselves to tort actions and a much greater likelihood of losing in court because they forego the right to the three common-law defenses: contributory negligence, assumption of risk, and negligence of other workers.

Some workers are covered by federal legislation. Under the Jones Act and the Federal Employers Liability Act, seamen and railroad workers are exempt from state workers' compensation laws. Such workers retain their right to sue their employers. Maritime workers are covered under the Longshoremen's and Harbor Workers Compensation Act. Federal employees also have a workers' compensation program. They are covered under the Federal Employees Compensation Act, which is administered by the U.S. Department of Labor.

FINANCING WORKERS' COMPENSATION

Employers can meet their requirements to provide workers' compensation insurance by insuring with private insurance companies, with state insurance funds, or by self-insuring. Six states do not permit employers to buy primary workers' compensation insurance from private insurance carriers. In the states that allow private property-casualty insurance companies to write policies, employers may insure with stock or mutual insurers, or, in some states, with reciprocal insurers.

Nevada, North Dakota, Ohio, Washington, West Virginia, and Wyoming have monopoly state insurance funds. Employers in North Dakota and Wyoming are required to purchase their insurance through the state monopoly. In the other four states they can either self-insure or buy insurance from the state fund. In thirteen states—Arizona, California,

Colorado, Idaho, Maryland, Michigan, Minnesota, Montana, New York, Oklahoma, Oregon, Pennsylvania, and Utah—the state has a "competitive state fund" that competes with private insurers for workers' compensation insurance business. Each of these 13 states also permits employers to self-insure.

Forty-seven states permit some form of self-insurance; Texas will become the 48th on January 1, 1993. Twenty states permit individual firms to self-insure. Firms that self-insure generally are required to meet minimum financial standards set by the state, and most employers are too small to qualify for self-insurance. Those firms that do self-insure generally are required to post a bond or deposit securities with a government regulatory agency (such as the Industrial Commission or the Workers' Compensation Board). Twenty-eight states permit employers, typically in the same industry and general line of business, to form groups for the purpose of self-insuring. Firms electing to self-insure, individually or in groups, may purchase excess insurance or self-insure for fixed amounts for individual or aggregate claims. This helps protect them against the cash drain that would accompany a large claim. Firms that self-insure are subject to different tax treatment than firms that buy primary coverage from a private insurance carrier. Private insurance carriers can deduct paid losses and the discounted present value of the change in loss reserves when calculating their tax liability under the Tax Reform Act of 1986. Firms that self-insure can deduct paid losses and expenses but not loss reserves. Hence, firms that self-insure lose the tax deduction for premiums paid they would get if they purchased a policy from a private insurance carrier, are subject to less-favorable tax treatment on incurred losses, and subject themselves to unlimited liability (unless they insure excess amounts of coverage with private carriers). Firms that self-insure may have some cash flow advantages and may reap the benefits of good claim frequency and severity experience.

Not all employers are able to secure coverage from private insurers at the posted regulated prices. Insurers do not expect to be able to earn the cost of capital by insuring such firms. In many of the states, such employers find themselves in the "residual" market or assigned risk pools. Although the percentage of the workers' compensation business in the pools is a function of the perceived adequacy of workers' compensation rates and varies by state, as of 1991 over 20 percent of the privately insured workers' compensation business was in the pools.

WORKERS' COMPENSATION PRICES

Workers' compensation insurance is regulated in every state. The state regulates solvency, forms, experience rating, dividend plans, and a host of other items. Most states also strictly regulate workers' compensation rates. Employers are charged workers' compensation insurance rates per hundreds of dollars of payroll. As the rate for some class codes (discussed later in the chapter) is well above $10 per $100 of payroll, workers' compensation insurance can be a major cost of doing business. Workers' compensation cash benefits increase every year in virtually every state. This is caused not only by changes in the state laws, but also by the fact that most current state laws tie workers' compensation benefits to the nominal statewide average weekly wage. As the statewide average weekly wage increases with inflation, new claimants are paid a fixed percentage of the higher nominal wage. Medical costs under workers' compensation also have increased more rapidly than for the medical component of the Consumer Price Index. Workers' compensation rate making is quite complicated, and the requirements differ by state. The scope of this chapter does not allow an exhaustive treatment of workers' compensation rate making, and the following is a brief overview.

The regulation of workers' compensation prices takes several forms. In many states, rating bureaus file proposed rates on behalf of members and subscribers. The state insurance department either approves the rates for use, or it orders a rate hearing at which a hearing officer attempts to determine if the proposed rates are adequate and not unfairly discriminatory. Although the issues to be resolved in such hearings are diverse, common themes include the accuracy of projected medical and cash claims, frequency and severity costs, the cost of capital and the allowed rate of return, and current and projected expenses. States that require insurance department formal review before insurance companies issue new policies at the proposed rates are called "prior approval" states. In other states ("file and use" states) insurers can file proposed rates and use them after a suitable period for insurance department review. Several states do not permit rating bureaus or rate making in concert. Currently, rating bureaus file proposed rates using losses, expenses, and a markup (a profit and contingency factor) that can be positive or negative. The National Association of Insurance Commissioners (NAIC) is working on a plan to require rating bureaus to file "pure premiums" or "loss costs" only. Such a plan, which is likely to be adopted, would enable rating bureaus to project future cash and medical losses only. Individual insurance companies could use their own expense experience and profit needs together with such bureau loss projections to file individual proposed workers' compensation rates with state insurance departments.

As a result of the McCarran-Ferguson Act, property-casualty insurance companies have been granted a partial exemption from the antitrust laws, and this exemption has enabled the companies to make rates in concert. Currently, the U.S. Congress is considering amendments that would repeal the exemption. If such amendments pass, and there is a good likelihood that they eventually will, the rating bureaus may be able to file the "pure premiums" discussed above. After a transition period, they would not be able to promulgate the "trend factors" discussed below.

Manual Rates

Manual rates are the starting point for an understanding of workers' compensation prices. Premium and loss data is collected for each employer insured by a private insurance carrier or competitive state fund. Firms are separated into three areas of economic activity: manufacturing, contract construction, and "all other," and then are classified further by the type of business in which they are engaged and assigned to one of more than 500 workers' compensation class codes (the number of classes varies by state). These codes are not the same as a standard industrial classification (SIC) or a census code. To determine what manual rates they will propose for a future time period, rating bureau actuaries examine all relevant available data to determine whether a rate increase, decrease, or no change is required. Projected costs and revenues are compared to make this determination, and the projected ratio of losses and loss-adjustment expenses is compared with a permissible loss and loss adjustment ratio.

Premiums collected during the time period for which data were gathered are adjusted to reflect development, subsequent changes in rates, and changes expected in payrolls during the future period in which proposed rates will be in effect. Losses also are adjusted to reflect loss development, benefit changes, and loss adjustment expenses. A ratio of these adjusted losses to premiums is compared with a permitted (the permissible) ratio to arrive at an indicated change in rates. The indicated change in rates is further adjusted to reflect both law amendments that will take effect during the period proposed rates will be in force and recent trends (called "trend factors") in adjusted loss ratios. These trend factors are derived through linear or nonlinear regression analysis. The overall change in rate level is determined for each of the three major subdivisions: manufacturing, contract construction, and all others. The rate change is then distributed to each of the workers' compensation class codes depending on the relative contribution or weight (class relativity) of the class within the major subdivision.

Small firms are charged these manual rates, which represent the average experience for their workers' compensation class code. Small firms also may be charged minimum premiums, loss constants, and expense constants. Loss constants are applied to small firms to attempt to stabilize loss ratios across all firm sizes. Expense constants reflect the fact that insurers must devote a higher percentage of each premium dollar from small policies to the cost of writing and processing that policy than they do for larger policies. Minimum premiums are charged because insurers do not want to subject themselves to unlimited liability unless they receive some minimum premium in return. Manual rates are the first step in workers' compensation pricing. There are many programs, some mandatory and others voluntary, that affect workers' compensation insurance prices.

Adjustments to Manual Rates

Insureds with premiums greater than $5,000 are given mandatory premium discounts that increase with the size of their manual premiums. These discounts can be close to 15 percent for premiums greater than $1 million. Where allowed, stock insurers and mutual insurers use different discount tables to reflect their different operating and policyholder dividend policies, but not all states permit the use of different discount tables. Stock company discounts are greater than mutual company discounts, and as can be seen from the example above, premium discounts can reduce workers' compensation prices substantially.

Firms with workers' compensation manual premiums in excess of $5,000 are subject to mandatory experience rating. Experience-rated firms have their manual rates adjusted up or down by a modifier (their "mod"), which is a weighted average of its experience and that of all other firms in its own class based on the firm's actual claims experience over the last three years. If a firm's experience is better or worse than the average or expected experience for its class, its manual rate will be reduced or increased accordingly. The weight given to the firm's own experience varies directly with the credibility of its data. Because of the paucity of claims and the inability to predict the nature of all work injuries, small (manually rated) firms have zero credibility. Large firms—for example, those with insurance premiums over $1 million—are fully credible and self-rated, that is, their modifier, and hence the price they are charged, is fully determined by their own experience. Experience-rating plans provide safety incentives for employers. Employers can reduce the price they pay for workers' compensation insurance by maintaining a safe workplace.

Firms that generate $25,000 of standard premium for a one-year policy, or $50,000 for three years, can elect to purchase a retrospective rating plan (retro). This option, which usually is selected by larger firms, is similar to cost-plus insurance. The employer pays the loss costs, subject to negotiated minimums and maximums, and an insurance charge. Insureds have several different plans from which to select, but each provides the opportunity to capitalize on above-average safety standards and good loss experience.

Most mutual insurance companies and many stock (participating) companies pay dividends to policyholders. Some of these dividend plans pay a flat percentage rate to all policyholders (flat-rate plans), while others pay sliding scale dividends based on the loss performance of the individual insured (sliding scale plans). Countrywide dividends to workers' compensation insureds have been in the 5–6 percent range recently, although they are much higher in some states and vary considerably by insurance carrier. Some stock companies pay smaller dividends but offer higher premium discounts.

Many states permit private insurance carriers to deviate from filed bureau rates, and such deviations can play an important role in the competition for workers' compensation business. Deviations can be up or down, and usually are in terms of flat percentages. Insurers may choose to deviate downward because they believe their expenses are much lower than average, or that their underwriting is superior. They may choose to deviate upward because they believe that the rating bureau has filed inadequate rates (or the regulatory authority has mandated them). Some insurers may own multiple insurance companies that write workers' compensation insurance in a state. One member of the group or fleet may deviate from bureau rates, while another does not.

"Scheduled rating" also is allowed in many states, and this can be a powerful underwriting tool. Insurers are allowed to reduce the rate charged to insureds to reflect characteristics of the insured (for example, strong management or outstanding safety programs) that are likely to result in lower-than-average loss costs. The state insurance department typically establishes the maximum scheduled rating credit that can be applied.

In some states employers can negotiate the amount and timing of deposits they pay insurers. These "deposit premiums" can be waived in some cases. As the timing of cash flows can be negotiated, the *real* (discounted present) value of an employer's workers' compensation premium is not necessarily fixed.

CLAIMS AND BENEFITS

There are five basic workers' compensation insurance claims. The five types include:

1. Noncompensatory Medical or Medical-Only Claims.
2. Temporary Total Disability Claims.
3. Permanent Partial Disability Claims.
4. Permanent Total Disability Claims.
5. Death Claims.

Explanations of each follow.

Noncompensatory Medical or Medical-Only Claims

"Medical only" claims result from injuries or occupational disease "arising out of and in the course of employment" that do not result in lost work time sufficient to generate cash benefit claims. These claims are by far the most common type, accounting for approximately 80 percent of all workers' compensation claims. Although the state workers' compensation laws provide for virtually unlimited medical coverage, most medical-only claims do not exceed $200, and they account for well under 10 percent of the cost of workers' compensation. The medical cost component of the cash claims described below are far more expensive. As the medical cost component of all workers' compensation claims, including the cash claims to be discussed shortly, now accounts for over 25 percent of system costs, states have adopted cost-containment strategies to rein in escalating medical expenses. Half of the states have adopted medical fee schedules that list the maximum amounts that will be paid for certain procedures. Many states limit the choice of medical care providers and the ability to switch providers after the initial choice has been made. States are beginning to adopt billing and utilization review procedures as well.

Temporary Total Disability Claims

Temporary total disability claims are those claims for injuries or occupational diseases serious enough to prevent someone from working but from which full recovery is expected. Most state laws have both waiting periods and *retroactive periods*. The waiting period in most states is between three to seven days. Injured workers begin to draw cash benefits if they have lost work time that exceeds the state waiting period. Should their temporary total disability result in lost work time that exceeds the state-mandated retroactive period—two to three weeks in most states—they receive retroactive cash benefits for the waiting period. Temporary total disability benefits are the most common form of cash claim accounting for roughly three of every four cash claims and 20 percent of workers' compensation costs. Although over one half of temporary total disability claims close within one month, some are long-duration claims, and others become permanent claims. States limit the amount of time that a temporary total disability claimant can collect benefits and in some instances the amount of cumulative cash benefits.

A typical state's workers' compensation law provides that workers who suffer temporary total disability receive cash benefits equal to two thirds of their pre-injury wage subject to maximum and minimum payments. The maximum generally is based on a percentage of the statewide average weekly wage, 100 percent being the most common. Consequently, workers who earned a wage greater than the statewide average weekly wage may have *replacement rates* that actually are less than two thirds. Similarly, virtually all states provide minimum cash benefits for temporary total disability. The most common method of determining the minimum payment is to use a percentage of the statewide average weekly wage or to specify the injured worker's wage as the minimum. In some states the minimum is as high as 50 percent of the statewide average weekly wage. Consequently, the replacement rate for low-wage workers can be greater than 100 percent. Because workers' compensation benefits are not taxable, it is not unusual for workers to receive larger amounts in cash benefits than their normal take-home pay. The higher the *real* (after-tax) replacement rate, the stronger the incentive both to file a workers' compensation insurance claim and to lengthen the duration of a nonwork spell. There is strong research evidence that a 10 percent increase in real workers' compensation cash benefits results in a 4 percent increase in claims filed.

Less than one quarter of the states adjust temporary total disability benefits for inflation, and several of these only after two or three years from the injury date. As most temporary disability claims close fairly rapidly, inflation does not have a chance to erode the value of cash benefits for the majority of temporary total disability beneficiaries. However, for long-duration cases and permanent claims, to be discussed below, the real replacement rate falls with the passage of time as inflation erodes the value of cash benefits.

The state workers' compensation statutes provide for vocational rehabilitation benefits for injured workers. More than one third of the states have special funds to finance the provision of vocational rehabilitation services. Over half the states have their own workers' compensation vocational rehabilitation sections, but most states refer injured workers to public or private providers for vocational rehabilitation services. Vocational rehabilitation services are used almost exclusively by long-duration temporary total disability claimants and permanent disability claimants. As temporary total claimants who will make the transition to permanent disability claimants can have the amount of their cash benefit determined by a disability rating (see below), they may have an incentive to forestall or forego rehabilitation services that could restore them to the world of work.

Permanent Partial Disability Claims

Permanent partial disability claims account for most of the costs of the workers' compensation program. Although these claims represent only 4 percent of all workers' compensation claims and 20 percent of cash claims, they constitute 60 percent of program costs. They also are responsible for a good deal of the litigation cases in workers' compensation. Permanent partial claims usually begin with a period of temporary total disability, but the claimants eventually are evaluated as having a permanent but *partial* disability. These partial disabilities can be quite severe, and some permanent partial disability claimants show up on the Social Security disability insurance rolls.

The method of evaluating the extent of permanent partial disability, as well as the rationale for awarding benefits, varies among (and sometimes within) states. Most permanent partial benefits fall into two broad categories, "scheduled" and "nonscheduled" benefits. States with scheduled benefits award a specific dollar amount depending on the nature of the injury. States that have schedules tend to list awards for amputations and loss of hearing. For example, the state of Connecticut pays about a quarter of a million dollars to a worker who loses his or her arm at the shoulder. A few states have no schedule but pay disability benefits on the basis of the "impairment," "whole man," or "wage loss" principles. As the amount of cash benefit to be paid varies directly with the disability rating assigned to injured workers under these three schemes, and for nonscheduled injuries in general, there is much contention over disability ratings.

Permanent partial disability benefits can be substantial. As lifetime awards can run well into the hundreds of thousands of dollars, there are incentives for both employers, as represented by their insurers, and employees to litigate these claims. Attorneys have incentive to litigate them on a contingency-fee basis because many states permit injured workers to receive lump-sum settlements called "redemptions," "wash-outs," or "compromise and release" in some states. In part to attempt to reduce litigation in the system, Florida adopted a wage-loss scheme. Workers receive a periodic payment based on their wage loss. The periodic payment lessens the incentive to litigate, as it is more difficult to interest attorneys in collecting one third of a weekly payment of $300 than one third of a lump-sum settlement of $120,000, but the system still has problems. Workers may suffer periods of reduced, or zero, wages unrelated to a work injury, and it is quite difficult to determine the cause of wage movements for individual workers. The wage loss can vary procyclically with the business cycle, for example, with the workers' compensation program carrying the burden for a soft economy.

Permanent Total Disability Claims

Permanent total disability claims are rare. Less than one half of 1 percent of all cash claims are permanent total claims. These claims tend to have the highest *average* claim cost, about $200,000 per claim, and account for about 5 percent of workers' compensation costs. Workers who receive permanent total awards are expected to remain totally disabled after maximum medical improvement. States tend to award benefits for life, or the duration of the disability. The replacement rates and inflation adjustments tend to be the same as those for temporary total disability, but a few more states provide inflation protection for permanent total cases.

Death Claims

Death claims are slightly more common than permanent total disability claims, but they still constitute less than one half of 1 percent of cash claims. The average cost of a death claim is lower than that of the average permanent total disability claim. Fatalities account for about 5 percent of workers' compensation insurance costs. Cash benefits are paid to surviving spouses and children. The replacement rates are similar to those paid for total disability claims, with two thirds of the pre-injury wage being a common benefit rate, but many states reduce the replacement rate substantially if a surviving spouse has no minor children.

Death benefits are subject to maximum and minimum weekly amounts, as well as to maximum lifetime amounts. The lifetime amount may be specified in the law or may be implied as the duration of benefit receipt is restricted in most states. Remarriage of a surviving spouse can result in the cessation of benefit payments, frequently with an accompanying lump-sum settlement. Actuaries use remarriage tables to reserve or price these claims. All states provide burial allowances for fatal injuries covered under the workers' compensation law.

COORDINATION OF BENEFITS

Because workers' compensation is one of a host of programs designed to assist people with work disabilities, it is not unusual to find workers' compensation cash beneficiaries receiving payments from one or more additional programs. The various Social Security benefits are those most commonly received with workers' compensation, but veterans' benefits, public assistance, private insurance, and other programs provide joint benefits as well. As mentioned previously, the workers' compensation laws were in force long before Social Security or unemployment insurance.

When workers' compensation was introduced, there was no need to consider offsets or coordination of benefits. When Social Security was introduced, there was no offset provision in the law, but one was initiated in 1965 and limits the combined workers' compensation and Social Security payment to 80 percent of pre-injury current earnings. Nineteen states have Social Security offset provisions in their state workers' compensation laws. The federal government has prohibited any further state offset provisions. Only nine states have offset provisions for unemployment benefits. Although there are exceptions, a good rule of thumb is that workers' compensation benefits are primary for other programs.

SUMMARY

Workers' compensation is a mandatory, no-fault social insurance program that provides medical and cash benefits and rehabilitation services to workers who suffer injuries or occupational diseases arising "out of and in the course of employment." The program is strictly regulated by the states. Employers pay for this program as an employee benefit, but there is research evidence that as workers' compensation costs increase for employers, employees bear the cost burden in a dollar-for-dollar wage tradeoff. Most employers, who tend to be small, pay manual rates, or close to manual rates. However, over 80 percent of covered payrolls are experience rated. There are many competitive pricing devices that have a major impact on the price of workers' compensation insurance.

Most workers' compensation claims are simple medical-only claims, and the most frequent cash claims, temporary total disability claims, usually close within a month. Unfortunately, permanent claims that result from serious injuries are expensive and prone to litigation. Medical benefits are virtually unlimited in all states, but cash benefits usually are capped. Federal law limits the combined workers' compensation and Social Security benefit to 80 percent of pre-injury earnings. Less than half of the states offset Social Security, and even fewer offset unemployment insurance. In most other cases workers' compensation is primary.

CHAPTER 7

FUNDAMENTALS OF UNEMPLOYMENT COMPENSATION PROGRAMS

George E. Rejda

Unemployment compensation is an important employee benefit. Weekly cash benefits are paid to workers who are involuntarily unemployed who meet certain eligibility requirements. The weekly cash benefit enables unemployed workers to maintain their consumption and reduces the economic insecurity that results from extended unemployment.

The primary purpose of this chapter is to discuss the fundamentals of unemployment compensation programs. Unemployment compensation in the United States consists of several distinct programs. First, regular state unemployment compensation programs exist in all states, the District of Columbia, Puerto Rico, and the Virgin Islands. The regular state programs came into existence as a result of the Social Security Act of 1935. Second, a permanent extended-benefits program also is available that pays additional unemployment benefits in states with high unemployment. In addition, separate government-provided programs exist for civilian employees of the federal government, for ex-service members, and for railroad employees. Private employers may provide unemployment-related benefits such as severance pay and, in conjunction with unions through collective bargaining, supplemental unemployment benefits (SUBs). These are covered in Chapter 28 of the *Handbook*.

The treatment in this chapter is limited to the regular state programs and the permanent program of extended benefits. More specifically, the following areas are discussed: (1) objectives of unemployment compensation; (2) state unemployment compensation provisions; (3) extended benefits program; (4) financing unemployment compensation; (5) administration of unemployment compensation; and (6) unemployment compensation problems and issues.[1]

OBJECTIVES OF UNEMPLOYMENT COMPENSATION

Unemployment compensation programs have several objectives. The most important include the following:

- Provide weekly cash benefits during periods of involuntary unemployment.
- Help stabilize the economy during recessions.
- Encourage employers to stabilize their employment.
- Help unemployed workers find jobs.

Unemployment can cause great economic insecurity. Thus, the primary purpose of unemployment compensation is *to pay weekly cash benefits to workers who are involuntarily unemployed*. The benefits paid provide for the partial replacement of earnings to workers who are involuntarily unemployed for temporary periods and thus help the unemployed workers to maintain their previous standard of living. As a result, economic insecurity from involuntary unemployment is reduced.

Unemployment compensation programs *help stabilize the economy during business recessions*. Unemployment compensation is a powerful automatic stabilizer. During business recessions, when unemployment increases, unemployment benefits also increase in a desirable countercyclical manner. Thus, personal income and consumption spending can be maintained, which reduces the severity of the business recession and helps stabilize the economy.

Another important objective is *to encourage employers to stabilize their employment*. This is done by experience rating in which employers with favorable employment records pay reduced unemployment compen-

---

[1]The material in this chapter is based largely on George E. Rejda, *Social Insurance and Economic Security*, 4th ed. (Englewood Cliffs, N.J.: Prentice-Hall, Inc., 1991), Chapters 14 and 15, and Committee on Ways and Means, U.S. House of Representatives, *Overview of Entitlement Programs, 1990 Green Book*, Background Material and Data on Programs within the Jurisdiction of the Committee on Ways and Means (Washington, D.C.: U.S. Government Printing Office, 1990), pp. 443–522. The author drew heavily on these sources in preparing this chapter.

sation tax rates. Experience rating is an important financing issue that will be discussed later in the chapter.

Another important objective is *to help unemployed workers find jobs*. Applicants for unemployment benefits are required to register for work at local employment offices, and officials assist unemployed workers in finding suitable employment. The unemployed benefits give the unemployed workers time to find jobs that are consistent with their education, skills, and experience. Computer job banks are especially helpful in matching the available jobs in the community with the skills and experience of unemployed workers.

STATE UNEMPLOYMENT COMPENSATION PROVISIONS

The characteristics of regular state unemployment compensation programs vary widely among the states. Each state is free to determine coverage, eligibility requirements, and benefit amounts, subject to certain minimum federal standards. However, certain common provisions are present in all programs.[2]

Covered Occupations

Most occupations today are covered for unemployment compensation benefits. About 97 percent of all wage and salary workers or about 87 percent of all employed workers are covered by unemployment compensation programs.[3]

The Federal Unemployment Tax Act (FUTA) requires coverage of certain occupations under state unemployment compensation programs if the state wants to qualify for the 5.4 percent federal tax credit (discussed later). *Private firms* are covered if they pay wages of at least $1,500 during any calendar quarter or employ at least one worker on at least one day of each of 20 weeks in the current or prior year.

Agricultural firms are covered if they pay cash wages of at least $20,000 for agricultural labor during any calendar quarter or employ 10 or more workers on at least one day in each of 20 different weeks in the current or prior year. *Domestic service employers* are also covered if they

---

[2]Rejda, *Social Insurance and Economic Security*, pp. 329–45.

[3]*Overview of Entitlement Programs*, p. 458.

pay cash wages of $1,000 or more for domestic service during any calendar quarter in the current or prior year.

Most occupations in *state and local government* also are covered for unemployment compensation benefits. However, state and local government employers are not required to pay the federal unemployment tax and have the option of reimbursing the state for any unemployment benefits paid to laid-off employees rather than paying regular state unemployment compensation contributions.

Nonprofit organizations of a charitable, religious, or educational nature are covered if the nonprofit organization employs at least four workers for at least one day on 20 different weeks in the current or prior year. Like state and local governments, a nonprofit organization is exempt from FUTA taxes and has the option either to pay the state unemployment tax or to reimburse the state for the benefits paid. Many jurisdictions have expanded coverage of nonprofit employers beyond that required by federal law. At least 21 jurisdictions now cover nonprofit organizations that employ one or more workers rather than four or more.[4]

Finally, the states can elect to cover certain occupations not covered by FUTA, but most states have not expanded FUTA coverage significantly. Excluded occupations typically include (1) self-employment, (2) certain agricultural labor and domestic service, (3) certain student interns, (4) service of patients in hospitals, (5) certain alien farm workers until January 1993, and (6) seasonal camp workers.[5] Railroad workers are not covered under state programs, but have their own program under the Railroad Unemployment Insurance Act.

Eligibility Requirements

Unemployed workers must meet certain eligibility requirements to qualify for unemployment benefits. Eligibility requirements vary among the states. However, the most common eligibility requirements include the following:

- Earn qualifying wages.
- Be able to work and be available for work.

---

[4]Rejda, *Social Insurance and Economic Security*, p. 330.

[5]*Overview of Entitlement Programs*, p. 459.

- Actively seek work.
- Satisfy a waiting period.

Unemployed workers must earn a certain amount of qualifying wages during their *base period* to receive unemployment benefits. Most states (47) define a base period or base year as the first four of the last five completed calendar quarters before the unemployed worker receives benefits. Most states also require employment in at least two calendar quarters in the base period. The purpose of the qualifying-wages requirement is to limit benefits to workers who have a current attachment to the labor force.

The amount of wages earned during the base period determines the benefits that are paid during the benefit year. The *benefit year* usually is a 52-week period during which the claimant can receive benefits. In 1990, qualifying wages for minimum weekly benefits ranged from $150 in Hawaii to $3,640 in Oklahoma. Qualifying wages for maximum total potential weekly benefits ranged from $4,400 in Puerto Rico to $23,500 in New Hampshire.[6]

Unemployed workers also must be able to work and available for work. *Able to work* means the unemployed worker is physically and mentally capable of working. *Available for work* typically means being ready, willing, and otherwise prepared to work. Registration for work at a public employment office provides some evidence that the unemployed worker is available for work.

In addition to registration for work, unemployed workers must actively seek work or make a reasonable effort to obtain suitable work. Suitable work generally is work in a worker's customary occupation that meets certain safety, moral, and labor standards. An unemployed worker is not required to take any job. However, if the claimant refuses suitable work, he or she may be disqualified. In general, as the length of unemployment increases, the claimant is required to accept a wider range of jobs.

In most states, unemployed workers also must satisfy a one-week waiting period. Eleven states have no waiting period. The purposes of the waiting period are to hold down claim costs, reduce administrative expenses by eliminating short-term claims, and give claims personnel time to process claims.

---

[6]*Overview of Entitlement Programs*, p. 462.

Weekly Benefit Amounts

A weekly cash benefit is paid for each week of total unemployment after the worker meets the waiting period. The benefit amount depends on the amount of wages earned during the base period, subject to certain minimum and maximum amounts.

Several methods are used to determine the weekly benefit amount. Most states compute benefits based on a fraction of the worker's high-quarter wages. For example, some states use the fraction one twenty-sixth, which results in a weekly benefit of 50 percent of the full-time wage for a worker who is employed 13 weeks on a full-time basis. Thus, if a worker earns $400 weekly or $5,200 during his or her high quarter, one twenty-sixth of this amount produces a weekly benefit of $200. Many states use a lower fraction to provide relatively higher benefits to low-wage workers.

In virtually all jurisdictions, regular weekly benefits can be paid up to a maximum of 26 weeks. However, under the extended-benefits program (discussed later), benefits can be paid up to 13 additional weeks.

In fiscal 1989, the national average weekly benefit was $152, and the average duration of benefits was 13.3 weeks. In 1989, minimum weekly benefits ranged from $5 in Hawaii to $62 in Alaska. Maximum weekly benefits ranged from $96 in Indiana to $408 in Massachusetts.[7]

Finally, reduced benefits can be paid for part-time work. A part-time worker is eligible for a partial unemployment benefit if the amount earned from the regular employer or from odd jobs is less than the weekly unemployment benefit or the weekly benefit plus some amount ranging from $5 to the weekly benefit amount (in Montana, it is two times the weekly benefit amount). The partial unemployment benefit usually is the weekly unemployment benefit less wages earned, but with a certain amount of earnings disregarded in computing the benefit.[8]

Disqualifications

Unemployed workers can be disqualified for unemployment compensation benefits for a variety of reasons. The most important are the following:

---

[7]*Overview of Entitlement Programs*, p. 469.

[8]Rejda, *Social Insurance and Economic Security*, p. 336.

- Not able or available for work.
- Voluntarily quit without good cause.
- Refusal of suitable work without good cause.
- Unemployment as a result of direct participation in a labor dispute.

Disqualification for one of the above reasons can result in (1) postponement of benefits for a certain period or until certain conditions are met, (2) cancellation of benefit rights, or (3) a reduction in benefits that otherwise are payable.

Disqualification rates are relatively high. Of the 14.2 million workers who were "monetarily eligible" for initial unemployment compensation benefits in fiscal 1989, 24.3 percent were disqualified for some period. This percentage is broken down as follows:[9]

5.9%	Not able or available for work
6.8%	Voluntarily quit without good cause
4.1%	Fired for misconduct on the job
0.3%	Refusal of suitable work
7.2%	Other disqualifying acts

In addition, unemployed workers can be disqualified for benefits if they receive certain types of *disqualifying income*. This includes severance pay, holiday pay, back pay, wages in lieu of notice, and workers' compensation for temporary partial disability. Also, unemployment benefits must be reduced by the amount of any public or private pension based on the worker's own work, which includes a primary Old-Age, Survivors, and Disability Insurance (OASDI) or Railroad Retirement benefit. However, only the pension benefit paid by the most recent or chargeable employer is considered, and the state can reduce the unemployment compensation benefit by less than a dollar-for-dollar basis to take into account the employee's contributions into the private pension plan.[10]

Finally, certain groups are disqualified from receiving benefits. These groups include employees of educational institutions during summer months and other vacation periods if they have a reasonable assurance of reemployment, professional athletes between seasons, and

---

[9]*Overview of Entitlement Programs*, p. 466.

[10]Rejda, *Social Insurance and Economic Security*, p. 337.

aliens not legally admitted to work in the United States. Many states also have disqualification provisions that apply to students while attending school or to individuals who quit work to attend school.

Taxation of Benefits

As a result of the Tax Reform Act of 1986, all unemployment compensation benefits are now subject to federal income tax. Between 1979 and 1987, only part of the unemployment benefits was subject to taxation. About 88 percent of the unemployment compensation recipients were affected by the taxation of benefits in 1990. About 16 percent of the total benefits were recovered by taxation. However, this latter figure should be interpreted with caution because of the significant under–reporting of income by recipients.[11]

EXTENDED BENEFITS PROGRAM

Many unemployed workers exhaust their regular benefits and are still unemployed. In 1970, Congress enacted a permanent state-federal extended benefits program that pays additional benefits to workers who exhaust their regular benefits in states with high unemployment. The weekly extended benefit amount is identical to the regular state benefit. *Claimants can receive up to 13 additional weeks of extended benefits or one-half of the regular benefits that have been received, whichever is less.* However, the duration of both regular and combined benefits is limited to a maximum of 39 weeks. The cost of the extended benefits program is financed equally by the states and federal government.

Extended benefits can be paid only if the state's insured unemployment rate exceeds a certain level. The *insured unemployment rate* is the ratio of unemployment insurance claims to total employment covered by unemployment compensation programs. The insured unemployment rate is substantially below the total unemployment rate because some unemployed workers have not met the eligibility requirements, have not satisfied the waiting period, have exhausted their benefits, or are not covered for unemployment compensation benefits.

---

[11]*Overview of Entitlement Programs*, p. 468.

Extended benefits can be paid in a state only under certain conditions: (1) the state's 13-week average insured unemployment rate (IUR) in the most recent 13-week period is at least 120 percent of the average of its 13-week IUR's in the last two years for the same period and its current 13-week average IUR is at least 5 percent; or (2) at the state's option, the current 13-week average IUR is at least 6 percent. All but 13 states have adopted this second option. No state paid extended benefits during the first week of 1989.

FINANCING UNEMPLOYMENT COMPENSATION

State unemployment compensation programs are financed by a payroll tax on the covered wages of employees. In five states, the employees also contribute (Alabama, Alaska, New Jersey, Pennsylvania, and West Virginia). All unemployment tax contributions are deposited in the federal Unemployment Trust Fund. Each state has a separate account, and a state's unemployment benefits are paid out of that account.

In 1991, each covered employer paid a federal unemployment tax of 6.2 percent on the first $7,000 of wages paid to each covered employee. However, if the state program meets certain federal standards and the state has no delinquent federal loans, employers are eligible for a maximum tax credit of 5.4 percent, which reduces the federal tax rate to 0.8 percent (including a special temporary surcharge of 0.2 percent). The 0.8 percent that is paid to the federal government is used for administrative expenses, for loans to states that have depleted their unemployment reserve accounts, and for the federal government's share of the cost of the extended benefits program.

Because of a desire to strengthen their unemployment reserve accounts, the majority of states have a taxable wage base in excess of $7,000. As of January 1990, 36 states had a taxable wage base higher than the federal wage base. The higher state tax bases ranged from $8,000 in eight states to $21,300 in Alaska.[12]

All states use experience rating to determine individual employer tax rates. There is considerable variation among the states with respect to experience rates. In 1990, only 15 jurisdictions used the standard 5.4

---

[12]*Overview of Entitlement Programs*, pp. 453–54.

percent rate as the maximum tax rate subject to experience rating. In 38 jurisdictions, maximum tax rates were much higher, ranging from 6 percent to 10 percent. Minimum tax rates for some employers with low unemployment were as low as zero percent in 15 jurisdictions. The estimated average tax rate was only 2.2 percent of taxable wages in 1989.[13]

Various experience rating formulas are used to determine employer tax rates. The most common is the *reserve-ratio method.* Under the reserve ratio method, each employer has a separate account. The total benefits paid since the program became effective are subtracted from the total employer contributions over that period. The balance is then divided by the employer's taxable payroll (usually an average of the last three years). The higher the reserve ratio, the lower the contribution rate. The reserve-ratio formula can be summarized as follows:[14]

$$\frac{\text{Total employer contributions} - \text{Total benefits paid}}{\text{Taxable payroll (usually an average of last three years)}} = \text{Reserve ratio}$$

Experience rating is a controversial subject. The major arguments for experience rating are (1) experience rating encourages firms to stabilize their employment; (2) the costs of unemployment are allocated to the firms responsible for the unemployment; and (3) employers have a greater interest in unemployment compensation programs.

The major arguments against experience rating are (1) some cyclical and seasonal firms have little control over unemployment and should not be penalized by higher tax rates; (2) employers may oppose an increase in unemployment benefits because of higher tax rates; and (3) experience rating may result in inadequate income to finance the system.[15]

ADMINISTRATION OF UNEMPLOYMENT COMPENSATION

Each state administers its own unemployment compensation program. The majority of states administer their programs through employment security offices in the department of labor or some other state agency. Other states have independent boards or commissions to administer their programs.

---

[13]*Overview of Entitlement Programs,* pp. 453–54.

[14]Rejda, *Social Insurance and Economic Security,* p. 342.

[15]Rejda, *Social Insurance and Economic Security,* pp. 339–41.

State agencies operate through local unemployment insurance and employment offices. The local offices process unemployment compensation claims and provide a variety of job placement and job development services. Federal law provides that personnel who administer the programs must be appointed on a merit basis except for personnel in policy-making positions.

The federal functions of unemployment compensation programs are the responsibility of the Employment and Training Administration, Unemployment Insurance Service, in the U.S. Department of Labor. The Internal Revenue Service collects the FUTA taxes, and the Treasury Department maintains the unemployment insurance trust fund. The Unemployment Insurance Service determines annually whether the state programs conform to federal requirements and also provides technical assistance and statistical data.

Most states collect quarterly wage data from employers that are used to calculate unemployment benefits. Massachusetts, Michigan, and New York obtain the necessary wage data only after a claim is filed. In general, claims must be filed within seven days after the week for which the claim is made unless there is a good cause for a late filing. The unemployed worker files a weekly claim form at the same office. In most cases, claims may be filed by mail and in some cases by telephone. The benefits are paid weekly or biweekly after the waiting period is met.

In addition, all states have interstate agreements for the payment of benefits to workers who move to another state. All states also have special wage-combining agreements that apply to workers who earn wages in two or more states.

Finally, federal law requires that workers who are denied benefits must be given the opportunity of a fair hearing. Two levels of appeal exist (except in Hawaii and Nebraska, which have a single-level administrative appeal authority). The claimant can appeal first to a referee or tribunal and then to a board of review. The board of review decision may be appealed to the state courts.

UNEMPLOYMENT COMPENSATION PROBLEMS AND ISSUES

Unemployment compensation programs have numerous problems and issues that limit their effectiveness in reducing economic insecurity from involuntary unemployment. The most important are the following:

- Small proportion of unemployed who receive benefits.
- Inadequate financing in many states.
- Inadequate benefits for many unemployed workers.

One of the most serious problems at the present time is the relatively small proportion of the unemployed who receive benefits. *Only one third of the unemployed received unemployment compensation benefits in an average month in 1989.* This compares with a peak of 81 percent of the unemployed who received benefits in April 1975 and a low point of about 26 percent in October 1987.[16]

There is no single reason that explains the decline in the proportion of the unemployed who receive benefits. However, an econometric study by Mathematica Policy Research showed that the decline in the proportion of the unemployed who received benefits during the 1980s was due to the following factors:[17]

- Decline in manufacturing unemployment relative to total unemployment during the 1980s (4–18 percent).
- Shift in the geographic distribution of unemployment (about 16 percent).
- Partial taxation of unemployment compensation benefits (11–16 percent).
- Increased monetary eligibility requirements and reduced maximum potential duration of benefits under state programs (8–15 percent).
- Increase in disqualifying income denials (about 10 percent).
- Changes in other nonmonetary eligibility requirements (3–11 percent).
- More accurate measure of unemployment as measured by the Current Population Survey (1–12 percent).

The fact that only a relatively small proportion of unemployed workers receive unemployment compensation benefits during an average month violates a well-established and fundamental social insurance principle--*that of providing broad coverage of workers against well-*

---

[16]*Overview of Entitlement Programs*, p. 459.

[17]*An Examination of Declining UI Claims during the 1980s: Final Report* (Princeton, N.J.: Mathematica Policy Research, Inc., 1988), p. xiii.

defined social risks, including the risk of unemployment. Since only a small proportion of the unemployed receive benefits during a typical month, the effectiveness of unemployment compensation programs in reducing economic insecurity from unemployment can be seriously questioned.[18]

Inadequate Financing

Another serious problem is that many states have inadequate trust fund reserves. As a result, such states would be unable to pay unemployment benefits during a severe recession without borrowing from the federal government.

One common measure of the adequacy of a state unemployment reserve account is a complex measure known as the "high-cost multiple."[19] A value of 1 means that the state's current balance in its reserve account could support 12 months of payments at the highest unemployment rate historically experienced in the past. The U.S. Department of Labor has recommended a high-cost multiple of 1.5, which would enable a state to pay benefits for at least 18 months without a tax increase or borrowing from the federal government. However, for the third quarter of 1989, 30 jurisdictions had high-cost multiples below 1. Only six jurisdictions had a high-cost multiple of 1.5 or higher.[20] As the economy headed into a business recession during early 1991, jurisdictions with depleted or dangerously low trust fund balances included Arkansas, Connecticut, the District of Columbia, Massachusetts, Michigan, Missouri, Ohio, and West Virginia.

Several worthwhile recommendations have been made to improve the financing of unemployment compensation benefits. Such recommendations include (1) an increase in the taxable wage base, (2) higher

---

[18]Rejda, *Social Insurance and Economic Security*, p. 357.

[19]The high-cost multiple is determined by the following formula:

$$\text{High-cost multiple} = \frac{\text{Ratio of current net trust fund reserves to total wages in insured employment in the current year}}{\text{Ratio of highest state benefits during 12 consecutive months to total wages in insured employment during those 12 months}}$$

[20]*Overview of Entitlement Programs*, pp. 446–50.

maximum tax rates subject to experience rating, (3) greater refinement of experience-rating formulas to charge more of the cost of unemployment to those firms responsible for the unemployment, and (4) requiring employees to contribute to the program.

Inadequate Benefits

Another serious problem is that unemployment compensation benefits generally are inadequate for most unemployed workers, with the possible exception of low-wage earners. One common measure of benefit adequacy is that the weekly benefits should restore at least 50 percent of the unemployed worker's average weekly wage. This standard is not being met at the present time. The ratio of average weekly benefits to average weekly wages nationally has remained relatively constant over the years at about 35 percent. The average replacement rate was only 36 percent for the fourth quarter of 1989.[21]

Although national average replacement rates are useful, they are limited, since no meaningful information on workers with different earnings is provided. Thus, it is worthwhile to examine replacement rates for low-wage, average-wage, and high-wage earners. For purposes of illustration, we will assume that a low-wage earner earned $12,091 in 1989, which is the 1988 poverty threshold for a family of four. We will also assume that an average-wage earner earned $26,671 in 1989, which is the 1988 weighted average earnings from the U.S. Department of Commerce, Bureau of Census. Finally, we will assume that a high-wage earner earned $48,364 in 1989, which is four times the 1988 poverty threshold for a family of four.[22]

With respect to low-wage earners, the 50 percent standard generally is being met in most jurisdictions. In September 1989, the ratio of pre-tax unemployment benefits to pre-tax earnings for low-wage earners ranged from 41 percent in Indiana to 65 percent in Michigan and Oregon. Only seven jurisdictions did not meet the 50 percent standard.[23]

With respect to average-wage earners, a different conclusion emerges. Based on the 50 percent standard, unemployment benefits paid

---

[21]*Overview of Entitlement Programs*, p. 513.

[22]*Overview of Entitlement Programs*, p. 522.

[23]*Overview of Entitlement Programs*, pp. 520–22.

to average-wage earners are insufficient in most jurisdictions. In September 1989, the ratio of pre-tax benefits to pre-tax earnings for average wage earners ranged from only 19 percent in Indiana to 55 percent in the District of Columbia. The 50 percent standard was met in only six jurisdictions.[24]

With respect to high-wage earners, too, unemployment benefits are relatively low. In September 1989, the ratio of pre-tax benefits to pre-tax earnings for high-wage earners ranged from only 10 percent in Indiana to 30 percent in the District of Columbia. No state met the 50 percent standard. In the majority of jurisdictions, the pre-tax replacement rate was 25 percent or less.[25]

In summary, with the exception of low-wage earners, unemployment benefits paid in most jurisdictions are inadequate. As a result, during periods of extended unemployment, many unemployed workers will be forced to deplete their savings or go into debt. Thus, despite the payment of unemployment benefits, economic insecurity will still be present for many unemployed workers.

SELECTED REFERENCES

1. Committee on Ways and Means, U.S. House of Representatives. *Overview of Entitlement Programs, 1990 Green Book* (Background Material and Data on Programs within the Jurisdication of the Committee on Ways and Means). Washington, D.C.: U.S. Government Printing Office, 1990, pp. 443–522.
2. Myers, Robert J. *Social Security.* 3rd ed. Homewood, Ill.: Richard D. Irwin, Inc., 1985, Chapter 13.
3. Rejda, George E. *Social Insurance and Economic Security.* 4th ed. Englewood Cliffs, N.J.: Prentice-Hall, Inc., 1991, Chapters 14 and 15.
4. Rejda, George E., and Kyung W. Lee. ''State Unemployment Compensation Programs: Immediate Reforms Needed.'' *The Journal of Risk and Insurance,* 56, no. 4 (December 1989), pp. 649–669.
5. ''Social Security Programs in the United States.'' *Social Security Bulletin,* 52, no. 7 (July 1989), pp. 19–27.

---

[24]*Overview of Entitlement Programs,* pp. 520–22.

[25]*Overview of Entitlement Programs,* pp. 520–22.

PART 3

DEATH BENEFITS

Some form of death benefit is provided by almost all employers, large and small, for their employees. Death benefit plans must be designed in terms of employer and employee objectives.

Part Three begins with a discussion in Chapter 8 of some of the most important considerations involved in the design of a death benefit plan and an overview of the most popular method of providing death benefits—group term life insurance. Also included in Chapter 8 are permanent forms of group life insurance and their uses in employee benefit planning. This part of *The Handbook* concludes with Chapter 9 on Group Universal Life Programs, an increasingly popular form of death benefit plan that provides substantial flexibility for meeting certain employer and employee objectives.

CHAPTER 8

GROUP LIFE INSURANCE: TERM AND PERMANENT

William H. Rabel
Jerry S. Rosenbloom

INTRODUCTION

Death benefits are a nearly universal employee benefit in the United States. Almost all employers, regardless of size, provide death benefits for their employees as an integral part of their employee benefit programs, and they also are made available through public sector programs such as Social Security and workers' compensation. Some of the forms of death benefits provided through the employee benefit mechanism include the following:[1]

Group term life insurance.
Group paid-up life insurance.
Group permanent life insurance.
Group universal life insurance.
Group survivor income benefit insurance.
Group dependent life insurance.
Group accidental death and dismemberment (AD&D) insurance.
Group travel accident insurance.
Joint and survivor annuity benefits under retirement plans.

[1]See Jerry S. Rosenbloom and G. Victor Hallman, *Employee Benefit Planning*, 3rd Edition. (Englewood Cliffs, N.J., Prentice Hall, 1991), pp. 32–33.

Preretirement annuity benefits.

Supplemental executive death benefit plans.

The emphasis in this chapter is on group term life insurance—the most common means of providing death benefits as an employee benefit. This chapter and Chapter 9 review some of the permanent forms of group life insurance. Other chapters in the *Handbook* cover the forms of death benefits specific to their topic areas.

Traditionally, group life insurance has covered employees against death during their working years. The protection provided usually is one-year renewable group term life insurance with no cash surrender value or paid-up insurance benefits. However, a relatively small amount of permanent group life insurance is in force. Furthermore, with the growth of retirement plans other forms of death benefits, such as arrangements for the payment of a lifetime pension to the spouse of a career employee who dies before retirement, have developed.

In some cases, life insurance also is provided for dependents of employees, typically in small amounts such as $1,000 or $2,000, and some employee benefit plans may continue a reduced amount of death benefits on retired employees.

Survivor income benefit insurance (SIBI) plans also have become a part of employee benefit programs in recent years. These plans differ from traditional employer-sponsored death benefit plans in that a benefit is payable only to certain specified surviving dependents of the employee and only in installments. Additionally, mandated survivor benefits to spouses are available under certain conditions under the Employee Retirement Income Security Act of 1974 (ERISA). The Retirement Equity Act of 1984 (REA) also provides for a preretirement survivor annuity under pension plans for surviving spouses of vested employees who die in active service and who were not yet eligible for early retirement.

GROUP MECHANISM

While it is beyond the scope of this chapter to discuss fully the intricacies of the group mechanism, it is helpful to develop some basics to understand when the mechanism can be used. Five essential features of group insurance should be understood.

First, unlike individual insurance in which the risk associated with each life is appraised, group insurance makes use of group selection. In other words, an entire group is insured without medical examination or other evidence of individual insurability. For many years, state regulation and prudent practice have mandated stringent underwriting rules concerning such things as the minimum number of individuals in a group and the minimum proportion to be insured. However, in recent years, these rules have been relaxed somewhat as a result of competitive pressure and decades of experience with the group underwriting process.

A second feature of group insurance is that premiums on a plan usually are subject to experience rating. The larger the group, the greater the degree to which its cost of insurance reflects its own loss experience. Experience rating can either be on a prospective or retrospective basis. Normally, if experience has been favorable, an experience credit (sometimes called a dividend) may be paid at the end of the year to adjust the renewal premium for the next year (prospective basis), or credits may be applied to the current year's original premium (retrospective basis).

A third feature of the group mechanism calls for economies of administration. The plan is administered by an employer, a union, or some other agency positioned to obtain administrative efficiencies through payroll deductions and/or other centralized functions.

Group insurance makes use of a fourth feature—a master contract—containing all conditions concerning the coverage. Insured individuals receive a group certificate as proof that they are covered which shows the coverages provided and the amounts of those coverages. Often insureds receive a booklet (a summary plan description [SPD]) describing the plan in easy-to-read language.

The existence of a master contract indicates a fifth feature: that the plan may last long beyond the lifetime (or participation in the group) of any one individual.

GROUP TERM LIFE INSURANCE

The importance of group term life insurance in employee benefit plans is shown by the data in Table 8–1. This table reveals that at the end of 1989, group life insurance in force in the United States totaled $3,469.5 billion. While the amount of group life insurance in force continued to increase during the 1980s, the increase in group certificates has slowed, and group coverage has decreased as a percentage of life insurance sold. These figures suggest that the market is beginning to reach maturity.

TABLE 8–1
Group Life Insurance in Force in the United States (selected years: 1940–1989)

Years	Number of Master Policies	Number of Certificates	Average Amount per Certificate	Amount in Force (millions)	Percent of Total Insurance in Force	Purchases: Number of Certificates	Purchases: Amount (millions)	Percent of Total Insurance Purchases
1940	23,000	8,800,000	1,700	$ 14,938	12.9%	285,000	691	6.4%
1950	56,000	19,288,000	2,480	47,793	20.4	2,631,000	6,068	21.1
1960	169,000	43,602,000	4,030	175,903	30.0	3,731,000	14,615	19.7
1965	234,000	60,930,000	5,060	308,078	34.2	7,007,000	23,585	20.6
1970	304,000	79,844,000	6,910	551,357	39.3	5,219,000	46,590	26.5
1975	378,000	96,693,000	9,360	904,695	42.3	8,146,000	93,490	32.4
1980	586,000	117,762,000	13,410	1,579,355	44.6	11,373,000	183,432	31.2
1985	642,000	129,904,000	19,720	2,561,595	42.3	16,243,000	319,503	26.0
1986	612,000	135,157,000	20,724	2,801,049	41.7	17,507,000	312,941	25.1
1987	672,000	136,006,000	22,380	3,043,782	40.8	16,698,000	365,529	27.0
1988	625,000	138,071,000	23,409	3,232,080	40.3	15,793,000	410,848	29.2
1989	701,000	141,556,000	24,510	3,469,498	39.9	15,110,000	420,707	29.2

Note: Data includes group credit life insurance on loans of more than 10 years' duration; totals include all life insurance (net of reinsurance) on residents of the United States, whether issued by U.S. or foreign companies.

Source: American Council of Life Insurance.

Table 8–2 shows that while only 58.1 percent of group life insurance certificates in force at year-end 1988 covered members of employer-employee groups, they accounted for 88.3 percent of the total amount of group life insurance in force. The average amount of coverage per employee was $34,479. As shown in Table 8–3, survivor income and dependent coverages together accounted for $8.25 billion, or less than 2 percent of group life in force.

Benefits

Group term life insurance benefit amounts should be based on a plan designed to avoid or minimize possible adverse selection either by the employees or the employer. Factors to consider in the selection of a benefit schedule include (1) the employees' needs, (2) the overall cost of the plan, (3) the nondiscrimination requirements of the law, and (4) the employees' ability to pay if the plan is contributory. The interrelationship of these factors has resulted in the development of group term life insurance benefit schedules related to earnings, occupation or position, or a flat benefit amount for everyone covered. Benefit schedules that are a combination of these types of benefits schedules are also used.[2]

The most common benefit schedule bases the amount of insurance on the employee's earnings. An illustration of such a schedule is seen in Table 8–4.

Such a schedule would not discriminate in favor of key employees (including executives), thus making the plan eligible for favorable tax treatment if other conditions are met. The tax treatment and nondiscrimination requirements for group life insurance are discussed later in this chapter.

Financing

Any employee benefit program, including group term life insurance, may be financed on either a noncontributory basis (where the employer pays the total amount for the insurance) or a contributory basis (where the

---

[2]See Davis W. Gregg, "Fundamental Characteristics of Group Insurance," in *Life and Health Insurance Handbook*, 3rd ed., eds. Davis W. Gregg and Vane B. Lucas (Homewood, Ill.: Richard D. Irwin, 1973), pp. 357–58.

TABLE 8–2
Group Life Insurance in Force by Type and by Size Of Insured Group in the United States 1988

	Number of Master Units	% of Total (all groups)	Number of Members (000 omitted)	% of Total (all groups)	Insurance in Force		Average Amount of Insurance Per Member
					Amount (000,000 omitted)	% of Amount (all groups)	
Type of Group							
Related to employment or occupation							
Employer-employee	519,440	83.1	69,593	58.1	$2,399,516	88.3	$34,479
Union and joint employer-union	5,770	0.9	3,445	2.9	29,500	1.1	8,563
Multiple employer trusts	73,200	11.8	3,839	3.2	77,794	2.9	20,264
Professional society	870	0.1	794	0.7	51,940	1.9	65,416
Employee association	1,890	0.3	1,231	1.0	59,526	2.2	48,356
Other—related to employee benefit program	80	*	137	0.1	3,520	0.1	25,693
Other—not related to employee benefit program	40	*	26	*	1,046	*	40,231
Total	601,290	96.2	79,065	66.0	$2,622,842	96.5	33,173

TABLE 8–2 *(cont'd)*

Not related to employment or occupation							
Fraternal society	170	*	53	*	2,065	0.1	38,962
Savings or investment group	17,300	2.8	38,393	32.0	26,216	1.1	761
Credit card holders	270	*	267	0.2	3,727	0.1	13,959
Mortgage insurance	5,390	0.9	1,740	1.5	54,313	2.0	31,214
Other	900	0.1	300	0.3	5,947	0.2	19,823
Total	24,030	3.8	40,753	34.0	95,268	3.5	2,338
Total all groups	625,320	100.0	119,818	100.0	$2,718,110	100.0	22,685
Size of Group							
Fewer than 10 members	N.A.	N.A.	1,620	1.4	$ 25,868	1.0	15,968
10–24 members	N.A.	N.A.	2,983	2.5	54,131	2.0	18,146
25–99 members	N.A.	N.A.	8,009	6.7	150,599	5.5	18,804
100–499 members	N.A.	N.A.	13,028	10.8	250,453	9.2	19,224
500 or more members	N.A.	N.A.	94,178	78.6	2,237,059	82.3	23,745
Total all groups	625,320		119,818	100.0	$2,718,110	100.0	22,685

Note: Data exclude dependent coverage, Federal Employees Group Life Insurance, and Servicemen's Group Life Insurance. Group credit life insurance on loans of over 10 years duration is included.

* Less than .05% N.A. = Not available

Source: American Council of Life Insurance.

TABLE 8–3
Employee and Dependent Coverage Under Group Life Insurance in the United States 1989

	Number of Master Policies	*Amount (000,000 omitted)*
Purchased During Year		
Primary coverage, employee and other	175,522	$ 402,777
Survivor benefit coverage	N.A.	542
Dependent coverage	6,945*	7,709
Mortgage insurance issued through a lending agency	652	9,697
Total	176,174	$ 420,707
In Force at End of Year		
Primary coverage, employee and other	696,431	$3,301,086
Survivor benefit coverage	N.A.	35,190
Dependent coverage	41,491*	82,189
Mortgage insurance issued through a lending agency	4,341	51,033
Total	700,772	$3,469,498

* These policies cover employees as well as dependents and are also included with employee master policies.
N.A. = Not available.

Source: American Council of Life Insurance.

employees share the cost with the employer). A number of advantages are claimed for each approach. The following advantages are claimed for the *noncontributory approach:*[3]

All Employees Insured. All eligible employees who have completed the probationary period and are actively at work have coverage. Thus, the plan has maximum participation and minimizes adverse selection.

Tax Advantages. Under conditions described later in this chapter, employer premium costs are deductible as an ordinary business expense

[3]Gregg, op. cit., pp. 358–60.

TABLE 8–4
Sample Schedule Basing Benefits on Amount of Employee Earnings

Monthly Earnings	*Group Term Life Insurance*
Less than $1,500	$25,000
More than $1,500 but less than $2,000	30,000
More than $2,000 but less than $2,500	35,000
More than $2,500 but less than $3,000	40,000
More than $3,000 but less than $3,500	45,000
More than $3,500	50,000

for federal income tax purposes, whereas employee contributions under a contributory plan are not unless under an Internal Revenue Code (IRC) Section 125 flexible benefit plan up to a maximum of $50,000 of life insurance.

Simplicity of Administration. Records for individual employees are easier to maintain than under contributory plans primarily because no payroll-deduction procedures are involved.

Economy of Installation. Since all employees are covered, it is not necessary to solicit plan membership among individual employees.

Greater Control of Plan. The employer may have more control over changes in benefits under noncontributory plans because, in the absence of collective bargaining, unilateral action may be more feasible when employees are not sharing in the cost of the plan.

The *contributory approach* to financing group term life insurance also has certain claimed advantages.[4]

Larger Benefits Possible. More liberal benefits are possible if employees also contribute.

Better Use of Employer's Contributions. A contributory plan, provided enough individuals participate to meet the nondiscrimination

[4]Ibid.

requirements, may permit the employer to direct group term life insurance funds to the employees with the greatest needs. Employees who elect not to contribute, and hence who are not covered, tend to be young, single individuals who may have few life insurance needs and among whom employee turnover also may be high. In such a case, a contributory plan allows employer funds to be used most effectively by sharing the cost of benefits for the employees who have greater needs for life insurance and who also are most likely to be long-service employees.

Employees May Have More Control. The contributory plan may afford employees a greater voice in the benefits, since they are paying part of the cost.

Greater Employee Interest. Employees may have a greater interest in plans in which they are making a contribution.

Important Group Term Life Insurance Provisions[5]

Beneficiary Designation

Under group term life insurance, an employee may name and change his or her beneficiary as desired. The only restriction is that the insurance must benefit someone other than the employer. If, at the death of the employee, no beneficiary is named, or if a beneficiary is named but does not survive the employee, the proceeds may be payable at the insurer's option to any one or more of the following surviving relatives of the employee: wife, husband, mother, father, child or children, or the executor or administrator of the estate of the deceased employee. If any beneficiary is a minor or otherwise incapable of giving a valid release, the insurer is able to pay the proceeds under a "facility of payment" clause, subject to certain limits.

Settlement Options

The covered employee or the beneficiary may elect to receive the face amount of the group term life insurance on an installment basis rather than in a lump sum. The installments are paid according to tables listed

---

[5]See William G. Williams, "Group Life Insurance," in *Life and Health Insurance Handbook,* 3d ed., eds. Davis W. Gregg and Vane B. Lucas (Homewood, Ill.: Richard D. Irwin, 1973), pp. 373–77.

in the group master policy. An insurer generally offers optional modes of settlement based on life contingencies. But the basis is seldom mentioned or guaranteed in the contract and is governed by insurance company practices at the time of death.[6]

Assignment

Group term life insurance generally may be assigned if the master policy and state law both permit. Assignment of group term life insurance is important as a means for an employee to remove the group life insurance proceeds from his or her gross estate for federal estate tax purposes by absolutely assigning all incidents of ownership in the group term life insurance to another person or to an irrevocable trust. In the past, this was an important estate-planning technique for some employees whose estates potentially were subject to federal estate taxation. However, because the Economic Recovery Tax Act of 1981 (ERTA) allows an unlimited estate-tax marital deduction, the attractiveness of assigning proceeds has decreased.

Conversion Privilege

If an employee's life insurance ceases because of termination of employment, termination of membership in a classification(s) eligible for coverage, or retirement, he or she may convert the group term insurance to an individual permanent life insurance policy. The employee must apply to the insurer in writing within 30 days of termination and pay the premium for his or her attained age, the type of insurance, and the class or risk involved; however, medical evidence of insurability is not necessary. Under the law, employers must notify employees of their conversion rights within 15 days after they take effect.

A more restricted conversion privilege may be provided for an employee if the group master policy is terminated or amended so as to terminate the insurance in force on the employee's particular classification. The employee may not convert more than $2,000 worth of coverage. The reason for such a limitation is to avoid the situation where an employer purchases group life insurance and quickly terminates the plan to allow individually uninsurable individuals to obtain by conversion large amounts of individual life coverage.

---

[6]Ibid., p. 376.

Thirty-One-Day Continuation of Protection

This provision gives a terminated employee an additional 31 days of protection while evaluating the conversion privilege or awaiting coverage under the group life insurance plan of a new employer.

Continuation of Insurance

The employer can elect to continue the employee's group term life insurance in force for a limited period, such as three months, on a basis that precludes adverse selection during temporary interruptions of continuous, active, full-time employment. Upon expiration of the continuation period, premium payments are discontinued, and the employee's insurance is terminated. However, in this event, the insurance, as well as the right to exercise the conversion privilege, is still extended for 31 days after termination of the insurance.

Waiver of Premium Provision

Because employees may become disabled, group life insurance policies generally contain a waiver-of-premium provision. Under a typical waiver-of-premium provision, the life insurance remains in force if (1) the employee is under a specified age, such as 60 or 65, at the date of commencement of total disability; (2) total disability commences while the person is covered; (3) total disability is continuous until the date of death; and (4) proof of total and continuous disability is presented at least once every 12 months.[7]

The waiver-of-premium provision is one of three types of disability benefit provisions used for group life plans. The second, the maturity value benefit, pays the face amount of the group term life insurance in a lump sum or monthly installments when an employee becomes totally and permanently disabled. A third type of disability provision, the extended death benefit, pays group life insurance death claims incurred within one year after termination of employment. It requires the employee be continuously and totally disabled from the date of termination of employment until death occurs.

Dependent Coverage

Dependent group life insurance may be offered either as part of the basic group term life insurance plan or as optional additional coverage. The

---

[7]Ibid., pp. 374–75.

growth of dependent group life insurance has been relatively slow, partly because of the taxation of amounts greater than $2,000. When provided, a typical schedule of benefits might give the dependent spouse life insurance equal to 50 percent of the employee's coverage but not more than $2,000. Typical benefits for dependent children often are graded from $100 between the child's age of 14 days to 6 months up to, for example, $1,000 or $1,500 between ages 5 and 19 years. Much larger amounts of coverage sometimes are offered under supplementary plans fully paid for by the employee.

The death benefit normally is payable automatically in one lump sum to the insured employee or, in the event of the prior death of the employee, either to the employee's estate or, at the option of the insurer, to one of certain specified classes of "order-of-preference" beneficiaries.

Coverage of Employees After Retirement[8]

Retired Employees

Upon retirement, a former employee's group term life insurance often is discontinued, and the high cost of conversion at the retiree's advanced age usually makes use of the conversion privilege impractical. Therefore, many employers are continuing reduced amounts of group term life insurance on retired employees under various types of reduction formulas. One formula reduces the insurance by 50 percent at retirement. Another uses a graded percentage system decreasing the amount of coverage each year after retirement age until a certain minimum benefit is reached; for example, 10 percent per year until 50 percent of the amount in force immediately prior to retirement is attained. Still other employers provide a flat dollar amount such as $15,000 or $20,000 at retirement. Taxation of the postretirement benefits is the same as for active employees. Because continuing group life insurance on retired lives is costly, employers may consider funding coverage for retired employees through some other means such as group paid-up, group ordinary, or a separate "side fund" to pay the premiums at retirement.

Active Employees

Coverage requirements for active employees after age 40 are strongly influenced by the Age Discrimination in Employment Act of 1967 (ADEA),

---

[8]See Jerry S. Rosenbloom and G. Victor Hallman, *Employee Benefit Planning,* op. cit., pp. 48–49.

as amended in 1978 and then by HR–4154, which became effective on January 1, 1987. This latest amendment to ADEA eliminated the age–70 ceiling on active employment. Essentially, employees aged 40 and above are considered the protected group. Plans may be "cut back," but individual plans must be actuarially analyzed to determine cost-justified reductions.

The U.S. Supreme Court in *Public Employees Retirement System of Ohio* v. *Betts* ruled that age-based distinctions in employee benefits were not prohibited by ADEA if they were not intended to discriminate in some nonbenefit facet of the employment relationship. This ruling seemed to allow employers to reduce benefits for older active workers without following previous Department of Labor and EEOC guidelines. However, with the passage of the Older Workers Benefit Protection Act amending ADEA in October 1990, the law seemed to restore the "equal benefit or equal cost" requirement for age-based differences in employee benefits.[9] The previous guidelines allowed cost-justified reductions that permit an employer to (1) reduce an employee's life insurance coverage each year starting at age 65 by 8 to 9 percent of the declining balance of the life insurance benefit, or (2) make a one-time reduction in life insurance benefits at age 65 of from 35 to 40 percent and maintain that reduced amount in force until retirement. The 8 to 9 percent annual reduction is justified by mortality statistics showing that, for example, the probability of death increases by that amount each year for the age-60-to-70 group. The one-time 35 to 40 percent reduction is justified by the difference in mortality expected, for example, by employees in the age-65 through age-69 bracket, compared with the mortality expected in the age-60 through age-64 bracket. An employer also may be able to cost justify greater reductions in group term life insurance benefits on the basis of its *own* demonstrably higher cost experience in providing group term life insurance to its employees over a representative period of years.

ADEA also permits use of a "benefit package" approach for making cost comparisons for certain benefits. This benefit package approach offers greater flexibility than a benefit-by-benefit analysis as long as the overall result is of no lesser cost to the employer and is no less favorable in terms of the overall benefits provided to employees.

---

[9] *A Special Report to Clients*, Hewitt Associates, October 16, 1990.

Advantages and Disadvantages of Group Term Life Insurance

In summary, employers and employees are interested in evaluating the relative advantages and limitations of group term life insurance as an employee benefit.[10]

Advantages to the Employer

From the employer's perspective the following might be considered advantages of including a well-designed group term life insurance program as one of its employee benefits:

- Employee morale and productivity may be enhanced by offering this element of financial security.
- The coverage is necessary for competitive reasons, since most employers offer this form of protection.
- The life insurance protection is an aid to attaining good public and employer-employee relations.

Advantages to Employees

Group term life insurance dovetails into an employee's financial security planning in the following ways:

- It adds a layer of low-cost protection to personal savings, individual life insurance, and Social Security benefits.
- It helps reduce the anxieties about the consequences of the employee's possible premature death.
- If the plan does not favor (key) employees, the employer's contributions are not reportable as taxable income to the insured employee for federal income tax purposes unless the total amount of group insurance from all sources exceeds $50,000; then the employee is only taxed on the value of amounts in excess of $50,000, as determined by a table in the Internal Revenue Code, less any contributions the employee made to the plan. However, if the plan discriminates in favor of key employees, the actual cost of all coverage (or the amount of its value as determined in the Code, whichever is greater) will be taxable to the employee. In other words, the employee loses the $50,000 worth of tax-free life insurance,

---

[10] See William G. Williams, "Group Life Insurance," op. cit., pp. 377–78.

and may end up paying a higher rate on amounts in excess of $50,000. However, even if the plan is discriminatory, "rank and file" employees will not suffer adverse tax consequences. A group term life insurance plan may be considered to discriminate in favor of key employees unless (1) the plan benefits at least 70 percent of all employees; (2) at least 85 percent of the participants are not key employees; (3) the plan is part of a cafeteria type; or (4) the plan complies with a reasonable classification system found by the Internal Revenue Service to be nondiscriminatory. In applying these IRS rules, part-time and seasonal workers as well as those with fewer than three years of service do not have to be considered. Employees covered by a collective bargaining agreement by which group term life insurance has been bargained for also may be excluded. Special rules apply to groups of fewer than 10 employees.[11]

- If employees are contributing toward the cost, their contributions are automatically withheld from their paychecks, making payment convenient and also reducing the possibility of lapse of insurance.
- The conversion privilege enables terminated employees to convert their group term life insurance to individual permanent policies without having to provide individual evidence of insurability.
- Liberal underwriting standards provide coverage for those who might be uninsurable or only able to get insurance at substandard rates.

Disadvantages

Despite its many advantages, group term life insurance has some disadvantages. First, the employee usually has no assurance the employer will continue the group policy in force from one year to the next. Group life insurance plans seldom are discontinued, but business failures can and do occur, and the conversion privilege upon termination of a group life policy may be of limited value to the employees because of the high cost of conversion on an attained-age basis.

Another limitation exists when employees change employers, because group term life insurance is not "portable." Only about one out of every hundred terminating employees uses the conversion privilege. However, most employees changing jobs expect to be insured for the

---

[11]For a detailed discussion of the tax aspects and nondiscrimination requirements of group life insurance and other welfare benefit plans, see Chapter 50, "Federal Tax Environment of Welfare Benefit Plans, of the *Handbook*.

same or a higher amount of group life insurance with their new employers. Group term life insurance provides "protection only," while employee needs, at least partially, may dictate some other form of life insurance that has a savings or cash-value feature. Also, with salary-related plans, coverage may be lowest when it is most needed (e.g., for a young employee with dependents). The next section looks at some permanent forms of group life insurance.

PERMANENT FORMS OF GROUP LIFE INSURANCE

Given the expense of providing retired employees with group term life insurance, it is not surprising that permanent forms of group life have engendered some degree of interest over the years. After all, even though most retired workers do not have dependent children, many of them have dependents, most often spouses, and some have problems of estate liquidity. Furthermore, a lifetime of work may not be sufficient to provide the legacy hoped for by many retirees, and their financial goals are made particularly elusive by the high level of inflation that has plagued most countries since World War II. Therefore, the thought of obtaining permanent insurance through the relatively low-cost group mechanism has a certain amount of appeal.

Several forms of group permanent life insurance have been developed over the years, mostly in response to government policies that have provided favorable tax treatment to group term life insurance. Among those to be examined here are group paid-up insurance and various forms of continuous premium coverage, including level-premium group, supplemental group, and group ordinary life insurance.

GROUP PAID-UP LIFE INSURANCE

First written in 1941, group paid-up life insurance allows all or part of an employee's scheduled group coverage to be written so that it will be fully paid up when the employee retires. During his or her working life, the employee makes a regular contribution that is used to purchase paid-up increments of whole life insurance. Each purchase increases the total amount of paid-up insurance owned. Figure 8–1 illustrates how units of paid-up insurance accumulate.

FIGURE 8–1
Interrelationship between Increasing Increments of Paid-Up Group Life Insurance and Decreasing Increments of Group Term Life Insurance

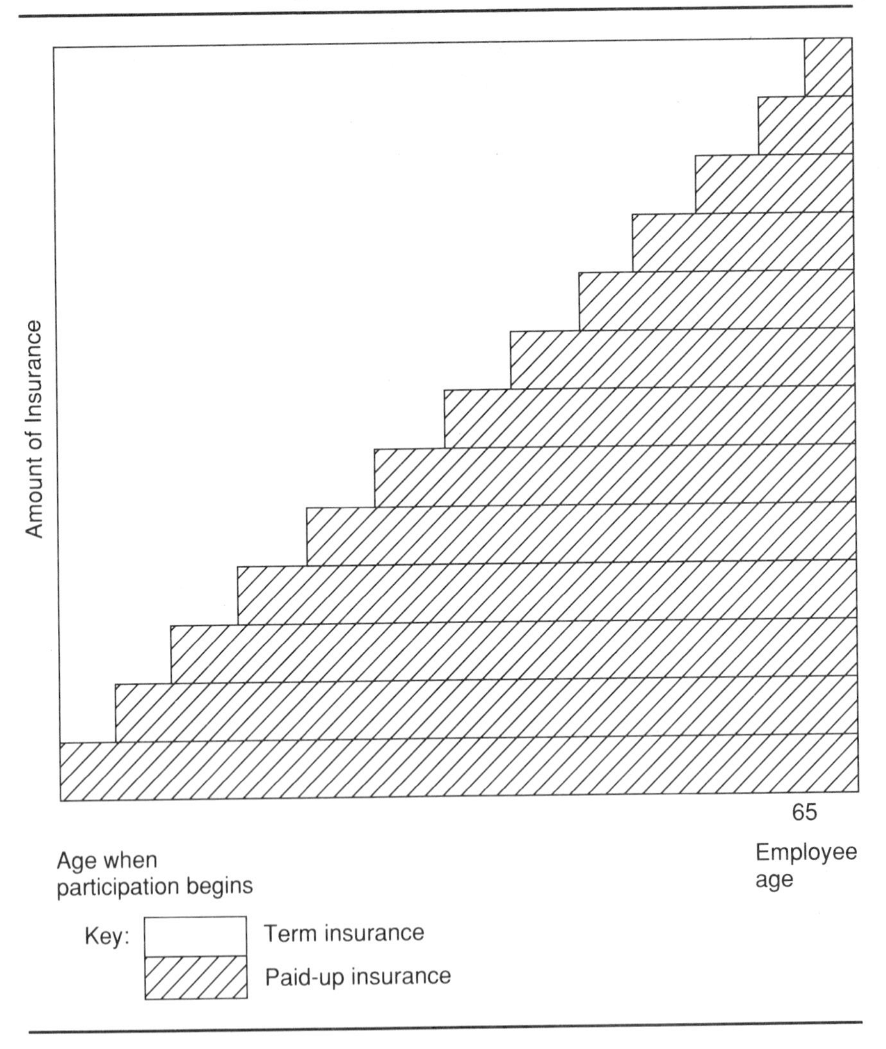

For tax reasons, discussed in the next section, employers do not purchase permanent insurance for their employees under this plan. Rather, they supplement the employees' purchases of permanent insurance with decreasing amounts of term insurance. After each contribution, the amount of term insurance decreases by exactly the amount by which the paid-up

TABLE 8–5
Accumulated Amounts of Paid-Up Insurance Based on $1 Monthly Contribution

	Number of Years in Plan				
Entry Age	*5*	*15*	*25*	*35*	*45*
20	$229	$609	$905	$1,139	$1,329
30	178	474	708	899	—
40	139	373	563	—	—
50	110	301	—	—	—
60	91	—	—	—	—

Source: Robert W. Batten et al., *Group Life Insurance* (Atlanta, Georgia: Life Office Management Association, 1979), p. 111.

insurance increases. Thus, the combined amount of both types of insurance remains constant at the amount set by the benefits schedule. Figure 8–1 illustrates the combination of coverages in this product.

Contributions

Employee contributions generally are designed to be level throughout the employee's working life. Naturally, because of actuarial considerations, the amount purchased with each contribution decreases as the employee gets older. Furthermore, costs are higher for individuals who enter the plan at older ages because they have fewer years in which to accumulate paid-up coverage. Therefore, in theory, a schedule of contributions should be graded for age of entry into the plan and anticipated length of service, and this is a common practice.

To provide certain minimum benefits for all employees and to encourage a high level of participation (particularly among older employees), some employers have set a single contribution rate for all employees. Table 8–5 illustrates the amounts of paid-up insurance that can be accumulated by workers at various ages with a monthly contribution of $1. When the flat contribution results in inadequate coverage for older employees, the employer may supplement the paid-up insurance by continuing the necessary amount of term insurance after the employee retires. Sometimes a flat contribution schedule is limited to those who have been with a firm for a minimum time when the coverage starts, while new employees pay according to an age-graded schedule. All such arrangements should be reviewed carefully to ensure that they do not run afoul of the nondiscrimination prohibitions in the tax laws.

Plan Provisions

As is normal for group insurance, benefits are determined by a schedule. In general, the provisions found in group term contracts apply to the term portion of the paid-up plan as well. These include conversion and disability (such as waiver-of-premium) benefits.

The employee-owned paid-up segment of the policy develops cash values, which are the greater of (1) the employee's contributions without interest, or (2) the standard nonforfeiture values as shown in the policy. In contrast to individual life policies, however, cash values are available only when the worker's employment terminates. Except in the case of termination, most plans do not permit surrender of the policy, and contracts do not contain a loan privilege.

The justifications for the constraints on loans and surrenders are that the cost of administering these benefits would offset some of the savings made possible through the use of the group technique, and that access to cash values could undermine the goal of the plan—to provide postretirement protection. Finally, it sometimes is maintained that access to policy values could subject insurers to adverse financial selection on a line of coverage for which contingency margins have not explicitly been added.

Under the provisions of some plans, the life insurance company may delay paying surrender values for a set period of time after employment is terminated. This provision is to prevent employees from quitting temporarily and then resuming their jobs just to obtain the policy surrender values. Obviously, there may be a great temptation to do so during a strike, layoff, or other period of economic stress for the worker. This restrictive provision is not applied when employees terminate with small amounts of coverage (e.g., less than $1,000). In such cases, policies are surrendered automatically for purposes of administrative simplicity.

Coverage is not automatically surrendered if the master contract terminates. Paid-up coverage remains intact as long as employment is not terminated and for life unless it is surrendered. Term coverage is convertible under the same rules as under a group term plan.

Premium Rates and Experience Rating

Group term policy owners (usually an employer) normally receive a dividend or "experience credit" each year if plan experience has been favorable. As a result of revenue rulings beginning in 1971, the term account may not subsidize the permanent account, or vice versa. In other words, each account must stand on its own feet. Thus, favorable experience credits must be allocated to the account from which they originate, whether it is the term or the paid-up account. Favorable experience may be passed on to the paid-up account in the form of a dividend to insureds or as reduced rates for future purchases.

All normal or customary practices in experience rating are subject to change under the pressure of competition. When competition is intense, insurers may expand their tendency to pool the underwriting experience of different coverages or even different lines (e.g., group term and group permanent, or group life and group health). Pooling may lead to changes in the experience-rating practices.

Uses of Group Paid-Up Insurance

Group paid-up tends to appeal to firms with fewer than 500 employees. Furthermore, it generally is underwritten only for groups that display certain characteristics. As a first requirement, only those employers that provide stable employment can purchase group paid-up. Since strikes and layoffs interrupt employee contributions and therefore interfere with the accumulation of paid-up coverage, such events must be most unusual for the industry in which the policy owner operates. Furthermore, some carriers will not underwrite a case until the firm has been in business for a minimum period (e.g., three years).

Insurers also require that turnover be very low for the employer. To a degree, the turnover problem can be controlled by a long probationary period. However, the underwriting rules of some carriers exclude employers that have an annual turnover rate in excess of 5 percent. In addition, some establish minimum-age requirements for participation (e.g., 30–35).

Advantages of Group Paid-Up Life Insurance

Adherents of group paid-up life insurance claim it provides several advantages to employers or employees, or both. First and foremost, as contrasted with group term, it does provide permanent protection. Related to this is the advantage of cash-value accumulations by the insured that can be made available when employment terminates. Both these features are related to a third, which is that group paid-up provides a scientific way to fund postretirement coverage over the working life of the employee.

Group paid-up plans facilitate the conversion by long-service employees of any term coverage remaining at age 65, because it usually is a relatively small proportion of the scheduled amount and because converted coverage is purchased at net rates. Thus, for these two reasons, retirees may end up being able to afford even more permanent coverage than they had anticipated.

A sixth advantage to group paid-up is that employers electing to continue all or part of the coverage on retirees find the scheduled amount of term reduced well below the amount needed in the absence of paid-up insurance. This smaller financial burden may be easier for a business to justify.

A seventh advantage, when group paid-up is compared with other forms of permanent group coverage (discussed below), is that the status of these plans is well established with the Internal Revenue Service. They are a known commodity, and no serious modification of existing plans has been required by tax rulings to date. Therefore, it is highly unlikely that they will be subject to unfavorable rulings in the future. Another important tax factor is that the employer-purchased term coverage receives the favorable tax treatment accorded to all group term coverage.[12]

The group paid-up system provides still other advantages. Being contributory, the plan encourages participation only by those who need insurance. At the same time, in contrast to group term plans, employees may be more willing to contribute to the cost of group paid-up because they can see a permanent benefit growing out of their premiums.[13]

It is worth noting that insurers may be willing to offer higher limits on group plans containing permanent coverage than on term alone. The amount at risk for each individual continually diminishes throughout his or her working life. Furthermore, margins in interest earnings on reserves may support a more liberal benefit schedule.

---

[12]See: William H. Rabel and Charles E. Hughes, "Taxation of Group Life Insurance," *Journal of Accounting, Auditing, and Finance,* 1, no. 2, p. 177, for a thorough discussion of this topic.

[13]For a discussion of the advantages of contributory group life plans, see Robert Batten et al., *Group Life and Health Insurance* (Atlanta, Georgia: Life Office Management Association, 1979), p. 42.

Disadvantages of Group Paid-Up Life Insurance

Among the greatest disadvantages of group paid-up insurance is that the type of employer that can use it is limited, as explained above. Another drawback is the relatively high cost of administering the plan, when compared with term insurance, because more professional advice is needed in designing, installing, and operating it. Furthermore, changes in benefits, eligibility status, and the like often require more record changes than would be required for term. A third disadvantage is that employer costs are higher in the early years of the plan than they would be for group term. Thus, the employer may delay the plan until it can be afforded. The high cost in the early years is caused by start-up costs as well as the need to fund coverage for employees approaching retirement. In some cases, the employer may decide not to purchase a term plan to provide temporary protection with the result that there is no protection at all.

Finally, the principal advantage of group paid-up is also its principal weakness. Employee contributions purchase permanent coverage, and therefore afford less current protection for each premium dollar.

LEVEL PREMIUM GROUP PERMANENT LIFE INSURANCE

In exploring various approaches to providing postretirement coverage through the group mechanism, it was only a matter of time before someone suggested taking standard, level-premium, whole life insurance and writing it on a group basis. The idea was to have the employer pay all or part of the premium and to have the employee pay any amount not paid by the employer. However, before this approach could develop much of a following, the Treasury Department quashed it for all practical purposes in a 1950 tax ruling (Mimeograph 6477). The ruling required employees to include as current taxable income any employer contribution toward the cost of permanent insurance, unless the insurance is nonvested and forfeitable in the case employment is terminated. As a result of this ruling, the use of traditional level-premium group life insurance has been limited principally to qualified pension plans or to forfeitable group life plans. However, an adaptation of the concept has begun to emerge in the form of supplemental group life.

GROUP ORDINARY LIFE INSURANCE

In the mid-1960s, a new type of permanent coverage was introduced; it purported to allow employers to contribute to permanent policies because of some newly introduced standards in the tax law. Over the years these products have varied widely in design, but are known collectively as "group ordinary" or "Section 79" plans.

In concept, group ordinary allows employees to elect to take all or a part of their term insurance as permanent coverage. In effect, the contract is divided into protection and savings elements. Employer contributions are used to pay only for the term insurance component of the permanent contract, while employee contributions are credited to cash values. The plan can be limited-payment (e.g., life paid up at 65) or ordinary whole life. Had plans been limited to this simple design, the taxation of group life insurance would be less complex than it is today.

However, inherent in the group ordinary concept is the fact that premium contributions will vary from year to year, as the amount at risk under the policy and the insured group's death rate vary. This variability of premium limited the attractiveness of the product, and companies began to seek ways of smoothing or leveling the premium. Of course, such designs fly in the face of the tax rules providing that payments can be used to purchase term insurance only; premium leveling by its very nature creates a reserve. Furthermore, the IRS suspected that some products were designed so that employers were paying more than their fair share of expenses under the contract. (This practice had been common under group paid-up, and was never brought into question until the IRS began to scrutinize group ordinary.) As a result, during the 1960s and 1970s a tug-of-war developed in which the IRS would write regulations and carriers would try to design plans that would comply while still being attractive in the marketplace. The final result is that today all group permanent insurance issued must meet stringent, complex rules that ensure that (1) employer contributions are not used to purchase permanent insurance and (2) employee-owned benefits are self-supporting. A few group ordinary plans remain in force under these circumstances, but the coverage is not widely marketed.

FUTURE OF PERMANENT GROUP LIFE INSURANCE

In 1974 permanent forms of group insurance constituted eight tenths of one percent of the total amount of group insurance outstanding, and they constitute a similar percentage today (Table 8–6). Group paid-up continues to attract a low but steady level of interest; other forms of group permanent business, especially group universal life, are growing rapidly after years of decline.

The group insurance business is a dynamic, ever-changing arena. Large purchasers are highly sophisticated and are constantly seeking better products and services for their money. By the same token, carriers compete fiercely for the business and are always innovative in their products and administrative procedures. As time passes, the distinctions among various product lines will continue to blur, and it appears likely that in the near future scholars and practitioners will have to begin developing an entirely new taxonomy for describing the group life insurance business.

RETIRED-LIVES RESERVE

Another approach used to fund life insurance benefits for retired employees is a retired-lives reserve plan. A retired lives reserve arrangement can be set up as a separate account through a life insurance company or through a trust arrangement for providing group term life insurance for retired employees. Such an approach provides for the funding of retiree life insurance over the employees' active employment period.

Retired-lives reserve plans were once a popular mechanism for providing life insurance for retired employees because of very favorable tax implications for the employer. Restrictions imposed by the Deficit Reduction Act of 1984 (DEFRA) have limited the previous favorable tax aspects of retired lives reserve plans for both employers and employees, and such plans have decreased in importance.

TABLE 8–6
Group Life Insurance In Force in the United States: 1989, 1985

Plan of Insurance	1989			1985		
	Number of Policies (000 omitted)*	*Amount (000.000 omitted)*	*Percent of Amount*	*Number of Policies* (000 omitted)*	*Amount (000.000 omitted)*	*Percent of Amount*
Term						
Decreasing	3,000	$ 78,800	2.3	2,200	$ 58,100	2.3
Other	137,100	3,360,500	96.8	126,600	2,494,600	97.4
Permanent						
Whole Life						
Premium paying	800	27,100	0.8	500	6,400	0.2
Other (including paid-up)	600	2,500	0.1	600	2,000	0.1
Endowment and retirement income with insurance	100	600	††	†	500	††
Total group	141,600	$3,469,500	100.0	129,900	$2,561,600	100.0

Note: Includes credit life insurance on loans of more than 10 years duration.

* Includes group certificates.

† Less than 50,000.

†† Less than .05%.

Source: American Council of Life Insurance.

ACCIDENTAL DEATH AND DISMEMBERMENT (AD&D) INSURANCE

In addition to providing group term life insurance or some form of group insurance with cash values, employers typically also provide accidental death and dismemberment insurance. The AD&D benefit usually is some multiple of the amount of group term life insurance provided the employee under the plan's benefit formula. AD&D insurance is payable only if the employee's death is a result of accident. Percentages of the AD&D coverage amount are payable in the event of certain dismemberments enumerated in the contract or employee booklet.

SUPPLEMENTAL GROUP LIFE INSURANCE

In the past few years, interest has been kindled in an employee-pay-all approach to providing permanent insurance, which has some features of both group and individual insurance. Sometimes called supplemental insurance, it may be provided under a master policy with a certificate being issued to each employee. Alternatively, sometimes individual policies are issued when the coverage is written. Premiums are paid through payroll deduction, and do not receive favored tax treatment. Depending on competitive factors and amounts available, coverage may be purchased with minimal individual underwriting. Since the employee owns the coverage, it goes with him or her if employment is terminated.

Supplemental group life insurance appears to be giving way to "mass marketed" or "wholesale" life insurance. This approach involves the issue of individual insurance through the endorsement (and sometimes the administrative support) of a third party. Over $45 billion of mass marketed insurance is now in force, including almost $9 billion that has been issued through employers. It seems likely that much of this coverage would have been sold as supplemental group if the mass-marketed coverage were not available.

GROUP UNIVERSAL LIFE PROGRAMS

Interest in supplemental protection has been substantially increased through the addition of group universal life (GULP) in the mid-1980s.

GULP is a permanent form of insurance that (like individual universal life) has two separate parts: (1) pure term protection, and (2) an accumulation fund. The employee contributes periodically to the fund, which is credited with interest at a competitive rate. Each month the carrier deducts the cost of pure term protection for the amount at risk under the policy and the cost of administering the policy. The insured may elect to increase the face amount of the policy, provided that certain requirements are met. Like other insurance products, reserves accumulate on a tax-deferred basis and are tax-free if paid as a death benefit. Since GULP is becoming such an important form of benefit for many employees, Chapter 9 covers this subject in detail.

CHAPTER 9

GROUP UNIVERSAL LIFE PROGRAMS[1]

Everett T. Allen, Jr.

Group universal life insurance—permanent life insurance dressed up in new clothes—attests not only to the staying power of permanent life insurance coverage, but also to the ingenuity of the life insurance industry.

During the 1970s, sellers of individual whole life policies faced considerable pressure from disciples of the "buy term and invest the rest" concept. To meet this challenge, the industry developed individual universal life insurance and then forged ahead in the next decade with the group universal life product. Each of these refinements proved to be a boon for consumers in that the cost of coverage decreased while flexibility increased. In fact, growing interest in group universal life programs (GULP) suggests that they may become a major new benefit in the 1990s. This chapter examines GULP's structure and operation, explores its pros and cons in general terms, and discusses relevant tax and legal considerations.

BACKGROUND

To understand GULP, it is helpful to begin with a look at its direct forebear—individual policy universal life (UL). This form of permanent life insurance, in just a short period of time, has become a major product line for almost all life insurers (accounting for more than 50% of some insurers' newly issued individual policy business).

[1]This chapter is reprinted herein with the permission of Towers Perrin.

The hallmark of UL is flexibility. Among its distinguishing characteristics are the following:

- Policy holders decide on the amount and timing of premium payments. They can, for example, fund the policy up front with a single premium and make additional payments at irregular intervals and in irregular amounts. They can also arrange premium "holidays" for any payments scheduled at a specific time.
- Premiums—minus mortality charges and expenses—create policy cash values that are credited with interest, typically at current rates for new investments with some applicable guaranteed floor amount (e.g., 4 percent). This interest accumulates tax-free (as it does with most forms of permanent life insurance) and can totally escape income taxes if ultimately paid out as a death benefit.
- Policy holders can usually choose between a *level death benefit* (i.e., the policy's cash value plus whatever amount of term insurance is required to provide the level benefit selected) and an *increasing death benefit* (i.e., a level amount of term insurance plus the policy's cash value). They may also be able to increase their amount of term insurance—subject to some controls to prevent adverse selection.
- Policy holders can withdraw or borrow against cash values or use the money to purchase paid-up life insurance. If they do not pay future term premiums, both mortality charges and administrative expenses (including premium taxes) are withdrawn from the cash values. If cash values are used up for any reason, leaving nothing to cover term premiums due, the policy is terminated.

In essence, UL offers individuals the chance to "buy term and invest the difference." GULP provides the same opportunity, but with a key difference: coverage is available on a group basis in a form similar to the coverage available under an employee benefit plan. Thus, GULP can be written as a supplement to, or replacement for, an existing group term life insurance plan. In addition, GULP may well have other important applications for employers. These include:

- Funding ERISA-excess and top-hat plans (both defined benefit and defined contribution), and
- Replacing coverage lost under discriminatory postretirement life insurance plans.

ABOUT GULP

Although GULP works much the same way that individual UL does, there are some differences:

- Because GULP is underwritten on a group basis, mortality charges may or may not be based on the underlying experience of the group. In addition, coverage amounts are guaranteed up to some limit without evidence of insurability. These limits vary from plan to plan, depending on plan provisions, the size of the participating group and the insurer's underwriting standards.
- Rates are set on a prospective basis (although the experience of the group may be used for this purpose) and the contracts are generally *nonparticipating*.
- Group underwriting requirements are used to avoid adverse selection and may limit GULP's flexibility to some extent. Actively-at-work requirements, for example, generally apply, and some formula is used to determine amounts of coverage available (e.g., one or two times pay). Health statements or other proof of insurability may also be required in some situations—for example, if participation falls below some predetermined level. In addition, while an individual UL policy holder may be able to choose between a level or increasing death benefit, a GULP purchaser may be limited to one of these choices. But despite such constraints, overall plan design remains significantly more flexible than that available through a traditional supplemental group insurance contract.
- GULP is not typically sold by insurance agents and is therefore available on a no-commission basis. (Individual UL policies, by contrast, are sold by agents who receive commissions for their sales and service efforts, even in cases where an employer permits "mass marketing" of such policies to employees).
- Charges for any administrative services provided by the carrier should be lower for GULP than for individual coverage.

Finally, note that GULP is written on an employee-pay-all basis. Introducing employer contributions could eliminate most of its advantages, particularly its status under Section 79 of the Internal Revenue Code (IRC or Code). This and other Section 79 issues are discussed in the Tax and Legal Issues portion of this chapter.

SPECIFIC GULP FEATURES

Coverage Options

Under GULP, the purchase of term insurance can be separated from the savings or cash-value element. Thus, employees can buy only term insurance or whatever combination of term insurance and savings best meets both their death benefit and capital-accumulation objectives.

Employees select an amount of term insurance from the choices available—either a flat amount or a multiple of pay. In the latter case, the plan could provide for coverage to increase automatically in relation to pay. Although some plans limit coverage to employee life insurance, it is possible to include accidental death and dismemberment insurance and dependent coverage for spouses and children. Typically, children are covered only for term insurance, but spouses may be able to accumulate cash values. It is also possible to add waiver-of-premium coverage (payable in the event of an employee's disability) to the term insurance.

Payment Arrangements

Employee contributions for both the cost of the term insurance and administrative expenses are automatically withheld from after-tax pay. Employees who wish to add a savings element authorize an additional amount to be deducted from pay as well. In theory, these latter contributions can be variable, but in practice, design and administrative considerations may require regular savings. Even so, employees might be able to change their rate of savings, suspend savings contributions from time to time or contribute lump-sum amounts (called "drop-ins"). In many respects, given these features, GULP more closely resembles a defined contribution plan than it does a traditional life insurance "product."

Insurance Rates

Premium rates for term insurance are negotiated based on the experience and characteristics of the participating group and can be quite attractive. (Table 9–1 illustrates the rates used for one existing plan). Generally, the rates are guaranteed from one up to three or five years, with higher rates presumably applicable for coverage with extended guarantees.

TABLE 9–1
Illustrative Term Insurance Rates (Per $1,000)

Age	*Monthly Rate*
Under 30	$ .069
30–34	.089
35–39	.099
40–44	.152
45–49	.259
50–54	.428
55–59	.669
60–64	1.040

While rates (even though guaranteed) can be designed to increase each year by age, linking rates to five-year age brackets is possible. Premiums can also be lower for nonsmokers than for smokers. Or nonsmokers might be given additional term insurance (e.g., 20 percent more) for the standard premium.

Cash Values

The interest credited to cash values varies depending upon current rates for new investments and insurer practices. Once a rate is declared, moreover, it may apply for a limited period such as one year. A permanent guaranteed floor rate of interest (e.g., 4 percent) is also set for purposes of state insurance and federal tax laws.

Table 9–2 illustrates the buildup in cash values over a 10-year period for a 25-year-old employee with level term insurance of $70,000 plus a savings contribution of 10 times the term premium. The illustration is based on sample rates and expense charges furnished by a major insurer. A credited interest rate of 9.5% is assumed.

As noted earlier, participating employees may withdraw cash values at any time and may replace them later with supplemental contributions. Employees may also be able to borrow from the insurer, using their cash values as collateral security. The interest charged for such loans exceeds the rate being credited to cash values—possibly by 1.5% or 2%. In addition, a withdrawal or loan transaction may trigger a transaction charge (e.g., $10 or $20) against the cash value.

TABLE 9–2
Illustration of Cash-Value Buildup*

End of Year	*Attained Age*	*Term Contribution*	*Fund Contribution*	*Expenses*	*Deposit*	*Interest*	*Fund Balance*	*Total Death Benefit*
1	26	$ 84	$ 840	$ 37	$ 803	$ 41	$ 844	$70,844
2	27	168	1,680	74	1,606	162	1,768	71,768
3	28	252	2,520	112	2,408	371	2,779	72,779
4	29	336	3,360	149	3,211	676	3,887	73,887
5	30	420	4,200	186	4,014	996	5,010	75,010
10	35	841	8,410	372	8,038	5,086	13,124	83,124

*Assumptions:
$70,000 of term insurance.
Fund contribution of ten times term premium.
Interest at 9.5%.

Benefit Portability

An attractive feature of GULP is that individual coverage may be portable when insured employees terminate employment or retire. Specifically, some insurers would permit employees to continue coverage on a premium-paying basis—making payments directly to the insurance company—for the full duration of the mortality table (e.g., to age 100). In such a case, different mortality costs and expense charges may apply to continued coverage because all nonactive insureds are "lumped" for experience purposes. In any event, if coverage is continued, it is important to clarify whether the subsequent experience of former employees will be charged back to the employer group and reflected in future premium levels.

As the above discussion illustrates, GULP is not a product. Rather, it is a highly flexible type of coverage that involves many of the design and financial issues applicable to other employee benefit plans. Some of these issues are:

- Selecting eligibility requirements.
- Establishing insurance schedules.
- Fixing contribution schedules.
- Obtaining competitive bids and negotiating contract provisions.

Clearly, given these considerations, the insurance "product" ultimately used is not "off the shelf," but rather is the result of a careful design and negotiation process. Moreover, an insurer's underwriting and administrative requirements can influence design or become a factor in carrier selection. (See the Administration/Design Checklist at the end of this chapter for a more extensive list of administrative and design considerations).

TAX AND LEGAL ISSUES

Internal Revenue Code Section 79

It is generally advantageous for broad-based life insurance plans to be covered under IRC Section 79, which governs the tax treatment of group term life insurance provided to employees. This is not, however, true for

GULP. One reason is that Section 79(d) nondiscrimination requirements do not apply if GULP falls outside the purview of Section 79. Equally important, imputed-income problems can be avoided.

To illustrate the effect of Section 79's imputed-income requirements, consider a traditional supplemental group life program, set up on an employee-pay-all basis, where the term insurance cost for a 60-year-old executive is $0.85 per month per $1,000 of coverage. The executive has $500,000 of coverage costing $5,100 per year. The imputed cost for this coverage (based on Table I rates of the IRS) is $7,020. Assuming basic coverage of at least $50,000, this executive faces $1,920 of imputed income *even though* he has paid the full cost of the insurance. If, however, the plan were not subject to Section 79, he would have no additional imputed income.

Compounding the above problem in the case of permanent life insurance is the manner in which the IRS determines the cost of permanent benefits provided. Although common sense would suggest that this cost equal the yearly side-fund contribution, the prescribed formula is:

$$\text{Cost} = NSP_B \times (CV_E \,/\, NSP_E - CV_B \,/\, NSP_B)$$

where NSP is the net single premium, CV is the policy cash value, and B and E represent beginning and end-of-year values.

The following example, based on typical values provided by a large insurer, points up the impact of this formula:

Term Cost:	$ 125	
Side Fund Contributions:	375	
Side Fund Interest:	125	
CV_B:	1,000	
CV_E:	1,500	
NSP_B (50):		.42334
NSP_E (51):		.43558

Cost = .42334 × (1,500/.43558 − 1,000/.42334), or $457.85

In this case, because the total employee contribution is $500, only $42.15 would be allocated to group term life insurance and available as an offset to Table I imputed income. And this is true even though the actual term cost is $125!

Clearly, there are sound reasons for removing GULP from the scope of Section 79. The next question is: How can it be done?

Section 1.79-1(a) of the Income Tax Regulations provides, in part, that life insurance is not group term life insurance for purposes of Section 79 unless:

1. It provides a general death benefit that is excludable from gross income under Section 101(a).
2. It is provided to a group of employees.
3. It is provided under a policy carried directly or indirectly by the employer.
4. The amount of insurance provided to each employee is computed under a formula that precludes individual selection.

Since GULP meets conditions 1, 2, and 4, to escape Section 79 treatment it must *not* be "carried directly or indirectly by the employer." What would this entail? Under Section 1.79-0 of the Regulations, a life insurance policy is carried directly or indirectly by an employer if:

1. The employer pays any part of the cost of the life insurance directly or through another person; or
2. The employer or two or more employers arrange for payment of the cost of the life insurance by their employees and charge at least one employee less than the cost of his or her insurance, as determined under Table I of Section 1.79-3(d)(2), and at least one other employee more than the cost of his or her insurance, determined in the same way.

The first requirement can be met by setting GULP up on an employee-pay-all basis. The second requirement can be met in one of two ways. One is to ensure that term premiums are always greater or less than Table I rates at all ages. The other is to write GULP through an independent trust arrangement established by an insurer or other third party (e.g., a consulting or brokerage firm), thereby ensuring that the employer has no part in arranging for the coverage.

Under this latter approach, the trustee becomes the policy holder and fees and commissions are paid by the trust or the insurer. The fact that the employer withholds and remits employee contributions and permits descriptive materials to be given to employees does not bring the program within Section 79. However, the employer could not participate in the insurer selection process or in the development of premium rates.

The question of paying for the cost of life insurance is very important. In the opinion of many experts, amounts paid directly by an employer to a third party for items such as communication and enrollment would *not* invoke Section 79 treatment. In preparing specifications, it may be prudent to specify the third party's role and to isolate the insurer's expense load for any services included in the insurer's expense level. These charges should then be removed or paid directly to the third party by the carrier on a fee-for-service basis. Presumably, fees paid by the employer in excess of the expense load would be permissible since they are not part of the cost of insurance.

Employers should also be aware that some tax counsel view the issue of GULP and Section 79 in far more simple terms. Their view is that group universal life insurance does not come within the scope of IRC Section 79 in the first place. Therefore, as long as an employer pays no part of the cost of insurance, Section 79 is inapplicable. The IRS has not yet taken a formal position on this question, however, and employers should research this issue carefully lest Section 79 be applied in a remedial fashion to a GULP arrangement.

Life Contract Defined

To avoid taxation on the buildup of cash values, a life insurance product must meet the definition of life insurance as specified in Section 7702(a) of the Code. In general, life insurance contracts must meet one of two tests, the cash-value accumulation test (7702[A][1]) or the guideline premium requirement test (7702[A][2]).

Under the cash-value accumulation test, the cash-surrender value may not at any time exceed the net single premium required to fund future benefits under the contract. To meet this test, therefore, insurers using it have to stipulate that when the cash-value limit is reached, all or part of the cash value will either be used to purchase paid-up insurance or refunded to the employee.

Under the guideline premium requirement test, the sum of the premiums paid under the contract must not at any time exceed the greater of the guideline single premium as of such time or the sum of the guideline-level premiums to such date.

Accumulated premiums paid must also meet the cash-value corridor test of Section 7702(A)(2)(B), which states that the death benefit must never be less than the applicable percentage of the cash surrender value.

The "applicable percentage" is 250 percent, but it is reduced, after the insured reaches age 40, in accordance with the Table 9–3.

Insurers using this test could automatically increase the amount of term insurance to comply with the cash-value corridor requirement. They will also return premiums to employees to avoid violating the guideline premium limitation. In addition, insurers are likely to impose some overall maximum on the amount an employee can contribute to build cash values, thereby avoiding IRS limitations for a considerable time period. Plan design should recognize this issue.

The insurer must be relied on to make certain that the contract can be classified as life insurance. Thus, it is important to understand the differences between these two approaches and to ensure that the carrier's administrative system is capable of "warning" employees before an automatic purchase of additional insurance (term or paid-up) is made or cash values or premiums are refunded.

Employee Retirement Income Security Act of 1974 (ERISA)

Although neither a Section 79 nor an employer-sponsored plan, GULP seems to fall within the broad definition of welfare plans under Title I of ERISA and would be subject to this law's reporting, disclosure, and fiduciary requirements. If, as is likely, GULP replaces an existing group

TABLE 9–3
Reduction Schedule for Applicable Percentage

In the case of an insured with an attained age, as of the beginning of the contract year, of:		*The applicable percentage decreases by a ratable portion for each full year:*	
More than:	*But not more than:*	*From:*	*To:*
40	45	250%	215%
45	50	215	185
50	55	185	150
55	60	150	130
60	65	130	120
65	70	120	115
70	75	115	105
75	90	105	105
90	95	105	100

term life plan, this administrative burden will be no more onerous than under the conventional approach. But there may be additional fiduciary implications because of the "investment" aspects of the program.

Taxation of Withdrawals and Loans

If an employee withdraws cash values, the amount withdrawn is not subject to tax until it exceeds the employee's cost basis or investment in the contract (i.e., the sum of all term insurance premiums, all net additions to the side fund, and administrative costs). Thereafter, the withdrawal is taxable as ordinary income. Table 9–4 illustrates the effect of these tax considerations on the after-tax yields available under GULP (using the data previously shown in Table 9–3).

Loan proceeds are not subject to income tax unless and until cash values are used to repay the loan. At that time, the transaction is treated as a withdrawal.

TABLE 9–4
Illustration of Effective Aftertax Investment Yields*

				Effective After-tax Yields at Various Marginal Rates	
End of Year	*Fund Contribution*	*Investment in the Contract***	*Fund Balance*	*40%*	*25%*
1	$ 840	$ 924	$ 844	0.8%	0.8%
2	1,680	1,848	1,768	5.0	5.0
3	2,520	2,772	2,779	6.5	6.5
4	3,360	3,696	3,887	6.2	6.6
5	4,200	4,620	5,010	6.2	6.7
10	8,410	9,251	13,124	6.3	7.2

*To determine after-tax yields, it was assumed that deposits to the side fund were made at the beginning of the month in which the after-tax value of the withdrawal equalled the fund balance (at a given point in time) less the marginal tax rate times the excess of the fund balance over the investment in the contract. Note that the after-tax yields are net of administrative expenses levied against the side fund.

**Sum of the term premium plus gross contribution to fund.

Modified Endowment Contracts

Special rules apply to contracts entered into on or after June 21, 1988, as well as contracts materially changed after that date. In order to avoid accelerating taxation on distributions from the contract, it is necessary to avoid designation as a modified endowment contract under IRC Section 7702(A). Under the Code, if the accumulated amount paid under the contract at any time during the first seven contract years exceeds the sum of the net level premiums that would have been paid up to that time if the contract provided for paid-up future benefits after the payment of seven level annual premiums, then amounts withdrawn under the policy will be taxed on an earnings-first basis under Section 72(e)(10). Moreover, an additional 10 percent tax would also apply to such taxable distributions under Section 72(v) under certain circumstances.

Taxation of Death Benefits

The full amount of the proceeds payable at death (term insurance and cash values) is considered life insurance and therefore not subject to income tax. However, the proceeds are includable for estate tax purposes unless the employee's incidents of ownership have been assigned at least three years prior to death, or if it can be proved that assignments within three years of death were not made in contemplation of death.

ADVANTAGES AND DISADVANTAGES

GULP offers a number of advantages to employers. Specifically:

- A successfully implemented plan may relieve pressure on the employer to provide postretirement life insurance coverage.
- GULP is a low-cost "benefit improvement," much like an unmatched 401(k) plan.
- GULP offers a way to move away from an existing subsidized flat-rate plan.
- Significant benefits are available for key employees.
- Because GULP is generally sold on a group basis, there is no need for individual insurance agents to solicit employees.

- If an employee continues coverage after termination of employment, the employer will not face conversion charges.

GULP also offers many advantages to employees. Among them are the following:

- Employees can consolidate all coverages for themselves and their dependents under one contract.
- Upon termination of employment, the coverage may be portable.
- Premiums are flexible in amount and timing.
- Investment income is on a tax-deferred or tax-free basis.
- GULP appears to be a very low-cost way to purchase term or permanent life insurance.
- GULP is a convenient way to purchase insurance; premium payments are made on a payroll-deduction basis.
- Guaranteed issue amounts are available at levels sufficiently high to cover most employee needs.
- Cash values offer a source of funds for emergencies. This may be very attractive because withdrawals from qualified defined-contribution plans are often limited and may be subject to excise taxes.
- Employees receive periodic reports and are kept up-to-date on the status of their life insurance program.
- Upon retirement, employees can use their cash value to purchase paid-up insurance.

The appeal and versatility of GULP notwithstanding, employers should be aware of certain potential disadvantages before adopting such a program for any reason. Among the major issues to consider are the following:

- Employees may view GULP as a more attractive savings vehicle than an employer-sponsored 401(k) plan. If that occurs and precipitates a drop in 401(k) participation, the 401(k) plan could have trouble meeting ADP tests for nondiscriminatory participation by higher-paid employees.
- GULP cannot be funded with before-tax employee contributions if it is to remain outside the scope of Section 79. Thus, it cannot be a direct part of a flexible benefit program.

- Although employers are not technically involved in operating GULP, they may well bear the brunt of employee dissatisfaction if servicing problems arise.
- To preclude financial selection, insurers may move toward short-term interest guarantees. In such a case, the interest credited to individual accounts will probably depend on when the moneys are invested. Although the yields on current investment vehicles are likely to be as good as or better than those available from other investment vehicles, there is no guarantee that the total cash value will enjoy similar results, especially in a period of rising inflation.
- Changes in law, regulations, and rulings could bring GULP within the purview of Section 79 or make taxable the buildup of cash values.
- As with any form of permanent life insurance, participants could face adverse financial results if coverage is surrendered early.
- Low GULP participation may saddle employers with administrative burdens and no offsetting advantages.
- The feasibility and consequences of terminating the master policy and/or obtaining coverage with another insurer remain unclear. For example, can individual units of coverage continue after termination of the master policy? If so, will there be any change in the structure of premiums, cash values, interest credits, and other policy provisions? Can reserves be transferred to another insurer and, if so, would this be a taxable transaction?

Communicating GULP to Employees

GULP's very flexibility necessitates careful employee communication. After all, employees are being offered an opportunity to participate in a program with many choices—generally without the benefit of face-to-face explanations and enrollment by insurance agents or insurance company personnel. Although insurance carriers will undoubtedly provide communication assistance (at no additional specified cost), bear in mind that they want to sell the product. Generally, therefore, it will be up to employers to ensure their employees receive a balanced presentation and understand both the advantages and disadvantages of participation.

Pretesting the concept with employees in focus groups can help employers determine the magnitude of the communication challenge. Based on this information, employers can then prepare appropriate written and audiovisual communication materials to explain how the program works and the various options available to employees. Trained employer personnel should also be available to answer questions and help employees make appropriate choices. Although strategies and techniques will be much the same as those used for other employee benefit plans (particularly savings or 401(k) plans), employers may have to place extra emphasis on communicating initial and ongoing choices and their implications. Employers who wish to encourage participation for a specific area (e.g., to replace postretirement life insurance) may also have to use specific ''selling'' techniques.

ADMINISTRATION/DESIGN CHECKLIST

Administration

Administration of GULP can be complicated, combining the record-keeping and systems requirements of both group insurance and defined-contribution plans. That is, in fact, one of the main reasons that some carriers may not be in a position to offer GULP. It also points up the importance of evaluating administrative capability in selecting a carrier.

Administrative requirements include the following:

- Linking with payroll systems to accommodate withholding.
- Establishing coverage amounts and contribution levels and allocating these amounts to term and savings elements.
- Collecting and remitting contributions to the carrier with appropriate allocations between savings and term insurance coverage.
- Maintaining individual account balances (including charges and credits).
- Processing such transactions as:
  —Changes in beneficiary, coverage amounts, contribution levels and address/location.
  —Contribution suspensions.
  —Addition or deletion of participating employees.
  —Loans, withdrawals, and claims.
  —Transferring administration for terminating and retiring employees.
  —Producing annual reports.

In addition, plan administration encompasses the experience-rating process, the resolution of underwriting questions, and the preparation and filing of tax reports (e.g., Form 1099) and financial reports to the employer and employees (e.g., Form 5500 and SARs).

Although third parties are likely to offer GULP administrative services, utilization of such services may be inappropriate for several reasons:

- Insurers are developing their own administrative capability and are not receptive to the idea of using an outside administrator.
- The costs would be redundant and therefore unattractive.
- It does not appear that any third-party "system" would be distinguishable from or superior to the ones developed by insurers.
- Significant interaction with individual policy holders would be required—an unnecessary and costly role for any third party.

Design

What follows is a list of the issues involved in designing GULP—many of which have to be negotiated with the insurer and must be included in the competitive bidding process. Key considerations include the following: Eligibility requirements (age, service, minimum pay level, employment classification).

Coverage to be included:

—Term only.
—Term plus savings.
—Accidental death and dismemberment.
—Declared interest rate.
—Policy loan interest rate.
—Regular administrative charges.
—Transaction fees.
—Reserve basis for paid-up insurance.

Underwriting:

—Guaranteed issue amount.
—Evidence of insurability requirements.
—Open enrollment availability.
—Dependent coverage.
—Waiver of premium.

Term coverage amounts to be included:

—Number of choices.
—Flat amounts.
—Multiples of pay:
Initially frozen.
Automatically increased with pay.

Savings provisions:

—Number of choices.
—Maximum contribution level.
—Regular contributions.
—Variable contributions.
—Floor rate of interest.
—Declared rate of interest.

Other provisions:

—Withdrawals.
—Policy loans.
—Paid-up insurance options.
—Portability.

Premiums and other financial considerations:

—Level.
—Guarantees.
—Renewal rating process.
—Floor interest rate.

THE FUTURE

Many employers have already utilized GULP—either in addition to or as a replacement for conventional group life insurance. They have done so to achieve a number of the advantages previously described but, in particular, to avoid the tax implications of Section 79. GULP has also proven to be an effective way of providing additional benefits for highly compensated employees. Its value in allowing employees to continue meaningful amounts of coverage after retirement is also a significant factor. And, of course, the savings opportunities presented are important to employees at all pay levels.

Employers still must consider the potential disadvantages of using GULP. Also, they need to recognize the additional and somewhat complicated administrative issues that GULP entails. At this stage in the development of GULP, however, it does not appear that these disadvantages outweigh the positive results, both for employers and employees, that this coverage creates.

As more and more experience with GULP is acquired—in terms of underwriting, rates, administration, and employee acceptance—it seems possible that it will be used to a significant extent as an alternative to conventional group life insurance plans.

PART 4

MEDICAL AND OTHER HEALTH BENEFITS

In this part the critically important topics of medical and other health benefits are explored. Of prime importance in any discussion of medical benefits is the subject of cost containment—a topic so important today it is referred to either explicitly or implicitly in all the chapters in this part.

Part Four opens with a discussion of the environment of medical expense plans in Chapter 10. Following this stage-setting chapter, hospital and medical care expense plans and surgical/medical expense and major medical/comprehensive plans are analyzed in Chapters 11 and 12, respectively. Chapter 13 presents an overview of medical care cost containment techniques used by medical care risk bearers to limit medical care expenses.

Health maintenance organizations (HMOs) and preferred provider organizations (PPOs) have grown extremely popular as alternative approaches to handling the medical care expense risk in a more cost-effective way, and the nature, advantages, and disadvantages of these approaches are explored in detail in Chapters 14 and 15. The concept of managed care which encompasses all approaches to medical care cost containment appears in Chapter 16 and completes this series of chapters.

Other health-related benefit plans such as dental, vision care, prescription drug, and hearing care plans and the nature and issues involved in such plans are discussed in Chapters 18 and 19.

Also included in this part is a review in Chapter 17 of the issues involved in long-term care insurance—probably the most needed health benefit not widely provided either through the private or governmental sectors of the economy. Many experts believe the employee benefits mechanism is the appropriate vehicle to broaden this coverage.

CHAPTER 10

THE ENVIRONMENT OF MEDICAL BENEFIT PLANS IN THE 1990s

Charles P. Hall, Jr.

"The severe and continuing escalation of medical care costs over the past decade is a matter of growing concern to virtually all segments of our society. It has caused great financial stress to both public and private sponsors of medical expense benefit plans, with the private sponsors being especially hard hit. Yet despite much rhetoric, there is little evidence of lasting solutions being developed." That opening statement from the first two editions of this *Handbook* is equally true today despite enormous changes that have taken place in the delivery, financing, and organization of medical care over the past decade.

The issue of cost containment continues to occupy center stage at both the public and corporate policy levels. While some of the benefit innovations described in the earlier editions have become "traditional" in their own right, others have virtually disappeared, and a whole new lexicon of terms has emerged to describe yet another generation of innovations. Moreover, since the overall inflation rate has remained relatively modest, it is painfully clear that in comparable terms medical care costs have continued to be out of control. In 1990 alone, the United States spent over $666 billion on health care—12.2 percent of gross national product—up from 11.6 percent in 1989.

Continued double-digit inflation in the medical care sector has given rise to new and increasingly insistent calls for action at both the federal and state levels, and a growing number of business leaders have begun to lend their support to some form of national health insurance, though few believe that such a move will solve the cost problem. It would, however, address the continuing problem of more than 30 million uninsured Americans, a blight that has drawn intense media attention for the past several years.

It remains true that there are only a few basic approaches that will effectively control the cost of medical expense benefit plans. Cost containment can be accomplished either by controlling the factors that affect the costs of these plans or by designing the medical expense benefit or plan to minimize the impact of increases in the cost of medical services.

This chapter identifies some of the major factors that must be taken into account in the design of employee medical expense benefit plans if there is to be any hope for meaningful cost containment.

PUBLIC POLICY ISSUES

Anyone responsible for the design of employee medical expense plans should pay close attention to public policy issues relating to health care. This has been a politically charged arena for decades and, if anything, has become more so in the last few years. Widespread shifts in government policy have had an enormous impact on the private sector. Employers have found that "cost containment" from the point of view of the government frequently translates into "cost shifting" to the private sector as a means of saving on the costs of public programs such as Medicare and Medicaid while at the same time avoiding politically unpopular tax increases or added pressure on the federal deficit. At both the state and federal levels, legislators have been far more willing to grant "entitlements" than they have been to fund them. A widely used and even more frequently proposed "solution" from government's point of view has been to "mandate" that employers provide those benefits which government sees as desirable but is unable or unwilling to fund directly.

Unfortunately, mandates have perhaps done as much to exacerbate the problem as they have to solve it. More than 700 state-level mandates now exist, and there is no question they have helped to increase the cost of medical insurance. In trying to avoid the higher premiums thus produced, as well as to avoid the payment of premium taxes that typically range from 2 to 3 percent in every state, more and more large employers have shifted to self-insurance. They have discovered that by taking advantage of the preemption provision of the Employee Retirement Income Security Act of 1974 (ERISA), they can cover their workers with benefits that are exempt from both the state mandates and taxes. The savings for large employers can be substantial, but reducing the pool of privately insured plans, to which providers have traditionally shifted costs resulting from deficits under government programs or other bad debt, accelerates premium increases and may force many small employers to drop their coverage. Thus, mandates often produce not only fewer regulated health insurance plans, but fewer insured persons. While the impact of mandates varies from state to state, it has been estimated that as many as 64 percent of the uninsured in Connecticut owe their uninsured status to state mandated benefits.[1] Ironically, then, mandates designed to extend medical insurance benefits may unintentionally result in decreased access to coverage.

Congress changed the Medicare ground rules several times in the 1980s, with each change adding costs to the private sector. Examples include changing reimbursement from a retrospective cost-related basis to a prospective system based on diagnostic related groups (DRGs) in 1983 and legislating Medicare as secondary coverage to employer-sponsored benefits for workers over age 65, while also requiring that employers retain benefits for such workers at the same level as for younger workers. Whereas employers formerly utilized "carve-out" provisions designed to make their group benefits responsible only for those items not covered by Medicare for over-65 workers, the employee benefit plan is now primary for all active workers regardless of age. In other action, the Consolidated Omnibus Budget Reconciliation Act (COBRA) made it mandatory effective July 1, 1987, that companies with at least 20 employees make medical benefits available at group rates for at least 18 months after an employee leaves employment regardless of whether the worker left voluntarily, retired, or was dismissed. Furthermore, an employee's family members may be entitled to continued coverage even if the employee dies or gets divorced, and the right to such coverage for an employee and the employee's family members may be extended for up to three years. These and other actions have had a profound and lasting impact not only on the financing of care

---

[1]Goodman, John C., and Gerald L. Musgrave, "Freedom of Choice in Health Insurance," *NCPA Policy Report No. 134,* The National Center for Policy Analysis, Dallas, November 1988.

but also on the access to insurance and on the organization and delivery of medical services. There is no question that they gave rise to redoubled efforts on the part of employers to search for ways to protect themselves against federal cost shifts and to discover meaningful cost-control measures of their own.

For the prudent benefits planner or manager, then, it makes sense to keep a close watch on emerging issues with a view to anticipating changes and designing plans that will minimize any undesirable impact on the employer or its employees. It also may be possible to lobby successfully either for or against proposals that are of direct concern. There are, at present, several such issues.

The Uninsured

Although the figure of 182.3 million insureds reported for 1988 in the *Source Book of Health Insurance Data*[2] was up from the 179.7 million reported for 1987, the 1987 figure was the lowest number since 1976, and the 1988 count was still considerably less than the all-time high of 188.2 million in 1982. Indeed, the total number covered had declined in each of the five years between 1982 and 1987, a fact that focused the attention of the nation on the growing problem of the uninsured and spurred renewed interest in some form of national health insurance or, in its absence, a federal policy that would mandate private coverage. Except for 1976, these were the only years in which the total number of insureds declined since the Health Insurance Association of America (HIAA) started publishing data in 1940.[3]

Factors that contributed to the sharp decline from 1982 to 1987 include, but are not limited to, medical care cost increases, which caused many small firms and individuals to drop their coverage; the changing composition of American industry and the American work force, discussed later in this chapter; and a rapid growth in the service sector, characterized by relatively small, nonunion firms dominated by white-collar workers. Indeed, the dramatic increases in new jobs and employment during this period were heavily concentrated in small firms.

---

[2]*Source Book of Health Insurance Data,* Health Insurance Association of America, 1990.

[3]Note that some of the numbers for years 1975 and later have been adjusted downward from earlier reports because of new data on average family size.

If not for the federal budget deficit and growing U.S. trade deficit, both of which scuttled most proposals for expanded social programs in recent years, the magnitude of the increasing number of uninsureds might already have produced a national health insurance plan or at least a policy assuring universal access to insurance. Instead, the current Congress is considering, as did its predecessor, a plethora of new bills that offer a range of alternative approaches to "solving" medical care problems. Unfortunately, Congress restricted its ability to act in this area at the end of the last session by imposing a requirement that any new federal program must be budget-neutral unless it specifies the new tax that will support it, and it now seems unlikely that any major initiative will be successful before the presidential election in 1992.

Political winds do have a way of shifting suddenly, however, and with the American Medical Association's (AMA's) unexpected call in May 1991 for the federal government to guarantee basic medical insurance to all Americans, stating that it is "no longer acceptable morally, ethically, or economically" for millions of citizens to live with inadequate or nonexistent health insurance, the long stalemate on this topic may soon be broken. It may be recalled that in a similar break from long-standing opposition to early proposals for Medicare, the AMA unwittingly triggered passage of both parts A and B of that legislation in 1965. Of course, there is still much to be done before any agreement is reached on exactly how the desired universal coverage is to be achieved, what it should include, and who will pay for it. Those questions have not changed, and there remain advocates for solutions that range from a British-style national health service, to a Canadian-style national health insurance, to a public-private partnership that would involve a combination of employer mandates plus various reforms of existing federal programs, to name just a few of the options. The most crucial question that must be resolved before any real progress can be made is the precise definition of the benefits to be included in "universal access."

At this writing (summer 1991) several bills already have been introduced to the first session of the 102nd Congress that would mandate all employers to provide certain health benefits. The House Ways and Means Subcommittee on Health held extensive hearings in early May 1991 on the reform of private health insurance, and Senate hearings were expected to follow quickly. It is anticipated that most of the proposals would result in an immediate increase in group medical plan expenditures for many employers, but the most serious impact would likely be on smaller employers, many of whom might be forced either to lay off workers or go out of business. A recent survey highlighted the concerns of small business owners regarding health care costs.[4] Given the substantial changes in the structure of American industry that occurred in the 1980s, when small firms became the primary sources of new employment, these concerns cannot be dismissed lightly. Meanwhile, despite many calls for a more drastic, government-run program with universal access, such as the Canadian-style program recommended by the Pepper Commission and others, there are few who believe that such a plan can possibly overcome seemingly insurmountable political hurdles any time soon.

Retiree Coverage

For several years now some courts have shown a tendency to find that certain postretirement health benefits extended by some companies to their workers, often as a gesture of goodwill, are now fully guaranteed as vested contractual rights with no residual right on the part of the employer to reduce the benefits either by increasing the retirees' contributions via premium, deductible, or coinsurance modifications or by eliminating any previously covered benefits. So, while Congress can make such changes in Medicare provisions, some courts may be holding private employers to a higher standard.

Any problem from such court decisions pales, however, in comparison to the requirement that all firms must account fully on their balance sheets for their projected liabilities under postretirement health plans by no later than January 1993. In the past, these liabilities have been handled on a pay-as-you-go basis, and the potential impact of this change could be staggering to many firms. With continued rapid increase in the over-65 population, growing life expectancy, and increasingly costly medical technology for dealing with the diseases of the elderly, many firms now find themselves faced with potentially catastrophic unfunded liabilities in this area. There are sure to be dramatic changes—most likely cutbacks—in the future level of employer coverage for retired workers, at least for acute-care services, as a result of these developments. At the very least, retiree

---

[4] *Small Business and Health Care: Results of a Survey,* Charles P. Hall, Jr., and John M. Kuder, NFIB Foundation, Washington, D.C., 1990.

medical care benefits will be described in very careful contract language to protect the employer from unanticipated and unwanted commitments. This response, however, could generate further Congressional mandates.

Catastrophic Coverage

After years of debate, Congress finally enacted the Medicare Catastrophic Coverage Act in 1988, only to repeal it a year later under considerable pressure from an extremely vocal and politically active minority of the elderly who would have been required to contribute to the added cost of the benefit based on their income. This sequence of events left many in Congress confused about what should be done for senior citizens. To some extent they felt betrayed, since they had consulted with the American Association of Retired Persons (AARP) before enacting the legislation and thought they had its support. Unfortunately, the AARP had misread the attitudes of some of its most vocal members.

While the proposed premium contribution was a major point of contention in the now-repealed law, another concern was that it focused exclusively on *acute* medical care services. The prevailing view of most health economists and the elderly themselves is that the most pressing need is for an acceptable form of long-term care insurance that provides adequate protection for nursing home and home health services as well as some basic social services that, presumably, would cost less and enable elderly persons to maintain some degree of independence. With nursing home costs currently averaging from $2,500 to $3,000 per month, few people could support lengthy stays in the absence of insurance, and not many wish to be faced with the spend-down provisions of Medicaid in order to become eligible for those benefits. This has led to a growing interest in long-term care insurance by the private sector in recent years. Long-term care is discussed briefly later in this chapter and in detail in Chapter 17 of the *Handbook*.

Other Current and Emerging Issues

Some of the other areas relating to medical care benefits in which Congress has shown recent interest suggest that the field will remain volatile and controversial for years to come. For example, the Congressional Office of Technology Assessment (OTA) has been looking into the possible impact that rapid technological development in the field of genetic testing would have on insurance and employment. At issue is whether Congress should establish regulations dealing with the use of such tests for either insurance underwriting and rating or employment decisions.

Concern over AIDS continues, and various efforts have been made either to mandate coverage or to limit traditional underwriting controls available to private insurers. There can be no doubt that the impact of AIDS on private life and health insurers is potentially catastrophic, especially as the epidemic spreads. Continued sparring can be anticipated in both legislative and court actions before a "final solution" is found.

Widespread interest also exists in both public and private circles for providing more extensive mental health benefits. Concern ranges from specific conditions such as senile dementia and Alzheimer's disease, which primarily strike the elderly, to the pervasive problems with various forms of substance abuse, including both alcohol and drugs, which seem to have their most severe impact among our youth and young adults.

Occasionally, initiatives also are presented in Washington that might actually save employers money on their employee benefit plans. One such example was the Health Maintenance Organization Amendments Act of 1988, which softened the community rating requirements for federally qualified health maintenance organizations (HMOs) and permitted employers' contributions to be based on the projected claims experience of employees joining the HMO.

State-Level Issues

In addition to extensive activity at the federal level, a good deal of public policy action has taken place at the state level. While the trend toward the enactment of state-mandated health benefits peaked in the late 1970s, there continue to be various special interest groups lobbying for this type of legislation, and more than 700 mandates currently exist nationally. As noted, state mandates spurred the rapid movement toward self-insurance in the 1980s, since most such mandates can be avoided in self-insured plans under the ERISA preemption of state laws. Because self-insurance is not an option available to all firms, once again the smaller firms suffer. Recent court decisions have found that some such state laws are not in conflict with ERISA, and this may result in renewed activity. In general, employers have fought these mandates, not always successfully. On the other hand, some states have tried to remedy the small-group access problem by passing laws to exempt small groups from mandates in order to improve their access to viable insurance markets. Eleven states had taken this step by early 1991, and similar legislation was pending in eight other states. Moreover, 33 states had either created (26) or were considering (7) the creation of state risk pools to guarantee the availability of insurance to individuals who normally would be uninsurable. These and other steps have been strongly supported by both HIAA and the Blue Cross/Blue Shield Association as part of their proposed strategies to eliminate the problem of the uninsured in America.

In an effort to curb, or at least rationalize, the many proposals for mandates while at the same time trying to control the escalation of medical care costs, some states have established various commissions and review panels to provide legislative guidance. In Pennsylvania, for example, the creation in 1986 of a Health Care Cost Containment Commission carried with it the establishment of a Mandated Benefits Review Panel charged with responsibility for reviewing all proposed mandated benefits in accordance with explicit criteria spelled out in the law. Composed of "experts" from the fields of biostatistics, health economics, and health research, the panel reports to the commission, which also obtains input from the insurance commissioner and the secretary of health. The commission then makes a recommendation to the legislature as to the desirability of specific proposals. Several other states have adopted or are studying similar proposals. One of the most controversial of all state initiatives to date has been the legislation in Oregon that for the first time would establish an overt program of rationing the availability of care under the state's Medicaid program. After an elaborate process of hearings involving representatives from all segments of society, the legislature recently passed a law to rate medical services on their effectiveness, cost, and benefit to society. Based on a weighted average of these factors, it would establish a hierarchy of services and designate those available to Medicaid recipients. Certain services would not be made available. The program has not yet been implemented, since a waiver of normal Medicaid rules is required from the federal government before it could be started. It also is likely to face a series of court challenges. Nevertheless, some feel that this law represents the wave of the future, and though it currently is applicable only to Medicaid recipients, if successful, it may have spill-over effects on the private sector.

Though critics of the Oregon plan abound, it is difficult to say if it is any more irrational or insensitive than what other states have done to control Medicaid spending. For example, when as the result of a federal mandate California recently was required to include an additional service, it simply redefined ''poverty'' by changing the income level for Medicaid eligibility. The result was that all Medicaid-eligible persons were entitled to the new benefit, but there was a substantial reduction in the number who were eligible for *any* Medicaid services.

Other states are considering alternative approaches. The Ohio legislature, for example, is considering a state-level Canadian-style program. Such a plan would virtually eliminate the private health insurance industry, except for any supplemental benefits not covered in the state's plan.

In summary, ''Washington watching'' and ''state capital watching'' will continue to be very important in the design of medical care expense plans.

ENVIRONMENTAL FACTORS

Following one of the most extended periods of peacetime prosperity in the nation's history, the recession that began in the fourth quarter of 1990 raised many concerns about unemployment, renewed inflation, unstable interest rates, growing federal deficits, persistent foreign trade imbalances, and fluctuations in the value of the dollar. While many originally predicted that the recession would be shallow and short, others were less optimistic, and serious economic uncertainty continued to persist as 1991 came to a close.

It now seems clear that the widely proclaimed ''peace dividend'' anticipated as a result of recent dramatic political and social upheavals in Eastern Europe is not likely to materialize. The combined impact of the Gulf War and its aftermath of chaos in the Middle East, natural disasters in Bangladesh and several other Third World countries, and growing economic problems in the Soviet Union and many of its former satellite nations had already combined to prevent any significant ''dividend'' from being realized by the spring of 1991. While the stock market rebounded briefly to reach historical highs in early fall, it again plunged as the steel, airline, automobile and retail industries continued to report losses, layoffs and reduced sales in the closing months of the year. Rapidly deteriorating ethnic strife in Yugoslavia and the sudden political disintegration of the U.S.S.R. in late 1991 further complicated matters, with President Bush finding his attention to foreign policy matters increasingly criticized by those who were demanding more attention to very real domestic problems.

THE WORK FORCE

Some of the major changes in the characteristics of the American work force over the past decade have been important in their impact on employee benefits. After a sharp increase in the total number of employed workers during most of the 1980s, accompanied by a marked shift in the nature of American industry, unemployment soared in 1990–91. The traditional "smokestack" industries so dominant in the years after World War II have, at least in relative terms, declined dramatically in importance as the pressure of foreign competition and the rapid shift of American industry from a manufacturing to a service orientation has progressed. This change is of enormous importance from the standpoint of medical care expense plans for several reasons. The traditional manufacturing giants typically were large employers with a heavily unionized work force, and while their employees never accounted for a majority of the labor market, the negotiated benefits they obtained often became the pattern for other employers to emulate. The majority of the workers were blue collar, and most were from single-income families. Over the past decade, changes in the workplace have been characterized by a shift from manufacturing to service industries, from large to small firms, from heavily unionized blue-collar to minimally organized white-collar positions, and from a male-dominated to an almost gender-balanced work force. More important, a larger proportion of the work force now comes from multiple-income households, and a significant proportion of workers are employed on a part-time basis. One result of these changes is that a very significant portion of the "uninsured" in the United States (by some estimates, up to two thirds) actually are fully employed workers and their dependents, whereas historically the uninsured were concentrated among the unemployed.

DEMOGRAPHICS AND TECHNOLOGY

The "graying of America" continues, with both average life expectancy and the average age of the population increasing as the Baby Boom generation matures. There also has been a noticeable increase in the birth rate.

It is a well-known fact that from a medical viewpoint the first and last six months of life are the most expensive. Increasingly sophisticated medical technology now makes it possible to preserve the lives of babies who only a few years ago would have had no chance of survival. At the other extreme, the ability to extend life, though not necessarily to improve its quality, has become both a blessing and a curse. This applies, as well, to the vast majority of the population not at the extremes of age. The technology in question is both extraordinarily expensive and controversial, and those who design and sponsor medical care expense plans face hard decisions as to the criteria they will establish for coverage. Should everyone be eligible for organ transplants? Intensive care? Experimental treatment? These questions continue to be addressed on an ad hoc basis under many benefit plans, while others have established formal policies.

RECENT MARKET TRENDS

Any discussion of recent market trends in health insurance must start with the continued rise in costs and the increasing difficulty of providing a viable market for individuals and small groups. HIAA data show that commercial insurers cover over nine times as many people under group as opposed to individual medical expense insurance policies. In 1984, the ratio was about five to one. Most of these group policies are part of an employee benefit plan and provide more generous benefits than are available under individual policies. The majority of Blue Cross/Blue Shield coverage also is in the form of group contracts, and the same is true for HMOs and other plans. As was already mentioned, it has been estimated that as many as two thirds of the uninsured are fully employed workers and their dependents, mostly employees of small employers that do not provide group health insurance benefits. While many small businesses would like to provide these benefits, it is often beyond their financial capacity to do so. Not only small groups are in trouble, however. Many leaders of the largest American firms have voiced their alarm at the spiralling costs of medical care, and some, departing from a long-standing tradition among business leaders, have called for some form of national health insurance and now believe that no other approach can control the crushing burden of medical care expenses on the private sector.

In the wake of renewed calls for national health insurance and congressional hearings on the crisis of availability of health insurance among small businesses, the HIAA and the Blue Cross/Blue Shield Association responded in the spring of 1991 with similar proposals to reform the small-group market. Both groups propose to stabilize the market with a series of commitments regarding treatment of underwriting, pricing, preexisting conditions, and renewal in exchange for certain state and federal government actions regarding the provision of reinsurance, risk pools, and waivers of state benefit mandates. They also call for certain tax concessions and the expansion of Medicaid. However, these attempts to define an acceptable and affordable "minimum benefits" policy have been attacked by some as being totally unacceptable.

Aside from the particularly acute problems encountered in the small-group market, the overall trend in recent years has gone overwhelmingly in two directions: (1) managed care programs, with a constantly expanding array of offshoots from the original HMOs and preferred provider organizations (PPOs), and (2) a continuing trend toward self-insurance.

Managed Care[5]

Managed care in all its manifestations tends to focus on two main goals—reducing or controlling costs and assuring patients appropriate care. Ways of accomplishing these goals vary, but in most cases several methods are employed. In both the HMO and PPO models, a major factor is in the development of a network of providers who, in theory, are dedicated to both cost containment and quality care. Usually, they have been contracted to provide services at a fixed fee or at an agreed discount from normal charges. Often, managed care programs incorporate the concept of a primary-care "gatekeeper" physician or some other pre-authorizing mechanism for any nonemergency service. There often are incentives for providers if certain targets are met in terms of the number of referrals made, and there usually is a prescribed list of services, such as some surgeries, that must be performed on an outpatient basis. Even the few remaining indemnity products incorporate various elements of managed care such as utilization review and pre-authorization. According to the HIAA's *Source Book,* by 1990 there were nearly 600 operational

---

[5]Managed care is covered in detail in Chapter 16 of the *Handbook.* HMOs and PPOs are the subjects of Chapters 14 and 15, respectively.

HMOs and almost 700 PPOs in the United States. Together, they accounted for more than 60 million insureds. In a general sense, HMOs and PPOs represent opposite extremes of the managed care spectrum, with the HMO offering a ''closed system'' with very complete coverage within the network but essentially no coverage for services obtained outside the network except in cases of emergency. This lack of ''freedom of choice'' for the insured has traditionally been one of the major complaints against HMOs. At the other extreme, a pure PPO normally allows the insured complete freedom of choice of physician or institutional provider while providing financial incentives to use providers from within the network. While care can be sought from outside the network, it usually carries a ''penalty'' in terms of a lower coinsurance—for example, 90 percent coverage for services within the network versus 70 percent for services from non-network providers. An alphabet soup of intermediate versions, such as individual practice associations (IPAs), exclusive provider organizations (EPOs), point-of-service (POS) plans, and others, has emerged in recent years. In general, it can be said that employers and employees favor greater choice, but that preference sometimes succumbs to the desire for greater control. There has been a tendency for the distinctions between the two polar prototypes, HMOs and PPOs, to blur over time, with HMOs introducing elements of choice at the margin and PPOs incorporating elements of coverage that go beyond the usual diagnostic codes and include such items as well-baby care and free physical examinations, items originally introduced by HMOs.

In general, financial incentives such as coinsurance provisions in managed care programs sponsored by commercial insurers do not exceed a 20 percent differential between network and non-network services. That is because most states provide for much more stringent regulation of so-called disincentive plans than of ''incentive plans.'' For example, a plan that uses a coinsurance differential of 20 percent or less would be regulated only by the state insurance department in Pennsylvania, whereas a disincentive plan that used larger coinsurance differentials would be subject to regulation by both the insurance department and the health department, as is currently true for HMOs. This is because regulators believe patients need more protection under disincentive plans. Most states have similar provisions, and most insurers try to avoid getting involved in dual regulation.

After a period of rapid growth in the mid 1980s, both HMOs and PPOs have recently undergone a period of consolidation and retrenchment. The explosion of new organizations and new subscribers frequently resulted in over-expansion in particular geographical areas. That, combined with inexperience, inadequate capital, questionable regulation, and, in some cases, poor management, led to a series of bankruptcies and mergers in recent years. At the present time, the numbers of persons covered under various managed care programs continue to grow, but the growth of new organizations has slowed as the weaker systems have either shut down or merged with stronger organizations.

The Surge in Self-Insurance

One of the most important changes in the medical expense insurance market has been in the rapid growth of self-insured medical expense benefits in the past decade, especially among larger employer groups. While there is no single published source of data on this matter (the HIAA's *Source Book* lumps self-insured statistics together with self-administered plans, plans employing third-party administrators, and HMOs), there is little doubt that growth has been substantial. There are many possible explanations, but the major reasons probably are related to concern with the continued rapid escalation of costs. As health benefit costs go ever higher, savings on premium taxes alone provide some incentive to self-insure. While the premium tax typically is modest in terms of percentage (2–3 percent), for large firms the actual dollar amount can be staggering. In addition, as previously noted, ERISA preemption of state mandates can also provide a self-insurer with substantial savings in some states. More important, the fact that PPOs and other managed care arrangements can be set up independent of an insurer—especially if a firm has a large concentration of workers in a given market—may have encouraged some employers to try their hands at holding the cost line. In some cases they must have believed that it would be difficult not to improve on the records of their insurers. Another factor may be the increase in the number of third-party administrators (TPAs), which has made the market more competitive than ever before. Finally, as employers have awakened to the fact that there are possible ways to effectively "manage" health care costs, they may feel that their own management skills are up to the task, after many years of virtually abdicating any responsibility in this regard. So far, however, the benefits provided under self-insured plans tend to be very similar to those offered by commercial insurers.

Commercial insurers often become the TPA for accounts they lose to self-insurance and, in addition, they may offer the self-insured firm a stop-loss policy to protect against unexpectedly large losses. (For a more detailed discussion of such "alternative" insurance company arrangements, see Chapter 47 of the *Handbook*).

Long-Term Care

With the growing recognition that Medicare does not adequately address the full range of health care needs of the elderly, a private market for long-term care insurance began to emerge in the mid-1980s. Private policies now are available in all 50 states, though the range of benefits differs greatly, and no significant market penetration has been achieved by any product. Many insurers are understandably reluctant to enter this arena, because so little is known about it and the long-term risks appear to be substantial, but since public solutions are not likely to be offered in the immediate future, the private sector, with encouragement from legislators at both the federal and state levels, has been stepping up its efforts to develop products to address this need. Some home health services have already been added to existing policies.

For several reasons, it is unlikely that individual policies will ever be able adequately to address the growing long-term non-acute care needs of the elderly. As a result, some believe this area will represent the next major frontier for the development of employee benefits. That may seem strange at a time when most employers are concerned about excessive benefit costs and are attempting to cope with accounting for their existing postretirement health-care obligations under the new accounting rules, but something will have to emerge to meet this growing need, and an employer-based group approach does have some merit in the absence of a national plan. If, as has been stated in the past, "a major underlying purpose for employee benefit plans is satisfaction of employee needs," then surely this is an area that is ripe for development. Whether this happens through a formal insurance program or through sponsorship of some form of elder day care is yet to be determined. The day-care approach could either be linked with the growing network of child day-care centers that have arisen to meet the changing needs of the American work force, or centers could be set up as independent units dealing strictly with the elderly.

CONCLUSION

This chapter has identified some of the major factors to be taken into account in the design of medical expense benefit plans. Chapter 11 reflects the importance of these factors in the way in which the design of such plans has changed since the *Handbook*'s first edition in 1984.

ADDENDUM

The closing months of 1991 did, indeed, see a remarkable shift in the political winds in the United States. Nowhere was this more evident than in the special Senatorial election in Pennsylvania in November, when former popular Republican Governor Richard Thornburg was soundly defeated in his bid for the seat of the late Senator John Heinz by Democrat Harris Wofford, a political neophyte who had been appointed to temporarily fill the position by Governor Casey. Most observers felt that the main issue that propelled Wofford to victory was his vigorous support for immediate major reform in U.S. health care policy, to include universal coverage. His message clearly hit a responsive chord which was quickly picked up on by politicians of both parties. Realists still predict that no major reform will occur before the presidential election in 1992, but health care will clearly be occupying center stage in the major political debates of the coming year. The fear is that the debate will generate more heat than light. In any case, it is likely that failure to read the daily newspaper will put observers out of date with regard to the rapidly emerging proposals.

CHAPTER 11

HOSPITAL AND MEDICAL CARE EXPENSE PLANS

Charles P. Hall, Jr.

Until recently, it was easy to describe group medical care–expense insurance products by using the traditional and relatively straightforward classifications of hospital, surgical, medical, major medical, and comprehensive policies. Although some blurring in the area of comprehensive coverage existed, the lines of demarcation between the different products generally were clear. This is no longer the case. The dramatic changes described in Chapter 10 have led to similarly sharp product modifications. In addition to the "traditional" indemnity products and benefits of the past, many commercial insurance companies and Blue Cross/Blue Shield plans now offer employers a wide variety and mix of managed care options along with administrative services only (ASO) contracts and stop-loss protection for those that wish to self-insure. It is clear if this type of comprehensive insurance package succeeds to the degree anticipated, the traditional classification of hospital expense insurance will become meaningless except in the smallest markets. While a few "traditional" products still exist, they account for a dwindling share of the market, and any discussion of hospital plans is now primarily of historical interest. Nevertheless, it is useful to trace the historical development of group hospital and medical expense coverage to understand how they evolved to their present forms and to set the stage for the remaining chapters in this section of the *Handbook*.

HOSPITAL INSURANCE

Because it was the earliest form of health insurance and because the hospital was the most costly setting in which to be treated, hospital insurance was for years the most widely held form of medical care insurance protection in the country. From the 1940s until 1986, the Health Insurance Association of America (HIAA) reported separately on the number of persons insured under hospital, surgical, and basic medical insurance plans. In 1986, HIAA combined surgical and medical plans under the heading "medical other than hospital expense" but retained separate reports on major medical and dental insurance. In the 1990 edition of its *Source Book of Health Insurance Data,* which reported on data from 1988, even those distinctions have been dropped, and only the number insured under all private plans combined is listed. The remaining distinctions are between commercial insurance companies (broken down by group and individual plans), Blue Cross/Blue Shield plans, and "other plans," which are noted to include self-insured plans, self-administered plans and plans involving third-party administrators (TPAs), and health maintenance organizations (HMOs). There is a separate report on the number of persons covered under Medicare and Medicaid, and there is a brief note that 23 million senior citizens, or 70 percent of the Medicare enrollees, supplemented their Medicare coverage with private "medi-gap" policies in 1988. No other information on these sometimes-controversial policies is presented. One reason for combining the various forms of coverage for reporting purposes is that today virtually no one is interested in buying only hospital expense insurance, and it is almost unheard of today to purchase hospital coverage except in combination with other medical benefits. Thus, while HIAA continues to describe briefly the various coverages offered in today's market, the breakdowns it uses include hospital/medical as one category, along with major medical, disability income protection, dental expense, and long-term care insurance. The 1990 *Source Book* also describes self-insurance and has a lengthy discussion of the evolution of the managed care concept, some of which is now incorporated into almost every health insurance plan.

Group hospitalization insurance was the first of the now-diverse medical expense employee benefits to appear in the United States.

Though there are a few isolated earlier examples, it is customary to identify the modern origin of medical care expense insurance with the Baylor University Hospital prepayment plan that emerged in the late 1920s and ultimately gave birth to Blue Cross. In general, commercial insurance companies were not active in any medical care expense insurance until about a decade later. There were some good reasons for their reluctance; traditional insurance theory suggested that health was not a very desirable subject of insurance.

In the 1940s, growth of employer-based health insurance plans accelerated, spurred by such factors as the wage and price stabilization programs of World War II and the identification of medical care benefits as appropriate matters for collective bargaining just after the war. Because of their pioneering role, the early Blue Cross plans had a profound and lasting impact on the nature of hospital benefits. Aside from insisting on distinguishing their "prepayment" method from traditional commercial insurance, they were philosophically wedded to the concepts of *service benefits, first-dollar coverage,* and *community rates.*

Service Benefits

Service benefits were possible because of the special relationship Blue Cross plans had (and have) with hospitals. Blue Cross operated through contracts with both subscribers and hospitals. Typically, the hospital fixed the price for its services in its contract with Blue Cross, thus enabling Blue Cross to compute an appropriate subscription fee (premium) for its members while defining benefits in terms of days of coverage. Not all Blue Cross–hospital contracts were the same. In some cases, they were based on actual hospital costs, while in others they were based on charges. A considerable difference often existed between the two. The determining factors included the strength of the Blue Cross plan vis à vis the local hospitals (determined in large part by the market share of Blue Cross subscribers) and by the philosophy of local Blue Cross leadership. In general, cost-based contracts were more common in the northeastern and upper midwestern states where labor unions were strongest and Blue Cross penetration was greatest. Blue Cross plans often enjoyed some discount allowance on the strength of their presumed role as a "quasi-social insurance plan," which offered open enrollment periods each year, thus allegedly lowering the hospitals' level of bad debt by making insurance more readily available to all comers.

Commercial insurers, lacking direct contracts with hospitals, typically promised insureds a stated maximum dollar allowance per day up to a specified number of days. Plans of this type were known as indemnity plans. The clear result of this disparity was that Blue Cross subscribers always knew exactly how many days of hospitalization were available to them without cost, while commercial insureds knew only how many days they would be eligible to collect up to some stated number of dollars. They had no assurance that the number of dollars available would be adequate to pay the hospital in full. As a result, commercially insured patients carried a residual financial risk avoided by Blue Cross subscribers—at least until they had exhausted the total days of coverage provided in their contract.

Many consumers preferred the relative certainty of full-service contracts, and by the end of the 1970s, most commercial insurers offered a quasi-service benefit in the form of full coverage for the cost of semiprivate room accommodations, up to some maximum dollar limit. This still entailed some pricing problems, but they could be handled by the insurer under experience-rated programs, though at considerable risk to the employer, who typically paid the bulk of the premiums.

When Medicare was introduced in the mid 1960s, the basic benefit to the elderly was in the form of a service benefit for 60 days of hospitalization, but it was modified with some indemnity principles in the form of an initial deductible and a coinsurance arrangement for stays in excess of 60 days. Most important for later developments, however, the government, like Blue Cross before it, had two separate commitments—the promised benefits to participants, and a reimbursement arrangement with the hospitals. The latter was tied to a retrospective cost-based formula.

Rapidly escalating medical care costs, a growing number of elderly, and sharp increases in the utilization of medical care services, especially among the elderly, all combined to propel government expenditures for the Medicare program far higher than even the most generous predictions of actuaries. At the same time, both the federal and state treasuries were facing additional strain from the mounting costs of the massive Medicaid programs. In efforts to control the mounting cost of the programs, "allowable costs" to hospitals were progressively reduced by Congress. Not surprisingly, many Blue Cross plans tried to redefine the costs they were responsible for to match the Medicare definition, since in many cases Blue Cross was the administrative agency for Medicare.

As the proportion of patients covered by cost-based contracts grew, so did the financial problems of hospitals. Clearly, no organization can stay in business, even with full cost reimbursement, if it cannot spend money to replace its physical plant and keep up with technological change. Thus, some hospitals faced serious financial shortfalls as they found themselves with increasing numbers of patients under less than full cost coverage. To remain solvent, they had to make up the shortfall from charge-based (primarily commercially insured) patients. As the number of cost-based patients increased, the proportion of charge-based patients from which the hospitals were able to recover dwindled, and the revenue differential between cost-based and charge-based patients got out of hand, in some cases exceeding $100 per day for identical services by the end of the 1970s.

This trend had a devastating impact on the ability of commercial health insurers to compete in the marketplace. The aggregate Medicare/Medicaid ''shortfall'' (underpayment to hospitals) had reached nearly $6 billion in fiscal year 1982. Though this constituted cost saving for the government programs, it was merely cost shifting for society and represented an enormous hidden tax on parts of the private sector.

In 1983, with costs still escalating at an unacceptable pace, Medicare switched to a prospective reimbursement system based on *diagnostic related groups (DRGs)*. Hospitals are now reimbursed a fixed amount, based on the allowable length of stay for the patient's entering diagnosis. If the patient leaves the hospital in less than the allowable time, the hospital benefits, but if the patient overstays that time, the hospital is at risk for the additional costs. From the participant's point of view, however, Medicare still basically provides a service benefit.

For years, commercial insurers and self-insured employers remained quite passive in the face of the increasing cost shifting described above. Though they were not hesitant to voice their complaints, they did little else to fend off the added burden. There were several reasons for their passivity. They had neither the geographic monopolies enjoyed by the Blue Cross plans nor the ''clout'' inherent in government programs. While there were a few exceptions (for example, in ''company town'' situations where they were able to negotiate discounts), employers were reluctant to push for concessions for the same reason they avoided collective action against hospitals—fear of antitrust prosecution.

Much of that fear dissolved with the introduction of the preferred provider organization (PPO) concept in California in 1982. Specific legislation in California authorized this concept of contracting with medical care providers for preferred status in terms of price, utilization review, and quality control. The concept was an outgrowth of the pro-competition school of thought, and was initially proposed as a means for the state to gain control over its wildly escalating Medicaid costs by contracting with low-cost providers to service the poor. When the legislature specifically authorized private sector payers to do the same, it opened the floodgates to some of the most dramatic changes ever seen in the financing of medical care in this country. The PPO movement is covered fully in Chapter 15 of the *Handbook*. The point in mentioning it here is that one of the strong incentives that have made PPOs popular with insureds is their promise, in many cases, of full service benefits to those who use their designated providers.

First-Dollar Benefits

Initially, Blue Cross plans were at least as interested in assuring hospital solvency as they were in protecting patients from financial strain. This suggested full coverage for all charges. Furthermore, the plans tried to distinguish their operation from traditional insurance by emphasizing that they were prepayment plans, providing service benefits from the first moment of hospitalization. Their direct contractual relationship with hospitals helped make this feasible.

Initially, commercial insurers followed rather blindly the same pattern of first-dollar benefits, but later they introduced some cost-control devices such as deductibles and coinsurance. Nevertheless, the pattern of first-dollar coverage had been established and, perhaps because of the incorporation of these benefits in many of the early union-negotiated contracts, the pattern persisted on a wide front. By the early 1980s, there were increasing allegations that, though originally well-intentioned, such benefits were uneconomical and also promoted overuse (misuse) of benefits. It was claimed that by not requiring any point-of-service financial responsibility from patients, the insureds neither knew nor cared about the increasing costs of medical care, and care providers thus were spared any pressure from their patients to hold down costs.

The economic slowdown of the early 1980s resulted in a historical first: massive union "give-backs" of benefits under their medical expense coverage. These included reintroduction of and/or increases in deductibles, changes in coinsurance provisions, and, in some cases, a return to contributory rather than noncontributory premium plans. Despite the fact that the economy rebounded, data reported in the *Source Book of Health Insurance Data* for that period showed marked increases in deductibles after the early 1980s. It has been widely claimed that these changes are perceived to be among the most effective cost-containment techniques available to insurers, and even many Blue Cross plans began to make wider use of cost-sharing provisions in a departure from their earlier commitment to first-dollar benefits. However, while allegedly producing cost-containment by reducing "unnecessary utilization," these moves were primarily a means of cost shifting from the employer to the employee under group insurance plans.

Oddly enough, many insurers, at the same time they were nominally increasing their cost-sharing provisions, were offering to waive them altogether if the insureds used "network providers" identified with PPOs. Among other things, this movement points to the clash of traditional insurance techniques with the rapidly emerging concept of "managed care," discussed in detail in Chapter 16 of the *Handbook*.

Community Rating

Community rating, a uniform rate for all subscribers or insureds in a given area, though still the philosophical favorite of many, especially in Blue Cross ranks, has long since become insignificant in the group insurance market. The competitive pressures from corporate insurance buyers and unions to obtain rates commensurate with their real or perceived "preferred risk" status were simply too great to be resisted in most cases. Most Blue Cross plans still use community rates for their individual subscribers, and some also may use them for small groups, but all have some form of experience rating available to large group customers. In order to be qualified, HMOs originally had to adhere to specific rules regarding community rating, but those were finally relaxed somewhat in the 1988 amendments to the Health Maintenance Organization Act.

Scope of Hospital Expense Benefits

Though few straight hospitalization plans currently exist, it may be worthwhile to describe the general scope of hospital expense benefits as they now exist under some of the more common combination policies.

Covered hospital expense under a comprehensive major medical policy (subject to any deductible, coinsurance provision, maximum payment limit, and/or exclusions), typically might include charges made by a hospital for the following items:[1] Hospital room and board charges, including charges for a semi-private room, meals, general nursing, and all other services and supplies needed for care of an inpatient. For a private room, coverage normally would be limited to the hospital's semi-private room rate. If the hospital has no semi-private rooms, coverage might be limited to some percentage (say 80 percent) of the lowest-priced private room. If the hospital charges a flat daily rate for all expenses, a percentage (say 60 percent) of that rate may be considered for room and board and if the flat rate decreases with the length of stay, a higher percentage (say 90 percent) of the lowest daily rate may be considered to be for room and board. Certain policies also allow services in some less expensive settings, such as skilled-nursing facilities, and home health services sometimes also are included.

From this example, it can be seen that hospital coverage, though seldom handled via separate policies today, tends to be quite broad under whatever comprehensive package an employer may use, and the basic parameters of the coverage are very similar regardless of who is bearing the risk, although details such as duration of the hospital coverage, the amount of the deductible and coinsurance, and stop-loss arrangements will vary by plan. These variations often result from labor-management negotiations.

Exclusions

Even with the changing circumstances of the past few years, most of the old standard exclusions continue to appear in today's hospital/medical expense insurance policies. Among them are occupational illness or injury eligible for benefits under workers' compensation laws; convalescent or rest cures, custodial or domiciliary care; services not ordered by a physician or not reasonably necessary for diagnosis and treatment;

---

[1]Detailed coverage of the many and varied hospital benefits provided under the wide variety of broader medical care expense policies currently available is beyond the scope of this chapter, and this brief example is used for illustrative purposes only. Variations within HMO and PPO contracts, for example, may relate benefits to the DRG formula now operating under Medicare.

procurement or use of special appliances or equipment; services a patient is entitled to receive under the laws or regulations of any government or its agencies and war- or service-connected injuries or diseases. These examples are not exhaustive, and the specific list of exclusions, of course, must be checked in the case of each individual policy or plan.

General Provisions

All group insurance contracts contain a range of general provisions, many of which are almost universal, whether by law or by custom. Examples include the 31-day grace period for payment of premiums, a clause on incontestability, an entire-contract clause, which also specifies how valid changes may be accomplished, and a provision to adjust benefits automatically whenever and wherever they conflict with statutes. Another whole set of provisions has to do with claims submission and payment procedures. These provisions often apply equally to a whole set of employee benefits, from life insurance to medical care expense insurance.

Provisions specific to hospital insurance that deserve mention are those dealing with the definition of a benefit period of confinement and coordination of benefits. The latter is a cost-containment mechanism to prevent duplication of benefits and is discussed in detail along with other cost-containment techniques in Chapter 13 of the *Handbook*. A single benefit period under hospitalization insurance typically is considered to be any one or more periods of confinement of the insured, unless separated by a return to full-time employment for at least one week, or unless subsequent confinement is due entirely to causes unrelated to the previous confinement. For dependents, unless the causes are unrelated, a subsequent confinement in less than three months' time generally is considered a continuation of the previous hospital stay. Some insurers apply the harsher three-month rule to primary employee insureds as well.

An important provision to check in any medical care expense coverage is the definition of ''dependent.'' The term normally encompasses the spouse and all unmarried children, including those who may have been legally adopted, up to age 19. An extension of coverage up to age 24 or 25 usually is granted for children who are full-time students. Naturally, the specific ages may vary by company and policy.

A brief comment is in order about insurer attitudes toward the coverage of new and costly medical technologies, such as organ transplants, open-heart surgery, and infertility services, such as in vitro fertilization. No blanket statement can be made with great certainty. Most policies will not cover procedures that are considered ''experimental,'' but there is no single, universally accepted definition of when a procedure changes from experimental to accepted practice.

More than likely, cases at the margin will continue to be discussed with the insured employer before a decision is made, because it is often true that the political or public relations cost of refusing a claim will be far greater than the economic cost of providing the benefit. Since these ''at the margin'' decisions often deal with life-and-death issues, it may at times be prudent to pay the claim even if it is not technically covered by the contract. Again, the decision is sometimes taken out of the insurer's or employer's hands, as when the state decides to mandate certain benefits. As noted in Chapter 10, these mandates have been a factor in some companies deciding to self-insure to avoid the cost of the mandated benefit via the ERISA preemption.

Other Hospital Insurance

One other type of hospital insurance has acquired fairly wide acceptance. It is the so-called hospital indemnity policy. Patterned somewhat after disability income policies, these plans are not really indemnity policies at all. They could more appropriately be called ''status'' policies. They pay stated dollar amounts on either a daily, weekly, or monthly basis for people confined in a hospital. In some cases, skilled nursing facilities also are covered. They pay the predetermined amount without regard to actual charges incurred or income lost and, perhaps more important to many buyers, without regard to any other insurance holdings. Some of the popularity of these policies undoubtedly can be attributed to consumers' fears about the continued rapid escalation of health care costs. They see these policies as providing an added buffer, in case their medical expense reimbursement coverages fall short.

HOSPITAL INSURANCE SUMMARY

Group hospitalization insurance, as the earliest and most widely held of the medical expense employee benefits, was for many years also the easiest to describe. Its provisions were quite straightforward, and almost everyone understood what it was all about. The dramatic changes that have occurred over the past decade, however, have virtually eliminated the pure hospital benefit policy from the marketplace. Hybrid versions that are fully integrated in comprehensive major medical policies seem to be the order of the day now, and most managed care plans focus on minimizing inpatient treatment whenever possible.

MEDICAL CARE EXPENSE INSURANCE

After the initial breakthrough in hospital insurance, a series of ''named peril'' medical expense insurance coverages followed—first, surgical benefits, and then nonsurgical medical benefits both in and out of hospital settings. Blue Shield emerged in these areas as the prepayment counterpart to Blue Cross. In the late 1940s a few companies also introduced ''dread disease'' policies, with quite high limits of protection for a very narrow range of conditions—often only one disease (e.g., polio).

Note that medicine as we know it today was almost nonexistent before World War II. Hospitals were primarily places in which to die, not to get well. The majority of doctors were general practitioners, not specialists. The first major inroads in many infectious diseases were made in the late 1930s, with the discovery of sulpha drugs and penicillin, but they were not widely available until after World War II. Because virtually all mental illness treatment was performed in state hospitals in that era, mental illness was not covered in early Blue contracts, whose member hospitals did not provide the service.

Before commercial insurers could become established in the medical expense insurance area, Blue Shield had established a strong foothold in the field and had put its philosophical stamp on the health insurance industry. As with Blue Cross, Blue Shield's trademarks were service, as opposed to indemnity, benefits, first-dollar coverage, and community rates. Blue Shield could promise payment for certain surgical procedures and office visits, though its arrangement with physicians usually included income limits on service benefits; that is, if the subscriber earned more than a stipulated amount, the physician could ''balance bill'' an amount over the Blue Shield benefit. Commercial insurers seldom dared even to think about direct contracting on price until the 1980s, when the emergence of PPOs seemed to free insurers from the threat of antitrust action from direct contracting. Until then, however, commercial medical care expense insurance was basically an indemnity product, though the distinction became less significant in later years when benefit limits soared and assignment of benefits agreements meant that claims usually were paid directly to providers.

By the end of the 1940s, once the negotiation of so-called fringe benefits, including medical expense insurance, had been given the status under the Taft-Hartley law as properly subject to union wage negotiations, commercial insurers were aggressively promoting it, and developed the concept of major medical insurance, which was to change the face of the market significantly in the next decade. Major medical was typically characterized by high limits, front-end deductibles, and coinsurance clauses. In addition, it was the first ''all-except'' coverage in health insurance, replacing what had been exclusively ''named peril'' coverage of hospital, surgical, and medical expense policies. It could be issued either as a stand-alone policy or, more commonly, as a supplement to basic coverage from either the Blues or commercial insurance companies. Shortly thereafter, comprehensive major medical policies, which incorporated basic and major medical coverage in a single policy with differential internal limits, was introduced, and this comprehensive model clearly dominates the market today. Supplemental major medical and comprehensive plans are discussed in Chapter 12 of the *Handbook*.

Medicine also changed during the 1940s. Particularly significant advances in emergency and trauma care grew out of techniques developed during the war. Widespread availability of antibiotics also had a profound effect. Then, in the 1950s, successful vaccines for polio were developed, and the trend toward medical specialization continued.

Another surge of growth in medical insurance took place in the early 1950s, when the Korean war led to another wage-price freeze. By the mid 1950s, commercial insurers were making serious inroads in the Blues' business, and the Blues were forced to set up national organizations and go to experience rating of some groups in order to remain competitive on large corporate accounts. In addition, the nation woke up to the fact that there was a serious problem with availability of medical insurance benefits for senior citizens. It wasn't until then that the full impact of the 1935 Social Security law, which had, in effect, institutionalized age 65 as ''old'' really was felt. But with 65 having become the standard retirement age—often on a compulsory basis—and with most medical expense insurance tied to places of employment, retirees suddenly discovered they were hard-pressed to find available and affordable coverage. This gave rise to increasing pressure for a political solution, including calls for national health insurance. To forestall any such action, insurers promoted so-called "state-65 plans," starting in Connecticut in 1961. Their success, however, was both limited and short-lived, and the federal government then acted, first with the Kerr-Mills bill, which provided benefits on a means-tested basis, and then with the Medicare program, an insurance program for all citizens 65 and over in 1965. The companion program, Medicaid, is a welfare plan for the categorically needy. Both were implemented in 1966, and it was not long before the full retrospective cost reimbursement of hospital costs under Medicare would lead to unprecedented increases in medical care costs.

Over the first 30 years, insurers had behaved largely as fiscal funnels for benefits. Employers had been quite passive in accepting whatever benefits the insurers offered. Changes, however, were constantly taking place. Early "scheduled benefits" under hospital and surgical plans gave way over time to "usual, customary and reasonable" (UCR) benefits, and hospital benefits changed from straight dollars per day to "semi-private room" with a maximum dollar limit. Both of these changes made commercial indemnity policies look a bit more like the "service benefits" of the Blues.

With the exception of a few special areas, such as dental insurance and, more recently, separate plans for prescription drugs, vision care, and substance abuse or other psychiatric services, most of the changes in medical expense reimbursement coverages since the late 1950s have merely been refinements reflecting pressure for broader coverage brought on as a result of some combination of the rapid escalation of medical care costs, changes in medical technology, or changes in consumer demand.

Even in the special areas mentioned, where separate plans frequently emerged as the result of special-interest advocacy groups, sometimes aided by support from providers of the specialized services, the benefits often were simply included in expanded basic plans. In some cases, notably mental health benefits, special restrictions in the form of larger coinsurance or more stringent limits on the days of coverage became common. Expanded mental health benefits frequently were included in the basic plan as the result of state legislation mandating the coverage. By the early 1960s, insurers were becoming concerned with escalating costs, and some early utilization review programs were instituted. Meanwhile, medical technology continued to develop, and advanced surgical techniques were introduced along with a whole new generation of psychotropic drugs that would change forever the treatment of mental illness. Various government initiatives, especially in the mental health field, produced new pressures on the private sector for both treatment and financing of care. The number and variety of state mandates expanded dramatically during the 1970s and early 1980s, but most were ''wrapped around'' the basic insurance plan, rather then emerging as separate policies. Other obvious exceptions, such as the emergence of so-called medigap policies after the enactment of Medicare have resulted from federal policy actions.

Health Care Coalitions

Organizations holding a special interest in health care issues initially emerged in the mid-1970s and continued to grow in strength and influence during the 1980s. While corporate employers continue to dominate most such groups, membership has broadened to include representatives of providers, unions, insurers, and others. They concern themselves with virtually the entire spectrum of health-related issues, and they have become increasingly sophisticated in their understanding of those issues. While cost of care remains a dominant concern, especially on the part of employer members, quality of care is also a primary goal. Many of the coalitions are actively involved in the design of employee health benefits, legislative analysis, and legislative advocacy. Many are involved directly in the development of or analysis of health data such as cost evaluation and utilization patterns. They are often able to provide valuable assistance in the design of effective benefits.

Benefit Provisions

Some significant changes in benefit plan provisions have occurred in recent years. Most of those changes have been triggered by a response to the many public policy and environmental issues discussed in Chapter 10. While relatively few totally ''new'' provisions have emerged, there have been some major adjustments in existing provisions.

Alternatives to Inpatient Care

Preadmission testing (PAT) was a relatively new concept just a few years ago; it is now not only available but mandatory under most medical expense benefit plans. There is a general consensus that a well-administered plan does effectively reduce the average length of stay (LOS) for patients, and physicians seem more comfortable with the concept than they were when it was first introduced. The same applies to preadmission certification.

Ambulatory surgical benefits have by now achieved almost universal recognition as both an effective and safe way to reduce benefit costs. Indeed, a growing tendency exists for benefit plans to identify an extensive list of surgical procedures that will be compensated only if performed on an outpatient or ambulatory basis. This surgery may be performed in a hospital short-procedure unit (SPU), a surgi-center that may or may not be directly tied to a hospital, or sometimes even in a physician's office. There is some variability among plans as to which locations will be covered. However, while ambulatory surgery was once viewed as a definite cost-containment tool, some feel it is losing ground, since outpatient services are not subject to the strict limitations that govern reimbursement under inpatient DRGs.

The growth of HMOs, PPOs, and other forms of managed care arrangements has led to more widespread coverage of a range of outpatient services that often were not covered in the past. Because these plans have resulted in much closer association between plan managers and health care providers, a relationship of trust seems to be emerging. It has been widely noted that employers, insurers, and providers recognize themselves to be more interdependent than in the past. Providers, at a time of projected physician surplus and declining utilization of inpatient facilities, are very much interested in capturing a guaranteed market share. Employers and insurers often are able to deliver a guaranteed market share, but in return they are demanding provider cooperation in terms of quality and utilization controls as well as, in most cases, cost/charge concessions. Nevertheless, costs of ambulatory services have been rising more rapidly than inpatient services since the introduction of DRGs, and this trend has become a matter of concern. Many believe that the introduction of the resource-based relative-value scale in 1992 will be a major tool in the effort to get some control over physicians' fees. In addition, by 1991, even the American Medical Association had endorsed the concept of developing ''treatment protocols'' in an effort to achieve greater standardization of treatments and costs. However, it will take some time before any agreement is reached in this matter.

In earlier editions it was noted that, in contrast to the ''front-end'' ambulatory services discussed above, home health services offer an opportunity for early discharge and the possible savings that can accrue because of the substantial cost differential between inpatient and home health services. It was noted, too, that it would be necessary to educate the consuming public as to the desirability and effectiveness of such services. Since most Americans had a perception of hospital services as the "best" services, it was suggested that they might be reluctant to accept the substitution—especially since, for many, there were virtually no point-of-service payments required to obtain the hospital care. It is still true that many providers and patients underestimate the quality of available home health services, and there remain some benefit plans that do not reimburse for them. Nevertheless, there has been some expansion of coverage, and modifications to many deductible and coinsurance provisions for inpatient services have generated more interest in the alternative treatment.

Inpatient Alternatives to Acute Care

There have been no dramatic changes in the level or type of coverage for skilled-nursing facility (SNF) services in recent years. It remains a supplement to hospitalization benefits, usually on a 2-for-1 basis in terms of days of protection. Most plans continue to have a requirement of at least three days of prior hospitalization as a prerequisite to eligibility.

As has been noted above, one of the emerging areas of potential catastrophic exposure, particularly for the elderly, is long-term care of a nonacute variety. The care may involve a minimum of medical services. The coverage in question has not traditionally been provided through either private benefit plans or Medicare, except to a very limited degree. Individual purchases are not likely to accomplish much, because of the potential for adverse selection and the resulting high costs, and this area may indeed be the next frontier for employee benefit plans as the graying of America continues and more and more people find themselves in need of this coverage.

There has been relatively little progress in the provision of hospice benefits in recent years, though some dramatic results have been obtained in some sectors, especially for AIDS. It remains a limited and experimental coverage, with no good data currently available. It remains possible that the soaring cost of dying that accompanies our high-tech medical interventions will, at some point, generate a sharp upsurge in interest for hospice care—especially if the United States, as a society, can come to terms with some of the ethical, legal, and moral dilemmas of caring for the dying.

Other Provisions

Second surgical opinions are now a standard benefit in most plans. Though there is still some question as to the exact payoff, the "sentinel effect" is judged to be worthwhile by most benefits managers. Whether other specific benefits ranging from dental, vision, prescription drug, and preventive care to mental health and substance abuse are included is most often determined by the specific needs and demands of individual worker groups, the biases of the employer, the cost of benefits as they relate to the resources available, and, as when state mandates prescribe one or more of these benefits, the location.

Cost-Sharing Provisions

After remaining static for many years, the cost sharing provisions under most medical expense benefit plans were adjusted in the late 1980s. After a decade or more of expanding benefits to more and more comprehensive levels, during which time there were strong incentives under the tax law to have noncontributory health plans, employers have significantly changed their approach. They discovered, belatedly, that many workers were so insulated from the cost of medical care that they not only failed to appreciate the benefits that were available, but they tended to abuse them, or at the very least not use them wisely.

There has, therefore, been a swing back to contributory plans, accompanied by a sharp increase in deductibles under most plans. These deductibles, then, along with various coinsurance provisions, are increasingly being used in conjunction with PPOs to shape the utilization of services by the insureds. The waiver of a deductible provision can be used as a positive incentive to direct patients to cost-effective and high-quality practitioners and facilities while nominally retaining their "freedom of choice," the absence of which under HMOs had slowed their growth.

It must be pointed out, however, that after major benefit "give-backs" in the early 1980s, most unions have become increasingly militant in recent years about their medical expense benefits. It has been estimated that over 85 percent of all work stoppages in recent years have been largely the result of disputes over health-related matters. Unions not only object to further cuts in benefits, but they want earlier cuts restored. Employers, on the other hand, have been increasingly intransigent in demanding that the workers share in the costs.

MEDICAL CARE EXPENSE PLAN SUMMARY

It should be clear from the preceding discussion that medical care expense plans exist in a volatile and rapidly changing arena, over which benefit managers exercise little effective control. To a significant degree, then, they are forced to react to environmental and political factors that shape the nature of treatment, the cost of care, and our perceptions about both. Despite a plethora of new delivery and financing mechanisms and a multitude of specific benefit provisions, there is little evidence that any significant degree of cost containment or control in the medical care expense sector has yet been achieved after years of trying.

In fact, as has been noted, by some measures, costs are more out of control than ever before. If nothing else, this poses a monumental challenge for the future. In the meantime, it is interesting to speculate where costs would be if the cost-containment initiatives of the past decade had not been developed. Would it have made a difference?

CHAPTER 12

SURGICAL/MEDICAL EXPENSE BENEFITS AND MAJOR MEDICAL/COMPREHENSIVE PLANS

Zelda Lipton

Just as it is useful to be aware of the historical development of hospitalization coverage to better understand today's benefit plans, so too is it of value to look at why and how other medical benefits were originally designed and have since developed. Although today's packages may look different, all or most of the early components are still there with varying degrees of medical management aimed at providing the most appropriate level of care on the most cost-effective basis. Managing the cost of medical care clearly was not the issue in the early years that it has more recently become, and its cost is fast outpacing the ability of many Americans to pay for it.

The rise in the medical care component of the consumer price index has almost consistently exceeded the rise in prices for all consumer goods and services combined. It has been driven primarily by hospital costs—the largest single item in the delivery of medical care. Although hospital costs therefore offer the greatest opportunity for cost control, design of the remaining benefits in a health insurance plan can influence significantly the utilization of the entire package. This is particularly true as more services previously provided on an inpatient basis are moved out of the hospital in an effort to reduce their cost. Physicians' fees alone represented $105.1 billion or 22 percent of the total personal health care dollar spent in 1988. Equally important, however, physicians themselves are key to the most effective use of the health care system and therefore directly influence the cost of medical care.

This chapter traces the development of surgical and medical expense benefits and supplemental major medical and comprehensive plans to meet the need for such protection as it evolved. Although some of the plans described are not commonly in use today, the history sets the stage for the current variations that are referred to here and described in greater detail in other chapters of the *Handbook*.

SURGICAL/MEDICAL EXPENSE BENEFITS

Plans to cover the cost of physicians' services were first introduced in 1920 by county medical societies. Although Blue Shield plans didn't begin until 1939 with the California Medical Association Plan, they were at the forefront of the development of physicians' services plans. They attempted to follow the same full-service philosophy as Blue Cross did for hospital expenses. Physicians contracted with Blue Shield, which paid an agreed-upon level as full payment for services provided to subscribers. However, physicians had long been accustomed to charging patients based on their incomes. As a result, Blue Shield modified its early approach to allow a physician to charge patients with incomes above a stated level the difference between the Blue Shield reimbursement and the physician's usual fee.

At the same time, private insurance companies were developing indemnity contracts, which reimbursed the insured person for services provided by a physician up to the agreed amount in the contract. Physicians would look to the patient, rather than the insurer, for payment. Otherwise patterned after Blue Shield plans, the insurance plans paid first-dollar coverage for a limited number of medical services. Together with hospital benefits, these came to be known as basic benefits. Many insurers soon developed procedures for reimbursing the provider directly, should the buyer prefer that approach.

SURGICAL EXPENSE BENEFITS

The earliest of these basic benefits for physicians' charges covered surgical expenses, because those represented comparatively large expenditures and were believed to be more easily defined and controlled. Surgical expense benefits provide coverage for the cost of surgical procedures required as a result of accident or sickness wherever the surgery is performed.

Surgeons' Fees

Plans were designed to cover surgeons' fees on either a scheduled or reasonable and customary basis.

Dollar-Fee Schedules

Typical early surgical schedules listed about 100 procedures in such major categories as abdomen, heart and blood vessels, chest, mouth, and obstetrics.

For each procedure, a specific maximum-dollar payment was allowed. Each maximum depended on the value of that procedure, compared with others, and the overall maximum for multiple procedures by which the schedule is usually identified. The level of overall maximums available has historically ranged from as low as $200 to $1,000 and more. Payment to the insured was the charge made by the surgeon, up to the maximum payment allowed in the schedule for the procedure performed. For an unlisted procedure, reimbursement was based on its relative difficulty, compared with those listed.

If an employer desired to avoid encouraging escalation of charges, schedules were set to reimburse at a level below the usual charges in an area. Such scheduled plans did contribute toward control of the cost of a plan, since, regardless of inflation, reimbursement for any procedure remained constant. Furthermore, since the patient was directly responsible for the difference between the plan payment and the charge, fees did not escalate as rapidly. However, such a plan very quickly becomes outdated in a rising-cost environment and results in large out-of-pocket expenses for the insured.

Relative Value Schedules

These schedules were developed in the 1950s, with California Medical Services leading the way. The first California Relative Value Schedule was designed in 1956 and revised twice, in 1969 and 1974. It served as a model for many insurance plans. Relative value schedules attach a unit value to a large number of surgical procedures. The relationship of the unit values to each other typically is a function of the relative difficulty of the procedures. The maximum amount payable for a procedure is its unit value multiplied by a dollar amount purchased by the employer that is commonly referred to as a conversion factor. Payment was subject to an overall schedule maximum. A wide range of conversion factors were available; but, the conversion factor was intended to produce no more than the usual charges in an area.

A relative value schedule permitted greater flexibility, particularly for employers with more than one location. Appropriate conversion factors could be applied to the schedule to produce the level of reimbursement reflecting regional differences in cost. Schedules were kept current by adjusting the conversion factor as costs changed.

Some insurance plans continue to include relative value schedules based on each insurer's own nationwide charge data.

Reasonable and Customary Fees

Alternatively, surgical plans were designed to reimburse for a surgeon's fee up to the reasonable and customary charge for the procedure performed without any identified schedule. "Reasonable and customary" reflects both the charge usually made by the physician for the procedure and the range of charges made by physicians for that same procedure in the locality where performed. Typically, it is set to cover the full charge of 85 or 90 percent of all physicians in a geographical area. Differences arise because of different charge data bases and area designations.

Reasonable and customary surgical plans have the advantage of automatically adjusting to inflation without plan change. For the same reason, however, they build inflation into the cost of a medical care plan and are accused of encouraging continually increasing charges by surgeons.

Multiple Procedures

Scheduled surgical benefit plans usually limit reimbursement for multiple procedures, depending on whether they are performed at the same time and/or in the same operative field. Although reasonable and customary plans often do not include similar language, they may apply similar rationale in evaluating the reasonable charge for multiple procedures.

Associated Benefits

Regardless of the approach to reimbursement of the surgeon, surgical expense benefits plans may cover other physicians' charges associated with surgery.

Assistant Surgeon

Some plans reimbursed for charges for an assistant surgeon on a scheduled basis. In that case, a dollar amount was identified for each procedure; it usually was determined as a percent of the maximum payment provided for the surgeon's fee for the same procedure. Most relative value plans excluded any assistant surgeon benefit for a surgical procedure with less than 35 units, since such surgery should not require an assistant.

Anesthesiologists

The charge for an anesthetic generally was included in the hospital or outpatient facility charges in connection with a surgical procedure. It was considered part of necessary services and supplies.

However, charges for the administration of anesthetics have been reimbursable in different ways. Some plans considered them part of the hospital benefit, regardless of whether they are billed by a hospital or by a provider who works independently. Another approach offered coverage for administration of an anesthetic by a physician who was not a salaried employee of a hospital under the surgical benefit. In that case, charges were reimbursed as a percent, such as 20 percent, of the surgical allowance, as a specified unit value, or on a reasonable and customary basis.

Pregnancy

Historically, pregnancy expense benefits had been provided, excluded, or limited at the option of the policyholder; because, at least, normal pregnancies were considered budgetable but represented a relatively high-cost portion of the total health care package. Through the years, several states have mandated coverage at least for complications of pregnancy in all insurance policies.

Complications have been variously defined. A typical definition includes expenses incurred as a result of an extrauterine pregnancy, a pregnancy that terminates by cesarean section or miscarriage, or expenses incurred as a result of sickness caused or contributed to by pregnancy.

Federal legislation, effective October 31, 1978, changed much of that. It required that, by May 1, 1979, employers with 15 or more employees engaged in interstate commerce (i.e., employers who are, or become, subject to Title VII of the Civil Rights Act of 1964) provide the same benefits for pregnancy as for any other sickness. The law does not require an employer to provide benefits for abortions "except where the life of the mother would be endangered if the fetus were carried to term or except where medical complications have arisen from an abortion.'' The burden of compliance rests with the employer and need not be insured even if other benefits are. However, most employers now include equal coverage for pregnancy in their health care insurance plans.

This approach changed the historical treatment of most insured pregnancy benefits. It eliminated the extension of pregnancy coverage for a pregnancy that began while insured and was therefore covered, even if the individual was no longer insured under the plan when the pregnancy terminated. To match the treatment of any other sickness, an insured must be totally disabled as a result of the pregnancy when coverage terminates or the pregnancy is not covered under the extension provisions.

The equal treatment for pregnancy requirement also affects the benefit amount provided to the obstetrician in the surgical schedule of a health insurance plan; it must follow the relativity of the schedule for other procedures. Thus, if surgery is covered on a reasonable and customary basis, pregnancy also must be covered on a similar basis.

Although the law itself left the status of pregnancy benefits for dependents unclear, most consider it impractical to provide different pregnancy benefits for employees and dependents.

Special Features

Second Surgical Opinion Programs

Past studies have questioned the necessity for a large number of surgical procedures being performed throughout the country. In early efforts to reduce costs by eliminating unnecessary procedures, insurance companies urged insureds to obtain a second and even a third opinion to verify the need for the surgery. To encourage that, most insurance plans cover the cost of these consultations without any additional cost to the patient.

Some plans still leave the decision to seek a second opinion up to the insured. Others require a second opinion for elective surgery and/or specified common procedures or payment for the surgery either will be reduced or eliminated. Indications are that savings are greater with a mandatory program.

More recently, verification of the need for recommended surgery has been incorporated into hospital utilization review programs discussed in detail elsewhere. These are designed to ensure that the patient receives the level of medical care most appropriate to his or her condition. They attempt to eliminate unnecessary or inappropriate services. As part of a hospital pre-admission process, for example, an insurer may request a second opinion as to the appropriateness of recommended surgery before the hospital admission is agreed to.

Surgi-Centers

Surgical plans always have covered surgery wherever it was performed. In the interest of further discouraging hospital confinement and its associated high cost, most insurance plans cover the charges for a type of facility variously referred to as a surgi-center, freestanding or ambulatory surgical facility, or one-day surgical facility. It provides an appropriate setting for certain types of comparatively simple surgical procedures that don't normally require overnight confinement and may or may not be part of a hospital. In either case, the charges for use of the surgi-center generally have been covered under the plan's hospital benefits.

Limitations and Exclusions

Surgical expense benefits have not covered the cost of cosmetic surgery and have commonly excluded dental surgery unless it is the result of an accident.

PHYSICIANS' VISITS EXPENSE BENEFITS

It was a logical next step, after surgical benefits were added to insurance plans, to address coverage for physicians' charges for other medical services. Thus, physicians' visits coverage was developed and, together with other nonsurgical benefits, often was referred to as basic medical expense insurance. It remained a comparatively limited first-dollar benefit.

Two types of first-dollar physicians' visits plans were offered, providing benefits (1) in the hospital only, or (2) in either the hospital, home, or office.

In-Hospital Visits Only

Following the early direction of medical insurance, physicians' expense benefits plans at first were designed to cover only fees for visits made while the patient was confined in the hospital. Benefits had a specified maximum-dollar amount for each period of hospital confinement and often a maximum per day. The daily amount sometimes varied depending on the day of confinement on which the visit was made; if so, it was most often higher on the first day, to reflect the greater involvement of the physician at that time.

The benefit period normally coincided with the benefit period for hospital expense benefits.

Hospital, Office, and Home Visits

It wasn't long before plans were expanded to cover physicians' visits in the office or home, as well as in the hospital, but total disability often was required. Such plans, for example, provided $10 for an office visit, $15 for a home visit, and $15 for a hospital visit with an overall maximum, such as $600. This limit applied to all visits for the care and treatment of any one injury or sickness, or in the case of sickness, all visits in either a calendar year or in 12 consecutive months.

When purchasing a plan to cover physicians' fees in and out of the hospital, the policy holder selected the visit when benefit payments began, usually any visit from the first to the fourth. If hospital confinement was required, payment often started with the first visit in the hospital, regardless of when it otherwise would have begun. Benefits normally were restricted to only one visit per day.

Compared with hospital-only coverage for physicians' charges, this broader benefit was not as commonly included on a first-dollar basis. It can result in many small claims, which some believed were more appropriately covered under major medical on a shared basis.

Limitations and Exclusions

Neither of the two types of plans described for physicians' visits expense benefits normally covers charges for a visit after surgery if it is made by a physician connected with the surgical procedure, since a surgeon's charge usually includes postoperative care. Similarly, physicians' visits for pregnancy are not separately covered, because they normally are included in the obstetrician's charge for managing the total pregnancy. In addition, physicians' visits made for dental treatment commonly are excluded from this part of a plan, as are examinations for the prescription or fitting of eyeglasses or hearing aids.

Special Features

Well-Baby Care

The question of whether expenses for normal, healthy babies should be covered from birth under an insurance plan has been debated through the years on much the same grounds as has normal pregnancy. It became even a bigger issue as the pregnancy laws changed and the costs for care of the healthy baby escalated. As coverage for newborns developed, they first were covered only for accidents or sickness after 14 days of age. Soon, however, this was extended to include children with specific abnormal conditions at birth and then to cover a defined number of days of nursery charges for the normal child. Before the federal pregnancy legislation, some plans did the latter only to the extent the mother did not otherwise use her entire pregnancy allowance.

Other charges for a healthy baby, such as a pediatrician's visits, whether the first, usually in the hospital, or subsequently in the office, and immunizations are now often covered either as part of the basic plan or in a preventive care benefit.

Preventive Care

Preventive care was not part of early health care plans, but it has become a buzz word in this era of increasing interest in how it might improve the health of the nation and decrease the cost of medical care for all. In the course of its development, its definition has moved from annual physical examinations for everyone to more sophisticated approaches. Newer concepts address the cost effectiveness of the procedures recommended, the intervals at which they are performed, and even more basically, methods for changing lifestyles that contribute toward illness. Many approaches continue to be evaluated. The jury is still out, but in the meantime, medical benefit plan designers are involved heavily in how best to provide preventive benefits.

DIAGNOSTIC X-RAY AND LABORATORY EXPENSE BENEFITS

This coverage is designed to complement other first-dollar medical expense benefits already discussed. Without it, X-ray and laboratory analyses normally would be covered as hospital services and supplies, but only if the services are performed when the insured is hospital confined. This benefit, though, provides reimbursement for diagnostic X-ray and laboratory examinations made in a doctor's office, in an independent laboratory, or in an outpatient department of a hospital on an ambulatory basis. As with surgical plans, benefits have been covered on a scheduled or nonscheduled basis.

Scheduled

A scheduled plan is a more controlled approach to first-dollar coverage of diagnostic X-ray and laboratory expenses typical of early designs for each new benefit as it developed. Plans of this type itemize the maximum allowance for each examination—as a dollar amount or as a unit value to be multiplied by a conversion factor. Benefits are provided up to an overall schedule maximum, such as $200 or $250, either for all examinations for any one accident or sickness or for all accidents or sicknesses during any one year. In early plans, a two-part schedule sometimes was used. The first part provided coverage for diagnostic X-ray and radioisotope studies, and sometimes was written as a separate coverage. The second part provided payment for diagnostic laboratory services, and generally was written only in conjunction with the first part of the schedule.

Nonscheduled

A nonscheduled plan is a less-restrictive approach since it eliminates maximums for each service. Instead, it provides reimbursement for the actual fee charged for each service, subject to the reasonable and customary test.

As for scheduled plans, overall maximums are set, for example, at $100 or $200, either for all examinations for any one accident or sickness, or for all accidents or sicknesses during any one calendar year. These first-dollar maximums have remained comparatively low because major medical covers expenses that exceed them.

Limitations and Exclusions

Early plans did not cover diagnostic X-ray and laboratory examinations for pregnancy. Since the 1979 Federal Maternity legislation, however, this is no longer true; but the benefit continues to exclude costs for fitting of eyeglasses or of hearing aids or for dental treatment, unless the examination is made to diagnose an injury caused by an accident.

RADIOTHERAPY EXPENSE BENEFITS

Coverage for radiotherapy as a first-dollar benefit developed as the treatment became more prevalent and the cost more significant. However, charges continued to escalate and the first-dollar portion became an ever smaller part of the total cost. Like diagnostic benefits, the balance was covered under major medical. Many plans even eliminated the first-dollar radiotherapy benefit as it became less meaningful and instead covered the cost only under major medical.

First-dollar plans used a schedule that assigned a maximum-dollar amount or a unit value to identified services. The cost of covered radiological treatment (e.g., radium or cobalt therapy) included (1) administration of the treatment, (2) materials and their preparation, and (3) the use of facilities. The maximum payment for all treatments received during any one day often was limited to the largest payment provided in the schedule for any one of the treatments.

Whether a dollar-amount or unit value schedule was used, the total amount payable for all treatments for the same or related injury or sickness was the overall schedule maximum. Maximums that were available ranged from as low as $200 on a dollar-amount schedule to $1,500 or more on a unit value schedule. In some plans this approach was modified to apply the maximum to all treatments for the same or related injury or sickness in a calendar year. The benefit was intended to cover treatment and, therefore, excluded diagnosis.

SUPPLEMENTAL ACCIDENT EXPENSE BENEFITS

This coverage also is variously referred to as additional accident or special accident expense benefits. The concept was first developed to provide an extra, limited amount of first-dollar coverage for medical expenses resulting from an accident. Although that was long before the current concern with cost containment, the benefit does address that issue somewhat; it avoids the penalty of the major medical deductible and coinsurance, because treatment for a minor accident is received in a doctor's office and not in a hospital outpatient department.

The coverage usually provided payment toward the cost of the following services as a result of an accidental injury: (1) treatment by a physician, (2) hospital care, (3) registered graduate nursing care (RN), and (4) X-ray and laboratory examinations. Benefits were payable for covered medical expenses that exceeded the amount the insured otherwise was entitled to under the rest of the basic medical care plan, up to a maximum for any one accident. The most common maximums were $300 and $500. Most plans required that the costs be incurred within 90 days of an accident that happened while the individual was insured.

EXTENSION OF BENEFITS

A key provision of basic benefits from the beginning, which added significantly to their value to the insured, was the extension-of-benefits provision. Under its terms, if an individual's insurance terminated for whatever reason, covered services received within three months of termination were still covered. But the service must be for an injury or sickness that caused the individual to be totally and continuously disabled from the day his or her insurance terminated until the day the service was rendered. Thus, disabled persons were not left without coverage for an existing disability because their insurance ended.

CONVERSION PRIVILEGE

Similarly, the conversion privilege offers a way to fill what might otherwise be a gap in coverage for terminating employees. It allows an individual whose insurance terminates after being insured for at least three months to convert to a personal medical care policy without evidence of insurability. Many states require this provision, and even specify the levels of coverage that must be available. Many insurers include it in all plans. The converted policy usually provides somewhat more restrictive benefits than those under the terminating group coverage, and experience proves individuals most likely to use the plan take advantage of it. The privilege is not generally available to individuals who terminate coverage for failure to pay premiums, are eligible for

Medicare, or become insured under another group medical plan within 31 days of termination. In addition to the conversion privilege, continuation of coverage is now mandated for certain individuals under the Consolidated Omnibus Budget Reconciliation Act, explained in Chapter 50.

SURGICAL/MEDICAL EXPENSE BENEFITS: SUMMARY

The development of basic benefits started with hospital coverage—since it represented the greatest cost of an illness. Additional benefits were developed as other costs increased and as health care plans expanded to satisfy the buyer.

A variety of such benefits have evolved through the years as a result of the continuing demand for fuller coverage. Some, such as the prescription drug benefit, have developed along somewhat different lines, because special administrative issues made the use of participating providers and of a third-party administrator cost-effective. Interest in the vision care benefit has grown, and plans have been written on either a scheduled or participating provider basis. Other benefits, such as home health care and skilled nursing facilities, offer alternatives to hospital confinement and may be covered as either basic or major medical benefits. All are discussed in detail elsewhere in this text.

Furthermore, several limitations not yet mentioned do often apply to basic benefits. These are designed to avoid payment for custodial care, duplicate coverage, illegal or unnecessary charges, etc. Because many also affect major medical benefits, they are discussed separately.

SUPPLEMENTAL MAJOR MEDICAL/ COMPREHENSIVE PLANS

Although the scope of basic medical care benefits has been expanded through the years, adding such alternatives to hospital confinement as home health care and skilled nursing facilities, it remains primarily hospital oriented and geared toward acute care. Benefits usually are first-dollar, but limited both in the services and charges covered. As medical technology advanced and costs increased, the need for additional coverage for a variety of expenses not covered under the so-called basic benefits and for protection against the financial catastrophe of serious and prolonged illness became increasingly apparent.

In response to that need, major medical insurance plans were introduced in 1949. They grew rapidly, covering more than 32 million people by 1960, and approximately 163 million persons by the end of 1985. Today, most plans include major medical in some form.

Major medical provides broad coverage and substantial protection from large, unpredictable, and therefore unbudgetable medical care expenses. As might be expected, with hundreds of companies involved in the development of benefits, many variations in design appeared. Difficult as it is to call anything typical, patterns emerged. From the start, most plans covered a wide range of medical care charges with few internal limits and what was then considered a high per person overall maximum benefit, such as $10,000. Both the range of charges covered and the maximums have increased steadily through the years, but the early requirement that the insured participate to some extent in the cost of care through deductibles and coinsurance remains a conviction for most designers. Although the coverage was born as a supplement to basic medical care plans, that too has changed—and now two approaches to major medical exist: (1) supplemental major medical over some form of basic benefits, and (2) the stand-alone package, referred to as a comprehensive plan. Most of both have had a variety of cost-containment features incorporated.

APPROACHES DEFINED

Supplemental Major Medical

A supplemental major medical plan pays benefits when the basic benefits are exhausted. The claimant is reimbursed first for any charges covered by specific formulas in the basic plan. Major medical covered expenses not reimbursed under the basic plan are covered under the supplemental major medical, subject to a deductible, payable by the claimant. After satisfaction of this deductible amount, a percentage of the remaining covered expenses are paid up to the supplemental major medical maximum. A commonly included provision caps the claimant's costs by paying 100 percent of major medical covered expenses after the insured has incurred the plan's out-of-pocket maximum.

Depending upon the basic benefits over which it was written, a supplemental major medical plan has come to be designated in several different ways:

1. With the insurer's own basic hospital, surgical, and medical benefits, the package is called a base-plus major medical plan.
2. Over another basic plan, such as Blue Cross or Blue Shield, the supplemental major medical more commonly is referred to as superimposed major medical.
3. Over Blue Cross only, the supplemental major medical is known as a wraparound. But even a wraparound can use different design concepts. Traditionally, a wraparound was written to include basic surgical and medical benefits supplemented by major medical. This is much like a base-plus major medical plan except that Blue Cross provides the basic hospital benefits. However, another wraparound design evolved with added simplicity and potential for cost control. It covers all benefits not covered by Blue Cross as part of the major medical subject to a deductible and coinsurance; the Blue Cross hospital benefits are the only basic benefits.

Coverage under the major medical portion of all these approaches differs only to the extent that it adjusts to the basic benefits over which it is written. The two-part basic and major medical coverage reflects the history of the development of medical insurance, in general, as well as the history of the particular plan—and sometimes the collective bargaining that gave rise to that plan. Over the Blues, the basic Blue Cross plan may even today have cost advantages in a particular geographical area, because of cost-reimbursement contracts with hospitals, making competition for basic hospital benefits difficult. More attention is being paid to the equity of different hospital charges based on the source of funding, but for now this remains a factor in some locations.

Whatever its form or the reason for using it, a two-part medical care plan with two carriers has some disadvantages. Administration becomes more difficult, since premiums and claims must be submitted to both carriers and benefits must be coordinated. Duplication may exist; however, there may be gaps in coverage caused by inconsistencies such as different definitions, reasonable and customary levels, and preexisting conditions limitations. Furthermore, when two carriers are involved, if the basic plan changes, the liability of the major medical carrier does also. Clear communication between carriers and with the insured is essential. Typical base-plus major medical, superimposed, and wrap-around plans are illustrated in Figure 12–1.

FIGURE 12–1
Typical Supplemental Major Medical Plan Designs

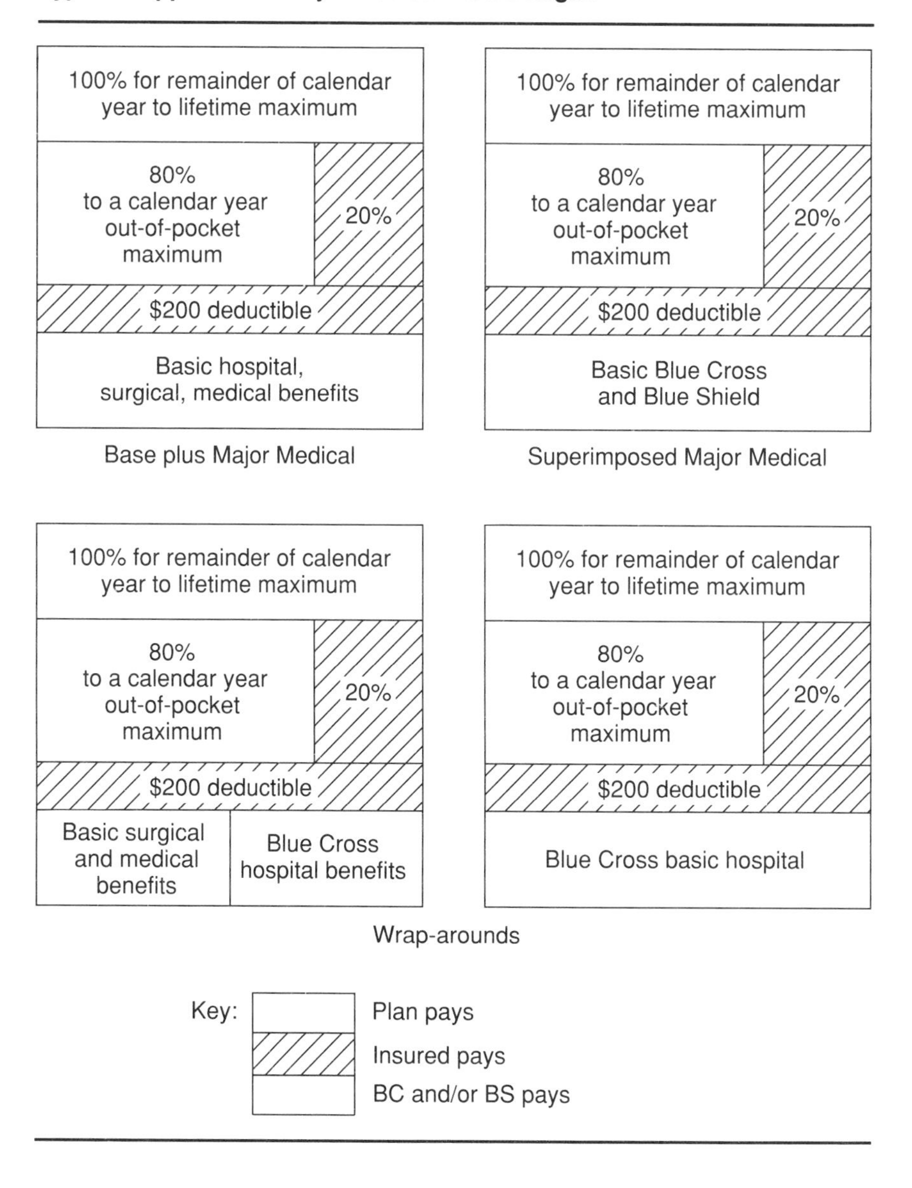

Comprehensive

The next step in the logical development of medical care plans was a single integrated program covering both basic and catastrophic costs—a comprehensive plan. The earliest of these were written in 1954. Their growth was slower than supplemental major medical plans at first, but by 1978 almost 37 million of those persons with major medical coverage in some form were covered by comprehensive plans, and the number grew to 63 million at the end of 1985. The trend continued, and it is the comprehensive plan design that serves as the basis for many of the cost-containment programs in place today.

A comprehensive plan is simpler to understand and easier to communicate. By applying one overall reimbursement formula to the total covered expenses, without attempting to distinguish between those that would have been eligible for basic or major medical benefits, it avoids the hazards of both the duplicate coverage and the gaps discussed earlier. Furthermore, since most comprehensive plans have few of the inside limits of a basic plan, the frequency of plan revisions is reduced.

The earliest and simplest form of comprehensive plan, a pure comprehensive, provided for reimbursement of a percent of all combined covered expenses in a calendar year after the deductible was met, up to an overall lifetime maximum. This design achieves the main purposes of the comprehensive approach; but its acceptance was at first limited because of the appeal of the first-dollar, full-pay coverages buyers had become accustomed to in basic plans. As a result, a variety of modified comprehensive designs were developed and are discussed later in this chapter. Typical comprehensive plans are illustrated in Figure 12–2.

Supplemental major medical and comprehensive plans have many common provisions. Their differences can perhaps best be identified by considering the supplemental features in detail, and then how some of those vary because of the comprehensive design.

FEATURES OF SUPPLEMENTAL MAJOR MEDICAL PLANS

Covered Expenses

Supplemental major medical plans cover reasonable and customary charges incurred for a wide variety of necessary medical services and supplies prescribed or performed by a physician. Reasonable and cus-

FIGURE 12–2
Typical Comprehensive Plan Designs

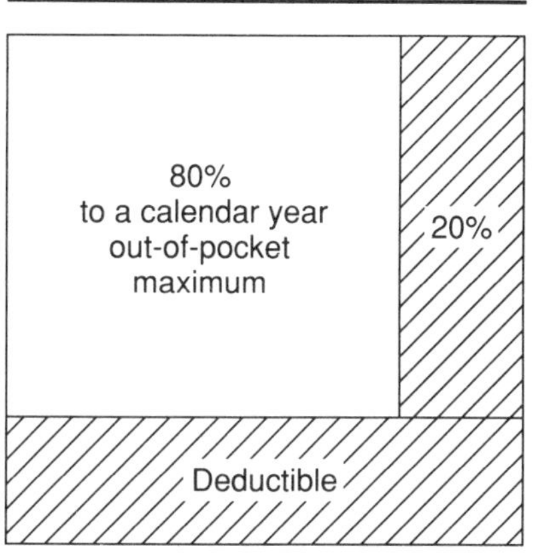

Pure Comprehensive

100% for remainder of calendar year to lifetime maximum

100% of a specified amount of covered hospital expenses

80% to a calendar year out-of-pocket maximum

20%

Deductible

Modified Comprehensive

Key: Plan pays

Insured pays

tomary charges may be interpreted differently by different carriers. Generally, however, they are the lesser of those charges normally made by a provider for the service rendered or an amount large enough to cover the charges made by a percent of the providers in a given geographical area for a similar service. The percent is set by each insurance carrier and applied to the best data available. A carrier with a data bank of its own large enough to be valid will use it. Otherwise, industry-compiled charge data often is used, since its size makes it more credible. The insurer establishes a contractual liability and the patient assumes the obligation to pay any charges exceeding the benefit maximum that results.

From the beginning, supplemental major medical plans included some out-of-hospital benefits; in fact, that was part of the reason for their development. Continuing advances in medical technology have resulted in new and sophisticated outpatient procedures to deal with many conditions that formerly required hospitalization. At the same time, although all medical care costs have continued to escalate faster than the consumer price index, hospital costs remain among the worst offenders. As a result, the trend in recent years has put even greater emphasis on coverage for outpatient services in the hope of containing costs by reducing or eliminating hospital stays.

Although specific covered expenses and their descriptions vary from plan to plan, the following illustrates the broad scope of services and facilities for which charges typically are covered as well as some of their limitations and rationale.

Professional services of physicians or surgeons and other recognized medical practitioners.

Hospital charges for semiprivate room and board and other necessary services and supplies.

Private room charges usually at the most common semiprivate room rate to discourage use except if medically necessary. Confinement in an intensive care unit may be at two or three times the most common semiprivate room rate or even the actual charge.

Preadmission testing prior to a scheduled hospital confinement.

Ambulatory surgical facilities to encourage one-day surgery when medically advisable.

Mental illness or alcohol and drug abuse treatment centers for a limited number of days, such as 28, either per confinement or per calendar year. This is based on the concept that short-term therapy in such facilities is beneficial, but long-term treatment often is custodial in nature and not intended to be covered.

Skilled nursing facilities that meet prescribed requirements. This is limited to a specified number of days, such as 30, per confinement or per calendar year, and was covered, at first, only if it followed a hospital stay of at least 3 consecutive days. The intent was to provide for the person who no longer needed acute care in a hospital but did still need intermediate care and monitoring. The prior hospital confinement requirement has been eliminated in many plans.

Home health care for a defined number of visits per calendar year, such as 40 or 80, by physicians, nurses, and home health aides. Care must be under a plan supervised by a home health agency.

Anesthetics and their administration.

X-rays and other diagnostic laboratory procedures wherever performed.

X-ray or radium treatments.

Oxygen and other gases and their administration.

Blood transfusions, including the cost of blood if charged.

Prescription drugs.

Professional ambulance service to or from the nearest hospital where care can be provided.

Rental of equipment required for therapeutic use.

Casts, splints, and initial prosthetic appliances, trusses, braces, and crutches.

Deductible

The deductible is the amount of covered major medical expenses that must be incurred by the insured before supplemental major medical benefits become payable by the insurer. Its basic purpose is to lower costs by reducing unnecessary utilization and by eliminating small claims and the expense of handling them. It attempts to accomplish this by giving the insured some interest in the up-front cost of medical care.

Levels

Through the years, the most common individual deductible has been \$100. Recently, however, many employers have opted for higher deductible amounts, such as \$200, \$500, \$1,000, even \$2,000. Some of this reflects an effort toward further control of utilization and, therefore, of premium during a period of rapid inflation.

Some consideration also has been given to relating an insured's deductible amount to income, either as a percent of earnings or by identifying a different deductible amount for various earnings ranges. The premise is that a higher-paid employee can afford to cover a larger part of medical expenses and, unless the deductible is significant enough, it will have little effect on utilization. Earnings-related deductibles could become more prevalent in the future in spite of the difficulties with administration of many individual deductible levels on each account that also could change every year.

Type

There are two types of supplemental major medical deductibles: (1) corridor and (2) integrated. The former is by far the more common.

Corridor. This type of deductible is so named because it serves as a corridor between the basic benefits and the supplemental major medical plan. It is applied to covered major medical expenses that exceed amounts covered under the basic plan. Benefits payable under the basic plan are not counted toward satisfaction of the corridor deductible.

Integrated. An integrated deductible was an early approach to the application of the deductible in a supplemental major medical plan. It is rarely used today. The deductible is the greater of (1) a fairly high amount, such as $1,000, or (2) the basic plan benefits. For example, if the basic plan paid $1,250, a $1,000 deductible would be satisfied and supplemental major medical benefits would be payable for the remaining covered expenses with no further deductible. However, if the basic plan only paid $800, the balance of $200 needed to satisfy the deductible would be paid by the insured before supplemental major medical benefits would be payable.

Basis for Application

In conjunction with the deductible, an accumulation period feature is included in one form or another. The accumulation period is that time during which covered medical expenses sufficient to satisfy the deductible must be incurred. It was designed originally as a device to further insure that only relatively substantial claims would be covered. In addition to the length of the accumulation period, the basis for application of the deductible and the benefit period to which it applies vary according to the needs of the policyholder and the underwriting requirements of the insurer.

The following are the two common deductible bases and illustrate how the above features can be combined in a variety of ways.

All-Cause Deductible. Under the all-cause approach, all expenses incurred by an insured, regardless of the number of illnesses or accidents giving rise to the expenses, are considered for purposes of satisfaction of the deductible. Although it is possible to combine the all-cause deductible with various accumulation periods and benefits periods, the calendar year is almost universally used for both (e.g., a $200 deductible applies to each calendar–year benefit period and must be satisfied between January 1 and December 31). As a result, this all-cause deductible approach often is referred to as a calendar-year deductible.

Its most important advantages are that it is simple to administer and is considered the easiest for the insured to understand. Benefits are paid, following the satisfaction of the calendar-year deductible, for expenses incurred during the remainder of that calendar year. To reduce the seeming inequity between insureds who incur expenses early in the year and those who do so late in the year, a carry-over provision has been included. This permits expenses incurred in October, November, or December, which are applied toward satisfaction of the deductible for that year, to be used toward satisfying the deductible for the next calendar year as well. Insurers have been moving toward elimination of this feature.

A policy year or a running 12 months may be substituted for a calendar year. The former is a period beginning with the date each year on which the policy was effective; it is sometimes referred to as the plan year. The latter is any period of 12 months, beginning with the date the first charge is made, counting toward an individual's deductible. These approaches are no longer commonly used because of the difficulty of administering a different period for each individual under the plan.

Most plans also have a special deductible modification known as the common-accident provision. It provides that only one deductible will be applied to the total covered expenses incurred when two or more insured persons of the same family sustain injuries in a single accident.

In addition, to reduce the financial effect of the deductible on large families if several members have major expenses in one year, a "family deductible'' provision usually is added with an all-cause deductible. This provision can operate in several different ways. The deductible may be waived for any further family members after either any two or any three of them have individually satisfied their deductibles in the same year.

Another approach waives any further deductible for the year when any combination of family members has satisfied a total of two or three times the individual deductible amount. The latter may be modified by requiring that at least one family member satisfies the individual deductible.

Per-Cause Deductible. The per-cause deductible was common in early major medical plans but has not been very popular for some time. Under this approach, all expenses incurred by an insured because of the same or related causes were considered for purposes of satisfaction of the deductible. An accumulation period most often was included, in which case the deductible for each cause had to be satisfied within a specified period, typically 60 or 90 days, from the date the first expense was incurred.

In such a plan, the benefit period for each cause started with the first expense used to satisfy the deductible, and normally ended one or two years after the date it started or two years from the date the deductible was satisfied. When benefit periods longer than one year were provided, it was common to include an alternate cutoff date that terminated the benefit period. This might be the end of a period of 60 or 90 days, during which less than a certain amount of expenses (such as the deductible amount) is incurred. Once a benefit period ends, the deductible must be satisfied again to start a new one.

The chief advantage of the per-cause approach is that claims for minor, unrelated illnesses can be eliminated. However, an individual may have to satisfy two or more deductibles in any 12-month period. This approach is more difficult to understand and can cause administrative problems since it often is difficult to distinguish among causes of diseases. This is especially true in cases of chronic illness, diseases of advancing age, and those related to the immune system, such as AIDS.

Coinsurance

Coinsurance provides further participation by the insured in part of the cost of medical care. By reimbursing for less than 100 percent of ongoing expenses over the deductible, coinsurance reinforces the objective of retaining the insured's financial interest in the cost of medical services. Thus, it is one more tool in keeping plan costs down.

Levels

By far the largest majority of plans use 80 percent for most reimbursements, but other levels are available. However, since even with 80 percent reimbursement the cost of a catastrophic illness can cause financial disaster, many plans eliminate coinsurance and reimburse at 100 percent after a certain dollar amount is reached. This amount has come to be most often expressed as the out-of-pocket maximum (e.g., $1,000) paid by an insured as a result of deductible and coinsurance provisions. For even further protection, a family out-of-pocket maximum equal to two or three times the individual amount often is included.

Mental Illness and Alcohol or Drug Abuse

Although reimbursement for charges for treatment of inpatient mental and nervous disorders or alcohol and drug dependency is at the same coinsurance level as for other inpatient charges, an overwhelming number of plans require greater participation by the insured in the cost of these services on an outpatient basis. A variety of coverage designs and levels are available. Coinsurance for outpatient care may, for example, be set at 50 percent subject to a maximum payment under the plan each calendar year, such as $1,000. This may apply separately to (1) mental illness and (2) alcohol and drug dependency, or to all combined.

It also is still common, for mental illness and nervous disorders, to limit outpatient coverage to a specific maximum number of visits per year (e.g., 30) and a maximum covered charge per visit (e.g., $50) for even further control. Neither inpatient nor outpatient charges generally are included in out-of-pocket maximums, and they are rarely if ever payable at 100 percent.

Maximum Benefit

Except for specifically identified coverage limitations, reasonable and customary charges for all eligible expenses are covered by the plan provisions up to the overall maximum benefit of the plan. In the 1960s, a $10,000 maximum was common; today $1 million is common, and many plans are written as unlimited. Consistent with the application of the deductible, the overall maximum benefit may be written as either (1) lifetime (all-cause) or (2) per-cause.

Lifetime

Under the lifetime approach, the overall maximum benefit applies to all covered expenses during the entire period of coverage. However, major medical plans, from their beginning, typically included a reinstatement provision to avoid penalizing insureds who have either partially or wholly exhausted their benefits, but who have recovered to the extent of again being acceptable insurance risks. This provision might provide that after a minimum amount of benefits (e.g., $1,000) is used, the maximum may be reinstated to its original level by submitting evidence of insurability satisfactory to the insurance company. In addition, some plans provide a form of "automatic" reinstatement. For example, benefits paid in a calendar year may be reinstated automatically as of January 1 of the following year for amounts from $1,000 to as much as $25,000. Some plans allow continued reinstatement each January 1 until the full amount is restored.

For further control, it is not unusual to include a separate lifetime, nonreinstatable maximum for all mental and nervous disorders, such as $25,000 to $50,000 lifetime. This is in addition to the coinsurance and the per-visit and maximum-dollar amount or duration limits discussed earlier.

Per-Cause

Under the per-cause approach, the overall maximum benefit applies to each cause. Thus, if an insured individual is receiving benefits under a per-cause plan for the treatment of both diabetes and a heart condition, a separate overall maximum benefit would be applicable to each illness, as would a separate deductible amount. A typical per-cause reinstatement provision states that when a covered person has received benefits for any one accidental injury or any one sickness equal to the overall maximum benefit, major medical benefits for that injury or sickness terminate and can only be reinstated if satisfactory evidence of insurability is submitted to the insurance company. Another approach reinstates some or all of the maximum if the insured does not incur medical expenses for the injury or sickness of more than a specified amount, such as $500, during a given period, such as six months.

With the very high maximums being written today, especially on lifetime all-cause plan designs, the maximum benefit reinstatement provisions no longer have the significance they did in the past. Nevertheless, they typically continue to be included unless the maximum benefit is unlimited.

Limitations and Exclusions

The following describes the charges and services most commonly limited or excluded from medical insurance coverages today, with a brief explanation of the reason for each. Those which apply to major medical only are so identified.

Preexisting Conditions

Because of the potential for selection against the plan, it is common practice to pay major medical benefits for preexisting conditions only after certain requirements are met. A typical preexisting conditions limitation might read:

> A preexisting condition is defined as a condition resulting from an injury or sickness for which expenses were incurred during the three months prior to the effective date of insurance. For such a condition, benefits will be payable only (1) after the completion of a period of three consecutive months ending after insurance becomes effective, and during which the individual received no care or treatment for the condition, or (2) after the individual has been covered for major medical benefits for a period of one year.

In the case of a plan transferring from one carrier to another, however, many plans universally apply a "no loss—no gain" or "hardship" provision required in some states. It usually provides that an insured will be reimbursed under the new plan at the lesser of the amount that would have been payable under the terminated or the new plan regardless of any preexisting conditions limitations or active service requirements of the new plan.

Duplicate Coverage

In many households today, more than one family member is employed. As a result, a person may be covered under more than one group medical care insurance plan and could profit financially from an illness. Thus, in the interest of cost control for all concerned, a coordination of benefits (COB) provision routinely is included to avoid overinsurance. At first, it followed the guidelines recommended by a health insurance task force and adopted by the National Association of Insurance Commissioners (NAIC) in 1971. That version of the NAIC Model Group COB Provisions and Guidelines established the order in which carriers were responsible for reimbursement. The provisions allowed a claimant to recover as much of his or her medical care expenses as coverage under each plan permitted, up to 100 percent of charges for expenses allowable under any of the plans. When a plan provides benefits in the form of services rather than cash payments, the reasonable cash value of the services is considered both an "allowable charge" and a benefit paid. To the extent any plan, therefore, did not need to pay its full liability, benefit credits were accumulated and available if they should be needed to cover expenses later in the benefit period.

Beginning in June 1984, the NAIC proposed several changes to the 1971 guidelines. First, instead of the father's plan always paying first for a dependent child, the plan of the parent whose birthday falls earliest in the year pays first. Similarly, the plan of an active employee or that employee's dependent pays before the plan of a retiree or an employee on layoff. If one plan has the birthday rule and the other does not, the latter determines the order of payment. The retiree/layoff rule is ignored unless both plans include it.

In addition, rather than always covering up to 100 percent of allowable charges under either plan, thereby removing any incentive to contain costs, the secondary carrier can retain the deductibles and coinsurance of the most generous plan. Reimbursement from both plans must be at least 50 percent of allowable charges for alcoholism, mental and nervous expenses, or cost-containment features, such as second surgical opinion, and at least 80 percent of all others.

Medical care plans coordinate benefits not only with other group medical insurance plans and health maintenance organizations, but also may do so with at least the mandatory benefits under state no-fault automobile laws and Medicare, which until recently had always been primary.

In 1982, the Tax Equity and Fiscal Responsibility Act (TEFRA) amended the Age Discrimination in Employment Act of 1967 (ADEA) to require employers with 20 or more employees to offer active employees age 65 through 69 and their spouses of the same age, the same coverage offered to younger workers. The employee could choose for Medicare to be either primary or secondary.

The Deficit Reduction Act of 1984 extended those provisions to include 65- through 69-year-old dependent spouses of active employees under age 65. The Consolidated Omnibus Budget Reconciliation Act of

1985 (COBRA) further extended the provisions to include active employees and their dependents who are age 70 or older.

For those employees who choose to continue their employer's plan as primary, Medicare is secondary and coordination of benefits applies. For active employees who choose it and for all covered retirees, Medicare is primary; there is no additional benefit under the employer's plan.

Another approach is often used in place of coordination of benefits to avoid duplicate coverage particularly in the case of Medicare. Normal liability under the insured plan is determined and directly reduced by the amount paid by Medicare for the same expenses. This is commonly referred to as carve-out. It attempts to provide the individual eligible for Medicare with the same reimbursement under the insured plan and Medicare together as any other insured would receive under the group medical care insurance plan itself. This same approach also may be applied to "no-fault" benefits.

Other variations have been developed to coordinate benefits for the same charges under several plans. For example, in some cases, a plan is designed to specifically fill the gaps in coverage under the primary plan. This was, at first, a common way to supplement Medicare, but is more difficult to keep current. Whatever the variation, all such approaches have the same objective—cost control by elimination of overinsurance.

Other Limitations and Exclusions

Care Received in Federal or State Hospitals

Experience revealed many of these hospitals furnish free service except when a patient has insurance coverage, in which case some make a charge for services rendered. Since the existence of insurance coverage should not affect the way a hospital's charges are billed, it is the practice of insurers to honor such claims only when an unconditional requirement exists for a person to pay for the services provided, without regard to the existence of insurance. This type of exclusion is very common, although most government hospitals no longer base their charges on the existence of insurance.

Cosmetic Surgery

This is only covered if it is necessary to correct injuries caused by an accident that occurred while insured, or to correct a congenital anomaly in an insured newborn infant. Elective cosmetic surgery is excluded.

Custodial Care

Since the purpose of health insurance is to provide benefits for the treatment of an injury or sickness, various exclusions and limitations are included to terminate benefits when institutionalization of the patient becomes custodial in nature (i.e., there is no longer any medical care being provided).

Dental Care and Treatment

Care or treatment of teeth and gums is usually excluded, except for treatment required because of accidental injury to natural teeth and charges for hospital confinement for dental treatment. With the rapid growth of group dental expense insurance, care must be taken to avoid duplicate coverage.

Elective Items

There are many services, such as television, telephone charges, air conditioners, swimming pools, bath massagers, and trips to different climates, that a patient can elect to use, which can relate to the illness or injury being treated, but which do not contribute materially to the cure of a patient. Charges for many of these might be billed by a medical care provider, such as a hospital or a physician, or secured with a prescription. Because of the questionable relationship of many of these expenses to medical treatment, they usually are excluded.

Routine Health Examinations

Since there is no illness, these budgetable expenses for years have been expected to be paid by the covered person. However, in the interest of cost control it has become common to include preventive care benefits, such as periodic examinations and immunizations, either as part of the basic coverage as described or under the major medical plan.

Occupational Accidents and Sicknesses

No benefits are payable for any medical care expenses resulting from an occupational accident, or from sickness covered by any workers' compensation law or similar legislation. Workers' compensation benefits cover the medical care expenses of most workers for job-related accidents and sicknesses.

Purchase or Fitting of Eyeglasses or Hearing Aids and Examinations for Them

These services are considered routine care not expected to result in significant expense to the individual, and for years were not reimbursable. No illness in the usual sense is involved in the majority of cases. Nevertheless, in response to demand, plans have been developed covering these services either as basic or major medical benefits. This is particularly true of vision care, for which plan designs vary from fixed-dollar reimbursement for examinations and glasses to full-pay provider network arrangements.

War

Injuries or illness because of war, whether declared or undeclared, are excluded from coverage because a substantial catastrophic risk that is beyond the scope of group health insurance is created.

Extension of Benefits

As with basic benefits, major medical benefits will be continued after insurance terminates for an injury or sickness that causes the insured to be totally disabled from the date of termination. However, unless the individual is or becomes covered under another group plan for the same injury or sickness, major medical benefits will be extended for one year rather than the three months provided by basic plans. This extension terminates when the individual is no longer totally disabled by the injury or sickness, if that is earlier than one year from termination.

Survivor Coverage

Although not a standard coverage included in all plans, this provision often was available and added considerably to the value of a medical expense benefit plan. It provided for the medical care insurance in effect for dependents on the date of an employee's death to remain in force, usually without payment of premium, for some specified period ranging from six months to two years from the date of the employee's death. Coverage terminated before the end of that period if the surviving spouse remarried, in which case the coverage for all dependents terminated or if any dependent became insured under another group insurance plan, became eligible for Medicare, or no longer qualified as a dependent according to the terms of the contract. Alternatively, some carriers allowed an employer to maintain coverage on dependents of a deceased employee by continuing to pay the required premium.

This survivor coverage, designed to protect surviving dependents from the sudden termination of benefits as a result of the employee's death has been replaced and broadened by the requirements prescribed by COBRA. The law is effective for the ERISA plan year of each employer that begins on or after July 1, 1986. Broadly speaking, an insured or uninsured plan is required to provide the option to continue benefits for employees and dependents who lose group health benefits because of termination, death, or divorce. The cost of continuation can be passed along to eligible participants up to 102 percent of the cost of benefits to the plan for similarly situated active employees. The continuation period varies based on the reason for loss of benefits, but does not exceed 36 months. Coverage may continue, as long as the policy is in force, until the end of the continuation period or the individual fails to pay the required premium, becomes eligible for Medicare, or is insured under another group plan, whichever is earliest.

Handicapped Children Provision

As early as 1965, states began to require continuation of coverage on handicapped children beyond the age limit provided by the contract. Today, most states have such mandates and most insurers provide the benefits on all plans nationwide. The child must be unmarried, incapable of self-support because of mental or physical handicap, and primarily dependent upon the employee for support. This provision provides a vehicle for coverage of a group of individuals otherwise likely to be uninsurable.

Conversion Privilege

When insurance terminates under previously described circumstances, the right to convert to a personal medical care policy without evidence of insurability generally is available and mandated by some states. At first, only limited hospital, surgical, and medical benefits were required to be included in the converted policy. Since 1973, however, a few states have legislated the availability of major medical benefits as well.

COMPREHENSIVE PLAN VARIATIONS AND DIFFERENCES FROM SUPPLEMENTAL MAJOR MEDICAL

Single Formula

As described earlier, a comprehensive plan, in its simplest form, is a medical care benefit design that covers under one formula those expenses earlier considered basic benefits as well as those included in supplemental major medical benefits. In a pure comprehensive, that formula is applied to reasonable and customary charges without the inside limits of basic benefits, such as maximum hospital days or surgical schedules. Although a comprehensive plan can be written on a per-cause or policy-year basis, the all-cause calendar year approach is used almost exclusively. The features described as applying to that type of supplemental major medical plan also apply to a calendar-year comprehensive plan. Their differences are discussed below.

Deductible and Coinsurance

Unlike supplemental major medical, a comprehensive deductible generally is referred to as an "initial" deductible rather than integrated or corridor, since, at least in the pure comprehensive, the insured must bear expenses up to the deductible amount before the insurance carrier begins to reimburse for any charges. Further participation by the insured through coinsurance until the out-of-pocket maximum is reached applies in a pure comprehensive just as it does in a supplemental major medical plan.

However, to satisfy the market need for a single easy-to-understand design, but with some first-dollar benefits, many other modifications have been made available in comprehensive plans either individually or in combination, depending on the products and underwriting practices of the insurer.

1. The deductible may be waived on all or on some portion of covered hospital expenses, such as the first $2,000, but applied to hospital expenses above that.
2. Coinsurance may be waived for the hospital expenses described above. Together with waiver of the deductible, this creates the commonly called "full-pay hospital" area.
3. The deductible may be waived on surgeons' fees.

4. Surgeons' fees may be payable according to a schedule, plus coinsurance for reasonable and customary fees in excess of the schedule with or without a deductible between.
5. The deductible and coinsurance may be waived in other areas—such as physicians' hospital visits, or diagnostic tests—to further match the base-plus major medical concept.
6. The deductible may be waived on certain outpatient services—such as ambulatory surgical facilities, preadmission tests, and second surgical opinions—to encourage their use and to avoid high cost hospital confinements if not necessary.
7. The coinsurance percent reimbursement level may be higher than the coinsurance level for the rest of the plan, increased even to 100 percent for some outpatient services to further encourage their use.

Clearly, as some first-dollar (no deductible) and full-pay (no coinsurance) benefits are built into a comprehensive plan, it becomes more like a base-plus major medical and loses some of its simplicity. Its potential for cost containment may be either diminished or increased depending upon the variation and its utilization.

Maximum Benefit

The overall maximum benefit and its reinstatement provisions apply to the entire comprehensive plan, since there is no separate major medical portion. With the rapid escalation of medical care costs, such earlier maximums as $100,000 or $250,000 typically have been increased to $1 million. Many plans even have an unlimited lifetime maximum.

Preexisting Conditions

The preexisting conditions limitation in supplemental major medical plans, from the beginning, only applied to the major medical portion of the total plan, because benefits under the basic portion were relatively limited. This allowed some reimbursement for a preexisting condition, but up to controlled maximums. Although basic benefits became so liberal that large amounts could be paid under that part of the plan for such a condition, the limitation continued to apply only to the major medical.

Application of the same limitation to a comprehensive plan would be much more restrictive, since it would apply to all benefits. A variation on the theme, therefore, was developed. It defines a preexisting condition in the same way as for a supplemental major medical plan and covers it from the effective date of insurance, but applies a dollar limit, such as $1,000, for the first year of coverage.

Extension of Benefits

The supplemental major medical one-year extension of benefits after termination for a totally disabling injury or sickness applies to the entire comprehensive plan. The confusion of 3 months for basic benefits and 12 for major medical is eliminated.

SUMMARY AND CONCLUSION

Medical care insurance plans have developed over the years so that most today include some form of major medical and cover an extensive array of services at least partially. To the extent they have been paid for with employer funds, the cost of coverage has been felt only very indirectly by the insured. However, the pressure driving medical costs upward grows relentlessly. As a result many employers have increased the employee's share of premiums. At the same time, there is even greater interest in medical plan designs aimed at maintaining the insured's concern with thecost of care by requiring that he or she share in it when service is received. The comprehensive plan design with higher up-front deductibles and coinsurance throughout fits that bill. However, clearly more was needed to control costs. Hospital utilization review programs that include preadmission certification, concurrent review, and discharge planning have become commonplace. They were the beginnings of what has come to be known as managed care and were designed to eliminate unnecessary confinements and reduce lengths of stay.

Various other arrangements for the delivery of health care have been developed aimed at cost control, without jeopardizing the quality of care, through the use of efficient providers. These are referred to as alternate delivery systems and include health maintenance organizations (HMOs) and preferred provider organizations (PPOs) in all their various forms.

HMOs began in the 1930s and got off to a slow start. Their growth was stimulated by passage of the HMO Act of 1973. It required that most employers offer a federally qualified HMO if one was available. By 1989, about 600 HMOs were operating throughout the country, covering almost 35 million members. An HMO provides defined comprehensive health care to enrollees in a specific geographic service area. The member must use an HMO physician, who in most plans coordinates all the care a patient receives and preauthorizes referrals to non-HMO providers if necessary.

HMOs are organized in a variety of ways:

Staff. Physicians are salaried full-time employees of the HMO

Group. Services are provided by an independent multispecialty group of physicians with whom the HMO contracts on a per capita or fee-for-service basis

Network. Like group, but more than one multispecialty group practice provides services to members

IPA. The HMO contracts with individual physicians or associations of individual physicians on a per capita or fee-for-service basis.

HMOs emphasize preventive care and have succeeded in reducing hospital stays significantly. Most services have been covered in full but, like comprehensive plans, in response to continuing increases in costs, copayments such as $5 or $10 for each office visit have been introduced by many plans.

PPOs have also proliferated, with 685 operating in 1989. Designed and managed in a variety of ways, with insurers, employers, providers, and administrators in diverse roles, these arrangements add provider discounts to utilization review to control costs. In the most common design, insureds can receive services from the provider of their choice but will have less out-of-pocket expense, and often full coverage, if a preferred provider is used.

Variations in the design of each of the managed care designs mentioned, as well as plans that combine two or more of them, have created gray areas in which it is difficult to distinguish between them. These more recent benefit designs and delivery systems provide the flexibility to best serve each participant's particular interests. The topics of health care cost containment, HMOs, PPOs and managed care are discussed in the next four *Handbook* chapters.

CHAPTER 13

MEDICAL CARE COST-CONTAINMENT TECHNIQUES: AN OVERVIEW

William G. Williams

It has been difficult over the past 20 years to pick up any general or trade publication without seeing some reference to medical care cost containment. The unprecedented rise in the cost of providing medical care is a problem in which we are all both victims and culprits. The dilemma is the result of living in a complex society with many conflicting objectives. We want everyone to have the best medical care. We want everyone to have the freedom to choose who will provide the care and to go to that provider as often as they want. We want every community, neighborhood, and religious group to have their own hospital. We want every medical facility to be equipped in the most modern fashion. We want every citizen to have access to care without money being a barrier. *And we want cost-containment.*

Problems are easy to identify; workable solutions are not. Nevertheless, continuing concern with the substantial increase in the money spent for medical care has focused the attention of employers, the public, government, and the providers of medical care services on finding ways to solve the cost problem.

Health care cost-containment techniques involve a set of interrelated components that produce cost savings for the employer. This chapter covers those components consisting of:

1. Benefit plan design ideas.
2. Claims review.

3. External cost-control systems.
4. Health education and promotion.

As it became clear that the early cost-containment techniques used alone could not produce sufficient savings, the idea of "managed care" came into being and has evolved rapidly in recent years. Managed care has been defined in many ways, but put in the simplest terms, it is any method or combination of methods of providing health care so that both cost and utilization are controlled. Health maintenance organizations (HMOs) and preferred provider organizations (PPOs), two of the earliest managed care innovations, are discussed here briefly in their early role of external cost control systems. Detailed discussions of HMOs, PPOs and of the whole spectrum of managed care alternatives are beyond the scope of this chapter and are found in Chapters 14, 15, and 16 of the *Handbook,* respectively.

BENEFIT PLAN DESIGN IDEAS

Changes in health benefit plans have taken place over the years because of legislative mandates, changes in medical care institutions, emergence of new types of providers, development of new methods of medical care and treatment, and continuing health care cost increases. As the effects of these changes impacted the overall costs of medical benefit plans, plan design changes were introduced in an effort to control the escalating costs. Such benefit plan design ideas as deductibles, coinsurance, cost sharing, coordination of benefits, subrogation, preadmission testing, emergency room treatment, weekend admissions, incentives for outpatient surgery, medical necessity language, skilled nursing care, home health care, preventive care, second surgical opinions, hospice care, and birthing centers serve this function.

Deductibles

A deductible, which is the cost of medical care expenses a covered person must incur and pay before medical care benefits become payable under a plan, may be expressed as a dollar amount ($100, $200, $500, $1,000), a percentage of the insured employee's income (1 percent), or both. Traditionally, they have been expressed in fixed-dollar amounts; however, there recently has developed a tendency to adopt or to consider income-related deductibles, because such deductibles adjust automatically to inflationary trends and may serve as a health care cost-containment technique.

Deductibles eliminate the high costs of investigating and paying for small claims, they lower employer costs for a medical care expense plan and employee costs for a contributory plan, and they help to discourage misuse of medical care, because the user's financial involvement encourages scrutiny of the amount and type of treatment received. However, the use of deductibles may pose a financial impediment to treatment, and the costs of care may increase if treatment is postponed. Employees may be dissatisfied with insurance plans that have deductibles and may opt for alternative plans, such as HMOs and PPOs, which usually do not use deductibles. The combination of a deductible and other cost-sharing features (such as coinsurance, copayment, or inside limits) also may impose a financial hardship on insured persons. Modifications of the deductible principle that have evolved in response to these concerns include benefit designs that involve separate deductibles, maximum family deductibles, common accident deductible provisions, and deductible carry-over provisions.

To encourage insureds to seek less expensive alternatives, deductibles can be waived for preadmission testing, outpatient surgery, and second surgical opinions.

Ultimately, the impact of deductibles applied to inpatient care is likely to be limited to discouraging frivolous admissions. When applied to outpatient care, however, this technique may discourage prompt diagnosis and treatment of legitimate illnesses, with a result that the higher cost of later treatment may outweigh the savings accrued through the intended avoidance of nuisance claims.

Coinsurance

Another way to assure that an individual participates in sharing a risk is to require that his or her participation in the payment of covered medical care expenses be a continuing one. A coinsurance provision typically indicates the insurance plan will pay a specified percentage (usually 80 percent) of all or of certain covered medical care expenses in excess of any applicable deductible. The remaining percentage (20 percent) is borne by the insured. In many plans today, a coinsurance limit or ''cap'' eliminates the coinsurance factor for the balance of the calendar year, after the insured has paid a fixed amount in expenses (e.g., $1,000, $1,500, $2,500).

Variable coinsurance percentages are found in many major medical expense insurance plans. In one plan, for example, inpatient and outpatient benefits are payable at 80 percent of all covered medical care expenses incurred during any one calendar year, in excess of any deductible, until the out-of-pocket maximum is reached; thereafter, 100 percent of all additional covered expenses for the balance of the year is paid. These features (where permissible) do not apply to the expenses incurred for outpatient treatment of alcoholism, drug addiction, and mental and nervous disorders, which are payable at 50 percent of the charges incurred and limited to a total maximum amount each calendar year (e.g., $1,000).

In order to influence insureds to obtain medical care on an outpatient basis (i.e., ambulatory surgery and ambulatory care), reimbursement could be 100 percent of usual, customary, and reasonable (UCR) charges instead of 80 percent. Also, to discourage elective hospital admissions on Fridays and Saturdays, coinsurance factors can be increased (e.g., from 20 to 50 or 60 percent).

Those who favor the use of deductibles and coinsurance say the following:

1. They may lead to a reduction in the use of health services and, hence, reduction of costs.
2. They reduce premiums because, for a given set of benefits, the insurance company pays less of the bill. Savings are eventually passed on to the employer and employee, although the effect is really to shift some of the cost burden from the employer to the employee.
3. They are equitable in the sense that the amount insured persons pay is related to the health services they use.

But those who oppose their use argue:

1. They may not reduce utilization of health services because physicians, not consumers, make such decisions.
2. To the extent they do decrease utilization, they may discourage needed preventive care.
3. For some employees they may present a financial barrier to receiving necessary care.

The use of deductibles and coinsurance as disincentives to overutilization and unnecessary care probably will continue to increase, resulting in an immediate containment of premium costs. However, there does not seem to be any optimum deductible amount or coinsurance rate at which excessive utilization is reduced but people are not discouraged from getting necessary care. Whatever the amount or percentage, there must always be some trade-off in the efforts to balance the two competing objectives of coverage adequacy and cost control.

Cost Sharing

Cost sharing, a key issue in medical benefits design, usually takes four different forms:

1. Deductibles.
2. Coinsurance.
3. Copayment (i.e., a specified dollar amount per day of inpatient care or per unit of service).
4. Premium contributions by employees.

Although cost sharing reduces medical care expenditures, many experts believe employees who share in medical care costs should do so at the point of service (i.e., by utilizing deductibles, coinsurance, and copayment) rather than through increased contributions by employees, which lower the employer's medical care costs, but do not affect the overall cost of medical care.

Coordination of Benefits (COB)

Very simply defined, coordination of benefits (COB) is a process by which two or more insurers, insuring the same person for the same or similar group medical insurance benefits, limit the aggregate benefits he or she receives to an amount not exceeding the actual amount of loss, that is, not more than 100 percent[1] of allowable expenses.

---

[1] Since June 1984, the National Association of Insurance Commissioners (NAIC) rules permit an option for plans to coordinate at less than 100 percent of allowable expenses, provided that the percent of allowable expenses for COB purposes is never less than 80 percent.

Coordination of benefits was developed as a cost-containment technique to prevent duplication of benefits, which occurred, with the rapid growth of overinsurance. Overinsurance exists when a person is insured under two or more insurance policies and is eligible to collect an aggregate of benefits that exceeds his or her actual loss. The following are the most common circumstances causing overinsurance:

1. Both husband and wife employed and eligible for group medical insurance benefits.
2. Persons employed in two jobs, both of which provide group medical insurance benefits.
3. Association group plans, especially among salaried and professional people who usually already have group medical insurance benefits through their employers.

COB is an arrangement among several group insurance plans to predetermine responsibility for coverage so the total of all "coordinated" benefits paid will not exceed 100 percent of allowable expenses, so it is necessary to determine which insurer is to pay any claim first. If only one plan has a COB provision, the plan *without* the COB provision pays its benefits first and the plan *with* a COB provision pays second; that is, it coordinates its benefits based on the benefits paid by the primary plan. However, when both plans have a COB provision, both have the right to reduce their benefits based on the benefits paid by the other plan. To prevent the possibility of an insured being caught in the middle of a dispute between two insurers, and to provide a consistent and simple order of benefit determination (i.e., who pays first), the great majority of states now follow the National Association of Insurance Commissioners' (NAIC) model insurance provision guidelines (including the "birthday rule"). The NAIC model sets out the following system:

1. The plan covering the patient as an employee pays before the plan covering the patient as a dependent.

2. If the patient is a dependent child of parents who are *not* separated or divorced, the plan covering the parent whose birthday falls earlier in the year pays before the plan covering the parent whose birthday falls later in the year. If both parents have the same birthday, the plan that covered the parent longer pays before the plan that covered the other parent for a shorter time. While it is unlikely since the adoption of the NAIC model guidelines by most states that one plan uses the birthday rule and the other uses the old "male/female" rule, in this event, both plans will follow the "male/female" rule whereby the plan covering the male parent pays first. This fallback provision avoids the possibility that under different rules, both plans will be primary or both plans will be secondary.

3. If the patient is a dependent child of parents who *are* separated or divorced:

a. The plan or the parent with custody pays first,
b. The plan of the spouse of the parent with custody (the stepparent) pays next, and
c. The plan of the parent without custody pays last.

If the specific terms of a court decree state that one of the parents is responsible for the child's health care expenses, and the entity obliged to pay or provide the benefits of that parent's plan has actual knowledge of those terms, that plan pays first. If any benefits are actually paid or provided before that entity has actual knowledge, this "court decree" rule is not applicable. If divorced parents have joint custody of a child and neither parent is specifically responsible for the child's health care expenses, the birthday rule applies.

4. A plan that covers the patient as an active employee (one who is not laid off or retired) or that employee's dependent pays before the plan that covers a laid-off or retired employee or that employee's dependent. If neither plan has this rule, and if, as a result, the plans do not agree on the order of benefits, this rule is ignored.

5. If one person is covered under the continuation-of-coverage provisions of the Consolidated Omnibus Budget Reconciliation Act (COBRA), the plan of the person who is covered as an employee (or as the employee's dependent) pays first.

6. If none of the above rules determines the order of benefits, the plan that has covered the patient longer pays before the plan that covered that person for a shorter period of time.

The following claim example illustrates what occurs in the absence, and the presence, of a COB provision:

> Mrs. Jones has filed a claim for $600 with both company A and company B. Company A insures Mrs. Jones as a female employee under a plan covering 80 percent of eligible expenses after a $100 deductible is satisfied.

Company B insures her as a dependent spouse under a plan providing 75 percent of eligible expenses after a $100 deductible is met. In the absence of COB both companies would have to pay Mrs. Jones as follows:

Company A		*Company B*	
Allowable expenses	$600	Allowable expenses	$600
Less deductible	100	Less deductible	100
	$500		$500
× 80% coinsurance	.80	× 75% coinsurance	.75
Benefit payable	$400	Benefit payable	$375

In the absence of a COB provision, both insurers would pay the full benefits payable under the plans which in this example totals $775. In this case the insured, Mrs. Jones, would have made money to the extent of $175 as a result of her medical care expenses.

Using our example again, here is how the payments would be calculated with the presence of a COB provision in both plans:

Company A		*Company B*	
Allowable expenses	$600	Allowable expenses	$600
Less deductible	100	Less Company "A"s benefit	400
	$500	Company B pays	$200
× 80% coinsurance	.80		
Company A pays	$400		

Thus under COB, company B paid only $200, producing a benefit saving of $175. This amount is credited to Mrs. Jones, to be applied to any future claims she might have against company B during the claim determination period, generally a calendar year. This credit can be used to provide benefits that would not otherwise have been paid. If, for example, the policy with company B provides psychiatric outpatient benefits, but only to a maximum of $500 in a claim determination period, and Mrs. Jones incurs $750 of psychiatric outpatient expenses in that same claim determination period, then the $175 credit could be used to extend benefits beyond the $500 maximum. The effect of COB in Mrs.

Jones's case, then, is that, between the two insurers, she received reimbursement of the full $600 of expenses and has a $175 credit with company B.

Coordination of benefits is a necessary cost-containment technique used to prevent duplicate payments for covered services and thereby limit the potential of a net financial gain to the person seeking medical care. It is estimated the use of COB saves approximately 4 to 8 percent in claim payments that would otherwise have been made.

Subrogation

In general, subrogation means the substitution of another party, in this case the employer or the insurer, in place of a party (the employee or a dependent) who has a legal claim against a third party. Thus an employee benefit plan that includes subrogation provides the employer or insurer with rights with respect to claims that a covered employee or dependent might have against third parties, such as negligent tortfeasors in automobile accidents, and the employer's insurer receives reimbursement if the employee or the dependent receives a liability recovery from a third party. Insurers may be reluctant to include specific subrogation provisions in group insurance contracts because of the time delays involved in settling claims.

Preadmission Testing (PAT)

The purpose of preadmission testing is to help contain hospital costs by reducing the number of in-hospital patient days through having the necessary X-rays, laboratory tests, and examinations conducted on an outpatient basis, prior to a scheduled hospital admission, and reimbursed as if on an inpatient basis. It is important to note PAT is not an outpatient diagnostic benefit program but is offered as an inpatient reimbursement alternative to a longer hospital confinement or, in some cases, to an unnecessary hospital confinement.

Advantages to Patients

The advantage for the patient being admitted for medical care is that treatment can begin immediately. This is far better than admitting the patient a day or two ahead of time to have tests run and then waiting for the results before treatment is begun.

PAT reduces the possibility of patients being admitted on weekends for routine or elective surgery and necessary tests scheduled for the following week. It allows the patient to become familiar with the hospital before admission, and means an alleviation of anxiety as well as less time away from home and job.

Advantages to Physicians

Getting test results early—especially in cases where there is a history of heart disease, diabetes, and the like—is a great advantage to the patient's physician. It helps the provider get a jump on planning the course of treatment. Should there be negative test results, the admission can be canceled before the patient comes to the hospital.

The physician who is able to confirm a diagnosis and develop a plan of treatment before the patient is admitted is able to begin treatment promptly upon the patient's arrival. Once the test results are available and the physician is sure of the admission, the admitting department need only type the bed assignment and date of admission on the admission form and wait for the patient's arrival. Because all the paperwork can be prepared in advance, the admissions process is effectuated promptly and smoothly.

The tests also are available for the anesthesiologist's evaluation prior to the patient's arrival for surgery. This enables the anesthesiologist to determine the proper type and amount of anesthesia in an unharried atmosphere.

How PAT Works

In general, this is how preadmission testing works:

1. After the diagnosis has been established, the procedure scheduled, and the patient's room reserved by the hospital, the attending physician orders those tests and examinations he or she considers necessary before the procedure can be performed.
2. The patient is instructed to report at a scheduled time and specified place in the hospital where the tests are to be completed. The results of the tests are reported to the attending physician and are made a part of the patient's hospital chart at the time of admission.
3. Charges for the tests are billed by the hospital to the insurer as a part of the bill for in-hospital care according to the benefit provisions of the patient's insurance plan.

4. The time period prior to admission, during which the tests and examinations are to be made, is determined by the attending physician. Most tests are made as close to the admission date as practicable so the test results are completely dependable and acceptable.
5. When the admission must be cancelled or postponed for any reason outside the patient's control, the insurer will still make payment for the tests and when the admission is rescheduled will make the same benefits available again.
6. The above procedures apply to elective surgical admissions and medical confinements.

How is PAT's Cost-Containment Potential Compromised?

PAT's cost-containment potential can be compromised in the following ways:

1. By the pattern of medical practice in the community. For example, providers in a fee-for-service setting lack the financial incentive to use PAT. In addition, some providers admit their patients several days prior to surgery to allow for their adjustment to hospitalization.
2. By the often-mistaken assumptions of the patient, doctor, or hospital that the patient's insurer provides more comprehensive coverage for inpatient care.
3. By the desire of hospitals to keep their beds filled. Hospitals with low occupancy, on the one hand, have strong financial incentives to fill beds and to render all possible services on an inpatient basis. On the other hand, hospitals with high occupancy have strong incentives to reduce the length of hospital stays and make beds available.
4. By the physician's time involvement in the scheduling of tests.
5. By the matter of convenience to both physician and patient. For example, some patients find it difficult to go back and forth to the hospital on an outpatient basis; other patients are very sick or elderly and cannot go back and forth to the hospital.
6. By the mistaken notion of the patient that testing on an inpatient basis is more thorough.
7. By the lack of coordination in the scheduling of tests and the availability of beds and operating rooms. Inefficient scheduling of all elements in this process leads to delays which offset any PAT savings.

8. By the reluctance of hospitals and physicians to participate because of the specter of malpractice suits. This attitude probably is the result of concern about any testing done in facilities outside the hospital, such as an ambulatory care center, independent clinical laboratory, or physician's office. In addition, in many cases hospital-based laboratories are contracted out to a physician or group of physicians. Since their reimbursement formula often is dependent upon utilization, it would not be in their interest to encourage the use of "outside" facilities.

Conclusions

PAT benefit programs, which are relatively easy to add to existing benefit plans, are provided at no additional cost to employers or employees. Effectively utilized, they can generate cost savings. PAT programs alone can help to reduce hospital lengths of stay. When combined with a hospital utilization review program evaluating the necessity of a hospital admission, the quality of care, and the length of stay for a given diagnosis, PAT has considerable potential to encourage hospitals to improve their admission and presurgical testing procedures. Ultimately, it usually is the physician who decides whether to use PAT, but the decision can be influenced by the patient concerned about the escalating cost of medical care who asks, "Can't my presurgical or medical tests be done on an outpatient basis?"

PAT programs offer the potential for reducing both the cost per hospital admission and the time lost from work. At the same time, PAT can help reduce the need for more hospital bed construction.

Emergency Room Treatment

To discourage the unnecessary use of hospital emergency rooms (i.e., in lieu of a doctor's office), a deductible can be utilized (e.g., $50) or the coinsurance could be 50–50 rather than 80–20 percent. Usually a physician can advise whether an individual should utilize the services of a hospital emergency room.

Weekend Admissions

Hospitals, like many businesses, reduce their activities on weekends. In many cases a patient admitted on a Friday or Saturday and another person admitted the following Monday receive the same treatment and both leave the hospital on the same day. Because of unnecessary elective (nonemergency) admissions to hospitals on Fridays or Saturdays, insurers are either not providing benefits or are requiring a substantial deductible (e.g., $250, $500) or imposing 50–50 or 60–40 coinsurance. Necessary weekend admissions (e.g., childbirth or a life-threatening or potentially disabling emergency) would be reimbursed like any other days and no disincentives would be applied.

Incentives for Outpatient Surgery

Insureds are provided with incentives to utilize outpatient surgery, when it's medically feasible. The deductible is waived and the surgery is reimbursed at 100 percent instead of 80–20 percent. Outpatient surgery is being performed at hospital outpatient facilities, free-standing surgical centers, or in doctors' offices. Utilization review programs review medical information and evaluate it against medical criteria to determine medical necessity and appropriateness of inpatient admission and the proposed treatment plan. For example, could the proposed treatment be delivered in a more cost-effective setting without any sacrifice in quality of treatment or the anticipated result?

Medical Necessity Language

Medical care and treatment is "medically necessary" if it meets all the following conditions:

1. The care and treatment is appropriate given the symptoms, and is consistent with the diagnosis, if any. "Appropriate" means that the type, level, and length of service and the setting are needed to provide safe and adequate care and treatment;
2. It is rendered in accordance with generally accepted medical practice and professionally recognized standards;
3. It is not treatment that is generally regarded as experimental, educational, or unproven; and
4. It is specifically allowed by the licensing statutes that apply to the provider that renders the service.

With respect to confinement in a hospital "medically necessary" further means that the medical condition requires confinement and that safe and effective treatment cannot be provided as an outpatient.

Skilled Nursing Care

Skilled nursing care refers to care that usually is furnished in a skilled-nursing facility (SNF) and can only be performed by, or under the supervision of, licensed nursing personnel. The care in an SNF includes room and board charges, registered nursing services, physical therapy, drugs, supplies, and equipment. Intermediate care and respite care may or may not be covered, and custodial care generally is not covered.

The shift in emphasis today to out-of-hospital care (i.e. less-costly alternatives to hospitalization without sacrificing the quality of the care) has resulted in development of a concept sometimes referred to as progressive care. In this environment, a patient proceeds through various levels of care, as dictated by his or her health condition, not necessarily beginning with a hospital confinement. For example, these levels could include intensive care, normal acute inpatient hospital care, confinement in a skilled-nursing facility requiring limited medical attention, and home health care.

It is well-recognized that the latter days of a hospital confinement require a lower level of care than that provided in a general acute care hospital. Accordingly, if a plan includes skilled nursing care and home health care, the patient with the concurrence of the attending physician could be prevailed upon to transfer to a lesser level of care. The obvious cost savings relative to these levels of care is the greatly reduced per diem charge, compared with a hospital's room and board charge.

Home Health Care

Like skilled nursing care (care in an extended care facility, nursing home, or convalescent home), home health care is an alternative to costly inpatient hospital care. A comprehensive range of medical care services (e.g., part-time or intermittent nursing care provided under the supervision of a registered nurse, physical therapy, occupational therapy, medications and laboratory services, and part-time or intermittent services of a home health aide) can be provided to a patient at home. Decisions to use home health care benefits are based on such factors as family capabilities and patient desires. Home health care programs are appropriate for chronically ill or disabled persons as well as for patients who require only monitoring during rehabilitation or maintenance care.

Home health care provides supportive care at costs considerably less than hospital confinement and in an atmosphere often far more restful to the patient.

Preventive Care

Traditionally, medical care has focused on treatment rather than on prevention of illness. However, many health experts today believe the incidence and/or severity of illnesses such as heart disease, stroke, and cancer can be greatly reduced through proper preventive care and early diagnosis.

Preventive care can take many forms, some of them being periodic physical examinations to minimize complications through early detection, well-baby care (under two years; including immunizations), well-child care (2–15 years; including immunizations), and patient counseling by physicians for non-illnesses (e.g., smoking cessation, weight control, diet counseling, physical fitness, nutrition). Insurers are increasingly involved in examining the value of all these forms to determine which preventive measures are health and cost effective. For example, some differences of opinion exist, even within the medical profession itself, concerning the value of annual physical examinations versus cost and the most effective use of physicians' time. Those who approve the concept of preventive physical examinations lean toward providing specific tests periodically, the frequency being based on age and sex. Ultimately, say the experts, preventive care may reduce a company's health care costs, though results are difficult to measure.

Second Surgical Opinions

''Second opinion'' has been defined as a prospective screening process that relies on a consulting physician's or surgeon's evaluation of the need for surgery that another surgeon has recommended. Thus, anyone for whom elective, nonemergency surgery is recommended is well-advised to obtain a second opinion before proceeding. While one doctor may recommend surgery, another may recommend medication or postponing an operation. A second opinion encourages doctors to review the necessity and advisability of surgery, instills patient confidence by reducing anxieties, and discloses alternatives that may avoid or postpone surgery. The decision whether to accept surgery or alternative treatment is still the patient's.

What Kinds of Surgery Are Suitable for Second Opinions?

The following are typical procedures often suitable for a second surgical opinion:

Dilatation and curettage (D and C).
Surgery of the thyroid, tonsils, or adenoids.
Surgery of the back, hip, or knee joint.
Surgery of the colon, duodenum, or stomach.
Surgery of the gallbladder or prostate.
Surgery for hernia.
Hysterectomy.
Surgery of the breast.
Surgery for hemorrhoids.
Surgery of the heart, veins, or arteries.

This is a partial list, because many observers say that almost 90 percent of all surgery can be categorized as elective and nonemergency. It is important to remember second surgical opinion programs do not cover second opinions for the following:

Normal pregnancies.
Elective abortions.
Occupational accidents or diseases.
Surgery involving local infiltration anesthesia.
Second opinions rendered while confined in hospital.
Surgery that may be performed in a doctor's office, such as incision and drainage of an abscess.
Cosmetic surgery.
Dental surgery.
Sterilizations.

How Are Second Opinions Reimbursed?

In specifically designed second surgical opinion programs, the manner of reimbursement may be as follows:

1. One hundred percent of the first $100 of such charges and 80 percent of the balance of such charges. No cash deductible applies.
2. A fixed fee (e.g., $50) to the consulting surgeon if he or she agrees to accept the fee as payment in full. Charges for necessary X-rays and laboratory tests, up to a fixed limit (e.g., $75) will be reimbursed in addition to the fixed fee payable to the consulting

surgeon. No deductible or coinsurance provisions are applicable to this benefit.

3. One hundred percent of usual, customary, and reasonable charges incurred in seeking a second (and third) opinion from a consulting surgeon, prior to being hospitalized for the proposed elective surgery. This surgical consultation benefit also includes any charges for additional necessary X-rays, laboratory tests, and other diagnostic studies. No deductible or coinsurance provisions are applicable to this benefit.

Voluntary versus Mandatory Second Surgical Opinion Programs

A second surgical opinion program is instituted either on a voluntary or a mandatory basis. The major problem with the voluntary program is underutilization. Indeed, many employees do not understand the second surgical opinion option. The degree to which voluntary programs are used often hinges directly on the enthusiasm of management in promoting the concept and the inclusion of an incentive. For example, surgery without a second opinion is reimbursed at 50 percent, whereas surgery following a second or even a third opinion is reimbursed at 100 percent.

Mandatory programs, which require patients to seek a second opinion before insurance will pay for the surgery, have been subject to many objections. They concern the denial of payment if second opinions are not obtained; payment of a reduced benefit if the claimant has surgery without getting a second opinion or after receiving a nonconfirming second opinion; regimentation that takes away the patient's right of free choice; and possible adverse effects on the physician/patient relationship. Enforcement is a problem for mandatory programs, as well as denial of payment, which can cause employee dissatisfaction. Despite the objections and concerns, mandatory second surgical opinion programs may serve as an effective cost-containment technique.

Under either type of program, and regardless of the consulting surgeon's opinion, the final decision whether to go ahead with the operation lies with the patient. The potential for cost savings in a second surgical opinion program lies primarily in the following areas:

Surgeries not confirmed and not performed.

Surgeries performed on an ambulatory rather than an inpatient basis, as initially recommended.

General reduction in surgical claims because of physician awareness of the program. This result is known as the "sentinel" effect.

Hospice Care

Hospice care is a mode of care aimed at providing terminally ill patients (i.e., patients whose prognosis for life expectancy is six months or less) with an alternative to traditional modes of treatment. The hospice concept gradually emphasizes palliative care (medical relief of pain) rather than curative care for patients for whom there is no chance of a cure. While there is no standard definition of a hospice, there are four basic principles that distinguish hospices from the traditional health care system:

1. Patient and family, not the patient alone, are considered the unit of care.
2. A multidisciplinary team, which may include a physician, nurse, home health aide, social worker, psychiatrist, psychologist, clergy, and trained volunteers as well as family members, is used to assess the physical, psychological, and spiritual needs of the patient and family, develop an overall plan of care, and provide coordinated care.
3. Pain and collateral symptoms associated with the terminal illness are controlled, but no heroic efforts are made to cure the patient.
4. Bereavement follow-up is provided to the family to help them with the grieving process.

Hospice care currently is delivered through a variety of program models, including:

1. The free-standing hospice, with or without direct affiliation with a hospital.
2. The hospice unit within a hospital.
3. The hospice team within a hospital.
4. The hospice unit in a skilled-nursing facility.
5. The so-called "hospice without walls" or home health care provider exclusively.
6. The case manager model, which provides home health care services but through existing service providers rather than through its own personnel.

Proponents of hospice care have historically argued that this form of treatment for the terminally ill is less costly than care provided in the typical hospital setting. They acknowledge that hospice care may not be a total substitute for hospital care, in that the terminal patient may at some point need to be admitted to a hospital, but they feel that hospice care has the potential to reduce the overall length of a general hospital stay and thereby reduce costs. Realistically the selection of hospice care as an alternative may depend on the specific needs of the patient and family, variables that cannot always be controlled by the mere existence of a hospice program.

Birthing Centers

These centers are a popular, cost-effective alternative to acute hospitalization for low-risk deliveries and postpartum newborn care. The centers, usually owned and operated by obstetricians or nurse-midwives, are located close to a full-service hospital–which allows easy transport for any complications that may arise during the childbearing process. Because of the popularity of these centers, hospitals have been creating these facilities within the walls of the hospitals.

CLAIMS REVIEW

The usual claims review by insurance carriers is a process in which medical care expense claims are examined before payment. Such analyses of claims do reduce the policyholder's medical care costs by identifying claims that the policyholder is not obligated to pay because of:

- Ineligibility of the employee.
- Ineligibility of a particular service.
- Duplicate reimbursement due to coverage by more than one health plan.
- Discrepancies between the services claimed and the services actually performed.
- Claims that exceed usual, customary, and reasonable charges.

Today, the claims review process generally includes two additional cost-containment techniques: utilization review and hospital bill audit programs.

Utilization Review

Utilization review (UR) is designed to reduce the incidence of unnecessary or inappropriate hospitalization. The procedure, used for both cost and quality control, involves the use of locally determined criteria to establish guidelines for appropriate admissions, hospital lengths of stay, and course of treatment. These criteria are based on age, sex, and diagnosis. The actual review process is either done by independent review organizations or, for a few large insurers, by in-house programs. In addition, some insurers are also utilizing professional review organizations (PROs), which have been established in the states by federal law to monitor the health care services provided by the Medicare and Medicaid programs. A thorough utilization review program involves preadmission certification, concurrent or continued stay review, retrospective review, and discharge planning.

Preadmission Certification

This is a process whereby an insured is required to obtain an authorization from the review program in advance (prior to admission) that an elective or nonemergency hospitalization is necessary and will be provided in an appropriate facility. The review and authorization are performed by qualified health care professionals utilizing accepted medical care criteria in order to determine the medical necessity and appropriateness of an inpatient stay and the proposed treatment plan. The result of this review is an assurance that only patients with a medical need for hospitalization are certified for admission, that the proposed treatment is customary for the diagnosis, and that opportunities for treatment to be received in more cost-containing settings (e.g., skilled-nursing facilities, outpatient surgical facilities, the home, hospices) have been identified.

In order for preadmission certification to be effective, participation must be ensured. This is done by providing a benefit design that requires a reduction in benefits for nonparticipation. For example, here is a contractual option that is being utilized:

> If preadmission certification (PAC) is not received, a per admission penalty of $300 will be imposed. This penalty is in addition to any per confinement or other deductible required by the plan and cannot be applied to the out-of-pocket.

If PAC is performed, room and board payment for any days of hospitalization not certified as medically necessary will be reduced by 50 percent.

Payment for any confinement for which outpatient care facilities were recommended will be reduced by 50 percent.

Concurrent or Continued Stay Review

Concurrent Review

This on-site review, takes place when a patient is confined to a hospital. Concurrent review is typically carried out by a nurse coordinator (i.e., a review program employee) who reviews patients' charts within 24 hours of admission, and then at designated intervals until discharge occurs in order to:

- Assess the need for admission to the hospital.
- Assign an initial length of stay and assess the medical need for any extensions.
- Assess the appropriateness of the level of care provided.
- Generally assess the progress and efficiency of the care being given.
- Abstract data for retrospective quality assessment in comparison with medical care criteria.

The nurse coordinator is allowed to authorize care that falls within predetermined explicit quality and length-of-stay guidelines. These guidelines usually are based on common practice and experience. When necessary, the nurse coordinator requests additional information from the attending physician or a decision from a physician who serves as medical adviser (also a review program employee). While the nurse coordinator assigns a diagnosis-specific length of stay, the maximum and any extensions are the purview of the medical adviser consulting with the attending physician. The date representing the minimum length of stay is flagged on the patient's chart; on that date, the patient's length of stay is reviewed and the nurse coordinator, after looking at the patient's chart, may assign a new review date. On that review date, the nurse coordinator may determine that the patient is ready for discharge. Subject to approval by the medical adviser, the nurse coordinator can also recommend that all future reimbursement be canceled; however, the absence of "medical necessity" language in an insurer's contract will void this cancellation.

Continued-Stay Review
This off-site medical review process is conducted, while the patient is hospitalized, by telephone with the treating physician at designated intervals until discharge occurs. Again using established medical criteria and length-of-stay norms, the review program professionals determine medical necessity and appropriateness of both the treatment plan and the inpatient stay.

Retrospective Review

This is after-the-fact review that applies the same medical criteria as concurrent or continued-stay review, but only after the patient is discharged. Obviously, there is more potential for controlling costs while they are occurring, but a retrospective review can still limit costs by identifying medically unnecessary bed days and treatment charges and, where appropriate, isolate unrelated charges.

This type of claims review allows an employer to establish a utilization profile to use in monitoring trends. Included in such a profile would be diagnoses, the kinds and prices of medical services purchased by each employee, where they were provided, and the portion paid by the company. Appropriate action could then be taken in excessively high-cost areas.

Discharge Planning

This process occurs when it is apparent that the patient will be leaving the facility. For patients who have not recovered, arrangements are made for continuing care (e.g., in a skilled-nursing facility; for home health care). The attending physician documents and explains the care and treatment needed after discharge.

A basic objective of any utilization review program is to ensure that the patient is not located in a setting of care that exceeds medical necessity. Far too many beds are filled with patients who should be in a nursing facility, outpatient facility, or at home. Achievement of this objective would result in great cost savings. An important result of an effective UR program is the reduction of ''defensive medicine,'' where physicians tend to overuse medical services for fear of malpractice suits. Accepted utilization criteria define the necessary tests and services for common diagnoses.

Employer interest in UR (i.e., to scrutinize claims to determine the appropriateness of the care and services rendered, and to determine the costs eligible for coverage) is being expressed individually and through employer coalitions. The potential for implementation of such programs continues to be contingent on the density of insureds in a given geographic area and on the contractual commitment of an area's hospitals to participate in a private-sector utilization review program. Ultimately, it is the individual physicians who control the resources of a hospital. If any UR system is to have an impact, the behavior of the physicians who have demonstrated consistent patterns of high utilization and excessive lengths of stay by diagnosis must be changed.

Hospital Bill Audit

Hospital bill audit programs exist because insurers have long been aware that good medicine and good accounting do not necessarily go hand in hand. To deal with this problem, insurers use independent or internal (sometimes both) auditors to conduct a continuing series of audits of hospital claims most likely to be in error. These include: bills exceeding a certain amount (e.g., $10,000), room and board charges less than 40 percent of the total bill, certain lab tests (e.g., complete blood counts, urinalyses, SMA–12/60s, and sodium potassium levels) listed more than once every 24 hours, therapy sessions (physical and occupational) prescribed more than normal, bills that show evidence of treatment for nonrelated conditions, drug charges that are large and frequent, patients who are hospitalized longer than necessary (the number of days confined does not relate to the diagnoses involved), and a high number of charges for whole blood and blood derivatives without any credits given for donated replacements.

Some of the most prevalent errors are in pharmacy, laboratory, radiology, inhalation therapy, and occupational therapy. Auditors check the doctors' orders, the nurses' notes, pharmacy records, the total charges for therapy divided by the recorded number of hours spent by the therapist, and radiology and lab records, as well as the room and board charges and length of stay for a given diagnosis. Insurers have found that every dollar spent on hospital bill audit programs saves almost two dollars in overcharges. It is important to note that hospitals underbill as well as overbill, and it is hard to get a hospital to cooperate in an audit if an insurer won't agree to reimburse on underbillings.

EXTERNAL COST-CONTROL SYSTEMS

External medical care cost-control systems include such elements as ambulatory care facilities, HMOs, PPOs and large claim management.

Ambulatory Surgical Centers

A significant portion of the diagnosis and treatment provided to hospital inpatients can be rendered more economically on a "walk-in" basis when appropriate facilities and adequately trained personnel are available. Thus, ambulatory care facilities such as ambulatory surgical centers, emergicenters and urgicenters, free-standing diagnostic radiology centers, facilities for the treatment of end-stage renal disease, comprehensive outpatient rehabilitation facilities (CORFs), and independent clinical labs serve this purpose.

Recognition that many surgeries could be performed on a same-day, outpatient basis (e.g., cataract removal, tonsillectomies, simple hernias, removal of noncancerous cysts, minor gynecological procedures, and biopsies of various kinds) led to the development of ambulatory surgical centers. The concept was fostered by the development of new surgical techniques and by the discovery of faster-acting anesthetics that wear off sooner and leave fewer aftereffects.

Two types of ambulatory surgical centers are in operation today: those independent and separate from any hospital—commonly referred to as free-standing ambulatory surgical centers (FASCs) and often called "surgicenters"—and those operating under the auspices of a hospital and known as short-procedure units. In any case, the purpose of these facilities is the performance of surgical procedures considered too demanding for a doctor's office, but not serious enough to warrant an inpatient hospital stay. However, the benefits for ambulatory surgery usually are treated as an extension of inpatient hospital benefits with the same level of coverage as if the surgery had been performed on an inpatient basis.

What Are the Savings in the Ambulatory Surgical Concept?

It is estimated the percentage savings for procedures performed under this concept can range from 15 to 40 percent. Incidentally, the proponents of free-standing (i.e., not hospital-based) surgical facilities point to two reasons for such savings. First, they state they operate more efficiently than do hospitals and thus can handle more patients at lower average cost.

Second, they need not provide extensive ancillary and support services, nor 24-hour staffing, and thus are not obliged to redistribute costs for expensive procedures and services to the minor surgical patients.

The counterargument of hospitals is certain services must be provided to the community (e.g., emergency room, open-heart surgery, burn treatment, intensive care) and the revenues to fully support these and other expensive services must be obtained by distributing the costs throughout the spectrum of hospital charges. The development of competing, low-cost free-standing surgical facilities therefore is indicated as contributing to higher community costs. Furthermore, some hospital officials assert independent free-standing day surgery services further worsen hospital finances by neglecting to handle a proportionate number of medically indigent patients. In today's world, competition has tempered these hospital arguments as hospitals are erecting free-standing facilities.

It also should be noted in this ''savings debate'' that some nonsurgical procedures are appropriate in a day surgery setting. For example, among the most frequently performed procedures are chemotherapy and extensive radiological examinations. Finally, it is estimated that between 20 and 40 percent of all surgical procedures could be performed on an outpatient basis.

What Are Some of the Advantages of the Ambulatory Surgical Center Concept?

1. Lower cost than inpatient surgery as a patient forgoes a two-to-three day hospitalization by having surgery performed on an outpatient basis
2. Less time away from home and work, because this type of surgery is less disruptive and permits a patient to return to a regular schedule more quickly.
3. Frees hospital beds for more acutely ill patients.
4. Scheduling is quick and relatively easy, as opposed to the process of securing a hospital bed for inpatient surgery, which may require a wait.
5. Offers great convenience to physicians and patients.
6. The environment is conducive to high patient morale and faster recovery.
7. May obviate the need for the expansion of hospital beds.

By eliminating overnight (or longer) confinement, the cost of a surgical procedure is reduced drastically, while the traumatic effect of hospital confinement on a patient is minimized. Thus, coverage of ambulatory surgery serves to lower a company's health care expenditures in the short term. However, unless community hospitals respond to the decreased patient load by reducing beds, labor, and assets, hospital rates undoubtedly will rise and effectively negate any savings.

Other Ambulatory Care Facilities

Emergicenters and urgicenters (which provide 24-hour, 7-day-a week service to treat minor conditions such as cuts, bruises, and removal of sutures), free-standing diagnostic radiology centers, facilities for the treatment of end-stage renal disease, comprehensive outpatient rehabilitation facilities (CORFs), and independent clinical laboratories all have become more common in recent years. Employers can encourage the utilization of these less costly ambulatory care facilities by waiving plan deductibles and coinsurance.

Health Maintenance Organizations (HMOs)

An increasingly popular form of alternative health care delivery is the health maintenance organization, which refers to any public or private organization providing a full range of health services to an enrolled population (generally through employer-sponsored plans) within a defined geographic area in return for a fixed, prepaid premium for all services provided. The two major types of HMOs are distinguished by the manner in which their physicians are organized and are called individual practice associations (IPAs) and prepaid group practices.

Individual Practice Associations

An IPA is composed of a central administrative component (e.g., a foundation sponsored by a medical society, an insurer, or a hospital) and a group of physicians in a community. The participating physicians continue to practice in their own offices and are reimbursed on a fee-for-service basis according to agreed-upon fee schedules. The HMO, however, receives a prepaid premium from its enrollees, and it is thus "at risk" financially for providing the stipulated health care services to its subscribers. The individual physicians are also "at risk" in the sense their fees from the plan may be reduced in the event of poor overall plan experience. Conversely, they may share in any plan profits.

The IPA's greatest strength, physicians practicing in their own offices, is also its greatest weakness because it lacks the peer interaction and physician selection that facilitates control of utilization and costs. IPAs usually do succeed in lowering inpatient hospital utilization rates, but they seldom attain the levels associated with effective prepaid group practices.

Prepaid Group Practices

A prepaid group practice may be a medical group model, in which the plan contracts with an existing or forming group practice, or a staff model, in which physicians are hired by the plan and paid a salary. The participating physicians represent the various medical specialties and practice as a team. Primary patient care is provided in multispecialty clinics usually associated with the HMO's own hospital or with participating hospitals. The HMO receives a prepaid premium from its enrollees and is "at risk" for the costs of the covered health care services because it must provide them for the predetermined premiums as well as meet their financial obligations to their closed panel of physicians.

Employers normally want to provide adequate health care benefits to their employees and their dependents in an effective, economical manner. Following are some of the advantages and disadvantages of HMOs for employers and their employees.

Advantages of HMOs

- Broader coverage with emphasis on preventive care.
- Less administrative work.
- Coordinated services at one location (only true for prepaid group practices).
- Lower hospitalization rates, i.e., hospital days per 1,000 insureds.
- Potential for greater cost effectiveness through incentives to the primary care physicians to constrain health care expenditures.

Disadvantages of HMOs

- Loss of freedom of choice of doctors and hospitals.
- Limitations in choosing specialists as HMO primary care physicians control access.
- Lack of, or inadequate, cost and utilization data collection system.

- Geographically limited.
- Employee misunderstandings (communication problems).
- Out-of-plan area coverage problems.
- Loss of personal physician relationship.
- Location of HMO facilities (transportation, accessibility problems).
- Concern about the fiscal condition of HMOs.
- The expense of offering an HMO option (which can be material).
- Insignificant overall savings. (This has been experienced by many who have been insured under HMOs.)
- Satisfaction with existing systems of health care delivery by health care consumers.

Despite the disadvantages, HMOs offer a potential solution to problems found in many traditional health care plans. Such problems include

1. Difficulty in finding satisfactory medical care services: an HMO provides access to a team of doctors of all specialties available at most times.
2. The fragmentation of services, e.g., services are at various locations and communication is poor: an HMO team works together at a single location, where patient records and histories are readily available (true for prepaid group practices but not IPAs).
3. The high cost of services.

High inpatient benefits encourage the use of high-cost hospital facilities. The money saved by an HMO in limiting hospital confinements goes, in theory, to provide preventive care and comprehensive outpatient benefits.

Today, with the emphasis of insurers on managed health care, many of the elements that at one time were unique to HMOs are now included in insurance company health insurance products. For example, insurers are routinely offering preadmission certification, concurrent or continued-stay review, retrospective review, and discharge planning. In addition, insurers are providing increased benefits for the use of preadmission testing, outpatient care and treatment, home health care, and hospice care. Many insurers are now including HMOs as well as PPOs in their product lines. In fact, "triple options" (i.e., traditional insured health care plan/an HMO/a PPO) are being offered by many insurance companies, enabling employers to negotiate with one entity rather than three; an influx of employees into the HMO or PPO doesn't distort the demographics or experience of the traditional insured plan.

Preferred Provider Organization (PPOs)

Simply stated, a PPO is a network of hospitals and/or doctors organized to provide a range of health care services for fees specified in a formal contract and performed according to agreed-upon standards.

This recent type of alternative delivery system came into being because many providers are unwilling to assume the financial risks of HMO participation and many employees are unwilling to limit their choice of providers to HMO-participating doctors and hospitals.

Hospitals are organizing PPOs in order to maintain occupancy rates in areas where HMOs and (PROs) private review organizations are reducing hospital utilization. Physicians are affiliating with PPOs in order to maintain patient volume in areas where there are too many physicians and where other health care delivery systems are taking patients away. Employers support PPO development in order to control both inpatient and outpatient utilization in areas where health care costs are escalating out of control.

Participation in a PPO enlarges a provider's patient base (i.e., increased market share) and at the same time creates a minimal financial risk for providers who have agreed to a fee schedule. The PPO option is described and included in an employer's existing medical care benefits plan, but unlike an HMO, no prepayment or capitation amount is paid to the providers. A PPO offers many of the advantages of an HMO, but unlike an HMO it offers freedom of choice for the patient relative to doctors and hospitals. For example, under the most popular type of PPO arrangement known as a point of service plan the covered person can choose to receive care from either a PPO provider or a non-PPO provider. If a non-PPO provider renders care, the benefits usually are reduced (i.e., a deductible is required; increased coinsurance is required).

While PPOs are not an all-purpose remedy for current problems in the health care marketplace, all new opportunities for cost containment should be explored, developed, and utilized if effective from quality and cost standpoints.

Large-Claim Management

Traditionally, employers haven't had the opportunity to review catastrophic and high-risk claims from the perspective of total management, that is, addressing the care needs of the patient and family, the health care services provided, and the costs of the care. Today, large-claim management programs (also called medical case management) are available to policy holders from independent review organizations or from a few large insurers by in-house programs. The initial stage of a serious illness (e.g., neonatal high risk infant, severe stroke, Lou Gehrig's disease [ALS], multiple sclerosis) or injury (e.g., major head trauma, spinal cord injury, amputations, multiple fractures, severe burns) is the point at which the outcome for better or for worse can be most dramatically changed.

Medical case management firms do a comprehensive assessment of a case, taking into account the patient's needs and treatment plan, committing resources available, and evaluating the work environment and family situation. These case management professionals have the ability to work with medical care providers to implement alternatives if and when they are appropriate. Savings in a large claim management program are generated in three ways:

- Alternative care—movement from a high-cost acute care facility (hospital) to a skilled-nursing facility, a rehab facility, or a home health care program.
- Accelerated care—care provided through a specialized facility, additional or intensive therapy, patient and family training, or early home care.
- Reduction of medical complications—complications (e.g., digestive or respiratory problems, skin diseases, or circulatory complications) can often be reduced or prevented through proper care and patient or family education.

Of course, the patient and his or her attending physician always have the last word on the plan of treatment.

HEALTH EDUCATION AND PROMOTION

In today's environment, the support of health education/promotion activities is considered a universal good. Health education/promotion has been defined as "efforts to encourage healthy lifestyles, discourage risk-associated behavior, and educate individuals about health care and the appropriate use of health services." There is a growing belief that healthy lifestyles can improve health status. In this regard, the public has become increasingly cognizant of the impact of lifestyle—smoking or excessive drinking, uncontrolled hypertension, poor diet, lack of exercise, and the like—on the incidence of disease and injury. Individuals have begun to assume more responsibility for their own health, with the understanding that changes in lifestyle can significantly reduce risk factors associated with premature death and disability.

A new philosophy also has emerged regarding the role of the employer in promoting well-being or wellness. There is growing opinion among at least major employers that they have a distinct responsibility to help improve the quality of health of their employees, and company-sponsored programs in health education/promotion offer a promising means to carry out that responsibility.

Health education includes a combination of learning experiences (both informational and educational) that help people to make informed and voluntary decisions about their health and safety, and about the health resources available to them. It provides individuals and families with the knowledge for making their own choices and pursuing their own actions about what is important for health and prepares them to accept the consequences of their decisions just as they would in any form of endeavor.

A health promotion program uses a variety of educational/behavioral strategies (e.g., health risk appraisal, one or more risk-reduction components, health education) to foster changes in daily life habits that could lead to better health. It attempts to integrate the concepts of disease prevention and lifestyle modification with the more traditional practice of treating diseases after they occur. The expectation is that such a program will benefit not only employees and their families but the employer as well by effecting reduced absenteeism and turnover, improved employee morale and productivity and savings on insurance and other employee benefit costs—important objectives of any employer. The program costs might be considered an investment in a company's human resources. The following examples of health promotion programs vary in difficulty to start, in the effort, equipment, and dollars required, and in their benefit:

Smoking cessation.

Hypertension recognition and control.

Stress management.

Weight control.

Employee assistance programs.

Exercise fitness.

Alcohol/drug abuse control.

Cancer risk reduction.
CPR training.
Accident risk reduction.
Self-care.
Emergency medicine.
Glaucoma screening.
Wise utilization of medical care benefits.

This new philosophy is consistent with the mounting intensity of interest in and expectations for health promotion activities. It also coincides with efforts to more effectively contain the escalation in the direct and indirect health, economic, and social costs associated with accidents and illness.

Is There Evidence that Health Education/Promotion Programs Reduce Health Costs?

In all fairness, it is difficult, at this time, to obtain hard data on cost savings, because of the short time in which these programs have existed. To see the effects of risk factor intervention on morbidity and mortality will take years. However, common sense alone suggests that prevention is preferable to curing, that staying healthy is less expensive than being sick, and that improved lifestyles should improve a person's health and longevity.

CONCLUSIONS

There are no "quick fixes" to the problem of rising health care costs; no magic solutions that lie near at hand. It is self-delusion to believe that major cost-containment results can be achieved in the short term or middle term without inflicting unacceptably high levels of discomfort and discontent on the public, the providers, and the payors (Medicare, Medicaid, health insurance companies, Blue Cross/Blue Shield plans, HMOs, PPOs, self-insureds, and self-pay patients). Total care costs are essentially a product of volume of service and cost of service. To make significant inroads on either of these factors requires major structural changes in the system, or major behavioral changes on the part of the populace and the providers, or both. There is little sign to date of major behavioral changes, and no established method for producing such changes in large populations.

In the final analysis, the physician continues to be the primary decision maker in the medical care system. The choice of what needs to be done, how much needs to be done, and where it is to be done generally is under the physician's control. Therefore, review by physicians of physicians' practices for propriety, i.e., the provision of services that are medically indicated, may be the best possibility for controlling system-wide health care costs, as the goal of cost containment should be the promotion of an adequate supply of reasonably priced and rationally distributed resources.

All these health care cost-containment techniques are still experimental, and their cost effectiveness has not yet been fully determined. They do however, contribute to cost containment in two ways:

1. They tend to increase the cost consciousness of patients or physicians or both.
2. They tend to foster increased interaction and cooperation among the insured, the insurer, and often the hospital or physician.

It is unlikely that any one health care cost-containment technique will produce large savings for an employer. However, when a number of these techniques are put into effect together, significant cost reductions can be achieved.

CHAPTER 14

HEALTH MAINTENANCE ORGANIZATIONS IN THE 1990s

Alfred F. Meyer

An analysis of the origins, status, and near-term future of health maintenance organizations (HMOs) in the United States is shaped by certain constraints. The past is reasonably clear, the present somewhat clouded, and the future only partially visible. HMOs have evolved dramatically in recent years, from a collection of mostly small, financially vulnerable companies that were part of a "movement" into a more mature "industry" dominated by major national and regional organizations that have incorporated many of the previously independent plans into corporate systems competing against each other in various markets around the country.

This chapter covers a range of topics, including:

- The origins of HMOs.
- Various model types and structures.
- Organizations that are similar to HMOs and compete for the same business (preferred provider organizations [PPOs]).
- HMO benefit designs offering coverage for out-of-plan services (point-of-service [POS]) products.
- The role of physicians and hospitals in the development and operation of HMOs.
- How HMOs are marketed.
- The role of state and federal regulators.
- Benefit design and rating issues.
- The features of HMO operations that may make it possible for them to offer a comprehensive set of benefits at prices usually

below traditional indemnity programs that sometimes offer less comprehensive benefits.

Finally, this chapter addresses briefly the challenges currently facing both the industry and those who must make decisions about buying services from companies active in the industry.

ORIGINS

The HMO concept is not new. It has existed throughout this century in a variety of forms and in various parts of the country. Prepaid group practices were established in the Pacific Northwest, Oklahoma, and California during the first three decades of this century. In 1929, for example, the Ross-Loos Clinic of Los Angeles signed a contract with the Los Angeles water and power departments to provide medical care to employees of the departments. The success of this initial contract resulted in its expansion to include other employees in Los Angeles. The early prepaid group practice plans were resisted by many physicians in private practice and by local medical societies. At this time, the concept of health insurance per se was in its infancy in the United States. What would evolve into the Blue Cross concept of hospitalization began in 1929 in Texas. In this context, then, the early prepaid group practice developments were very significant.

During the early 1930s, what would become the Kaiser Permanente Health Plan was started by Sidney Garfield, MD, to serve workers building an aqueduct to bring water from the Colorado River to Los Angeles. Dr. Garfield's association with the Kaiser organization grew to include the provision of health care to workers and their families at construction and shipbuilding sites in various locations in California and Washington state. By the end of the Second World War, Dr. Garfield had developed a delivery system that served many thousands of Kaiser company employees and family members. When the Kaiser Permanente Health Plan was opened to the public following the war, it was well-received and began a pattern of steady growth that would take it at last count to a national system of approximately 6 million members in 16 states and the District of Columbia.

In addition to the programs that arose in the West, programs that resembled in many respects what are now regarded as HMOs were started in Washington, D.C., New York City, Minneapolis-St. Paul, and a few additional areas in the United States. As with the programs in the West, the prepaid group practice programs that were started elsewhere in the country encountered heavy opposition from many proponents of fee-for-service medicine.

Notwithstanding this early work, it would be fair to note that HMOs as they now are known were barely visible on the American landscape into the late 1960s and early 1970s. The major period of growth of HMOs in the United States can be measured from the mid-1970s, due largely to a federal program initiated pursuant to P.L. 93-222, the HMO Act of 1973. This statute was the cornerstone of what was called the "health maintenance strategy." This strategy, which Dr. Paul Ellwood named and promoted, consisted of federal grants and loans to organizations to investigate the feasibility and plan the development of what would be called "federally qualified HMOs." The program was viewed by the federal government as a potential solution to the growing problem of health care cost escalation, which had become acute by the early 1970s.

Spurred by a substantial legislative and financial initiative on the part of the federal government, what can be characterized as the activist phase of the federal "health maintenance strategy" lasted from approximately 1974 through the early 1980s. With the advent of the Reagan administration in 1981, there was a major change in federal policy with respect to the financing of HMOs. While continuing to support the concept of HMOs as a cost-effective vehicle for delivering high-quality health care, the federal government encouraged HMOs to look to private sources of capital. Prior to eliminating the federal government as a source of grants and loans, the Department of Health and Human Services issued several hundred million dollars in grants and loans to HMO start-ups. As a result of this initiative, the HMO industry has grown dramatically into a multi-billion dollar enterprise serving more than 35 million people in 46 states and the District of Columbia.

TYPES OF HMOs

A general discussion on the origin of health maintenance organizations serves to introduce the subject. To understand more fully what HMOs are and how they work, one must examine the various types of HMOs and the basic characteristics that distinguish one form of HMO from another.

There are three basic types of health maintenance organizations. They are referred to as group, staff, and individual practice association (IPA) models. In addition, there is a hybrid form, the mixed-model HMO, a combination of the basic models. The primary distinguishing feature of each model is the relationship between the HMO company and the physicians who deliver the health care to the members of the HMO. All the other features are in some way or another shaped by this basic relationship.

Group Model HMO

In the case of the group practice model *HMO*, illustrated in Figure 14–1, the distinguishing feature is the distinctive contractual tie between the HMO company and a medical group controlled and operated by physicians. The contractual relationship is likely to be complex and enduring. It addresses a variety of economic and service issues that have the effect of linking the financial well-being of the HMO company and the medical group. In a group model, the medical group is at financial risk for providing or arranging for the provision of a comprehensive range of services to be used by the subscribers who join the HMO.

The economic aspects of the contract are likely to be driven by fairly objective actuarial assumptions on the types and extent of services that will be used by the population served. The amounts budgeted for the services at risk typically are adjusted to reflect the age and sex of the individual subscribers and covered beneficiaries. Depending on the size of the medical group and the population served, the contract may contain risk-sharing and stop-loss arrangements that protect the medical group from catastrophic or "shock" claims that occur randomly in a population.

The size of the medical group may range from a handful to several hundred physicians. In its purest form, the medical group exists primarily for the care of subscribers who belong to an HMO. To the extent that fee-for-service medicine is practiced, it typically is not the dominant feature of the practice and often is an economic expedient allowed to cover unused capacity or accommodate patients who no longer are covered by the insurance mechanism of their employer or other group coverage arrangements. In the case of long-established group model HMOs, the medical groups are major organizations with well-structured mechanisms for doing the business of medicine in a cost-effective manner. In the Kaiser organization, for example, the medical groups typically are mature, well-established organizations with formal hierarchies and strong administrative-support mechanisms.

FIGURE 14–1
HMO Group Practice Model

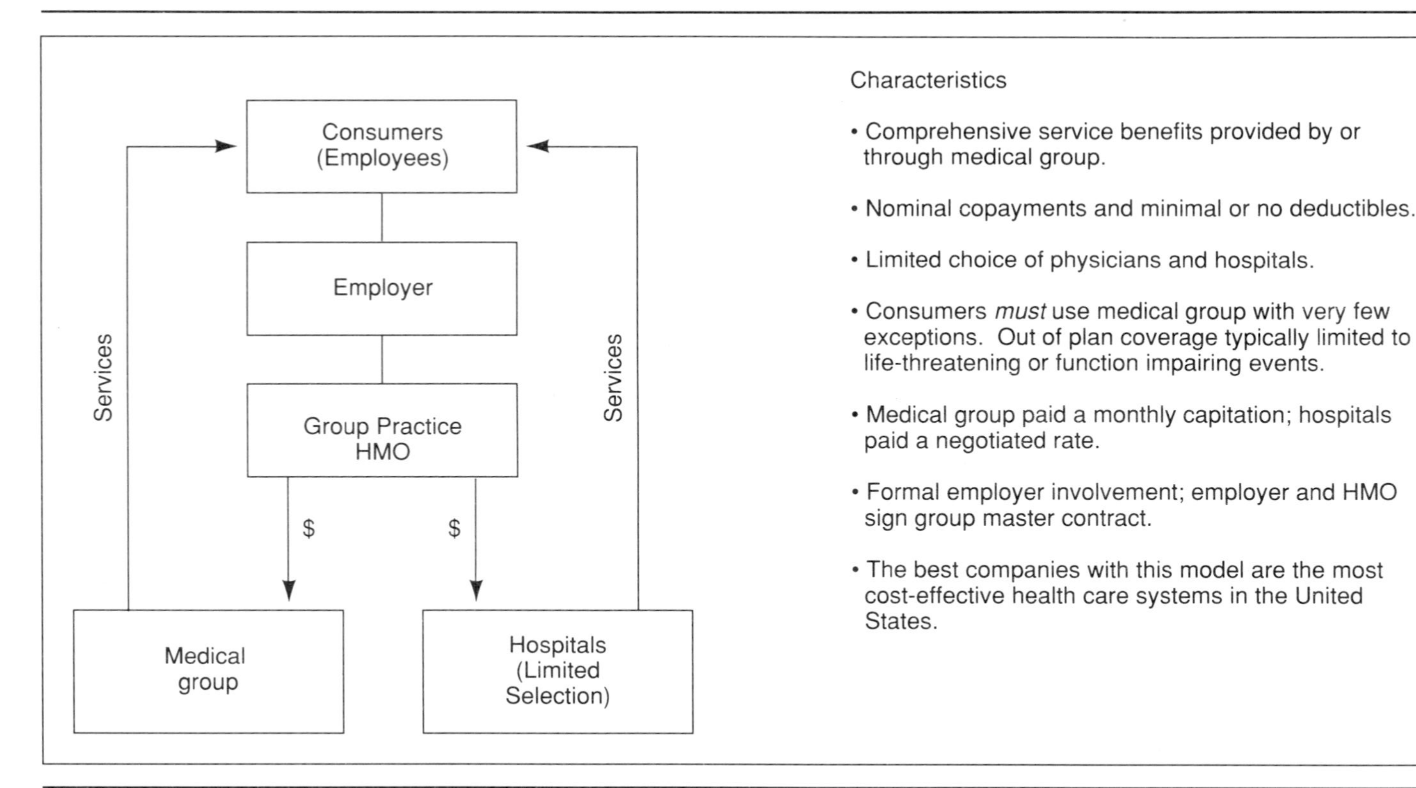

Characteristics

- Comprehensive service benefits provided by or through medical group.
- Nominal copayments and minimal or no deductibles.
- Limited choice of physicians and hospitals.
- Consumers *must* use medical group with very few exceptions. Out of plan coverage typically limited to life-threatening or function impairing events.
- Medical group paid a monthly capitation; hospitals paid a negotiated rate.
- Formal employer involvement; employer and HMO sign group master contract.
- The best companies with this model are the most cost-effective health care systems in the United States.

In group model HMOs, new physicians are recruited into the organization for a trial period during which they are given an opportunity to demonstrate their compatibility with the goals, objectives, and values of the medical group. Those who successfully complete a qualifying period of several years may become partners in the group. The salaries paid to the physicians who practice in a medical group are established by the group and reflect such things as productivity, specialty practiced, and amount of administrative work performed.

Depending on the age and size of the medical group and the population served, the physician members include representatives from all the primary care specialties and many of the medical and surgical specialties and subspecialties. Once a medical group becomes well established and gains a reputation for clinical competence, it should be able to recruit skilled physicians easily. Many physicians are attracted to a group practice HMO by the opportunity to practice in a colleagial setting that emphasizes the practice of high-quality, cost-effective medical care. In addition, physicians in a group model HMO are free to concentrate on the practice of medicine without the business and administrative distractions that typically accompany private practice.

The subscribers who join a group model typically do so at work, where they have an opportunity to select among health insurance options offered by their employer. Subscribers who select a group model HMO typically are required to obtain their care at a health center, clinic, or other designated service site. These centers are the focus for almost all primary care and much of the ambulatory specialty care provided by the HMO to the subscriber and covered dependents pursuant to the group master contract between the HMO and the subscriber's employer. Hospital-based care on both an inpatient and ambulatory basis is arranged by the medical group through hospitals with which the group is affiliated or with which the group has contractual ties.

The subscribers and their covered dependents may select a personal physician and develop a relationship similar to that with a physician in private practice. The patient may make appointments with a specific physician at the health center and in all important respects rely on that physician for the care required. As in private practice, patients in a group model HMO may change physicians within the medical group for any reason. Depending on the size of the medical group, there may be more or less opportunity to find a compatible fit between physician and patient.

In the case of needed specialty care, the primary care physician or other members of the staff arrange for referrals to physicians who are members of or under contract with the medical group. Depending on the age of the HMO and the size of the medical group, referrals for obstetrical care, dermatology, and other services may be within the group or to private-practice physicians in the community who have agreed to treat HMO members on referral. Outside specialty care arrangements typically are with a small panel of physicians and may be of limited duration until the medical group generates enough volume to bring the required medical specialty on board.

In general, the use of hospital emergency rooms is restricted to cases that are life threatening or seriously impair function. Subscribers are expected to use the health center for all care unless otherwise authorized. Group model HMOs typically have comprehensive coverage arrangements and extended hours that permit urgent care to be delivered at the health center or other authorized location.

Staff Model HMO

To an employer considering offering a variety of HMO options to its employees, a staff model HMO, illustrated in Figure 14–2, may appear to be identical to a group model HMO: patients receive care from physicians engaged primarily in the care of HMO subscribers and covered dependents; care is delivered at one or more health centers; the administrative arrangements of enrolling in the HMO and receiving health care appear to be identical; and the restrictions on using non-HMO physicians are the same.

The critical difference, however, is that the major part of the care provided in a staff model HMO is performed by physicians who are *employees* of the HMO company. Unlike their counterparts in a group model, physicians at a staff model HMO are paid a salary established by the HMO. The salary is likely to reflect some differentiation among physicians based on the local market for physicians in various specialties. In other respects, however, staff model physicians practice medicine in a setting much like that of their colleagues in a group model setting. Depending on the size of the HMO, the medical administrative hierarchy contains one or more medical directors, several department heads, and often a physician who is an elected officer of the HMO corporation. This individual, the chief medical officer, is responsible for the oversight of the health care delivered to subscribers and often is directly accountable to

FIGURE 14–2
HMO Staff Model

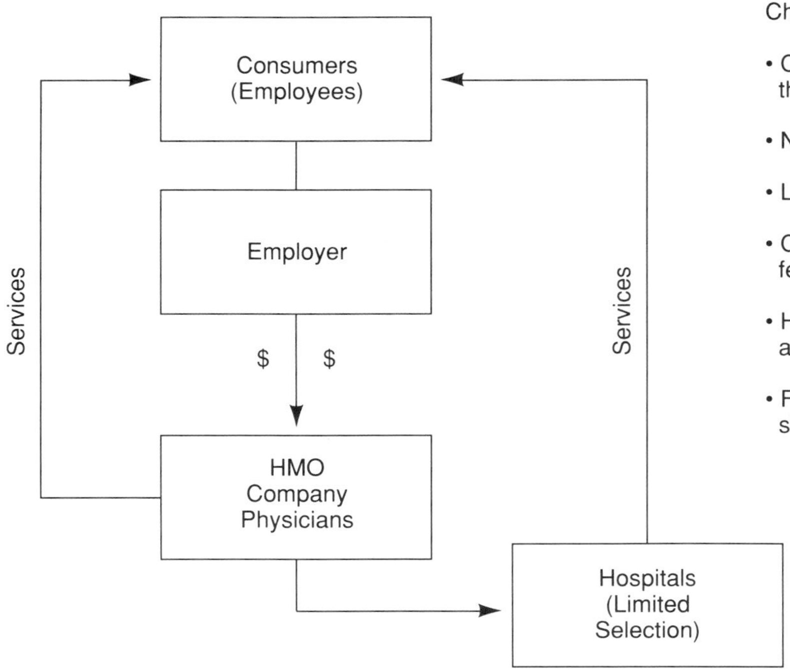

Consumers (Employees)

Employer

$ $

HMO Company Physicians

Hospitals (Limited Selection)

Services

Services

Characteristics

- Comprehensive service benefits provided by or through staff physician.
- Nominal copayments and minimal or no deductibles.
- Limited choice of physicians and hospitals.
- Consumers *must* use HMO's staff physicians, with very few exceptions. Out of plan coverage typically limited.
- HMO's staff physicians paid a salary; hospitals paid a negotiated rate.
- Formal employer involvement; employer and HMO sign group master contract.

the board of directors of the HMO company for the quality of medicine practiced.

Given the similarity in practice styles and settings, it is not surprising that a number of staff model HMOs have been transformed into group models through an agreement between the HMO company and the participating physicians effecting the change.

IPA Model HMO

The individual practice association (IPA), illustrated in Figure 14–3, is the most difficult type of HMO about which to generalize. The classic IPA Model had its origins in the Foundations for Medical Care, established by physicians in private practice in California, Oregon, and Washington. Originally, the Foundations were established by county medical societies to perform a number of functions, including protecting private practitioners from the erosion of their business by group model HMO activity. In the late 1940s and 1950s, the success of the Kaiser Permanente plans in attracting patients away from physicians in private practice motivated several county medical societies to establish an alternative to group models (also called "closed panel plans"). The alternative, foundation plans (or "open panel plans"), served as the model for what are now called IPA model HMOs, the most numerous HMO form in the United States at present.

The essential feature of the health care delivery system in an IPA is the dominant role of private-practice physicians in the provision of both primary and specialty care. The HMO may contract with one or more IPAs and through the IPAs have access to large numbers of private-practice physicians, or it may contract directly with private-practice physicians.

In many cases, the HMO contracts with physician-owned corporations that have a large number of physician shareholders, who elect officers to represent their interests in negotiations with the HMO. Some of the more well-established IPAs retain managerial, legal, and accounting professionals to advise them on day-to-day operations and in negotiations with the HMO.

For the employer and the potential subscriber, the IPA may offer a number of advantages over other HMO models. Depending on the number of physicians participating in the IPA, the subscriber may not have to change physicians. This makes it easier for the employer to

FIGURE 14–3
HMO IPA Model

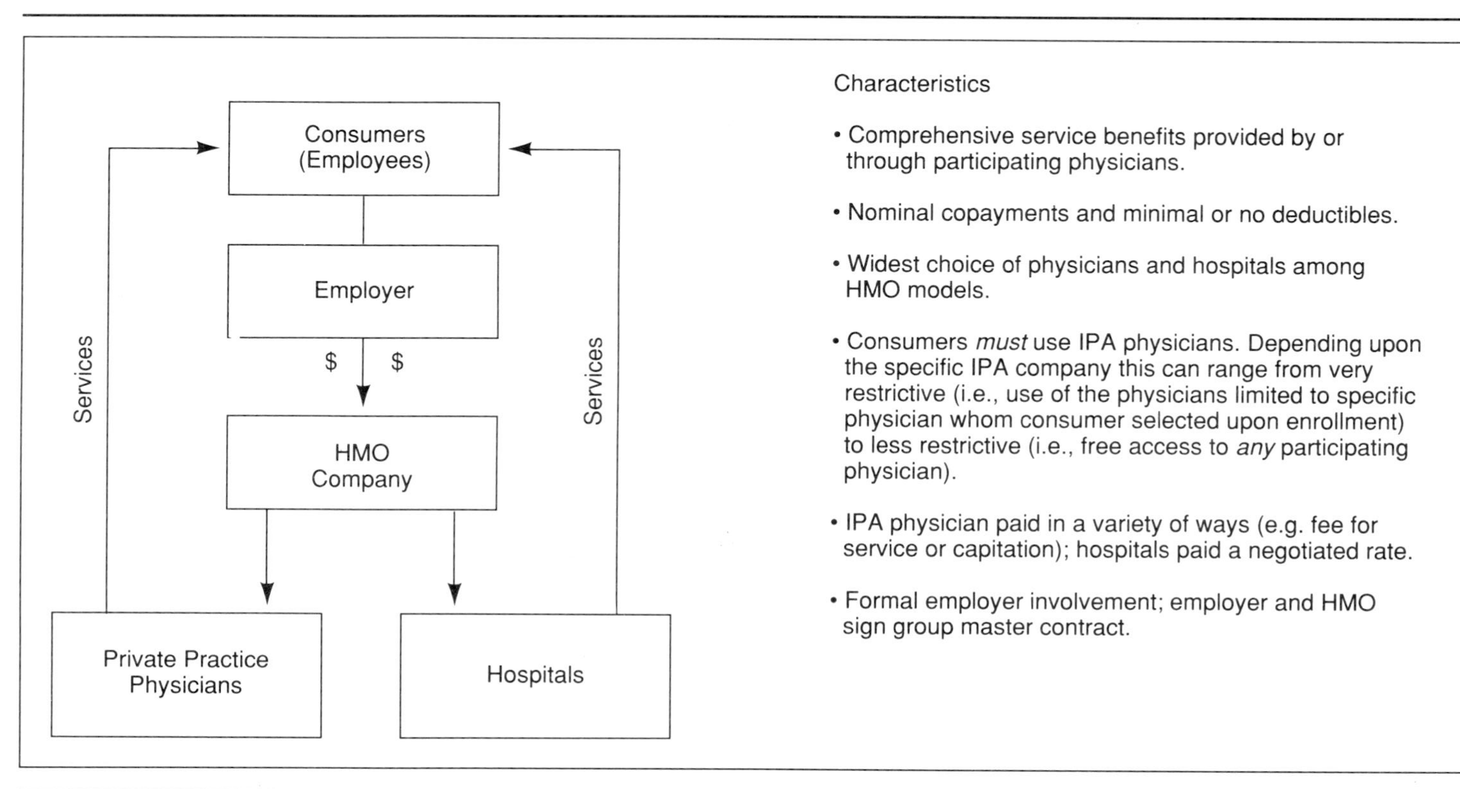

introduce the IPA to its employees than if the HMO option entails a disruption in care experienced by the employees and covered dependents. Aside from what typically is a modest copayment, the subscriber receives care from a private-practice physician at the physician's office without paying the normal fee for service. In most cases the patient must use a participating physician except for genuine emergencies. In this respect, the IPA is like the other models.

Unlike those other models, the IPA lends itself to multiple HMO companies recruiting the same doctor to serve patients under a variety of HMO labels. In larger, urban settings, a physician in private practice may "join" two or more organizations that contract directly with HMOs or insurance carriers. This benefits the physician who is trying to build a practice. To the extent that each HMO company or insurance carrier has different administrative procedures or benefit designs, it significantly complicates the physician's office activities. It also may make for confusion on the part of the employer, especially where competing HMOs charge somewhat different premiums for access to some of the same physicians and hospitals.

Mixed Model HMO

With the increasing complexity of the health care delivery system and the growing competitiveness of the health insurance market, the mixed model HMO has evolved. This model combines aspects of the health care delivery system of two or more of the traditional models. The mixed model HMO typically is a network based on a variety of contractual relationships linking together a variety of providers, including physicians in group practices and solo practitioners.

From an employer's perspective, the mixed model HMO may have a number of distinct advantages. Depending on the community served, the mixed model may offer a wider variety of service sites than either a group or staff model. To the extent that the mixed model combines group practice sites as well as one or more groups of private-practice physicians organized into IPAs, it is likely to appeal to employees. On the other hand, mixed models may incorporate the economic and operational disadvantages that arise when a health care delivery system is built around diverse physician groupings lacking any strong philosophical or clinical linkage.

Point-of-Service Product

Since the mid-1980s, a number of HMOs and insurance carriers sponsoring HMOs and HMO-like products have offered what generally is called a point-of-service (POS) product. (See Figure 14–4.) This product permits subscribers and covered dependents who belong to the HMO to avail themselves of the comprehensive benefits typically associated with an HMO and, in addition, go outside the HMO-provider system for services normally covered only if received within the system. In return for this flexibility, the HMO usually charges an added premium. In addition, a variety of cost-sharing features exist that require the subscriber who goes outside the system to shoulder some of the cost in the form of fee-schedule limits and coinsurance. As of 1991, the POS product has achieved a degree of popularity, particularly to the extent that it is incorporated by consultants to major companies in requests for proposals (RFPs) that solicit bids from insurance carriers and HMOs for health insurance quotes.

Preferred Provider Organizations (PPOs)

As of 1990, there were more than 700 PPOs (see Figure 14–5) of various types operating in the United States. Since corporate benefits and human resource decision makers often consider PPOs in the same context as HMOs and other forms of alternative delivery systems (ADSs), they are mentioned here briefly. For a more detailed discussion of PPOs, see Chapter 15 of the *Handbook*.

PPOs have realized considerable growth in the last decade because the PPO often features the breadth of benefits associated with a health maintenance organization with some added flexibility in out-of-system services. In addition, PPOs have been promoted as cost-effective health care delivery alternatives by various groups, including commercial insurance carriers, Blue Cross/Blue Shield plans, benefits consultants, third-party administrators (TPAs), and hospital systems.

PPOs resemble IPAs in some respects. The provider system typically consists of hospitals in the community and physicians in private practice. Often a PPO consists of a health care delivery system that has contracted with one or more insuring entities for services to the covered employees and dependents of a number of employers in a given area. The system

FIGURE 14–4
Point-of-Service Product (Open-Ended or Leaky HMO)

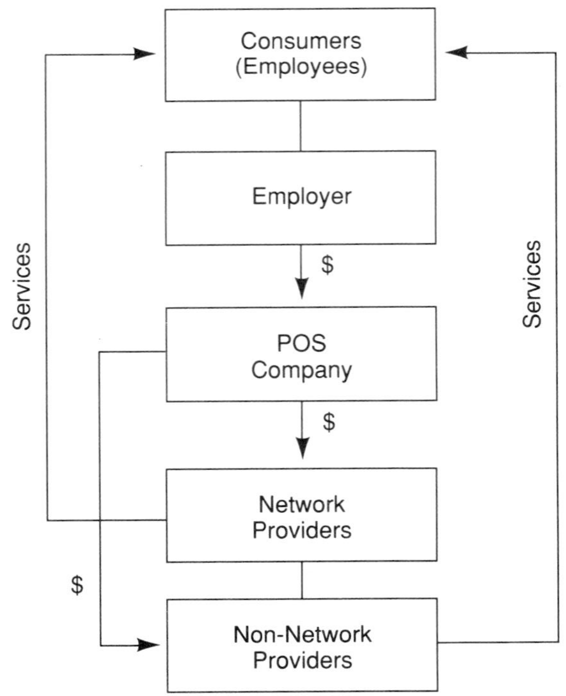

Characteristics

- See previously-listed characteristics of HMO's.
- Consumer has ability to access non-network providers for specialty care, subject to deductibles and coinsurance.
- Role of primary care physician varies, depending on plan design.
- More flexible for consumer and more expensive.

FIGURE 14–5
Preferred Provider Organization (PPO)

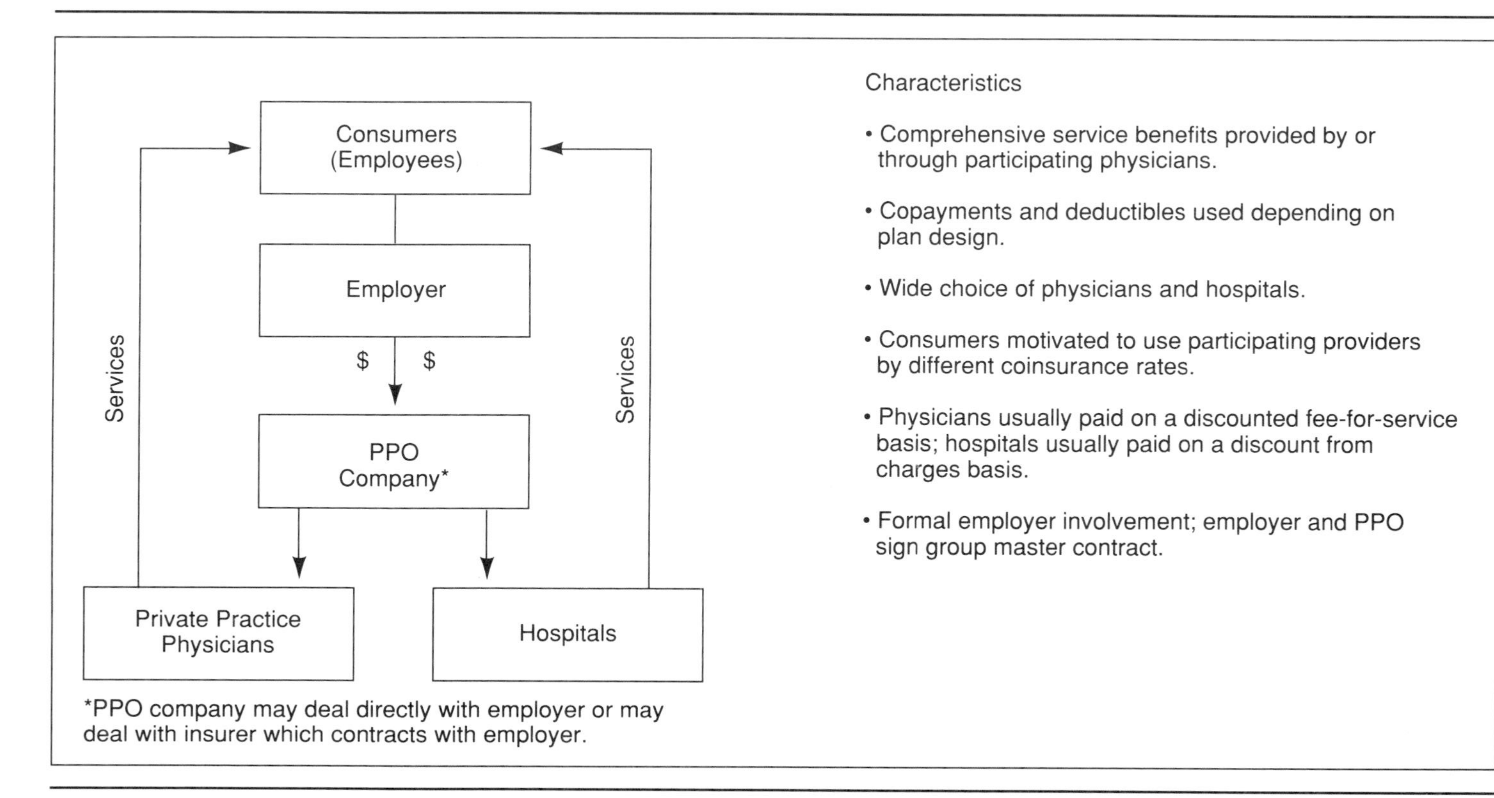

may include a number of participating hospitals and some or all of the physicians on their staffs. The hospitals and physicians typically agree to discount their charges in return for an expected increase in volume of business from the people who join the PPO.

PPOs often are discussed in the context of a "triple option" of plans offered by a single carrier to an employer. The three health insurance options include a traditional indemnity plan, an HMO, and a PPO. Conceptually, the "triple option" has several clear advantages. The employees are likely to better comprehend the coverage options offered by a single carrier, particularly if the employer and carrier initiate a program that clearly explains the options and the distinguishing features of each. Employers also assume, especially where the experience of the three products is pooled by the single carrier, that the selection bias many associate with community-rated HMO products is likely to be reduced.

Opponents of the PPO concept argue that the PPO model and associated insuring assumptions may not endure, especially with the emergence of the point-of-service feature in the HMO industry. One criticism is that if the PPO has a weak managed care program and rich benefits, it is likely to be expensive compared with comprehensive major medical plans and HMOs with a strong managed care component, and this may negate the attractiveness of a PPO (either in a free-standing context or as part of a triple option) both to employers and potential subscribers. The critics argue further that to the extent the PPO introduces a managed care component that restricts the behavior of subscribers and providers, it will resemble closely an IPA Model HMO. Their final argument is that the advantages of packaging and explaining the features of multiple-option products by a single carrier do not require three different products. It may be done effectively with two, and when those two are indemnity coverage based on a comprehensive major medical plan and an HMO with a point-of-service feature, a PPO may not be needed or desirable.

THE REGULATION OF HMOs

Typically, HMOs are regulated by one or more state agencies. The statutory and regulatory oversight is focused on a range of issues including financial solvency, rates charged, mandatory benefits, and quality of care delivered. In New York and Pennsylvania, for example, the regulatory responsibilities are divided between the states' insurance departments and health departments. The divided and occasionally overlapping jurisdiction of HMOs by multiple state agencies is more the rule than the exception and adds a note of complexity to HMO operations. It also limits the extent to which HMOs can respond to requests by employers for variations in benefit design and rating formulas.

In addition to the role of state agencies in the regulation of HMOs, the federal government plays a major role in the regulatory process, particularly in the case of federally qualified HMOs under the terms of the HMO Act of 1973 and its subsequent amendments. This act, the regulations promulgated pursuant to it, and the programs associated with the early years following its enactment have been the major driving force in the HMO industry over the last 15 years. It is fair to say that federal policy has influenced all HMOs, including those regulated solely by state agencies, because the existence of hundreds of federally qualified HMOs has influenced the industry in general and the expectations of the public about HMOs.

From the mid-1970s through the early 1980s, the position of the federal government was that of active promoter, banker, and demanding regulator of HMOs. Since the first term of the Reagan administration, the position of the federal government has shifted, especially in the area of financing. In keeping with the philosophical orientation of the Reagan administration, the federal government encouraged HMOs to look to the private sector for development and operational capital. As a result, HMOs evolved from what could accurately be characterized as a cottage industry in the late 1970s and early 1980s into an industry that includes HMOs operating under the aegis of a number of major national and regional companies consisting of commercial insurance carriers, Blue Cross/Blue Shield plans, and publicly traded HMO companies.

In the several amendments to the HMO Act of 1973, the Congress has sought to introduce greater flexibility into the statutory and regulatory control over HMOs without abandoning a substantive role for the federal government. Thus, while federally qualified HMOs must continue to adhere to a rather specific set of minimum benefits and abide by limits on out-of-pocket expenses paid by subscribers in the form of copayments, the federal government has responded to requests for flexibility in a number of areas, including rating methodologies. In this specific context, HMOs are no longer required under the HMO Act to use community rating as a basis for pricing the products sold. Based on the most recent set of amendments to the Act, federally qualified HMOs may use adjusted community rating—a method of rate setting that permits the HMO to set a rate for a rating period based upon an actuarially derived estimate of what the HMO calculates will be the actual experience of the particular account in question.

These changes in federal law and regulation, when they are not otherwise limited by state statutes, regulations, or administrative policies, have permitted federally qualified HMOs to be somewhat more responsive to the complexity and volatility that have characterized the market for group health insurance and related employee benefits in the last 15 years.

Unlike the somewhat vulnerable collection of predominantly small, independent HMOs that served a few million people in a handful of locations during the 1970s, the HMO industry enters the 1990s in basically sound fiscal health, serving more than 30 million Americans in hundreds of markets around the country. In significant measure, the supportive role played by the federal government in the 1970s and 1980s made this possible. This evolution has prompted some to suggest that it is time for the federal government to conclude its statutory and regulatory oversight of HMOs and leave that responsibility to the states, the traditional regulators of the insurance industry.

HOW MEDICAL AND HOSPITAL CULTURE SHAPES HMO OPERATIONS

An HMO, regardless of the model, is a complicated business built upon a foundation of relationships that determines where subscribers will receive services as well as what the HMO will pay for those services. Since health care delivery in the United States is shaped by the unique social and clinical culture that has grown up around an area's physicians and hospitals, it is necessary to understand this culture in designing and operating a successful HMO.

The number of physicians in an area in relationship to the general population is a starting point. The ratio between primary care and specialty care physicians also is important. Depending on the number of physicians practicing in various specialties and subspecialties, how busy these physicians are, and how influential particular groups of physicians are on hospital medical staffs, the HMO may have more or less success in organizing a cost-effective delivery system in a community. In some settings, the role of the local medical and specialty societies may influence the response of physicians to the prospect of an HMO in the community. Regardless of whether one is developing a group or staff model HMO or an IPA, the condition of private-practice medicine and its relative strength and cohesiveness influences the approach to be taken in developing an HMO.

From the perspective of many physicians in private practice, fee-for-service medicine is superior to all forms in which there is oversight by an outside party or insurance carrier. As a practical matter, however, the ''golden age'' of fee-for-service medicine may be over for many physicians in private practice. Except for a few physicians who are the beneficiaries of geographic or other anomalies, most physicians have some piece of their practice paid for, directly or indirectly, by insurance carriers or government. And since medicine is never as ''organized'' or monolithic as it may appear to the lay world, it is possible for HMOs to develop successful programs over time, even in the face of resistence on the part of many segments of the medical community.

Notwithstanding the various positions taken by physicians in a given community toward an existing or proposed HMO, the interests of the local hospital or hospitals may diverge substantially from that of the medical staff. If a hospital is running a high census of private-pay patients, it may have no interest in encouraging an HMO to develop, lest the HMO reduce the aggregate number of hospital days generated in the community. Conversely, if a hospital is running well below capacity in terms of private-pay patients, it may well be interested in developing a relationship with an existing or proposed HMO, especially where the HMO will generate additional use of the hospital's ambulatory and inpatient services. In this case, the hospital is more likely to endure criticism from some segments of its medical staff because it has no reasonable alternative if it hopes to survive as a viable institution.

The reaction of a particular hospital to the prospect of doing business with an HMO ultimately will be shaped by a variety of factors, including the attitude and policy perspective of the hospital board of directors, the financial position of the hospital, whether it is a free-standing institution or part of a system, the sponsorship and reputation of the HMO in question, and any experience the hospital administration has had with HMOs.

The attitude of the medical and hospital community toward a particular HMO or HMOs in general is significant to corporate decision makers for a number of reasons. To the extent the individuals representing corporate purchasers of health insurance or HMOs select one or more options built upon unstable medical or hospital support, it is likely that the subscribers who select such options will encounter problems that ultimately will translate into employee relations problems. Accordingly, it is always advisable for employers or other organizations considering doing business with HMOs and related organizations to be aware if any substantial strains exist in the relationship between the HMO and the physicians and hospitals that will be used to any extent by the HMO.

THE "SELLING OF HMOs"

The marketing and sales activities associated with HMOs have much in common with other forms of group health insurance product sales. Many HMOs have a direct sales force that exists exclusively for the development of prospects and closing of sales with group purchasers of health insurance. Typically, the HMO salesperson is seeking to have the particular HMO product he or she represents added to the list of options an employer will offer. Much of the ongoing HMO sales activity is quite professional and typical of what is found in most forms of group insurance sales. The successful HMO salesperson recognizes the necessity for developing a collaborative relationship with the decision maker at the account. This consultative sales approach is now the norm and is typical of the HMO sales approach as HMOs have matured and entered into the mainstream of health insurance options.

In addition to the direct sales force most often associated with free-standing HMO operations, HMOs also are marketed by commercial insurance carriers and Blue Cross/Blue Shield plans as part of a menu of products offered to the marketplace. Depending on the market and the client, the HMO product may become part of a comprehensive set of products presented to a given account through a direct sales force or through brokers and consultants. Since the successful installation and initial operation of the HMO product requires the development and presentation of an effective program of employee communications, the sales cycle and associated activities usually are more complicated with an HMO than with traditional health insurance products.

DO HMOs MANAGE PRUDENTLY?

In spite of the many attempts of individuals in academic and professional circles to address definitively the question of the relative efficiency of HMOs in comparison with fee-for-service medicine and traditional insurance approaches, the issue remains in dispute. Selection bias is suggested as a major factor in the apparent efficiency of HMOs. Whether a given HMO saves a given employer money or, as some suggest, simply takes the better risks and leaves the employer's indemnity plan with the sicker population is something that lends itself to objective analysis.

Many major employers now require HMOs to provide reports on the utilization of HMO services by the employees and their covered dependents who enroll through the employer in a given HMO. The major trade associations of the HMO industry, the Group Health Association of America (GHAA) and the American Managed Care and Review Association (AMCRA) have developed standard formats for the dissemination of such data and have urged HMOs to cooperate with employers who request account-specific utilization information, provided patient confidentiality is protected. This information, along with greater use of variable rating formulas, will not only address the selection question, but will permit major employers, at least, to be charged rates that reflect the experience of their employees and covered dependents. As this occurs, and as larger insurance carriers offer an employer the opportunity to pool its experience across health insurance lines, the selection issue should diminish in importance.

Without resolving the selection issue, it is clear that in a number of critical areas HMOs operate differently from traditional insurance carriers. HMOs use a number of specific, patient care management techniques that produce efficiencies without adversely affecting the patients in question. The application of the techniques employed vary from one HMO model to the next and within model types from one HMO to another. While much depends on the local medical and hospital environment, the following two patient management principles are observed by most successful HMOs.

Specialty Care

Referrals for routine specialty care for HMO patients are controlled and focused on participating specialists whenever possible. In an IPA model HMO, this often is done formally through a process that requires a written approval, often on a multipart form developed by the HMO for this purpose. The form authorizes a specific specialty care physician to see a specific patient for a specific and often narrowly defined purpose. In addition to serving as an authorization document for the specialist, the form often is incorporated into the billing process of the HMO and permits both the early financial accrual by the HMO of the services likely to be provided and timely payment to the specialist who attaches the authorization form to the bill submitted to the HMO. In group and staff model HMOs, the process typically is less complicated and may simply require the patient to secure an appointment at the health center for the required consultation or treatment by a specialist on staff at the HMO or one who is on contract with the HMO for a specific number of sessions each month. Of course, in emergencies or urgent cases, the primary care physician will arrange for an immediate consultation and necessary treatment.

While restrictive use of specialists is common enough in the case of group or staff model HMOs, IPAs also are increasingly sharply limiting the panel of participating specialists in a number of specialty areas, including allergy, podiatry, dermatology, radiology, and psychiatry. HMOs that have employed this smaller panel of participating specialists in specific areas have found it cost effective. The requirement for feedback by the specialist to the primary care physician or his or her surrogate is an essential characteristic of the referral control process. The feedback not only permits the primary care physician to follow the progress of his or her patient, but also ensures that the HMO is able to further develop its referral process as a result of patient reaction and clinical outcomes.

Hospital Care and Alternatives

The major source of health care expenses in all forms of health insurance is hospital stays. HMOs have demonstrated a propensity to avoid certain hospital stays altogether and to manage effectively those stays that are necessary. Efficiencies achieved in the area of inpatient care make it possible for HMOs to offer comprehensive benefits at prices that are competitive with less inclusive forms of health insurance.

The mechanism through which an HMO member is admitted to a hospital is significantly different from that used by most traditional insurers. It is this mechanism that not only reduces the number of admissions of HMO patients to a hospital in comparison to community averages but also reduces the number of days that HMO patients once admitted to a hospital stay for a particular diagnosis. Most HMOs use a specific authorization process when the participating physician wishes to admit an HMO patient. The process is mandatory, except for emergency admissions. It requires the physician to be precise concerning why an HMO member is going to be admitted to a hospital. If it is for tests or for procedures that can be performed on an ambulatory basis, the physician will be queried why he or she is proposing to admit the patient to a hospital given more cost-effective alternatives. In an HMO with a number of participating hospitals, the HMO may suggest that the physician admit the patient to a particular hospital and to a specific specialist's service for the treatment of a diagnosis.

This dialogue requires a great deal of sophistication on the part of the HMO's managed care team. It typically involves trained nurses and, when necessary, HMO physicians who discuss a particular case with their colleagues. Once a patient is in the hospital, the HMO's managed care staff keeps on top of treatment plans, anticipated length of stay, and impediments to discharge. To the extent the HMO can provide support to the physician and patient to ensure a timely discharge, it will do so. This support often takes a variety of forms, including home care and related services that ensure that a patient's recovery is not impeded.

CONCLUSION

HMOs are not a panacea for what ails the American health care delivery system. HMOs are part of the solution. Given the magnitude of the challenge, Americans will have to undertake a major departure from traditional forms of financing and delivery of health care in the United States within the next few years. The lessons HMOs have learned about efficiency, effectiveness, and quality of care are portable to a variety of financing and delivery mechanisms. To this extent, then, HMOs are likely to have a major impact on the decisions reached by those who purchase or influence the decisions to purchase health care during the next decade.

REFERENCES

Mayer, Thomas R., and Gloria Gilber Mayer. "HMOs: Origins and Development." *The New England Journal of Medicine,* 312, Feb. 28, 1985, p. 590.

"Health Care Hall of Fame." *Modern Healthcare,* Sept. 10, 1990, pp. 78 and 85.

Susan J. Palsbo. "HMO Market Penetration in the 30 Largest Metropolitan Statistical Areas, 1989." *GHAA Research Briefs,* December 1990, no. 13.

HMO Act of 1973, P.L. 93-222, Dec. 29, 1973.

HMO Amendments of 1976, P.L. 94-460, Oct. 8, 1976.

HMO Amendments of 1978, P.L. 95-559, Nov. 1, 1978.

HMO Amendments of 1981, P.L. 97-35, Aug. 13, 1981.

HMO Amendments of 1988, P.L. 100-517, Oct. 24, 1988.

CHAPTER 15

PREFERRED PROVIDER ORGANIZATIONS (PPOs)

Sarah H. Bourne
Susan M. Garrahan

During the 1980s, spiraling health care costs moved the issue of health care cost containment from the primary domain of employee benefits managers to the top of the agenda of senior executives, the federal, state, and local governments, union leaders, individual citizens, and all health care providers. While overall health care costs remain largely untamed today, it is not through a lack of effort on the part of employers and various third-party payors, who—in an attempt to stem this upward trend—have developed and implemented many new approaches to health care delivery and financing during the last decade. ''Managed care'' has become a standard part of the health care vernacular, along with ''utilization review'' and ''quality assurance.'' These programs are an integral part of most employers' medical plans today. Utilization review and quality assurance are discussed later in this chapter. Managed care is discussed here briefly and is covered in detail in Chapter 16 of the *Handbook.*

This period of great frustration and experimentation has seen the explosive growth of the preferred provider organization (PPO). In 1983, the American Hospital Association estimated there were 115 PPOs.[1] By 1990, that number had increased to almost 700, according to the

[1]Dorothy L. Cobbs, *Preferred Provider Organizations: Strategies for Sponsors and Networks* (Chicago: American Hospital Publishing, Inc., 1989), p. 9.

American Association of Preferred Provider Organizations (AAPPO). It is estimated that approximately 60 million employees and their dependents nationwide have access to a PPO today.[2]

This dramatic growth in PPOs resulted from the interaction of several key factors:

1. With the advent of the federal prospective payment system in 1983, hospitals found their Medicare reimbursements significantly reduced and in turn sought to increase their private-pay caseload to make up this deficit by contracting directly with payors (insurers and employers).
2. Physicians were trying to control the growth of restrictive managed care approaches by developing a model with which they could live.
3. Employers and other payors were experiencing double-digit cost increases, and were not realizing the cost control that they expected from health maintenance organizations (HMOs).
4. Individuals were resistent to the restriction on choice of provider characteristic of an HMO.
5. Federal regulations that governed the development of PPOs were few compared with those that governed HMOs.

In the latter part of the 1980s, the nation's major insurance carriers played—and continue to play today—a significant role in the development and expansion of PPOs. These carriers have made heavy capital investments in the purchase and development of PPO networks, which has led to aggressive PPO marketing to employers, often to the exclusion of promoting their traditional indemnity business.

PPOs have thus become an integral part of the health care landscape. Many employers have incorporated PPOs into their benefit plans, some have considered but chosen not to add a PPO, and others continue to analyze such a change. Making an informed decision—whether or not to offer a PPO and how to structure it—amid the variety and complexity of products and services available requires a commitment of time and resources as well as a carefully planned blueprint for action. An employer's first step is to understand the design elements of a PPO and

---

[2]Louise Kertesz, *Business Insurance*, December 1990, p. 1.

the various forms each element can take. Next, an employer must assess its internal objectives regarding benefits in general and managed care in particular. The employer then must analyze its own claims history to understand its employees' pattern of health care utilization. In addition, the employer must review the geographic distribution of its employees to gauge the accessibility of available networks. Based on this analysis, the employer can assess the suitability of available PPOs or custom-designed networks for its employees. And, finally, the employer must determine how best to integrate the PPO into its existing medical benefit plan in order to realize expected utilization and cost control.

BACKGROUND

The preferred provider organization is one of the most common forms of managed care today. The term "managed care" can be defined as an approach to delivering health care services in which a person's access to care is controlled by the health care provider, employer, or insuring organization with the expectation that cost control will result. That is, the managed care approach assumes that there is a tradeoff between free access to providers and the cost of services delivered. As managed care mechanisms have matured, quality also has become a major focus, since poor quality care may result in the need for additional services and expense.

The basic health care delivery mechanisms in operation today vary greatly in the degree of access and cost control offered. Traditional indemnity insurance without managed care mechanisms offers free choice of providers but virtually no cost-control potential outside of the effects of cost sharing through deductibles and coinsurance. On the other side of the spectrum, staff model HMOs allow access only to staff providers and are purported to offer the greatest cost control. Occupying the middle ground of this continuum is the PPO.

The first generation PPO, which featured negotiated service arrangements and the preservation of both choice of providers and fee-for-service payment, was introduced in the early 1980s. These PPOs were composed primarily of a panel of physicians and hospitals, a negotiated payment mechanism, and benefit incentives to use PPO providers. Little variation from this simple model was available. *Sponsorship* typically was by a provider group, either a hospital, a physician group, or a specialty practice, such as a mental health care practice. Payors followed providers in sponsoring PPOs, waiting to see the concept accepted by the marketplace before proceeding. The state of California may be considered the first payor to sponsor a PPO. In 1982, state legislation was passed (AB799) that enabled California's Medicaid program, MediCal, to contract selectively with providers for the care of its beneficiaries.[3]

The *network of providers* normally was a simple panel of primary care physicians, selected acute care specialists, and hospitals. Little consideration was given to the quality of care provided by the physician or institution, or to whether their practices were cost effective. If a physician belonged to an association that was to be included in the PPO, the physician, too, would be included regardless of his or her willingness to support the managed care concept. In addition, the inclusion of ancillary services, convalescent care, mental health services, or alternative treatment facilities was uncommon.

The *payment mechanism* was a discount from normal fee-for-service charges, under which the payor continued to bear all risk. While negotiated discounts varied from region to region, hospital discounts could average from 15 to 25 percent and physician discounts from 5 to 15 percent.[4] Since any losses incurred by providers through discounting their services could be regained through increases in utilization, the call for utilization review (UR), in which a third party participates in the decision about appropriateness of care, was made quite early. However, because the appeal of a PPO to many participating physicians was maintaining freedom in the practice of medicine, they demanded that UR be conducted by local, physician-run UR services rather than by independent UR organizations.

The *incentives* used to channel patients to network providers were enhanced benefits (perhaps 100 percent coinsurance) if the individual used network providers, and the pre-existing level of benefits if the individual used a non-network provider. This so-called incentive arrangement was not very successful at containing costs (most of the discounts were given away in the form of increased benefits), yet it was acceptable to many employers at the time as an intermediate step to ease employees into managed care.

---

[3]Cobbs, *Preferred Provider Organizations*, p. 10.

[4]Marianne G. Brackey, et al., *Fundamentals of Flexible Compensation: 1990 Supplement*, Hewitt Associates, p. 150.

PPO DESIGN TODAY

Despite the dramatic growth of PPOs in the late 1980s, many employers never achieved the cost savings they were anticipating from their PPOs. It became readily apparent that discounts alone would not necessarily yield savings. Many lessons have been learned about what it takes to manage health care costs and utilization since the first generation PPOs were introduced. It is now a widely held belief that health care cost control can be realized only through comprehensive plans that provide the appropriate level of care in the appropriate setting. There also must be systems in place for monitoring utilization, quality, plan performance, and individual satisfaction and well-being.

PPOs have continued to add services in order to demonstrate to employers that they are no longer just discounting mechanisms and to respond to employer demands for proof of savings. A PPO can take on many forms today. It can appear as a tangible, independent organization (one that markets a network of provider services and administration to employers or other payors) or as a less tangible, contractual relationship (between providers and payors) to establish a network. The key elements of PPOs are described below.

Sponsorship

While providers, third-party administrators, employers, or combinations of these in joint ventures are sponsoring PPOs, the predominant sponsor today is the national insurance carrier. Through the development of new networks and the purchase and combination of existing networks, some of the major carriers today have in excess of 100 networks in every major metropolitan area across the country. The large networks cover between 1 and 2 million individuals, while some networks are larger still. Due in part to the significant capital investment in these networks, carriers continue aggressive marketing of PPOs to employers.

Other PPO sponsors include regional Blue Cross/Blue Shield plans that are combining what were local networks into national affiliations; independent PPOs merging with one another to better serve the multistate employer; national hospital chains in ventures with local physician groups; universities with affiliated hospitals and medical school faculty; and large national employers with providers in areas where there are high concentrations of employees.

While there was a movement to develop national health care delivery systems in the 1980s, the trend today is toward regionalized health care, including that provided through PPO networks. Network sponsors have realized that while services must be available on a national scale to serve national employers, the delivery of health care is best described as a local business. Thus, in addition to the common prerequisites for success (understanding the health care market, developing an appropriate panel of providers, incorporating the necessary managed care mechanisms into the network, etc.), PPO sponsors must manage their networks locally as well as control them centrally. The major carriers have an advantage here, given their experience and the national scope of their business, which has helped them achieve the significant role they now play in the sponsorship of PPOs.

Comprehensive Panel of Providers

PPOs today are including not only primary and acute care services in their networks but also ancillary services such as home health care, outpatient rehabilitation, skilled nursing care, and mental health services. By offering a comprehensive range of delivery settings, the PPO can ensure that individuals are treated within the network in the most appropriate and cost-effective setting. If comprehensive services are not offered, individuals may remain in a more costly setting because the service they need is not offered through the network and must be obtained from a non-network (i.e., nondiscounted) provider. The AAPPO considers a comprehensive, managed panel of services one of the most important elements of a progressive PPO and makes it a priority in granting accreditation.[5]

Gatekeeper Approach

Some PPOs are incorporating the *gatekeeper approach*—seen previously only in the HMO model—whereby primary care physicians (internal medicine, family practice, pediatrics, etc.) act as the point of contact for all health care services, particularly specialty care. While the cost-savings potential of the gatekeeper approach continues to be debated, some PPOs have begun to add this feature to help contain costs.

---

[5]Cobbs, *Preferred Provider Organizations,* 1989, p. 3.

Number and Mix of Providers

The number of providers needed to build a comprehensive panel may vary a great deal. At one time the "25 percent rule" was an accepted standard. This rule suggested that a PPO network should include 25 percent of a service area's physicians and hospital beds. It was believed that this would maintain a high degree of exclusivity yet ensure adequate service and geographic coverage. Exclusivity was important to providers who wanted assurance that the PPO would yield patient volume. Adequate access to specialists and convenient access to provider offices was important to employers to meet employee needs. These interests are still important yet can be met by a well-constructed panel, with more regard paid to the mix of specialties represented than to the sheer number of providers included. For example, a university that contracts with its associated hospital for primary and acute care services and uses one or two other provider groups in the area for specialty care can adequately serve the needs of both providers and subscribers. Thus, the "25 percent rule" itself is less important than ensuring that the number and mix of providers meets the needs of a particular employer or payor.

Payment Mechanisms

Mechanisms for reimbursing providers have changed dramatically since the first generation PPOs and now more commonly include *risk-sharing arrangements*. Some of the various mechanisms that currently are used to reimburse hospitals and providers are shown in the following table.

Payment Mechanisms/Risk-Sharing Arrangements

Hospitals	*Physicians*
Discounted Fee-For-Service (FFS)	Discounted FFS
Per diem	Fee schedule
Diagnostic Related Group (DRG)	Group capitation

Payment mechanisms have changed over the years in an effort to better control total costs. To assure that providers do not "game" the system by increasing utilization or inappropriate admissions, PPOs have sought providers who support the managed care philosophy, accept reimbursement through a mechanism that controls utilization as well as cost, and will share risk through arrangements such as fee schedules or DRGs. While risk sharing with hospitals has been a standard feature, PPOs are increasingly sharing risk with physicians, too, through fee schedules and group capitation arrangements.

Payment mechanisms also have evolved in response to the belief that PPOs place too great an emphasis on reducing costs through discounts. Such an emphasis actually may detract from what is now considered the top priority—cost-effective care. If Provider A performs a procedure with excellent results, even if he or she charges more for that initial procedure than Provider B, total costs may be lower if follow-up costs are less than they would be with Provider B. The belief is that the highest quality care is the most cost-effective care.

Channeling Incentives

Channeling incentives—establishing different levels of benefits for network and non-network care—typically are designed to meet the needs of individual employers. In some cases, however, providers dictate the nature and extent of incentives needed to capture increased patient volume. While early "incentive only" structures may have been designed to ease individuals into managed care alternatives, employers now are using a combination of incentives and disincentives to more aggressively channel employees to network providers. Examples of typical incentives and disincentives are presented later in this chapter.

Utilization Review (UR), Quality Assurance (QA), and Provider Selection and Monitoring

Progressive PPOs are capitalizing on UR and QA activities to provide high quality, cost-effective care. A provider selection and monitoring program is another characteristic that the AAPPO looks for in an accredited "managed care PPO."[6] An effective program requires tremendous commitment from the utilization management staff as well as data collection, analysis, and reporting capabilities to support their efforts. It might involve a retrospective review of a physician's practice patterns at the local hospital as a requirement for acceptance into the network. Once

---

[6]Ibid, p. 4.

accepted, the physician would agree to be reviewed concurrently to ensure that he or she continues to practice high quality, cost-effective medicine. Then, if problems in practice patterns were identified, the PPO would work with the physician to correct the situation. Likewise, hospitals in the network would agree to similar reviews that would ensure that the most appropriate, cost-effective treatment was being delivered.

Data Collection, Analysis and Reporting Services

The effectiveness of a PPO can be demonstrated only by the information it produces. Therefore these services are becoming increasingly sophisticated as PPOs mature. Data is being used routinely for UR and QA functions and is essential to support provider selection and monitoring programs. An equally important purpose for excellent data collection and analysis is to monitor the performance of the PPO in managing costs. Employers should be able to examine and compare claims experience after PPO introduction with their experience before PPO introduction to determine how extensively the PPO is being used, if it is controlling utilization, and if it is saving health care dollars. PPOs able to demonstrate cost savings (or an attributable improvement in experience) to employers will have a competitive advantage and may begin to share risk with the employers (e.g., charging fees as a percent of savings).

Demonstrating savings is neither an easy task nor an impossible one. By comparing providers' non-network (full) charges with their network (discounted) charges, an employer can calculate the savings that accrue from network utilization. Admittedly, providers may increase the volume of services provided to recoup the losses they incur because of discounts, which could offset the savings the employer otherwise would realize from the discounts. However, if the right panel of providers has been selected to begin with—one supportive of the managed care concept and committed to providing only appropriate care—and if the proper utilization controls are in place, an employer can expect to reduce costs through the use of the PPO.

Comprehensive Case Management

A relatively novel design element for PPOs, comprehensive case management focuses on high-cost, catastrophic cases and seeks to ensure the delivery of high quality, cost-effective care in the most appropriate setting. It involves management of all aspects of an individual's care and coordination of the many services that might be needed, including alternative treatments. Acting within the context of a PPO, a case manager would manage an individual's case so as to keep the individual within the network if possible (if the needed specialty were available) or direct him or her to the next best, non-network alternative based on appropriateness, cost effectiveness, and accessibility.

PPOs/HMOs—SIMILARITIES AND DIFFERENCES

In spite of the growth and evolution of managed care networks, it is readily apparent that the health care market has not settled on the perfect managed care model. PPOs and HMOs can in many ways be considered transitional products; in fact, the distinctions between PPOs and HMOs are disappearing as each model adopts features typically attributed to the other.

PPOs are increasingly entering into risk-sharing payment arrangements with their providers and are adopting provider selection and monitoring programs and gatekeepers, features that have long been the hallmark of the HMO. Meanwhile, some HMOs are dropping their capitation payment arrangements in favor of various fee-for-service arrangements; others are no longer using the gatekeeper approach to service delivery. In fact, the fastest-growing HMO model today is the open-ended HMO (OEHMO), which in many ways is more similar to a PPO than to a true HMO. Largely as a response to employers' and employees' demand for provider choice, OEHMOs have gained in both number and popularity by combining the cost management of an HMO (through the use of gatekeeping primary care physicians) with point-of-service choice (the ability to seek care outside the network and still receive benefits).

While the distinctions between PPOs and OEHMOs are disappearing, tangible differences between them remain that deserve mention:

- OEHMOs can both finance and deliver health care services and are true alternative delivery systems. PPOs deliver but do not finance health care services, and represent a modification to the traditional indemnity approach.
- Individuals have no claims-filing responsibilities under the network side of OEHMOs but typically do under PPOs (although some PPO networks require providers to handle claims filing).

- Benefits for preventive health care (well-child care, annual physicals and mammograms) are prevalent among OEHMOs, yet are less common or less generous among PPOs (they can be designed into the plan, however).
- OEHMOs are more regulated at both the federal and state level than PPOs, since the network benefit typically is filed as an HMO.

PPOs and OEHMOs are jointly referred to as point-of-service plans. The most appropriate model for a given employer obviously depends on the employer's unique situation. Because the models are so similar, it is incumbent upon an employer to understand its own objectives and needs as well as the different features of point-of-service products before selecting a model type for its medical benefit plan.

EMPLOYER INTERNAL ANALYSIS

Objectives

As with any significant change to a benefit plan, the decision to offer a PPO option must follow careful consideration by the employer of its benefit objectives. Certainly the objective of controlling costs is paramount to most employers. In theory, this objective is met by the PPO concept. The managed care philosophy also must fit with the company's culture and approach to providing employee benefits.

The degree of provider choice that an employer wishes to offer is another important philosophical consideration. How much choice is available to employees currently? Are all employees in a single indemnity plan with no choice among coverage options but free choice of provider? Is the plan a flexible indemnity plan that offers choice among different levels of deductibles and coinsurance? Or does the plan offer employees a choice between indemnity coverage and an HMO (suggesting that the employer believes that some limits on choice are acceptable)? To what extent will the employer encourage use of the PPO over indemnity coverage? Will the PPO be confined only to certain services such as mental health, or will it encompass a full range of health care services? By offering a PPO, an employer is indicating a willingness to become involved in the patient/physician selection decision; this must be considered within the context of the employer's objectives concerning choice.

Successful implementation of a PPO option must begin with this internal assessment of benefit objectives to ensure that the necessary fit exists between the concept and approach of a PPO and the employer's objectives.

Employer Experience

In general, employers are well served by having a detailed understanding of their claims history, the providers currently being used by employees, and the demographics of their employee population. This information is essential to the effective ongoing management of a medical benefit plan. The need for this understanding is even more pronounced when a major change such as the addition of a PPO to the benefit plan is being contemplated. Without this knowledge, an employer has no way of knowing which PPO and which implementation strategy is best suited to meet its particular needs and may risk forgoing any significant improvement a PPO could make to the plan's overall performance.

Claims History

Detailed claims information probably is the most important data requirement of any employer large enough to use this information well. In addition to frequency, cost, and average-length-of-stay information, employers must be aware of the most prevalent inpatient and outpatient procedures, the highest-cost procedures, and the longest episodes of care occurring among their employees. This information conveys, on a procedural basis, not only where employer dollars are being spent but also where utilization problems exist currently and where they may arise in the future.

Coupling this information with demographic statistics and comparing it with normative data allows for timely recognition and resolution of health care problems. With respect to network development, it ensures that a breadth of appropriate specialties is represented in the new network based on the services needed by employees. Without this fundamental—albeit detailed—information, an employer is forsaking a tool that is essential to selecting or designing a successful PPO network.

Provider Experience

Employers must determine which providers are most commonly used by their employees. This indicates, on a provider-specific basis, where employer dollars are being spent. More important, this knowledge enables an employer to select a network that includes a significant number of currently used providers which will increase network utilization. This "disruption analysis" can help an employer avoid one of the greatest barriers to managed care acceptance: the need for employees to switch providers in order to receive favorable network benefits.

Employee Distribution

Knowing the geographic distribution of employee residences also is important to assessing the accessibility of a network by a particular population. This "network match" determines if the geographic distribution of providers overlaps sufficiently with that of employees. Successful PPO implementation depends in part upon the employees' perception that providers in the network are accessible.

PPO NETWORK SELECTION

In selecting a network, an employer needs to know what health care services it wants to offer through the network, in which locations it is going to offer a PPO, and how to purchase the array of network services.

Scope of Services

Comprehensive data analysis will suggest to the employer what services should be included in the PPO. For example, either a full range of medical/surgical services could be included, or the network could be limited to mental health and substance abuse care for the employer wishing to address high psychiatric and chemical dependency claims only. Philosophy and current circumstances of the employer also may influence the scope of services included. An employer comfortable with the concept of managed care may be willing to endorse a full-service PPO, whereas an employer whose only experience is with traditional indemnity plans may opt for a more limited network at the outset.

While a limited approach may have appeal to some employers, these specific preferred provider arrangements—by focusing on only a single high-cost area—may or may not reduce an employer's overall health care costs. If careful data analysis reveals that this particular high-cost area is the only trouble spot, the approach should prove successful. If, however, other problem areas exist, the preferred provider arrangement alone cannot be relied on for long-term cost reduction. Additional controls will have to be imposed in conjunction with the preferred provider arrangement to yield an improvement in total health care costs.

Whatever the scope of services to be included, a PPO must be set up not as a means to restrict access to care but rather to ensure that appropriate care is delivered. Otherwise, health care problems will persist and perhaps worsen. If care is delayed, treatments ultimately will be more expensive, and other hidden costs such as absenteeism and lost productivity may arise. Thus the focus must truly be to *manage* care.

Locations to Be Served

Based upon the concentrations of employees in different geographic locations, the employer must determine how many of these locations are to be serviced by a PPO network. Is a limited introduction preferred, or a more broad-based introduction encompassing as many employees as possible? This is a philosophical consideration as well as an administrative or practical one. With target locations established, an employer must determine which locations presently are serviced by a network. Some large carriers have developed national networks, but it is unlikely that any single network will ever fully cover all regions of the country. Moreover, since health care is regarded as a local business, employers may have to use a combination of both national and local networks.

Bundled vs. Unbundled Services

Once the scope of services and locations to be served is determined, the employer must decide how the services will be purchased. An employer electing the bundled approach is seeking to get as many services as possible (i.e., access to a network, contract negotiations, UR, QA, claims administration, and reporting) from the fewest number of vendors or perhaps from a single vendor, such as a large insurance carrier or network sponsor. A bundled approach simplifies administration by reducing the number of vendors and contracts to be managed. For example, the employer may wish to bundle all medical plan services together under the triple-option approach. This typically includes an indemnity plan, an HMO, and a PPO and may be delivered by a single vendor or carrier for administrative ease.

Under the unbundled approach, the employer opts to contract directly with a variety of organizations for different services and may even develop its own network through direct negotiations with providers. Different companies may be used for UR and QA, while claims payment may be placed with an insurance carrier or third-party administrator. Or, the employer may wish to handle these functions internally, hiring the appropriate staff to assume these responsibilities. A perceived advantage of the unbundled approach is the ability to obtain an array of the best-quality services from different vendors. An obvious disadvantage to this approach is the added administrative complexity that results.

At present, most employers find themselves somewhere in the middle between the purely bundled and the purely unbundled approach to the purchase of services. For example, the employer already involved in managed care may contract with one carrier to insure the indemnity plan and one or more HMOs and/or PPOs to serve the employer's different geographic locations.

EVALUATION OF AVAILABLE PPOs

Having developed a clear understanding of what is needed, an evaluation of available PPOs must be undertaken by the employer to determine whether any existing networks fit its needs.

Provider Panel

The PPO must include the appropriate providers, specialties, and services needed by the employee population, including as many as possible of the employees' currently used providers. It also must ensure a good geographic match between network providers and employees.

Provider Selection

Consideration must be given to how providers are selected for the network. Are acceptable, objective criteria used? Is there a credentialing and recredentialing process? Are physician profiles examined to assess adherence to appropriate practice patterns and standards of care? Are the providers philosophically disposed to the managed care concept and willing to participate in utilization review?

Gatekeeper Approach

Are primary care physicians used to control access to care? While the cost savings associated with gatekeepers are difficult to quantify, a gatekeeper approach could be incorporated into the network. On the other hand, it also is felt that selection of the proper providers and implementation of a strong UR program together obviate the need for a gatekeeper approach. This decision ultimately is contingent upon the employer's confidence in the existing provider panel and UR programs.

Payment Methodology

The network's payment arrangements require careful review. Generally, most PPOs pay physicians on a discounted fee-for-service or scheduled basis and pay hospitals on either a discounted, per diem, or DRG basis. Discounted fee-for-service reimbursement does not place physicians at economic risk for the services they deliver. Thus, there has been a movement from discounts to fee schedules, which are more successful at controlling physicians' costs.

In addition to payment methodology, attention must be paid to the equity of reimbursements made to individual practitioners. Providers must be compensated fairly for the services they deliver. This is particularly true in capitated environments, where a fixed charge per member per month is paid regardless of the quantity of services provided. Furthermore, under capitation arrangements a physician's level of compensation and bonus can be adversely affected by the number of specialty referrals he or she makes. There should not be an incentive to "undertreat." Clearly the focus cannot simply be on reduced payments to providers, but must be on an overall payment approach that ensures that effective, high-quality care is delivered.

Utilization Review and Quality Assurance

The network's approach to utilization review and quality assurance must agree with the employer's philosophy about and expectations for these network elements. These programs, combined with the appropriate payments, are essential to ensuring that the PPO offers a comprehensive approach to cost management. The guidelines followed for UR and QA, as well as the qualifications of the professionals conducting these programs and the vigilance with which they enforce the guidelines, must be carefully scrutinized.

Direct Contracting

An employer may find that no network exists in its target locations or may determine through the evaluation process that existing networks are unsuitable. If so, it might consider developing a network through direct provider negotiations either on its own or in conjunction with other area employers. Again, the network may encompass a full range of health care services or may be limited in scope (for example, including only mental health and chemical dependency or only maternity care). This strategy typically befits the larger self-insured employer, which has a negotiating advantage because of its size and which might have prior experience with managed care.

Liability

Employers offering a PPO—especially one that has been contracted directly by the employer—should be aware of the potential exposure they may face in offering such managed care arrangements. Plaintiffs have recently employed several theories to impose liability on third parties in medical negligence actions. Under the theory of "corporate negligence," for example, courts have imposed a duty upon hospitals to verify the credentials of their providers and to monitor the quality of care rendered. Courts also have found that hospitals and HMOs can be held liable, under the "apparent agent" theory, for the negligent acts of network providers if employees have reason to believe that the providers are agents of the hospital or HMO.

Where a PPO network is involved, plaintiffs could attempt to hold a "deep pocket" employer liable for the treatment decisions and outcomes of the network's providers. An employer's development and use of a network, including the use of incentives to encourage network utilization, might imply endorsement by the employer of the participating providers. Moreover, courts may impose a duty on an employer to conduct a thorough review of the qualifications of the providers.

While much uncertainty remains as to the liability exposure facing employers who use PPOs, careful review of physician credentials and quality-assurance efforts, as well as clear documentation that health care services are rendered by independent practitioners, could minimize this exposure.

Financial Stability

Prior to entering into a contract with a PPO, an employer must assess the organization's financial stability. This is particularly important if the PPO itself is assuming the risk for care (e.g., a physician-sponsored PPO as opposed to an investor-sponsored PPO, which assumes no risk but serves mainly as a "middle man"). Considerations include the length of time the network has been in operation, the volume of individuals handled by the network, historical and expected growth, and the adequacy of the capital resources backing the network.

State Law and Regulations

Seen largely as a positive competitive influence in the nation's health care market, the PPO has been relatively unburdened by federal regulations. In part because of this virtual absence of federal regulation, a patchwork of state laws and regulations pertaining to certain PPO arrangements exists.

Many states regulate the activity of insured PPO arrangements. These regulations typically address the extent to which individuals can be required to seek care from participating providers and the degree to which different rates can be charged and benefit levels provided to comparable groups. In some states, for example, the difference between the network and the non-network benefit levels may not exceed a specified percentage, nor may the difference in deductibles exceed a given dollar amount. Other states require the review of the PPO's standards for quality assurance and utilization review.

In contrast to employers who use insured arrangements, employers who self-insure their health benefits have considerable latitude in the design and implementation of their benefit plans, including the use of PPOs, under the preemption afforded by the Employee Retirement Income Security Act of 1974 (ERISA). Employers seeking the services of an insured arrangement, however, must be aware of the particular laws and regulations affecting PPOs in those states where PPOs will be offered.

INTEGRATING THE PPO INTO THE CURRENT MEDICAL BENEFIT PLAN

An extensive and thoughtful evaluation of available PPO networks will reveal whether a network or networks exist that can realistically serve an employer's population and whether the opportunity exists to realize meaningful savings. Carefully integrating the PPO into the existing health benefit plan is the employer's next challenge.

Point of Service Plan

For most employers, the PPO is integrated with an existing indemnity plan. Employees continue to be enrolled in the indemnity plan but can at the point of service decide whether to use network providers to receive higher benefits. Indemnity-like benefits are provided through the network but at a more generous level than the existing indemnity plan offers, as the following example illustrates.

Indemnity	*PPO Network*
$200 deductible	$200 deductible
70 percent coinsurance	90 percent coinsurance

A dual-option or enrolled plan might also be constructed; it is similar to the point of service plan though less prevalent. Under this approach, employees must enroll each year in either the indemnity plan or the PPO. Again, all benefits are indemnity-like in design, with the network coverage being the most favorable. The indemnity coverage is the same as or less than that offered through the network.

Triple Option

For the employer that currently offers both indemnity coverage and HMOs, the addition of a PPO results in a triple option plan. The PPO serves as the middle ground between the free choice of the indemnity plan and the restricted choice of the HMO. The basic benefit structure of the triple option plan might be as follows:

Indemnity	*PPO Network*	*HMO*
$200 deductible 70 percent coinsurance	$200 deductible 90 percent coinsurance	$10 office visit 100 percent coinsurance

PPO with Flexible Benefits

The addition of a PPO to a flexible benefit (flex) plan enhances the employer's ability to control costs *and* grant employees choice in selecting the appropriate level of medical coverage as well as the desired provider. A managed flex plan might offer the following benefits:

Option	*Network*	*Non-Network*
1.	$150 deductible 90 percent coinsurance $500 out-of-pocket	$150 deductible 70 percent coinsurance $1,000 out-of-pocket
2.	$300 deductible 90 percent coinsurance $1,000 out-of-pocket	$300 deductible 70 percent coinsurance $2,000 out-of-pocket
3.	$500 deductible 90 percent coinsurance $2,000 out-of-pocket	$500 deductible 70 percent coinsurance $4,000 out-of-pocket

Many of the guidelines that hold true for successful operation of a flex plan also contribute to the success of the managed flex plan. The design of the new plan must maintain significant differences among options. Effective flexible benefit plans offer employees distinct coverage choices that have noticeable differences in value. The addition of a PPO can complicate this task. Therefore, caution must be used to be sure that (1) these differences are perceived by employees, and (2) employees are encouraged, through benefit design, to use the network for the majority of their first-dollar expenses. It also is essential to keep as many of the high utilizers within the network as possible. A relatively small number of high-risk employees typically generate a large percentage of an employer's total medical costs. Thus, incentives must be in place that will steer these cases to network providers, where the high claims will be paid at a discount and the episodes of care will be managed more closely.

Incentives and Disincentives

Perhaps the most critical factor to the success of the newly integrated plan—whether a point of service, triple option, or managed flex plan—is the extent to which employees are encouraged to seek care from network providers rather than from non-network providers. Varying the deductible and/or coinsurance levels sufficiently between network and non-network coverage generally is required to produce the desired channeling.

In the design of the incentive structure, how the new network and non-network benefit levels will compare with current benefit levels must be determined. If non-network benefits mirror current coverage and the network benefits are enhanced (i.e., provide lower deductibles and coinsurance levels), the potential for increased cost arises from the improved benefit—the incentive—on the network side. However, if proper controls are in place, including discounts and adequate utilization review, this initial run-up in costs may be checked.

If, on the other hand, network benefits match current coverage and non-network care is subjected to higher deductibles and coinsurance levels—the disincentive—the employer's cost-containment objectives may more readily materialize. However, employees may react negatively to the design as a pure take-away.

A compromise design would offer network benefits higher than current coverage and non-network benefits less generous than current coverage. This design might have a neutral effect on short-term costs, but might provide a more palatable design with which to introduce the new program to employees. These three approaches are summarized in the table below:

	Network Benefit	*Non-Network Benefit*
Incentive	Better	Same
Compromise	Better	Worse
Disincentive	Same	Worse

Network use can be encouraged through any of the above designs. Overall, the network coverage must be sufficiently better than the non-network coverage to encourage employees to seek care from network providers. However, it should not be so generous (e.g., 100 percent coinsurance) as to promote unnecessary utilization, which might offset the savings that the discounts would otherwise yield. In addition, the benefit differential should not be so great as to leave those employees who seek non-network care feeling unduly penalized for their decision, or worse, discouraged from seeking needed care altogether. The most popular differential in coinsurance is 20 percent (as noted in the previous benefit structure illustrations), though it may be greater. In some instances, insurance carriers promise their network providers a minimum differential, which leaves little or no discretion to the employer over this design element.

For employees living outside the network service area, the employer must decide upon benefit design. Is uniform design a high priority, or is some design variation acceptable? Depending upon the employer's objective, benefits can be designed accordingly.

COMMUNICATION

All changes to an existing benefit plan should be well communicated in a timely fashion to employees. This is particularly true when significant changes are taking place, such as the addition of a new option. The degree to which employees understand a new PPO option could well determine its success. If employees don't feel that the PPO represents an acceptable option—offering them access to high-quality health care at a reasonable price—they will not embrace the concept and will retain their current coverage.

Just as implementation of the network requires thoughtful planning and analysis (which can take months of time), a communications campaign also must be carefully planned and presented to employees, allowing them enough time to learn and appreciate what may well be a completely new subject—managed care. This important step—fostering employee understanding and acceptance of the PPO—must not be handled casually.

PPOS IN THE 1990s

As the search for solutions to the health care cost crisis continues, PPOs will continue to be a part of many employers' cost containment strategies. There will continue to be fewer clear distinctions between PPOs and HMOs as each of the models evolves, seeking to become the product that has broad appeal and ensures access to high-quality, appropriate health care at an affordable price. Growth in the number of networks and key network sponsors likely will taper off as competition intensifies and network consolidation takes place; overall PPO membership, however, may continue to increase. Providers' negative reactions to the complexity of dealing with a multitude of networks may foster network consolidation. Providers increasingly will drop their affiliations with those networks that represent only a negligible portion of their overall patient load.

As PPOs intensify their provider recruiting in order to serve their growing membership, the value of the discounts they obtain from providers will diminish. As more providers join a given network, each individual provider will have less guarantee of increased patient volume. This will result in far more reluctance to grant the discounts that networks request and have historically received.

Cost-shifting effects may intensify as providers aim to recoup lost revenues from nondiscounted payors. Those employers who succeed in channeling more of their employees into scheduled payment arrangements through a PPO will be somewhat protected from the effects of this cost shifting.

The 1990s will bring an increased focus on data analysis and the importance of projecting and quantifying cost savings. Quality assurance activities and outcomes-measurement will be a high priority of network sponsors and employers alike. This enhanced focus on quality care could in turn lead to more selective provider recruiting by the networks. In summary, PPOs will continue to evolve—as they have over the past decade—to better meet the needs of employers and employees.

CHAPTER 16

MANAGED CARE ALTERNATIVES

Phillip D. Pierce

The critical burden of medical care benefit costs, which continue to rise despite traditional efforts at cost containment, has forced companies and public-sector employers to seriously evaluate the variety of "managed care" alternatives that have evolved over the past two decades. Starting with the 1973 Health Maintenance Organization (HMO) Act, which provided federal guidelines for the establishment of HMOs, many other alternatives, such as preferred provider organizations (PPOs), exclusive provider organizations (EPOs), and the newer point-of-service (POS) programs, have emerged and gained the serious attention of both private and public-sector benefit sponsors. Yet, despite the intense focus on "managed care" alternatives, there is little agreement among employers, medical care providers, insurance companies, and third-party administrators (TPAs) who deal with medical care on how to define managed care or outline its parameters. This chapter provides a general framework within which to understand and compare the fundamental components of the more commonly discussed managed care alternatives available, particularly as they compare to elements of the more traditional indemnity benefit plans. It is not an exhaustive study of all the managed care variations available in the market today. Virtually all medical care vendors—whether insurance carriers, TPAs, HMOs, PPOs, or direct medical care vendor coalitions—have developed unique products and services associated with their particular managed care offerings, and new variations are being introduced to the marketplace daily. Nor does the chapter try to authoritatively answer the question of whether managed care programs will best serve to control the ever rising costs of medical care plans in the United States. There is growing consensus throughout the employee benefit industry that managed care alternatives—at least in the aggregate—offer greater opportunity to control the cost of delivering medical care coverage than traditional fee-for-service indemnity plans. However, many of the alternatives are still relatively young, and data are still being evaluated to make clear comparative evaluations of the cost effectiveness of managed care plans versus fee-for-service plans.

ECONOMIC TRENDS FACING THE EMPLOYER[1]

Entering the 1990s, both public and private employers in the United States face multiple economic and financial challenges. Powerful economic trends are forcing corporations to reduce operating costs and improve productivity in order to survive in an increasingly competitive global environment. Simultaneously, employers face shrinking labor markets in areas that are critical to their growth and development. Creative and flexible approaches are needed to attract, retain, and motivate the talented people necessary to help corporations and public-sector employers meet the economic realities they face.

Federal Government Cost Shifting

In spite of federal deficit-cutting efforts, the U.S. debt is expected to continue to grow, profoundly impacting all sectors of the economy and threatening the ability of private employers to grow and prosper in the 1990s. As the federal government competes with private employers for the available funds in the investment marketplace, the resulting higher interest rates mean less available capital to replace plant and equipment and for investment in new technology needed to compete effectively. Attempts to lower the federal deficit have shifted costs to state and local levels and to the private sector. A prime example of the latter that directly affects employer-sponsored medical care costs can be seen in the limited

---

[1]For a detailed discussion of the environment of medical care expense plans in the 1990s, see Chapter 10 of the *Handbook*.

annual increase in provider reimbursements under Medicare. As hospital and physician reimbursements are squeezed under Medicare, many medical care providers are forced to more rapidly increase their charges to other payors to make up for lost revenues. At the same time, federal laws have moved large portions of medical care costs previously funded through Medicare directly onto private plans. The Consolidated Omnibus Budget Reconciliation Act (COBRA) allows active employees over age 65 to select either Medicare or their employer's health plan as the primary source of benefits, and since group plans typically provide much broader benefits and easier access to medical providers, most employees continue to use the employer's plan as their primary coverage. As a result, employers have been forced to accept greater responsibility for financing the medical care costs of an aging population.

Competitive Global Environment

Corporations also face pressure from the emergence of new global competitors. In addition to dominant economic players in western Europe and Japan, new entrants from the Third World and even eastern European nations will play a greater role in international production in the 1990s. New alliances among foreign capital markets, such as the European Economic Community pact in 1992, will test the ability of U.S. companies to compete with the collective strength of nations linked by free-trade agreements.

Virtually all medical care in foreign countries is provided primarily through governmental programs (some countries, such as Canada, permit supplemental plans to enhance governmental benefits). Since these programs typically are funded by national or regional governments, their costs are less directly identifiable as a company's costs of production. In contrast, employer-sponsored medical care plans in the United States are completely funded through revenues of the employer and its employees. Thus, employers can see the immediate impact of uncontrolled costs, and they have a real incentive to investigate alternatives that can lower these costs while maintaining an attractive level of benefits for employees.

Shrinking Work Force

Both private and public employers will have to operate in the 1990s and beyond with an increasingly tighter supply of trained labor. Since the 1970s, most industrialized nations—including the United States—have faced negative net population growth. In addition, the demographic bulge of the Baby Boom generation is now in mid-life and will start to enter retirement age in the next 10 to 15 years. Confronting a shrinking work force, employers will be forced to pay premium wages and enhanced benefits to attract qualified employees who will be in greater demand and shorter supply. Acute shortages are projected in the areas of science and technology, health care, and hospitality services. With today's pre-adult populations facing lower education levels, trained people will be even more precious to corporations. Given the dynamic changes in technology and the emergence of totally new products and services, corporations must invest in retraining current workers to meet their human resource needs.

From a long-term perspective, employers stand to gain the most competitive advantage—and best chances for economic survival—by maintaining a stable and highly trained work force. Attracting and retaining such a work force will continue to require an enticing and well-developed package of compensation and employee benefits. Therefore, employers must successfully balance the need to control medical care costs with the need to gain employees' acceptance of potentially new forms of delivery.

THE GROWING NEED FOR MANAGED CARE

As noted above, controlling medical care cost increases and their resulting financial impact on employer-sponsored medical benefit plans without severely diminishing the value of plans to employees is one of the most critical problems facing private and public-sector employee benefit plan sponsors in the '90s. Even the most casual observer of employee benefits trends is acutely aware of the magnitude of the crisis.

National Resources Spent on Health Care

As shown in Figure 16–1, total 1990 national health care expenditures are estimated to exceed $600 billion, an increase of 273 percent over the $220 billion spent in 1980. While these total dollar expenditures seem staggering, perhaps more startling is the fact that health care costs, which accounted for about 5.2 percent of gross national product (GNP) in 1960, will consume over 12.6 percent of GNP in 1991. In other words, national

FIGURE 16–1
Growth in Total Personal Health Care Expenditures (273% Increase Over the Decade)

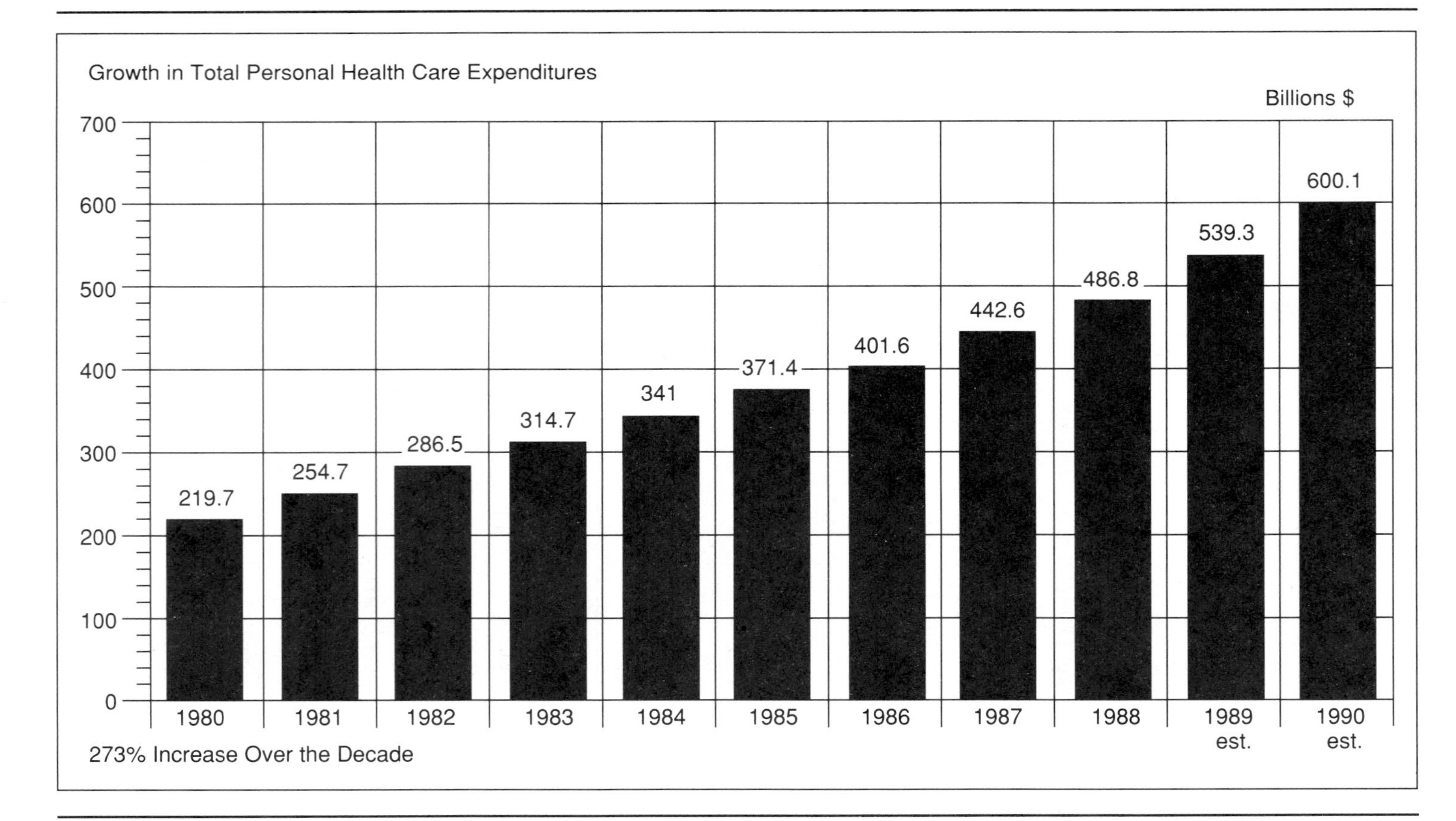

Source: *Bernstein Report*

health care expenditures are taking a greater and greater proportion of available resources.

While little argument exists about the importance of accessible, high-quality health care, this shift in priorities is hardly the result of national deliberation. Whether intentional or not, health care dominates other areas of national interest, including education of the population and investment in new technology and research, which are so essential to keeping American companies competitive in the global economy.

Impact on the Plan Sponsor

For private and public-sector employers, the impact is closer to home and increasingly pressing. Nationwide, medical benefit costs increased an average of 21.6 percent in 1990, after a 20.4 percent jump in 1989.[2] That level of increase has prevailed for much of the last 20 years, and the cumulative results are seen clearly on the "bottom line." Health care benefit costs represented about 4 to 6 percent of corporate profits in the 1960s; those figures increased to between 25 percent to 50 percent of earnings in the 1990s.[3] For many smaller, growing companies, this financial burden can threaten the very financial survival of the firm. But the problem is by no means limited to smaller firms, and most of the country's largest corporations have actively pursued new and dramatic means of delivering their employees' health care in an effort to better manage the long-term costs of such plans.

History of Cost-Control Attempts

In the 1950s and 1960s, insurers and other providers of medical care plans concentrated on expanding the level of coverage and number of customers. However, as costs began to spiral, the industry was compelled to address directly the concerns of employers. Encouraged by an Act of Congress in 1973, HMOs distinguished themselves by their use of a closed network of providers, provider risk sharing, and tight control over

---

[2]Survey of more than 1,950 companies and private-sector employers conducted by A. Foster Higgins, a national benefit consulting firm, *The Wall Street Journal*, January 29, 1991, p. A20.

[3]"Corporate Chiefs See Need for U.S. Health-Care Action," *New York Times*, April 8, 1991, p. D4.

delivery of care. Their growth continued throughout the 1970s and 1980s, some with more success than others. Most traditional medical plan vendors made little effort to develop products to compete directly with HMOs, preferring to encourage clients to use plan design techniques (discussed in Chapter 13 of the *Handbook)* to control cost increases. For years, insurance companies, TPAs and the consulting community recommended a variety of refinements—from greater employee contribution arrangements to expanded coverage for "cost effective" forms of treatment, such as home health care or generic drugs—in an effort to provide at least short-term relief from the upward trend of health care costs. These efforts have met with some success, but there is little evidence to show that tinkering with plan design within the traditional fee-for-service indemnity arrangement leads to long-term substantial flattening of costs and utilization.

In the 1980s, PPOs (covered in Chapter 15 of the *Handbook)* grew in acceptance, as a means of providing both cost control for employers and higher benefits for participants who used "preferred" physicians and hospitals with whom the payor had a negotiated fee. Employers have accepted both HMOs and PPOs as viable means of delivering health care benefits, and the growing consensus is that managed care programs, in whatever format, will continue to dominate the health care benefit marketplace.

In 1988, the first national point-of-service (POS) plan was established for the employees of Allied Signal Corporation. These POS plans—which have become increasingly popular as a "hybrid" between the PPO and HMO approach—vary from the standard PPO arrangement in that employees are required to select a primary care physician (PCP), who then handles basic medical services for the plan participant and also oversees access to more specialized levels of care, including hospitalization.

Over the last decade there has been a dramatic shift from traditional indemnity plans to managed care programs. In 1980, only about 4 percent of all participants covered by group health plans were enrolled in a managed care plan. Today, it is estimated that 30 percent participate in HMOs and PPOs. When members covered under managed indemnity plans that provide structured utilization-review programs are included, the estimated coverage extends to over 51 percent. Health industry analysts project that 50 percent of health care enrollees could be participating in an HMO, PPO, or other form of structured managed care program by the year 2000, as indicated in the following table:

Plan Type	*1990 Estimated Members (Millions)*	*Percent Total*	*2000 Estimated Members (Millions)*	*Percent Total*
HMO	32.5	13.0	55.0	20.0
PPO	42.2	16.9	82.5	30.0
Managed Indemnity	52.5	21.0	27.5	10.0
Traditional Indemnity	17.5	7.0	13.7	5.0
Government	55.0	22.0	68.8	25.0
Uninsured	31.0	12.4	13.7	5.0
Other	19.3	7.7	13.8	5.0
Totals	250.0	100.0%	275.0	100.0%

Source: *Medical Benefits*, 1990.

Managed Care Defined

For the purposes of this chapter, the term *managed care* encompasses programs intended to influence and direct the delivery of health care through one or more of the following techniques:

1. Plan-design features, including incentives and disincentives in the level of coverage, intended to redirect delivery of medical care.
2. Access restricted to a specified group of preselected providers.
3. Utilization management programs intended to pre-authorize certain forms of medical care use and/or concurrently monitor the use of more expensive forms of care such as inpatient treatment.

Essentially, this includes the broad array of ''managed'' indemnity plans—HMOs, PPOs, and the newer POS plans. The specific definition used for the term *managed care* is not as important as having an understanding of the context in which it is applied. Some people use the term exclusively in the context of HMOs, while others may regard managed care as any plan that deviates in any manner from a traditional fee-for-service arrangement.

The provider community, an integral player in managed care plans, often uses the same term in a different context, referring to a patient's integrated treatment program rather than to a specific benefit design or provider reimbursement method. The ultimate definition, according to some industry analysts, may need to be one that embraces some financial risk and responsibility, a particular set of benefits, high-quality care mechanisms, and payment initiatives. Unfortunately, employers, payors, consumers, providers, and plan managers all see their own piece of the puzzle based on their own experience, often without seeing the other pieces. In short, they view plans through the lenses of their own self-interest.[4]

MANAGED CARE SPECTRUM

Understanding the complexities of various managed health care alternatives may be simpler by viewing their components along a continuum. Figure 16–2, referred to as the Managed Care Spectrum, illustrates the major managed care alternatives in terms of those components other than specific plan design that distinguish their method of operation, provider involvement and reimbursement, and claims administration.

A new language is needed to understand these programs, and a greater attention to detail is required to properly evaluate the degree of cost effectiveness and employee satisfaction proposed by various health care vendors. The purpose of illustrating these alternatives along a spectrum is to help provide the reader with a basic understanding of that new language and a basis for evaluating specific types of managed care programs.

The horizontal scale of the spectrum shows the major types of managed care alternatives and compares those to a traditional fee-for-service comprehensive medical plan. The following discussion examines each of these alternatives in detail. The vertical scale lists fundamental components, aside from specific plan-design features, that distinguish the operation of the various alternatives, including the following:

1. Degree of freedom in the participants' *choice of providers.*

2. Degree of *"steerage"* incorporated in plan design as a means of encouraging plan participants toward certain providers.

3. *Claims handling* responsibilities between the patient and the provider.

---

[4]*Medical Benefits,* Vol. 8, No. 4, According to *HMO Magazine,* Jan/Feb 1991 article by Maria R. Traska.

FIGURE 16–2
Spectrum of Managed Care Alternatives

	Primary Managed Care Plan Alternatives				
Key Features	*Standard Indemnity*	*Managed Indemnity*	*Preferred Provider Plan*	*Point-of-Service Plan*	*Health Maintenance Organization*
Choice of Provider	Maximum	Maximum	Moderate	Moderate	Limited
Degree of Plan's "Steerage"	None	Limited	Moderate	Considerable	Maximum
Claims Handling	Patient	Patient	Provider/Patient	Provider/Patient	Provider
Utilization Management	None	Limited	Limited	Considerable	Maximum
Referral Management	None	None	None	Yes	Yes
Negotiated Pricing from Providers	None	None	Yes	Yes	Yes
Provider "Risk Sharing"	None	None	None	Varies	Maximum
Experience Rating and Financial Alternatives	Full	Full	Full	Varies	Varies
Expected Net Savings	None	$	$$	$$$	$$$$

4. Degree of external *utilization management* (UM) or *utilization review* (UR) typically administered by an insurance carrier or other third-party vendor, to preauthorize, monitor, and/or review the necessity of care rendered.

5. *Referral management,* whereby any levels of specialty care that cannot be rendered by the primary care physician must be referred by the PCP and typically approved in advance by a separate UM manager (often the same vendor who performs the other UM functions). This is more comprehensive than the typical UM programs, which generally are limited to the overview of hospital confinements and selected outpatient procedures.

6. *Negotiated pricing* from providers, either through a discount from standard fees or through an established "capitation" payment to those providers who are selected by plan members as their primary care physician.

7. *Provider "risk sharing,"* whereby providers in the network—typically the primary care physicians—have part of their regular reimbursement payments withheld to be paid later in the form of a bonus, depending on whether they meet targets on controlling utilization of services and maintain satisfaction among their patients.

8. *Experience rating and financial alternatives,* whereby the net costs of the managed care program, that is, claim payments and administrative expenses, are directly accountable to the plan sponsor and whether the payment of those costs can be handled in a manner to give the employer preferential cash flow advantages.

9. *Expected net savings,* which, while difficult to predict, tend to reflect the expected ''value'' of the combined network discounts and utilization controls incorporated in the managed care alternatives.

With these components briefly identified, we can examine how they compare in the traditional fee-for-service, or standard indemnity, plans and the various managed care alternatives.

Standard Indemnity

The term *indemnity plan* is used somewhat broadly within the benefit industry to encompass the diverse array of plans that have dominated the delivery of group health benefits for the past 30 years. Technically, indemnification refers to the guarantee of one party to secure another against the risk of a loss and reimburse certain values if the first party suffers the prescribed loss. Insurance carriers are traditional hosts to indemnification plans and have played a large role in the development of the more common fee-for-service plans. Insurers are also playing a central role in the development of many managed care alternatives described later in this chapter. The traditional fee-for-service, or standard indemnity, plan, still widely used by corporate and public employer-sponsored medical programs, usually involves a combination of deductible and coinsurance, with some level of catastrophic coverage for the individual participant. Some programs continue to use a combination of basic medical benefits superimposed with major medical benefits, while most others have evolved to use the comprehensive plan design approach. Both these approaches are described in Chapter 12 of the *Handbook* and are included in the ''standard indemnity'' category in this chapter.

This category also includes the wide number of self-insured plans, which may be administered by an insurance carrier or a third-party administrator. In such plans, the final guarantor of benefits is the plan sponsor. In a sense, the employer agrees to indemnify the plan's participants directly without the supporting guarantee of a third-party insurer. Although self-funded plans can purchase individual and/or aggregate forms of stop-loss insurance to limit their financial exposure, it is important to note that these stop-loss policies are issued to indemnify the *employer* against risks of excess liability within the plan and not the individual plan participant. The distinction between insured and self-insured becomes more apparent later in the analysis of managed care alternatives because not all programs offered today allow employers the full array of self-funding arrangements available with traditional fee-for-service plans.

Also included in this category are the traditional prepaid plans such as Blue Cross and Blue Shield, a major source of group benefits for many employees nationwide. Technically, these are neither insured nor self-insured plans, and in the strictest sense of the definition most Blue Cross and Blue Shield plans could be considered a form of managed care because they have preexisting contractual arrangements with established providers. However, many of the Blues have developed specific HMO, PPO, and other managed care programs in addition to their more common prepaid plans, and for simplification their traditional arrangements are included here in the standard indemnity category.

As mentioned earlier, indemnity plans have undergone their own cost-containment evolution—mostly through plan design—but these rarely dictate the *choice of providers*. As long as the physician or health care facility is duly licensed and operating within the scope of that license, the indemnity plan typically covers the expense. While most claims payors apply a variety of controls and edits to eliminate unnecessary or excessive charges, there is no specific distinction in benefit levels between different providers, and *plan steerage* to precontracted physicians or hospitals does not exist.

Claims submissions generally are handled by the participant or, in some instances, by the provider as a convenience for the patient who submits a detailed listing of charges and appropriately completed claim form to the insurance carrier or third-party administrator for review and processing. Claims handling has been considerably refined over the past 30 years, and most claim operations today are computerized at least to some extent. Most major insurance carriers participate in the National Electronic Information Corporation (NEIC), which serves as a clearinghouse to receive claims information electronically from providers. Most

Blue Cross and Blue Shield organizations have automatic reimbursement systems established with their participating providers. A few employers still handle claims processing internally or at least assist employees in preparing claims for submission and certifying their eligibility for benefits. Nonetheless, it is still *ultimately* the employee's responsibility to make sure the employer receives all necessary claim information.

There is no structured *utilization management* or *referral management* under the standard indemnity plan. As noted above, although claims payors should continuously review and scrutinize submitted expenses to ensure that reimbursements are within the scope of the plan documents, these steps rarely include any prospective or concurrent intervention in the delivery of health care.

Similarly, providers are under *no negotiated-pricing* or *risk-sharing* arrangements with the claims payor. Most plans pay charges that fall within the range of prevailing fees based upon type of service and geographic area in which the service is performed. Although claims payors may not cover excessive charges, the provider is free to pursue the plan participant for any nonreimbursed balances. The elimination of this potential for ''balance billing'' by providers is one of the important attractions to employees of many managed care alternatives.

For the most part, standard indemnity plans have a complete array of *experience rating* and *financial alternatives* available. Although small plans often are pooled, the premiums for medium- and large-employer plans usually are based on the prior experience of the plan. In addition, such plans can take advantage of various funding arrangements such as retrospective premium, deferred premium, or minimum premium, which can improve the cash flow associated with funding benefits. As mentioned earlier, a large number of plan sponsors self-fund their indemnity plans, sometimes using individual and aggregate stop-loss insurance to limit their financial exposure.

Managed Indemnity Medical Plans

Essentially, these are identical to standard indemnity plans, but with some degree of third-party intervention during the process of health care delivery referred to as utilization management. Many plan sponsors incorporated basic utilization management techniques within their standard indemnity plans in the 1980s and have experienced some relief in the advancement of their health care costs.[5] The distinction between the cost-containment benefit enhancements discussed earlier and the more structured managed indemnity plans is the broader use of these utilization-management programs, which generally are designed to provide pre-authorization and/or concurrent review of certain types of treatments. Some industry experts would argue that such programs are not truly in the managed care category because they do not include the establishment of prearranged contractual obligations between providers and payors. However, they are listed as part of the spectrum in this discussion because the use of UM procedures signifies the first structured attempt of the plan sponsor (or claim payor on behalf of the plan sponsor) to actively intervene in the delivery of health care either prior to or during its actual delivery. The most common UM programs center around precertification of hospital admissions and concurrent stay review designed to ensure that confinements are appropriate and that the length of stay is no longer than medically necessary.

Generally, the UM process is employee driven and involves little provider commitment. The employee must contact the UM administrator prior to admission or treatment. Most insurance carriers and administrators offer combined UM and claim services, greatly simplifying the final process of benefit payment. Precertification notice may come from the provider, but this does not bind the provider to accept the level of reimbursement allowable under the plan, nor does it establish any other contractual obligation between medical provider and claims payor. Failure to adhere to the UM requirements typically reduces the benefit payable for a procedure. For example, if a participant fails to get precertification of a scheduled hospital stay, there may be a penalty of either a flat-dollar deductible or a higher coinsurance percentage of the total charges. Another example is the possible reduction of benefits payable for certain elective surgical procedures not preceded by a second surgical opinion.

---

[5]Based on ''Managed Care,'' presented by Joseph Duva, director of employee benefits, Allied Signal Corporation, at the International Foundation of Employee Benefit Plans Symposium, December 5, 1989. Allied Signal incorporated hospital precertification and mandatory second surgical opinion programs in the early 1980s, and medical plan cost increases were considered ''under control'' for 1983–1986. Mr. Duva stated for most larger plan sponsors the initial inclusion of such programs should produce a two-to-three year ''leveling off'' of cost increases but that such relief is transitory without further intervention in the basic delivery of health care to the employee population.

There is no formal focus on the quality management of care delivered, since there is no pre-established provider contracting involved in the program. While UM managers may provide suggestions on alternative types of care, they typically do not recommend specific providers.

Preferred Provider Organizations (PPOs)

In PPOs we start to see a structured network of preselected providers, to whom plan participants are encouraged to go for their health care. A common PPO plan may cover preferred providers at 90 percent, often with little or no annual deductible, while nonpreferred care is covered at 70 percent with higher annual deductibles and out-of-pocket limits. PPOs also tend to reimburse for office visits for specific illness and often for routine and preventive care at 100 percent after the participant makes a modest copayment such as $5 or $10 per visit. Office visits to nonpreferred providers typically are covered at the reduced coinsurance level and after the annual deductible.

As noted on the spectrum, there is some limit placed on the *choice of providers* if the participant wants the highest benefits under the plan. This results in *steerage* of plan participants to the preferred providers in the network. It is important to note that the degree of benefit difference between preferred and nonpreferred care is directly related to the degree of steerage utilization between network and non-network providers. The higher the benefit differential, the greater the percentage of participants who seek ''preferred'' care. While this point may seem intuitive, it is an important fundamental consideration for the plan sponsor who wishes to establish any managed care program that steers employees to certain providers. A minimum benefit differential of 20 percent generally is required to achieve adequate steerage of plan participants. However, the trade-off is measured by the level of employee satisfaction with plan benefits. For example, consider an employer who currently offers an 80 percent indemnity plan for all medical care and who is considering a PPO plan that provides 90 percent reimbursement for preferred care and 70 percent reimbursement for nonpreferred care with 20 percent higher out-of-pocket expenses. Certain employees will be forced to change their physicians to avoid reduced benefit levels. Other employees whose physicians already contract with the PPO network will see a net increase in benefits. (The question of network adequacy in terms of employee coverage is an important evaluative tool in comparing competing managed care programs and is discussed later in this chapter.) If the employer wishes to minimize possible adverse employee reaction, the PPO plan may use 100 percent for preferred and 80 percent for nonpreferred care. However, then there is no benefit cost savings for nonpreferred, plus a substantial increase in actual benefit payments for preferred care. While provider discounts and utilization-management controls in the PPO network will offset most of these additional benefits, the net savings may be negligible, especially when the employer also considers the higher administrative costs of the PPO plan and the internal costs of installing the new program.

As with *any* employee benefit program, a critical fundamental step is the proper analysis of plan design in terms of the plan sponsor's overall compensation/benefit objectives and financial parameters. This is especially true in the adoption of any managed care program where employees are offered incentives to change providers.

The provider is responsible for all *claims handling* in the preferred network, which often is a very real attraction to employees. The lack of claim forms and any balance billing eases overall administration for the participants and helps "sell" the PPO concept to employees.

Utilization management is similar to the managed indemnity plans, where all hospital admissions and certain prescribed outpatient courses of treatment are subject to pre-authorization and/or concurrent review by the UM administrator. Typically, preferred physicians will handle UM procedures as part of their agreement with the PPO network manager, and some networks penalize providers for noncompliance. Participants who select nonpreferred providers are responsible for following UM requirements, and any penalties for noncompliance are borne by the participant.

In contrast to other managed care arrangements, there is no formal *referral management* process among preferred providers, and the participant is responsible for selecting network providers for all levels of care. While PPO providers are encouraged to refer specialty care to other PPO physicians, they typically are under no contractual obligation to do so.

Providers join PPO networks to attract and retain patients. In return they agree to *negotiated pricing* arrangements with the PPO network manager, usually in the form of discounts from standard fee-for-service charges, although these reimbursement arrangements typically do not require participating providers to accept any structured *risk sharing* with regard to utilization of plan services. However, the provider is expected to adhere to all claims handling and UM requirements as noted above.

Typically, since benefits are priced as discounted fees, there is a full array of *experience rating* and *financial alternatives* available to the plan sponsor similar to those available for standard indemnity programs.

Point of Service (POS)

As discussed earlier, this is one of the newest forms of managed care arrangements, and it has received considerable attention in the last few years. In simplest terms, the POS blends aspects of the PPO and HMO approach. Like the PPO, there is an established network of providers that, by way of benefit differentials, the participant is encouraged to utilize. An important distinction is that the participant need only select a primary care physician (PCP), who then acts as the "gatekeeper" for all levels of care required by the participant. Therefore, the *choice of provider* is somewhat more limited than in a PPO, but this can be viewed positively since the plan participant need only select the "front line" of medical care and is removed from selecting providers for more specialized health care. *Steerage* disincentives in the form of reduced benefits apply to *any* care in or outside the network if it is not coordinated through the PCP. Typically, nonreferred care is reimbursed at a substantially lower level of benefits, and the differential is often greater than under a PPO, with a 30 percent minimum differential being common.

It is this more intense level of *referral management* that helps tighten the overall cost control of *utilization management* under the POS arrangement. The PCP is strictly required to properly refer care within the established network. Effective communication and coordination between the PCP and the POS network manager is critical to assure that the patient receives appropriate care promptly and in the most cost-effective setting.

Normally, each family member can select a different PCP. For this reason, many networks identify general practitioners (GPs), family practitioners (FPs), and pediatricians as available primary care physicians from which members can select. Some networks also include gynecologists (GYNs) as primary care physicians, although this often is handled administratively by covering routine GYN services at the "preferred" level even if a female family member uses a non-network provider.

In addition to *negotiated pricing agreements,* most PCPs also participate in some form of structured *risk-sharing arrangement* with the POS network manager. This may take the form of bonus pools, financed by amounts "withheld" from regular service payments. If, during the contract period, the PCP demonstrates effective utilization management and meets other criteria such as member satisfaction levels, supplemental bonuses may be paid to the PCP. This provides additional incentive to the provider to actively participate in the established medical management guidelines of the network and to provide a satisfactory service level to network participants. This latter point is vital to the plan sponsor, since the most visible aspect of POS plans to the participants is their interaction with the primary care physician and his or her staff. Another common form of provider reimbursement is capitation, under which the PCP receives a flat monthly reimbursement per member. This cap fee is in lieu of specific discounted payments for each service rendered to the participant. The cap fee also may include a risk-sharing bonus arrangement if the PCP meets certain criteria during the evaluation period. Whether the underlying reimbursement system uses discounted fees or capitation, the plan sponsor must be assured that there are sufficient and well-established UM techniques that assure consistent, high-quality care for participants.

The extent of *experience rating* and *financial alternatives* available to a plan sponsor depends largely on the method of provider reimbursement. Some managed care companies have built their POS products from existing HMO network arrangements because the contractual obligations of referral management are nearly identical. Since most HMO networks operate on a capitated basis of reimbursement for the provider—which often is also used in the POS approach—there is less need to experience-rate claims or to fund benefits outside of the conventional method. Essentially, capitation payments are the claim costs of the plan. Whether the total monthly capitation reimbursements are deducted from the conventional monthly premiums or handled through minimum premium wire transfer, the cash flow is nearly identical. Likewise, as long as premium payments are based on the level of expected capitation costs, experience rating is redundant. Not surprisingly, many insurance carriers offer their POS products on a prospectively rated basis, although for competitive reasons they typically offer full financial arrangements upon request. Similarly, some HMO organizations that have developed POS-like products (often called "swing-out" HMOs) offer them on either a conventional or alternatively funded basis.

Regardless of the funding method used, many employers are requesting that the managed care companies they are considering demonstrate the value of their proposed networks through various financial guarantees. These can take the form of specified per capita claim cost projections or caps on the level of subsequent annual increases relative to a common benchmark. The original POS contract between Allied Signal Corporation and CIGNA Insurance Company, for example, included a three-year rate guarantee, from 1988 through 1990, whereby annual premium increases could not exceed 15 percent. The contract was renewed for one year in 1991, although CIGNA no longer guaranteed costs for those Allied employees who are not eligible under the POS arrangement.[6]

Health Maintenance Organizations (HMOs)

At this point, the reader can appreciate the interrelational nature of the various fundamental components on the managed care spectrum. The degree of choice (or limit) is linked to plan steerage; the level of UM is linked to the type of referral management; the extent of provider risk sharing depends on its level of responsibility for guiding care delivered in the program.

HMOs, perhaps the most commonly found forms of managed care alternatives, lie at the far end of the spectrum. HMOs are discussed in detail in Chapter 14 of the *Handbook,* and this chapter only highlights their primary differences from other managed care arrangements.

Choice of provider is most restricted in the HMO, since the participant must select all care from only those providers with whom the HMO contracts. There generally is *no* non-network coverage (except for certain emergency services rendered out of the service area of the HMO). Furthermore, the choice of provider is made once each year, at the time of annual enrollment, so that plan *steerage* is not an issue. It is totally steered since the employee is eligible only for HMO-provided services.

Claims processing is done entirely within the HMO without paperwork for participants. This is a real attraction of HMO plans and is why PPOs and POS plans mimic this feature as much as possible.

Utilization management and *referral management* are internal to the HMO with the medical staff handling all procedures with network specialists. There are two primary types of HMOs: the individual practice association (IPA) model and the group practice (clinic) model. For the

---

[6] "Allied Signal–CIGNA Deal Extended Without Rate Pledge for Indemnity," *Medical Benefits,* February 28, 1991, p. 6. Based on an article by Phoebe A. Eliopoulus in *Managed Care Report,* January 21, 1991.

purposes of this comparison they operate essentially the same as other managed care alternatives.

Most HMOs use a capitation basis of *physician reimbursement,* although certain specialists may be handled on a discounted fee-for-service basis, since they need to be attracted into the network in order to provide adequate service coverage. As such, providers normally are in some type of *risk-sharing* arrangement with the HMO either through a bonus arrangement or, often, an equity participation.

Fully pooled, or community-rated pricing is quite common among HMOs, fitting in line with the provider reimbursement style. However, for competitive reasons some HMOs have been restructured to offer some elements of experience rating and retrospective accounting. In certain states this has required revised provider contracting and different contract filing requirements with applicable state agencies. This has led to the development of the exclusive provider organization (EPO), which operates in virtually the same way as an HMO except for the provider reimbursement and the ability to offer the employer an experience-rated product.

EXPECTED NET SAVINGS

Rather than trying to describe the expected net savings associated with each managed care arrangement, the discussion is combined here for easier comparison between and among arrangements.

"Does managed care save money?" "Should our plan move into managed care?" Few employee benefit questions are getting more attention than these today, and this chapter would not be complete without at least trying to answer them. First, these are separate and distinct questions. While cost savings are the primary reason for the development of managed care alternatives, there are other fundamental considerations that the plan sponsor must consider such as the impact of restricted choice on employee satisfaction.

The managed care spectrum indicates that net expected savings increase as the plan sponsor moves along the continuum toward the HMO side. This is not intended to reflect an expected *reduction* in costs but, rather, a deceleration in the rate of medical care cost increases. While lower actual costs are possible, they are more likely attributable to random claim fluctuations than to the impact of implementing managed care.

To understand the impact of managed care alternatives on the average costs of medical care, it is important to review the basic components that define medical care costs to the plan sponsor: Gross Medical Care Cost = Average Unit Price of Care × Number of Units Purchased. In other words, overall medical care costs are a direct reflection of average price of supplies and services times the degree of utilization of those supplies and services by plan participants. Therefore, to the extent a managed care plan affects price (for example, through discount payments), utilization (for example, through precertification and concurrent review of various procedures), or the proportion of net benefits paid by the plan sponsor, there is the potential for reducing cost increases in the future. Let's examine these in terms of each of the managed care alternatives.

Clearly, the standard indemnity fee-for-service plan provides the least chance for cost control. Although there should be measurable savings from various cost-containment controls applied during claims processing, these are typically retrospective in nature and offer little opportunity to alter the price of care or the degree of benefit usage. For example, many insurers and third-party administrators limit covered expenses to those charges considered to be reasonable and customary (R&C). These limits are based on available data (either internal or obtained through industry databases such as the Health Insurance Association of America), which help determine the prevailing fee—for the type of service and area in which it has been rendered. However, the database that supports prevailing fees is based upon nonmanaged claims. Therefore, prevailing fee levels are bound to increase at the same general trend rate as all other costs associated with nonmanaged care plans, and while the use of reasonable and customary guidelines is an important tool to reduce the excessive charges of specific providers, it is not an effective means of controlling overall increases in physicians' charges.

Consider another example regarding hospital charges. Most fee-for-service medical plans pay hospital room and board charges at the "most common semi-private" rate for a given hospital. While this saves the plan from incurring additional costs of private rooms and special services, the plan is still subject to non-negotiated average charge increases for hospitals and other facilities. In fact, this "pay as billed" approach inherent in fee-for-service plans makes them vulnerable to shifting of costs by providers between one type of payor and another. As mentioned previously, recent reforms in Medicare's reimbursement procedures have shifted a disproportionately greater share of hospital costs onto private plans. In 1982, Medicare adopted a national diagnostic related group (DRG) method of hospital reimbursement. Under DRG, the level of reimbursement is predetermined for approximately 500 established types of confinements. The hospital receives a flat payment for each admission based on the established DRG for the admitting diagnosis. While there are variations in DRG allowances from area to area, the overall level of reimbursement is considerably lower than the actual charges for handling those admissions. In many instances this encourages the hospital facility to raise the actual charge level (i.e., for room and board and ancillary services) for other payors to recoup the lost revenue under Medicare DRG. While several individual states, notably New Jersey, have instituted a uniform DRG reimbursement method for hospitals, most areas of the country have little in the way of regulatory mechanisms to counterbalance the impact of Medicare cost shifting onto private payors, and managed care arrangements in which medical care providers enter into private negotiated payment arrangements are the only viable method in many areas for private payors to control costs.

As noted on the spectrum, the *managed indemnity* plan incorporates basic utilization-management techniques, notably hospital precertification and other forms of authorization control. There can be incremental savings associated with these programs, although results vary. Many plan sponsors have found that inpatient precertification programs have reduced the average length of stay of hospital confinements, although outpatient charges have exploded at the same time.

Similarly, certain early forms of UM programs have not proven to provide the expected impact on cost controls. For example, many employers initially adopted voluntary second surgical opinion programs to reduce the number of unnecessary operations. These provisions quickly gave way to mandatory second surgical opinion requirements that include some form of benefit penalty for noncompliance. However, these provisions typically only require the plan participant to seek a second opinion—the final decision on whether or not the surgery is performed still remains with the plan participant.

While preferred provider organizations improve the potential for net cost savings through the inclusion of discount provider pricing and tighter UM controls, it is important to understand that the pricing discounts achieved by the initial introduction of a PPO plan (as well as other discounted arrangements, such as POS) is a one-time savings. Also, the degree of net savings from the PPO depends on the level of benefits used for in-network and out-of-network usage as well as the percentage of employees who end up using network benefits.

Figure 16–3 is a sample pricing model showing the components that impact the net expected costs an employer can expect when transferring

FIGURE 16–3
Sample PPO Pricing Model

Assumptions—Existing Plan

All employees covered under 80% standard indemnity (fee-for-service) with no network arrangement or utilization management programs. All employees located in one region, such that the proposed PPO network would be available to all employees.

1. 1990 Recorded Medical Claims	$1,000,000
2. Average Number of Employees	500
3. Average Annual Per Capita Claims (Line 1/Line2)	$2,000
4. Normal Projected Existing Plan Costs (@23%)	$1,230,000
Projected PPO In-Network Benefit Costs	
5. Average Annual Per Capita Claims	$2,000
6. Projected 1991 PPO Trend	×119%
7. Projected PPO Per Capita Before Adjustments	$2,380
8. PPO Adjustments	
a. Benefit Increase (90% Preferred)	×107%
b. Network Discounts	×88%
c. UM Adjustments	×95%
9. Projected PPO Per Capita After Adjustments	$2,129
10. Expected Average PPO Participants	×400
11. Net Projected PPO Annual Costs	$855,600
Projected Non-Network Benefit Costs	
12. Average Annual Per Capita Claims	$2,000
13. Projected 1991 Standard Trend	×123%
14. Projected PPO Per Capita Before Adjustments	$2,460
15. PPO Adjustments	
a. Benefit Decrease (70% Non-Preferred)	×92%
b. Network Discounts	×n/a
c. UM Adjustment	×97%
16. Projected PPO Per Capita After Adjustments	$2,195
17. Expected Average PPO Participants	×100
18. Net Projected PPO Annual Costs	$219,500
19. Combined 1991 Projected Costs (Lines 11 & 18)	$1,075,100
20. Expected Net Savings from PPO Implementation (Line 4–19)	$ 154,900
	12.6%

from a fee-for-service indemnity plan to a PPO (or other managed care alternative) and helps illustrate some of the basic pricing components used to evaluate the net cost advantage of establishing such a managed care plan. The numbers used in the illustration are actual 1990 and projected 1991 figures available at the time this chapter was written (summer 1991) for a sample plan sponsor, with 500 employees incurring $1 million in recorded medical benefit costs in 1990 and for which projected claims in a completely unmanaged environment were expected to increase commensurate with the level of "trend" (expected cost increase) for fee-for-service plans. Recent surveys of the largest U.S. group insurance companies showed they projected that of all their medical expense products their traditional fee-for-service indemnity plans would have the highest average trends in 1991, ranging from 20 percent to 25 percent over comparable 1990 plan costs. Those same carriers expected their PPO plans to average increases in the 15 percent to 19 percent range in 1991, about one fifth less than standard indemnity plans. The lowest rate of expected cost increases in 1991 was attributed to HMOs, both stand-alone and insurance-company-based. Of 11 companies surveyed, ranging from staff model HMOs to insurance-company-based HMO plans, average cost increases in 1991 were expected to range between 10 percent and 15 percent.[7] Hence, assuming a nonmanaged care trend rate of 23 percent in Figure 16–3, the resulting annual costs for the existing plan would increase $230,000 in 1991.

With implementation of a 90 percent preferred/70 percent nonpreferred PPO, the net expected plan costs would be a combination of adjusted in-network and non-network benefits. Steps 5 through 11 illustrate how the PPO network is valued. Using the starting point of historical indemnity claims, Line 6 shows a lower expected trend of 19 percent, as compared with the 23 percent for nonmanaged plans. The PPO adjustments reflect the specific expected impact on projected claims caused by the implementation of the PPO.

Line 8a shows the estimated additional costs for the higher benefit levels payable under the preferred PPO, generally payable at 90 percent coinsurance rather than 80 percent under the former plan. The actual adjustment will vary, depending on other plan features, although it typically is not worth a full 10 percent, since both plans eventually cover

---

[7] *Medical Benefits,* Vol. 8, No. 2, January 20, 1991, quoting Michael Schachner in *Business Insurance,* December 17, 1990.

expenses above the coinsurance limits at 100 percent for catastrophic benefits. Network discounts are reflected on Line 8b. Here, too, the exact value of discounts will vary among networks, although this adjustment reflects the full value of various discounts over the entire array of covered expenses. Therefore, even if the PPO network has an average hospital discount of 20 percent, this will only cover about half of total benefits, the balance going to physician, prescription drugs, and ancillary services. For our illustration, we show an overall 12 percent discount adjustment; again, this is a one-time adjustment in the level of expected paid claims, and future years' costs are influenced only by the continued impact of utilization management procedures, except for minor adjustments in average discount levels negotiated by the PPO manager.

Line 8c reflects the expected value of reduced utilization brought about by the various precertification and concurrent review programs associated with the PPO. Similar savings might be expected under stand-alone UM programs, although many PPO operations provide somewhat stricter UM protocols and controls than those used in conjunction with indemnity plans.

The net value of these adjustments is a reduction of 11.5 percent from the trend adjusted claims for 1991. The expected usage of the PPO network is 80 percent, so the claims of an average of 400 employees (and their covered dependents) will flow through the network side of the equation. The actual degree of network utilization will depend largely on the success of employee education about the PPO plan and the accessibility of network providers to employee locations. While the illustration assumes 100 percent availability of PPO network providers, this assumption is generous, and in the majority of instances there will be some employees who live outside the available service area and who receive "neutral" benefits of 80 percent.

Therefore, the expected net per capita benefit costs under the PPO network plan is only 6.5 percent more in 1991 as compared with 1990—considerably better than the projected 23 percent increase under the nonmanaged care plan.

However, that is only half of the story. The plan sponsor needs to understand that non-network benefits also are impacted, as shown in Lines 12 through 28. The trend is based on the higher nonmanaged care level of 23 percent. The PPO adjustments include a net benefit decrease (Line 15a) because of lower reimbursement levels and penalties for noncompliance, no adjustment (Line 15b) for network discounts since these are not applicable, and a smaller adjustment (Line 15c) for UM features, since the stand-alone programs generally are not as comprehensive as those integrated into the PPO plan operations.

Again, the actual adjustments will vary from plan to plan and among different vendors within the same geographic area. The non-network PPO plan is expected to have increased costs of 9.8 percent compared with 23 percent for nonmanaged care, although much of this reduction is attributable to the cost shifting onto plan participants in the form of reduced benefit payments.

Assuming 20 percent non-network usage among eligible participants, the combined plan costs are increased about 7.5 percent on average from 1990 to 1991, versus 23 percent with no changes. As mentioned above, this pricing model is illustrative. Exact network discounts and UM adjustments will vary among networks and vendors, and the point here is to understand some of the components that impact the value of PPO plan pricing.

Point of service plans can be valued using an essentially identical pricing model although the level of network discounts may vary. The most significant pricing differential should be in the added UM savings brought about by the internal referral management process whereby preferred care is received only if accessed through the primary care physician (PCP). The net difference can be significant, since this added referral management more directly controls utilization of medical services.

Health maintenance organizations net savings are not as easily evaluated using the above pricing model, especially where the primary method of provider reimbursement is capitation. *Capitation* essentially means that part of or all provider reimbursements are fixed, usually as a dollar amount per member per month, regardless of the number of services a member uses. With provider revenues capped, the frequency of services (utilization) is a more direct concern for the provider; the greater the frequency of services performed on average, the fewer members a physician can accept, which directly reduces overall revenue. Therefore, the provider must carefully balance the extent of care in the most cost-effective way.

In contrast, under all indemnity and most PPO plans, providers receive a discounted fee for their services, but it is the responsibility of the managed care company to control plan utilization through plan features (incentives/disincentives or case management). Point of service (POS) plans can offer either capitated or fee-for-service reimbursement arrangements.

When capitation reimbursement is used, however, the traditional methods of experience-rating evaluation (as shown in the pricing model) and the use of alternative funding arrangements become more obsolete. The fixed revenue of capitation translates into a fixed level of paid claims. In fact, if all providers within an HMO are capitated, the financial arrangement becomes one fixed prospective payment with no cost accounting, no (or little) experience rating, and less need for using the various funding arrangements (e.g., minimum premium, premium deferral, administrative services only) that evolved in the last two decades in the indemnity employee benefits business. An important question being debated in many circles of the employee benefit field today is this: Are long-term health care costs better controlled under capitated arrangements (where the provider absorbs the risk of overutilization) or under a discounted fee-for-service arrangement with tight outside-utilization controls?

Studies are showing that HMOs are expected to produce better control over trend levels than other forms of managed care alternatives. Indeed, several national insurers that operate both PPO and HMO plans are expecting lower average premium increases among their HMOs.[8] Regardless of the precise program used, there is wide agreement throughout the employee benefit industry that virtually *any* form of managed health care should be less expensive than nonmanaged health care.[9] While this has often been an intuitive assumption on the part of plan sponsors, there is growing statistical data supporting the view that managed care plans offer greater potential for lower cost increases.

Large corporations that have entered into national managed care programs have done so with the conviction that such programs stand a significantly better chance of financial viability than fee-for-service plans. This was a critical aspect in the decision of Allied Signal Corporation when it decided to adopt the point of service approach nationwide in 1988.[10]

---

[8] Ibid.

[9] For example, in a speech at the 1990 Certified Employee Benefit Specialist Conference, Patricia M. Nazemetz, director of benefits for the Xerox Corporation, expressed a strong feeling that managed care, over the long term, can produce savings over the fee-for-service indemnity business, although "that side of the business (fee-for-service) is in such a very bad state of repair that almost anything should be able to improve that process."

[10] Joseph Duva, op. cit. According to Mr. Duva, in 1987, using a managed indemnity approach, health care costs for Allied Signal rose 39 percent. Initial results for the 1988 plan year, the first year of the point of service plan using the gatekeeper primary care physician approach, showed overall average increases of 4 percent.

OTHER ISSUES AND CONSIDERATIONS

Other Hybrid Plans

While the managed care spectrum is intended to outline the primary forms of health care alternatives, there are some variations that do not fall neatly on the continuum. For example, insurance companies frequently offer a combined package of an HMO plus an indemnity plan (''dual option'') or an HMO plus an indemnity plan and a PPO (''triple option'') plan. Employees have the same choices they would have without the integration of the program, but these arrangements can offer integrated administrative and financial advantages to the plan sponsor. The vendor handles joint billing, enrollment, experience rating, renewal accounting, and management reports for both plans. Financial experience results often are cross-applied between programs, so that the employer essentially has one common plan, much like a flex plan.

The benefits of these integrated multiple-option plans are several: (1) the employer saves internal administrative duties since the carrier combines several tasks of enrollment and billing together; (2) experience rating of the plans allows the employer to enjoy the benefits of better-than-average claims experience, especially for the managed care portions; (3) combined reporting gives the employer a more consistent picture of how each plan option is operating and allows for easier comparative study between the HMO and the other options offered to employees; (4) the carrier often is more willing to offer flexible financial arrangements and better overall pricing for the employer because it can cross-apply financial results between the various options and does not have the adverse-selection problems associated with competing stand-alone HMO plans; and (5) employees still have the flexibility of choosing the benefit plans that best suit their budgets and family medical care needs.

Network Development and Management

Network configuration and adequacy are important criteria for plan sponsors to examine when considering various managed care products. After deciding what type of managed care alternatives best fit a plan sponsor's benefit objectives and cost considerations, the next critical step is selecting a managed care network that provides an acceptable match between employee locations and provider locations. Managed care companies place great importance on establishing networks of providers that are well-dispersed geographically and also include the necessary medical disciplines to be able to deliver high-quality care at all levels. That is a difficult challenge in many parts of the country. Plan sponsors, often through the help of a qualified broker or benefit consultant, must be comfortable that employees will have relatively easy access to network providers, whether the underlying plan is a PPO, POS, HMO, or other hybrid arrangement. It can be expected that some employees will need to select new physicians and possibly travel some distance, especially to receive certain specialty care. Nonetheless, a thorough evaluation of provider/employee site matches early in the process of comparing managed care providers can save considerable time later in the request-for-proposal (RFP) process.

The degree of managed care network development has varied significantly across the United States. Differences in population demographics, availability of *medical care and hospital facilities,* the influence of local provider associations, and the statutory regulations of medical providers all have influenced the ability of managed care vendors to build viable, cost effective networks and products.

Managed care acceptance is considerably higher in West Coast areas, especially in California, than in most northeastern states. A 1989 study of HMO membership, as a percentage of eligible insured population, within the 300 largest metropolitan statistical areas (MSAs) showed that within the top ten MSAs, West Coast cities account for four of the top ten, with 46 percent HMO penetration in the San Francisco/Bay Area and 32 percent in the southern California areas of Los Angeles/Anaheim/San Diego.[11]

In contrast, in the greater New York City and northern New Jersey area HMO penetration was 11 percent, ranking 24th in percentage of HMO market penetration among MSAs.[12] Pockets of significant HMO market presence also exist in such diverse areas as Minneapolis/St. Paul, Boston, and Washington, D.C., all of which are in the top ten MSAs. To

---

[11]"HMO Market Penetration in 30 Largest MSAs, 1989," from a study by the Group Health Insurance Association of America (December 1990) in an article by Susan J. Palsbo, *Medical Benefits,* January 30, 1991.

[12]Joseph Duva, op. cit. Mr. Duva indicated that Allied Signal's new POS health plan was easier to establish in West Coast cities and certain other pockets, including Kansas City, than it was in the corporate headquarters location in Morristown, New Jersey.

the extent HMO market penetration is indicative of the availability and acceptance of managed care alternatives, it shows that managed care plans are evolving at different paces across the country. This presents a very real challenge for the plan sponsor who has multiple locations across the country and yet wishes to maintain a uniform approach to its health care plan.

Although most national managed care vendors are able to provide uniform administrative systems for managed care plans, the underlying delivery platform may vary from area to area, in order to conform to accepted practices within those areas. Plan sponsors need to be aware of these possible differences in advance of committing to a given managed care product so they can make plans to modify plan design or product offerings based on what can yield the best quality of care at the most reasonable cost in each geographical area.

In the development of an RFP for a managed care plan, it is very common for the plan sponsor (or adviser) to request detailed information regarding the managed care manager's network operations and extent of coverage. Employee census, which has traditionally been included in RFPs for evaluation of financial ratings, is now included largely for the managed care vendor to estimate a site match between network providers and employee locations. These site matches often show the percentage of total employees who can be serviced by the proposed network, or networks if there are multiple employee locations. It is important that employee home addresses be used in this evaluation process, so that the site match results will produce a clearer indication of the availability of providers where employees typically use services—nearer their homes than their place of employment.

Provider Contracting & Credentialling/Quality Assurance

Assuming that general network configuration matches well with employee locations, it is equally important, regardless of the product offered, that the plan sponsor understand how the managed care company contracts with and credentials its network providers. In many ways, the network provider is the "front line" with plan participants, and their degree of overall satisfaction with the managed care plan is determined largely by their interaction with the providers. This point cannot be overstated, since the principal new element within managed care plans is the deliberate restriction of provider selection and limited access to services.

Therefore, especially for a plan sponsor who is first starting a managed care plan, it is important to ask several questions of prospective managed care vendors such as the following:

1. Exactly what process is used in *selecting* providers? What formal certification (beyond state licensing) is required? How often is it updated and checked? What steps are taken if inadequate providers (especially within certain specialties) exist?
2. How do these processes assure *high-quality* providers? What ongoing measurement processes does the manager use to evaluate membership satisfaction with providers and to measure the outcome of care delivered to participants? What percentage of providers are reviewed and eliminated each year? What independent organizations does the manager use to verify information obtained directly from the provider?
3. What are the manager's methods of *measuring the outcomes* of treatment delivered by network providers, and against what benchmark are these results compared? What are the quantifiable differentials that these providers provide in delivering cost-effective care?

Credentialling processes help ensure that providers meet acceptable levels of professionalism. While each managed care company has its own sets of credentialling requirements, the following are representative of some of the standard areas considered for physicians and hospitals.

Sample Hospital Guidelines:

Joint Commission on Accreditation of Hospitals (JCAHO) accreditation.

Contractual warranty of state license.

Agreement to participate in the various utilization control programs.

Sample Physician Guidelines:

Graduation from an accredited medical school.

Valid state license.

Valid Drug Enforcement Administration (DEA) registration if needed to deliver care (for example, to prescribe medications).

Clinical privileges at a licensed participating hospital.

Adequate professional liability insurance.
No mental/physical restriction on performing necessary services.
No prior disciplinary action.
No prior involuntary termination of employment or contract.
No prior criminal conviction or indictment.
No evidence of inappropriate utilization patterns.
Agreement to follow utilization programs, including periodic on-site review of procedures and adherence to contractual obligations.

While thorough credentialling cannot fully guarantee perfect medical care, it is an important indicator of the manager's commitment to provide high-quality levels of care for plan members.

Mental Health/Chemical Dependency

Clearly the fastest growth area in costs, among various types of health care services, is that of mental health and chemical dependency (MH/CD). MH/CD costs, both inpatient and outpatient, average 10 percent and can run as high as 35 percent of total health care costs, and the growth rate is over twice that of medical/surgical costs. Many presumed reasons exist for this recent trend, but essentially there is less uniformity associated with accepted patterns of treatment for mental health and substance abuse than for other physiological causes.

Most standard indemnity plans deal with excessive MH/CD costs through plan feature limitations. For example, outpatient benefits may be payable at 50 percent up to preset calendar-year limits such as $1,000. Similarly, there may be an overall lifetime limit placed on combined inpatient and outpatient benefits—for example, $100,000. Many managed care plan designs also handle this part of the cost equation through limitation rather than through focused utilization control. Many HMO plans, for example, simply do not cover certain psychiatric or substance abuse costs.

Unfortunately, limiting benefits in many ways fails to address the underlying problem and may lead to longer term cost for the employer. For example, an alcoholic employee who receives limited coverage under his or her benefits may forgo additional needed treatment, which can lead to much more costly long-term medical expenses as well as lost productivity and value to the plan sponsor. Similarly, an employee who has to deal alone with the cost of helping an emotionally disturbed spouse or child cannot reasonably be expected to be of the same value to his or her company as one who is unburdened by such distractions.

Many employers, recognizing at least the need to care for the tangible impact of such problems, have established and maintained employee assistance programs (EAPs). The form and functions of EAPs are described in greater detail in Chapter 24 of the *Handbook* and they are discussed here only as they relate to managed care. Many forms of managed care programs are looking to more closely integrating EAP-style programs into the structured health care plan in order to maximize the usefulness of identifying potential problems and dealing with them in a more managed environment.

Figure 16–4 is an adaption of the Managed Care Spectrum, showing the various methods available to deal with mental health/chemical dependency access and treatment. *Indemnity benefits* are shown on the left-hand side of the chart, with no incentive for use (or, more precisely, benefit limitations, as described earlier). Treatment is selected by the plan participant as desired. Any resulting benefits are incorporated into the overall plan experience, although there are no negotiated prices and no expected savings for such benefits other than those imposed by the plan features.

Standard EAP programs, as shown next on the chart, provide access to professional resources by providing early and controlled intervention to personal problems to help decrease unnecessary admissions and promote appropriate use of outpatient services. The EAP program gives incentives, often in the form of free short-term counseling, to employees. Most programs are prepaid, capitated arrangements and therefore not experience rated through claims, but the pricing can vary in accordance with the program utilization. Most EAPs do not include negotiated pricing at inpatient or outpatient facilities.

EAP gate operates the same as the standard EAP, except that the use of the EAP by plan members also is encouraged by health plan design, thus directing more clients to managed care. For example, for maximum MH/CD benefits to be received members must recertify through the EAP in all but emergency situations. However, like the standard EAP, such costs are typically prepaid and involve no formal network of prenegotiated facilities. However, through better utilization control, there are more expected savings than with the standard EAP.

FIGURE 16–4
Mental Health/Chemical Dependency Access and Treatment Options

Services Provided	Indemnity	EAP	EAP Gate	MH/CD Network	MH/CD Network with EAP Gate
Employee Incentives for Use	No	Free short term counseling	EAP and Plan	Plan Design	EAP and Plan
Treatment Approach Consistent with Managed Care Philosophy	Maybe	Yes	Yes	Yes	Yes
Experience Rating	Yes	No	No	Yes	Yes
Negotiated Pricing at Facilities	No	No	No	Yes	Yes
Expected Savings	None	$	$$	$$	$$$

A formal *MH/CD network* introduces the use of prenegotiated pricing and provider contracting. Such providers are selected on the basis of their clinical expertise, cooperation with utilization management procedures, and preferential prices. Such networks typically consist of special inpatient facilities (hospitals and clinics), outpatient providers (MDs, PhDs, and masters-level therapists), and alternative care resources (nonacute residential centers, structured day/evening programs, and halfway houses). By itself, the network does not offer employee short-term counseling but relies on plan-design incentives to encourage employees to use network providers. However, this approach does have the added advantage of being experience rated and having preferred pricing arrangements with providers.

MH/CD network with EAP gate combines the benefits of simple and early mental health access with experience rating and preferred pricing arrangements. Such arrangements are offered in conjunction with the established medical/surgical plan, although some vendors now offer stand-alone managed mental health/EAP services, which are ''carved out'' of the rest of the health care benefit. Either way, the best long-term costs savings are expected from this combination of EAP and network, since there is consistent utilization control from initial identification of the problem through treatment and outcome.

CONCLUSION

Clearly, few employee benefit topics today receive more focused attention than controlling the rapid escalation of medical care costs. Many employers are now considering whether their group medical expense benefit plans, which originally were intended to increase the attractiveness of a company's total compensation program, will place the future financial viability of the firm in serious jeopardy. With medical care expense plan costs eating up more and more corporate earnings and with increasingly greater shares of our nation's gross national product being devoted to medical care, it is expected that any solution that shows the promise of controlling costs will receive serious consideration.

As mentioned in the introduction to this chapter, ''managed care'' in its various forms is not widely seen as the panacea for controlling medical care costs, nor in guaranteeing accessibility to health care for all citizens.

The latter problem, which includes the pressing dilemma of finding affordable and appropriate care for millions of uninsured Americans, may in the final analysis play a larger role than just cost of care in determining to what extent governmental intervention will proceed.

An increasing number of this country's largest private corporations acknowledge that a fundamental rebuilding of the U.S. medical care delivery system is needed. According to a survey of chief executive officers conducted for the Robert Wood Johnson Foundation,[13] the majority still favored the existing employer-based structure of health care delivery, but there was a growing consensus that the federal government needed to play a greater role of intervention in the system, a position that was rarely expressed among U.S. corporations in recent years.

Various forms of government intervention are supported, including increasingly selective purchasing of medical services by Medicare and Medicaid programs, the establishment of tax incentives for smaller employers to offer comprehensive health coverage, the establishment of federal standards for medical care programs, and the expansion of current programs to cover the uninsured population, as well as the adoption of a universal payment system for all medical providers to be used by both government and private payors.

However, until fundamental changes are made to the U.S. system of medical care delivery, it is up to the individual plan sponsor to work with available tools to control cost while continuing to provide meaningful benefits to employees. As with any facet of an employee benefit plan, it is important for the plan sponsor to consider the value of "managed care" alternatives within the context of its own human-resources objectives and culture. The functional approach to analyzing benefits, as described in Chapter 2 of the *Handbook,* is most helpful in this context. The plan sponsor must consider and carefully balance the impact of any managed care plan on employee relations with its true potential for cost control. Remember that the local medical care environment plays a critical part in this evaluation. The reader should be aware by now that a standard "managed care product" is not necessarily the appropriate direction in which to go, regardless of the initial cost savings of the program. Implementing a managed care plan can have a more profound impact on

---

[13]*New York Times,* April 8, 1991, p. D1.

FIGURE 16–5
Fundamental Approach to Managed Healthcare

Customer Need/Behavior	Traditional Indemnity	PPO	Point of Service	HMO
Planning Orientation	Short term	Short term	Long term	Long term
Motivation to Satisfy Overall Employee needs	High degree	Moderate to High degree	Moderate degree	Low to Moderate degree
Motivation to Control Costs	Low to Moderate degree	Moderate degree	High degree	High degree
Need to Provide Freedom of Choice in Plan Design	High degree	High degree	Moderate degree	Low degree
Need for a Broad Range of Cost Control Features	Low to Moderate degree	Moderate degree	High degree	High degree
Desire for Financial Accountability in Form of Management Reports	Low to Moderate degree	Moderate degree	High degree	Low to Moderate degree
Premium Sensitivity	High	High	Moderate	Moderate

the way in which employees view their benefits (and their employer) than any other single benefit program. Therefore, a thorough evaluation of employee needs, employee benefit philosophy, and other aspects outlined in the functional approach are critical before adopting any managed care plan. Figure 16–5 may prove helpful in this evaluation.

CHAPTER 17

LONG-TERM CARE[1]

Anthony J. Gajda

WHAT IS LONG-TERM CARE?

Long-term care (LTC) usually is thought of in the context of old people in nursing homes, but actually it is a much broader concept. Frequently it is needed because of a medical problem, but often it encompasses services beyond those covered by most medical plans because they are not "medically necessary." It often is not oriented toward rehabilitation. It may be needed by people of all ages, and it can be provided through a wide range of delivery systems and in a variety of settings.

Long-term care can be defined as a system of health and custodial services to support people who have chronic, or long-term, nonremediable physical or mental conditions. Under this umbrella definition, there are many kinds and classifications of long-term care. One classification is by *level of service*—skilled, intermediate, or custodial—differentiated by the degree of medical care involved. Another basic distinction is between *informal services*—provided by family and friends—and *formal services,* purchased from individuals or institutions. Somewhere between 60 and 80 percent of the long-term care provided in the United States still falls into the category of informal services.

Within the category of formal services, the market is diverse and fragmented. The list of providers includes nursing homes; long-term care units in hospitals; continuing care retirement communities; home health

---

[1]Adapted, with permission, from *Long-term Care: The Newest Employee Benefit,* William M. Mercer, Incorporated, 1988.

agencies; adult day-care centers; and social health maintenance organizations, an experimental system that includes some prepaid long-term care services along with traditional medical services. Even such unusual players as the hotel and real estate industries are exploring business opportunities in long-term care, through residential facilities that offer some health and support services.

Why Is Long-term Care Suddenly a Big Issue?

Long-term care has become an important public concern for several reasons:

1. *Medical advances,* ironically, have helped to convert many critical short-term health problems into long-term health problems. New techniques and technology permit us to "save" the lives of heart attack and stroke victims, premature babies, and many other people whose diseases or injuries would have been fatal in the past. Yet while modern medicine prevents death, in many cases it cannot restore health. Particularly for older people, life-saving medical treatment often is the threshold to months or years of custodial care.

2. *The demographics of the Baby Boom* mean that we are on the verge of a population explosion in the higher age groups. In 1986, more than 30 million people, 12 percent of all Americans, were older than 65. By 2030, that age group will have grown to 66 million, more than 20 percent of the population.

People who think long-term care "won't happen to me" stand on increasingly shaky ground; for example, at age 65, there is a 40 percent probability of being in a nursing home before death.

3. *Changes in the way we live* have made it less likely that long-term care can be provided at home by the patient's family. Now that most women are employed, they are not available to care for their ailing parents or husbands. Children frequently live far from their parents, and few people enjoy the built-in support system of a large extended family in the same city, let alone the same house. This distance also means that parents cannot as easily get help from their children for nonmedical affairs, such as financial paperwork, meal preparation, or transportation.

4. *Existing medical coverage is inadequate* to pay for long-term care. Neither government nor private insurance health programs cover much long-term care, and long-term care can be staggeringly expensive.

Nursing homes can cost $20,000 to $40,000 a year; three home health visits a week can cost $5,000 to $8,000 a year. In 1988 Americans spent $47.5 billion on long-term care, of which $40 billion went for nursing home care for the elderly. These figures do not include the value of informal services.

5. *Public awareness* about the risks and costs of long-term care has traditionally been low. Unless one's own family has seen the financial effects of a long nursing-home stay, one is likely to believe that Medicare or Medigap insurance policies will cover long-term care. Typically surveys find that about half the population has this misunderstanding.

While none of these factors appeared overnight, they were all brought into focus by the Bowen Report in 1986. Dr. Otis Bowen, secretary of Health and Human Services, observed in his report that catastrophic illness could wipe out a family's entire savings and pointed out many of the gaps in existing medical programs. Following Bowen's report, other government task forces were asked to study the problem. In 1990, the Pepper Commission proposed a federal long-term care program at a projected cost of $70 billion, and a federal study released in 1991 projected that nearly half of all Americans who turn 65 in 1990 would spend some time in a nursing home before they die.

As the public becomes more aware of the problems of long-term care, many people look to government programs as a possible solution. Several legislative proposals have been made to add long-term care to Medicare. Because the cost would be enormous, passage of any publicly funded comprehensive long-term care program seems unlikely in the near future. For many reasons, it is much more difficult to try to cover long-term care through social insurance than it is to provide basic medical services. If there is a public solution, it will be expensive, complex, and, no doubt, imperfect.

That leaves the bulk of the long-term care problem firmly in the lap of the private sector—the responsibility of individual families. While more than 130 insurance companies and Blue Cross plans offer individual LTC coverage, many policies provide low levels of coverage, and the product is so new that pricing and marketing change rapidly, bewildering consumers who try to purchase coverage. The good news is that an important new participant—the employer—has joined the game on the side of the individuals. This new player could make a big difference in the final outcome.

LONG-TERM CARE AS AN EMPLOYEE BENEFIT

In recent years, employers' interest in long-term care has increased dramatically for many reasons:

1. *Protecting employees' financial security* has been a traditional employer concern, since destitute employees and retirees are bad for morale, productivity, and public image. Long-term care insurance can protect against financial devastation, just as pensions and life insurance do.

2. *Increasing employee satisfaction* with benefits is an important concern as employers try to make benefit dollars go farther. As people become aware of the need for long-term care, they will appreciate LTC coverage, and as more employers offer LTC benefits, organizations may want to match their competitors.

3. *Cutting medical costs* may be possible through long-term care programs if they enable patients to be treated at home or in a custodial facility more cheaply than in a hospital or skilled nursing facility. Far more compelling, adding LTC coverage to the benefit menu may be an effective way to restructure post-retirement medical benefits and satisfy retirees while limiting employer liabilities.

4. *Changing the emphasis of benefits* from covering routine expenses to protecting against catastrophic occurrences has become a necessity now that medical costs are soaring and employers can no longer afford to take a paternalistic view of the employment relationship. LTC coverage can limit the potential devastation of an extended period of care without providing expensive routine or first-dollar coverage.

5. *Preventing productivity losses* may be a significant benefit of an LTC program from the employer's standpoint, although this may not be apparent at first glance. Many employees are responsible for providing care to older or disabled people, a responsibility that often cuts into work time and creates stress, fatigue, and even illness.

6. *Government pressure* on employers to provide LTC benefits may be an alternative to publicly funded long-term care coverage. Some employers feel that if they take the initiative in helping employees provide for their own long-term care protection, they can stave off federal attempts to require action in this area.

7. *Union pressure* also is beginning to grow for LTC benefits—the 1987 United Auto Workers contracts with Ford and General Motors include custodial care—and employers may want to anticipate demands and present their own plans first.

According to the Health Insurance Association of America, as of June 1990, more than 150 employers had adopted group long-term care insurance programs covering nearly 80,000 employees and retirees. At present, most of the plans are paid for entirely by contributions from employees or retirees, with the employer's involvement limited to selecting an insurance carrier and handling communication and administration. Beyond that, there is little uniformity in how the programs operate, since few standard policies exist, and the pioneering employers have, in effect, required carriers to tailor the coverage to the employer's specifications. Although they want to proceed with LTC plans, some employers feel that the insurance market for such plans is too immature to work in. But the market is changing so rapidly that employers determined to wait and see won't have to wait long.

COORDINATION OF LONG-TERM CARE WITH OTHER BENEFITS

Benefit managers may find that managing long-term care coverage is far more difficult than managing traditional medical benefit programs. Provider availability is one reason. The country has a severe shortage of nursing home beds, nurses, and support staff to tend the beds. Some regions also have shortages in other delivery systems such as home health agencies and adult day-care centers. The vast majority of beds are occupied by Medicaid patients—in some areas of the country, as much as 95 percent. In addition, some states are not allowing new beds to be provided. To make things even more complicated, employers must be concerned about availability not just in the area of their plant or office but anywhere in the country to which retirees might move. Geographical pricing and benefit design may be required. For instance, the Alaska LTC plan sets higher reimbursement levels for facilities in high-cost Alaska than in the rest of the United States.

In long-term care, some of the traditional benefit plan assumptions do not work the same way they do for medical plans. As with many new benefits where lack of care has existed, an LTC program may not cut costs. Indeed it may actually raise costs in the near term. In traditional medical plans, costs can be managed by substituting one type of formal medical service (such as a visiting nurse) for a more expensive one (such as a hospital). But long-term care can mean substituting a formal service (the visiting nurse) for an unpaid, informal one (the daughter-in-law). Or it can mean substituting home health services for institutional care at only a modest savings—more than offset by the administrative expenses of the care manager.

Probably the single best piece of advice to the benefit manager embarking on LTC deliberations is to be sure to consider long-term care as part of an integrated health care benefit program, not in isolation. Deficiencies in supply or quality of nursing-home care, for instance, have a direct effect on hospitalization and, therefore, on medical plan costs. If minor medical care cannot be provided at the nursing home, or the nursing staff doesn't detect health problems in time, patients may be hospitalized unnecessarily. On the other hand, many patients are kept in hospitals longer than medically necessary, because nursing home beds are not available. This integrated view is important because the lines between acute-care medical benefits and long-term care benefits are arbitrary. Add government benefits to the picture, and it becomes even more complicated.

For example, consider an employee who suffers a stroke. He immediately is admitted to a hospital, where for several weeks he receives aggressive treatment to stabilize and improve his condition. He then may be transferred to a skilled-nursing facility, where he continues to receive medical attention from physicians and registered nurses. This treatment is covered by the medical plan because it is "medically necessary." Later, the patient may be transferred to a rehabilitation center for various kinds of therapy, which also generally would be covered by the medical plan. At some point, however, whether in the hospital, the skilled-nursing facility, or the rehabilitation center, the doctors may decide they have done as much as they can and the patient will never fully recover. Perhaps he can return home, where he can manage with the help of occasional home health visits and help with bathing, dressing, walking, or other daily activities; perhaps he must be put into an intermediate-care or custodial institution. In either case, the medical plan will not cover the expenses unless they are considered medically necessary. The patient has now slipped over the line between acute care and long-term care, with little change in physical condition, but immense financial effects. If the patient cannot return to work, he will qualify for Social Security disability coverage and after two years on disability will become eligible for Medicare. The employer plan then will become the secondary payor, picking up any medically necessary expenses that are not covered by Medicare. From the patient's standpoint, however, Medicare coverage will do little to improve his financial outlook, unless he needs to go into a skilled-nursing facility, in which case the

Medicare coverage may be better than the employer plan. If the patient goes through all his resources paying for care and help, he eventually will qualify for Medicaid coverage. In some states this will include intermediate care or care in custodial institutions. If the patient still can get along at home with some help in daily activities, but can no longer afford it, his only alternative may be to enter a nursing home anyway—perhaps at much greater cost to the taxpayers.

Principles of Long-Term Care Plan Design

In designing a long-term care plan, the benefit manager should keep several principles in mind:

1. The plan should be coordinated with medical and government coverages to minimize gaps and make the most of benefit dollars. Any opportunities to save money through LTC programs come only if the LTC plan is carefully coordinated with other medical coverage and with long-term disability coverage, so the most cost-effective methods of care can be used.

2. The plan should be coordinated with the existing provider marketplace, lest demand for long-term care services, far greater than the supply of such services, set off economic chaos and fuel inflation. When installing an LTC plan for its 7,000 retirees, for instance, the state of Alaska discovered that only 600 nursing home beds exist in the entire state, the great majority of which were used by Medicaid patients.

3. Levels of coverage should be both adequate and appropriate. As in any emerging insurance market where no rules of thumb have yet been established, it is difficult to determine how much insurance is enough.

4. The plan should share risk appropriately among employer, provider, and beneficiary. As experience builds and various types of coverage are tried, it will be easier to understand and quantify these risks.

5. A quick-fix solution to the problem simply does not exist. Off-the-shelf insurance programs are not likely to satisfy either employer or beneficiaries. Employers should recognize that the LTC plan installed this year will unquestionably need revisions, perhaps major ones, as the laws and the marketplace change. They also should recognize that premiums may rise in the future as health care costs and utilization increase and that coverage levels may have to be increased to provide adequate protection.

6. A single approach to employer-provider LTC does not exist, either. Employee needs and preferences differ from one workplace to another; health care supply varies by geography; corporate culture also is a great variable. The plan that works for one employer may fail dismally at another organization.

Despite all the uncertainties, employers should try to get everything right the first time. It is harder to make changes in an LTC insurance plan than in the typical medical group plan, because in LTC plans employees generally begin building reserves with their first premium payments. These reserves greatly complicate the process of changing carriers or benefits.

Furthermore, participants may be upset if the plan is changed and their reserves are tied up in a program they do not like (because of benefit cutbacks) or cannot afford (because of benefit enhancements).

What Should a Long-Term Care Insurance Plan Include?

The employer beginning to design an LTC program has many choices to make. From the benefit side, the choices include the following:

1. How will benefits be paid? Will the plan reimburse for a given service at a fixed rate, or pay a certain percentage of care costs? Will there be a deductible?
2. What level of coverage is appropriate? Should it be defined as a daily maximum, a lifetime maximum, or in some other way?
3. Will the plan include an inflation escalator?
4. What kinds of services are covered? Will the plan cover just nursing home stays, and, if so, what kind? Will it cover services such as home health visits, adult day care, or respite care? Will inpatient and outpatient services vary?
5. Are certain diseases and conditions excluded from coverage?
6. Will the plan take an HMO or preferred provider (PPO) approach, encouraging or requiring the use of certain providers? Will access to care be granted or facilitated?
7. Should benefits vary by geographical area?
8. Who will be eligible for coverage? Will the plan be offered to all employees, or just to retirees? To increase the size of the group and thus spread risk, will employees be allowed to enroll their parents or children as well as themselves and their spouses?

9. Will the plan require a hospital stay to trigger benefits? This is a commonly used ''gatekeeper'' mechanism intended to determine whether the benefit is really needed, yet it may encourage unnecessary and expensive hospital confinements or prevent legitimate use of the plan.
10. If employees leave the employer, will they be able to convert their coverage to an individual policy? If not, will past premiums be refunded wholly, or in part? What, if any, benefits will be payable upon death?
11. What utilization controls will be in effect? Will the plan include practices typical in medical plans, such as preadmissions screening or advance certification of treatment? Will it include case management? Will the employer or a third party attempt to monitor quality of care?

There are important decisions to be made on the financing side of LTC plan design as well as on the benefit side. Among them are these:

1. How will the reserves built up from the policy be valued? The plan may want to move them from one carrier to another in the future, and it may want to offer certain portability options to participants. This issue may be complicated because of limits on reserves set by the Deficit Reduction Act of 1984.
2. Will premiums vary by age brackets? In general, the plan probably will want to charge lower premiums if employees enroll at early ages, to minimize adverse selection. But there are many variations in how steeply the steps go up with age of entry, and in turn, how quickly reserves will build up.
3. Will coverage be paid up at retirement, or will retirees continue to pay premiums? Will premiums be waived while the participant is collecting benefits?
4. Should the plan be insured or self-funded? In the infancy of the group LTC market cycle, employers will no doubt want to transfer risk to an insurance company, but the long-run trend probably will parallel that of medical coverage, where employers eventually look to self-funding as a more efficient technique.
5. What underwriting guidelines should be used in deciding which applicants will be permitted to enroll? Will the plan cover for

pre-existing conditions or establish a waiting period? Will medical examinations or tests be required? State insurance laws will affect the options and decisions on these issues.

6. What actuarial assumptions will be used? How will the costs of future care and utilization be projected, especially since availability of coverage may increase utilization?

Funding and Financing of Long-Term Care Programs

Until recently, group long-term care plans were strictly employee-pay-all plans. But now a handful of employers contribute to the cost of their plans. This practice may continue for several reasons. As mentioned earlier, labor unions are beginning to look at LTC benefits. Even if long-term care doesn't come up as a bargaining issue, employers may want to introduce it themselves as a pre-emptive move. Another impetus toward employer contributions may be the growing concern over skyrocketing liabilities for retiree medical coverage. With the issuance of Financial Accounting Standards Board Statement 106 putting retiree medical liabilities on corporate balance sheets, employers are looking for ways to cap these commitments. Under present court interpretations, it is difficult if not impossible to cut back on a promise to provide medical care to retirees—but retirees can voluntarily agree to a new arrangement. In such a situation, long-term care could be an incentive for retirees to reopen the discussion and, in return for LTC coverage, accept a less expensive medical plan.

Employer contributions to LTC plans, however, have a major potential problem that could outweigh the benefits. The tax consequences of an employer-provided LTC benefit are unclear. Long-term care is not a statutory welfare benefit, and thus if it is paid for by the employer, employees apparently cannot receive it tax-free, nor can it be included in a cafeteria plan.

Whatever their reasons for contributing to LTC plans, employers, learning from their recent experience with medical plans, probably will prefer a "defined contribution" approach to plan funding rather than a "defined benefit" approach. In other words, they will express their financial commitment as a certain dollar amount, rather than promising to cover a share of all costs. The amount may well vary by length of service.

THE INSURANCE COMPANIES' VIEW

Long-term care coverage is a totally new market for the insurance industry, and carriers are testing the waters cautiously. LTC coverage is a curious hybrid, which in some ways resembles several different kinds of traditional insurance products.

1. LTC resembles medical insurance because it involves health services and health facilities.
2. LTC resembles disability insurance because in many cases, the insurance benefit is simply a daily or monthly amount, paid to a nursing home rather than directly to the beneficiary when disabilities or inabilities to function reach a certain level.
3. LTC resembles life insurance because the risk curves have the same shape, and many years pass before the carrier has good information on experience and pricing.
4. LTC resembles deferred annuities because reserves build up over many years before payout, making long-term investment decisions an essential factor in pricing and profitability.

As a result, carriers wanting to enter the LTC market have many different models to look at for guidance—but LTC is unlike any single one of them, based on past experience.

Insurance companies have been issuing individual LTC policies for about 15 years, but only about half a million have been sold, most within the last three years, so that very little credible experience is available to analyze. During that period, of course, the health care delivery system has changed radically, making it more difficult to predict costs and utilization with a great degree of confidence.

Within the industry there is no standard policy form, making it difficult to compare the experience that is available. Nor have rule-of-thumb underwriting approaches been developed through trial and error. Some companies have suggested including LTC coverage in other policies such as life and disability or annuities. The National Association of Insurance Commissioners has written a model act regulating LTC coverage, which is being adopted by some states, but others have developed their own regulations that may differ greatly; this complicates the position of the insurance company that wants to market its LTC products widely.

Finally, the tax status of LTC reserves—which directly affects profitability—has not been clarified by the IRS, and while this uncertainty exists, carriers are justifiably nervous. Similarly, the tax situation for beneficiaries and for employer-funded plans also is questionable, putting more barriers into the path of potential customers.

But many new companies are entering the market, and products offered are improving in breadth of coverage and choices for the buyer. The insurance industry sees the challenges, the opportunities, and the needs of society, and is working to develop appropriate responses.

A few years ago, carriers were just as reluctant about another new product, group universal life insurance—everybody talked about it, but for a long time nobody marketed it. Once somebody opened the door, however, all the insurance companies rushed through. We may see the same pattern with group LTC coverage, although the potential liability and duration of LTC claims are certainly worrisome to insurers.

Legal and Tax Issues

As itemized by the Department of Health and Human Services task force on Long-Term Care Insurance, there are several legal and tax impediments to the development of employer-sponsored LTC benefit plans, whether insured or self-funded.

1. LTC insurance is not defined in the Internal Revenue Code as a statutory employee benefit, thus employers cannot deduct LTC premiums and employees cannot exclude from income any payments from an employer-provided LTC policy.
2. The tax status of insurance company reserves in LTC policies is uncertain: Insurance carriers are operating as though such reserves, set aside to pay claims that may not be incurred for many years, are a deductible charge against current premiums.
3. Employers cannot legally prefund LTC plans over the working lifetime of employees, as they can with pensions.
4. LTC benefits cannot be included in a cafeteria plan.

The task force recommended changes in these areas to encourage employer-sponsored LTC plans. It also recommended changes in the tax code that would encourage individuals to purchase LTC coverage on their own, by allowing people to use funds from their individual retirement accounts, qualified pension plans, or accumulated cash values in life insurance contracts to buy LTC insurance without first having to pay income tax on the distributions.

Several employers have asked for private letter rulings from the IRS on various aspects of LTC plans. Legislation also has been drafted to change the tax code to permit employers to sponsor insured and self-funded LTC plans and to encourage individual purchase of LTC insurance.

COMMUNICATION—THE MAKE-OR-BREAK ELEMENT IN LTC PROGRAMS

The evidence is already strong that the success of a group long-term care plan—defined as the level of employee participation—depends on how well it is communicated to employees. As mentioned earlier, the American public generally is not informed of the facts about long-term care—either about the probability that they will need such care or the adequacy of existing insurance to pay for it. Unless people understand these facts, they are not likely to want LTC coverage. In turn, low participation tends to create adverse selection and drives up costs, thus making the program even less attractive. The first step in successfully introducing long-term care coverage, therefore, must be education. As with life insurance, people's reluctance to contemplate their own decline or demise presents an obstacle, but the subject can be made more palatable by broadening the focus from nursing home care to other services such as adult day care or home health assistance.

Employers can further diffuse the denial response by including LTC in a much wider context: that of wellness, health promotion, and disease intervention. The United States is behind many other countries in its approach to health issues of aging; we tend to regard physical and mental decline as inevitable instead of looking for ways to prevent or retard it. Unfortunately, few physicians are knowledgeable about geriatric care and few see their responsibilities to older patients in preventive terms.

While some employers have been disappointed in participation levels for their LTC plans, others have been amazed by how well employees responded. The state of Alaska, for instance, after an aggressive education and promotion campaign that included newsletters and a retiree survey, signed up 3,400 out of 7,000 eligible retirees. Owens-Corning Fiberglas recently surveyed employees about their interest in LTC coverage. The survey was accompanied, however, by information about the incidence and costs of nursing home care, and about Medicaid spend-down requirements. Before the survey, the company thought interest would be higher among older employees, those with lower incomes, and those who had recently been hospitalized or whose general health was poor—people who might consider themselves more likely to need help. To Owens-Corning's surprise, none of these factors made any difference in employees' response. Across the spectrum of age, income, and health, employees were all concerned about LTC and interested in the availability of LTC coverage.

Surveys are an essential tool in making good pricing decisions, as well as deciding what levels of coverage to offer in the first place. But communication cannot stop after the initial enrollment, nor focus solely on plan details. If people have unrealistic expectations about the risk of long-term care expenses and the ability of the plan to protect against it, they may be disappointed, and this can jeopardize the continued appeal of the plan for new participants. Continuing communication with both active employees and retirees is critical to getting the most out of an LTC program.

CAREGIVERS—ALSO IN NEED OF ASSISTANCE

The recipients of long-term care benefits generally are thought of as the people who must receive custodial care. But another type of benefit program has as its recipients the people who provide care to family members or friends. Across the country, the best research indicates that 20 to 25 percent of employees are responsible for taking care of aged or disabled parents or spouses. Employers are coming to realize that it is in their best interests to help caregivers with these responsibilities, which can erode productivity.

Various studies have attempted to quantify the burdens of caregiving upon people and their employers. Among the statistics:

—Caregivers to brain-damaged older people lost an average of 9.3 hours every month from their jobs.

—Twelve percent of employed caregivers had to quit their jobs; 55 percent had to reduce their work hours.

—Caregivers tend to get sick themselves as a result of the physical and emotional strain of their responsibilities; they were 25 percent more likely to be under physicians' care, almost twice as likely to have frequent headaches, and almost three times as likely to have frequent anxiety or depression.

—Thirty-five percent of employed caregivers said their work is affected; 13 percent had to decline overtime work, and 18 percent had to pass up training opportunities.

The cost to employers of their employees' caregiving responsibilities, therefore, is significant. Employees simply cannot operate at top quality if they are exhausted from nursing an invalid at night or visiting the hospital or nursing home every day. They cannot put in a full day's work if they are on the phone arranging Grandma's doctor appointments, handling her legal affairs, getting her into a nursing home, or checking whether she ate a decent lunch. The situation can be even more difficult if Grandma lives 1,000 miles away.

In their own interest, employers are beginning to look for ways to ease these burdens, through a wide variety of programs that have come to be described by the term *eldercare*. Eldercare activities fall into two categories—indirect and direct. Indirect programs are those that may help many employees, not just those with caregiving responsibilities. Such programs can provide emotional support and reduce conflicts between work and caregiving. They include flextime, liberal personal-leave policies, job sharing, employee assistance programs, and dependent-care spending accounts. Use of spending accounts for pretax payment of dependent care expenses, unfortunately, is quite restricted. Under IRS regulations, the employee must claim the older person as a dependent for income tax purposes and provide at least 50 percent of support. The dependent must spend at least eight hours a day in the caregiver's home, and the care purchased through the spending account must be necessary to allow the employee to work.

Direct programs are designed specifically to help caregivers, and include several types:

Information programs can include printed materials, seminars and meetings, or fairs to which many local agencies send representatives.

Direct service programs might include support groups or individual counseling services for caregivers, an adult day-care center affiliated with the employer, or subsidized slots in a community center.

Referral and linkage programs put caregivers in touch with community agencies, geriatric case managers, nursing homes, day-care programs, or other resources that can help the caregivers or the patient.

Reimbursement programs subsidize various services for caregivers, such as respite care to allow the caregiver time away from the patient.

Eldercare programs often are perceived by employees as being far more valuable than their costs might indicate. Employed caregivers, above all, lack time in which to gather information or investigate alternative arrangements or even to take care of their own emotional or physical health.

In addition, there are no tax problems involved in most eldercare benefits, since many of these programs are similar to employee assistance programs and do not provide any tangible, thus taxable, benefits.

CONCLUSION

While long-term care is a hot issue and likely to get even hotter, employers need to be especially careful in making decisions. The environment in which LTC plans operate, including the insurance marketplace, tax and accounting treatment, and supply of services, is still unclear and undefined. Of those vast areas of uncertainty, the question of supply is perhaps the most troubling, and employers should make this a top priority as they consider LTC benefits. The most generous LTC plan in the world will mean little if there are no support services available when beneficiaries need them, so the employer who fails to think about supply can't help but be disappointed in the eventual effectiveness of the plan. Feasibility studies must include an assessment of care facilities—not just institutions but home health agencies, hospices, adult day-care centers, and other support resources. If the assessment is bleak, employers may decide to use their clout to help increase supply. Corporations in some cities have funded adult day-care centers and referral agencies. Just as employers are banding together in coalitions to control hospital costs and encourage alternative delivery systems for acute care, they could work together to encourage new nursing homes or health agencies. They also could provide financial support for education of geriatric nurses or physicians.

Of course, the current legislative and regulatory situation may need changing before significant improvements can be made in the situation.

As mentioned earlier, the tax status of LTC benefits is unclear, and it does not appear that existing benefit vehicles can be used to fund LTC plans. From the insurance carriers' standpoint, there are also questions about the tax treatment of LTC reserves.

In addition, many state health licensing boards have tried to control medical costs by keeping a tight lid on beds and facilities.

As the need for long-term care increases, the government will certainly respond—in some way or another. Employers who have carefully researched their own resources and options and who are clear about their own goals will be in an excellent position to lobby for a response that will make the situation better, not worse.

Currently, long-term care benefits probably are feasible only for relatively large employers who can negotiate tailor-made programs with their insurance carriers. The experience of these pioneering organizations will be eagerly watched by both employers and insurers as they consider whether they, too, should enter the LTC arena. While LTC is still in its infancy as an employee benefit, it is clear that long-term care is a growing health care issue that is coming into the full limelight of public attention. Employers who do take initiatives in the area will find them well-received by employees, retirees, and the public.

CHAPTER 18

DENTAL PLAN DESIGN

Ronald L. Huling

Dental plans have become one of the nation's most popular employee benefits. In 1990, more than 100 million individuals were covered by workplace-based dental benefit plans. These individuals represent a significant portion of the United States' full-time work force.

It is not surprising that dental plans are so popular. Most of the U.S. population visits a dentist at least once each year.

The Difference between Medicine and Dentistry

Medicine and dentistry have many differences, and sound dental plan design recognizes these. Two of the more important differences relate to the location and nature of care.

Location

The practice of the typical physician is hospital oriented, while dentists practice almost exclusively in an office setting. Partly because of these practice differences, physicians tend to associate with other physicians with greater frequency than dentists with other dentists. This isolation, along with the inherent differences in the nature of medical and dental care, tends to produce a greater variety of dental care patterns than is the case in medicine. In addition, practicing in isolation does not afford the same opportunities for peer review and general quality control.

Nature of Care

Perhaps contributing more significantly to the differences in medicine and dentistry are the important differences between the nature of medical and dental care. Medical care usually is mandatory, while dental care often is elective. In medicine, except in the case of routine examinations, the patient typically visits a physician with certain symptoms—often pain or discomfort—and seeks relief. Whether real or imagined, the patient's perception is that delay can mean more pain and, under certain circumstances, even death. Under these circumstances, the physician's charge for treatment historically has not been an issue, perhaps from fear of alienating the individual whom the patient has entrusted with his or her care or perhaps in gratitude for the treatment.

Dental treatment, on the other hand, often is elective. Again, unless there is pain or trauma, dental care often is postponed. The patient recognizes that life is not at risk and as a result has few reservations about postponing treatment. In fact, postponement may be preferable to the patient—perhaps because of an aversion to visiting the dentist, which was rooted many years in the past when dental technology was less well developed.

As a result, dentists' charges for major courses of treatment often are discussed in advance of the treatment when there is no pain or trauma and, as with any number of other consumer decisions, the patient may opt to defer the treatment to a later time and spend the money elsewhere.

A second difference in the nature of care is that while medical care is rarely cosmetic, dental care often is requested for cosmetic purposes. A crown, for example, may be necessary to save a tooth, but it also may be used to correct only minor decay because it improves the patient's appearance. Many people place orthodontia into the same category, although evidence exists that failure to obtain needed orthodontic care may result in major gum disease in later life.

A third major difference between the nature of medical and dental care is that dentistry often offers alternative procedures for treating disease and restoring teeth, many of which are equally effective. For example, a molar cavity might be treated by a two-surface gold inlay, which may cost 10 times as much as a simple amalgam filling. In these instances, the choice of the appropriate procedure is influenced by a number of factors, including the cost of the alternatives, the condition of the affected tooth and the teeth surrounding it, and the likelihood that a particular approach will be successful.

There are other significant differences in medical care and dentistry that will have an effect on plan design. These include the cost of the typical treatment and the emphasis on prevention.

Dental expenses generally are lower, more predictable, and budgetable. The average dental claim check is only about $100. Medical claims, on the average, are much higher.

The last difference of significance is the emphasis on prevention. The advantages of preventive dentistry are clearly documented. While certain medical diseases and injuries are self-healing, dental disease, once started, almost always gets progressively worse. Therefore, preventive care may appear to be more productive in dentistry than medicine.

Providers of Dental Benefits

Providers of dental benefits generally can be separated into three categories: insurance companies; Blue Cross and Blue Shield organizations; and others, including state dental association plans (e.g., Delta plans), self-insured, self-administered plans, and group practice or HMO-type plans. Insurance companies and Blue Cross/Blue Shield plans cover the largest share of the population. However, enrollment in self-administered, self-insured plans, plans employing third-party administrators, dental association plans, and HMOs is in an upsurge.

Insurance company–administered dental benefits and most self-insured, self-administered plan benefits are provided on an indemnity or reimbursement basis. Expenses incurred by eligible individuals are submitted to the administrator, typically an insurer, for payment; and, if the expense is covered, the appropriate payment is calculated according to the provisions of the plan. Payment generally is made directly to the covered employee, unless assigned by the employee to the provider. When benefits are provided on this basis, the plan sponsor normally has substantial latitude in determining who and what is to be covered and at what level.

The dental benefits of both dental service corporations and Blue Cross/Blue Shield plans generally are provided on a "service" basis. The major differences between indemnity and service benefits relate to the roles of the provider and the covered individual. Service benefits are payable directly to the provider, generally according to a contract, which fixes the reimbursement level between the dentist and the plan. In some instances, this payment actually may be lower than what would be charged to a direct-pay or indemnity patient. Despite the differences between the indemnity and service approaches, plan design plays an equally important role in both.

Under the group practice or HMO-type arrangement, a prescribed range of dental services is provided to eligible participants, generally in return for a prepaid, fixed, and uniform payment. Services are provided by dentists practicing in group practice clinics, or by those in individual practice but affiliated for purposes of providing plan benefits to eligible participants. Some individuals eligible under these arrangements are covered through collectively bargained self-insurance benefit trusts. In these instances, trust fund payments are used either to reimburse dentists operating in group practice clinics or to pay the prescribed fixed per capita fee. Group practice HMO-type arrangements generally offer little latitude in plan design. As a result, the balance of this chapter, since it is largely devoted to the issue of plan design, may have limited application to these types of arrangements.

Covered Dental Expenses

Virtually all dental problems fall into nine professional treatment categories:

1. *Diagnostic*. Examination to determine the existence of dental disease or to evaluate the condition of the mouth. Included in this category would be such procedures as X-rays and routine oral examinations.
2. *Preventive*. Procedures to preserve and maintain dental health. Included in this category are topical cleaning, space maintainers, and the like.
3. *Restorative*. Procedures for the repair and reconstruction of natural teeth, including the removal of dental decay and installation of fillings and crowns.
4. *Endodontics*. Treatment of dental-pulp disease and therapy within existing teeth. Root canal therapy is an example of this type of procedure.
5. *Periodontics*. Treatment of the gums and other supporting structures of the teeth, primarily for maintenance or improvement of the gums. Quadrant scraping is an example of a periodontic procedure.
6. *Oral Surgery*. Tooth extraction and other surgery of the mouth and jaw.

7. *Prosthodontics.* Replacement of missing teeth and the construction, replacement, and repair of artificial teeth and similar devices. Preparation of bridges and dentures is included in this category.
8. *Orthodontics.* Correction of malocclusion and abnormal tooth position through repositioning of natural teeth.
9. *Pedodontics.* Treatment of children who do not have all their permanent teeth.

In addition to the recognition of treatment or services in these nine areas, the typical dental plan also includes provision for palliative treatment (i.e., procedures to minimize pain, including anesthesia), emergency care, and consultation.

These nine different types of procedures usually are categorized into three or four general groupings for purposes of plan design. The first classification often includes both preventive and diagnostic expenses. The second general grouping includes all minor restorative procedures. Charges in the restorative, endodontic, periodontic, and oral surgery areas are included in this classification. The third broad grouping, often combined with the second, includes major restorative work (e.g., prosthodontics). The fourth separate classification covers orthodontic expenses. Pedodontic care generally falls into the first two groupings. Later in this chapter plan design is examined in greater detail, with specific differences evaluated in traditional plan design applicable to each of these three or four general groupings.

Types of Plans

Dental plans covering the vast majority of all employees can be divided broadly into two types: scheduled and nonscheduled. Other approaches discussed below are essentially variations of these two basic plan types.

Scheduled Plans

Scheduled plans are categorized by a listing of fixed allowances by procedure. For example, the plan might pay $40 for a cleaning and $350 for root canal therapy. In addition, the scheduled plan may include deductibles and coinsurance (i.e., percentage cost-sharing provisions). Where deductibles are included in scheduled plans, amounts usually are small, or, in some cases, required on a lifetime basis only.

Coinsurance provisions are extremely rare in scheduled plans, since the benefits of coinsurance can be achieved through the construction of the schedule (i.e., the level of reimbursement for each procedure in the schedule can be set for specific reimbursement objectives). For example, if it is preferable to reimburse a higher percentage of the cost of preventive procedures than of other procedures, the schedule can be constructed to accomplish this goal.

There are three major advantages to scheduled plans:

Cost Control. Benefit levels are fixed and, therefore, less susceptible to inflationary increases.

Uniform Payments. In certain instances, it may be important to provide the same benefit regardless of regional cost differences. Collectively bargained plans occasionally may take this approach to ensure the "equal treatment" of all members.

Ease of Understanding. It is clear to both the plan participant and the dentist how much is to be paid for each procedure.

In addition, scheduled plans sometimes are favored for employee-relations reasons. As the schedule is updated, improvements can be communicated to employees. If the updating occurs on a regular basis, this will be a periodic reminder to employees of the plan and its merits.

There also are disadvantages to scheduled plans. First, benefit levels, as well as internal relationships, must be examined periodically and changed when necessary to maintain reimbursement objectives. Second, where participants are dispersed geographically, plan reimbursement levels will vary according to the cost of dental care in a particular area, unless multiple schedules are utilized. Third, if scheduled benefits are established at levels that are near the maximum of the reasonable and customary range, dentists who normally charge at below prevailing levels may be influenced to adjust their charges.

Nonscheduled Plans

Sometimes referred to as comprehensive plans, nonscheduled plans are written to cover some percentage of the "reasonable and customary" charges, or the charges most commonly made by dentists in the community. For any single procedure, the usual and customary charge typically is set at the 90th percentile. This means that the usual and customary charge level will cover the full cost of the procedure for 90 percent of the claims submitted in that geographical area.

Nonscheduled plans generally include a deductible, typically a calendar-year deductible of $25 or $50, and reimburse at different levels for different classes of procedures. Preventive and diagnostic expenses typically are covered in full or at very high reimbursement levels. Reimbursement levels for other procedures usually are then scaled down from the preventive and diagnostic level, based on design objectives of the employer.

There are two major advantages to nonscheduled plans.

Uniform Reimbursement Level. While the dollar payment may vary by area and dentists, the percent of the total cost reimbursed by the plan is uniform.

Adjusts Automatically for Change. The nonscheduled plan adjusts automatically, not only for inflation but also for variations in the relative value of specific procedures.

This approach also has disadvantages. First, because benefit levels adjust automatically for increases in the cost of care, in periods of rapidly escalating prices cost control can be a problem. Second, once a plan is installed on this basis, the opportunities for modest benefit improvements, made primarily for employee-relations purposes, are limited, at least relative to the scheduled approach. Third, except for claims for which predetermination of benefits is appropriate, it rarely is clear in advance what the specific payment for a particular service will be, either to patient or dentist.

Other approaches are, for the most part, merely variations of the two basic plans. Included in this list are combination plans, incentive plans, and dental combined with major medical plans.

Combination Plan

This simply is a plan in which certain procedures are reimbursed on a scheduled basis, while others are reimbursed on a nonscheduled basis. In other words, it is a hybrid. While many variations exist, a common design in combination plans is to provide preventive and diagnostic coverage on a nonscheduled basis (i.e., a percentage of usual and customary, normally without a deductible). Procedures other than preventive and diagnostic are provided on a scheduled basis.

The principal advantage of a combination plan is that it provides a balance between (1) the need to emphasize preventive care, and (2) cost control. Procedures that traditionally are the most expensive are covered on a scheduled basis, and, except where benefit levels are established by a collective bargaining agreement, the timing of schedule improvements is at the employer's discretion. Preventive and diagnostic expenses, however, adjust automatically so the incentive for preventive care does not lose its effectiveness as dental care costs increase.

The combination approach shares many of the same disadvantages as the scheduled and unscheduled plans, at least for certain types of expenses. Benefit levels—for other than preventive and diagnostic expenses—must be evaluated periodically. Scheduled payments do not reimburse at uniform levels for geographically dispersed participants. And dentists may be influenced by the schedule allowances to adjust their charges. Also, actual plan payments for preventive and diagnostic expenses rarely are identified in advance. Finally, it can be said that the combination approach is more complex than either the scheduled or unscheduled alternatives.

Incentive Plan

This type, a second variation, promotes sound dental hygiene through increasing reimbursement levels. Incentive coinsurance provisions generally apply only to preventive and maintenance (i.e., minor restorative) procedures, with other procedures covered on either a scheduled or nonscheduled basis. Incentive plans are designed to encourage individuals to visit the dentist regularly, without the plan sponsor having to absorb the cost of any accumulated neglect. Such plans generally reimburse at one level during the first year, with coinsurance levels typically increasing from year to year only for those who obtained needed treatment in prior years. For example, the initial coinsurance level for preventive and maintenance expenses might be 60 percent, increasing to 70 percent, 80 percent, and, finally 90 percent on an annual basis as long as needed care is obtained. If, in any one year, there is a failure to obtain the required level of care, the coinsurance percentage reverts back to its original level.

The incentive portion of an incentive plan may or may not be characterized by deductibles. When deductibles are included in these plans, it is not unusual for them to apply on a lifetime basis.

The incentive concept, on the one hand, has two major advantages. In theory, the design of the plan encourages regular dental care and reduces the incidence of more serious dental problems in the future. Also, these plans generally have lower first-year costs than most nonscheduled plans.

On the other hand, there are major disadvantages. First, an incentive plan can be complicated to explain and even more complicated to administer. Second, even in parts of the country where this design is more prevalent, little evidence exists to suggest that the incentive approach is effective in promoting sound dental hygiene. Finally, this particular plan is vulnerable to misunderstanding. For example, what happens if the participant's dentist postpones the required treatment until the beginning of the next plan year?

Plans Providing both Medical and Dental Coverages

The last of the variations is the plan that provides both medical and dental coverage. During the infancy of dental benefits, such plans were quite popular.

These plans generally are characterized by a common deductible amount that applies to the sum of both medical and dental expenses. Coinsurance levels may be identical, and, sometimes, the maximum applies to the combination of medical and dental expenses. However, recent design of these plans has made a distinction between dental and medical expenses so each may have its own coinsurance provisions and maximums.

The advantages of this approach are the same as for the nonscheduled plan (i.e., uniform reimbursement levels, adjusts automatically to change, and relatively easy to understand). But this approach fails to recognize the difference between medicine and dentistry, unless special provisions are made for dental benefits. It must be written with a major medical carrier, whether this carrier is competent or not to handle dental protection; it makes it extremely difficult to separate and evaluate dental experience; and it shares the same disadvantages as the nonscheduled approach.

ORTHODONTIC EXPENSES

With possibly a few exceptions, orthodontic benefits never are written without other dental coverage. Nonetheless, orthodontic benefits present a number of design peculiarities that suggest this subject should be treated separately.

Orthodontic services, unlike nonorthodontic procedures, generally are rendered only once in an individual's lifetime; orthodontic problems are highly unlikely to recur. Orthodontic maximums, therefore, typically are expressed on a lifetime basis. Deductibles, which are applicable only to orthodontic services, also are often expressed on a lifetime basis. However, it is quite common for orthodontic benefits to be provided without deductibles, since a major purpose of the deductible—to eliminate small, nuisance-type claims—is of no consequence.

Because adult orthodontia generally is cosmetic, and also because the best time for orthodontic work is during adolescence, many plans limit orthodontic coverage to persons under age 19. However, an increasing number of plans are including adult orthodontics as well, and many participants are taking advantage of this feature.

The coinsurance level for orthodontia expenses typically is 50 percent, but it varies widely depending on the reimbursement levels under other parts of the plan. It is common for the orthodontic reimbursement level to be the same as that for major restorative procedures.

Reflecting the nature of orthodontic work, and unlike virtually any other benefit, orthodontic benefits often are paid in installments, instead of at the conclusion of the course of treatment. Because the program of treatment frequently extends over several years, it would be unreasonable to reimburse for the entire course of treatment at the end of the extended time.

FACTORS AFFECTING THE COST OF THE DENTAL PLAN

A number of factors, including design of the plan, characteristics of the covered group, and the employer's approach to plan implementation affect the cost of the dental plan.

Plan Design

Many issues must be addressed before a particular design that is sound and reflects the needs of the plan sponsor can be established. Included in this list are the type of plan, deductibles, coinsurance, plan maximums, treatment of preexisting conditions, whether covered services should be limited, and orthodontic coverage.

An employer's choice between scheduled and nonscheduled benefits requires a look at the employer's objectives. The advantages and disadvantages of scheduled versus nonscheduled plans, combination plans, and others have been described earlier in this chapter.

Deductibles may or may not be included as an integral part of the design of the plan. Deductibles usually are written on a lifetime or calendar-year basis, with the calendar-year approach by far the more common.

Numerous dental procedures involve very little expense. Therefore, the deductible eliminates frequent payments for small claims that can be readily budgeted. For example, a $50 deductible can eliminate as much as 30 percent of the number of claims. A deductible can effectively control the cost of claim administration.

However, evidence exists that early detection and treatment of dental problems will produce a lower level of claims over the long term. Many insurers feel the best way to promote early detection is to pay virtually all the cost of preventive and diagnostic services. Therefore, these services often are not subject to a deductible.

Some insurance companies are advocates of a lifetime deductible, designed to lessen the impact of accumulated dental neglect. It is particularly effective where the employer is confronted with a choice of (1) not covering preexisting conditions at all; (2) covering these conditions, but being forced otherwise to cut back on the design of the plan; or (3) offering a lifetime deductible, the theory being, ''If you'll spend *X* dollars to get your mouth into shape once and for all, we'll take care of a large part of your future dental needs.''

Opponents of the lifetime deductible concept claim the following disadvantages:

- A lifetime deductible promotes early overutilization by those anxious to take advantage of the benefits of the plan.
- Once satisfied, lifetime deductibles are of no further value for the presently covered group.
- The lifetime deductible introduces employee turnover as an important cost consideration of the plan.
- If established at a level that will have a significant impact on claim costs and premium rates, a lifetime deductible may result in adverse employee reaction to the plan.

More and more dental plans are being designed, either through construction of the schedule or the use of coinsurance, so that the patient pays a portion of the costs for all but preventive and diagnostic services. The intent is to reduce spending on optional dental care and to provide cost-effective dental practice. Preventive and diagnostic expenses generally are reimbursed at 80 to 100 percent of the usual and customary charges. Full reimbursement is quite common.

The reimbursement level for restorative and replacement procedures generally is lower than that for preventive and diagnostic procedures. Restorations, and in some cases replacements, may be reimbursed at 70 to 85 percent. In other cases, the reimbursement level for replacements is lower than for restorative treatment.

Orthodontics, and occasionally major replacements, have the lowest reimbursement levels of all. In most instances, the plans reimburse no more than 50 to 60 percent of the usual and customary charges for these procedures.

Most dental plans include a plan maximum, written on a calendar-year basis, that is applicable to nonorthodontic expenses. Orthodontic expenses generally are subject to a separate lifetime maximum. Also, in some instances, a separate lifetime maximum may apply to nonorthodontic expenses.

Unless established at a fairly low level, a lifetime maximum will have little or no impact on claim liability and serves only to further complicate design of the plan. Calendar-year maximums, though, encourage participants to seek less costly care and may help to spread out the impact of accumulated dental neglect over the early years of the plan. The typical calendar-year maximum is somewhere between $1,000 and $1,500.

To put things in perspective: In 1986, only about 14 percent of people visiting a dentist spent from $300 to $999 annually, including insurance company payments, and just 3.5 percent spent $1,000 or more, including insurance company payments. Most claims are small (50 percent spent $100 or less), and, therefore, the maximum's impact on plan costs is minor.

Another major consideration is the treatment of preexisting conditions. The major concern is the expense associated with the replacement of teeth extracted prior to the date of coverage. Preexisting conditions are treated in a number of ways:

- They may be excluded.
- They may be treated as any other condition.
- They may be covered on a limited basis (perhaps one half of the normal reimbursement level) or subject to a lifetime maximum.

If treated as any other condition, the cost of the plan in the early years (nonorthodontic only) will be increased by about 6 to 10 percent.

Another plan design consideration is the range of procedures to be covered. In addition to orthodontics, other procedures occasionally excluded are surgical periodontics and temporomandibular joint (TMJ) dysfunction therapy. It is difficult to diagnose TMJ disorders, and many consider them a medical and not a dental condition. Claims are large, and the potential for abuse is significant.

Although rare, some plans cover only preventive and maintenance expenses. These plans are becoming more common in flexible benefit plans where employees often may pick a preventive plan or one more comprehensive.

Orthodontic expenses, as noted, may be excluded. However, where these are covered, the plan design may include a separate deductible to discourage "shoppers." The cost of orthodontic diagnosis and models is about $175, whether or not treatment is undertaken. The inclusion of a separate orthodontic deductible eliminates reimbursement for these expenses. Also, orthodontic plan design typically includes both heavy coinsurance and limited maximums to guarantee patient involvement.

An indication of the sensitivity of dental plan costs to some of the plan design features discussed can be seen in the following illustration. Assume a nonscheduled base model plan with a $25 calendar-year deductible applicable to all expenses other than orthodontics. The reimbursement, or employer coinsurance, levels are:

- Diagnostic and preventive services (Type I): 100 percent.
- Basic services (Type II), including anesthesia, basic restoration, oral surgery, endodontics, and periodontics: 75 percent.
- Major restoration and prosthodontics (Type III): 50 percent.
- Orthodontics (Type IV): 50 percent.

There also is an annual benefit maximum of $1,000 for Types I, II, and III services, and a lifetime maximum of $1,000 for orthodontics. Based on this base model plan, Table 18–1 shows the approximate premium sensitivity to changes in plan design. If two or more of the design changes shown in this table are considered together, an approximation of the resulting value may be obtained by multiplying the relative values of the respective changes.

The change in deductibles has a significant impact on cost, as much as a 23 percent reduction in cost to increase the deductible from $25 to $100. The change in benefit maximums has some impact, but it is minor. Coinsurance has a definite effect, especially changes for restoration,

TABLE 18–1
Model Dental Plan

	Relative Value (in percent)
Base model plan	100%
Design changes	
Deductible	
Remove $25 deductible	108
Raise to $50	92
Raise to $100	77
Benefit maximum (annual)	
Lower from $1,000 to $750	99
Raise to $1,500	101
Coinsurance	
Liberalize percent to: 100–80–60–60*	108
Tighten percent to: 80–70–50–50*	91
Orthodontics	
Exclude	89

*For Types I, II, III, and IV services, respectively.

replacement, and orthodontic portions of the plan, all of which represent about 80 to 85 percent of the typical claim costs. Finally, the inclusion of orthodontics in the base plan is another item of fairly high cost.

Characteristics of the Covered Group

A second factor affecting the cost of the dental plan is the characteristics of the covered group. Important considerations include, but are not limited to, the following:

- Age.
- Gender.
- Location.
- Presence of fluoride in the water supply.
- Income level of the participants.
- Occupation.

The increased incidence of high-cost dental procedures at older ages generally makes coverage of older groups more expensive. Average charges usually increase from about age 30 up to age 75 or so and then decline. One possible explanation for the decline from age 75 is the existence of prosthetic devices at that point and the generally poor dental habits of the current older generation.

Gender is another consideration. Women tend to have higher utilization rates than men. One study showed that women average 1.9 visits to dentists per year, compared with 1.7 for men. These differences probably are attributable to better dental awareness by women rather than to a higher need.

Charge levels, practice patterns, and the availability of dentists vary considerably by locale. Charge levels range anywhere from 75 to 125 percent of the national average, and differences exist in the frequency of use for certain procedures as well. There is evidence, for example, that more expensive procedures are performed relatively more often in Los Angeles than, say, in Philadelphia.

Interestingly, the presence of fluoride and the time it has been in the water supply also are important. One recent study showed that the prevalence of tooth decay was 40 percent greater in areas with negligible fluoride than in optimal fluoride ones.

Another consideration is income. One study shows that dental care expenditures per participant were 6 to 8 percent higher for members of families with higher incomes.

Essentially four reasons may account for income being a key factor. First, the higher the income level, the greater the likelihood the individual already has an established program of dental hygiene. Second, in many areas there is greater accessibility to dental care in the high-income neighborhoods. Third, a greater tendency exists on the part of higher income individuals to elect higher cost procedures. Last, high-income people tend to use more expensive dentists.

Another important consideration is the occupation of the covered group. While difficult to explain, evidence suggests considerable variation between blue-collar plans and plans covering salaried or mixed groups. One possible explanation is higher awareness and income-level differences. One insurer estimates that blue-collar employees are 15 to 20 percent less expensive to insure than white-collar employees.

Sponsor's Approach to Implementation

The last of the factors affecting plan costs is the sponsor's approach to implementation. Dental work, unlike medical care, lends itself to "sandbagging" (i.e., deferral of needed treatment until after the plan's effective date). Everything else being equal, plans announced well in advance of the effective date tend to have poorer first-year experience than plans announced only shortly before the effective date. Advance knowledge of the deferred effective date easily can increase first-year costs from 20 to 25 percent or even more.

Employee contributions are another consideration. Dental plans, if offered on a contributory basis, may be prone to adverse selection. While there is evidence that the adverse selection is not as great as was once anticipated, most insurers continue to discourage contributory plans. Most insurance companies will underwrite dental benefits on a contributory basis but some require certain adverse selection safeguards. Typical safeguards include:

- Combining dental plan participation and contributions with medical plan participation.
- Limiting enrollment to a single offering, thus preventing subsequent sign-ups or dropouts.
- Requiring dental examinations before joining the plan and limiting or excluding treatment for conditions identified in the exam.

The last item to be addressed is claims administration. The nature of dentistry and dental plan design suggests that claims administration is very important. While several years may lapse before an insured has occasion to file a medical claim, rarely does the year pass during which a family will not visit the dentist at least once. Therefore, claims administration capability is an extremely important consideration in selecting a plan carrier—and might very well be the most important consideration.

One key element of claims administration is "predetermination of benefits." This common plan feature requires the dentist to prepare a treatment plan that shows the work and cost before any services begin. This treatment plan generally is required only for nonemergency services and only if the cost is expected to exceed some specified level, such as $300. The carrier processes this information to determine exactly how much the dental plan will pay. Also, selected claims are referred to the carrier's dental consultants to assess the appropriateness of the recommended treatment. If there are any questions, the dental consultant discusses the treatment plan with the dentist prior to performing the services.

Predetermination is very important both in promoting better quality care and in reducing costs. These benefits are accomplished by spotting unnecessary expenses, treatments that cannot be expected to last, instances of coverage duplication, and charges higher than usual and customary before extensive and expensive work begins. Predetermination of benefits can be effective in reducing claim costs by as much as 10 percent. Predetermination also advises the covered individual of the exact amount of reimbursement under the plan prior to commencement of treatment.

CHAPTER 19

PRESCRIPTION DRUG, VISION, AND HEARING CARE PLANS

Eugene J. Ziurys, Jr.

Rounding out a benefits package, prescription drug, vision care, and hearing care plans are becoming increasingly visible. Prescription drugs have received new attention throughout the benefit marketplace because of continuing prescription drug price inflation, the introduction of new drugs, and increased outpatient drug therapy. Vision and hearing care benefits continue to complement a medical care package without a major outlay of premium dollars in comparison to the basic medical products.

PRESCRIPTION DRUGS

Inpatient prescriptions are covered by basic hospital, major medical, or comprehensive medical plan benefits. This chapter concentrates on prescription drugs strictly in an outpatient environment, and the discussion essentially is limited to federal legend drugs or state-restricted drugs which cannot be dispensed without a prescribing physician or dentist.

Until recent years, prescription drugs seldom drew attention, as they constituted a very small portion of the health care dollar. Drug price inflation lagged behind the consumer price index (CPI) until the 1980s, when it soared, and now drugs are outpacing not only the CPI, but its medical component as well.

New "wonder" drugs are on the market, and in most cases they are expensive. Counteracting the increasing expense of these drugs, new generics are entering the marketplace, and the use of generics is increasing

Consumer Price Index (CPI)

Year	CPI	Medical	Prescription Drugs
1990	5.4	9.0	10.0
1989	4.8	7.7	8.7
1988	4.1	6.5	7.9
1987	3.7	6.6	8.0
1986	1.9	7.5	8.8

Source: U.S. Department of Labor

continuously as a percentage of the total prescription drug market. Anti-substitution laws have been repealed in all states and the District of Columbia, and the passage of the 1984 Drug Price Competition and Patent Restoration Act (Hatch/Waxman) accelerated the introduction of generic products. It is estimated that over 20 percent of prescriptions dispensed in 1990 were generics. Several states mandate that some of the substitution savings be passed on to the consumer. Generic substitutes have a wide price variation, often from close to that of the innovator to substantially lower. In a mail-order benefit plan, the average brand-name drug can be up to five times the cost of the average generic drug.

The matter of generic drug quality continues to surface from time to time. However, the Food and Drug Administration (FDA), charged with monitoring the quality and safety of all prescription drugs, has reassured the American public periodically of generic integrity. Several leading research drug manufacturers also produce generic drugs, and some research companies purchase generic drugs and sell them under their own label.

Prescription drug benefit programs can be designed in various ways to encourage the use of generic drugs. The simplest is patient incentive, offering a lower copayment (two-tier) when a generic is dispensed. A pharmacy can be paid a surcharge for the use of a generic, and some health maintenance organizations (HMOs) mandate their use.

There are several modes of reimbursing outpatient prescriptions. One is a traditional indemnity product as part of a major medical or comprehensive medical benefits package. Others stand as a distinct benefit from these basic plans. They are service-type card plans with per-prescription cost sharing, mail-order programs, and managed care arrangements through HMOs in which a patient's selection of a pharmacy is limited.

Traditional Indemnity Approach

In the traditional indemnity environment, drugs are covered under major medical or comprehensive medical policies. The majority of outpatient drug benefits still are provided in this way despite new administrative benefit packages on the market.

To obtain prescription drug benefits under these plans, the employee must fulfill an annual deductible and thereafter is subject to coinsurance, usually at 20 percent. The total charge is paid at the pharmacy, and the patient files a claim. The convenience of having the prescription filled by any retail provider (pharmacy) is an advantage, but the total charge almost always is the usual and customary one, and the beneficiary participates in prescription drug price inflation by contributing a percentage of the total cost through the 20/80 percent coinsurance provision. Because of the still relatively low cost of drugs compared with other medical expenses, many claims are never submitted to the payor. This is commonly known as the "shoebox effect." While the extent of this is impossible to quantify, it is guessed that between 15 percent and 17 percent of prescription drug charges are never claimed under traditional plans.

Prescription drug claims submitted separately from other charges are expensive to process when compared with the total cost of the drug. For example, since the cost of issuing a check ranges between $5 and $7, a prescription-only reimbursement could cost more to process than the drug itself. In addition, claims for some noncovered drugs may slip through the system with relative ease.

Card Plans

The impetus for service-type card plans was a result of collective bargaining between the Big Three auto makers and the United Auto Workers in the late 1960s. Prior to that time, few health plans had separate prescription drug benefits. In a card plan, an insurance company, Blue Cross organization, or administrator (also called a clearinghouse or fiscal intermediary) solicits pharmacies nationwide or on a regional, as-needed basis to join the plan. While under a master contract, the pharmacy usually has the latitude to accept or reject a particular offering.

The covered employee is issued a plastic identification card, has a selection of participating pharmacies, and can obtain a prescription drug by paying a modest per-prescription copayment. Today, this generally ranges from $5 to $10. The card is similar to a credit card and gives the pharmacy ample information to process the claim transaction.

Employees electing to patronize a non-network pharmacy must pay for the prescription out of pocket. A claim form must be completed (a portion by the employee and the balance by the pharmacy) and mailed to the insurance company or clearinghouse. Provided that the employee and the drug are eligible, reimbursement less any per-prescription copayment will be sent to the employee's residence. In many cases, these prescriptions are tested for reasonableness, and a charge beyond the copayment may be made. Some plans have an additional penalty if a nonmember provider is used within a designated service area. Claims processed through a non-network pharmacy are called direct or nonparticipating reimbursements.

Reimbursement Level

The reimbursement level is decided by insurers or employers when contracting directly with an administrator. A common reimbursement formula has these components:

Ingredient cost + professional (dispensing) fee + state sales tax (where applicable) − cost sharing (coinsurance or copayment)

The ingredient cost usually is based on the published average wholesale price (AWP). Recently more plans have been taking discounts off the AWP as pharmacies often are able to purchase drugs below these published prices. The professional fee paid to the pharmacy is a flat amount. This fee usually is set by region or state based partly on the cost of doing business in that particular part of the country.

Covered Costs and Exclusions

Benefits under a card plan most often cover:

- Federal legend drugs.
- State-restricted drugs—In several states, some drugs that are nonlegend under federal law must have a physician's prescription to be dispensed.
- Compound items containing a federal legend drug or state restricted drug.
- Injectable insulin—Needles and syringes often are covered when purchased with injectable insulin.

Quantity limitations often are the greater of a 34-day supply or 100 units.

Common exclusions are contraceptive medication, drugs for investigational use, drugs covered under federal and state workers' compensation programs, immunizing agents, cosmetic drugs, and the administration of drugs. However, plans do differ. In certain states, contraceptives must be covered, while in others coverage can be offered voluntarily by the employer.

Claims Processing

The pharmacist processes the prescription claim by making an imprint from the identification card on a universal claim form (UCF), completing the drug information and asking the employee to sign the form acknowledging receipt of the prescription, assigning benefits (beyond the copayment amount) to the pharmacy, and authorizing release of information should the payor request it. In automated pharmacies, information is keyed into the computer, and the employee signs a log in lieu of a claim form. Periodically (for example, weekly), the pharmacy sends claims to the insurance company or clearinghouse or arrangements usually are made to send a tape to the insurer or clearinghouse.

Most card plan claims are processed by gigantic clearinghouses/ fiscal intermediaries. The fiscal intermediary receives claims via paper or electronic transmission tape, processes them, and sends checks or wires funds to its network of pharmacies. Funds are transferred from the insurer (payor) to the intermediary for these prescriptions. Modern computerized technology lends itself well to handling the high volume of claims combined with the still relatively low charge per prescription. Economies of scale apply, and the administration usually costs substantially less than $1 per claim.

Advantages and Disadvantages

Certain features make card plans desirable. An important consideration is the ability to place a ceiling on the provider reimbursement. Useful statistics have emerged from the highly mechanized procedures and include pharmacy and employee profiles, particular therapeutic classes of drugs being dispensed, and average costs per prescription and per employee. These statistics benefit the employer and can be the basis of pharmacy audits.

On the negative side, in the absence of an annual deductible, *all* prescriptions are covered (less the per-prescription copayment), and many claims are paid. If the benefit package is not designed with ample exclusions and realistic copayments, the net payout could be higher than traditional indemnity plans. Also, there is speculation in some circles that card plans result in increased drug utilization.

Mail-Order Prescription Programs

Prescriptions by mail began after World War II with the U.S. Veterans Administration and the American Association of Retired Persons (AARP) Pharmacy Service Programs. The private sector got off to a slower start, and mail-order programs did not become an employee benefit to an appreciable segment of the population until the 1980s. The practicality of the mail-order market is for maintenance drugs in the treatment of chronic conditions. It is estimated that up to 70 percent of the number of prescriptions and prescription expenditures are for chronic conditions. Mail order has a special relevance for the senior citizen population, as over half of those 65 and older have at least one such chronic condition, and the convenience of ordering by mail is appealing to the aged. Complete self-addressed packets are provided, simplifying the mail-order process. With the first order, information is requested to create a patient profile. The pharmacy usually fills prescriptions quickly, at a 10- to 14-day turnaround (from residence, to pharmacy, back to residence). Home delivery is a convenience rarely offered by the retail pharmacy today. Toll-free 800 phone numbers for both patient and physician are commonplace in a typical mail-order plan.

Plan Design

A mail-order benefit program can be an add-on to a major medical or comprehensive medical plan. Such a plan usually waives the annual deductible and imposes a modest per-prescription copayment or coinsurance amount as an incentive to use the mail-order arrangement. An additional incentive is a more liberal quantity allowance, typically up to a 90-day supply, compared with the 30- to 34-day arrangement at the retail level. For example, the employee can receive up to a 90-day supply for $10 per prescription. In a traditional indemnity plan, the same employee would have to fulfill the annual deductible and pay a 20 percent coinsurance charge thereafter for a lesser quantity. Another method of designing a mail-order plan is to integrate it with a card arrangement with a lower copayment as an incentive to use the mail-order option. While some plans mandate use of the mail-order segment after one or two refills, most still only offer an incentive to use it.

Advantages and Disadvantages

Because of pharmacy volume buying, substantial discounts off the AWP are commonplace. The employer and insurer can add to these savings by negotiating a discounted reimbursement formula with the mail order (central fill) pharmacy. In addition, the professional (dispensing) fee is lower than in a retail setting, and most mail-order pharmacies are committed to fill prescriptions generically whenever legally permissible, further managing benefit dollars.

Although the unit price virtually always is lower at a mail-order pharmacy, some difference of opinion exists on whether a mail-order plan produces savings to the employer. The matter of "wastage" often is debated. Being able to obtain up to a 90-day supply of a needed medication is beneficial. However, should the employee's drug regimen change after a week, for whatever reason, there would be substantial extra cost. An employee also might terminate employment after "stocking up" on several prescriptions, thereby receiving an extended benefit. However the plan is designed, instituting realistic cost-sharing amounts while simultaneously providing incentives to use the mail-order plan increases the savings potential.

The Future

Although there are about 35 pharmacies operating mail-order facilities, fewer than 10 are major players, filling thousands of prescriptions daily from a single facility. With the aging population and pressures to manage health care costs in general, mail-order arrangements are expected to become a larger segment of the prescription drug market.

Managed Care Techniques

Maximum Allowable Cost (MAC)

MAC programs reimburse only up to a certain threshold on selected, often-dispensed generics. This maintains a substantial price differential between the innovator drug and generic ceiling. MAC programs were initiated by the U.S. Health and Human Services Department and are used in many state Medicaid programs and are becoming more common in the private sector.

Formularies

Basically, a formulary is a listing of drugs approved for dispensing. A formulary mandates specific innovators and generics within therapeutic classes to limit inappropriate utilization and to aggressively price frequently prescribed formulary drugs. Formularies are in general use in hospitals and managed care health plans that utilize a primary care physician (PCP) or ''gatekeeper.'' Some formularies have drugs tied to manufacturers' rebates once certain thresholds are reached. The formulary considerations are both medical and economic and are set by panels of physicians and pharmacies. Step-care protocols utilizing a sequence of drug therapy lend themselves well to such medical management techniques.

Drug Utilization Review (DUR)

With the advent of managed care, a DUR system connects drug utilization to a medical condition on a per-case basis. This is especially crucial with the increased use of a primary care physician. Computerized on-line prescription profiles link both the retail pharmacy(ies) and the mail-order house with the patient's record. Vital interventions can be made not only on drug interactions but unnecessary prescribing as well. DUR can be utilized on a prospective, concurrent or retroactive basis.

In-House Pharmacy

Most staff model HMOs have in-house drug dispensing units. Here the ideal situation occurs when drugs are prescribed by a primary care physician and dispensed using strict formularies, thus minimizing ''dispense as written (DAW)'' situations that often result in the use of more expensive drugs.

Individual practice association HMO's (IPAs) commonly give a pharmacy chain with major presence in a service area exclusivity at a discounted reimbursement in exchange for channeling a large segment of eligible participants to the provider.

Some employers with large facilities have on-site pharmacies as a convenience to employees and tie-in incentives to utilize the ''company pharmacy.''

Point-of-Sale (POS)

State-of-the-art telecommunication has enabled administrators to have on-line prescription drug claim adjudication conducted while the beneficiary is present at the pharmacy. This has administratively opened up the ability to have a separate annual prescription drug deductible and/or annual maximum per patient.

Today, the vast majority of pharmacies are connected with one or more data centers. In a matter of seconds, the pharmacist can tell if the employee has prescription drug coverage, whether the drug prescribed is covered and appropriately priced, and the exact amount of copayment to collect. In addition, some plans add on DUR and alert the pharmacist to a possible drug interaction or early refill detection.

VISION CARE

The most common response to a questionnaire on the relative importance of the five senses would be to rank vision first. Yet our vision is often neglected. Eye surgery is covered by most major medical and comprehensive medical policies, but a large segment of those with fairly complete health benefits still must purchase routine vision examinations, lenses, and frames on an out-of-pocket basis. Vision care often is compared to dental care because of its frequently elective and predictable nature.

Providers

Typically, a vision care program deals with three different health professionals:

Ophthalmologists are medical doctors (MDs) specializing in the total care of the eye, including diagnosis, treatment of eye diseases, and surgery. Many perform eye examinations and prescribe corrective lenses. Some also dispense corrective eyewear. An ophthalmologist typically completes four years of premedical training, another four years of medical school, and subsequent internship/residency.

Optometrists are doctors of optometry (ODs) who are licensed to test the eye and related structures for vision defects by performing various diagnostic procedures. They are trained to detect eye disease and/or symptoms requiring the attention of ophthalmologists. In addition to performing vision examinations and prescribing lenses, most optometrists dispense glasses and contact lenses. An optometrist typically completes undergraduate work and is graduated from a college of optometry.

Opticians fit, adjust, and dispense eyewear (lenses, frames, and contact lenses) prescribed by ophthalmologists and optometrists. They are eyewear retailers and provide advice on what lenses and frames are most appropriate. Many grind and fabricate eyewear, verify the finished products, and repair and replace various ophthalmic devices. Optician certification, licensure, and registration varies by state, as does training and/or apprenticeship.

Vision Care Plans

Eye disease, treatment, and surgery traditionally are covered under hospital, surgical, major medical, and comprehensive medical policies. However, most of these plans bypass routine vision examination and eyewear. Separate (free-standing) vision plans cover services such as routine examinations and materials (products) such as lenses, frames, and contact lenses. In a purist sense some do not consider this coverage *insurance* because of the absence of illness or disease. Nevertheless, the need for appropriate vision care is real, as over half our population wears corrective eyewear. A routine vision exam not only confirms whether prescription eyewear is necessary but may detect unrelated problems such as diabetes, high blood pressure, and renal abnormalities. Aside from the obvious medical benefits to employees, vision care plans have the potential of reducing accidents and increasing production, factors that are important to the employer as well.

Vision Examination

A thorough review includes a history of general health and vision complaints and an external and internal eye exam. Other services may include various ocular tests usually including but not limited to coordination of eye movements, tonometry, depth perception (for children), and refraction testing for distance and near vision. In addition to the possible needs of corrective eyewear, the exam could detect cataracts, glaucoma, diabetes, and brain tumors.

Lenses

The lens is the heart of sight-corrective material. Single vision lenses are the most widely used, with multivision lenses (bifocal, trifocal) also being dispensed in large quantities. Plastic is replacing glass as the predominant lens material, and a wide array of lenses, such as oversized, photochrometric, and tinted, are available. Most plans consider these "cosmetic extras" and outside normal plan limits. Contact lenses have gained strong popularity, and a large segment of contact lens wearers wear them for cosmetic rather than medical reasons.

Many dispensers have an in-house laboratory for grinding and fabrication of the more routinely prescribed eyewear, while others use full-service labs for all their needs.

Frames

The cosmetic element is much more obvious in the area of frames than in lenses. Frames are increasingly being selected for cosmetic purposes, and at times are part of a fashion wardrobe featuring "signature" types. The cost can run into hundreds of dollars for plastic or metal frames of almost limitless sizes, shapes, and colors. Herein lies a dilemma for the payor. The frame is a must, but how does one avoid paying for fashion while giving a fair reimbursement for utility? Certain plans make allowances up to a specified dollar figure, while others approve a limited selection, for example, 50 frames each for men, women, and children.

Marketing

Since the mid-1970s, aggressive competition among dispensers ensued as a result of the removal of advertising restrictions by the Federal Trade Commission. Since advertising by various media has increased appreciably, such things as two-for-one deals and "glasses in an hour" have become popular promotions, and full-page newspaper ads for them are commonplace. A wide range of prices is especially prevalent in metropolitan areas with optical outlets in shopping centers, some of which are members of regional and national chains.

Plan Design

Coverage

The typical vision care plan provides either a measure of reimbursement or pays in full after a modest copayment.

Frequency Limits

To control unnecessary use and keep administrative costs down, plans limit the frequency with which a participant may utilize the plan for covered expenses. Typical frequencies are as follows:

	Month Intervals			
Exams	24	12	12	12
Lenses	24	24	12	12
Frames	24	24	24	12

Schedule-of-Benefits Approach

This type of plan has maximum allowances for each service and material and a limit on the frequency of use. A typical schedule pays the lesser of the claimed or schedule maximum:

Service/Material	*Maximum Allowed*
Examination	$ 40
Lenses (pair)	
Single vision	60
Bifocal	90
Trifocal	110
Lenticular	140
Contacts	100
Frames	40

Schedules can be national or regional, based on a geographical percentage of usual, customary, and reasonable (UCR) charges. A variation of a straight schedule is a group of providers accepting the above basic amounts as "payment in full."

Advantages of a schedule-of-benefits plan are that it is easy to understand, has no restriction on the choice of provider, and encourages the thrifty employee to "shop." The employer is cognizant of premium outlay, as the schedule ceiling does not change with inflation, and administration is simplified for the insurer or administrator because the frequencies and caps are determined in advance.

Participating Providers

Participating provider plans steer employees to a network of providers where a modest copayment is made for a routine examination and eyewear. An employee simply shows an identification card, which can be subject to confirmation at the provider's place of business, or the employee can mail a request for vision services and materials to the administrator and receive a benefit form stating which benefits are available, for what length of time, and the extent of the copayment. The cost-sharing amount is modest, usually ranging from $5 to $15.

Providers are solicited by the insurer or administrator with the expectation of an increased volume of patients. In return, the provider agrees to reimbursement of discounted material costs plus dispensing fees. Some plans also mandate the use of specific laboratories. Various quality-control measures are inserted into these plans, and peer review is common. In some plans, participating providers can charge the regular retail price for certain extras, while others call for reduced charges for oversized or tinted lenses, designer frames, and other extras.

Many plans allow reimbursement even when a participating provider is not utilized. In these instances, the employee must pay the provider's charge and file a claim. Reimbursement is based on a schedule or UCR determination. When a nonpanel provider is used, the employee's out-of-pocket expense almost always is greater than it would be from a participating provider.

Reasonable and Customary (R&C)

These plans usually follow a medical plan pattern, with a percentile of the charges in a given area prevailing. A higher figure is allowed for examination and lenses and less for lenses of a cosmetic nature. Inflation is shared by the employee with a percentage coinsurance applied along with the medical reimbursement. A separate means of administration is unnecessary.

Flex Plans

Flex plans are a growth area for various ancillary benefits including vision. They enable an employee to choose among various coverages, taking into account such factors as overall health and any separate spouse coverage available, and place vision care in competition with other coverages. Some plans allow an examination at 12- or 24-month intervals, and it is up to the employee to arrange for eyewear if needed.

An exam-only plan also is featured by some HMOs. Other plans provide for material reimbursement as well, with varied copayment provisions.

Flexible Spending Accounts (FSAs)

Under an FSA arrangement, the employee has the opportunity to reduce taxes by funding benefits such as vision care with pretax dollars. A salary deduction is made and placed into a special account making needed funds available to meet various health care expenses. Care should be exercised in the amount put aside, as amounts not used in a given period are forfeited by the employee.

Video Display Terminals (VDTs)

The increased use of VDTs is introducing a new segment of vision care programs into the marketplace. These programs educate employees on things such as the most effective distance one should be from the screen when using the display unit, and provide financial assistance for eye examinations and eyewear. Some programs require a certain frequency of display unit use for eligibility.

Occupational Safety and Health Administration (OSHA)

OSHA requires employers to provide protective eyewear to employees in positions exposing them to the danger of eye injury. These "safety glass" programs usually are outside the normal health benefit package.

HEARING CARE

While an increasing number of employers are providing hearing care benefits, a majority of benefit packages still do not contain this coverage. The aging population, coupled with a generally noisy contemporary society, contribute to the prevalence of hearing loss/impairment, and it is estimated that over 10 percent of the population is affected. Despite the generally acknowledged increase in the number of hearing impaired persons and the substantially improved technology of hearing-aid instruments available, many would rather continue with this impairment than bear the stigma of wearing a hearing aid in public.

Coverage

Surgical procedures affecting the ear normally are covered in standard medical policies. Beyond this, some major medical comprehensive policies include hearing aids. However, more complete coverage is afforded by plans designed specifically to cover hearing care.

Hearing Care Benefits

A common benefit package includes an 80 percent reimbursement of services and materials up to a ceiling of $300 to $400. The frequency of benefit availability usually is every 36 months. Items often covered are:

- Otologic examination (by a physician or surgeon).
- Audiometric examination (by an audiologist).
- Hearing instrument (including evaluation, ear mold fitting, and follow-up visits).

Preferred provider plans in which access to a panel would result in discounts for audiologist fees as well as hearing-aid instruments also are available. Several administrators have developed service plans in which copayments apply when participating providers are utilized. Material costs can be reimbursed on a cost-plus dispensing-fee basis. However, identical procedures vary by geographic areas and even within specific metropolitan areas.

As with vision care expenses, a flexible spending account is a convenient vehicle through which to budget for hearing care expenses in the absence of benefit coverage in this area.

CONCLUSION

While still a small segment of the health care dollar, the cost of prescription drugs is growing relative to the total bill. New technology combined with managed care is quickly tracking the use of drugs for more effective use. In many cases, a year of proper drug therapy still costs less than a one-day hospital stay, but the increased percentage of the health care dollar being spent on prescription drugs is one of the newer targets for managed care, and insurer intervention is increasing.

Vision care in traditional benefit plans or as an elective part of a flexible benefit plan is growing. It is a frequently used benefit with a relatively low cost. Barriers to the growth of the coverage are the lack of awareness by many employees of their possible need for vision care and the relatively affordable cost of vision care.

Hearing care benefits are still absent from the majority of benefit packages, but this coverage, too, is growing.

Employees are receptive to programs that reimburse for prescription drugs and vision and hearing care. Taken as a single expense, any one of these items probably is affordable for most people in the employed population. However, when incurred in combination, particularly for individuals with families, the total expense can represent a large financial commitment for the employee.

PART 5

DISABILITY INCOME PLANS

In addition to the medical costs associated with an illness or accident discussed in Part Four, the potential loss of income associated with such loss exposures is a critical component of an employee's financial security. Chapter 20 provides an overview of the disability loss exposure and the various types of disability including the consequences of short and long-term exposures.

Chapter 21 covers in depth the assorted disability income plans available through employee benefit arrangements and the key provisions inherent in each approach. Coordination of private disability plans with government-provided plans which is so essential to the sound functioning of a disability income program also is covered in this chapter.

CHAPTER 20

GROUP DISABILITY INCOME BENEFITS

Donald J. Doudna

Losing the ability to work can be devastating to a family's emotional and financial well-being. Yet, the exposure of disability, with its accompanying loss of income, often is neglected by families in their financial planning and not dealt with sufficiently by employee benefit plans. After a brief analysis of the disability exposure, this chapter focuses on issues in providing disability income coverage for employee groups and the various approaches available to meet this loss exposure. Chapter 21 expands on the discussion of the disability exposure, explains the relationship and integration of private and public sector disability income programs and benefits, and outlines how an employer can best provide coverage to its employees in a cost-effective manner.

POSSIBILITY OF DISABILITY

The possibility of losing earnings due to an accident or illness is significant. In 1987, 32 million persons, 13.5 percent of the U.S. civilian noninstitutional population, suffered a limitation of activity because of one or more chronic conditions.[1] It is estimated that one out of four adults between ages 55 and 64 is so severely disabled, they cannot work regularly if at all.[2]

---

[1] *1989 Source Book of Health Insurance Data* (Washington, D.C.: Health Insurance Association of America, 1990), p. 70.

[2] *Transactions, Society of Actuaries,* Report of the Committee to Recommend New Disability Tables for Valuation (individual rate) vol. XXXVII, 1985, p. 574.

TABLE 20–1
Group Long-Term Disability Insurance Crude Rates of Disablement per 1,000 Lives Exposed (Three-Month Elimination Period: Calendar Year of Issue Excluded; Calendar Years of Experience 1976–80)

All Experience Units Combined			
Attained Age	*Life Years Exposed*	*Number of Claims*	*Rate of Disablement per 1,000 Lives*
	All Experience, Males, Females, and Sex Unknown		
Under 40	552,098	1,153	2.09
40–44	103,139	390	3.78
45–49	92,824	584	6.29
50–54	83,973	722	8.60
55–59	66,678	970	14.55
60–64	40,471	805	19.89
All ages	939,183	4,624	4.92

Source: *Transactions, Society of Actuaries,* 1982 Reports of Mortality and Morbidity Experiences, 1985, p. 297.

Table 20–1 indicates the probability of a disability lasting three months or longer for various age groups.

Although results vary among employee groups, it is evident that the possibility of disability is an exposure that should be considered thoroughly. This chapter provides some historical perspective on disability insurance, an overview of available disability coverages, an analysis of issues in plan design, and a discussion of administration and cost-saving procedures of the plans.

GROUP COVERAGES AVAILABLE

Historical Perspective

Following the adverse claims experience of the 1930s, insurers were reluctant to provide disability income coverages again until about three decades ago. Some of the adverse claims experience in the early years of disability insurance, of course, can be attributed to the Great Depression. Even if the economy had been stable, the probability of negative disability income insurance results was high for several reasons. First, the definitions of disability in the early contracts were extremely liberal, and thus an inordinately high number of cases received benefits. Second, insurers in the disability income market used a flat rate structure. Prices were charged per unit of income replaced, with the same premium sometimes being applied to all ages. Third, insurers neglected to use underwriting safeguards, such as a maximum cutoff age for benefits, and some disability income benefits that should have been terminated earlier, continued for life. These reasons, accompanied by the economic pressures caused by the Depression, encouraged overfiling, and insurers in the 1930s found themselves with inadequate reserves and several years of substantial losses.

Although hospital indemnity policies were revived and became profitable in the early 1950s, disability income protection was not readily available until the 1960s, when it became available from two primary sources. The Social Security program initiated a disability income program for disabled workers over the age of 50, and by 1960 an amendment had been passed to provide this protection to workers of all ages. The Social Security disability income program was characterized by a very strict definition of disability and a six-month waiting period. To be eligible for benefits, a claimant had to be incapable of performing any substantial gainful employment, and many persons, though ill or injured, could not meet the ''definition-of-disability'' or ''waiting-period'' requirements of this program. When collective bargaining units across the country became aware their disabled members might not be able to collect governmental benefits, they encouraged insurers to make coverage available for the varying needs of their members. Therefore, products were designed to cover a worker who could not perform his or her *own occupation* with benefits that could start after a waiting period of as little as one day and could continue until retirement. Thus began the emergence of short- and long-term disability income coverages as we know them today. The following section describes short- and long-term coverages available today through private insurers or by self-funding.

Short-Term Disability

Short-term disability income benefits apply to cases in which the injured or ill worker is unable to perform the duties of his or her current position. Benefits may be paid for as short a period as one week or may continue for as long as 26 weeks. Although some short-term plans provide income beyond 26 weeks (some for as long as 52 weeks), 26 weeks normally is considered the break point between short-term and long-term plans.

Benefit duration often is dependent upon the length of time an employee has served the employer. Income replacement for short-term disability is available from four major sources: (1) self-funded sick leave plans; (2) insured income replacement plans; (3) state-mandated plans (found in California, Hawaii, New York, New Jersey, Rhode Island, and Puerto Rico); and (4) workers' compensation.

For short periods of disability, say between 1 and 10 days, the employer may continue the worker's entire salary as though the worker had been on the job. This arrangement, called a sick leave plan, normally is self-funded. It is common in such a plan to allow an employee to carry unused benefit days from one year to the next (usually up to some maximum number of days), thereby enabling an employee to "bank" or "save" days to be used in the event of an extended illness or disability. Some sick leave plans provide additional days of sick leave as the length of service with the employer increases. For example, an employer might provide 10 sick leave days the first year and an additional 10 days for each year of service up to a maximum of 180 sick leave days. Unused sick leave days could be carried forward to arrive at the maximum more quickly. Sick leave plans are common for salaried personnel and often are combined with insured long-term disability plans. Although sick leave plans are self-funded, the benefits provided should be communicated in written form as part of the overall benefit package.

Another plan is a group insured or self-insured income replacement plan. To qualify for short-term disability benefits under this group plan, an employee must be unable to work and be off the job, usually for a minimum of five working days because of illness, or one day because of accident (not job related). Waiting periods vary, but the general intent is to discourage staying off the job. An attempt is made to ensure that the benefit program is not abused because it provides too much income replacement. Income replacement is stated in terms of hundreds of dollars per week or, more commonly, as a percentage of salary. A common benefit agreement replaces 50 to 66.6 percent of gross salary for up to 26 weeks. Newer plans may give a benefit based upon take-home pay or spendable income. Short-term disability insurance plans tend to be very expensive, and thus this exposure often is self-insured.

In both insured and self-insured cases payments are considered wages and thus subject to income, Social Security, and unemployment taxes. Social Security and unemployment taxes are not applicable after six months of benefit. However, income tax continues on both short- and long-term benefits paid for by the employer.

Long-Term Disability (LTD) Insurance

Long-term disability plans provide income replacement on an insured or formalized self-insured program for a period usually starting after six months and lasting for the duration of the disability (or until normal retirement age). The definition of disability under the long-term plans usually is broken into two parts. During the first two years of disablement, employees must be disabled to the extent they cannot perform the duties of their own occupations. To quote from a standard contract, "Total disability for the purposes of this policy means the complete inability of the person due to accidental bodily injury or sickness or both during the first 24 months of such disability to perform any and every duty pertaining to his or her own occupation." If the person remains disabled after 24 months, the second part of the definition applies: "Benefits will continue during any continuation of such disability following the first 24 months of disability if the person is unable to engage in any work or occupation for which he or she is reasonably fitted by education, training, or experience."

Most long-term disability programs have either a three-month, six-month, or one-year waiting period. The most common waiting period historically has been six months. After the waiting period, long-term disability plans provide benefits to injured or ill employees until the point they are able to return to work. However, benefit payments for long-term disability usually end at retirement age and cease earlier if the disabled participant should die. Because of amendments to the Age Discrimination in Employment Act (ADEA), coverage for active employees cannot be terminated because of age.

The amount of income replaced by LTD benefits usually is based upon gross salary, with some monthly limitation or maximum. In long-term plans, income is often replaced at a rate of 50–66.6 percent, but can be as much as 75–80 percent of gross income.

ISSUES IN DESIGN

Eligible Groups

Whether a group of employees or labor union members can afford and obtain disability benefits depends upon a number of factors. Key factors in eligibility and affordability are group size, sex, age, occupation, and income.

Group Size

Many long-term disability carriers restrict their group disability policies to groups with a minimum of 10 participants. If smaller groups desire coverage, individual underwriting applies, and other lines of coverage often must be purchased to obtain long-term disability for small groups. Although smaller groups may require individual underwriting, claims experience indicates ''jumbo'' groups with more than 5,000 participants also may produce a high incidence of disability. As the group becomes extremely large, there may be a loss of employer control or interest, or both. Thus, groups at both ends of the spectrum may produce a higher incidence of disability and cost the employer more.

Gender

Discussion has arisen over the reason for rate variation based upon the number of women in a group. Table 20–2 demonstrates the statistical difference in incidence of disability for males and females.

As can be seen from Table 20–2, women have a higher incidence of disability than men at younger ages, but a lower incidence at older ages, and their overall morbidity factor is approximately 10 percent greater than for men. Thus, in some organizations with a high percentage of young female workers, disability rates may increase by as much as 25 percent.

Some insurers are concerned about the movement toward the unisex mortality and morbidity table. There may be valid reasons for using this table in long-term disability insurance, but these reasons probably do not apply for short-term. Maternity and related illnesses increase group rates for groups that have short waiting periods, but group plans with at least a six-week waiting period are not affected as much by this morbidity factor.

Age

Age is a key factor in the eligibility of a group for both short- and long-term disability coverage, and is even more important in determining the rate to be paid than are group size and gender. The Society of Actuaries *Reports on Mortality and Morbidity Experiences* show that disabled rates vary significantly from the younger to older ages. See Table 20–3.

The ages of participants in a group affect the number of claims that will occur over the years. Young workers (between ages 20 and 40) have a small probability of disablement and a great capacity for retraining. Young workers have significant incentive to regain their capacity and,

TABLE 20–2
Group Long-Term Disability Insurance Rate of Disablement in Men and Women per 1,000 Lives Exposed (Calendar Years of Experience 1976–1980)

Six-Month Elimination Period	*Male Experience*	*Female Experience*
Under 40	1.02	1.39
40–44	2.02	3.04
45–49	3.56	4.52
50–54	6.33	7.41
55–59	12.20	10.88
60–64	16.63	12.98
All ages	3.78	3.40
Three-Month Elimination Period	*Male Experience*	*Female Experience*
Under 40	1.70	2.83
40–44	3.41	4.84
45–49	5.75	7.67
50–54	8.35	9.50
55–59	15.41	13.30
60–64	21.26	17.63
All ages	4.85	5.24

Source: *Transactions, Society of Actuaries,* 1982 Reports on Mortality and Morbidity Experiences, 1985, p. 279.

therefore, little moral hazard of malingering exists. In most cases, the cost of insuring groups of young employees should be reasonable. However, a large claim reserve may be required to cover the possibility of a young worker becoming seriously disabled.

The probability of sustaining a disability is much greater at older ages. About 80 percent of disabilities in older people are caused by sickness or disease and not by accidental injury. Therefore, if the mean age of the insurance group is high, the probability of disablement caused by sickness is high. Claims tend to last longer among older workers, because of lower educational levels and inability to be trained for other positions.

While the increase in retirement age and the passage of amendments to the Age Discrimination in Employment Act (ADEA) could have a significant impact on disablement rates, it is too early to know what the exact impact will be. As more workers continue in their jobs after age 65,

TABLE 20–3
Group Long-Term Disability Insurance Crude Rates of Disablement per 1,000 Lives Exposed (Six-Month Elimination Period; Calendar Years of Experience 1976–1980)

Attained Age	*Life Years Exposed*	*Number of Claims*	*Rate of Disablement per 1,000 Lives*
	All Experience: Males, Females, and Sex Unknown		
Under 40	2,154,087	2,491	1.16
40–44	440,458	1,009	2.29
45–49	427,019	1,620	3.79
50–54	396,023	2,611	6.59
55–59	314,773	3,717	11.81
60–64	177,339	2,708	15.27
All ages	3,909,699	14,156	3.62

Source: *Transactions, Society of Actuaries,* 1982 Reports of Mortality and Morbidity Experiences, 1985, p. 279.

increased claims may occur. The ADEA, as amended, prohibits forced retirement, but in benefit programs it is still possible to provide for shorter benefit durations without discriminating against an older person. For example, if a working person at age 69 became disabled, the benefits could still be cut off at retirement at age 70.[3] Therefore, the reserve and the cost for that disabling condition would be minimal. If disability occurred between the ages of 62 and 65, a stated number of months of disability income might be provided. Under some plans, if the person becomes disabled prior to age 62, benefits under the disability program are limited to 60 months. In another example, if the person becomes disabled after reaching age 62, the amount of benefit will be based on a sliding schedule as demonstrated in Table 20–4.

In summary, if the group has a high percentage of persons over the age of 60, the potentiality for an increase in disability incidence is present. However, the duration of that disability can be limited by a benefit cutoff age.

---

[3]Under a 1987 ADEA law change disabled employees 70 years of age or older must receive a minimum of 12 months of disability benefits.

TABLE 20–4
ADEA Option for Benefits

Employee Attained Age at Disablement	*Maximum Months of Income Replacement*
62	42
63	36
64	30
65	24
66	21
67	18
68	15
69	12

Source: Group Contract, The Principal Mutual Life Insurance Company, Des Moines, Iowa.

Occupation

Claim frequencies vary from one occupation to another, and each class of occupation demonstrates a distinctive accident and sickness frequency. That is, working with steel is more hazardous than working with a computer and thus produces more disabilities. Although workers' compensation provides benefits for occupational injuries, group disability plans may still be affected. In some jurisdictions, workers' compensation income replacement does not begin until after a three- to seven-day waiting period, and thus claims could be paid out of a short-term sick leave plan. Additionally, some workers' compensation benefits are inadequate, and the group plan would be needed to supplement income replacement. A long-term disability program may be affected further because of the susceptibility of certain occupations to various chronic conditions. For instance, people employed in mining or chemical industries may develop serious heart or lung conditions, and these ailments may or may not be ruled to have resulted from occupational hazards. If workers' compensation benefits are not awarded, group disability benefits probably will be paid.

Job classification of the employee also may affect disability plans. Historically, hourly paid and lower-paid workers either were declined or rated very heavily. This rating may be attributable to overinsurance problems, discussed later in this chapter. Whether a group is insurable may depend on the percentage of workers in hourly paid or lower-paid positions and the type of job performed. Each insurer has a different underwriting standard, but it is not uncommon, for example, to decline groups involved in agriculture, fishing, chemicals, entertainment, or construction.

Duration

Certain employees may be considered ineligible for coverage because of their age or occupational status. It is common to exclude seasonal or part-time employees from disability plans, as well as persons who have been working for the firm a short time, even if they are employed on a full-time basis. If qualification procedures have been met, there generally is a waiting period before disability income benefits begin. However, some plans pay benefits immediately in the case of a non-job-related disabling accident. Waiting periods for short-term disability range from 0 days because of accident, and 7 days because of illness, to 7 days because of accident, and 14 days because of illness. In long-term plans, waiting periods range from one month to one year.

Disability income benefits continue as long as the definition of disability is met and are paid according to the contractual provision until one of several things occurs. First, disability contracts require that the participant be under the care of a physician and that statements to that effect be made on a regular basis. Payments terminate when the participant stops receiving this care. Death of the participant, of course, will terminate disability benefits. In short-term plans, most disability benefits are terminated when the employee has returned to work or has been paid for the maximum number of weeks, and in long-term plans, benefits are terminated when the definition of disability can no longer be met. Because of the two-stage definition of disability discussed earlier, it is normal for an individual to go off benefit status at the end of the 24-month "*own* occupation" definition of disability. If such person continued to be disabled under the "*any* occupation" definition, disability benefits could continue to age 65 or 70 depending on how the benefit package is coordinated with any pension plan that may be in effect. If the pension plan is so set up that retirement income can begin at age 65, disability income stops at that point. If there is no pension plan, disability income should continue until age 70 or until contractual provisions are met. Proper drafting of a disability and pension plan should include some provision for accrual of pension benefits during disablement. If no disability program exists, pension plans often allow early retirement benefits because of disability.

Amount of Benefits

Two perspectives on the amount of income to be replaced by disability income benefits may be valid. Some benefit managers believe disability income should be high enough to allow disabled persons to continue in their normal lifestyle, while others believe disability benefits should be closer to a subsistence level, thereby encouraging employees to return to work. In either case, the goal is to control overall income in a way that discourages malingering. Historically, some firms did not consider that income might be available to participants from several sources, and that participants might collect from various other plans as well as from the employer-provided disability plan. Today, target replacement is in the range of 60 to 70 percent of gross salary, with an offset for benefits received from other sources such as workers' compensation and Social Security. Even at this level, overinsurance may result if the disabled party is collecting from several sources. For example, an employee might have an 80 percent replacement of spendable income under workers' compensation and a minimum payment from a disability income plan. This might provide more real income after disability than before. Contributory disability plans should be analyzed carefully, because benefits received as a result of participant premiums are received income-tax-free. Thus, the benefit manager faces the task of determining an income replacement level that allows the disabled party to live in a reasonable fashion, but not to the extent that the worker will have so much income that no incentive exists to return to work. The problem is particularly acute for young hourly paid and lower-paid workers because of the amount of income potentially available from Social Security. A high-income replacement percentage from Social Security, combined with a benefit from a disability income plan, may cause an overinsurance problem.

The increase in cost attributable to the overinsurance is not easily quantified. Insurers agree, however, that overinsurance increases both frequency and duration or continuation of claims. Some figures are available concerning cost consequences of increasing the aggregate income level from a 50 percent benefit to a 60 or 70 percent benefit. In a typical group, an increase from 50 to 60 percent of gross income might increase premiums by as much as 50 percent. An increase from 50 to 70 percent could increase premiums by as much as 90 percent. This change of premium reflects an increase in both annuity value and in claims frequency. Careful analysis should be made to assure all offsets are known, and managers need to explicitly state offsets for primary and family Social Security benefits, workers' compensation benefits, and pension and other group insurance benefits. All salary continuation benefits or sick leave plans also should be taken into consideration.

A topic related to the percentage of monthly income to be replaced is the maximum amount of such income to be replaced. In older plans it was common to replace a maximum of $2,000 to $3,000 per month, while newer plans are shifting to $5,000 and $10,000 monthly limits. It is desirable to provide a higher level of income because of inflation, but a reasonable maximum should still be selected. For highly compensated employees, particularly if a plan is contributory, $10,000 per month may cause a problem. On the other hand, if a person were earning $7,000 a month prior to disability, a $2,500 maximum benefit could cause a severe economic strain on the person's family. In cases of highly compensated employees, individual insurance with a higher limit may be purchased or self-insurance may be used to supplement the group plan.

Limitations and Exclusions

Group disability plans have some limitations and exclusions. Some plans have a preexisting clause. That clause could say, "We the insurance company will not pay for disabling conditions that commence within 12 months after the effective date of the person's insurance if the person received treatment or service for such disability during the 3-month period preceding the effective date of his or her insurance." The time periods may vary, but the concept is the same. If a person has been receiving treatment or has been off work because of disabling conditions, or both, he or she may not have group coverage benefits available until the coverage has been in effect for a minimum of 12 months. In addition, a limitation for disability because of intentional or self-inflicted injury is found in most contracts. It also is common to have a limitation or exclusion for disability because of war or any act of war, declared or undeclared.

In the past, disability contracts had two-year benefit limitations for alcoholism, drug addiction, and mental and nervous disorders; but such limitations are being used less frequently now; in many accident and sickness policies, alcoholism is treated as any other illness.

ADMINISTRATIVE AND FINANCIAL ISSUES

Cost Sharing—Contributory versus Noncontributory

As with other employee benefits, it is important to consider whether disability benefits should be paid for on a contributory or noncontributory basis prior to the installation of the plan. The amount of cost sharing affects benefit levels and the taxability of benefits received under disability plans. Benefits attributable to an employee's contributions are received tax free without limit. Therefore, if an employer is asking an employee to contribute a significant portion of the disability insurance premium, the percentage of income replaced must be decreased to take into consideration the tax-free status of benefits received, or an overinsurance problem can result.

An additional issue in contributory versus noncontributory plans is the minimum benefit. If an employee is required to contribute, should a minimum benefit be paid from the disability plan even though overinsurance problems might result? In many plans, whether contributory or not, a minimum benefit of $50 per month is provided. As the contribution level rises, employees could reasonably request a higher minimum payout from the plan.

Small employers may find that flexible benefit plans offer the best solution for providing disability benefits. Employees then may choose appropriate benefit levels or decline the benefits entirely.

Claims Administration

Claims administration in the group disability area can have a very large impact on the cost of the program. A variety of claims administration techniques exist, and each technique and form has advantages and disadvantages. The three main types of administration can be characterized as regional, centralized, and combined.

Regionalized Administration

Some large insurers have totally decentralized claims administration and control, in which the claims investigation and claims decision and monitoring take place at a local or regional level. Claims examiners in each state or sales region of the country handle all claims administration for disability in that area. In some cases, when disability income insurance volume is too small to make it efficient to have a claims examiner who specializes in disability claims, a claims examiner may deal in a number of different types of coverages, including disability. It is the responsibility of the claims examiner in the specific region to collect medical data and make a decision on the qualification of a claimant for disability benefits. The claims examiner must have a working knowledge of the various group contract provisions and be able to interpret medical and personal data.

Centralized Administration

The second type of claims administration is the centrally located claims department. In this type, claims work and investigation are performed from a central office. The group policy holder files claims applications directly with the home office. Backup investigations may be performed by independent claims adjusters or by credit bureaus. However, most information about the claim is gained by mail or telephone directly from the policy holder and physicians involved; there usually is no personal interview with the claimant. Generally, the claimant fills out the entire claim form, and payment usually is made directly from the home office, but in some instances it is made by the employer in the interest of better employee relations. Continued monitoring of the data is performed at the central location.

Combined Administration

To obtain the advantages of both the claims contact of regional administration and the cost savings of central administration, certain large insurers have claims systems that use regional claims people but keep the decision process in the home office. Local claims people are used for investigative purposes and to contact the claimant and his or her employer. Employees make claims to the home office, but regional personnel deal with the policy holder. The regional claims people bring together all pertinent claims information and make a personal call on the claimant if it is considered necessary. Compilation of a claims file takes place at the regional outlet. Regional office personnel may make a recommendation on the claim, but approval or denial comes from the central office.

Third-Party Administrators (TPAs)

If the disability exposure is self-insured, an outside administrator may be chosen to manage claims. Independent claims professionals will be used to adjudge eligibility and suggest rehabilitation. The TPA will make claims payments.

An employee benefit manager must decide what type of claims administration is appropriate for its organization. Because of the delicate nature of disability claims, whether short- or long-term, it seems desirable in most cases that claims administration be handled by a third party and that the third party have a centralized or combined system for adjudicating claims. Claims services may be procured from insurers or specialty firms that monitor and control claims. Then, in the event an employee is dissatisfied, the dissatisfaction is aimed not at the employer but at another entity. In any event, it is important to have quick processing of claims and to have claim investigations started immediately.

Not only should proper claims processing be started for the private coverage, but a system to encourage disabled employees to file for Social Security disability income benefits should be in place. The number of people who receive Social Security disability benefits has changed drastically in the last decade. In the period between 1957 and 1969, it was not uncommon for the percentage of disability claims approved by Social Security to be above 50 percent, and in some years the percentage of claims approved by Social Security for disability benefits was above 60 percent. Because of massive changes in the economy, the percentage of persons who applied for and received Social Security awards dropped drastically in the 1970s. In the period 1970 to 1974, the percentage of applicants approved was less than 50 percent, usually between 40 and 50 percent. In the 1980s, the approval rate for Social Security disability claims dropped into the 30 percent range. It is important to understand that the increased cost to integrated plans resulting from a lower percentage of Social Security disability claim approvals must be borne by the group policyholder. Thus, for potential cost savings, claims should be followed to their completion. Careful application and possibly reapplication should be made under Social Security if it seems at all possible the claimant could qualify for Social Security disability benefits.

Rehabilitation

Another important part of an employee benefit manager's responsibility in the disability area is to make sure the rehabilitation process gets started as soon as possible. Rehabilitation services may be provided on a local basis or may be provided by an insurance company. The employee benefit manager should aid the insurance company or private rehabilitation firm.

Benefit managers can help identify employees who could benefit from rehabilitation and motivate these employees to seek rehabilitative services. Several disability insurers now have trained rehabilitation specialists who will help locate services at the local level. Rehabilitation programs first seek to put the person back in the job he or she was performing prior to the disabling condition. This may be accomplished by restructuring that job or by moving the employee into a slightly different work environment. If restructuring does not work, the next step is retraining for a position in the same company. In each case, early help is most important in getting people back into the production process. The best rehabilitation programs stress existing skills. If it is not possible to go back to the existing workplace, the insurance company involves the claimant in vocational rehabilitation. This is required if a claimant is to receive Social Security benefits. In addition, specific workshops and other education and training can be considered. The employer and the benefit manager must compare the cost of rehabilitation with the cost of keeping the person on the disability rolls. If the insurance carrier is not providing rehabilitation services for people on disability, services should be sought independently. Rehabilitation is a cost-effective device—both in human terms and in dollar terms—and should be part of the plan design.

SUMMARY

This brief overview of the types of coverages available for short- and long-term disability provides background for the material that follows in Chapter 21. Proper underwriting and claims administration help assure the employee benefit manager that the firm's employees are well protected at an acceptable cost.

CHAPTER 21

DISABILITY INCOME BENEFITS

Waldo L. Hayes

Chapter 20 provided background information on disability income benefits, including risk elements and relevant plan-design considerations. The focus of that overview was on the issues surrounding provision of coverage and the demographic elements constituting the loss exposure of disability. This chapter expands on the significance of the disability exposure not only to the employee (from a claimant's perspective) but also to the employer in terms of providing a high-quality program to its employees at reasonable net costs. First, the potential consequences of such a loss—the magnitude of risk—is established; then the various types of protection currently available for losses of income due to disability are analyzed. The emphasis in this chapter is on long-term disability (LTD).

POSSIBILITY OF DISABILITY

The chances of a disability in a lifetime are significant. As noted in Chapter 20, 32 million persons, 13.5 percent of the U.S. civilian noninstitutional population, suffered a limitation of activity because of one or more chronic conditions in 1987. It is estimated that one out of four adults between ages 55 and 64 is so severely disabled they cannot work regularly if at all. Table 20–1 indicated the probability of a disability lasting three months or longer for various age groups. Gross disablement rates rise rapidly with age. An average incidence is 3.5 per 1,000 lives exposed for a disability lasting three months or longer. The rate can be as low as 0.5 per 1,000 at the younger ages (where accident claims are most prevalent) to as high as 20 per 1,000 near age 65.

TABLE 21–1
Crude Rates of Disablement per 1,000 Lives Exposed Experience by Employee Class (Six-Month Elimination Period; Calendar Year of Issue)

Employee Class	*Ratio Act/Exp* *
At least 75% salaried, majority executive	73%
At least 75% salaried, majority nonexecutive	91
50%–75% salaried	120
At least 50% salaried (exact percentage unknown)	121
Subtotal (majority salaried)	97%
At least 50% hourly	103
50%–75% hourly	165
At least 75% hourly	176
Subtotal (majority hourly)	169%
Indeterminate	89%
Total	102%

*Actual claims versus what would be expected from a tabular risk.

Source: *Transactions,* Society of Actuaries, 1984 Reports, p. 253, excerpts.

These are average incidence levels for all industries, all occupations, and all salary levels. The rates obviously vary by demographic makeup of an employee group: women versus men, hourly employees versus salaried and manufacturing industries versus financial service industries. Occupational levels with the highest incidence are those that involve manual labor. Table 21–1 indicates the experience expectations based on broad occupation/class data. The greater the number of hourly employees, the higher the ratio of actual claims to the tabular disablement rates of all exposed units. In sum, disability is indeed a fairly likely event, and it is one that can critically impact the disabled person's current standard of living.

SIGNIFICANCE OF DISABILITY

A disabling event has the obvious potential of ceasing all or a portion of the required income flow to maintain one's standard of living. Disability has long been recognized as a pure risk deserving of full attention by various insured, mandated social-insurance and assistance programs. The pure dollar potential loss is vast when viewed through to an age such as 65. Pure dollar losses can be quickly appreciated in Table 21–2.

Fortunately, all these dollars are not lost to the disabled, even in those disabling situations that are permanent and total with no return to meaningful employment.

First, there are federal, state, and city income taxes and FICA contributions for OASDI that never would have been part of the disabled individual's disposable income. Second, not all long-term disability events continue through to an advanced age such as 65. Table 21–3 indicates the gross recovery rates or death for all disabilities with durations of six months or longer for various ages of disablement, male and female.

On average, long-term claims last between 18 months and 5 years. The shorter average is for claims with 30-day elimination periods; the longer average is for long-term disability plans with 180-day (elimination) periods. These averages can be deceptive because a majority of the claims last less than one year. In essence, there is a batching effect at work on the recovery patterns. A significant number of claims last less than a year or continue through to age 65. A third cluster of recoveries is in the 18- to 24-month period and likely is tied to the change in definition of disability wording that occurs in many contracts at the two-year point—that is, the change in definition of disability from "own occupation" during the first 24 months to "any occupation" after 24 months. In sum, a majority of the claimants do not continue for full duration to incur the level of income loss illustrated in Table 21–2.

TABLE 21–2
Potential Lost Salary (000s) due to Disability at Various Ages of Disablement—to age 65

Gross pay at Disability	*Age at Disability*			*Estimated Composite FIT & FICA Rates (%)*
	25	*40*	*50*	
$ 7,500	$ 906	$ 358	$ 162	12
18,000	2,174	859	388	17
50,000	6,040	2,386	1,079	21

Assumes a 5 percent salary increase per year if disablement had not occurred. For example, if disabled at age 40 with a salary of $18,000, then future earnings lost would be $859,000 to age 65.

TABLE 21-3
Crude Termination Rates per 1,000 Claims Exposed to Death or Recovery
(Six-Month Elimination Period; Calendar Years of Experience 1962–81)

	Age at Disablement				
	Under 30	*30–39*	*40–49*	*50–59*	*60–64*
Male Only:					
1st year (last 6 months)	311.5	238.5	177.1	117.1	80.5
2nd year	307.3	241.5	156.9	112.0	95.0
3rd year	217.1	145.7	97.1	73.0	65.5
4th year	114.8	88.4	57.6	54.1	56.1
5th year	49.7	52.6	41.1	49.4	34.9
8th year	19.8	27.5	42.2	37.6	21.5
Female Only:					
1st year (last 6 months)	313.4	227.5	196.6	124.4	96.0
2nd year	287.7	223.3	188.4	120.0	89.1
3rd year	210.3	132.1	108.8	69.6	60.9
4th year	63.6	52.3	51.2	39.1	33.5
5th year	62.3	40.4	37.0	30.4	26.9
8th year	17.5	32.0	18.4	28.7	30.1

Source: *Transactions,* Society of Actuaries, 1984 Reports, p. 271, excerpt.

Finally, and fortunately, there are federal and state programs in place that mitigate the level of income lost because of severe disabilities. These programs provide for partial-income payments to disabled individuals.

TYPES OF CURRENT PROTECTION

This section describes the various federal and state income replacement programs that exist in the public sector. The intent is to provide a succinct description of each program and level of income replaced (replacement ratios). An understanding of the level of benefits available from public-sector programs coupled with the frequency of benefit availability leads to a discussion of the need for insured and self-insured benefit programs in the private sector.

Current Public-Sector Programs

Public-sector programs include the following:

- Old-Age, Survivors and Disability Income (OASDI).
- Workers' compensation.
- Supplemental Security Income.
- Veteran's benefits.
- State retirement systems (disability rider).
- State-mandated (short-term) plans.

In evaluating a particular program, it is important to understand four key elements of the program to understand its benefits and its limitations. This overview generally will comment on:

(1) Eligibility.
(2) Benefit levels in terms of approximate replacement ratios.
(3) Duration of benefits.
(4) Definition of disability.

Where appropriate, certain specified limitations and exclusions are pointed out.

OASDI (Social Security Disability)

Chapter 5 of the *Handbook* described the compulsory/optional categories of individuals participating in the OASDI program and discussed fully insured status, eligibility conditions, the OASDI definition of disability, and benefit levels based on the primary insurance amount (PIA). Advantages of attaining disability status (freeze provision for retirement formula, or qualification for Medicare benefits) also are covered in that chapter. Disabled employees receive 100 percent of the PIA, with each auxiliary beneficiary receiving 50 percent of the PIA subject to a maximum family benefit. Benefits are payable to age 65, normally modified (lowered) by payments from workers' compensation. While those descriptions of the program are well stated, it is difficult to appreciate, in a general sense, what average replacement of "current income" is provided and what are the average approval rates of the Social Security system.

Social Security Approvals. The Social Security Disability Income approval process is a series of applications, approvals, denials, and, frequently, reapplications. The process obviously begins with the initial application. This is a series of forms completed by the claimant and one or more of his or her attending physicians. Claimants usually receive an approval or denial of this application within 60 days. Of all initial applications, only 36 percent are approved at the initial-application stage. If the claim is denied, the claimant's next step is the reconsideration level. This consists of a second review of the information already presented in the initial application; no new information is reviewed. Fourteen percent of these reapplications are approved upon this resubmission. If the reconsideration decision is still unfavorable to the claimant, the next step is to have the claim reviewed by an administrative law judge (ALJ). Claimants usually are represented by legal counsel for this hearing and can appear before the judge to present expert testimony if they desire. Fifty-seven percent of these reviews are approved. Finally, claimants denied at the ALJ level can have their claims reviewed by the Social Security Appeals Council, which can uphold the ALJ's decision, approve the claim, or remand the case to the judge for review. If the decision is upheld at the Appeals Council level, the claimant can bring suit against the Social Security Administration in federal court. Five percent of the Appeals Council reviews result in approvals.

Overall, the process is a bit complicated and results in approximately 50 percent of all initial claims, including all appeals, finally being approved. But, what is the income replaced by Social Security when a claim is approved? Table 21–4 illustrates potential replacement levels as a percentage of current predisability income.

For example, a person who was age 45 would have 32.4 percent of income replaced by Primary Social Security (PIA) if predisability income was at the $2,500 per month level in Table 21–4. It is important to note that in the majority of applications claimants receive only the primary award because of nonqualifying family status. Also, the table is a simplification, and the actual results depend on many variables of each individual disabled—i.e., number of dependents, work/salary history, and actual covered quarters. However, the table is illustrative of relative income replacement levels. In sum, most workers are eligible for Social Security Disability Income, but not all claims are approved, because the definition of disability is severe. The disability must be expected to continue for at least 12 months or to result in prior death. Basically, about 50 percent of the claims are ultimately approved, and then the percentage of current income replaced by Social Security Disability Income is adequate only in the lower income brackets.

TABLE 21–4
Social Security Disability Income Crude Replacement Ratios (Percent of Income Replaced)

Current Monthly Income	*Primary Social Security*			*Family Social Security*		
	Sample Ages					
	25	*45*	*55*	*25*	*45*	*55*
$ 400	75.3%	72.8%	72.8%	76.8%	69.8%	69.8%
600	59.8	57.2	57.2	76.7	69.8	69.8
800	52.0	49.5	49.5	76.7	69.8	69.8
1,000	47.4	44.8	44.8	71.1	67.2	67.2
1,500	41.2	38.6	38.7	61.8	57.9	57.9
2,000	38.1	35.5	35.1	57.2	53.3	52.6
2,500	34.0	32.4	31.4	51.0	48.7	47.1
3,000	30.6	28.4	27.4	45.9	42.6	41.1
3,500	28.2	25.2	24.1	42.2	37.8	36.1
4,000	25.3	22.3	21.2	38.0	33.5	31.9

Workers' Compensation

Workers' compensation provides reasonable income and medical benefits to work–accident victims, or income benefits to their dependents, regardless of fault. The first state workers' compensation laws were enacted in 1911, and today all 50 states have workers' compensation programs. While there is broad agreement that coverage under the acts should be universal, in fact, no state law covers all forms of employment. In 1984, the proportion of all wage and salary employees covered by job injury laws was 87.5 percent, and while the intent of state laws is to cover all work-related injuries and diseases, interpretations have not resulted in completely uniform coverage of injuries and diseases. These compensation laws are compulsory or elective. Under an elective law, the employer may reject the act, but if it does so, it loses the three common-law defenses: assumption of risk, negligence of fellow employees, and contributory negligence. Practically, this means that all the laws, in effect, are "compulsory." Coverage is still elective in only three states: South Carolina, New Jersey, and Texas. Most states require employers to obtain insurance or prove financial ability to carry their own risk. Self-insurance is permitted in 47 states. Employers may set up a reserve fund for self-insurance to pay compensation and other benefits.

Benefits Provided. Because workers' compensation imposes an absolute liability upon the employer for employee disabilities caused by employment, the benefits payable to the injured employee attempt to cover most of the worker's economic loss. Specifically, the benefits provided are:

Cash benefits, which include both impairment benefits and disability benefits. The former are paid for certain specific physical impairments, while the latter are available whenever there is an impairment and a wage loss.

Medical benefits, which usually are provided without dollar or time limits. In the case of most workplace injuries, only medical benefits are provided, since substantial impairment or wage loss is not involved.

Rehabilitation benefits, which include both medical rehabilitation and vocational rehabilitation for those cases involving severe disabilities.

Cash Benefits. Four classes of disability are used: (1) temporary total, (2) permanent total, (3) temporary partial, and (4) permanent partial. Most cases involve temporary total disability (the employee, although totally disabled during the period when benefits are payable, is expected to recover and return to employment). "Permanent total disability" generally indicates that the employee is regarded as totally and permanently unable to perform gainful employment.

In general, most states provide payments extending through the employee's lifetime on permanent total disability. Replacement ratios vary somewhat by various states but are always reasonable and are a percentage of "current" predisability income. The data below are a brief consolidation that demonstrates benefit levels that are relevant to predisability income for most workers, subject to the maximum weekly payments.

1. *Percent of Wages.* Forty-five states have a 66.66 percent of salary benefit. Formulas of other states are 60 percent or 70 percent of salary, with one state at 80 percent of spendable earnings.
2. *Maximum Weekly Payments*

Less than $250 per week	$250 to 350	$350 to 500	$500+
16 states	28	6	2

Maximum weekly payments vary by state-perceived need.

3. *Duration of benefits.* Forty-two states cover for the full period of disability. Thirteen states cover for specific time periods ranging

from a low of 208 weeks to a high of 600 weeks; most are in the 400- to 500-week range. Ten states cover permanent and total disabilities for life.

The workers' compensation coverage is significant. Most employees have a solid replacement level of income for a good to excellent duration of benefit payments for disabilities that result from work-related injuries and diseases. However, these work-related disabilities represent less than 10 percent of all disabilities that occur to the employee population.

Supplemental Security Income

This program, administered by the Social Security Administration, is a "need based" program that provides social assistance. The payments are based on individually determined needs financed from general government funds. The basic payment amount, before reduction for other income, for 1991 was $407 per month for one recipient and 50 percent more for an eligible couple. Such payments have no fixed durations and are intended as a financial support until other programs are available to the disabled. In addition, some states pay supplements to Supplemental Security Income.

Veterans Benefits (Disability Income)

Members of the military are provided with a noncontributory pension plan. Retirement is provided for after 20 years of service. If a member is disabled before retirement, he or she becomes eligible for veterans compensation, provided such disability is service-connected. Compensation varies by degree of disability, ranging in 1990 from $76 per month for a 10 percent disability, to $1,370 per month for 90 percent and $1,847 for 100 percent. Severely disabled individuals (i.e., amputees, blinded persons) receive additional amounts that can bring the total to $3,461 per month. Additional allowances are paid for dependents of those with at least a 30 percent disability; these allowances are computed as flat amounts varying with the number of dependents and the percentage of disability. These veterans disability benefits are currently paid in addition to disability benefits that might be payable under the OASDI program.

Retirement Systems (Disability Features)

Pension programs, especially public employee retirement systems (PERS), frequently have a disability component to protect the income of disabled members. The PERS programs are usually "instead of" the OASDI program of Social Security (i.e., state and local governments can opt out of the Social Security system if their employees are covered by their own retirement system). The PERS programs are individually established by the states to provide for the retirement and disability income needs of their employees. The eligibility point for disability benefits generally varies from immediate to five years; in some states 10 years of service is required in order to be eligible for benefits. Thirty-three states require a 5- or 10-year employment period before an employee is eligible for the disability income benefit. The benefit levels frequently are based on a service-type formula such as 2 percent of salary for each year of service times a final average salary (FAS), to a maximum percentage of salary. Other states provide for straight formulas such as 50 percent of FAS or 62.5 percent of average monthly salary (AMS). The number of years required in these averages varies by state, but the most frequent requirements are "latest *x* years," or all years since a certain date, excluding the five years of lowest earnings. In general, replacement ratios are not applied to current incomes prior to disability, and benefit levels generally are in the range of the Social Security Disability Income programs with some exceptions. The benefits usually are paid through to normal retirement (age 65) under the program. The definition of disability usually is permanent and total disability. The approval rates on PERS programs (i.e., of the claims submitted, how many are approved for payment by the PERS) generally are not available. However, since the definition of disability is permanent and total, similar to that of the Social Security Disability Income system, there probably is a sizeable declination rate that may be more severe than that of Social Security.

State Mandated (Short-Term Disability) Plans

The states of California, Hawaii, New Jersey, New York, and Rhode Island and the territory of Puerto Rico have passed legislation that provides or requires nonoccupational disability benefits for workers. These programs all provide benefits for short-term disabilities. The maximum benefit duration of most plans is 26 weeks. Most plans only provide modest levels of coverage (e.g., New York's DBL benefit is 50 percent to a maximum of $145 per week. Table 21–5 provides a brief synopsis of the mandated short-term disability programs.

TABLE 21–5
Mandated Short-Term Disability Programs—Abbreviated Summarization

State/Territory	*Enactment Date*	*Elimination Period (days)**	*Max.*	*%*	*(Duration)*
California	1946	7	$224	55/60	52
Hawaii	1969	7	223	55	26
New Jersey	1948	7	226	66⅔	26
New York	1949	7	145	50	26
Puerto Rico	1968	7	113/55	60	26
Rhode Island	1942	7	236	60**	30/defined

* Generally 7 days, but various modifiers based on in-hospital or duration considerations.
** Plus 5 percent/$5 per week for each dependent child up to five children (defined).

In summary, these various public sector type programs can be viewed to provide a modest yet very important foundation of disability income protection to the working population.

• The most comprehensive level of coverage is provided by the workers' compensation programs. However, those apply only for work-related disabilities, and, as mentioned previously, work-related disabilities represent less than 10 percent of total disabilities that lasted more than 90 days.

• Social Security Disability Income provides protection for both occupational and nonoccupational disabilities, but its strict definition of disability and general benefit levels are not intended to support all disabilities at all income levels. Similarly, state retirement systems usually apply in lieu of participation in the Social Security Disability Income system, with relative replacement ratios and claim approval rates.

• The state-mandated (short-term) programs likewise are modest and by definition are operative in the high-frequency, short-duration protective area.

• Veterans benefits can be very meaningful depending on the degree of disability. These benefit levels are normally provided regardless of benefits received from other programs.

The foundation of public sector programs is critical, yet all disabilities are not covered or are not covered at a level of benefits approximating predisability income needs. As such, additional disability income protection is a basic need to be provided within the private sector in the form of insurance or self-insurance.

INSURANCE/SELF-INSURANCE PROTECTION

In Chapter 20, disability programs were discussed in terms of design, process, and standards. It is important to restate here that generally all programs described are integrated with any benefits resulting from the previously described public-sector programs. Integration means that the benefits of an insured or self-insured program generally are reduced by benefit amounts resulting from the public-sector programs. Insured/self-insured programs also generally integrate with other disability income benefits from any government or employer group programs. The exception to this is veterans benefits, which government and insurers have thus far been reluctant to consider as an offset source.

Basically, the private-sector programs guarantee a level of reliable protection to the members of the group. This applies generally to all disability programs. If, for example, the benefit level is 66.66 percent, the eligible claimants receive that amount less any integrated benefit amounts from other sources. As discussed in Chapter 20, employers choose the level of protection desired, taking into account the employer's/ employees' disability program objectives, taxation-of-benefit issues, and the desired net costs of such a disability program. Those program objectives consider not only replacement ratios and benefit maximums and durations, but also the key factors of definition of disability, underwriting restrictions and limitations, and claims-management considerations.

Having looked back briefly at those program parameters, the remainder of this chapter elaborates further upon the concepts of self-insurance decisions and preemptive claims-management considerations.

Self-Insurance—Disability Claims Expertise

Chapter 47 of the *Handbook* provides a comprehensive discussion of conventional insurance versus alternative insurance arrangements. Discussed here are additional considerations unique to long-term disability coverages.

A general discussion of when it is wise to insure versus self-insure is appropriate, with the main considerations being a reiteration of the concepts of the law of large numbers, financial dependability, and avoidance of catastrophic fluctuations. In essence, long-term disability is a catastrophic type coverage—that is, few events, but most events potentially quite large.

Employers generally should not fully self-insure a low-frequency and catastrophic-type coverage, such as the long-term disability exposure. Self-insurance should be utilized primarily in areas of shorter-term, high-frequency claim activities with inherently higher predictability of incidence. High credibility on the expected experience levels would be the desirable self-insured scenario. And, even there, the precaution of stop-loss insurance on nonhomogeneous design components, such as a very high maximum benefit on one or a few highly paid employees, should be taken. In sum, consider the benefits of self-insurance on the more predictable portion of the loss exposures, and consider transferring to an insurance company pool the unpredictable, catastrophic, and volatile portions of benefit programs.

One can argue that a firm's *total* LTD coverage is catastrophic in nature and should be fully insured with the possible exception of the very largest groups. However, if a smaller firm were to self-insure a portion of its LTD risk, the prevalent tendency is to self-insure the relatively higher-frequency claim area of the first two or the first five years of a claims duration. This "front end" period satisfies certain employer desires to have some control on the early claims period of their employees. Further, employers sometimes feel they can maximize their participation in any favorable claims experience during this high-visibility control period by monitoring their employees. Finally, there normally is a real concern by employers to self-insure the back end of claims durations: i.e., the volatility of, say, the liability of claims in excess of five years.

At any rate, no employer should fully self-insure either the front end or the back end of claim liabilities without carefully evaluating and limiting its maximum benefit exposure on any given disabled individual. Similar to the life insurance pooling concepts discussed in other chapters, it is wise to limit the catastrophic size of (monthly) claim payments. In essence, any interest of employers to participate in perceived advantages of self-insurance on long-term disability should be limited to the most predictable windows of claims experience. On long-term disability, this window might be framed as the first $2,000 of monthly benefit, the first two years of claim duration, and only for larger employer groups.

Partial (versus total) self-insurance is also important for the employer because it continues a risk-profit incentive for the insurer. The claims management expertise of insurers should be allocated to those disability risks where recovery or rehabilitations have a direct impact on bottom-line (insurer) profit levels. It is distinctly in the insurer's best interest to fully manage any front-end self-insured portion of these risks. Recoveries within this window create the insurer's desired experience results for the catastrophic insured portion of the claim duration; i.e., claim payments in excess of that two-year limit are the liability of the insurer. The insurer's full expertise, and resources including rehabilitation resources, should come to bear as early as feasible and within the self-funded period. This maximizes the effective management of the "front-end" employer-funded period.

The long-term disability insurance product itself is critically dependent on the true expertise of claims management. *Management* is a key word here. Claims administration, claims examiners, or processing have no relevance to a controlled employer net cost, or to equitable treatment for the insureds; professional management is the key concept and key element to a successful program. Because of the nature of the coverage and its relatively brief evolution in the employee benefit arena, virtually all competent claims expertise resides with active long-term disability insurance carriers. Very few third-party administrators have the ability to create the desired net cost and employee equity. The claims management on long-term disability is truly complex and demanding.

Preemptive Claims Management

The normal complexities of professional disability claims management can be significantly affected by the individual characteristics and the relative sense of values of the employee population.

As discussed previously, such items as replacement ratios, multiple-source overinsurance, and adverse selection concerns are involved in the potential of making attainment of disability status more desirable than working. Strategies in this area normally view the financial comparisons of predisability income versus postdisability health and welfare status. These are normal analyses since they are relatively obvious concepts and can be somewhat mechanically measured, even though not totally controlled.

There is, however, another major area of impact that should be considered in the evaluation of the long-term disability product. Employee motivation is the element that keeps net cost for the long-term disability product at its most efficient levels. Satisfied and motivated workers choose to work rather than stay home regardless of certain disabling conditions. Thus, the employer's environment and culture is a major source of productivity, not only for the employer's product or service but also for the ultimate costs of all the employer's employee benefit programs. An employer's overall employee benefit program should include some investments by management to identify individual physical or emotional situations at their earliest stages and be geared toward individual correction for overall employee satisfactions and equity. Positive company attributes such as wellness programs and accommodations for the handicapped can truly bolster the desire to work and can influence the choice to work versus not to work. The savings in the collective areas of company productivity and employee benefit net costs normally will far outweigh the additional infrastructure and management costs of programs to address early warning signals of the employee. The concept is obvious: deal with the disability issue before a claim is filed, before the employee makes choices on work versus nonwork, and comparisons of preclaim financial status and stress. Once a claim has commenced, claims management, including the rehabilitation initiatives, goes to work. However, stopping that initial claim submission is a critical key to the total program management, and whether to file a claim or not is frequently rooted not only in the value system of the employee (work ethic), but also in the degree to which this employee values his or her work and employer.

SUMMARY

A significant likelihood of disability exists for the working population, and loss of income obviously has significant economic effects. There are several sources of public income provided for the disabled, but they do not cover all employees nor all types of disabilities. Thus, private-sector coverage is needed to provide an adequate level of reliable protection, either on an insured or self-insured basis. Such private programs usually integrate with the public programs before remitting the additional income support to the insureds.

Self-insurance of the long-term disability exposure is not a normal solution for employers because of the catastrophic and volatile nature of the coverage. The lowest net cost of these employee benefits plus the highest productivity of the employer are best served by a progressive and preemptive approach to employees' motivations and attitudes.

PART 6

OTHER WELFARE BENEFIT PLANS

Part Six consists of seven chapters dealing with the design of various employee benefit plans and several service type plans.

Chapter 22 covers the pressing issue facing employees in today's environment of providing for child care and eldercare needs. This chapter explores the several approaches that have been developed as employee benefits to help meet the financial and emotional needs of employees for this growing concern.

Chapter 23 presents a discussion of the increasingly important subject of family leave programs. Such programs are being provided by more and more employers to allow for the many employee situations where family leave is desirable.

Employee assistance programs are not only an important employee benefit by themselves but often function in tandem with other employee benefit programs particularly those related to medical benefits. Employee assistance programs are especially useful in conjunction with managed care approaches to health care cost containment, and are discussed in Chapter 24.

The nature and uses of legal service plans provided through the employer are covered in Chapter 25. The various types of plans and the advantages and limitations of each are evaluated.

Financial planning as an employee benefit is the subject matter of Chapter 26. Chapter 27 presents a brief review of property and liability insurance as an employee benefit and deals with such issues as the types of coverages offered, the kinds of programs under which they are offered, advantages and disadvantages to the employee, the role of the employer, and regulatory issues.

Part Six concludes with an often overlooked but significant and often costly portion of employee benefits; namely, payments for nonproduction time, time not worked and miscellaneous benefits. The many benefits that fall into this category are reviewed and their usefulness to employees analyzed.

CHAPTER 22

DEPENDENT CARE

Ann Costello
Kathleen Hunter Sloan

Increasing numbers of employers are offering dependent care as an employee benefit because they have come to recognize that many employees experience a conflict between work and family that stems from dependent care responsibilities. Although usually thought of as assistance for child care, dependent care benefits encompass employer support for the care of other dependents, including elderly parents, elderly, ill or disabled spouses, and dependent adult children. An employer that offers dependent care benefits usually considers them an important element of its human resources policy directed at maintaining or improving its competitive position.[1]

In the 1980s, the benefit portion of employee compensation began to change in a number of ways in response to social and demographic changes in the American family. The stereotypical family composed of working father, housewife, and two or three children was rapidly being replaced by a family unit that reflected workplace and demographic realities. By 1988, both husband and wife worked in 63 percent of families, an 11 percent increase from 1980.[2] In 1990 over half the mothers of young children were employed.[3] The number of single mothers who

---

[1]See Kathleen H. Sloan and Ann Costello, "Employer Integration of Dependent Care Into Employee Benefit Plan Designs: Politics, Public Policy, and Planning," V *Benefits Quarterly* 40 (1989).

[2]Stephanie L. Hyland, "Helping Employees With Family Care," *Monthly Labor Review,* 22 (Sept. 1990).

[3]*Households, Families, Marital Status and Living Arrangements: March 1988, Current Population Reports, Series P–20, No. 432* (Advance Report) (Bureau of the Census, September 1988).

were heads of households increased 23 percent from 1980, and many were employed.[4] In many cases, the grandmothers of the children of working mothers also were participating in the labor force and thus not available to care for their grandchildren. Employed parents were confronted with an urgent need for child care, and the younger segment of the grandparents group often had difficulty in coping with the responsibilities of working because they had to help care for their elderly parents.[5] With far more of the adult population participating in the labor force, the need for some accommodation on the part of employers for employees' dependent care needs came forcefully to both the public's and employers' attention.

Thus, employers who recognized they had human-resource management problems—such as recruiting and retention of certain categories of workers, high turnover rates, high rates of absenteeism, and requests for time off the job—turned to employer-supported child care as a problem-solving technique.[6] Growth of dependent care benefits was stimulated by several factors, including information given to employees by labor organizations, media attention to child care as a highly significant issue, and a gradual understanding that dependents other than children required similar care and that employers could increase management efficiency by assisting their employees to solve these problems.[7] Also, the granting of tax-preferred status to employee-benefit dependent care and the use of flexible spending accounts have encouraged the growth of these plans.

DEPENDENT CARE AS A WORK-FAMILY ISSUE

The increased awareness of the broader nature of employees' dependent care responsibilities led to a new focus on these obligations as a component of the general issue of work-family conflict. The other elements, seen as benefits that would alleviate work-family conflict, included family leave, maternity leave, paternity leave, flexible work-hour and workplace poli-

---

[4]Ibid., p. 23.

[5]Roy S. Azarnoff and Andrew E. Scharlach, "Can Employees Carry the Eldercare Burden?" *Personnel Journal*, 60 (1988); Kathleen Glynn, "Providing for Our Aging Society," 67 *Personnel Administrator*, 56 (1988).

[6]See Joan P. Fernandez, *Child Care and Corporate Productivity* (Lexington, Mass.: D.C. Heath, 1986).

[7]Allan Halcrow, "IBM Answers the Elder Care Need," *Personnel Journal*, 67 (1989); William H. Wagel, "Eldercare Assistance for Employees at the Travelers," *Personnel* 4 (1987).

cies, and flexible benefit options. At the heart of work-family issues, however, remained the changes brought about by the influx of women into the work force. To the younger women's problems of balancing work and child care was added the older women's problems of balancing work and eldercare—and some women experience both.[8] Some women are able to work, but feel they must accommodate the need for before- or after-work care for an elderly relative and may need to help with the shopping and the household chores as well. Men, too, may be called upon to give care and attention to elderly relatives. Unmarried men, or those who are married but who for personal reasons take on the role of caregiver, have been shown, in employer dependent-care surveys, to be more frequently involved in the care of elderly relatives on an ongoing basis than with child care. However, an increasing number of men are single parents, and many married men share in child care responsibilities.

For the past two decades, the more troubling aspects of working parents and child care have received ever increasing attention. First, child care represents a considerable expense for the employed parent; second, the desired quality of child care may be difficult to obtain and too costly to be a realistic alternative; and, third, employers of working mothers have had to face the issue of either providing or subsidizing child care.

Child care costs can run between $50 and $400 a week or higher depending on the age of the child, location of care, geographic region, and services desired. The Conference Board estimated that child care is the fourth largest budget item for working parents, after food, housing, and taxes, and that it may represent 30 percent of the family budget.[9] Eldercare, depending upon the degree of skill needed in the caregiver, or for special treatments, can range from inexpensive for occasional at-home services to very expensive for a special day-care center with a nursing staff.

Both child care and eldercare can best be seen as part of the human-resource management challenge facing employers in the United States. Employers are challenged to provide the type of employee benefits that make the greatest contribution to overall productivity and employee morale and to do so in a cost-effective manner. Well-designed dependent child care and eldercare benefits offer an important means to meet the challenge.

---

[8]See Dana Friedman and Wendy B. Gray, "A Life Cycle Approach to Family Benefits and Policies," in 19 *Perspectives* 15 (The Conference Board, 1989).

[9]Dana Friedman, "Corporate Financial Assistance for Child Care," *The Conference Board Research Bulletin*, 1985, p. 6.

PUBLIC POLICY ISSUES AND LEGISLATION

On a national level, Congress has examined the question of what role the employer should play in providing dependent child care and what, if any, direct role the federal government should play, as well as the government's indirect role through providing tax credits to both employer and employee. State legislatures have both debated and enacted legislation to encourage employers to offer child care as an employee benefit. As in any public policy debate, conflicting ideological perspectives have shifted the focus of the debate from the questions of the responsibility of employers to provide dependent-child care to questions concerning the appropriateness of working mothers, the responsibility of society for children placed in day care, and the issue of whether parental leave from employment is a sounder approach than day care.

The recent enactment of the first major federal legislation on child care has done little to clarify the role that employers should play in the provision of the care.[10] The legislation establishes a three-year, $2.5 billion block-grant program for the states to distribute to parents and day-care providers who meet the minimum state health and safety standards. At least 75 percent of the grant money must go to the parents and day-care providers who meet the minimum state health and safety standards. At least 75 percent of the grant money must go to the parents who would be eligible for the federal aid, in the form of vouchers (as long as their incomes do not exceed 75 percent of the median income in their state of residence) or service providers. The remaining 25 percent of the funds are earmarked for preschool and after-school child care programs.

The public policy debates surrounding the child care legislation and the Family and Medical Leave Act that was passed by Congress and vetoed by President Bush on June 29, 1990, indicated both the widespread support for employer-sponsored family benefits and the lack of consensus on whether the benefits should be mandated by federal law or should directly involve the federal government. While policymakers in Washington and in the states debated work-family issues and sponsored "family friendly" legislation, employers continued to add, for the most

---

[10] Julie Rovner, "Congress Wraps Up Decision on Child Care Legislation," *Congressional Quarterly Weekly Report* 3605, *Washington Post*, Oct. 27, 1990; "Congress Passes Major Child-Care Legislation," *Hartford Courant*, Oct. 28, 1990.

part voluntarily, new benefits to provide family care support that met the existing needs of the new labor force.

Although employer-sponsored dependent child care benefits have been expanding fairly rapidly, they are not well-established or widespread among employers,[11] and according to the Bureau of Labor Statistics, of the estimated 1,126,000 firms in the United States with 100 or more employees, about 10.1 percent offer dependent care benefits.[12]

Public policies providing health and community services for the elderly were established during the 1960s, but it was not until the 1980s that the connection between increased numbers of women in the work force and the need for eldercare as an employee benefit was noticed.[13] Employers then began not only to pay serious attention to the need for child care benefits but also to investigate the need for eldercare benefits.[14]

TAX POLICY

The tax treatment of dependent care costs is governed by Internal Revenue Code (IRC or Code) Sections 21 and 129. Section 21 was passed by Congress in 1976 in response to rising dependent care costs and provides a tax credit on the individual's federal income tax liability. Also, important definitions such as ''dependent'' and ''employment related expenses'' required for Section 129 plans are stated in this part of the Code. The tax-preferred treatment of employer-provided dependent care assistance programs (DCAPs) was added in 1981 by Section 129 and amended several

---

[11]Cathy A. Cooley, ''1989 Employee Benefits Address Family Concerns,'' *Monthly Labor Review,* 60 at 61 (June, 1990); data from U.S. Dept. of Labor, *Employee Benefits in Medium and Large Firms, 1989* (Washington, D.C., 1990).

[12]Sloan and Costello, ''Employer Integration of Dependent Care,'' p. 44.

[13]*The Diversity and Strength of American Families,* Hearing Before the Select Committee on Children, Youth and Families, U.S. House of Representatives, 99th Cong., 2nd Sess. (1986); *Demographic and Social Trends: Implications for Federal Support of Dependent Care Services for Children and the Elderly,* Select Committee on Children, Youth and Families, U.S. House of Representatives, 98th Congress, 2nd Sess. (1984); Rhoda B. Gilinsky, ''Corporations Begin Studying Ways of Caring for the Elderly,'' *New York Times,* September 14, 1986, XXII 27:1.

[14]Dana Friedman, ''Eldercare: The Employee Benefit of the 90s,'' 23 *Across the Board* 44 (1986); ''New Benefit Looming (Eldercare),'' 31 *Personnel Administrator* 16 (1986); Leslie Stackel, ''Eldercare: An Emerging Phenomenon,'' 13 *Employment Relations Today* 359 (1986-1987); Fairlee E. Winfield, ''Workplace Solution for Women Under Eldercare Pressure,'' 64 *Personnel* 31 (1987).

times in the '80s. Under the provision, payments made in accordance with the tax law are deductible for the employer and excluded from the employee's gross income. The maximum exclusion for a tax year is the lesser of $5,000 or the earned income of the worker or spouse. Eligible expenses and the method for determining the earned income of a spouse who is disabled or is a student are set forth in Section 21 of the Code.

A dependent care program organized to meet Section 129 requirements can assist employees in securing services required for the supervision and care of children and of elderly or disabled dependents of the employee so long as the employee is employed full-time. The term "dependent care assistance" must meet the Code definition.[15] The Code requires that dependent care assistance be in connection with "employment-related expenses" incurred to enable the employee to be gainfully employed.[16] The expenses must be incurred for household services and the care for a "qualifying individual"[17] defined as (1) a dependent of the taxpayer under the age of 13; (2) a dependent who is physically or mentally incapable of caring for himself or herself; or (3) the spouse of the employee if the spouse is physically or mentally incapable of caring for himself or herself.[18] For services provided outside the home, dependents in the last two categories also must live at the taxpayer's residence each day for eight hours. If the dependent care services are provided by a dependent care center, to meet the Code requirements the center must comply with all applicable laws and regulations of a state or local government and receive a fee for the provisions of care for more than six individuals.[19] In addition, the DCAP must pass a special nondiscrimination test. The average employer-provided benefit for those not defined by the Code as highly compensated must be at least 55 percent of the employer-provided benefits given to those who are so defined.[20] Employees who are covered by collective bargaining agreements, who are under 21 years old, or who have less than one year of service may be excluded from the calculation. For plans that involve the

---

[15]IRC Sec. 129 (e) (1) and as defined under Section 21 (b) (2).

[16]IRC Secs. 129 (e) (1) and 21 (b) (A).

[17]IRC Secs. 129 (e) (1) and 21 (b) (2) (A).

[18]IRC Sec. 21 (b) (2) (c).

[19]IRC Sec. 21 (b) (2) (c).

[20]IRC Sec. 129 (d) (2). Section 129 (d) (8) as amended by PL 101-140 applies to plan years beginning after December 31, 1989.

use of salary reduction, employees with compensation below *$25,000* may be disregarded also. The reasoning for this provision is that the existence of the tax credit for dependent care would benefit this group of employees more than would a salary reduction.

In order to meet the requirements for the federal income tax exclusion, a DCAP must meet the following eligibility requirements:

1. The plan must be in writing.
2. The employee's rights under the plan must be enforceable.
3. Employees must be given reasonable notification of the benefits available under the plan.[21]
4. The plan must be maintained for the exclusive benefit of employees.
5. The plan must be established with the intention of being maintained for an indefinite period of time.[22]

Employees must be informed that they have to make a choice between use of the DCAP and use of the dependent care tax credit (DCC) in a given tax year, and employees are responsible for determining whether the tax credit offers them more tax savings than the use of the DCAP. Employers can assist employees in understanding which option provides the employee with the greater tax savings.

Currently, Section 21 of the IRC provides a credit against tax liability for individual income tax equal to 20 to 30 percent (depending on the taxpayer's adjusted gross income) for employment-related child care expenses.[23] The amount of the employment-related expenses incurred onbehalf of the qualifying dependent during any taxable year is limited to $2,400 for one dependent or $4,800 for two or more dependents of the taxpayer.[24] The dollar amount determined under Section 21 is reduced

---

[21]The notification must include a description of the dependent care credit (IRC Sec. 21) and the circumstances under which the credit is more advantageous than the exclusion.

[22]IRC Sec. 129 (d) (1) (B).

[23]IRC of 1986 Sec. 21. "Employment-related expenses" is defined by Sec. 21 (b) (2) to mean expenses incurred (9a) to enable the taxpayer to be gainfully employed and (b) for household service or for the care of a qualifying individual. Thus expenses can qualify for the credit even though incurred for domestic services such as cleaning and meal preparation, rather than actual care of a child or incapacitated person. Any amount paid for services outside the taxpayer's household at a camp where the qualifying individual stays overnight is excluded. This is *provided* the household includes a "qualifying" individual as defined by Sec. 21 (b) (1).

[24]IRC Sec. 21 (c) (a) (1) and (2).

dollar for dollar by the amount of expenses excludable from the taxpayer's income under the Section 129 dependent care exclusion.[25] Consequently, the employee who has the opportunity to make use of the DCAP benefit needs to assess carefully, based on his or her income or the combined income of a married couple, which exclusion provides the greater tax advantage.[26] If the employee's marginal tax rate is less than the percentage used in the tax credit formula, then the tax credit generally is more favorable than the dependent care spending account. For employees in the lowest income brackets, it is important to understand the additional tax benefits received through the earned income tax credit as the 1990 budget compromise legislation increased it.

The dependent care credit (Section 21) and the exclusion for employer-provided dependent care assistance benefits under Section 129 both require the taxpayer to report on his or her tax return the correct name, address, and taxpayer identification number of the dependent care provider.[27] If the taxpayer cannot report the required information, he or she must be able to prove to the Internal Revenue Service (IRS) that the taxpayer exercised due diligence in attempting to provide the information on the service provider; otherwise, the taxpayer may forfeit the Section 21 or the Section 129 exclusion.[28]

EMPLOYER OBJECTIVES

In the context of its overall benefit philosophy, an employer may decide to offer dependent care benefits when it finds it advantageous in order to meet its objectives. These objectives fall into three major categories:

---

[25]As amended by PL 100-485 which reduced the age of a dependent child from 15 to 13 effective for taxable years beginning after December 31, 1988.

[26]For example, if a taxpayer with one child incurred $6,500 of child-care expenses during a taxable year of which $3,000 is excluded under the DCAP, the amount excluded under the DCAP ($3,000) exceeds the expenses eligible for the DCC ($2,400) and no dependent care credit could be claimed for the taxable year. If the amount excluded under the DCAP was only $1,000, then the employee could claim $1,400 ($2,400 − $1,000) under the DCC.

[27]Taxpayers report this information on Form 2441, the current form on which the credit for child and dependent care expenses is computed. If the dependent care provider is exempt from federal income taxation under Sec. 501 (c) (3) of the Code, the taxpayer is only required to report the correct name and address of the exempt organization.

[28]IRC Sec. 21 (e) (9).

1. Employee needs.
2. Employer productivity goals.
3. Improved external relations.

Employee Needs

If the absence of available dependent care alternatives or the high costs of available care are creating hardships for employees, the employer may find it advantageous to offer dependent care benefits in recognition of employee needs. Personal considerations often dictate whether an individual accepts a particular employer's job offer or another's. Willingness to relocate is not as common as it was in the past, and family considerations are much more important. Individuals examine what the employer is willing to provide in total compensation, of which benefits are a major component. Employees see the employer's commitment to a benefit such as dependent care as recognition that employees are more than just workers, and assistance in finding high-quality dependent care or in reducing its cost bonds the employee to the company. The design of the actual benefit affects the level of freedom from concern, but almost any form of assistance provides some form of relief. An employee with dependent care concerns may see the need for and importance of such a benefit as greater than benefits such as a pension: the dependent care problem exists now; the others are something for the future.

Employee Productivity

With increasing health care costs and the passage of more restrictive and demanding employee benefit legislation, employers are hesitant to add benefits or increase existing benefits. An employer considering the addition of a benefit wants to know how the additional benefit will promote its goals. If the addition of dependent care benefits will contribute to productivity goals by reducing absenteeism and employee turnover and the attendant costs of hiring and training new employees, then the employer may decide potential improvements in productivity outweigh the additional costs of the benefit.

Three separate national surveys asked employers who offered child care services how the company had been affected by the addition of the benefit.[29] The respondents in two of the studies were predominantly employers who sponsored their own day-care centers. The data were of a subjective nature but did present a positive relationship between corporate child care and productivity, and improvements were seen in recruitment, employee morale, absenteeism, turnover, and employee work satisfaction.

Studies on eldercare and productivity have centered on employment problems, caregiver characteristics, and diversity of required caregiving. Similar work problems such as absenteeism, excessive phone calls, tardiness, high stress, and emotionalism have been cited. A Portland State University study of 9,573 employees of 32 companies found that 36 percent lost time because of caregiving, and the American Association of Retired Persons survey of 1,338 workers from five employers stated that 18 percent had lost work time.[30] Research by the University of Bridgeport Center for the Study of Aging of 504 employees noted that the average loss was 18 hours a year, while a Transamerica Life Companies study of 1,898 workers cited an average loss of 32 hours per year.[31]

Employers have started to realize that if an employee is late, absent, or disturbed because of a child care or eldercare problem, productivity will be affected. Someone else will have to perform the individual's duties, and this creates not only stress for other workers but also scheduling problems. Unforeseen problems, such as a late babysitter or a sick child, may mean that a project is not completed on time. At certain periods of the day, an employee's attention may not be on his or her work, but rather on whether the child has arrived at home after school or whether a parent is receiving medication.

The studies cited here and other recent studies suggest a positive relationship between employer-supported dependent care and productivity. Articles about firms that have adopted dependent care plans are

---

[29]The three studies that provided the surveys are: Sandra Burud, Pamela R. Aschbacher, and Jacquelyn McCroskey, *Employer Supported Child Care: Investing in Human Resources* (Boston: Auburn House, 1984); Renee Y. Magid, *Child Care Initiatives for Working Parents: Why Employers Get Involved* (New York: American Management Association, 1983); and Kathryn S. Perry, *Employers and Child Care: Establishing Services through the Workplace* (Washington, D.C.: Women's Bureau, U.S. Department of Labor, 1982).

[30]Donna L. Wagner, Margaret B. Neal, Janice L. Gibeau, Jeanne W. Anastas, and Andrew Scharlach (1989). "Eldercare and the Working Caregiver: An Analysis of Current Research." Unpublished research reported in Donna Wagner, Michael A. Creedon, Joan M. Sasala, Margaret B. Neal, *Employees and Eldercare* (Bridgeport, Conn.: Center for the Study of Aging, 1989).

[31]Ibid.

appearing constantly in the press, and individual firms are noting increased morale, increased employee retention, reduced recruiting costs, and reduced absenteeism as results. All of these appear to have led to increased individual employee productivity.

Improvements in External Relations

Besides productivity gains, an employer may gain additional advantages external to the organization. The installation of new benefits often is announced in the local press and industry publications. The image of a "caring" employer is reinforced; a message is transmitted that the company is progressive and a leader in its human resource management. Other firms may use the plan as a prototype for their benefit packages, and the company's name is often repeated as a trendsetter. Positive public relations may be furthered by actual involvement of the company in increasing the quantity and quality of dependent care in the community; this depends, however, on the actual design of the benefit.

OTHER ISSUES

While dependent care may offer many advantages to a company, there are major issues that affect its acceptance and are probably causing many firms to hesitate.

Equity

In a conventional employee benefit plan option such as health care coverage, an employee may or may not use the benefit during a given year; but all employees are eligible to use it any time, and over time all employees may have occasion to rely on it. However, dependent care may only be used by those who have "qualifying individuals" as dependents. Those employees who do use it will change over time. Resentment could arise among employees who have no need for such a benefit; compensation funds are being spent for something that does not help them at all. Equity is a fundamental issue in employee benefits, as can be seen from the nondiscrimination rules applicable to many benefits that exist to protect against a disproportionate amount of funds for a benefit being spent on top management, owners, and stockholders. The equity issue in dependent care benefits could lead to individual personnel issues, and the actual composition of the employee group is important in determining the size of the potential problem.

Upper Management

Decision-making about dependent care benefits is done by upper management. Some have argued that senior managers may be older and not really aware of the sociological changes that have affected the demographics of the labor force. Their sensitivity to the issue of dependent care may not be as acute as is necessary, and they may not be aware of the different options available for plan design.

Firm's Reputation

While there are positive outcomes for the reputation of a company offering dependent care, a risk manager would advise caution when considering the benefit from an external relations perspective. Firms do not want to be involved with a program that may be substandard, as the expected gain from such a substandard plan would be more than offset by the problems presented. Personnel complaints and, ultimately, liability suits could severely damage the company's reputation. A firm must be very careful about the qualifications of any day-care provider with which it associates and may decide to deal only with state-licensed or registered providers. As the majority of dependent child care in the United States is not licensed, that decision severely limits the possible use of the benefit by the employees. Attempts to limit liability by having a nonprofit foundation or a professional day-care chain control and manage the on- or off-site facility have been utilized. In plans that simply make referrals, the choices given have often been limited to licensed care; here the purpose is to inform, not to be the provider. Flexible benefits plans and reimbursement accounts merely provide financial aid; choosing the provider, within the requirements of the IRC, is left to the employee, and the employer would not be liable for the actions of the dependent care provider.

Dependent-Child Care Industry

One of the major obstacles to providing dependent-child care is the nature of the industry itself. High-quality child care requires dedicated and informed care providers who have an understanding of child development and the patience to provide the appropriate personal care in stressful situations. The ability to attract and retain qualified workers is difficult, for child care workers and teachers receive an average annual pay of only $9,000 and have a turnover rate of 42 percent, the highest of any occupation.[32] Quality of care is hard to maintain with such a high turnover. There also is a major shortage of available care. Connecticut, often cited among the states as having a highly progressive dependent care environment, still needs care for 40,000 more children. The market for child care is one of high demand and low supply—the seller exercises control because the parent needs the service. Parents who have to work are forced to look for acceptable alternatives, and an "underground" industry exists in which payments made to providers are not reported for income tax or Social Security tax purposes, thus making it impossible for parents even to use, legally, the federal tax credit. Child care is regulated by state agencies, and employers considering offering day care directly through their own facilities must meet state and local regulatory requirements.

EMPLOYER INITIATION OF THE DESIGN PROCESS

The Feasibility Study

In the process of designing or redesigning a benefit package, feasibility studies often are conducted to explore the possibilities of a particular benefit.[33] Employers considering adopting or modifying dependent care benefit policies need to research the specific needs and opportunities of their labor force. The analysis may be undertaken by management, but outside consultants often are used for their specific expertise. Expert assistance may be needed not only in the employee benefit field but in the child care and eldercare fields as well and may require the use of more than one consultant.

---

[32]Jeanne Saddler, "Low Pay, High Turnover Plague Day Care Industry," *The Wall Street Journal*, February 12, 1987, p. 27.

[33]Assistance for the portions of this section dealing with child care was given by Barbara P. Adolf, Associate Consulting Actuary, Buck Consultants, Harmon Meadows, New Jersey, in a telephone interview on March 13, 1987. For the section dealing with eldercare, see Wagner et al., *Employees and Eldercare*, 1989, with additional information from Dr. Donna L. Wagner, Center for the Study of Aging, University of Bridgeport, Bridgeport, Conn., in telephone interviews in fall 1990 and spring 1991.

The employer's overall employee benefit philosophy is the first consideration, after which the employer's objectives in adding dependent care should be established. With the objectives clearly defined and the need of the employees and their dependent care problems identified, those responsible for designing the new benefit may proceed.

The personnel problems that appear to diminish productivity should be reinforced by the benefit design. For example, to meet employer productivity objectives of reducing training costs, the level of acceptable turnover and the demographic characteristics of employees are important considerations. Some firms may accept a high turnover of employees, while others may spend large sums for recruiting and training and will want a very low turnover rate.[34] Some industries such as health care have predominantly female employees in their child-bearing years. The feasibility study should identify and further examine those relevant employee characteristics that suggest child care would meet the company's objectives, keeping in mind that while dependent care may not be useful for all employees, the productivity impact of dependent care problems on the entire organization may make alleviating those problems a priority.

Economic projections about future requirements for employees will help management to understand not only the immediate situation but also long-term implications as well. For example, a high-technology firm in Hartford, Connecticut, has implemented dependent care because of a tight employment market—both current and projected.[35] Data from personnel records are an important source of information. Examination of demographics of the employee group will show how many present employees are members of two-income families or are single parents; these data will assist in making projections as to future child care requirements. Comparative data about tardiness, absenteeism, and turnover can be collected for groups of employees with and without children. From this, the company can cost out the possible personnel problems as well as advantages associated with child care programs. Since the collected data are very limited, other techniques may be implemented. Adolf and Rose, in *The Employer's Guide to Child Care,* recommended

---

[34] "A Special News Report on People and their Jobs in Offices, Fields and Factories," *The Wall Street Journal,* June 30, 1987, p. 1.

[35] Susan Howard and Robert Weisman, "Shortage Demands New Ideas," *The Hartford Courant,* November 11, 1986, p. 1.

that a company use informal means and target groups for the feasibility study.[36] Information as to whether child care has been mentioned as a problem by employers is gathered from individuals by the personnel department and supervisors. Target groups involve discussions among a small number of specifically selected individuals led by an expert whose purpose is to elicit individual viewpoints concerning child care needs and propose alternative responses to the identified needs. The leader tries to keep the discussion focused on plan design options that would be acceptable to the company.

Analysis of personnel records will not disclose the need for eldercare, and the use of employee surveys is the most recommended tool. There may be a wide variation between the need and the types of care involved from one employee group to another. Also, the type of care needed may change drastically with the normal process of aging, and the "dependent" most likely will be involved in the selection and acceptability of the care. The survey may provide information totally unknown to management but of extreme importance to the worker, and the data will demonstrate which eldercare benefit options are viable.

Management and/or its consultant have the most current cost and tax implications of the different options available. To assist in choosing those possible for the firm, information must be available on dependent care in the local community. In a 1987 study, the Census Bureau stated that working women's children under five years of age were cared for most frequently in another home (37 percent), followed by in the child's home (31 percent), in organized child care facilities (23 percent), and at a parent's workplace (8 percent).[37] The employer tries to establish the existing availability of day-care homes and dependent care facilities. The ages of children and appropriate facilities for each age group are important considerations; children may be infants, toddlers, preschoolers, school-age, or those with special needs. Care for infants is the most expensive and often is in the shortest supply. Special children may be handicapped or temporarily sick; care of this type may not be available at all. Data are gathered about licensed or registered caretakers' costs, hours of operation, and services provided. If any other local businesses offer dependent-care assistance, their programs are examined.

---

[36]Barbara Adolf and Karol Rose, *The Employer's Guide to Child Care* (New York: Praeger Publishers, 1985), p. 88.

[37]U.S. Census Bureau, "Minding the Kids," *The Wall Street Journal*, May 26, 1987, p. 35.

As with child care, the availability of eldercare services is an important factor in the employer's decision-making process, and a similar study should be done for eldercare by an employer considering that benefit. The employer-supported benefit plan should not duplicate but complement any programs the community provides and to which the dependent may be entitled.

At this point in the feasibility study, company executives should be equipped to decide which design options are viable. Besides the obvious factor of cost, the firm must decide what level of involvement should exist in actually providing the dependent care. Low involvement would be a referral system; very high involvement would involve an on-site facility. A firm's ability to spend additional dollars on a new benefit will place constraints on acceptable alternatives. A flexible benefit plan that includes dependent care but also allows the employer more financial control thus may be attractive. For the child care benefit, after analyzing the possible acceptable options, the firm does a formal needs assessment. The firm should be seriously committed before doing this, as the employees' expectations may be raised, and negative feelings toward the employer could result if the process is not handled properly. Adolf and Rose state that the questionnaire should cover (1) demographics, (2) attitudes, (3) connection between child care needs and work problems, and (4) special needs.[38] Besides the normal demographics, the first section also would cover the types and operating features of dependent care currently available. This assessment data, similar to the eldercare survey data, will assist the firm in deciding which of the acceptable options would most satisfy employees' needs now and in the future. On completion of the feasibility study, the employer should have identified the dependent care needs and associated problems that inclusion of dependent care as an employee benefit may alleviate, thus meeting the employer's objectives.

TYPES OF EMPLOYER DEPENDENT CARE BENEFITS

Figure 22–1 shows a comparison of two forms of dependent care—child care and eldercare—as an employee benefit. While employer-provided benefits for child care and eldercare take different forms, they can be

---

[38]Adolf and Rose, *The Employer's Guide to Child Care*, p. 91.

FIGURE 22–1
Dependent Care as an Employee Benefit

	Child Care	*Eldercare*
Eligibility of dependent	Child under 13—worker claims as tax exemption	Mentally or physically incapacitated dependent or spouse of the taxpayer—lives in employee's home for eight hours a day
Annual limit	Lesser of $5,000 total; $2,500 if separate tax return of married individual or earned income of either spouse	Lesser of $5,000 total; $2,500 if separate tax return of married individual or earned income of either spouse
Tax Code	Section 129 subject to definition and requirements of Section 21	Section 129 subject to definition and requirements of Section 21
Care	Very routine—generally same type for almost all children of same age	Individualized with rapid change in needs—must be closely monitored
Decision-making as to care and type	Parent-employee for child	Employee in conjunction with dependent or spouse—level of resistance or resentment possible
Benefit Options	Straight benefit, flexible spending account (FSA), flexible benefits, vouchers, information and referral, employee assistance program (EAP), family day care, worksite day care	Straight benefit, FSA, flexible benefits, vouchers, information and referral, EAP, family day care, adult day-care center

placed on a continuum that represents the degree of employer involvement. A lesser degree of involvement usually implies lower employer costs. The cost of a program, however, should be viewed in relation to the cost of the problem it is attempting to address.

The classification of different types of benefits can be made according to the function or purpose of the program and according to ease of administration. The purposes of dependent-care programs include:

1. Financial assistance.
2. Information assistance.
3. Referral services.
4. Emotional support or counseling services.
5. Emergency or short-term services.
6. Direct or contractual provision of services.

Employers must consider the ease of administration, the cost/benefits and the risk of implementation of the particular form of the benefit. They must examine questions of employee equity that may arise so that employees do not feel that only limited numbers of their co-workers will benefit from dependent care. The six categories of employer-provided dependent care assistance serve different purposes, take different forms, and vary in relation to the nature of the dependent as children and the elderly differ in care giving and service needs. In any event, employers need to understand the nature of the forms of dependent care benefits that have been implemented by a variety of private and public-sector employers in the United States.

Financial Assistance

Dependent care assistance plans may be financed totally by the employer and treated as a separate benefit following Section 129 and Section 21 guidelines. However, if employee contribution is involved, Section 125 of the code allows this to be done on a pretax basis subject to the DCAP requirements. Flexible spending accounts and flexible benefit (Section 125) plans provide attractive options for dependent care.

Flexible Spending Accounts (FSAs)

FSAs, commonly referred to as reimbursement accounts, can be used to provide employees with dependent care benefits.[39] Such an account may be established at a very low or negligible cost to the employer, and employees can pay for dependent care expenses with pretax dollars by the use of a salary reduction program. Figure 22–2 illustrates the tax savings available through the use of an FSA for dependent care expenses. Money

---

[39]Assistance for the sections of this chapter on flexible benefits and FSAs was provided by Diane Luedtke, F.S.A., vice president, CIGNA employee benefits consulting actuary.

FIGURE 22–2
Usage of Flexible Spending Account Tax Savings On Eldercare or Child Care Expenses

Information: $9,000 eligible expenses
Head of household tax status (1990 rates)

	With a Dependent Care Assistance Plan	*Without a Dependent Care Assistance Plan*
Gross Income	$40,000	$40,000
Contributions to FSA (elder or child)	5,000	0
Taxable Income	$35,000	$40,000
Taxes (Fed. Income and Social Security)	9,085	10,867
Disposable Income	$25,915	$29,133
Elder or Child expense	4,000	9,000
Spendable Income after dependent care expenses	$21,915	$20,133
Increase in Spendable Income with FSA	$ 1,782	

going into the dependent care account must be kept separate from the other possible form of reimbursement account—accident and health. Employers may contribute to the account but often do not. The total amount of the dependent care account is restricted by the requirement of Section 129 of the Code—the total maximum amount that may be in the account is $5,000 for a single person or married couple filing jointly or $2,500 for a married person filing separately. This also is subject to the earned-income limitation. The employer pays no Social Security taxes or unemployment taxes on the amount of the employee's salary reduction.

As already discussed, *eligible employment-related expenses* provided for *qualifying individuals* by *approved caretakers* are governed by IRC Sections 129 and 21. While the plan may be funded by employee and employer contributions, if any form of salary reduction is used, the plan is subject to the Section 125 flexible benefit plan regulations. The amount of funds to be committed to the account must be decided in advance by the employee and must cover the whole period of the plan. Thus, an individual may not choose to participate for only 3 months rather than 12 months in order to protect the tax exclusion. A change in contribution amount is allowed only when there is a change in family status, such as a change in marital status, addition or loss of a dependent, or addition or loss of spousal employment. The plan also requires that any money left in an account at the end of the year is forfeited by the employee—"Use it or lose it"—and the employer must use the remaining funds for the exclusive benefit of the employees. This forfeiture requirement can strongly affect the desirability of such a benefit, and the employee should be conservative in estimating expenses. Also, it is essential that the employee do the comparison between the benefit of a salary reduction versus the tax credit of Section 21 discussed earlier. A Section 125 plan document is required for all salary-reduction plans, and the nondiscrimination rules and reporting requirements must be strictly adhered to.

The employer may administer the accounts or may contract with an outside organization such as a third-party administrator or an insurance company to provide the necessary expertise. Compliance with the IRC is essential, and the employer must have a payroll system able to handle the different accounts necessary for the calculation of withholding of income and Social Security taxes for the employee and unemployment and Social Security taxes for the employer. The timing of the eligible expenses during the year need not match the amount of the prefunded dollars in the individual account. For instance, if bills are reimbursed quarterly and there are not enough funds in the account at the end of the first quarter to reimburse all bills, a partial reimbursement can be made, or the employee can be reimbursed at the next period when there are sufficient funds.

The reimbursement account satisfies the equity issue so often raised about dependent care. Those not needing the benefit are not deprived of employer funds that could be used for some more desired benefit. Also, because the employer does not pay Social Security or unemployment taxes on the amount of the employee's salary reduction, these savings often are used to offset the administrative costs of setting up an individual account and reimbursing the employee, usually biweekly, monthly, or quarterly, for eligible expenses. Thus, in effect, the employee is paying for the cost of the benefit by trading Social Security and unemployment earnings credits for it, and the cost is borne only by those participating in the plan.

DCAP as Part of a Flexible Benefit Plan

While a dependent care assistance plan may be offered as a separate benefit, it also may be one of a choice of benefits under a Section 125 flexible benefit or "cafeteria" plan, and a growing number of employers have begun offering dependent care benefits this way. Employers have noticed that, in general, employees do not fully appreciate or understand the value of the conventional, no-options benefits package and gain a better sense of the value of the benefits portion of their compensation when they are directly involved in the process of selecting among the benefits available to them. Employers can use flexible benefit plans to limit the employer costs of benefit provision, and these plans also create savings by eliminating duplication of benefits between spouses or payment for unnecessary benefits. A cafeteria plan is a written plan under which participants may choose among two or more benefits consisting of taxable benefits and certain other permissible nontaxable benefits. Whether or not the flexible benefit plan offers the DCAP choice to employees, it must meet numerous requirements under Section 125 of the IRC that are beyond the scope of this chapter and are covered in detail in Chapters 29 and 30 of the *Handbook.*

The flexible benefit plan must follow the dependent care assistance plan rules of Section 129 for the DCAP to be a qualified benefit. The plan may allow for care of children, handicapped dependents, and elderly parents. Reimbursement accounts using salary reduction are governed by Section 125. Requirements for dependent care administration exist for salary-reduction plans as well as the flexible benefit program, both being governed by Section 129. Flexible benefit feasibility studies often are used to decide which qualified benefits should be included and which options offered, and the incorporation of a dependent care option often results from an examination of the whole benefit package rather than from a consideration of the need for dependent care benefits.

A flexible benefit plan provides an ideal situation for dependent care coverage. Recognizing that only a portion of employees need the benefit, the plan allows them to have it without depriving other employees of some portion of compensation. The employee who chooses dependent care elects it instead of some other benefit, thereby eliminating the equity issue. Also, the needs of employees change over time; some may want dependent care now but not in the future, and for others the reverse will be true.

Other Financial Assistance Approaches

Instead of or in addition to the methods just described, there are methods of more direct financial assistance for employees' dependent care expenses. These, by providing assistance through reduction of taxes, are employer-negotiated discounts at local day-care centers, subsidies, and child care or eldercare vouchers.

Employer Discounts and Subsidies

Certain national child care provider chains offer employers a discount (of 10 percent) on employee child care services if the employer meets the provider's requirements for use. The Department of Labor found that a number of employers match the discount with an equivalent subsidy. In 1987, the Conference Board estimated, only 25 employers were providing child care subsidies other than those linked to employer discounts at designated centers. The employer subsidy can be either a flat amount or a percentage of child care/eldercare expenses, and can be available for all employees or only for those employees in the lower income brackets.

Vouchers

Vouchers for eldercare services are relatively new and are used more widely for dependent-child care payments. Most voucher programs operate as Section 125 flexible spending accounts for dependent care, but they can be attractive to firms that cannot afford or choose not to adopt flexible benefits plans. The programs are limited to licensed care and are more common in the retail field.

Employers usually contract with a voucher vendor to administer the voucher program. Employees enroll in the program during an enrollment period and select a specific amount of pretax dollars to be deducted from each paycheck to cover all or part of the dependent care expenses. The employer advances monthly payments to the voucher vendor, who issues four vouchers per month to individual program participants. The voucher represents a fixed amount of available funds. The employee receives the voucher from the vendor and either endorses it over to the dependent care service provider or directly pays the provider and then turns the voucher in for reimbursement. To be reimbursed, the employee must submit identification information on the provider, as required by the IRC.

To implement a dependent care voucher program, an employer enters an agreement with the vendor firm and pays both a start-up fee (based on the employer's total number of employees) and a small monthly administrative fee (ranging from 3 to 7 percent of the total voucher amount). Major voucher vendors can provide a complete turnkey program that provides employer-employee summaries, communication kits, administrative forms, utilization statistics, and annual IRS reports. The fees paid to the vendor are structured so that the employer incurs little or no cost because of the savings on Social Security and unemployment taxes.

Dependent Care Information and Referral Services

Employers may choose to limit their dependent care assistance programs to the provision of information pertinent to their employees' needs or combine this with an actual referral service. The use of employer information and referral services for child care services has been well established, and while employer experience in using these services for employee eldercare is more limited, the results appear to be positive. The great contrast in the nature of the two different kinds of information and referral services means that very different types of community resources are involved in service provision.

For child care, the employer's objective in establishing an information service is to provide employees in need of child care services with a listing of available providers; these providers control the quality of care. Employers can exercise quality control only insofar as they limit information and referrals to state-licensed providers. Employers generally have to make a financial contribution to support the information system. Frequently, employers may contract with a nonprofit agency, such as the United Way, to provide the information service and to make referrals if that service is included. The nonprofit agency then has the responsibility to compile the listing of providers and, frequently, to attempt to ensure quality control through an on-site inspection process. The quality of service, however, is not guaranteed. The addition of referral services usually entails additional costs for the employer. If the information service is contracted out, it may mean an additional charge for the actual referral, since this involves the attempt to match the employee's need with the availability and type of service provided in the listings. If the employer is providing the referral system in-house, the additional time involved in finding an appropriate provider adds to the employer's costs for the service. This additional cost, however, needs to be weighed against the possible work time lost by requiring the employee to find a service provider, particularly when this is on short notice.

The service for eldercare is similar to that for child care. However, the range of community resources and the types of service provided may be much greater. Whether the service is provided in-house or is contracted out, it is of great importance that the information provider is knowledgeable about the various types of services and the special needs of the elderly. Unless the employer is of sufficient size to have specialists with gerontological knowledge and precise knowledge of community programs, the employer should look to contract with an external source for the provision of the service. In most U.S. communities of any size, a wide range of services exist to meet the needs of elderly persons, and since the enactment of the Older Americans Act in 1965, a network of community services has developed. Most communities in the United States have developed local agencies, called Area Agencies on Aging, to follow the mandate of the federal act as amended to plan, coordinate, monitor, and evaluate local services available to the elderly. Community services funded through the Older Americans Act are provided without charge, as they are an entitlement based on age. Other community-based services charge fees, usually based on a sliding scale to match the income of the elderly person.[40]

In a 1989 survey conducted by *Fortune* magazine and the John Hancock Insurance Company, only 18 percent of respondent companies indicated an interest in adding a DCAP component to include eldercare in their benefit plans, and 16 percent were considering adding information and referral services for eldercare.[41] The survey indicated that companies with existing child care assistance programs were far more likely to respond positively to adding eldercare benefits. Collective bargaining agreements may force employers to add information and referral services for elderly dependents of employees.[42]

Eldercare services, nevertheless, are quite different from child care services. The structure of the dependent care benefit for each of the two groups of dependents may be similar, but the specifics of services and

---

[40]For a comprehensive review of the scope of employers' involvement in eldercare as a form of dependent care employee benefit, see Wagner, Creedon, Sasala, and Neal, *Employees and Eldercare: Designing Effective Responses For the Workplace* (Bridgeport, Conn.: Center for the Study of Aging, University of Bridgeport, 1989).

[41]Ibid., at 17–18.

[42]Carol Perkin, "What's New In Elder-Care Benefits: Help for Workers Who Care for Their Parents," *New York Times*, June 4, 1989, p. F20.

programs differ greatly. The elderly dependent, unless mentally incapacitated, likely will want to be involved in the choice of service. Care arrangements may change more frequently in instances where the elderly dependent insists upon service changes or criticizes the care provider. This may add to the emotional stress of the employee.

As a result of these problems, an information and referral service may be linked to the employer's employee assistance program (EAP). The employer may structure the information service so that it is linked to a counseling service. This may facilitate the employee's ability to express the tension and frustration that often are found in a dependent care situation for an elderly parent. Some employers have made use of employee support groups for those employees who serve as care providers for elderly parents or other relatives.

Information services for either child care or eldercare are intended to provide information on the range of available services, their nature, their costs, their schedule of availability, and often the qualifications of the caregivers. The addition of a referral system provides assistance in matching the specific employee need with the available service. A hotline service may be included for either child care or eldercare to provide immediate information in the case of a crisis such as a sudden illness or the disruption of the existing dependent care services.

Emotional Support or Counseling Services

Employer establishment of EAPs has been most frequently associated with attempts to reduce employee problems with alcohol and drug abuse. As employers gained experience in EAP programs, their use was extended to other situations such as marital problems, spouse abuse, or problems with emotionally disturbed or substance–abusing children that might interfere with employees' job performance or ability to continue working. As employers began exploring the need for eldercare assistance with their employees, they came to realize that the emotional problems and tensions surrounding dependent care for parents, spouses, or elderly relatives were often destructive to an employee's well-being and ability to function on the job. It became apparent that extending EAP services to cover these problems might serve as a source of support to the employees and reduce associated productivity problems. Because the nature of the problems involved in eldercare are different, employers who wish to extend EAP services to assist their employees in coping with eldercare problems will need to add specialists trained to handle gerontological problems or contract out for such services.[43]

Emergency or Short-term Services

Even if parents have made satisfactory arrangements with a child care center to care for their child or children, a sudden illness can leave the working parents with the need to make alternative arrangements on short notice. In many cases, the demands of a job make it extremely difficult for a parent to stay at home to care for the sick child. In a few cases, employers have joined together to create an at-home emergency child care service that covers a wide variety of situations. For example, a New York pilot program managed to double the number of participating employers within a year.[44] For children who are ill or whose usual care arrangements are not available, some companies offer emergency child care in centers established for the care of sick children. Since 1981, more than 80 such day-care centers for mildly ill children have opened. The children are cared for in a safe environment with professional help, so that the parents are able to continue working. In certain industries that depend on large numbers of women to perform professional services, the need seems to be more acute, but they often are willing to share their sick-child care facility.[45] Employers indicate it is less expensive to pay for this service than to pay for temporary help or to bear the cost of absenteeism. In some communities, the Visiting Nurse Association attempts to coordinate the start-up of sick-child programs to service a number of cooperating employers in private or public organizations.

Emergency care for elderly dependents has not been a benefit given great consideration other than through the information and referral service that links the employee with existing resources in the community. Area Agencies on Aging provide information on service availability and also

---

[43]In Creedon (ed.), *Issues for an Aging America: Employees & Eldercare, A Briefing Book* (Bridgeport, Conn.: Center for the Study of Aging, 1987), the problems in EAPs and counseling are discussed with reference to their pilot project.

[44]Carol Lawson, "Emergency Child Care Program Grows," *New York Times,* October 25, 1990, p. F1. In most companies, employees can use the program up to three days at a time for a total of six days per year.

[45]"Hospital Day Care for Sick Children Makes Gains," *New York Times,* February 24, 1989, cites a report in *Pediatrician* magazine calculating that businesses lose 6 to 29 days annually for each parent of children under the age of 6 at a cost to employers of $2 to $12 billion.

coordinate many services. Local units of the Visiting Nurse Association can be contacted for the provision of nursing services in the home.

Contractual or Direct Provision of Services

For employees, there are obvious limitations to the financial-assistance programs employers may provide for dependent care because these programs depend on existing child care facilities which may or may not meet employee needs, and employers have no control over the quality of the care provided. If employees are not satisfied with the available services, the employer can attempt to find new providers, terminate the benefit program, or consider providing various dependent care services itself. Employers may directly provide or provide through a contractual arrangement an array of services ranging from information and referral or employee counseling programs to the provision of emergency care and even on-site day care services. While only a limited number of employers offer on-site eldercare services, there is a possibility that their use may expand in the future for those employers who have exceptional need for that type of service among their employees.[46]

Family Day-Care Home Support

In some communities day-care services for children and the elderly are available in family homes as well as in day-care centers, and some employers have made arrangements to make use of these facilities as an alternative to on-site care. Family day-care homes offer care for up to six children in a home by an individual. This form of care often is cited as being preferred for children from one to three years old, and many homes accept infants and toddlers. The family day-care home often is more convenient and less expensive than day-care centers and provides a homelike atmosphere. However, while these advantages make this an attractive option, estimates are that because 70 percent or more of the homes are unlicensed, the quality of care may vary greatly.[47] Employers in some localities have provided financial support to cover start-up costs

---

[46]Refer to Wagner, *Employees and Eldercare: Designing Effective Responses for the Workplace* (Bridgeport, Conn.: University of Bridgeport Center for the Study of Aging, 1989) for a thorough analysis of eldercare programs.

[47]Friedman, "Corporate Financial Assistance for Child Care," p. 2.

and assisted in the hiring of workers and the development of day-care homes. The homes usually agree to carry the necessary insurance and to act as independent contractors[48] and in some cases may agree to ceilings on their prices. The employer does not have management or financial control over the homes and is, therefore, not legally liable. The employer may or may not use some form of financial assistance to help employees with the cost of using the homes. (Vouchers, discounts, flexible benefit plans, and reimbursement accounts also can be used, subject to IRC requirements.

Workplace Child Care Centers

Analysis of the information gathered in a feasibility study may lead employers to establish a workplace child care center to meet their objectives. Child care centers provide institutional care for more than six children, from infants through school age (but normally over the age of three), and as many as 100 children may be cared for at one center. Centers usually are licensed, and extensive safety, health, and sanitation requirements are imposed on centers by local and state laws. If there are any educational services such as preschool or kindergarten, the programs must meet the appropriate educational standards of the community and state.

Employers may offer child care in one of the several ways identified by Adolf and Rose. Centers may be

1. Owned and managed by the employer.
2. Owned by the employer and operated by an outside group.
3. Contracted out to a nonprofit agency.
4. Contracted with a profit-making service.[49]

An employer may act alone or join a consortium of other firms. The consortium concept has been used by some employers in locating care in downtown urban areas, but difficulty in meeting varying employer objectives has limited its use. Another form that is relatively new is the building and operating of centers by developers for their office tenants.[50] The centers are used as a marketing technique to attract employers to lease space.

---

[48]Burud, Aschbacher, and McCrosky, *Employer-Supported Child Care,* p. 189.

[49]Adolf and Rose. *The Employer's Guide to Child Care,* p. 37.

[50]See Cathy Trost, "Toddling Trend: Child Care Near the Office," *The Wall Street Journal,* October 6, 1986, p. 33.

Employer-supported day-care centers may be at the work site or nearby, and the financial arrangements of the employers may vary. Some firms have supplied the start-up costs and expect the program to be self-sustaining; others have supplied full financial support and subsidized yearly center losses. Major employer concerns are cost, usage, and quality. These programs have high start-up costs, and attendance may fluctuate. In exchange for financial support, employers may want preferential treatment for their employees, reduced rates, or reserved spaces.[51]

The positive aspect of this option is that the center may be more flexible in providing the types of service required by the company's employees. The center may be open for different shifts of workers and be easily accessible during breaks and lunch, parents may be able to visit their children, and the available resources may permit children to have broader experiences than available with a babysitter or day-care home. The employer has the greatest amount of control with this arrangement, and the center may enable the employer to recruit new employees from a broader range of the community population and foster a positive image for the firm in the community.

However, there are negative considerations for the firm. The employer must be concerned with pricing. The benefit may be provided free to the employee; or, more commonly, the employee will pay part of the cost. The existence of other child care services in the community that offer lower prices and more desirable locations may offer competition for the center. If the center is located in an urban location, employees may not want to transport their children long distances daily or on public transportation. Also, the employer may incur extensive administrative and legal problems imposed by providing a center. Liability for the center may become a major issue and liability insurance may be expensive or unavailable. Some companies set up a 501(c)(3) nonprofit corporation to avoid financial loss, but a firm's reputation can be severely damaged by claims of injury to children.

The tax treatment of an employee's use of on-site facility care was provided by the Tax Reform Act of 1986 (TRA '86) in Section 129.[52] The utilization and the value of services determine the amount of tax exclusion

---

[51]Employee Benefit Research Institute, *Fundamentals of Employee Benefit Programs*, 2nd ed. (Washington, D.C.: Employee Benefit Research Institute, 1985), p. 202.

[52]IRC Sec. 129 (e) (8).

that is subject to the regular dollar constraints applied to other forms of dependent care.

CONCLUSION

Employers concerned with their responsibility to design benefits that both meet employee needs and contribute to productivity will continue to search for ways to integrate dependent care into their existing benefit plans. Employers have gained an increased understanding that parents in the labor force who have young children currently comprise and in the foreseeable future will continue to comprise a substantial portion of the labor force. An even greater number of employees have and will have eldercare needs. The high cost of good-quality eldercare and child care and problems with the continuing availability can contribute to the economic insecurity of those employees, particularly single parents and those with low incomes. Current evidence indicates that concerns over dependent care do affect employee performance detrimentally. Responsible employers will seek to improve their ability to analyze the dependent care needs of their employees and to design benefits that meet employee needs as well as employer objectives and that are administratively feasible. Any additional federal or state support legislated for dependent care will complement those employer-sponsored dependent care benefits.

CHAPTER 23

FAMILY LEAVE PROGRAMS

Kathleen Hunter Sloan

The importance of employee needs to balance work and family responsibilities has come to be recognized by increasing numbers of employers as an area for initiating a responsive family-oriented employee benefits program. While part of these needs may be met by an appropriate dependent care benefits plan, as discussed in Chapter 22 of the *Handbook,* employers have begun to implement, either voluntarily or as part of a collective bargaining agreement, more comprehensive human resource policies designed to reduce work-family conflicts. Such policies generally include a family leave benefit. Indeed, a number of states have enacted legislation that requires employers to offer unpaid job-protected family leave (sometimes called parental leave) for a stipulated period of time for designated reasons. These reasons usually are: to care for a newborn or recently adopted infant or young child; to care for a seriously ill child, spouse, or other dependent family member, including parents; or, if the legislation includes medical leave, to respond to the needs of an employee with an extended illness or medical condition that precludes working.

The purpose of family leave is to permit those employees whose family responsibilities necessitate their taking time off from work to have job protection for a specified period of time. Most family leave policies that have been developed voluntarily by employers grant employees unpaid leave with seniority continued and a guarantee of reinstatement in their former position or in an equivalent one. Other employee benefits, such as health insurance, may or may not be paid by the employer during the leave period. Length of time usually varies from 12 weeks to 6 months, although some employers permit up to a year.

Family leave has received a great deal of attention in recent years.[1] Much of the attention was stimulated by the legislative proposals considered by Congress and by a number of state legislatures as well.[2] When the Family and Medical Leave Act was passed by Congress in June 1990, it appeared that a national policy mandating employers to offer unpaid job-protected family leave would be in effect. However, President Bush vetoed the bill and the number of votes in Congress fell short of overcoming the presidential veto.[3] In most states, as a consequence, family leave remains discretionary with the employer. With a new proposed bill introduced in 1991, supporters of federal family leave legislation have indicated that they will continue to press for passage of such a measure, and employers should recognize the possibility of future Congressional passage of a federal mandatory family leave bill.

In any event, employers increasingly must consider whether or not they should adopt family leave as an employee benefit, and, if so, how the benefit should be designed to meet employee needs and be easily integrated with other available benefits. This chapter examines the need for the benefit, the development of the benefit, and considerations in the determination of employer adoption of the benefit.

THE NEED FOR FAMILY LEAVE

Although the reasons for family leave have been widely publicized and discussed, there are a number of reasons for employers to offer family leave benefits that need clarification. The three major reasons given by supporters of family leave are: first, the dramatic changes in labor force demographics; second, the economic pressure for both single parents and

---

[1]See, e.g., William J. Wiatrowski, ''Family-Related Benefits in the Workplace,'' *Monthly Labor Review*, 113 (3) 1990, 28–33; Dana Friedman, *Encouraging Employer Support to Working Parents*, Report Prepared for the Carnegie Corporation (NewYork: Center for Public Advisory Research, Inc., 1983); Conference Board of New York, *Corporations and Families: Changing Practices and Perspectives*, Report No. 868 (New York: Conference Board, 1985); Bradley K. Googins, *Work/Family Conflicts: Private Lives—Public Responses* (Westport, Conn.: Auburn House, 1991).

[2]Steven Holmes, ''House Passes Measure on Family Leave,'' *The New York Times*, May 11, 1990; Ellen Goodman, ''Success of Family Depends on Washington,'' *Hartford Courant*, July 31, 1990; Tamar Lewin, ''Battle for Family Leave Will Be Fought in States,'' *The New York Times*, July 27, 1990.

[3]Steven Holmes, ''Bush Vetoes a Bill to Give Workers Family Leave,'' *The New York Times*, June 30, 1990; ''Family Leave Veto Upheld,'' *Congressional Quarterly Weekly Review*, July 28, 1990.

two-earner families to retain employment in light of the decline in real income and job opportunities; and third, the changes in attitudes about family roles to permit both parents to share family caregiving responsibilities. It is really the combination of these changes that have led employees to request family leave and employers to begin to develop family leave as an employee benefit.[4]

Although the rapid increases in labor-force participation of women appear to be leveling off, there are substantial numbers of women with children in the labor force. In 1988, 71 percent of women between the ages of 16 and 44 were in the labor force, and 75 percent of the employed women held full-time jobs.[5] These employed women are more likely to remain in the labor force even after they give birth than were women in previous decades. Women have been confirming their commitment to lifelong careers by investing more time in their education, by delaying marriage and childbirth until further established in their careers, and by returning to work after having children.[6] This pattern is apparent in the other industrialized countries as well, and there is no indication that it will change in the future.[7] At the same time, the national birth rate is increasing in the United States.[8] In light of the decline in real earnings for workers, the indications are that women with children will continue to remain in the labor force but that more of them will need to interrupt their employment for childbirth and child care.

Related to the changes in women's employment patterns have been the much-noted changes in the American family. The majority of married couples are now two-earner couples; among married couples where the wife is between ages 18 and 44, in only 27 percent is the wife at home.[9]

---

[4]Carol Lawson, "Hope for the Working Parent: Company Care Plans Slowly Spread," *The New York Times*, March 15, 1990; Bureau of National Affairs, *Work and Family: A Changing Dynamic*, A Bureau of National Affairs Special Report (Washington, D.C.: U.S.G.P.O., 1986).

[5]U.S. Dept. of Labor, Bureau of Labor Statistics, *Employment In Perspective: Women In the Labor Force*, Report No. 747 (3rd. Qtr., 1987); Bureau of Labor Statistics, *Employment and Earnings* (January 1989).

[6]Susan E. Shank, "Women and the Labor Market: The Link Grows Stronger," *Monthly Labor Review*, March 1988, pp. 3–8.

[7]Constance Sorrentino, "The Changing Family In International Perspective," *Monthly Labor Review*, March 1990, pp. 41–56.

[8]"New Boom; No Panic," Editorial, *The New York Times*, December 9, 1990, E:16.

[9]"Changes in American Family Life," *Current Population Reports, Special Studies, Series P-23, No. 163*, August 1989 (Washington, D.C.: G.P.O.).

For many families, particularly young families, even with both parents working it is increasingly difficult to maintain an adequate standard of living.[10] Plant closures and job disruptions in many industries have made more couples aware of the need for both to keep working when employment is available. For single-parent families, work in most cases is an economic necessity. The United States has the highest rate of divorce and the highest incidence of single-parent households of any industrialized nation; these single-family households represent 27 percent of all family groups with children younger than age 18.[11]

The fact that the United States is the only industrialized country without a national maternity leave policy has received considerable attention.[12] Maternity leave is only one piece, albeit an important one, in the changing relationship between work and family life. Part of the support for family leave, as opposed to extended maternity leave, came from a recognition among dual-earner couples that both parents need to share the responsibilities of child care. If each parent took some time off, both could avoid prolonged disruption of work and could share in the child care duties and pleasures. In caring for a child with a serious illness, the same reasons held.

Family caregiving problems that create a need for employment interruptions can arise when employees have need to care for an elderly parent who is ill, or when a spouse becomes seriously ill. Surveys have indicated that a substantial number of employees have responsibility for the care of an elderly relative or spouse.[13] Without mandatory retirement ages, some workers remain active in the labor force until well into their seventies, increasing the likelihood that a spouse may become ill. Life expectancy is increasing, and as more persons live to older ages employees may have to take responsibility for elderly relatives and spouses as well as for children.

---

[10]Children's Defense Fund, *The Economic Plight of America's Families* (Washington, D.C., 1989); *Chicago Tribune,* "Young Parents Found Sinking Into Poverty," *Hartford Courant,* August 31, 1989, A:14.

[11]Sorrentino, "The Changing Family," pp. 41.

[12]See, e.g., Special Report, "Why We Should Invest in Human Capital," *Business Week,* December 17, 1990, pp. 88–90; Sheila Kamerman and Alfred J. Kahn, *Child Care, Family Benefits and Working Parents: A Study in Comparative Policy* (New York: Columbia University Press, 1981).

[13]Dana E. Friedman and Wendy B. Grey, "A Life Cycle Approach to Family Benefits and Policies," in *Perspectives,* No. 19 (The Conference Board, Inc.), 1989, p. 15.

Paradoxically, one of the major demographic trends of the past decade has been the decreased work-force participation of men, primarily due to early retirement.[14] Only slightly more than half of all men between ages 60 and 64 are currently in the labor force. A number took advantage of early retirement options; others elected to take Social Security at age 62.[15] After retirement, some may elect to work part-time. If, however, the men have spouses still actively employed, the latter may be faced with the need to interrupt employment if the husband becomes ill and needs care.

Employers have begun to adjust their employee benefits packages to better fit current needs of employees and adjust compensation policies to offer more support for employee family responsibilities. Dependent child care and eldercare are becoming more common, but they remain available only to a relatively small number of employees. Family leave, or more restricted types of leave for family-related caregiving, while becoming more common, is not available to the majority of workers. The Department of Labor found in its 1988 survey of employee benefits that unpaid maternity leave was available to 33 percent of employees in medium and large firms, with unpaid paternity leave benefits available to 16 percent of those surveyed.[16] Paid leaves for caring for newborn infants was rare in the survey. Nevertheless, by choice, through collective bargaining agreements, or because of mandated provisions in state legislation, family leave is becoming an important new benefit for employees, and it has significant implications for employers in designing compensation policies and employee benefits.

THE DEVELOPMENT OF FAMILY LEAVE AS A BENEFIT

The issue of family leave as an employee benefit began to receive public attention in 1984 when the Congressional Select Committee on Children, Youth, and Families held hearings on private and public-sector approaches

---

[14]George L. Stelluto and Deborah P. Klein, "Compensation Trends Into the 21st Century," *Monthly Labor Review*, February 1990, pp. 38–45, at 42.

[15]See Philip L. Rones, "The Retirement Decision: A Question of Opportunity?" *Monthly Labor Review*, November 1980, 14–17; Howard L. Fullerton, Jr., "New Labor Force Projections, Spanning 1988 to 2000," *Monthly Labor Review*, November 1989, pp. 3–12.

[16]*Employee Benefits in Medium and Large Firms, 1988*, Bulletin 2336 (Bureau of Labor Statistics, August 1989).

to child care and related problems. A number of witnesses testified about the problems that employed women experience in attempting to work and fulfill their responsibilities as parents, and many argued for the need for both parents to have more choice in parental care obligations. Testimony on the results of a survey, undertaken by Catalyst, on parental leave policies among large corporate employers indicated that 95 percent of the responding companies offered short-term disability benefits for mothers after childbirth, generally with reduced pay. Only a third of the respondents offered unpaid parental leave to fathers. In the hearings it became apparent that many women had experienced the loss of employee benefits and job seniority when taking leave for childbirth or other family caregiving responsibilities.[17]

In 1985, Representative Patricia Schroeder introduced the Parental and Disability Leave Act of 1985, the first attempt at Congressional legislation mandating parental leave. The bill provided for four months of unpaid, job-protected parental leave for either parent after the birth or adoption of a child or if the employee herself or himself needed leave as a result of a medical disability. The Schroeder bill did not win the approval of the House Education and Labor Committee, but another version, reflecting the broader nature of family leave, The Family and Medical Leave Act of 1986, gained committee approval.

Hearings on the bill received considerable attention and generated heated debate; opponents opposed federal ''mandating'' and intervention in employer-employee relations, while proponents emphasized the need for American families to meet the major changes in the labor force. These arguments have continued throughout each subsequent session of Congress on the same basic legislative proposal for family and medical leave. The Family and Medical Leave Act, vetoed by President Bush on June 29, 1990, would have required businesses with 50 or more employees to grant workers up to 12 weeks of unpaid, job-protected family or medical leave. A new version was introduced in October 1990, as a means of showing refusal to give up the fight for federal legislation; but no action was taken, since Congress was about to recess prior to the elections.

---

[17]See Congressional Quarterly, *1984 Almanac* (Washington, D.C., 1985); Select Committee on Children, Youth, and Families, *Families and Child Care: Improving the Options. A Report.*, House, 98th Congress, 2nd Session (1984).

STATE STATUTES MANDATING FAMILY LEAVE FOR EMPLOYEES

In the absence of a federal statute, some state legislatures passed laws requiring employers to grant employees job-protected family leave.[18] The state statutes mandating family leave and family and medical leave for employees vary considerably in definition of leave, employer and employee coverage, and the duration, timing, and requirements for the leave. The discussion of family leave often is confused by a blurring of definitions of the nature and purpose of the leave. However, "family leave" is most commonly used as the general term referring to employee leave for caregiving purposes. Some states have additional statutes requiring pregnancy or maternity leave. When the term *parental leave* is used, it generally refers to caregiving leave restricted to parents' care of children. The variation in definitions and specification of the key components of state family leave or family and medical leave statutes make it necessary for employers to understand fully the requirements imposed in the state or states in which the employer operates.

The following are the key components in the state statutes:

1. *Employer Coverage*. The definition of which employers fall under the requirements of the state statute distinguishes between public and private employers and usually focuses on the number of employees. For example, the recently enacted New Jersey statute defines employer as "a person or corporation, partnership, individual proprietorship, joint venture, firm or company or other similar legal entity which engages the services of an employee,"[19] and "the State, any political subdivision thereof, and all public offices, agencies, boards or bodies."[20] A number of the recently enacted statutes—including New Jersey's—phase in the coverage over a three-year period, with larger employers covered in the first year, then smaller employers in the second, and the smallest included after the third year.[21]

---

[18]See Steven K. Wisensale and Michael D. Allison, "Family Leave Legislation: State and Federal Initiatives," *Family Relations*, April 1989, pp. 182–189; S. Wisensale, "Family Policy in the State Legislature: The Connecticut Agenda," *Policy Studies Review* 8 (3), pp. 146–54.

[19]New Jersey Statutes, Chapter 34, Sec. 11B-3 (d).

[20]Ibid., 34:11B-3 (3).

[21]The New Jersey statute covers employers with 100 or more employees the first year, 75 the second year, and 50 the third year. The Connecticut statute covers employers with 250 the first year, 100 the second year, and 75 the third year.

2. *Employee Coverage*. The term *employee* usually is defined by exclusion of certain persons—"independent contractors" or "employer's parent, spouse, or child"—and by the length of time employed and the number of hours of service per week. Washington, for example, excludes independent contractors and requires employment "by an employer on a continuous basis for the previous 52 weeks for at least 35 hours per week."[22] Wisconsin, on the other hand, simply excludes an employer's immediate family members; while New Jersey stipulates 12 months "for not less than 1,000 base hours during the immediately preceding 12-month period."[23] The state statutes vary in their exclusions and inclusions.

3. *Duration and Timing of Leave*. The length of the job-protected leave period varies considerably from one state to another. The leave period generally ranges between 6 to 12 weeks within a stated period—usually 12 or 24 months. Some statutes specify that the leave may be intermittent within the specified time period. The Wisconsin statute permits six weeks of family leave for care of newborn or newly adopted children, but only two weeks for care of a seriously ill family member. Leave to care for a seriously ill family member may specify the relationship and the nature of the illness or health condition covered by the act. The state statute also may specify that the employee may substitute paid or unpaid leave of other types granted by the employer for the family leave. Such specifications are an attempt to reconcile differing employer leave policies. Since some employers grant paid disability leave for the initial weeks after childbirth, the question that arises is if the family leave is in addition to the disability leave or if the disability leave is subtracted from the total time period. When this is unclear in the statute, the state labor department may have issued regulations to clarify this for employers.

Some states limit the right to family leave to a certain time period following the birth or adoption of a child.[24] Some states limit the right of both parents to take family leave at the same time.[25]

---

[22]Washington Statutes 49.78.020 (3).

[23]Washington 49.78.020 (3); Wisconsin 103.10 2.(b); New Jersey 34:11B-3 (e).

[24]Wisconsin Stat. Ann. 103.10 (3) (b) (1) requires leave to care for a newborn or newly adopted child to begin within 16 weeks of the child's arrival (West Supp. 1989).

[25]For example, Oregon not only restricts the availability of leave for the 12-week period after birth but also grants availability to only one parent if the other parent is on parental leave. Oregon Rev. Stat. Ann. Sec. 659.360 (1) and (2) (1989).

4. *Medical Leave.* When the state statute covers medical leave for the employee who needs leave for her or his own illness, not only may the duration of the medical leave differ from that of family leave but also the employee may have to meet certain requirements for medical certification. The medical condition must render the employee incapable of performing the required duties of her or his job.

5. *Enforcement and Penalties.* The state statutes vary as to enforcing agencies, the penalties that may be imposed on employers found in violation of the statute, and the administrative process for securing enforcement against an employer. Employees usually are protected from employer actions or discrimination that result from availing themselves of the statutory right to family leave. The usual procedure is for the employee to file a complaint with the state labor department, which then investigates and, if necessary, conducts a hearing. Penalties usually are fines, but the agency may be granted the power to order reinstatement of an employee whom the employer attempted to terminate.

The state statutes can thus be seen to impose by law an employer policy for family leave and then to develop benefit design requirements. In those states with family leave statutes, the employer may add additional benefits such as extending the duration of the leave. Under most state statutes, the employer retains a great deal of discretion over the implementation of the family leave benefit. For example, the employer may choose to continue to pay for health benefits during the period of family leave. Because most state family leave statutes are recent, the statutes and state regulations may seem ambiguous as employers attempt to implement them. One area of potential ambiguity for those employers who offer disability benefits is the determination of when the period of disability leave after childbirth ends and family leave begins. Unless state statutes or regulations contain specific definitions and requirements, employers' policy directives for family leave should clearly define the terms and conditions of the family leave.

Legal Issues Arising From State Statutes

Employers usually are sensitive to the fact that the state laws and the employee rights created by them may result in litigation until the terms, definitions, and conditions imposed by the statutes and any accompanying administrative regulations become clear and understandable. Other possible legal issues that may arise are the question of Employee

Retirement Income Security Act (ERISA) preemption of state law, the question of reconciliation of state statutory requirements with the Consolidated Omnibus Budget Reconciliation Act (COBRA), and other benefit-continuation questions that arise when the employee is on family or medical leave.[26]

Employers should be aware that several states have recently enacted laws that grant employees the right to take leaves of absence for pregnancy and childbirth-related conditions. In 1987 the United States Supreme Court held, in *California Federal Savings and Loan Association* v. *Guerra,* that state laws mandating leave for pregnancy and childbirth-related disabilities do not violate Title VII of the Civil Rights Act of 1964, on the reasoning that the Pregnancy Disability Amendments to Title VII created a floor rather than a ceiling for the treatment of pregnant employees.[27]

Employers covered by recently enacted family leave statutory provisions in one or more states may find that as a number of employers experience difficulty in interpreting the statutes, state regulations or technical corrections amending the legislation may provide clarification during the next few years. Because state statutes make provision for an administrative hearing process for aggrieved parties, the adjudication of contested matters may lead to additional clarification of statutory requirements that facilitate employers' implementation.

DESIGN OF FAMILY LEAVE BENEFITS

In addition to compliance with any state statutory requirements, employers have a number of issues to consider in the design of family leave benefits. The various components of family leave legislation provide a guide to the areas where key design decisions have to be made. Issues of duration of leave, timing of leave, eligibility for leave, and whether or not the employer will continue to pay for benefits for the leave period require

---

[26]See Kenneth J. McCulloch, "State Family Leave Laws and the Legal Questions They Raise," *Employment Relations Today,* Summer 1990, pp. 103–109.

[27]479 U.S. 272 (1987). See Robert J. Nobile, "Leaving No Doubt About Employee Leaves," 67 *Personnel* (May 1990), pp. 54–60; Bureau of National Affairs, *Pregnancy and Employment, The Complete Handbook on Discrimination, Maternity Leave, and Health and Safety* (1987); Cynthia L. Remmers, "Pregnancy Discrimination and Parental Leave," 11 *Industrial Relations Law Journal,* 1989, pp. 377–413.

careful consideration and should be part of the total benefit planning process. Ideally, the planning process should begin with goal-setting based on analysis and should continue through the implementation period.

The Employer's Goals in Implementing Family Leave

First, the employer should be clear as to the goals in establishing family leave benefits. The goals for family leave should be congruent with overall business goals for profitability, productivity improvements, and enhancement of competitive position, as well as for fostering social responsibility. The goals may be part of a general strategy for improving human resource management, such as meeting employee needs more effectively; or the employer may have identified a specific problem, such as reducing the costs of recruiting and training new employees that result from the turnover associated with employees leaving their jobs for the caregiving purposes that would be covered by family leave. If business competitors have added family leave as a part of a well-publicized family-oriented benefits program, employers may feel that they need to make similar changes in benefits to remain competitive in the retention and recruitment of workers.[28]

Employers' goals should be based on careful analysis of existing leave and employee benefit use, and they should weigh the potential costs and benefits of alternative benefit policies. Alternative ways to create more family-oriented human-resource policies could include offering flextime, voluntary part-time, and working-at-home, along with the addition of dependent care, information and referral services, and employee counseling on family conflicts as additional benefits. The size of the employer, the nature of the business, the composition of the work force, and the distribution of employees among locations and job categories are major considerations in planning for an appropriate family leave benefit.

Initial Analysis of Existing Employee Benefits and Personnel Data

Employers need to examine their personnel records and analyze the data on absenteeism, turnover, requests for leave, use of sick leave and

---

[28]See Ray Collins and Renee Y. Magid, "Work and Family: How Managers Can Make a Difference," *Personnel,* July 1990, pp. 14–19; Kathleen Doherty, "Parental Leave: Strategies for the 1990s," 8 *Business and Health,* January 1990, pp. 21–23; Stanley Nollen, "The Work-Family Dilemma: How HR Managers Can Help," *Personnel,* May 1989, pp. 25–30.

personal days, and medical disability records in light of the demographics of the employer's work force. Careful analysis of this data may lead to identification of problem areas or clarify the employer's goals. It may demonstrate the need for a more comprehensive, written policy on all leaves of absence if analysis reveals an idiosyncratic use of leave or disparities in granting leave by supervisors. Employers need to devote time to this initial analysis in order to see the potential areas where changes in policy and in employee benefits may eliminate problems, lower benefit costs, and improve employee productivity and morale.

Analysis of personnel losses by usual risk-management methods should be an important part of the planning effort. Losses resulting from a high incidence of absenteeism during pregnancy, after childbirth, and among the parents of preschool children are areas deserving close scrutiny, as is absenteeism resulting from spousal or elderly parental care. Planning for reducing losses might include adding wellness programs for pregnant and post-partum mothers, adding information and referral services for related community services, adjustment of work duties and schedules, and providing better coverage for employees who choose to take family leave.

An employer, for example, with a work force with a high proportion of women of childbearing age may need to see if turnover or use of sick leave appears to be higher among women returning from maternity disability leave. If so, the employer may wish to consider implementing a family leave period of several weeks or months with the purpose of assisting employees to get through the early months after childbirth by permitting them to take unpaid but job-protected leave. With an extended period of leave, employers may decide to require employees to assume the entire cost of health benefits for the duration of the leave period so as to control employers' costs more effectively. Since longer leave periods may lead to the need for temporary or, in certain positions, permanent replacements, the full implications of the costs and benefits need to be considered. An employer with a high proportion of older workers may choose to concentrate on potential use of family leave for eldercare or family illness care, or on potential use of unpaid medical leave.

In any event, the employer should make sure that all applicable state and federal legal requirements are met. At present, no federal statute requires granting of family or medical leave. However, the Pregnancy Discrimination Act of 1978, which amended Title VII of the Civil Rights Act of 1964, requires employers to treat women affected by pregnancy, childbirth, or related medical conditions in a similar manner as the employer treats employees who are disabled for other medical reasons. The Equal Employment Opportunity Commission's guidelines on sex discrimination, in requiring employers to treat pregnancy and childbirth-related disabilities in the same manner as other disabilities, include written or unwritten employer policies regarding duration and availability of leaves of absence, accrual of seniority and other benefits and privileges during the leave period, and reinstatement in the same or similar position after a disability leave. Currently, federal law, although it generally does not require employers to grant job-protected medical disability leave for any reason, does require federal government contractors without written leave policies to grant employees "reasonable leave" for childbearing and to guarantee them reinstatement in their former jobs or comparable positions after such leave.

Assessment of Employee Needs

When the employer is clear about the purpose for change and has identified goals, a needs assessment of employees may add more information. In many cases, employers may find that consideration of family leave provides an appropriate opportunity to reevaluate their benefits package to integrate family leave with other existing benefits or other new benefits under consideration.

A needs assessment of employees can be based on a survey of employees, on the usage data, on interviews with focal groups of employees, as part of a special information seminar on family benefits, or, in some cases, on information collected through an existing employee assistance program. Employers who have conducted surveys often have been surprised to see the importance that employees place on the opportunity to take time off, even when unpaid, in order to fulfill family caregiving responsibilities. The desire of employees for unpaid leave may vary substantially with the nature of the work force and the average levels of pay. Lower-paid employees may acknowledge that unpaid leave realistically will not benefit them and thus may indicate a preference for paid time off. Employees generally prefer to be honest about their reasons for staying out of work; changes that permit them to assign the correct reason for an absence contribute to employee honesty and self-respect.

Information secured by a needs assessment then must be balanced with the information resulting from the initial analysis and the projected costs and benefits. In areas where family leave is mandatory, employers have found it to be fairly low in costs and relatively undisruptive.

Projected costs need to be compared with the cost of current benefits under existing plans. The needs assessment can lead to changes in plans for family leave, if, for example, lower paid employees wish a shorter period of unpaid leave combined with subsidized dependent care.

Design of Family Leave

Definition and Scope of Family Leave

As was the case in state statutes, the initial design requirement is the precise definition of family leave and the scope of its coverage. As family leave generally refers to unpaid but job-protected leave, the term must be defined clearly by the employer who is not meeting a statutory definition. While leave after the birth of a child is clearly necessary, an employer may wish to add age limits for an adopted child that requires leave: e.g., under the age of three years. When family leave includes the care of a seriously ill child, parent, spouse, or other family member, these terms need to be defined as clearly as possible. Serious-illness provisions may be limited to those that are life-threatening or be broadened to include those incapacitating the family member. The definition of family member may be limited by relationship dependency or by the status of the primary caregiver.

Because of the confusion between disability leave for recuperation from childbirth, which must grant the employee the same benefits as those for all other types of disabilities covered by the employer, and for parental leave, the two types of leave may need to be distinguished. Employers with short-term disability benefits should specify that the coverage includes all the same benefits as those for other disabilities, usually salary continuation for a specified period at a specified percentage and the continuation of payment of all group insurance premiums. Some employers may decide to extend a period of comparable paid salary and benefits to adoptive parents or may designate the primary caregiver of an adoptive child as eligible for paid salary and benefits for a comparable period of time as that for childbirth.

If medical leave for the employee is included, as is the case in some state statutes, the conditions covered should be delineated as unambiguously as possible.

Length of Family Leave

The total length of the family leave period must be specified. The inclusion of paid disability leave, paid sick leave, or vacation time, if

permitted to be applied, also must be specified. As some state statutes already specify, it should be stated whether the leave must be continuous or whether it can be taken in interrupted periods within certain time constraints; for example, 16 weeks in a given two-year period.

If different time constraints are set for different leave purposes, these should be identified clearly. For example, a total of one year might be set for care of a newborn or newly adopted child under five years of age, but the limit of time for care of a seriously ill child or relative might be set at a shorter period.

Eligibility for Family Leave

Eligibility requirements usually include permanent employees, a specific period of employment, such as one year or 1,000 hours, and a position that is either full-time or involves working more than a specified number of hours of work per time period. Excluded employees can be those on probationary status or under conditions of progressive discipline.

Conditions of Family Leave

The employer should specify that salary will not be paid or will not accrue and should identify any employer-paid benefits that will continue. If group insurance premiums are not paid by the employer, this should be specified; the employer also should provide information on benefits available at the employee's own expense. The employer may wish to state that while on unpaid family leave the employee may not take any paid employment of any kind from other employers or engage in paid consulting.

Notification and Planning for Family Leave

The employer needs to specify the notification and planning process and identify the responsibilities of the employee and the employee's supervisor, as well as those of the human-resource management department if it is involved. For family leave caused by the birth of a child, a longer advance notification and planning period is possible than may be the case for serious illness. The employee bears the responsibility for notification and the supervisor for the planning of coverage of the employee's job responsibilities while on family leave. The employer should designate who is to inform the employee of all the effects of family leave in relation to diminished compensation, such as lack of eligibility for short-term disability coverage while on family leave and no accrual of vacation time. Written policies and brochures are virtually essential to ensure mutual

understanding of all conditions of family leave. The employee needs to understand that in cases of business necessity jobs can be eliminated and, if such a position is eliminated, how notification of that decision will be made. The employee must be aware of his or her responsibility for returning to work on or before the date the leave is over and for participating in interim planning.

Employer planning for work coverage of the employee on family leave can make use of cross-training opportunities as well as reassignment of work. Some large employers create in-house agencies to make temporary job assignments as a part of ongoing employee development and training. Some positions will need to be filled with temporary employees or with retirees who serve as temporary replacements. In some cases a job will require permanent replacement, and the employee needs to understand that he or she will return to another comparable position. Some employers, such as law firms, may wish to specify in their descriptions of family leave the relation of the length of time to employees' promotional potential or advancement to partnership.

Development of a Comprehensive Family Benefits Policy

A comprehensive family benefits policy may best meet employer goals and employee needs and permit the addition of family leave to be integrated well with other benefits. The availability or the lack of a paid disability benefit for childbirth and recovery is a key element in the design of a family leave benefit. If a paid medical disability plan is in place, the employer may wish to include the disability period as a part of the total time limits on the period of family leave. For example, a six-week period of medical disability leave could be followed by a period of unpaid family leave, ranging from six or eight weeks to several months, with a limit set at any time from a period of twelve weeks to one year. Some employers have chosen to follow the six weeks of paid medical disability leave with an additional six weeks at half pay. The employee could still choose to take an additional period up to the aggregate limit of unpaid family leave.

The employer's overall paid leave policy for personal days, sick leave, and vacation days is an additional key element. Recently som employers have decided that these three types of leave should be combin as personal leave to give employees more flexibility and control over time. In any event, if the employer permits accumulated paid leav to be applied to family leave, the decision must be made that th

be part of the aggregate total time or be used in addition to the limit for unpaid family leave.

The employer may recognize that many employees cannot afford extended periods of unpaid family leave and consequently decide to include dependent care information and referral services, and employee counseling, to develop employee-support groups for new parents and those with eldercare responsibilities and to offer some form of dependent care benefits. A voluntary time-reduction policy that permits employees to return from family leave on a reduced time basis or to take family leave at periodic intervals is another way to assist employees in meeting their family caregiving responsibilities.

In any event, increasing numbers of employers are finding that a family leave benefit designed to meet their goals is an attractive new benefit to add either by itself or combined with other specifically family-oriented benefits. When well-designed, it should incur only modest additional expenses while providing employees additional job security and conveying to them that assisting employees to meet family responsibilities is a priority.

CHAPTER 24

EMPLOYEE ASSISTANCE PROGRAMS

Charles A. Weaver

THE CONCEPT

The problem of employees with alcohol and drug abuse or other personal problems has reached alarming proportions in our society. The associated economic losses to industry are estimated in the billions of dollars annually, and the social costs are beyond estimation. A few companies developed occupational programs in the early 1940s that concentrated on alcoholism alone and that were designed to identify the alcoholic in the workplace. Incorporated were traditional attitudes toward alcoholism as a self-inflicted disease denoting moral weakness, and a person was not considered an alcoholic until the final stages of the illness were reached. During the 1960s, it was discovered that employees who were not performing their work tasks satisfactorily were much easier to identify than were employees with alcohol problems. An approach evolved reflecting this observation—the employee assistance program (EAP). The concept of EAPs was simple. It was that a predictable number of employees will have declining job performance because of personal problems.

One corporate executive suggests as much as $100 billion per year is lost to American industry from combined alcohol- and drug-related problems—more than the combined annual profits of all the Fortune 500 companies.[1] While this figure illustrates the magnitude of the drug and alcohol abuse problem, it represents only a small percentage of the types of problems now addressed by EAPs, and it has been said that only 15 to 20 percent of troubled employees are in the category of alcohol-related problems while 50 to 60 percent have mental health–related problems having to do with stress, anxiety, depression, or family and relationship issues. The rest have to do with financial, legal, or medical difficulties.[2]

These employees are not "troublemakers." They are "troubled employees," and they often are among the best and hardest working employees an employer has when they work free from the burdens of their personal problems. Troubled employees appear at any level, from the executive suite to the assembly line. EAPs are designed to deal with these situations in the interests of both the individual employee and the organization.

Responsibility for identifying troubled employees in the workplace is a function of supervisors at all levels. It is not the responsibility of supervisors to *diagnose* or to *counsel* employees, only to deal with poor performance. Before supervisors can confront an employee with a job performance problem, several steps must be taken. These early first steps do not mention the EAP as a possible solution. During this phase supervisors are just getting a handle on the changes needed to bring job performance back into line. Supervisors, as well as the EAP coordinator, should take every opportunity to make EAP information available to employees on a continuing basis, but it is not part of solving job performance problems at this point. The second step is determining how the problem will be resolved. After supervisors have determined what changes are expected, they decide when this is to occur. Do they expect an employee to change immediately? If absenteeism is a problem, how many days may an employee be absent in what time frame? After this is done and the supervisor has decided that the employee can do the job as expected, he or she develops a plan of action to achieve the job performance change. During this process, supervisors make the employee aware of the problem, what is expected, and when. It may be best to

---

[1]Michael J. Major, "Employee Assistance Programs: An Idea Whose Time Has Come," *Modern Office Technology,* March 1990, 76, citing Allen Smith, executive vice president, General Motors Corporation.

[2]Ibid., citing Dr. Doug Adamek, president, Midwest Employee Assistance Programs, Inc.

develop a plan of action jointly with the employee. At this point, supervisors still use normal supervisory techniques, that is, the same things they would do without an EAP, and the EAP has not yet been mentioned. This is the point at which supervisors may want to mention the existence of the EAP and provide the employee with additional information on the procedures and on what to expect if he or she decides to try the EAP, stressing confidentiality and the voluntary nature of the program.

In the third step, supervisors periodically review employee progress and determine if further action is warranted. If the job performance has been corrected within the guidelines developed, the supervisor provides the employee with positive feedback. If the job performance has not been corrected, then supervisors move to step four.

If the plan has failed and job performance is still unacceptable the supervisor must decide if there are any other possible explanations for the unacceptable job performance. If the supervisor has covered all areas, it is now time to recommend the employee call the EAP coordinator and to urge the employee to use the EAP. Again, supervisors should spell out confidentiality guidelines and the voluntary nature of the program and should be specific about the consequences of unchanged job performance, including possible termination. Supervisors then report to the EAP office that a formal recommendation has been made.

The EAP provides an additional option for solving job performance problems. It helps employees resolve any personal problems interfering with job performance and often prevents termination. The earlier that problems are identified, the sooner they can be resolved, either through normal supervisory techniques or with the assistance of an EAP. Employees also may want to use the EAP for personal problems not yet affecting their job performance. In this case, supervisors and employees will be ahead of the game.

An EAP is a general term for a subsystem of interdependent components of the overall organizational system for solving or reducing problems that affect the employee's acceptable job performance by linking the employee with resources located within the community. The systems approach embodied in the EAP model accomplishes four major tasks:

1. It Guarantees Confidentiality. Diagnosis and referral of troubled employees is accomplished by a professional bound by strict rules of confidentiality. Program referral procedures are designed to guarantee no one is aware of the employee's problem except the employee, the diagnostic and referral person, and the community resource involved in the treatment program. Supervisors are removed from the task of inquiring into the nature of employees' problems and assisting them in dealing with those problems.

2. It Guarantees Professionalism. The supervisor's role includes responsibility for monitoring the performance of individuals under his or her supervision and confronting employees with any evidence of unacceptable job performance. In this way, supervisors perform job-oriented tasks: they supervise. If assistance is needed, the supervisor is not involved in such assistance. Rather, trained professionals from the community are utilized to assure professional treatment.

3. It Promotes Efficiency. Early intervention is a key to efficient problem solving. A program that focuses on indicators of problems while the problems are still relatively minor promotes efficiency in terms of individual problem solving and employer productivity.

4. It Helps Assure Utilization by Avoiding Stigmas. Because EAPs offer assistance for *many* problems, a particular employee's specific problem is not identified by participation in the program, and many of the negative implications of participating in a particular program are avoided.

INTEGRATING COMPONENTS OF EAPS

There are as many ways to conceptualize an EAP as there are people affected by a program. *Top management* may see it as a way to save money by maintaining a more efficient work force, as a way of providing an extra benefit to help employees live happier lives with no concrete monetary benefits resulting for management, or simply as one more problem management must deal with because someone has forced them to provide this service. *Supervisors* may view it as providing them with an additional tool to manage unacceptable job performance, as a device for graciously terminating an employee, or with indifference. *Employees* may view an EAP as a method for helping them obtain assistance for their personal problems or as something management developed to further control and intimidate them. Given this diversity of perceptions, it is vital to provide integrating components around which some consensus can be formed for the organization, the employee, and the community resources.

Broadly conceived, EAPs are a component of organizational human resources management systems. Therefore, a fundamental integrative concept is human resources management. Business and industrial organizations exist to make a profit. The three major variables that can be manipulated are direct cost, indirect cost, and overhead. Thus, the management of human resources is a vital area of business and of industrial productivity, efficiency, and profit. Employee assistance programs must be a part of that broad picture and be incorporated into the overall goals of the organization. Human resources management systems include many components in addition to an EAP (e.g., recruiting, training, promotion, wages, benefits, safety, supervisory practices, and so on), but an EAP might be vital to that system in several ways involving additional integrative concepts.

First, an employee assistance program can reduce losses and inefficiency related to distressed and dysfunctional employees. People suffering from emotional distress are less able to concentrate and work efficiently than those who are relaxed and dealing with stress effectively. In the work setting, distress may be manifested by such things as high absenteeism, low productivity, unsatisfactory workmanship, and disruptive interpersonal behavior. To reduce those losses at a cost less than the losses themselves saves an organization money. Cost/benefit, then, is a key to the integrative concept. This concept involves the identification of such employee problems and providing treatment that reduces or eliminates the cause of the dysfunctional behavior.

Another way an EAP might be vital to a human resources management system is in its potential as a problem-prevention tool. Preventive occupational mental health is, therefore, another integrative concept. Employees may be unconcerned with saving their employer's money; therefore, the risk management, cost/benefit model that appeals to employers cannot be presumed to motivate employees to support and participate in an EAP program. However, it generally is accepted that human beings are motivated to reduce painful distress in their lives when they have the means available. The system provided by an EAP supports mental health education and entry into community resources, making it easier for employees to gain assistance on a *voluntary* basis. Data indicate a majority of the employees using the system have done so on a voluntary basis, rather than as a result of a supervisor's recommendation related to poor job performance. However, voluntary participation also may lead to savings for the employer and meet the needs of the employee. This savings may be more difficult to measure, especially if large numbers of employees use the system *before* work-dysfunctional behaviors appear, but it would appear to be the ideal result of an effective EAP.

Integrating EAP components involves several concepts beyond human resources management, cost/benefit analysis, and problem prevention that include the following:

1. *Systems theory,* implied in developing an EAP, assumes an organization consists of an interdependent set of activities composed of subsystems that function within the larger set of parent institution and community. The step-by-step approach to EAP development (e.g., beginning with assessing management commitment and proceeding through implementation to evaluation) represents a systems approach. Each component affects the other components and the overall program affects the organization. The organization, in turn, affects the community.

2. *Participation management* is another key concept inherent in the model EAP development. It generally is an accepted organizational development principle that people more strongly support what they help create. Thus, committee involvement in setting policy, establishing goals, planning for employee education, and evaluating program effectiveness is viewed as a vital component of a successful EAP system.

3. *Human relations training for supervisors* is another integral concept in program development models. Supervisors are key members of the problem identification process. Vital to their facilitating worker problem resolution is their ability to listen to troubled employees with a nonjudgmental attitude and to convey a sense of compassionate understanding, yet, remain sufficiently detached to firmly confront employees with job performance inadequacies.

4. *Early detection based on job performance* is another integrative concept of EAPs.

5. *Utilization of existing community resources* is an integrative concept central to EAP philosophy. The use of existing community resources is viewed as an alternative far superior to creating internally based programs that duplicate existing resources.

6. *Integration with personnel management systems* is necessary for the EAP to survive and succeed because the EAP must be linked with the way job performance is evaluated, rewards or incentives are provided, health benefits are administered, and labor relations are managed. This is not to say that personnel managers should administer all aspects of EAPs, but that EAPs must be an integral part of all system elements that serve to interact with the organization's human resources.

7. *The use of self-help groups* is a basic aspect of an EAP. Self-help organizations should not replace professional diagnosis and treatment, but they are an important ingredient in creating the impetus for an individual to decide to seek help.

THE ROLE OF THE SUPERVISOR

The four-step process culminating in a supervisor's recommendation of an EAP to a troubled employee was discussed earlier in this chapter.

The matter of supervising a troubled employee is, however, considerably more complex, and three types of barriers provide special problems. One of the most basic problems is the absence of specific production goals or well-defined tasks to be performed by employees. EAPs are founded on the notion that the supervisor should not diagnose the employee's problems but should work only with job performance. When performance standards are vague or even nonexistent, the supervisor is put in a compromised position. The program must recognize those deficiencies and design training programs to assist the supervisor. *Close coordination is essential with other organizational training efforts.*

A second problem area is that of job stress related to role conflicts, work addiction, job obsolescence, or other work-related aggravations. The supervisor must learn to identify the factors that make work unrewarding. Training in recognizing the presence of those factors may be necessary in some work settings.

A third area involves the kind of social sanctions and expectations placed upon the employee about drinking on the job. Many organizations place employees in a role that seems to require drinking on the job or at least in related social settings. The supervisor needs to recognize situations where the risks of problem drinking are encouraged by the organization. This is especially difficult for the supervisor, and training may help the supervisor identify organizational roles and expectations that may contribute to performance problems.

A fourth point is that once a performance problem has been identified, the supervisor must determine whether the problem is caused by inadequate training of the employee or the lack of potential to perform the job, and the supervisor should check three organizational factors as possible reasons for the performance deficiency: (1) Is the desired performance punishing? (2) Is nonperformance rewarding? (3) Does performing really matter? If none of these factors is present, other external variables such as family, mental health, and alcohol or drug problems are likely causes. It is possible that organizational variables and personal/emotional variables may be interrelated, but when organizational and training factors can be eliminated, an offer of assistance from the EAP is indicated.

The emotional aspects of a supervisor's behavior in managing the troubled employee are important as well. Without proper training the supervisor's behavior can portray a pattern of interaction that parallels that of the spouse of the alcoholic. The pattern typically includes a process of ignoring the problem and hoping for a "miracle;" heart-to-heart talks, or reasoning; begging or pleading; and finally bleeding (transfer, fire, retire). The supervisor in this pattern feels anger, guilt, fear, and strong ego involvement with the successes and failures of the employee, and often is unwilling to recognize deviant behavior he or she is not prepared to handle. What this suggests is that the traditional training in the steps of the supervisor's role in the EAP is not enough. In traditional training programs, supervisors are given information they may not use immediately. The supervisor needs to recognize a connection between the employee's behavior, feelings, and resultant behavior and to seek out the EAP coordinator at the earliest sign of problems with an employee to learn specific procedures for dealing with the situation.

THE EAP COORDINATOR

Most EAPs depend on a small staff or a single person to implement the program, and the success of the program often depends on the capabilities and support of the coordinator. The role of the coordinator includes serving as a point of contact for troubled employees, discussing documentation and ways of handling unacceptable job performance with supervisors, maintaining confidential employee records for evaluation and follow-up purposes, and planning and implementing training programs for supervisors, education programs for employees, and orientation programs for advisory committees.

One of the basic functions of the EAP coordinator is to supply the organization with information to make decisions. In this capacity the coordinator is acting as a catalyst for change. This means demonstrating the need for an EAP in terms of its ability to improve production, reduce absenteeism, protect company assets, and, in general, produce a financial return on money invested in the program. Management also may be sensitive to the humanitarian aspects of EAPs as a secondary concern.

The impact of relevant information may not be immediate. Careful attention to detail and to development are appropriate for effective program planning. Hurried implementation may meet immediate needs but undermine the continuing success of an EAP. Alliances, timing, and coordinated efforts are important considerations. While the EAP coordinator may induce change by providing part of the solution to job performance problems during the development of an EAP, resistance can be generated by attempting to force a solution on reluctant, uninformed management or on community treatment resources. Furthermore, the demands of the coordinator's role often necessitate a full-time person with support staff, but in many situations the coordinator's role is secondary to his or her other responsibilities, such as personnel director. While certain circumstances may dictate the EAP coordinator perform several functions within the organization, the primary emphasis of the role is of great importance. The success of the program may depend on whether the EAP coordinator is personnel director first and coordinator second or vice versa. Ideally, the EAP coordinator's role is a full-time position with support staff, but a practical solution might be that of an EAP coordinator with some other secondary responsibilities.

The establishment of the EAP coordinator as a component of program planning is only part of the development process. The EAP coordinator can assume various roles. For example, a change agent is anyone who seeks to alter or modify the way organizations and people function. Ronald G. Havelock (1973) described four methods of being a change agent. He indicated a change agent may act as a catalyst to initiate change, provide solutions at timely moments, serve as a process helper in problem solving, and link resources with needs. The roles of a change agent are not mutually exclusive. The EAP coordinator must choose the appropriate emphasis for different circumstances that arise in the development of the EAP. The coordinator will act as a *catalyst* in starting an employee education program while *linking* and *developing* community resources to meet the needs of the EAP. The difficulty lies in the coordinator's ability to select and execute the proper role. A coordinator acting as a *change agent* can influence a management that does not view employee problems and job performance problems in the same light. To minimize resistance to EAPs as part of the *solution* to job performance problems, guidelines can be established. The coordinator's role is a demanding one in terms of the skills required and the level of involvement. According to Havelock, *process helpers* work with the system to recognize and define needs; establish goals and objectives; search for relevant resources; select, create, and match resources with objectives and needs; implement; and evaluate the model. For the program coordinator, process-helping skills are necessary to work with the advisory committee, community resources, management structures, and union officials, if applicable. The EAP coordinator should have group facilitation skills to perform this role. A model training program for committees promotes shared leadership rather than dominance or manipulation by the coordinator.

A key in the process-helping role is effective interaction among relevant groups, individuals, and the coordinator. Effective interaction may be viewed as part of the process-helping role, while management of information is part of the role of providing solutions. Switching from the providing solutions to the process-helper role should occur after corporate commitment has been obtained. As the EAP coordinator becomes a process helper, he or she should develop support for the program, facilitate involvement, and create joint ownership and leadership in the EAP.

For example, the needs and concerns of the organization should be determined prior to offering a solution. The EAP, as part of the solution, must be appropriate for the problem. This may mean determining if absenteeism or production problems are present in the organization, and then determining whether the EAP can assist in solving those problems. The EAP coordinator can assist management in establishing criteria for measuring the effectiveness of the EAP as part of the solution to job performance problems. Management, therefore, can determine if an EAP solves part or all of its job performance problems. The EAP coordinator should build a relationship with management based on trust to discuss problems, manage the adoption process, and promote sharing of knowledge. The coordinator should help establish the EAP in such a manner that the decision makers in the organization have ownership of the solution.

An issue for EAP coordinators is how to utilize their skills and ideas. The EAP coordinator should become a *resource* person for the system, while the advisory committee should discuss, evaluate, and adopt solutions for referral procedures, policy statements, supervisory training, employee education, and the like.

Finally, the coordinator can act in the capacity of *linking resources* with the needs of the EAP by providing access to community resources for employees. Services available in the community should not be duplicated; however, resources not currently available should be developed.

THE ADVISORY COMMITTEE

The advisory committee operates to give direction and guidance to other components of the EAP. While most advisory committees do not have decision-making authority, the committee can be influential in helping management in the decision-making process.

The advisory committee can be given responsibilities that will increase its influence and provide the groundwork for management/labor ownership of the EAP. It is suggested the inclusion of the advisory committee in the planning process increases the probability of a successful EAP, and the advisory committee can assist in such tasks as writing policy and procedure statements. Other areas in which the advisory committee can provide input include the goals and objectives for the EAP, strategies for implementing the EAP, reviews of proposed supervisory training and employee education programs, development of a strategy for publicizing the program within the organization and community, and monitoring the implementation and evaluation of the program. From this list, it should be evident the advisory committee is a vital component in the program-planning process, and that a committee satisfied with only marginal responsibilities will not be in the best interests of the EAP.

The committee must be committed to and have a thorough understanding of its role and responsibilities in the system. Issues and concepts must be discussed, and shared leadership is crucial to its growth. If one element (i.e., labor, management, or program coordinator) dominates the committee, its ability is diminished. Again, the committee should be representative of the major employee groups within the organization. A training program for advisory committee members in effective group decision-making is recommended to ensure shared leadership and committee vitality.

ESTABLISHING LINKAGES WITH COMMUNITY RESOURCES

When EAPs initiate linkages with community resources, tension is likely to exist because of uncertainties over roles and expectations. Great care should be exercised in selecting the community resources to be used, and the relationships with these resources should be in accordance with a set of prescribed guidelines and formalized in a written agreement with each resource.

The EAP–Community Resource Agreement

Prior to developing an agreement with a community resource, each party should have its individual needs focused and be able to accurately communicate them to the other. The overall purpose of such an agreement is to establish a clearly focused set of expected behaviors for the EAP and the community resource when employees are referred. These expectations should be communicated to all the employees in a general manner, and explicitly when an employee seeks assistance through the EAP.

The Referral Process

Referral is a common denominator in many EAPs because few of them can handle all aspects of an employee's problem. Therefore, referral to community resources is an essential element for EAPs, not promotion of an internally based program.

Referral is the process by which the EAP links an employee with the appropriate community resource, as opposed to the recommendation made by the supervisor to visit the EAP coordinator. The linkage resulting from the referral of an employee by the EAP coordinator may include assessment, diagnosis, information, and treatment. The task of referral is reserved for persons who have some expertise in determining the cause of problems and in choosing the appropriate community resource for handling the problem. If an EAP coordinator does not have this expertise, he or she should make a recommendation that an employee visit a centralized agency handling all assessments and making the appropriate referrals. Supervisors should *not* make a *referral* to the EAP, but rather should *recommend* the employee take advantage of the EAP. EAPs are voluntary programs, and the supervisor's role should be focused on the job performance of the employee. Referrals should be made by the EAP coordinator or the person performing the assessment or diagnostic function.

When an employee with a problem contacts the EAP coordinator or the person assigned to be the entry point into the community resource system, a number of actions take place. The employee should be clearly told about the EAP's policy and procedures, especially as they relate to pending disciplinary action. It should be made clear at the outset that the EAP is a means for employees to seek and receive assistance for problems affecting job performance and that it is not a shelter from disciplinary action. Making sure that the employee is made responsible for the consequences of his or her job performance actions is an essential element throughout the referral process both for the EAP and the community resource system. Additionally, it must be clear that utilization of the EAP will in no way affect future job security or advancement. The process of diagnosis, costs, and company insurance coverage should be explained to the employee. The process of making the appointment should be outlined. Having a specific person to contact is very helpful to the employee. Consent forms for authorizing release of information to the EAP coordinator should be available. Protection of confidentiality is essential in all elements of the referral process. Referral to a community resource should be made only after the EAP coordinator or the diagnostic agent has carefully explained the treatment options available to the employee.

To restate, the following should be discussed with the employee at the time of referral:

1. The extent of the company's insurance coverage for expenses incurred for services rendered by the treatment resource.
2. The assurance that the employee's promotion opportunities will not be hindered by the use of the EAP or any community resources.

The following points should be made clear:

1. Continued employment, pay raises, promotions, or disciplinary action will be based on job performance and not clinical progress.
2. Any type of communication about employee progress in a treatment program will be governed by confidentiality statutes that allow release of certain information only with the consent of the employee.

3. Receiving treatment during working hours will be handled according to the organization's general policy on absences for health reasons or statements on EAP procedures.

Motivating an employee to accept a referral may remain an ongoing problem. An even greater problem is created when the employee denies that a problem exists, even though job performance clearly indicates something is wrong and some action required. Dealing with these conditions requires a skilled interviewer.

Services to Be Provided by Community Resources

One of the first things the EAP coordinator, with the aid of the advisory committee, must do to establish linkages with community resources is to locate them. Many large cities have community service councils or other bodies for coordinating human resources. These organizations frequently publish directories of community resources or have information available. Other excellent sources of information are crisis-counseling centers, ministerial associations, police departments, and chambers of commerce. Other EAP or occupational program coordinators may have identified and compiled lists of community resources and should be consulted for advice and sharing of relevant information. Finally, state departments of mental health may offer assistance, and they often have directories of public and private facilities.

At least four basic categories of services should be identified.

1. Crisis Intervention. Included in this category are 24-hour ''hotlines'' and telephone counseling services, drop-in centers for immediate service without an appointment, and self-help groups, such as Alcoholics Anonymous.

2. Outpatient Services. These may include assessment, diagnosis, information, education, and ongoing treatment for a variety of problems, such as child abuse, child/adolescent problems, mental health counseling, marital counseling, family counseling, alcohol/drug dependency, debt management, career counseling, legal counseling, grief counseling, and family planning/sex education.

Outpatient services may be in the day or evening and usually are focused around a specific problem.

3. Inpatient Services. These services provide intensive care for employees with severe, chronic, and life-threatening problems. A continuum of inpatient services exists, ranging from hospital care to residential treatment. A number of intermediate services, such as halfway houses and day treatment centers, also are available.

4. Self-Help Groups. These groups focus on a specific problem and are operated by persons who have faced and overcome similar situations. The groups are effective in providing aftercare support, education, and crisis assistance. Self-help groups exist in such problem areas as: alcoholism, overeating, child abuse, death or dying, divorce, single parenting, gambling and other addictions, and chronic credit-problem management. Self-help groups are effective for ongoing support. However, they are not a substitute for professional diagnosis and treatment.

Evaluating Community Resources

The emphasis on accountability has spread to all aspects of society, including community resources. The reasons for evaluating community resources are to provide information for making decisions on program operation and to provide the best possible assistance to employees.

Criteria for determining effectiveness of community resources might include the opinions of certain individuals.[3] For example,

1. Direct users of the community resource both present and past.
2. Indirect users of the community resource, such as
   a. Families of the user.
   b. Community planning groups.
   c. Interest groups (mental health associations, counselors associations, and the like).
   d. Other community resources.
3. Administrators, board members, and staff of the community agencies.
4. State planning and regulatory agencies (mental health, public health, welfare, education, licensing agencies).

As a general rule, an EAP coordinator should have access to information that does not violate client confidentiality or employee

---

[3]Val D. MacMurray, *Citizen Evaluation of Mental Health Services* (New York: Human Services Press, 1976).

privacy, such as personnel records if the community resource receives public money from the local, state, or federal government. Private community resources are not obligated to disclose information. However, private resources may provide data, since the information will help referral sources make decisions on the use of services.

To summarize, the evaluation of community resources, therefore, has to be based on clearly stated needs and objectives articulated by the EAP coordinator and the employee. Community resource performance can be measured against the established criteria. Evaluation is not isolated from the community resources, linkages, and referral process but is a key to making good decisions on the appropriate use of community resources for the benefit of the employee.

CONCLUSION

Until recently most organizations did not provide a formal mechanism to respond to employees' job performance difficulties related to substance abuse and other personal problems, but that is changing with the awareness that such problems affect the organization through higher absenteeism and turnover, lower productivity, and increased health care costs. The rise in the popularity of EAPs reflects their ability to address job performance problems. In addition to their obvious benefits to employees, EAPs benefit management by eliminating or reducing the effects of employees' personal problems on the organization.

CHAPTER 25

LEGAL SERVICE PLANS

Claude C. Lilly III

ENVIRONMENT

Legal service plans are not a new development; they have been in effect since the early 1900s. In fact, insurance contracts providing legal benefits were available by 1907. However, legal benefit plans were relegated to a secondary role until the 1970s.

As an employee benefit, prepaid legal service plans made substantial gains in the 1970s and 1980s. Legal service plans are not as numerous as most of the traditional benefits. The growth of prepaid legal service plans has leveled off, and there probably will not be significant growth in this area in the short run.

THE PUBLIC'S LEGAL NEEDS

The public has always had a need for lawyers, even if it has not always sought legal help. A study done for the Association of American Law Schools in 1938 found in a sample of 412 families that 315 legal matters arose. However, legal advice was sought for only 35.2 percent of the 315 legal matters.[1] While comparable data are not available today, it is probably safe to assume that the legal needs of Americans have increased.

[1]Charles E. Clark and Emma Corstvet, "The Lawyer and the Public: An A.A.L.S. Survey," 47 *Yale Law Journal* 1276 (1938).

The United States seems caught up in a frenzy of litigation that affects every strata of society. For example, expenditures for legal services grew more rapidly than the national income account during the 1970s and the 1980s. Even in nonlitigious areas of legal practices (e.g., wills, real estate sales, and taxation), consumers are finding the services of a lawyer are needed more frequently.

FEDERAL LAWS

Three changes in federal laws have affected the growth of legal service plans. First, in 1973, Senators Williams and Javitz introduced S.1423. The bill modified the Labor Management Relations Act of 1947. The bill stated:

> Section 302(c) of the Labor Management Relations Act, 1947 is amended . . . by adding immediately before the period . . . or (8) with respect to money or any other thing of value paid by any employer to a trust fund established by such representative for the purpose of defraying the cost of legal services for employees, their families, and dependents.[2]

S.1423 was amended prior to enactment, but the basic provision cited above was not changed. The impact of S.1423 was to introduce prepaid legal service benefits into the area of collective bargaining.

The second federal change was initiated in 1974 by the passage of the Employee Retirement Income Security Act (ERISA). Since prepaid legal plans provided on a group basis are subject to ERISA, state insurance regulation over these plans is limited. Specifically:

> Neither an employee benefit plan described in Section 4(a), which is not exempt under 4(b) (other than a plan established primarily for the purpose of providing death benefits), nor any trust established under such a plan, shall be deemed an insurance company or other insurer.[3]

This allowed prepaid legal plans offered on a group basis (and subject to ERISA) to avoid state insurance regulations unless the group plan is offered by an insurance company.

---

[2]U.S. Congress, Senate, Subcommittee on Labor, "Joint Labor-Management Trust Funds for Legal Services, 1973: Hearings on S.1423," 93rd Congress, 1st session, April 10, 11, and 16, 1973, pp. 2, 3.

[3]Public Law 93-406, Section 514(b)(2)B.

The third, and perhaps the most important federal legislation was passed in 1976. Section 120 of the Internal Revenue Code was so modified that:

> Gross income of an employee, his spouse, or his dependents, does not include—
>
> (1) Amounts contributed by an employer on behalf of an employee, his spouse, or his dependents under a qualified group legal services plan (as defined in subsection (b)), or
>
> (2) The value of legal services, under a qualified group legal services plan (as defined in subsection (b)) to, or with respect to, an employee, his spouse, or his dependents.[4]

Section 120(b) defines a qualified legal service plan as:

> a separate written plan of an employer for the exclusive benefit of his employees or their spouses or dependents to provide such employees, spouses, or dependents with specified benefits through prepayment of, or provision in advance for, legal fees in whole or in part by the employer.

The law further stipulates that contributions can be made only to insurance companies, to qualified trusts, or to legal service providers.

The federal government is not the only governmental entity to exclude prepaid legal service benefits from gross income. Hawaii excludes from gross income "the value of legal services provided by a prepaid legal service plan to a taxpayer, the taxpayer's spouse, and the taxpayer's dependents."[5]

TYPES OF PLANS

The material that follows presents a brief discussion of the types of plans that have been developed.

Legal Service Plans

Legal service plans refer to any plans designed to offer legal services. The definition of a plan as set forth in the Texas statutes is typical of

---

[4]Internal Revenue Code, Chapter 26, Section 120.

[5]Hawaii Revised Statutes Annotated, s. 235-7.

the definitions in most states. A prepaid legal service plan is defined in the Texas statutes as:

> . . . a plan by which a sponsoring organization offers legal services benefits to its members or beneficiaries, which services are financed by direct financial charge in advance of need.[6]

Plans can be divided into several categories. These include:

1. Profit versus nonprofit.
2. Prepaid versus currently funded.
3. Group versus individual.
4. Closed versus open panel.

Profit versus Nonprofit Plans

Many states allow both profit and nonprofit organizations to provide prepaid legal service benefits. However, because of the perceived public nature of the benefits, some states restrict the provision of benefits to nonprofit organizations.

In Rhode Island, prepaid legal services plans have to be offered on a nonprofit basis. A nonprofit plan is defined as:

> . . . any plan whereby reimbursement for specified legal services is provided to participating attorneys or subscribers to the plan by a nonprofit prepaid legal service corporation. . . . [T]he plan shall be open for participation to all qualified, practicing members of the Rhode Island Bar Association.[7]

It should be noted Rhode Island not only requires that the plans be provided by nonprofit corporations but also that the plans have to be open to all members of the bar association.

Prepaid versus Currently Funded Plans

Legal service plans can be provided either on a fully funded basis (i.e., prepaid) or on a current funding basis where the cost of a plan is handled out of current income. Generally, only employer- or union-sponsored plans are available on a current basis.

---

[6] Vernon's Texas Statutes and Codes Annotated, Article 320b.

[7] General Laws of Rhode Island Annotated, s. 27-20.3-1.

Legal insurance contracts, some labor union plans, and some bar association plans can be classified as prepaid legal plans. One important distinction exists under a trustee plan (e.g., a union or a bar association plan): benefits may not be guaranteed. If the legal costs exceed the funds in the trust, benefits may be terminated. An insured plan is backed by the surplus of the insurance carrier and, therefore, could offer additional security to those purchasing legal service benefits.

Group versus Individual Plans

Legal service plans may be provided on either a group or an individual basis. Most coverage has been written on a group basis. There are several reasons. First, it is easier to obtain a spread of risk within a group. Second, administrative costs are held to a minimum. Third, and perhaps most important, the major impetus for legal service plans has come from labor unions for the benefit of their members or employers for the benefit of their employees. Many group plans require a minimum number of participants in each plan or a minimum participation percentage.

Individual plans are not available in all states. In Hawaii, for example, a prepaid legal service plan can be written only on a group basis.[8]

Closed- versus Open-Panel Plans

Union legal service plans, especially in the early stages of their development, usually were closed-panel plans. Under a closed-panel arrangement, a group of lawyers and paralegal personnel is hired by the unit providing the legal services. The individuals are paid salaries and are responsible for handling any legal matters set forth in the plan.

Funds are provided by employer contributions or by the union's membership through dues. The funds are invested by the union, and the funds plus the interest earned are used to defray the cost of legal services. This approach not only can provide quality control but also cost control. Under closed-panel plans, the specter of having the legal cost exceed the available funds may be offset because the lawyers are paid salaries. Thus, costs are fixed. (Even if expenses exceed the funds available, the

---

[8]Hawaii Revised Statutes Annotated, s.235-1.

employer or union often is responsible for any deficit.) However, the demands on the closed-panel lawyer can become excessive; as a result, in some plans, members may not be provided prompt service.

Another weakness of a closed-panel plan is that it may not provide the expertise necessary to handle all of the legal problems that arise. This can be overcome by hiring outside help as needed. The external counsel is paid from the closed-panel's funds. When this approach is used, the plan is called a "modified closed-panel plan." The term *modified closed-panel plan* has been given at least two definitions. In addition to the one just presented, a modified closed-panel plan has been defined as a panel where participants can choose between panel attorneys and external attorneys. If participants use an external lawyer, they are directly reimbursed for part or all of their expenses. To illustrate, a plan may sign up half of the attorneys in a city who agree to provide services for set fees. These are called "enrolled lawyers." If a participant does not want to use these enrolled lawyers, he or she can use another attorney. The benefits, however, may be reduced if a nonenrolled attorney is selected. Even if benefits are not reduced, that is, the same hourly rate is paid for a nonenrolled attorney, the amount of coverage may not be enough to pay the legal bill of the nonenrolled attorney.

Another method is available to handle the problem of not having adequate expertise. Instead of having an in-house closed-panel plan, an external closed-panel plan can be developed. In this situation, a group of lawyers is retained by a plan. The lawyers agree to work for a flat fee per hour or per case as long as the funds are available. They bill the plan directly for their services. If the funds are not adequate to meet all legal costs, the lawyers still provide services. The lawyers, therefore, become risk bearers; they guarantee services even if they have to work without compensation. Some lawyers find risk retention unacceptable. So, some plans have formed an external closed-panel plan. Lawyers work for guaranteed rates but are not required to provide services if the funds are not sufficient to cover the service demands.

In New Jersey, closed-panel plans can be offered by unions, but insurance companies cannot sell prepaid legal expense insurance. The situation arises because the state takes the position that plans are authorized by ERISA and therefore not subject to state control.[9]

---

[9]New Jersey Statutes Annotated, 17:46 C-1, historical notes.

Legal service benefits also can be provided under an open-panel plan. Under this approach, plan participants are permitted to select any lawyer they wish. The plan pays a schedule of benefits regardless of the cost of a lawyer's services. Benefits may be paid to plan participants or directly to the lawyers. Frequently, these types of plans provide participants with a list of lawyers who provide services for a fixed rate. Some states require that all lawyers that are members of the bar be allowed to participate in a plan. This is equivalent to having an open-panel plan for the entire state.[10]

TYPES OF BENEFITS

Schedule of Legal Services

Benefit packages vary significantly. Nearly all plans provide a schedule listing the covered legal areas. For example, a list of covered services might include

- Bankruptcy.
- Divorce.
- Wills.
- Adoption.
- Traffic violations.
- Felony representation.
- Misdemeanors.
- Juvenile delinquency actions.
- Condemnation.
- Real estate.
- Debt collection.
- Property damage.
- Small claims proceedings.
- Workers' compensation.
- Representation before governmental or administrative boards.

---

[10]See quote accompanying footnote 7 supra.

Coverage for Legal Services

Establishing which legal areas are covered is the first step in evaluating benefits. The next step is to ascertain the extent of the benefits in each category. A legal service plan may only provide advice. There may or may not be a charge to the plan participant for each visit or for each occurrence. These are called "limited access plans." They often provide a referral service, which will recommend lawyers who provide services for reduced fixed fees or hourly rates. In addition to advice, some plans afford services: a will may be drawn up, adoption papers may be processed, or defense advice on civil or criminal charges may be provided. Those plans that provide advice and a group of services (e.g., will preparation, adoptions, and the like) are called "basic plans." The amount of the benefit varies.

Plans that provide a broad range of benefits, including advice, basic services, and legal defense, are called "major plans." Closed-panel plans have the ability to offer full coverage for the legal service areas for which benefits are provided, but full coverage is rarely used.

Most open-panel plans and some closed-panel plans require a plan participant to share in the payment of legal costs, or the plans limit the maximum amount of benefits available in each legal service area. Sharing can be accomplished by:

1. A flat dollar deductible per year—open. (Open or closed indicates the type of plan that normally would use this limitation.)
2. A coinsurance provision—open. (Normally, the plan pays 80 percent; this generally would not apply to closed-panel plans unless outside legal talent had to be obtained.)
3. A maximum number of hours of legal service per year or per occurrence—open or closed. (An occurrence could be a visit or a sequence of visits resulting from the same legal problem.)
4. A maximum amount paid for each hour of legal service—open.
5. A maximum number of occurrences per year—open or closed.

Plans also may have waiting periods or internal limits. For example, there may be a six-month waiting period before divorce proceedings are covered or there may be a limit on the number of days of a trial that are covered.

Some plans provide legal checkups in addition to the benefits that have been described. Theoretically, these serve the same purpose an annual physical examination does under health insurance contracts. It may be more difficult to detect potential legal problems than existing health problems.

Exclusions

Most plans exclude some types of legal services. Possible exclusions include the following:

Criminal charges.
Business ventures.
Collection suits (as a plaintiff).
Charges not made except for existence of a legal service plan.
Class actions.
Tax return preparation.
Contingency fee cases.
Divorce (limited to one spouse per family).
Unreasonable charges.
When fees are paid by another source.
Appeals.
Fines and penalties.
Controversies with the plan.

While still included in many plans, the exclusion for criminal charges is slowly being eliminated. It has been found for many groups that the criminal coverage does not encourage criminal activities, as some early plan administrators had feared it might.

STATE REGULATION

Insurance Departments

Until the 1970s, state regulation of legal service plans was minimal. Most regulation was handled through the courts and aimed at obtaining jurisdiction over legal service plans. The first efforts by states to control legal service plans took place during the early 1900s. During this period, the

Physician's Defense Company offered legal and defense coverage to physicians. For an annual premium of $15, a physician could purchase a policy that had an annual aggregate limit of $10,000 and a per case limit of $5,000. Insurance commissioners in some states sought to regulate the company, but the company resisted. Several suits ensued, and the commissioners were generally successful in gaining jurisdiction over the company.[11] As a result, the company finally quit selling its policies. Following these cases, state regulation of legal service plans was fairly dormant until the *United Transportation Union* case in 1971. Following the decision, the states became interested in legal service plans.

Since 1971, insurance departments have had to deal with several problem areas associated with legal insurance plans. These include:

1. Language to be used (especially in view of the easy-to-read policy movement).
2. Difficulty in ascertaining if rates are appropriate.[12]
3. Agent's licensing procedures.
4. Premium tax collections.
5. Determination of whether legal insurance plans are life or property and casualty contracts.[13]
6. Determination of whether individual contracts should be written.

The National Association of Insurance Commissioners (NAIC) appointed a subcommittee to examine these and other legal insurance questions. The subcommittee met in 1973 and developed a model act

---

[11]See, *Physician's Defense Co.* v. *O'Brien,* 111 N.W. 396 (1907) and *Physicians' Defense Co.* v. *Cooper,* 199 F. 576 (1912).

[12]States have approached the rating and reserving problems from different directions. In Rhode Island, a prepaid legal service corporation's rates have to include a reserve element of at least 10 percent of the most recent 12 months of claims and operating expenses at the time of the filing, General Laws of Rhode Island Annotated, s. 27-20.3-1; in Texas, legal expense insurance plans are regulated like any other insurance coverage, Vernon's Texas Statutes and Codes Annotated, Article 5-13-1; in Georgia, a company must have a minimum capital of $5,000, deposit securities or post a bond for $25,000, and maintain minimum surplus (the surplus has to be at least 25 percent of a legal service plan's anticipated income over a two-year period based on ". . . estimates of premium writings for two-year and five-year periods which shall be filed . . . as a part of the . . . rate filing. . . .), Code of Georgia, s. 33-35-6.

[13]Some states let only property and casualty insurers write prepaid legal-expense insurance; other states allow life and health insurers, as well as property and casualty insurers, to write prepaid legal-expense insurance.

designed to serve as a guideline for the states. The model was adopted by the NAIC in 1974.[14]

Bar Association Control

Bar associations have been involved in the regulation of legal service plans since the inception of the plans. Regulatory oversight efforts by state bar associations have taken two forms. First, some state statutes give bar associations direct control over legal service plans. North Carolina is an example. In that state, a plan providing prepaid legal services cannot be implemented or operated without the prior and ongoing approval of the bar association.[15]

The second major way bar associations have had regulatory control is through advertising guidelines. While lawyers are permitted to pay for advertising, the nature of their advertising is limited. They cannot pay someone to channel business to them. Lawyers can avoid this problem if they participate in a prepaid legal service plan. Bar associations usually allow plans to solicit business that is channeled to lawyers.[16]

NONINSURANCE PLANS

Union Plans

Labor unions have been in the forefront of the legal services plan movement. While the Brotherhood of Railroad Trainmen is important

---

[14]In 1977, Spencer Kimball and Werner Pfennigstorf developed a model legal insurance act. The model act was:

> endorsed by the NAIC Prepaid Legal Expense (D5) Subcommittee prior to the subcommittee's dissolution as "accomplishing its objective of placing before the members of the NAIC alternative methods and approaches to the regulation of prepaid legal services. . . . (NAIC, *Model Laws, Regulations and Guidelines* [Kansas City, MO.: NAIC, updated service], pp. 685–91.)

Kimball and Pfennigstorf have offered additional ideas on model legal insurance laws. See Werner Pfennigstorf and Spencer L. Kimball, "Access Plans for Legal Insurance: How Far Should They Be Regulated?" *Journal of Insurance Regulation* 4, no. 4 (June 1986), p. 57.

[15]North Carolina General Statutes, s. 84-23.1.

[16]For example, see West Virginia Rules of Professional Conduct, Rule 7.2.

because of its initial efforts, the first modern-day plan to gain national attention was the Shreveport (Louisiana) Bar Association plan.

In 1969, Southwestern Administrators, Inc. (SA), agreed to operate a legal service plan for the Shreveport Legal Services Corporation (SLSC). SLSC was formed by the Shreveport Bar Association. The plan developed by SA afforded benefits for

1. Advice and consultation.
2. Conferences and negotiations.
3. Investigation and research.
4. Document preparation.
5. Litigation costs.
6. Major legal expense benefits.
7. Domestic relations benefits.

SLSC contracted with the Western Louisiana Council of Laborers, AFL-CIO, and one of its members, Local No. 229 of Shreveport, to enter into an open-panel prepaid group legal service plan. The plan started operation in 1971.

Many unions established plans following the success of the Shreveport program. The Amalgamated Clothing Workers of America instituted a plan in 1972 that provided benefits for consumer transactions, domestic relations, adoptions, landlord/tenant problems, real estate transactions, and wills.[17] In 1973, District Council 37 of the American Federation of State, County, and Municipal Employees entered into a program that was proposed jointly by the Columbia University School of Law, the Columbia University School of Social Work, and itself. Union legal service plans have grown significantly. Currently, the American Federation of State, County and Municipal Employees, the Minnesota Education Association, the Massachusetts Laborers' union, other major unions, and some local unions have prepaid legal service plans. The type of benefits do not vary as much between the plans as do the amounts of benefits.

---

[17]Amalgamated Clothing Workers of America, Chicago Joint Board, Prepaid Group Legal Service Plan, initiated in Chicago on April 1, 1972.

Bar Association Plans

Many bar associations have started or attempted to start legal service plans. For example, the Los Angeles County Bar Association attempted to start a plan in 1970 and 1971 with the California Teachers Association, but it was not successful.[18] The Monroe County Bar Association proposed a plan for Rochester, New York.[19] The New Mexico State Bar formed a prepaid group legal services corporation in 1973 to provide legal services.[20] As stated earlier, the Shreveport Bar Association formed the Shreveport Legal Services Corporation.

The Arizona Bar Association formed Arizona Legal Services (ALS), which offered what ALS termed a tri-open plan. Under this approach, members of the Arizona Bar Association provided services for ALS for the amounts set forth in the fee schedule. A plan participant selected a lawyer. If the lawyer operated as a member of ALS, he or she provided legal services for the fee agreed to in the plan schedule. If a plan participant elected to use the service of a lawyer who was not enrolled, the benefit payments were less than those for a participating lawyer.[21]

In addition to their oversight or regulatory role, bar associations are involved in the operation of some prepaid legal service plans. They may operate their own plans, but they often work with other organizations, e.g., labor unions, to develop or operate plans.

Other Plans

Legal service plans have been developed or sold by other organizations. Benefits have been offered to credit card customers. Some universities offer legal services to students, and some plans operate through the mail. Most of these plans have not had a major impact in the more complex

---

[18]Marshall A. Caskey, Director of Information, Los Angeles County Bar Association, letter, December 4, 1973.

[19]Edwin L. Gasperini and Max Schorr, "Prepaid Group Legal Services—Where We Are," 45 N.Y.S.B. *Journal* 76 (1973).

[20]Claude C. Lilly III, *Legal Services for the Middle Market* (Cincinnati: National Underwriter Company, 1974), p. 97.

[21]H. Lee Pickering, "Prepaid Legal Insurance—'Justice for All,' " *Management World* 7 no. 10 (1978), p. 18.

areas of legal services; instead, their success has been in offering limited programs.

INSURANCE PLANS

Contracts affording legal service benefits sold by insurers have several names. The terms most often used are *legal insurance, group legal insurance, prepaid legal insurance,* and *legal expense insurance.*

A review of legal insurance plans in the early 1970s indicated that the insurance industry planned to become deeply involved in the legal services movement. A tremendous gap existed between the initial insurance industry interest and the actual involvement. By 1973, CUMIS Insurance Society, Inc., Federated Insurers of Nashville, Inc., Fireman's Fund Insurance Company, Financial Indemnity Company, Insurance Company of North America, St. Paul Companies, Stonewall Insurance Company, Stuyvesant Insurance Company, and Midwest Mutual Company had designed legal insurance policies or plans, or both. Only Midwest Mutual and CUMIS ever took an active role in offering legal insurance policies.

The reasons for the reduction in the insurance industry's interest can be attributed to several factors. First, prepaid legal exposures do not meet all the criteria established by the industry in deciding what is an insurable risk. A loss may not be fortuitous in nature, and it can be difficult to verify. Payments for investigation, research, and trust preparation are examples. Obtaining a large number of homogeneous risks also is difficult.

Second, the industry also lacked the ready access to markets that was available to unions. This problem was compounded by the economic decline in the middle of the 1970s and the concomitant high inflation. Employees wanted increased pay, not legal service benefits.

Third, the industry encountered opposition from insurance regulators. Most of these obstacles have been overcome. When prepaid legal expense insurance was originally issued, it was designed primarily for individuals and families. The coverage was not intended to provide coverage for professional exposure. There has been a change in the last five years. Insurers are now offering on a regular basis prepaid legal expense insurance that provides defense-cost coverage for suits that arise when professional services are rendered. In addition, coverage for actions against professionals by regulatory authorities also is available.

THE FUTURE OF LEGAL SERVICES AS AN EMPLOYEE BENEFIT

The future of legal services as an employee benefit will be tied both to demand/pull and supply/push.

Demand for legal services will be affected by (1) demographic changes, (2) increasing litigation, (3) union pressures, (4) the economic environment, and (5) the elimination of the tax-exempt status of group prepaid legal service benefits. If the current demographic trends continue, the need for personal legal services will expand.

The litigious nature of our society has been discussed in numerous articles. It is sufficient to state that the existing attitude of the public can only mean the rate of growth of suits will increase.

The most important factor that can impact on legal service plans is the economy. If the economy slumps into a severe recession, there will be a greater push by workers for increased wages, rather than expanded benefits. Thus, a sluggish economy could result in a decline in the overall demand for legal service benefits. However, some of the potential decline in the demand may be dampened by the fact that economic downturns increase the public's need for legal services.

While the economy will be the major factor affecting the growth of prepaid legal services, part of the increase or decrease in the number of prepaid legal service plans will be a function of the marketing ability of some of the major providers of prepaid legal benefits. There are at least six plans that write coverage in a majority of the states. These are

1. Caldwell Pre-paid Legal.
2. Consumer Services Organization.
3. Lawphone.
4. Montgomery Ward.
5. National Legal Shield.
6. Pre-Paid Legal Services.[22]

To the extent these providers can convince the public that it needs legal services, the market for the legal service product will remain strong.

---

[22]Summary table of prepaid legal service plans developed by the National Resource Center For Consumers of Legal Services, 1990.

CHAPTER 26

FINANCIAL PLANNING AS AN EMPLOYEE BENEFIT

Charles E. Hughes
Robert T. LeClair

To make an informed decision on whether to offer financial planning services as an employee benefit, an employer must understand the elements of financial planning. The first part of this chapter provides background information on the need for financial planning and the role of the financial planner and then outlines the financial planning process. The chapter concludes with an examination of financial planning as an employee benefit, discusses the providers of the needed services, and looks at the cost factors involved in providing them.

FINANCIAL PLANNING

Personal financial planning is concerned with acquiring and employing funds in a manner consistent with established financial objectives. Since money is a limited resource that can be spent in an endless variety of ways with widely different results, financial planning plays a critical role in the satisfactory achievement of objectives.

Individuals or families experience problems with debt, current income and expenditures, protection, savings, investments, conflicting objectives, and haphazard or impulsive financial decisions. Perhaps most important, the individual or family may fail to meet needs and objectives in an economical and satisfactory way. Therefore, advice or consultation on the management of financial matters becomes a valuable service.

At one time a common belief existed that only the very wealthy needed to be concerned with personal financial planning. This no longer is the case. Increased income levels, taxation, sophisticated financial markets and instruments, increasing longevity, and the generally higher standard of living all have added to the complexity of managing finances. The growth and change of our economy and social structure have contributed to the widespread acceptance of the need for planning.

The need for and applicability of financial planning is much broader in our society today than most individuals realize. Many people look only at their bank accounts or investment portfolios in determining the extent of their wealth. They fail to consider other assets, including equity in a home, automobiles, furniture, paintings, cash value of life insurance, pension, profit-sharing programs, Social Security benefits, and other hidden assets as part of their financial position. Finally, a person concentrating on the demands of a career simply doesn't have time to explore all the possibilities for putting money to work and may fail to consider the consequences that can occur if financial planning is neglected.

The Role of the Financial Planner

The management of financial affairs has been changing through the years. There was a time when setting a budget for household expenditures was considered to be adequate financial planning. If adhering to that budget was difficult, or if carrying out the plan was impossible, an individual might have sought the advice of a counselor. Such an adviser would have reviewed the client's income and expenditures and devised a spending plan that made efficient use of the available income.

As income levels increased, larger amounts of surplus disposable income became available. Individuals and families sought ways of making money work harder for them. Various investments looked interesting, but the complexities of the securities markets appeared to be overwhelming. At this point, the counselor also was asked to take on the role of an investment adviser. However, investment opportunities were much broader than just securities. The adviser also was expected to be knowledgeable concerning real estate, tax-advantaged investments, and even such "hard" assets as gold or diamonds.

Added to this were the client's needs for an accountant to prepare tax returns, a lawyer to draft wills and other documents, and an insurance agent to assist in the protection, preservation, and distribution of an estate. Today, the adviser has become someone who counsels clients in all these areas and who serves as an intermediary in all these functions. From the growing needs of consumers has emerged a new professional, the financial planner.

The role of the financial planner is that of providing total financial management for individuals or families to enable these persons to realize the maximum enjoyment of their finances in an efficient and economic manner. The best means of accomplishing the financial objectives of a client is to develop specific plans to direct and control financial activity and progress. The financial planner must assess the client's current financial position, assist in establishing his or her objectives, consider all constraints and variables that bear on those objectives, and develop realistic projections and plans based on these factors. Financial planning, then, is an ongoing series of interrelated activities. It is a *process.*

The Financial Planning Process

It is most important to understand the concept of financial planning not as a product, or as a service, but as a process. Many persons claiming to engage in planning are really selling products and nothing more. A "good plan" is simply one that requires extensive use of their product whatever it may be. Similarly, a view of financial planning as a service provided at one point in time also is inadequate. This concept does not provide for the continuing needs of an individual or family for information, analysis, and review of its program.

Financial planning should be thought of as a series of interrelated activities a person participates in on a continuing basis. It is not something that is completed, even successfully, and then put away or forgotten. This is similar to the modern view of education that embraces learning not only through formal schooling but also throughout one's lifetime. In the same way, financial planning must be done regularly to take account of changes in an individual's circumstances, the availability of new products, and varying financial market conditions.

New tax legislation, fluctuating market interest rates, and the introduction of new or modified investment vehicles are examples of changes that can alter the way people and businesses handle money as well as the rates of return earned on liquid funds. As new products appear and market conditions change, even the best-prepared financial plan will tend to become obsolete. Changes in an individual's personal situation also may require adjustments in the overall plan. Births, deaths, marriage, divorce, or a new business venture can have a great impact on financial as well as personal planning.

The following activities in the process of financial planning must be carried out regularly and, when necessary, should involve qualified, professional advisers:

1. Gather background information.
2. Establish objectives.
3. Develop financial plans.
4. Execute and control plans.
5. Measure performance.

The flowchart shown in Figure 26–1 provides a summary of the individual activities involved in the process and shows the relationships among them.

Background Analysis

Financial planning requires comprehensive data on everyone participating in the program. Such information includes a record of income and expenditures as well as the current financial position of the individual or family. Prior to determining objectives, the financial planner needs information regarding the sex, health, age, lifestyle, tastes, and preferences of individual family members. Much of this information is subjective, and attitudes may shift considerably over the years. Such changes make it important that the financial planner maintain frequent contact with the client to be aware of important changes in these personal and family characteristics.

Another important area of background analysis is the client's attitude toward the degree of risk in the overall financial plan. Feelings about investment risk, personal financial security, and independence are just as important as the client's income statement or net worth. An awareness of risk attitudes permits realistic, acceptable objectives to be established with the individual or family. By ignoring these feelings, the adviser runs the risk of developing a "good plan" that is simply out of touch with the client's personality. Such plans are not likely to be accepted or implemented, and a great deal of time and effort will have been wasted.

FIGURE 26–1
The Financial Planning Process

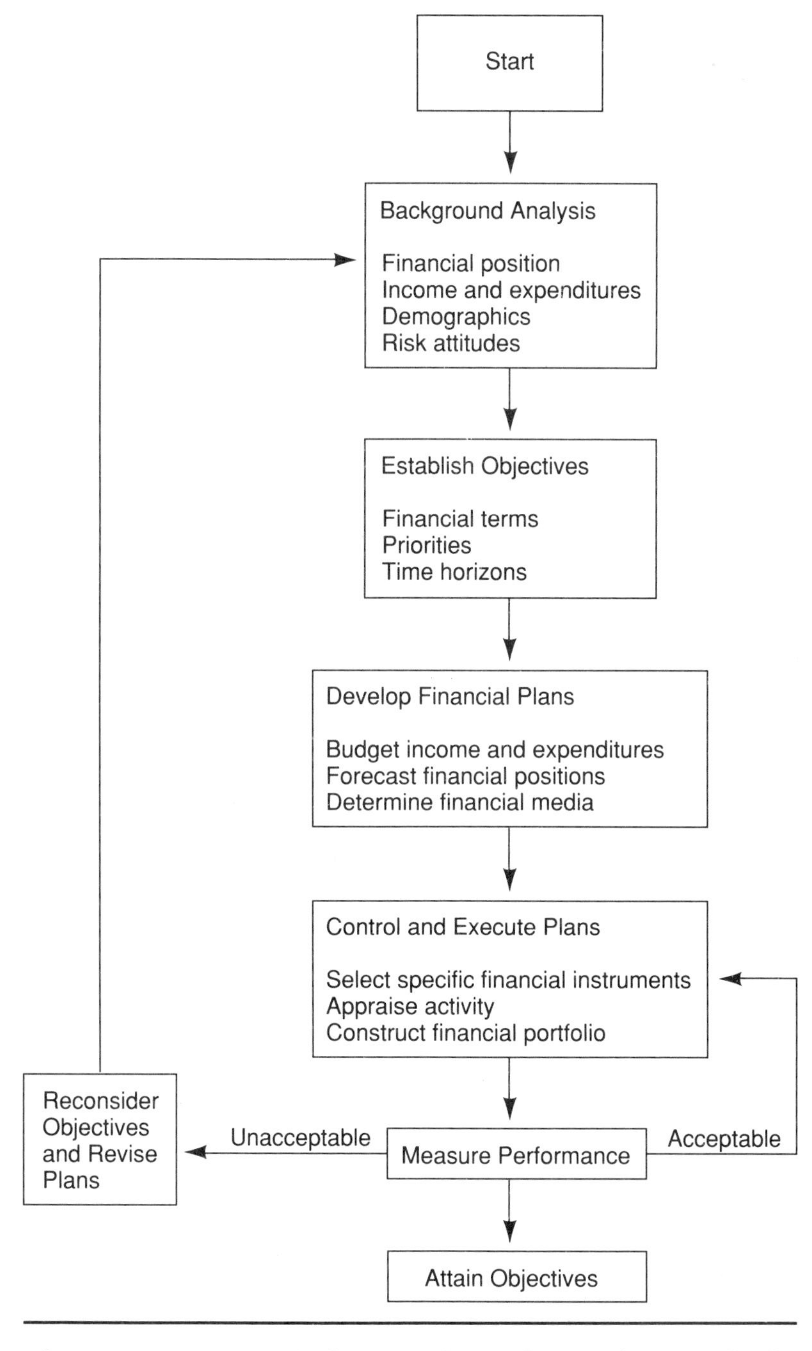

Source: "Introduction to Financial Counseling," *Financial Counseling* (Bryn Mawr, PA.: The American College, 1982), p. 133.

Unfortunately, for a number of reasons, attitudes toward risk are very difficult to measure or to judge. First, defining the nature of "risk" is highly subjective and varies considerably from one person to another. Second, attitudes about risk are likely to change dramatically over an individual's or family's life cycle. What seemed perfectly reasonable to the 25-year-old bachelor may be totally unacceptable to the 40-year-old father of four children. Finally, risk attitudes are a function of many personal, psychological factors that may be difficult for the financial planner to deal with. Yet, the counselor should try through discussions and interviews with clients to determine their feelings about risk and to be alert to significant changes which may occur in this area.

Setting Financial Objectives

Stating worthwhile financial objectives in a meaningful way is a difficult but necessary part of the planning process. One reason why many plans fail is that financial goals are not described in operational terms. Objectives often are presented in vague language that is difficult to translate into action.

Each objective statement should have the following characteristics. First, it should be *well-defined* and clearly understood by all participants, including members of the financial planning team. Unless individuals really know and understand what they are trying to accomplish, it is not likely they will succeed. Writing down objectives is one way of working toward a set of clear and useful statements. Such comments as "I want a safe and secure retirement income" do not provide much guidance for financial planners. They merely express an emotion that may be very real to the speaker but one that is hard to translate into effective terms and plans.

Second, good financial objectives generally are stated in *quantitative terms*. Only by attaching numbers to our plans can we know when the objective has been accomplished. This is a particularly important factor for long-term objectives, such as those concerning educational funding or retirement. It is desirable to measure progress toward these goals at various points along the way.

The goal of having a particular sum for retirement in 20 years can be reviewed annually to see if the necessary progress has been made. If earnings have been lower than anticipated, larger contributions may have to be made in succeeding years. If a higher rate of return actually has been realized, future contributions can be reduced. Such fine-tuning is impossible unless numbers are associated with plan objectives. Adding numbers to objectives also helps to make them more understandable to all members of the planning team as well as to participants in the plan.

Finally, each goal or objective should have a *time dimension* attached to it. When will a particular goal be accomplished? How much progress has been made since the last review? How much time remains until the goal is to be accomplished? These questions and similar ones can be answered only if a schedule has been established with objectives listed at particular points in time.

Some aspects of the plan, such as retirement objectives, will have very long timelines associated with them. Others, such as an adjustment to savings, may be accomplished in a few months or a year. Whether long-term or short-term in nature, the timing feature of objective statements is very important. Even long-term goals can be broken down into sub-periods that can coincide with an annual review of the plan.

After the objectives have been stated, they must be put in *priority order*. This ranking process is necessary since different objectives normally compete for limited resources. It is unlikely that a planner will be able to satisfy all the client's objectives at the same time. Some goals are more important, more urgent, than others. Critical short-term needs may have to be satisfied ahead of longer-range plans.

Once certain goals have been reached, funds may be channeled to other areas. An example would be the funding of children's education. After this goal has been met, resources previously spent on education costs may be allocated to building a retirement fund or some other long-range objective. Unless these and other goals have been assigned specific priorities, it is impossible to organize and carry out an effective plan. Conversely, a set of well-integrated financial objectives can make the actual planning process a relatively easy task.

Individuals and families should have workable objectives in each of the following areas:

1. Standard of Living. Maintaining a particular "lifestyle" normally takes the majority of an individual's financial resources. Setting an objective in this area calls for an analysis of required expenditures, such as food and shelter, as well as discretionary spending on such items as travel, vacations, and entertainment. If almost all income is being spent in this area, it is virtually impossible to accomplish any other objectives.

One widely used rule of thumb states that no more than 80 percent of income should be spent on maintaining a given standard of living. The remaining 20 percent of disposable income should be allocated among the other financial objectives. Obviously, this guideline varies from one person or family to another. But, unless a significant portion of income can be channeled toward the remaining objectives, those goals are not likely to be reached.

2. Savings. Almost everyone recognizes the need for funds that can be used to meet an emergency or other special needs. However, determining the ideal level of savings can be a complex problem. It is influenced by the nature of income received, individual risk attitudes, stability of employment, and other factors such as the type of health and dental insurance coverage.

It is recommended that savings balances should be equal to at least three months' disposable income. These funds should be maintained in a safe and highly liquid form where rate of return is a secondary consideration. Today, the typical bank money market account or money market mutual fund offers an excellent vehicle for maintaining savings balances. These funds offer a high degree of safety, ready access through the use of checks or telephone redemption of shares, and a good rate of return.

3. Protection. This objective incorporates property, liability, disability, life, and medical insurance coverage. It should be designed to provide protection against insurable risks and related losses. Objectives in this area should take account of coverage provided through public programs, such as Social Security, as well as group insurance offered as an employee benefit.

4. Accumulation (Investment). This is possibly the most complex objective in a number of ways. It relates to the buildup of capital for significant financial needs. These needs can be as diverse as a child's college education, a daughter's wedding, or the purchase of a vacation home. The sheer number and variety of such goals makes it difficult to define this objective and to set priorities.

Adding to the difficult nature of this area is the generally long time-horizon for planning that may encompass 20 years or more. Finally, the wide variety of possible investment vehicles that can be used in the planning process adds to the overall complexity. Regardless of the reason for building capital, the critical ingredients in this objective are the ability to quantify the needed amount and to state a target date for its accumulation.

5. Financial Independence. This objective may be thought of as a particularly important subset of the accumulation objective. It concerns the accumulation of assets over a relatively long time in most cases. Such independence may be desired at a particular age and may or may not actually correspond with retirement from employment. Many persons may wish to have complete financial security and independence while continuing to work at a favored occupation or profession.

Since the planning-horizon is such a lengthy one, this objective should be broken down into subgoals that can be evaluated, analyzed, and reworked over the years. More than most others, this area is affected by changes in government programs, such as Social Security, and in benefits paid by employers.

6. Estate Planning. Objectives in this area typically are concerned with the preservation and distribution of wealth after the estate owner's death. However, accomplishing such goals may call for a number of actions to be taken well before that time. Writing a will probably is the most fundamental estate planning objective, and yet thousands of persons die each year without having done so. These people die "intestate" and leave the distribution of their assets to state laws and the courts.

For larger estates, avoidance or minimization of estate taxes is an important consideration. These objectives can be accomplished, but call for careful planning and implementation prior to the owner's death. The use of various trust instruments, distribution of assets through gifts, and proper titling of property all can result in a smaller taxable estate. Carrying out such a program, however, takes time and should be considered as various assets are being acquired. This also is an area where professional guidance generally is necessary. If the financial planner is not an attorney, one should be consulted in drafting a will or in preparing a trust document.

Developing Financial Plans

Once a realistic, well-defined set of objectives has been established, the financial planner can begin to develop actual plans. This planning stage includes the budgeting of income and expenditures for the near term, along with a forecast of future activity. A projection of the client's financial position for the next several years also should be made.

These plans should identify the financial instruments to be included in programs to meet specific objectives. For example, specific savings media should be recommended for those who need more in the way of emergency funds. Should a family increase its regular savings accounts, purchase money market certificates, or buy shares in a money market fund? If an investment program is called for in the plan, recommendations should be made on the appropriate *types* of investments, such as securities, real estate, or tax shelters.

Executing and Controlling Plans

The next stage of the model calls for the financial planner to assist in setting the plan in motion. This may involve the purchase or sale of various assets, changes in life insurance protection, additional liability coverage, and other changes. All these activities should be monitored closely and appraised to see that they are effective in accomplishing the stated objectives. The outcome of some actions will be quickly apparent, while others may take a long time to produce results that can be evaluated.

Measuring Performance

The financial planner is responsible for gathering data on the plan's operations that are used to evaluate his or her performance and the actions of other professionals who may be involved. Such persons may include a banker, an attorney, a life insurance consultant, and an accountant.

This important step determines progress made toward the attainment of objectives. If performance to date is acceptable, no particular corrective action need be taken until the next scheduled review. However, if it is discovered that progress to date is unacceptable, several actions may need to be taken. These would include a review of the plans to see if they are still valid and analysis of the market environment to take note of unanticipated changes.

It also may be necessary to review and alter the original objectives if they are no longer realistic and desirable. When this occurs, the entire plan may have to be recycled through each of the stages described above. This model of financial planning is a dynamic one that is repeated continually as personal, financial, and environmental factors change.

FINANCIAL PLANNING AS AN EMPLOYEE BENEFIT

The array of programs, plans, and services that have been added to an employee's benefit package has expanded greatly over the past several years. Most benefits, by design, are selected or offered as part of a package for all employees; some are offered only to specific employees or groups of employees.

Financial planning is one benefit that has been limited to key executives or other highly compensated employees. This came about partly from the belief that aspects of the program dealing with estate planning apply only to those individuals who will accumulate sufficient wealth to be subject to significant estate taxes.[1] Also, since programs recommended by financial planners may include forms of tax shelters that contain considerable risk, employees other than top executives might not have sufficient assets or income to justify the amount of risk involved. Finally, from the point of view of the employer, the full financial planning process generally is expensive, and this inhibits extension to large numbers of lower-income employees.

Services Provided

Because of the relatively high cost many firms have opted for a partial financial planning service rather than the full process. These separate services include

1. Estate planning—disposition at death, insurance arrangements, minimization of taxes, estate liquidity.
2. Tax preparation—federal, state, and local returns; estate and gift tax returns.
3. Investment management—short- and long-term investment programs, tax shelters.
4. Compensation planning—analysis of options available, explanation of benefits.
5. Preparation of wills.

Some of these services may be provided by employees of the firm, while others are contracted for and performed by outside specialists knowledgeable in a particular area. As the number of individual services available expands, the need for full financial planning becomes more apparent. Many companies now are providing financial planning benefits to their top executives, and some have expanded it to middle managers as well.

---

[1]The Economic Recovery Tax Act of 1981 made major changes in the law relating to federal estate taxes. The size of estates not subject to tax increased to $600,000 in 1987.

Advantages

The major advantages of financial planning as an employee benefit are:

1. Many executives do not have sufficient time to devote to their own financial affairs. Financial planning as a benefit relieves them of having to spend time in financial planning and permits them to concentrate on business matters.
2. By reducing the likelihood a poor decision will be made on his or her own finances, the executive has greater personal peace of mind.
3. The employer probably is better able to screen and select financial planners. Thus, the executive is less likely to receive poor advice from unqualified planners.
4. Salaries offered may appear more attractive and competitive when such compensation is being used more efficiently to reach each executive's goals.

Disadvantages

Although financial planning as an employee benefit would appear to be attractive to both employer and employee, there are several reasons for not providing such services:

1. Financial planning might be construed as meddling in an employee's personal affairs.
2. There is a feeling the company might be held responsible for bad advice, since it has endorsed the services or employed the counselor.
3. Although the planning service is considered helpful to highly compensated employees, many companies are reluctant to provide benefits that are restricted to select groups of employees.
4. The cost can be substantial.

Who Provides Financial Planning?

Financial planning services are provided by numerous individuals and firms, including banks, insurance companies and agents, investment brokers, benefit consultants, lawyers, accountants, and others. The major firms specializing in financial planning services generally have staffs of professionals who are experts in investments, insurance, tax shelters, andso on, and who work as a team to provide the financial planning service.

Smaller organizations may concentrate on one area and hire consultants to complete the planning team.

The selection of a financial planning firm requires care. It is important that the objectives of the employer are satisfied, and, from the employees' standpoint, that their individual confidences be protected and the advice be in their best interests. Some employers have attempted to provide financial planning services through in-house personnel. This is most effective when the benefit is limited to a single service, such as tax advice. However, problems occur because many executives are hesitant to discuss details of their personal financial affairs with fellow employees.

The selection decision sometimes is simply one of identifying the best financial planning firm available. Generally, a firm that operates on a fee-only basis is the preferred type. However, the objectives of the employer may warrant consideration of product-oriented financial planners. For example, if the objective of the benefit is limited to advice on life insurance planning, a competent life insurance agent may be able to satisfy the need. Further, banks, brokerage firms, and life insurance companies have formed financial planning divisions that provide support services for their personnel. Therefore, although an adviser may be product oriented, he or she has substantial breadth of assistance available to analyze and design broad-based financial plans. In these cases, a fee may be charged even though commissions exist.

Individual professionals call themselves financial counselors, financial planners, or financial advisers. Many of these persons still depend solely on commissions for their income. However, since it is difficult for any single individual to give professional advice in all areas included in a comprehensive plan, the trend is to join together to form firms that are rich in experience and professionally qualified in all aspects of financial planning and that are compensated through fees or a combination of commission and fees. There exist today many quality individuals and firms that provide financial counseling. The most important ingredient, therefore, is to seek the individual or firm that understands financial planning as a process, one that can have important beneficial results for employers and employees alike.

Fiduciary Responsibility

As financial planners take on a wider range of responsibilities for their clients, a special fiduciary relationship develops between them. This arrangement arises whenever one person places confidence and trust in the integrity and fidelity of another. A fiduciary relationship is characterized by faith and reliance on the part of the client and by a condition of superiority and influence on the part of the financial planner.

The existence of a fiduciary responsibility does not depend upon the establishment of any particular legal relationship. Nonlegal relationships can be fiduciary in nature, especially where one person entrusts his or her business affairs to another.

When a fiduciary relationship exists, the fiduciary (adviser) has a duty to act in good faith and in the interests of the other person. A fiduciary is not permitted to use the relationship to benefit his or her own personal interest. Transactions between the client and counselor are subject to close scrutiny by the courts. Especially sensitive are transactions in which the fiduciary profits at the expense of the client. Fiduciaries must subordinate their individual interests to their duty of care, trust, and loyalty to the client.

The Investment Advisers Act of 1940 is particularly important in defining the nature of a fiduciary relationship. One objective of the act is to expose and eliminate all conflicts of interest that could influence an adviser to be other than disinterested. Congress thus empowered the courts to require full and fair disclosure of all material facts surrounding the fiduciary relationship. The adviser must disclose in a meaningful way all material facts that give rise to potential or actual conflicts of interest. For example, an adviser who receives commissions on products sold to clients, such as securities or life insurance, should disclose the amount of sales compensation received on recommended transactions.[2]

Cost

The cost of financial planning varies, based on the range of services to be provided and the type of individuals employed to provide them. A financial counselor or counseling firm may operate on a fee-only basis, a commission-only basis, or some combination of commissions and fees. The existence of commissions, which may eliminate or greatly reduce costs to the employer, can be a strong incentive for companies to seek product-oriented purveyors of financial planning services. It should be

---

[2]Robert W. Cooper and Dale S. Johnson, "The Impact of the Investment Advisers Act of 1940 on CLUs and Other Financial Services Professionals," *CLU Journal,* April 1982, p. 35.

understood, however, that insurance or investment advice given to employees could be heavily weighted in favor of products available from the counseling firm. For this reason, employers usually prefer financial counseling on a fee-only basis, since the belief is that this provides the most objective analyses and unbiased recommendations.

Since the financial planning process often is extremely detailed and complicated, costs of $3,000 to $6,000 or even higher per executive are common for a complete counseling program. Another approach used by some counseling firms involves seminars where the counseling process and available services are explained to groups of eligible employees. Some firms charge a separate fee of $1,000 to $3,500 for the initial data-gathering or fact-finding visit with the employee. In addition, if legal documents or certified financial statements are required, there may be additional legal and accounting fees. Finally, after the initial year of the program, the annual fees for maintaining and updating the program are based on required time and effort, generally averaging $1,000 to $2,000 per employee.

The relatively high cost of financial planning as an employee benefit has undoubtedly contributed to its limited availability to only highly compensated executives or perhaps to its adoption at all. The cost of financial planning to the firm can be reduced by offering the benefit to employees on a contributory basis.

The fees paid for financial planning generally are deductible by the corporation for tax purposes if the total compensation to the employee, including the counseling fee, is not considered unreasonable compensation by the IRS.[3] When this benefit is offered to highly compensated executives, the fee generally would be small, compared with the executive's total compensation, and it is unlikely that total compensation would be considered unreasonable.

The amount the employer pays to the planning firm for services performed for an employee is considered taxable income to the employee and is subject to withholding tax.[4] However, an offsetting tax benefit may be available to the employee since deductions are allowed for services directed to tax matters or allocable to investment advice.[5] Therefore, it

---

[3]IRC Sec. 106.

[4]IRC Sec. 61.

[5]Fees paid for *investment counsel* are deductible only to the extent that all *second tier* miscellaneous itemized deductions cumulatively exceed 2 percent of adjusted gross income.

could be possible for the employee to contribute the cost associated with those services allowed as deductions. The financial planning firm should indicate clearly the charge for these services as a separate item on its billing.

In addition to the tax aspects, when supplemental legal or accounting fees are necessary, these expenses should be borne by the employee. Overall, contributions by employees could reduce the cost to the employer and make it possible for the firm to offer financial planning an employee benefit.

CONCLUSION

Financial planning will become an increasingly important employee benefit. This will occur as more firms offer such services and as more employees qualify for eligibility. Another factor contributing to this growth will be the maturity of the financial planning industry itself. While the costs associated with offering financial planning services as a benefit are not insignificant, clear advantages exist for both the employer and the employee. There also are areas of concern, however, and firms should carefully analyze the nature of their employees and the qualifications of those offering to provide financial planning services for them.

CHAPTER 27

PROPERTY AND LIABILITY INSURANCE AS AN EMPLOYEE BENEFIT

Bernard L. Webb

While forms of property and liability insurance have been provided as employee benefits for many years, the practice was very limited until the late 1960s. There were reports of automobile insurance benefit plans as early as 1925, but few details are available. Because of the hostility of agent associations and insurance regulatory authorities, the plans were not discussed in public and were sold and serviced in an almost clandestine manner.

The practice received considerable attention at the 1926 meeting of the National Convention of Insurance Commissioners, the predecessor organization of the National Association of Insurance Commissioners.[1] Many commissioners issued regulations at that time prohibiting the practice of insuring employee-owned cars under fleet policies covering company-owned cars. One such ruling was challenged in the courts, but the commissioner's authority to issue it was upheld.[2] Little more was heard of property-liability employee benefit plans for 20 years, though it is clear that a few such plans persisted.

Such plans apparently began to spread in the middle 1950s, though progress was slow and not well-publicized. The major public manifesta-

---

[1]National Convention of Insurance Commissioners, *Proceedings* (Chicago: National Convention of Insurance Commissioners, 1926), pp. 117–20, 272–76.

[2]*Flat Top Insurance Agency* v. *Sims,* 178 S.E. 518, (W.Va., 1935).

tion of their growth was the activity of agents' associations in promoting administrative and legislative rules prohibiting the plans.

The first open promotion of property-liability employee benefit plans began in 1965, when the Continental National American Group (CNA) insurance companies announced their entry into the field. Other insurers followed, and plans proliferated until the middle 1970s. Severe underwriting losses at that time caused CNA and a number of other insurers to discontinue such plans. As this is written (1991), several insurers are active selling property-liability employee benefit plans, primarily automobile insurance.

KINDS OF BENEFITS

Virtually all kinds of property-liability insurance for individuals and families have been offered as employee benefits at some time. However, automobile and homeowners insurance (especially the former) have been most common.

Automobile Insurance

Automobile insurance has been the major property-liability insurance employee benefit for two reasons. First, it is compulsory (or virtually compulsory) for car owners in many states. Second, it is the largest single insurance purchase, in terms of premium, for most families.

In most cases, all automobile insurance coverages are offered, including liability, collision, comprehensive, medical payments, towing-cost coverage, and, in the states where applicable, no-fault benefits. The coverages offered under employee benefit plans usually are identical to those offered under policies sold to individuals. In a few cases, the medical payments coverage is modified to coordinate benefits with the employer's medical expense benefit plans. Also, where permitted by state law, a substantial deductible may be provided in the no-fault benefits, applicable only to the employee and family, to coordinate benefits with the employer's medical and income-loss plans.

Employees usually are permitted to select any reasonable limits of liability coverage, and are not restricted to predetermined limits as under group life and health coverage. The same right of selection usually is available for medical payments and no-fault coverage. Physical damage coverages (collision and comprehensive) usually are written for the actual cash value of the vehicle, and employees usually are permitted a selection of deductibles.

In most automobile insurance plans, coverage is provided under individual policies issued to the employees. Some insurers issue master policies to employers with certificates to employees, but the practice is not widespread and is prohibited by law in some states.

Homeowners Insurance

The second most important property-liability insurance employee benefit is homeowners insurance, including tenants coverage for those who do not own a home. It has proved less popular than automobile insurance for two reasons. First, the annual premium for homeowners is likely to be less than automobile insurance premiums for most families. Consequently, the potential savings are smaller. Also, many mortgage lenders require borrowers to pay the premium for homeowners coverage through monthly deposits to an escrow account. This requirement complicates the handling of homeowners policies through employee benefit plans.

Another complication in using homeowners insurance as an employee benefit is the wide variation in the coverages needed, even among families in the same income class. Some families own their homes, while others do not. Some families may need coverage for musical instruments, photographic equipment, golf or other sports equipment, stamp or coin collections, and a wide variety of other special personal property items, while others do not.

Personal Umbrella Liability Coverage

Several insurers offer personal umbrella liability policies under employee benefit programs. These policies offer high limits of liability coverage (usually in multiples of $1 million). The umbrella policy is excess over automobile liability and the liability coverage of the homeowners policy, and does not begin to pay until the limits of those policies have been exhausted.

Personal umbrella policies are especially popular among professional employees, executives, and other highly paid persons. Little variation exists in coverage needs from one person to another, so the administrative burden is much lighter for personal umbrella coverage than for automobile insurance and homeowners policies.

Other Coverages

Several other property-liability coverages have been offered as employee benefits. Boat insurance has been offered by several employers, and at least one airline offers insurance for the personal aircraft owned by its employees. Many employers provide coverage for employees' liability for their on-the-job activities.

KINDS OF PROGRAMS

All the coverages mentioned may be provided under three different kinds of programs. They are distinguished primarily by the relative cost and the amount of underwriting discretion retained by the insurer.

Franchise Plans

The earliest plans were franchise plans, in which the insurer charged the same rates it charged for its individual policies and retained its normal underwriting prerogatives. The principal advantage to the employee was the convenience of installment payment of premiums through payroll deduction. Insurers frequently did not charge interest for the installment payment privilege. In a few cases, the employer paid some or all of the premium, especially for sales personnel or other employees who used their cars for business purposes. Beginning in the late 1960s, franchise plans began to lose ground to mass merchandising plans.

Mass Merchandising Plans

Franchise plans and mass merchandising plans are similar in that the insurer retains the right to underwrite individual employees under both. However, they differ in one important respect because there is a price reduction (in comparison with policies issued individually) under the mass merchandising plans but not under franchise plans.

The extent of the price reduction varies among insurers. It also may vary according to the number of participants in the plan. The amount of expense saving in a particular plan also may affect pricing. The expense savings result primarily from reduction of the agent's commission, but the expense of premium collection and bad debts also may be reduced. Some have suggested better accident-prevention measures made possible by mass merchandising may reduce losses, providing another source of premium reduction. However, no statistical evidence of such savings has been made public.

Mass merchandising plans first appeared in substantial numbers around 1970. They still are the dominant form of property-liability employee benefit insurance, but the number of true group plans is increasing.

True Group Plans

Unlike franchise and mass merchandising plans, the insurer under a true group plan agrees to provide coverage for all eligible employees, without the right of individual underwriting. Of course, such an agreement would leave the insurer open to adverse selection in the absence of some method for compelling or enticing low-risk employees to participate in the program.

To avoid adverse selection, insurers that write group property-liability insurance require the employer to pay a part of the premium, a practice not common in franchise or mass merchandising plans. The amount of employer payment required varies among insurers. One insurer requires the employer to pay three or four dollars per week for each employee. Others require the employer to pay at least a specified percentage of the employees' premium, usually from 40 to 60 percent.

For automobile insurance, the insurer may require the employer pay a part of the premium for only one car for each employee. Employees who own more than one car would pay the full premium for the additional vehicles. Without some employer premium payment, the low-risk employees might be able to find insurance outside the plan at a cost equal to or less than the cost within the plan, since the rates within the plan are increased somewhat by the requirement that the insurer provide coverage for all eligible employees. The loss of low-risk employees to competitors, of course, would result in even higher rates for the remaining participants.

ADVANTAGES FOR EMPLOYEES

The advantages realized by the employees vary according to the kind of plan. Quite obviously, a true group plan offers more advantages than a franchise plan.

Lower Cost of Insurance

Both mass merchandising and true group plans offer the advantage of lower cost of insurance to the employee. The difference is especially noticeable under true group plans because the employer usually pays a part of the premium as a requirement of the plan. The magnitude of the premium reduction may vary from a negligible amount to 15 percent or more, not considering any premium payment by the employer. By definition, franchise plans do not offer any reduction in premium.

Greater Availability of Insurance

True group plans make insurance available to some employees who might otherwise be uninsurable. Under franchise and mass merchandising programs, the insurer retains the right to refuse insurance to employees who do not meet its underwriting requirements. However, it appears insurers are more lenient in underwriting individuals under such plans than they are for persons who apply otherwise. Consequently, even franchise and mass merchandising plans probably provide insurance for some people who would find it difficult to obtain in the absence of such plans.

Payroll Deduction

All the plans mentioned usually provide the advantage of installment payment of premium through payroll deduction. In many cases, the insurer does not charge interest or a service fee for the installment payment privilege.

DISADVANTAGES FOR EMPLOYEES

The disadvantages for employees appear to be small. The insurance may terminate when the employment terminates, though some insurers provide some form of conversion privilege. Also, the employees may not have the same flexibility in the selection of coverages that they would have if they purchased their insurance independently. Finally, some employees have expressed concern that their employers may obtain sensitive personal information through the processing of insurance claims or underwriting forms.

ROLE OF EMPLOYER

The role of the employer may vary from plan to plan. In some cases, the employer pays a part of the premium. The employer also may provide advice to employees on the kinds and amounts of insurance they should purchase. However, it is more common for the insurer or agent to provide such advice. It may be illegal in some states for any other person than a licensed insurance agent to provide such advice or to solicit applications for insurance.

In any case, the employer needs to give insurer or agency personnel access to employees for the explanation of the program and the negotiation of applications. The administration of property-liability insurance plans is substantially more complex than the administration of group life and health plans because of (1) the greater variation in the coverage provided, (2) greater frequency of changes, and (3) the complexity of handling claims, especially liability claims. For that reason, most employers prefer not to become involved in the detailed administration of the plan. The details of administration usually are delegated to the insurer or its representatives. Claims administration is seldom if ever performed by the employer, not only because of the complexity of the task but also because many employees would prefer their employer not have access to such detailed information about their off-the-job habits and activities.

In most property-liability insurance plans, the employer's role is limited to (1) selection of the insurer, (2) payment of the premiums from the employer's own funds, through payroll deduction or a combination of the two, and (3) mediation of disputes between the insurer and employees. The employer may be involved in notifying the insurer of needed changes in employees' coverage, such as changes of cars or increasing homeowners limits to reflect inflation. However, it is more likely the employees will handle such changes directly with the insurer or its representatives.

FEDERAL INCOME TAX CONSEQUENCES

Property-liability insurance plans do not enjoy the tax advantages that have been granted for pension plans, group life and health insurance, and prepaid legal insurance plans. This lack of tax incentive is a major reason for the slow growth of property-liability insurance plans.

Any property-liability insurance premiums paid by the employer on behalf of an employee are considered taxable income to the employee. It must be reported as income by the employee and the appropriate tax must be paid. Such payments by the employer are deductible expenses for the employer. Several bills have been introduced in Congress to grant property-liability plans the same tax advantage as other employee benefit plans, but none has been passed.

U.S. LABOR CODE

The U.S. Labor Code contains two provisions that may relate to property-liability insurance benefit plans. The first provision prohibits any employer from giving anything of value to any labor organization or an officer or employee thereof if such labor organization represents or could represent the employer's employees.[3] There is a specific exemption for payments into a fund to provide pensions, life insurance, or health benefits for employees. Payments into a fund to provide property-liability insurance for employees are not exempt, and would be illegal. Consequently, such plans could not be administered by labor unions if the employer pays any of the premium.

The second applicable provision of the labor code specifies the factors related to the employment concerning which the employer can be compelled to bargain in good faith with the union. Property-liability insurance plans are not specifically included among the bargainable items, but employers can be required to bargain over ". . . rates of pay, wages, hours of employment, or other conditions of employment."[4]

The National Labor Relations Board (NLRB) held in the *Inland Steel* case that: "The term 'wages' as used in Section 9(a) must be construed to include emoluments of value, like pension and insurance benefits, which may accrue to employees out of their employment relationship."[5] The NLRB's view has been supported by the U.S. courts in at least two circuts.[6]

---

[3]29 U.S.C. 186.

[4]29 U.S.C. 158(a), 159(a).

[5]77 NLRB 4 (1948).

[6]See *United Steel Workers* v. *N.L.R.B.*, 170 F.2d 247 (1948) and *W. W. Cross Co., Inc.* v. *N.L.R.B.*, 174 F.2d 875 (1949).

The interpretation adopted by the NLRB and the courts would seem to be sufficiently broad to include property-liability insurance. Consequently, it seems likely an employer can be compelled to bargain for such benefit plans.

STATE REGULATION

The primary responsibility for insurance regulation rests with the states. Historically, state regulation has been hostile to the use of property-liability insurance as an employee benefit. In many cases, regulatory prohibitions have been based on statutory provisions prohibiting unfair discrimination in insurance rating. In some cases, specific statutory prohibitions have been enacted.

Fictitious Group Regulations

Beginning in the 1950s, the insurance commissioners of 17 states adopted fictitious group regulations. The regulations differ somewhat from state to state, but the Florida regulation is reasonably typical:

> The Insurance laws of Florida require that any rate, rating plans or form of fire, casualty or surety insurance covering risks in this state shall not be unfairly discriminatory. Therefore, no insurer, admitted or non-admitted, shall make available through any rating plan or form, fire, casualty or surety insurance to any firm, corporation, or association of individuals, any preferred rate or premium based upon any fictitious grouping of such firm, corporation, or association of individuals, which fictitious grouping is hereby defined and declared to be any grouping by way of membership, license, franchise, contract, agreement, or any other method or means; provided, however, that the foregoing shall not apply to accident and health insurance.[7]

Unfair discrimination would seem to be a weak basis for such rulings. Group life and health insurance has been accepted as not unfairly discriminatory in all states for many years. No apparent reason exists to treat property-liability insurance differently.

---

[7]Fla. Ins. Dept., Bulletin No. 211 (1957).

Fictitious Group Statutes

In 1957, Florida replaced its fictitious group regulation with a fictitious group statute. The statute provided:

> (1) No insurer or any person on behalf of any insurer shall make, offer to make, or permit any preference or distinction in property, marine, casualty, or surety insurance as to form of policy, certificate, premium, rate, benefits, or conditions of insurance, based upon membership, nonmembership, employment, of any person or persons by or in any particular group, association, corporation, or organization, and shall not make the foregoing preference or distinction available in any event based upon any fictitious grouping of persons as defined in this code, such fictitious grouping being hereby defined and declared to be any grouping by way of membership, nonmembership, license, franchise, employment, contract, agreement or any other method or means. (2) The restrictions and limitations of this section shall not extend to life and disability insurance.[8]

Effectiveness of Regulations and Statutes

The fictitious group regulations and statutes seemed to be effective for several years after their adoption. However, by the late 1960s, several insurance commissioners had approved filings for franchise and mass merchandising programs in spite of the seeming regulatory and statutory prohibitions. Their actions were challenged in the courts by agent associations, but were generally upheld.[9] Although most of the fictitious group regulations and statutes remained on the books, they became increasingly less effective in controlling property-liability insurance plans for employees.

Enabling Legislation

Beginning in 1969, several states enacted legislation designed specifically to authorize the use of property-liability insurance for employee benefit plans. Minnesota was the first state to adopt such a statute. It reads as follows:

---

[8] Fla. Stat., Sec. 626.973 (1972).

[9] See for example, *Georgia Ass'n of Independent Ins. Agents v. Travelers Indem. Co.*, 313 F. Supp. 841 (N.D. Ga. 1970); *Independent Ins. Agents* v. *Bolton*, 235 N.E. 2d 273 (Illinois, 1968); and *Independent Ins. Agents v. Herrmann*, 486 P. 2d 1068 (Washington, 1971).

> One rate is unfairly discriminatory in relation to another if it clearly fails to reflect equitably the differences in expected losses, expenses and the degree of risk. Rates are not unfairly discriminatory because different premiums result for policyholders with like loss exposures but different expense factors or like expense factors but different loss exposures, so long as the rates reflect the differences with reasonable accuracy. Rates are not unfairly discriminatory if they attempt to spread risk broadly among persons insured under a group, franchise or blanket policy.[10]

The Minnesota statute was the model for several other states, but Hawaii took a slightly different route. It enacted a rather detailed enabling law specifically for automobile insurance.[11]

In 1977, the National Association of Insurance Commissioners (NAIC) adopted a model regulation for the control of mass marketing (mass merchandising) of property and liability insurance. The model regulation specifically authorizes mass merchandising. It has been adopted in only a very few states.

At its 1986 annual meeting, the NAIC adopted a model act for group property and liability insurance. The act specifically authorizes the writing of group property and liability insurance under a master policy, with certificates issued to individual participants.[12] The NAIC is an advisory body, so its model acts and regulations do not have any legal effect until adopted by state legislatures or state insurance commissioners.

Present Status

It appears that property-liability insurance can be used as employee benefit plans in all states. However, policy forms, rates, and rating plans must be filed with the insurance commissioner in virtually all states and must be approved before use in over half of the states. In early 1987, one insurer was offering its true group automobile insurance plan to employers in several states. Its plan provided for experience rating of each group, a feature that might complicate approval in some states. Several other insurers were also experimenting with group automobile insurance.

---

[10]Minn. Stat. Ann., Sec. 70A.04(4), (1981).

[11]24 Hawaii Rev. Stat., Sec. 431-751 et seq.

[12]For the text of the NAIC model act, along with annotations, see Vance C. Gudmundsen, ''Group Property and Casualty Insurance: Annotations to the NAIC Model Act,'' *Journal of Insurance Regulation* 5, no. 2 (December 1986), pp. 224–66.

SUMMARY AND CONCLUSIONS

Only a small percentage, probably less than 1 percent, of personal property-liability insurance is now sold through employee benefit plans. The practice is growing, though at a slow pace.

State regulation, which historically has been hostile to the use of property-liability insurance as an employee benefit, now seems less hostile. However, few states have specific enabling legislation.

Provisions of the federal Internal Revenue Code and the Labor Code place group property-liability insurance at a competitive disadvantage, relative to group life and health insurance and pension plans. Use of property-liability insurance in employee benefit plans is likely to grow slowly unless these federal laws are changed.

CHAPTER 28

PAYMENTS FOR NONPRODUCTION TIME AND TIME NOT WORKED AND MISCELLANEOUS BENEFITS

James C. Fee
Robert V. Nally

The U.S. Chamber of Commerce in its annual survey, *Employee Benefits,* defines employee benefits as any form of compensation paid to employees other than direct wages and divides them into seven categories. The first four—legally required benefits, retirement and savings plans, life insurance and death benefits, and medical and medically related benefits—are covered in other parts of the *Handbook.* This chapter discusses the final three: (1) payments for nonproduction time on the job, (2) payments for time not worked, and (3) miscellaneous benefit payments consisting of employer-subsidized activities and services, service awards and suggestion plans.

PAYMENTS FOR NONPRODUCTION TIME ON THE JOB

Every workplace typically has some nonproduction time during the workday in the form of rest periods, coffee breaks, lunch periods, get-ready time, wash-up time, clothes-change time, and travel time. Reporting pay and call-in pay also can be included among these. Their cumulative effect can be substantial, and their average cost is approximately 2.3 percent of direct wages. While many of these benefits are taken for granted by employees and typically not given much review and cost analysis by management, the average cost per employee can be several hundred dollars per year, and these benefits can be easily abused, even unintentionally, thereby increasing costs further.

Payments for nonproduction time on the job have largely been the product of collective bargaining, but union pressure is not the sole reason for their existence. There also are safety, production and morale based reasons for these benefits. The use of rest periods and coffee breaks for increased safety and morale is well-established, and some states mandate paid rest periods; for example, ten minutes after some specified continuous period of work such as four hours. Also, if a plant is operating eight-hour shifts, paid rest periods, coffee breaks, and lunch periods are dictated by the work schedule. Frequently, paid lunch periods are used in conjunction with the requirement that employees not leave the work place during lunch time to avoid problems caused by employees going out to lunch, such as drinking alcoholic beverages, returning late, or failing to return at all.

Paid get-ready time, clothes-change time, and wash-up time typically are used when these activities require substantial time either because special equipment must be worn or technical preparation must take place before work can begin. Paid time also often is granted for nonproduction periods if a job is particularly dirty or potentially harmful to health and for other reasons.

Paid travel time can come about in several ways. In mining operations, construction of underground tunnels, and the like substantial time may be required for employees to travel to their job sites after reporting to work, and they typically are paid for the time. Other jobs, particularly those involving the installation and servicing of equipment, require employees to travel to various customer locations, and the travel time is considered part of their normal workday. Also, some professional or technical employees such as "troubleshooters" do a considerable amount of traveling. While some of these are exempt employees under the federal wage laws and travel on their own time, many are compensated for travel time, which could amount to a day or more in a five-day workweek.

Reporting pay and call-in pay generally are restricted in use to production employees and are somewhat different from the traditional forms of paid nonproduction time. Reporting-pay provisions guarantee employees a minimum number of hours of pay for each scheduled day they report to their jobs whether or not there is any work to be performed. The guaranteed pay is approximately 50 percent of a normal day's pay, or four hours' pay, but some firms guarantee only one hour of pay, while a few guarantee a full day's pay. Employees who work the guaranteed minimum number of hours receive no reporting pay, and an employer usually can avoid paying reporting pay by notifying the employees not to report if there is no work for them. Typically, the notice must be given within the eight hours before they are scheduled to report for work. An employer is relieved of the requirement when the no-work situation is caused by such events as flood, fire, strike, or power failure. Under a call-in pay provision, employees who are notified by the employer to report to work at some time outside the normal work day or scheduled time period are guaranteed a certain number of hours of work at premium pay, usually time-and-one-half the normal rate.

Tax Treatment of Payments for Nonproduction Time on the Job

Because the cost to a firm of payments for nonproduction time on the job is difficult to determine precisely, such payments generally are treated as direct wages for accounting purposes, and as such are subject to federal income, Federal Insurance Contribution Act (FICA), and Federal Unemployment Tax Act (FUTA) taxes.

PAYMENTS FOR TIME NOT WORKED

The Chamber of Commerce survey generally indicates that payments for time not worked is an employer's costliest category of employee benefits. These benefits include vacation time, holiday pay, sick leave or sick days pay, various types of personal time off with pay, severance pay, and supplementary unemployment benefits. Today, these often are considered by employees as basic benefits, but paid time off other than vacation time was virtually unknown prior to World War II. Paid vacations generally were provided white-collar workers, but only half of the blue-collar workers had any vacations, and when a firm closed for a legal holiday employees typically lost a day of pay. This also was the case for time off because of sickness, a death in the family, jury duty, and the like.

Paid Vacations

Paid vacations are the most expensive type of payment for time not worked. They were first used by a few firms about seventy years ago to promote employee loyalty, health and safety, and productivity. These employers typically believed that if employees had one or two weeks of vacation per year for personal enjoyment and relaxation, they would be more productive during the other weeks. Vacations were viewed as instruments for recharging employees' physical and emotional energies, for building appreciation and respect among employees toward the employer, and for motivating employees to be more energetic and efficient in their jobs, but despite the fact that paid vacations were fostered by industrial psychologists and others on the basis of these considerable attributes, they were not widely granted prior to World War II. Now almost every organization has some form of vacation time.

Few, if any, firms continue to view paid vacations in the same simplistic context in which they were introduced into the employment relationship. Today vacations are considered by both employers and employees to be more a matter of employment rights and an ethical responsibility of the employer. Human-resource management people point out that paid vacations may not do much to improve morale and productivity directly, but their absence can be a deterrent to building effective employee relations.

A typical vacation policy grants employees two weeks off with pay after one complete year of service in the organization. Beyond the initial year of service, the length of vacation time generally increases with an employee's length of service. For example, some firms have a policy of two weeks for employees with one to five years of service, three weeks for employees with six to ten years of service, four weeks for employees with eleven to fifteen years of service, five weeks for employees with sixteen to twenty years of service, and six weeks for employees with more than twenty years of service. However, not all employers have such a rapid progression of increased vacation time, and many, particularly for production employees, have a maximum of four weeks vacation during a one-year period. Also, firms often have different vacation policies for specific employee groups such as production, supervisory, professional, and managerial employees. At one time, employees were required to schedule their vacations within specific months of the calendar year, but increased amounts of vacation time has helped to eliminate the concept of an official vacation period and has fostered the use of split vacations—for example, one week in the summer and one week in the spring or fall. In many instances supervisory approval of vacations is required, and a minimum time period such as a full week must be used in order for the employer to maintain an orderly flow of work. Some firms offer employees a cash bonus for each vacation week taken in the less popular vacation months such as January and February to help alleviate the scheduling pressures involved in providing acceptable vacation times for all employees.

Vacation pay is calculated in a manner consistent with an organization's overall compensation system. Normally, weekly salaried employees receive their base salary. Some people are paid 2 percent of their annual earnings for each week of vacation. Incentive workers may be paid on this basis, or on the basis of average weekly earnings or some shorter time period preceding the vacation.

In addition to establishing employees' vacation time entitlement, scheduling vacations and computing vacation pay, the vacation policy of a firm should include such things as qualifying dates for earned vacation, whether a carryover of unused vacation days to the next year is permitted, whether employees may take pay in lieu of actual vacation time, and a policy regarding sickness and holidays occurring during a vacation period. Vacation rules and rights should be objective, definitive, and clearly communicated.

Paid Holidays

Paid holidays have become a significant factor in employment relations in the past 50 years. By the 1950s a significant number of employees were provided with them, and today almost all employers offer paid holidays as part of their total compensation packages. As mentioned earlier, in the first half of this century, if an office or plant closed for a legal holiday the employees typically were not paid for the time. Thus, approximately six times a year employees had a day off without pay. This situation has changed dramatically. The Chamber of Commerce survey indicates that paid holidays rank second to paid vacations in terms of total employer costs covering payments for time not worked. The average employee receives approximately 10 paid holidays per year, and paid vacation and holiday time normally amount to one month per year for each employee.

The six most common paid holidays are New Year's Day, Memorial Day, Independence Day, Labor Day, Thanksgiving, and Christmas. A second group of holidays employers typically may include entirely or selectively is Martin Luther King, Jr. Day, Presidents' Day, Good Friday, the day after Thanksgiving, and Christmas Eve. Another group of holidays used on a selective basis by some firms includes New Year's Eve, Washington's and Lincoln's birthdays (Presidents' Day), Columbus Day, and Veteran's Day. Some regional holidays exist, such as Patriots' Day in Massachusetts, Lee's Day in the South, and Admission Day in California. The number of paid holidays varies along industry lines because manufacturers, banks, and retail stores serve different markets and adjust their holidays accordingly. Overall, however, the degree of uniformity among firms on their holiday policies and practices is greater than any differences. Religious holidays are treated separately in varying ways. Some firms provide extra days off, others allow time off without pay, and some permit employees to take time off on the condition they make up the time. The most equitable solution appears to be to allow each employee a few floating holidays. Some employers provide two or three such floating holidays, but the practice is not widespread. Additionally, some firms grant employees their birthdays as holidays. To facilitate work scheduling, whenever possible holiday observance is being shifted to a Monday, and the federal government has changed the official observance of four holidays, Presidents' Day, Memorial Day, Columbus Day, and Veteran's Day to Mondays. Labor Day always has been celebrated on a Monday, making a total of at least five Monday holidays a year.

Individuals typically are required to be full-time and permanent employees in order to receive holiday pay. Another common requirement is that an employee must work the day before and the day after the holiday to receive holiday pay. Employees required to work on a holiday are paid premium pay or given compensatory time off. In addition, some employers include appropriate shift premiums in the base calculation of holiday pay.

Sick Leave or Sick Days Pay

Sick leave or sick days pay, is provided to cover those one- or two-day periods when an employee cannot work because of some minor medical discomfort. Many employees do not receive it, but for some private workers, public school teachers, and many government employees sick leave is a significant benefit. Employers have experienced some abusive use of the sick days and as a response have developed some strategies to deal with the problem. For example, employees who do not use all their annual sick days allotment may be allowed to trade the unused portion for either cash or paid personal days off. A less-frequently used alternative allows employees to accumulate or bank sick leave. Some employers allow accumulation from year to year on a one-to-one basis (one day can be banked for each unused day in the previous year). Others permit only a partial carryover, such as one day bankable for every two unused days. One recent innovation is the use of sick leave sharing plans to deal with the problems of extended illness and/or the lack of any accumulated sick leave on the part of employees. A sick leave sharing plan is an employer-sponsored arrangement under which the unused leave of participating employees may be surrendered to a group bank of sick days. Employees with limited sick leave who suffer medical emergencies may use the sick leave that has been accrued by other employees and placed by them into the sharing plan. A medical emergency consists of an injury or illness that requires a prolonged absence from work and results in a loss of income for an employee whose accumulated sick leave has been exhausted.

Personal Time Off with Pay

Salary or pay continuance can be provided to employees for a variety of personal events. The most frequently recognized qualifying events for personal time off with pay include military reserve training, voting, jury duty, and a death in the family.

Military duty benefits permit employees to be absent for military reserve training duty with no loss of employment rights. Full pay for such time off usually is not granted, but a majority of companies keep the employee whole by making up any monetary loss because of lower military pay. A service eligibility of one year commonly is required for these benefits, and the maximum time period allowed for military duty absences typically is two weeks. Thus, if an employee who is in the military reserves is called into active service for an extended time period because of an international or military crisis these benefits have limited application. Usually there are other specific employment policies that cover the situation, and federal and state statutes protect the status of employees called into military service under these circumstances.

Allowing employees time to vote often is required by law. Over half of the states require time to be given, while approximately a third stipulate that employees must be paid for voting time.

Jury service typically is recognized by employers as a civic responsibility and thus they continue full pay for employees during the absence required for jury duty assignments. Sometimes the amount of the jury pay is deducted from the employee's base pay. Serving as a witness in court may be considered a basis for time off with pay, but this is not as widely applied as jury duty benefits.

A death in an employee's family usually is considered a legitimate reason for personal time off, and the time permitted generally is three days.

Other events also may qualify for paid time off. Election officials sometimes are granted time off with pay, typically receiving the difference between their base rate of pay and the amount earned as an election official. Time off for civic service is granted by a number of employers and provides a specified number of days off with pay to employees engaged in such activities as serving as a United Fund representative, teaching reading in a literacy program, or assisting in a disaster relief program. Illness in an employee's immediate family is recognized by some firms as a basis for granting one to five days off to allow the employee to care for the ailing family member. Some employers have instituted child care and eldercare programs to address this on a longer-term basis. Paid marriage leave of up to five days sometimes is granted to employees.

Paid maternity leave is provided by many employers by allowing employees to use sick leave and annual leave as paid time off for maternity, and some firms specifically grant maternity leave in the form of a set number of paid days off for maternity and/or an unpaid leave of absence. Organizations also must comply with the federal civil rights legislation concerning medical and sick leave coverages for pregnancy. A few employers grant paternity leave of up to five days off for a father to assist his wife after the birth of a child. Other employers permit new fathers to take an unpaid leave of absence of some specific duration. Additionally, paternity leave in some form is required by law in an increasing number of states. Family leave programs are covered in detail in Chapter 23 of the *Handbook*.

Personal days are being used as an emerging technique for dealing with the growing list of specific events for which days off with pay are granted. Under this approach each employee is given an allowance of two or more paid days off per year that can be used as the employee chooses. The number of days may vary on the basis of length of service, and this method frequently is used as an alternative to granting time off for such things as marriages, fatherhood, illness in the family, and regular medical and dental appointments.

Wellness leave is a relatively recent addition aimed at combating absenteeism. Under a typical program, each employee receives a half-hour of paid leave for each week of perfect attendance during all regularly scheduled work hours. Blood donations are encouraged by some employers, and employees are granted paid time off to donate blood. The time may vary from that sufficient to go to a mobile unit or up to four hours to go to a blood bank. Most unionized organizations permit time off with pay to employees who are involved in labor negotiations, grievance procedures, or certain other union activities specified in the collective bargaining agreement. Sabbatical leave is granted by a few organizations and generally is restricted to educational, research, professional, and religious settings. Employees who qualify are given up to one year of sabbatical leave at full or partial salary for performing work that has value to society or enhances the professional qualifications of the employee. A sabbatical leave should not be confused with a leave of absence for which an employer is not committed to continue any wage or salary payments and which is not considered part of an employee's benefit package.

Severance Pay

Employers may provide severance pay to terminated employees primarily in conjunction with the elimination of jobs as a result of technological changes, facility or plant closings, downsizing programs, site relocations, corporate mergers, and major reorganizations. Normally it does not cover people who resign voluntarily or who are discharged for cause. Severance-pay plans normally grant at least one week's pay, and larger amounts may be granted on the basis of length of service. Benefits may be paid as a lump sum or in weekly increments.

Supplemental Unemployment Benefits

During the late 1940s and early 1950s, unions were unsuccessful in their efforts to establish job security in the form of a guaranteed annual wage, and the supplemental unemployment benefit (SUB) plan was developed as an alternative approach to employment security. The first plans were negotiated in the mid-'50s with the basic automobile manufacturers and steel industry, and while they subsequently were introduced into many other industries as well, the total number of people in the work force covered by SUB plans has always remained relatively low. Most SUB plans in existence today cover employees in the manufacturing sector. Craft and service worker unions in nonmanufacturing industries tend to focus on other economic improvements and rely on the use of seniority to provide job security during low employment and recessionary periods. SUB plans exist exclusively in collective bargaining relationships to supplement the state unemployment insurance (UI) benefits of laid-off or terminated employees and continue payments to such employees after their state UI benefits have been exhausted. Some plans also permit employees who are working less than a full work week to draw SUB benefits during these slack work periods.

To be eligible for SUB benefits an employee must have worked for the employer for a specified amount of time, which varies among plans but is a minimum of one year. Employees usually start to accumulate SUB credits at the rate of one half unit for each week of work beginning with their date of employment and are credited with those units at the completion of the qualifying period. They then continue to accumulate additional units, generally up to a maximum of 52, which convert to 52 weeks of SUB benefits. Some benefit formulas integrate UI and SUB payments, with a combined amount under most formulas of 60 to 65 percent of average take-home pay. SUB plans are financed entirely by employer contributions, which range from 5 to 20 cents per work hour. The total liability of an employer at any point typically is limited to the amount of money accumulated by the plan, and each plan has a maximum amount of funds that can be accumulated. Contributions to some plans may cease when this point is reached but are resumed if the amount falls below the designated maximum. Alternatively, some SUB plans require that when the maximum level is reached, the employer must continue to make contributions, which are allocated to a savings and vacation plan and then again to the SUB plan until a designated amount is accumulated equally for each employee.

The overall experience of SUB plans reflects that they have been quite effective in dealing with periods of short-term unemployment, essentially the purpose for which they were designed, but less successful in cases of plant closings, mass layoffs, and long-term periods of unemployment, which have in the past decades taxed the assets and capabilities of the plans and forced affected employees to rely solely on UI benefits and ultimately on welfare benefits in some cases.

Tax Treatment of Payments for Time Not Worked

Generally, specific payments for time not worked are recorded as separate items in the accounts of an employer and in many cases are administered on a funded basis through periodic contributions. For example, SUB plans, as already mentioned, always are financed through contributions to a specific fund, and, in collective bargaining situations vacation, holiday, sick leave, and severance pay often are separately funded through joint (Taft-Hartley) trusts. In such cases, the full cost of these benefits can be clearly ascertained. Under the federal income tax laws, the costs to an employer of payments for time not worked are deductible business expenses to the extent such payments are reasonable, and they are taxable income for the employees who receive them, regardless of whether the payments are made directly by the employer or from a separate fund financed solely by the employer or on a multiemployer basis. The payments also are subject to FICA and FUTA taxes.

MISCELLANEOUS BENEFIT PAYMENTS

Employee benefits in the form of subsidized services and activities are diverse and are called miscellaneous benefits in the U.S. Chamber of Commerce *Annual Survey.* Various reasons exist for benefits that take the form of subsidized activities and services. Favorable treatment under Internal Revenue Code (IRC) Section 132 certainly plays a role in employers choosing to offer discounts and other noncash ''fringe'' benefits, while the basic reason for subsidizing employee transportation to and from work is to attract and retain capable employees. Counseling and physical fitness benefits usually are provided to improve efficiency, productivity, and morale. Educational subsidies and legal service benefits often have their genesis within collective bargaining, and credit unions, child care, and eldercare arrangements may be based on prevailing cultural and/or ethical values and possibly the presence of government-support mechanisms.

While the number of benefits in this classification is lengthy, the total amount of employer money spent for them is relatively small. However, this does not detract from their importance, particularly in specific employment settings, and some, such as child care services, are becoming increasingly important and costly for both employers and employees.

IRC Section 132

Many employer-subsidized services and activities are viewed as fringe benefits under Section 132 of the IRC and, as such, generally are deductible business expenses by the sponsoring employer and are not taxable income to employees. Specifically, IRC Section 132 provides that the following types of noncash benefits are excludable from an employee's gross income: (1) services that do not involve any additional costs for an employer; (2) qualified employee discounts; (3) working condition fringe benefits; (4) *de minimis* fringe benefits; and (5) the value of on-premises athletic facilities provided and operated by the employer. These benefits are excluded from gross income for purposes of FICA and FUTA taxes as well. In addition, IRC Section 132 benefits may be extended to retired and disabled former employees, to widows and widowers of deceased employees, to spouses and dependent children of employees, and to parents of employees in the case of air transportation.

A *no-additional-cost service benefit* is any service an employer normally sells to customers in the ordinary course of business and provides free to employees and their dependents at no substantial additional cost to the employer. Free stand-by flights to airline employees is an example of such a benefit.

A *qualified employee discount* is a discount given to employees on the price of "qualified" property or services offered by the employer to customers. To be qualified, the property or services must be those offered for sale to the employer's customers in the ordinary course of the business where the employee is working. Real or personal property held for investment is not qualified property. For property, the discount may not exceed the gross profit percentage of the price at which the property is offered for sale to customers. For services, the discount may not exceed 20 percent of the price the services are offered to customers.

A *working-condition fringe benefit* is any property or service provided to an employee that the employee would deduct for income tax purposes as an employee business expense had the employee purchased it. Such nontaxable working condition fringes include the value of the use of a company car for business purposes, subscriptions to business periodicals, on-the-job training, expenditures for business trips, and parking facilities.

De minimis fringe benefits are property or services so small in value that accounting for them is unreasonable or administratively impracticable. Some examples of *de minimis* fringe benefits include parties or picnics for employees, incidental supper money or taxi fare provided to employees who work overtime, traditional holiday gifts of small value, occasional tickets for entertainment events, and free coffee. A subsidized eating facility for employees is a *de minimis* benefit if it is located on or near the employer's business premises and the revenue generated by the facility normally equals or exceeds its direct operating costs.

To qualify for Section 132 treatment, an on-premises *athletic facility* must be operated by the employer, and substantially all use of it must be by the employees and their dependents.

Not all subsidized activities and services, or fringe benefits, are specifically set forth in IRC Section 132. The following is a list of the various types of subsidized activities and services, some of which have already been mentioned within the context of IRC Section 132:

1. Transportation and parking services.
2. Food services and subsidized meals.
3. Sports, recreation, and social activities.
4. Discounts on goods and services and purchasing assistance.
5. Credit unions.
6. Education subsidies.
7. Moving, housing, and relocation services.
8. Loans and home mortgages.
9. Charitable contributions and matching gifts.
10. Child adoption.
11. Clothing and tool reimbursement allowances.
12. Child care, eldercare and sick-child care.
13. Counseling.
14. Tax preparation and assistance.
15. Legal services.
16. Physical awareness and fitness programs.

Transportation and Parking Services

Transportation to and from work can be a major concern of employees and can result in considerable time and energy being devoted to organizing car pools and scrambling for parking spaces. Many employers have attempted to ease conditions by offering transportation in vans, and others provide free bus passes for employees. A few firms grant employees mileage allowances that are not considered a tax-favored employee benefit, while other forms of employer-provided commuting assistance already discussed may qualify for tax favored treatment as either a working condition or *de minimis* benefit under IRC Section 132. In addition, use of an employee's personal car for business may be reimbursed by the employer and generally results in a nontax result for employees.

Many employers provide free parking at the work site, some pay for employee parking at a private facility, and some give preferential parking treatment to employees who carpool frequently. On-site parking is a tax-free benefit under IRC Section 132. However, subsidized parking can result in a taxable benefit for the recipient employees if the parking allowance exceeds the amount spent for parking, and under those circumstances, the entire allowance is taxable.

Food Services and Subsidized Meals

One common arrangement for providing food services to employees is an employee cafeteria. The cafeteria may be directly operated by the employer or a separately owned and operated facility. Another approach is a room with vending machines and/or vending machines at various locations throughout the worksite, making food and beverages readily available for employees. A frequent complaint is that the vending machines do not offer sufficiently nutritious food.

Subsidized meals are provided wholly or partially by employers through in-house facilities for reasons that include inadequate outside eating facilities in the area, not wanting employees to leave the premises for lunch, and the belief that well-fed employees are better workers. A common feature in smaller companies, offices, and service types of businesses is free coffee, soft drinks, and snacks.

As previously discussed, the value of meals furnished on the working premises by an employer for the employer's convenience is not includible in the employees' gross incomes under specified circumstances (IRC Sections 132 and 119). Also, money provided by an employer to cover occasional meals for employees who are required to work overtime is not taxable income for the recipients under IRC Section 132.

Sports, Recreational, and Social Activities

Many organizations offer intraorganizational sports programs for employees, and some employers have representative teams in interorganizational and community athletic leagues as well. Social functions often are organized for employees and their families too. These include picnics, dance clubs, card and game parties, travel services, day trips, and group vacations. Employees frequently have a role in planning these programs to assure that the activities selected are what employees desire, will benefit employee relations, and are sufficiently varied to satisfy a wide diversity of employee interests. Thus, sports, recreational and social programs typically are designed to try and reach every employee in some way. Moreover, they enjoy tax-free status under IRC Section 132.

Discounts on Goods and Services and Purchasing Assistance

Various methods are used by firms to assist employees in purchasing merchandise more conveniently and at a savings. Many companies sell their own products at a discount to their employees, and sometimes items of other manufacturers are procured for the employee at a discount. A few firms have discount programs covering employee travel and entertainment expenditures for airline fares, vehicle rentals, tickets for amusement parks and sports events, motel and hotel rentals, and meals. Some organizations have equipment that must be replaced from time to time and sell the used equipment to employees at reasonable prices. As previously stated, qualified employee discounts in the form of reduced sales prices of products and services sold by the employer are excludable from the gross income of the recipient employees under IRC Section 132.

Credit Union

Credit unions are separate nonprofit entities organized to serve the financial needs of their members. Typically, the membership consists of the employees of a particular company or group of companies who elect to join the credit union. To become a member an employee usually must purchase shares for a minimal amount. These shares and additional savings deposits accrue interest at a rate determined by the board of directors. Generally, members can make savings deposits through payroll deduction as well as by direct deposits. A credit union member can apply for loans at a rate determined by the board of directors, and loan eligibility terms and rates of interest generally are more favorable than at commercial institutions. A credit union can be initiated by the employees themselves or with the aid of their employer. Various state credit union leagues and area chapters provide guidance to individual credit unions. Many of the larger credit unions have expanded their services in recent years by offering checking accounts, automatic teller services, and credit cards. While some employers may provide office space and a payroll deduction service for the credit union, the credit union is an activity operated by employees under federal and state legislation and supervision. Thus, as an employee benefit a credit union usually does not involve any federal income tax considerations for either the employer or the participating employees because the employer participation is considered *de minimis* under IRC Section 132.

Educational Subsidies

Educational benefit programs exist in the form of tuition aid and scholarship grants, and many firms conduct in-house educational programs ranging from basic literacy or remedial work to training aimed at improving job opportunities. Tuition-aid programs are based on the belief that education improves performance. Employees tend to use the programs, and they appear to be helpful in recruiting younger employees. College, high school, and vocational school studies typically are covered by tuition-aid programs, which normally provide total or partial payment of tuition and fees and books, or a flat fee per year. Payments of up to $5,250 per year received under an employer's educational assistance program may be excluded from gross income under IRC Section 127. Any excess is includible in the employee's gross income and is subject to income tax withholding. The plan must be in writing and be nondiscriminatory. The employer may pay the expenses directly, reimburse employees for their expenses or provide the education itself. Not covered as excludable assistance payments are tools or supplies the employee retains after completion of the course or the cost of meals, lodging, or transportation. Although the courses covered by the plan need not be job-related, courses involving sports, games, or hobbies may be covered only if they are relevant to the employer's business.

Some private employers provide college scholarships in the form of tuition, textbooks, and training material support for dependents of employees. These programs usually are administered directly by the sponsoring employer or through a trust. The costs of the benefits are deductible expenses for the employer and are taxable income for the employees who have participating dependents. However, the actual education can be provided by the employing institution or some other qualified organization. This extension of the tax-favored status to education benefits received at other institutions is included in IRC Section 117 in recognition of the fact that many colleges and universities have tuition exchange agreements with each other that complement their tuition reduction programs.

The amount of any qualified tuition reduction provided by an *educational institution* to its employees and/or family members may be excluded from gross income under specified circumstances under IRC Section 117. The tuition reduction must be provided to an employee of a qualified educational organization for the employee, his or her spouse, or dependent child. The reduction can only be used for education below the graduate level unless it is for the education of an employee who is a graduate student and who is engaged in teaching or research activities for his or her employer. Also, any qualified tuition reduction may be excluded only if it does not discriminate in favor of highly compensated employees.

Moving, Housing, and Relocation Services

Moving, housing, and relocation services provided in connection with transfers, promotions, or plant relocations include helping employees find living quarters, paying travel and moving expenses, and protecting employees from losses in the sale or purchase of their homes. Sometimes the employer will purchase the old home or provide a fixed fee for any differences incurred in mortgage costs. Some employers have an eligibility schedule listing the reimbursement a transferred employee receives, depending on the length of residence at the previous location and any cost-of-living differential between previous and new locations. These payments are made over a number of years. The federal income tax laws provide that any payment received by an employee, directly or indirectly, from his or her employer as a payment or reimbursement of moving expenses is income for the employee and subject to taxation under IRC Section 82. However, the employee is permitted to deduct the moving expenses to the extent they qualify as a deductible moving expense under IRC Section 217.

The high cost of housing has led some organizations to build homes, condominiums, and rental units with rental costs or purchase prices normally below existing market prices to attract individuals who might otherwise be reluctant to join or remain with the organization. When the housing involves a substantial subsidy by an employer, the participating employees have imputed income for this benefit.

Loans and Home Mortgages

Loans of various types are provided by individual firms to their employees, particularly when there is no credit union arrangement for employees. One service some employees find very useful is the opportunity to obtain emergency loans at little or no interest from their employer. To minimize any abuse of such a privilege, limits are set on the size and the number of times an employee can obtain such loans. Mortgage loans also are provided by or through employers at favorable interest rates. These often are made available to employees by banks and financial institutions. Some employers have found mortgage loan privileges a necessity for attracting and retaining employees, particularly in areas where critical residential housing problems exist. Additionally, federal legislation facilitates the use of mortgage or housing assistance trusts within collective bargaining relationships. These employer-financed trusts are used to provide employees with collateral mortgage assistance, direct subsidies for closing costs and fees, loans at favorable interest rates, and assistance with down payments. The trusts also can provide rental security deposits for those who elect to rent rather than buy housing.

Loans made by employers at below-market interest potentially can result in taxable income for the employee to the extent of the imputed interest. This is the difference between the applicable federal rate (market rate) and the interest charged by the employer. However, some of the imputed interest income on these loans may be treated as *de minimis* under IRC Section 132 because of the small dollar amount involved or may be nontaxable under the applicable rules for below-market interest loans under IRC Section 7872.

Charitable Contributions and Matching Gifts

Many employers match or supplement contributions made by employees to charities and/or educational institutions. There usually is a limit to the amount of such contributions that an organization will make to a specific charity or per year per employee. Matching gift programs are focused primarily on gifts to educational institutions, and a sponsoring employer usually requires the institution be an accredited college and the donor a full-time employee. The donors need not be alumni of the institution, and in many cases the participants are parents of students. Proof of the actual gift, rather than just a pledge, must be provided to the employer, and generally there is a limit of approximately $1,000 per employee per year. Employees do not receive any personal monetary benefit, and their reward is the satisfaction of donating to a charity with the help of their employer. Both the employer and employee have deductible charitable contributions for income tax purposes.

Child Adoption

Child adoption is one of legal services typically covered under legal service benefit plans which are covered in detail in Chapter 25 of the *Handbook*. However, a few firms provide employees with separate financial assistance for legal and other service costs incurred in adopting a child. One employer reimburses its employees as much as 80 percent of the adoption cost up to a maximum amount; another provides total reimbursement up to a maximum amount.

Clothing, Equipment, and Tool Reimbursement Allowances

Some companies require employees to wear safety clothing and may provide this free or at a discount or grant a purchase allowance for employees. Some employers grant clothing allowances or provide work clothing to employees, particularly in many types of rough and/or dirty work situations, and many service-related organizations provide their employees with well-styled clothing. Often employees are given a choice among a number of daily apparel options, and sometimes they even participate in the original design and selection of the items. Airlines, restaurants, banks, hotels, and automobile rental agencies, for example, feel that distinctive clothing permits the public to identify more easily with their employees.

Organizations that hire employees to do work that requires the use of small or hand tools frequently reimburse employees who must purchase these tools. Others grant employees an allowance for tool purchases.

The costs to an employee for the purchase and upkeep of a uniform, including laundering and cleaning, are deductible within limits as an itemized expense if the uniform is required as a condition of employment and is not adaptable for general wear. An itemized deduction also is allowed for special items required in an employee's work that do not replace items of ordinary clothing, such as special gloves for a fireman and boots required of a telephone company lineman. When an employee is reimbursed by the employer for such clothing, equipment, or tools, the reimbursement is not included in income if the expense is properly substantiated to the employer. Such reimbursement may be in the form of direct payments after proof of purchase by the employee, or as an annual reimbursement allowance account. If the expense is not substantiated to the employer, then the reimbursement is income for the employee. However, the overall federal income tax effect for the employee may be neutral because the employee is allowed to deduct the cost of the work-related expense within limits under the federal income tax laws.

Child Care and Eldercare

Child care benefits are increasingly a more common type of service provided by organizations. The benefits take many different forms and are both in-house and separately located facilities. Generally the value of dependent-child care assistance provided by an employer is not taxable income for the participating employees subject to a specified maximum under IRC Section 129.

Eldercare benefits are largely in the form of employee counseling and information concerning available community resources. A few organizations provide unpaid leave, and another small group supports day-care centers for elderly dependents. Sick-child care plans are designed to provide support to employees who have dependent children who are ill or otherwise incapacitated and in need of specialized temporary care.

Child care and eldercare plans are covered in detail in Chapter 22 of the *Handbook*.

Counseling

The types of counseling provided as employee benefits include medical, psychological, and family counseling services as well as others. Career-development counseling is made available to encourage employees to look toward the future and to pursue work opportunities. Outplacement counseling often is used to assist employees who lose their jobs involuntarily or who are disenchanted with their present jobs. The goal is to help these people to find new positions and/or careers. Employees frequently obtain various forms of counseling under medical expense benefit plans. Employee assistance programs (EAPs), legal service plans and retirement preparation programs have a counseling orientation as well. These programs are discussed in Chapters 24, 25, and 41 of the *Handbook,* respectively. Thus, many types of employment-related counseling are provided to employees on a tax-free basis, either as an employee benefit or as a human-resource activity of the employer. The major exception is personal financial planning/counseling which is discussed in detail in Chapter 26 of the *Handbook.*

Tax Preparation and Assistance

Tax preparation and assistance services help employees in meeting income tax requirements and may include advice concerning the reduction and/or deferral of tax liabilities. This benefit is provided on a very limited basis and usually only to executives as part of financial counseling services. However, even when financial counseling is provided as a benefit, tax preparation services may not be included as part of the financial services. The cost of tax preparation and assistance services provided to employees generally is deductible by an employer as a business expense under IRC Section 162, and is taxable income under IRC Section 61 to the employees who receive such services.

Legal Services

Legal service plans vary from the informal use of company counsel to structured formal plans with a specific set of scheduled benefits. Employer contributions for legal service plans as well as the value of legal services actually received under such plans are excludable, within limits, from the gross income of covered employees under IRC Section 120.

Physical Awareness and Fitness Programs

Some organizations provide educational and training programs to assist participants in understanding what they must do to improve their physical and emotional health. In addition, some organizations provide facilities and even grant time off to participate in physical fitness activities.

Employee Achievement Awards

Employee achievement awards are used by organizations to recognize individual employees for their special contributions to the organization and/or the community at large and also for their continuous years of service as valuable employees. The awards usually are in the form of an engraved clock or plaque, some property of personal interest to the recipient, extra vacation time, stock in the organization, or a sum of money. Typically the award is presented by an executive at a special ceremony, accompanied by a substantial amount of in-house participation and publicity. Awards programs require the presence of a well-administered employee information system to ensure that individual employees are given the recognition they deserve and serve as a demonstration of how an organization protects and rewards its human resources, particularly those who have accumulated some seniority. IRC Section 274 provides that an employer may deduct the cost of an employee achievement award up to $400 for all nonqualified plan awards and up to $1,600 for all qualified plan awards made to an employee during the tax year. Also, under IRC Section 274, employee achievement awards generally are excludable from an employee's gross income to the extent that the cost of the award is an allowable deduction for the employer. In order to obtain qualified status an employee achievement award program must be in writing and may not discriminate in favor of highly compensated employees as to eligibility or benefits, and the average cost of all qualified employee achievement awards may not exceed $400. Moreover, in order for an achievement award given for length-of-service to be excludable from income by an employee, it must conform to specific time and frequency requirements. Additionally, safety achievement awards that are based on safety accomplishments are not excludable from gross income when they are made to managers, administrators, clerical employees, or other professional employees or to an excessive number of employees within a tax year.

Suggestion Plans

Suggestion plans are formal programs designed to encourage employees to transmit their ideas for improving efficiency within the organization to management. Suggestions may cover a wide range of subjects such as work methods, equipment design, and safety devices and procedures, and employees who submit suggestions that are used are rewarded monetarily. These plans are based on a managerial belief that employees are capable of providing useful ideas and creative ideas when given the proper opportunity and encouragement. Along with cost-cutting advantages, several intangible benefits can be derived from a suggestion plan, such as improved overall morale, better communications between employees and managers, increased team spirit, and an impetus for employees to think about productivity, product quality and workplace safety.

Most firms pay employees a percentage of the net savings resulting from their suggestions, up to a maximum amount. A $1,000 top prize is typical for small companies, while large firms may pay as much as $100,000. The National Association of Suggestion Systems (NASS) reports that hundreds of thousands of suggestions are used annually by firms, and these result in savings of close to $1 billion.

Many employers allow employees 30 percent of the savings in the first year of using the suggestion, but, 15 to 20 percent is more typical. Others are more conservative, and some grant awards that are only minimal. Under some plans individual supervisors who help an employee in the development of a suggestion participate in the award, and where a formal group or several individuals working together have a suggestion accepted they jointly share the financial award.

Suggestion plans often have limited or only moderate success in generating meaningful ideas from employees, and a number of firms have installed suggestion systems and later discontinued them. Several reasons exist for this. Supervisors sometimes feel that such programs infringe on their time and may affect them adversely if employees make suggestions that they should have proposed. Some view all employee suggestions as undercutting their decision-making powers. Supervisors may also consider suggestions to be embarrassing to them because management's attention is drawn to matters where there is room for improvement. Employees sometimes look upon suggestion plans as potentially threatening to their job security. Productivity improvements by definition may constitute such a threat, and the potential financial reward may be viewed as meaningless when compared with keeping a job. Social considerations or group pressure also can be powerful dissuaders. Employees can, and have been informally, held responsible for terminating jobs of their co-workers through participation in a suggestion system.

Even in their administration, suggestion systems can pose problems. Employees whose suggestions have been rejected may feel they have been treated unfairly. Co-workers may be jealous or envious of those who have successfully participated, or an individual may claim a share of an award on the assertion that the idea was originally his or her own, and then subsequently was formally developed by the official recipient of the award. This is why under group suggestion systems, such as quality circles, all of the members share in an award. Even successful suggestion makers may not view their remuneration as fair, particularly if their suggestion, while accepted as an idea with merit, cannot be reduced to financial terms because it cannot provide tangible savings. The latter kind of suggestion, since it allows no estimate of first-year savings to share with the person submitting the idea, generally is rewarded by a one-shot bonus payment.

There are several rather well-established guidelines to be followed in developing and administering a successful suggestion plan. First, the backing of top management is essential. This means granting liberal awards, encouraging first-level supervision to solicit suggestions, and rewarding supervision in terms of the number of usable ideas generated from employees. Second, the evaluation of suggestions must be given to people of unquestionable objectivity and expertise. Usually a committee is used, and care must be taken to ensure that the committee is competent to evaluate suggestions. There also should be an understanding that the committee will defer suggestions to qualified people on those matters where it lacks the necessary background. Third, every suggestion must be handled with dispatch. Each suggestion received should be speedily acknowledged and reviewed, and the result should be communicated to the suggesting employee without delay. When a suggestion has been rejected, the communication of this also should contain an explicit explanation. Time limits can be set for each of these steps to move the process along. Fourth, the maximum possible publicity should be given to a suggestion program by the employer. Posters, bulletin board announcements, personalized letters from top management to employees' homes, and company newspaper or magazine announcements are all quite common as a means of gaining and maintaining employee interest in a program. Luncheons and banquets, in-house exhibits and public news releases honoring the winners also are useful. Most people appreciate attractive financial awards along with recognition for accomplishment, and awareness that co-workers have gained both can serve as a generator of suggestions from other employees.

Ultimately a plan will be evaluated in terms of the number of suggestions submitted, accepted, and rewarded, and also in terms of the savings generated. Undoubtedly, there are additional significant criteria, but these are the most obvious and pragmatic.

The payments made by an employer under a suggestion plan are treated as compensation. Thus, a firm has deductible ordinary and necessary expenses for such payments, and employees have gross income. However, some suggestion payments may be entitled to favorable income tax treatment as qualified achievement awards under IRC Section 274.

CONCLUSION

At first glance, the benefits described in this chapter may seem minor when compared with others such as pension and medical expense benefits. However, as already mentioned, payments for time not worked are an employer's largest outlay of funds for benefits (10.8 percent in 1989) of any category in the Chamber of Commerce's annual survey, and the three categories discussed here account for 13 percent of the 37.6 percent of annual payroll spent for benefits by all companies covered by the survey. On the more human side, these benefits serve to attract competent employees and to keep them satisfied in their jobs by improving the quality of their lives in more than just monetary ways.

PART 7

CAFETERIA BENEFIT PLANS

The tremendous diversity of today's work force which gives rise to dramatically different employee benefit needs is one of the forces behind the quest for more flexible benefit plans that can be tailored more to the individual needs and circumstances of employees. Also from an employer's perspective a flexible benefit approach can provide more efficiency in plan design and provide potentially better benefits at a more reasonable cost. Chapter 29 provides an overview of the reasons for the development of flexible benefit plans, the advantages and limitations associated with them and the regulatory structure under which they operate.

Chapter 30 discusses in detail how flexible benefit or cafeteria plans operate in practice. The design and administrative considerations in such plans are presented. Also discussed are flexible spending accounts which are frequently used as a valuable employee benefit planning tool along with a cafeteria plan.

CHAPTER 29

CAFETERIA APPROACHES TO BENEFIT PLANNING

Burton T. Beam, Jr.

Employee benefit plans that provide employees with some choice in the types and amounts of benefits they receive have become quite common. Traditionally, the cost of the optional or supplemental benefits made available under these plans was borne by the employee on an after-tax, payroll-deduction basis. Since the early 1970s, however, a steadily growing number of employers have established benefit programs in which all or a large segment of the employees are permitted to design their own benefit packages by using a prespecified number of employer dollars to purchase benefits from among a number of available options. Today it is estimated that almost a third of employers with more than 1,000 employees have full-fledged cafeteria (flexible benefit) plans. Still more of these larger employers and many small employers make flexible spending accounts (FSAs) available. FSAs are discussed later in this chapter. The popularity of these plans among employees, as well as continuing favorable tax legislation, has led most benefit consultants to predict that within a few years most employees will be provided benefits through a cafeteria plan.

While all employee benefit plans offering employee options might be viewed broadly as being flexible approaches to benefit planning, this chapter focuses primarily on those plans giving employees some choice in selecting the types and levels of benefits *provided with employer contributions*. The chapter first describes the structure of the plans available and continues by analyzing the reasons for employer interest in these plans, the barriers to their establishment, and the design decisions that must be made by employers.

TYPES OF PLANS

A cafeteria plan can be broadly defined as any employee benefit plan that allows an employee some choice in designing his or her own benefit package by selecting different types or levels of benefits funded with employer dollars. At this extreme, a benefit plan that allows an employee to select a health maintenance organization instead of an insured medical expense plan can be classified as a cafeteria plan. However, the more common use of the term *cafeteria plan* denotes something much more definite—a plan in which choices can be made among several different types of benefits and cash (that is, taxable and nontaxable benefits).

Prior to the addition of Section 125 to the Internal Revenue Code by the Revenue Act of 1978, the use of cafeteria plans had potentially adverse tax consequences for an employee. If an employee had a choice among benefits that normally were nontaxable (such as medical expense insurance or disability income insurance) and benefits that normally were taxable such as cash (or life insurance in excess of $50,000), the doctrine of constructive receipt resulted in the employee's being taxed as if he or she had elected the maximum taxable benefits that could have been obtained under the plan. Therefore, if employees could elect cash in lieu of the employer's medical expense plan, an employee who elected the medical expense plan would have taxable income merely because cash *could have* been elected. Obviously, this tax environment was not conducive to the use of cafeteria plans unless the only benefits contained in them were of a nontaxable nature.

Section 125 provides more favorable tax treatment to a cafeteria plan. As defined in that Code section, such plans are those under which all participants are employees and under which all participants may choose among two or more benefits consisting of qualified benefits and cash. Qualified benefits include most welfare benefits ordinarily resulting in no taxable income to employees if provided outside a cafeteria plan. There are some exceptions, and the following benefits cannot be provided under a cafeteria plan: scholarships and fellowships, transportation benefits, educational assistance, no-additional-cost services, and employee discounts. However, one normally taxable benefit—group term life insurance in excess of $50,000—can be included. In general, a cafeteria plan cannot include retirement benefits other than a 401(k) plan.

Recent IRS regulations define the term *cash* as being broader than it would otherwise appear. In addition to the actual receipt of dollars, a benefit in a cafeteria plan is treated as cash if two conditions are met. First, the benefit is not specifically prohibited by Section 125. This means that the benefit cannot defer compensation or be among the list of previously mentioned exceptions. Second, the benefit is provided on a taxable basis. This means that either (1) the cost of the benefit is paid by the employee with after-tax dollars on a payroll-deduction basis or (2) employer dollars are used to obtain the benefit, but the employer reports the cost of the benefit as taxable income for the employee. This recent change, for example, would allow the inclusion of group automobile insurance in a cafeteria plan, with the value of the coverage being reported as taxable income for each employee who selected the benefit. It also allows long-term disability coverage to be provided on an after-tax basis so that disability income benefits can be received tax-free.

As long as a cafeteria plan meets the Section 125 requirements, the issue of constructive receipt is of no concern. Employees have taxable income only to the extent they elect normally taxable benefits.

Core-Plus Plans

Probably the most common type of cafeteria plan is one that offers a basic core of benefits to all employees, plus a second layer of optional benefits from which an employee can choose the benefits he or she will add to the basic benefits. These optional benefits can be "purchased" with dollars, or credits, given to the employee as part of the benefit package. If an employee's credits are inadequate to purchase the desired benefits, the employee can make additional purchases with after-tax contributions or with before-tax reductions under a flexible spending account.

The following is an example of the plan of one employer. The basic benefits provided to all employees include term life insurance equal to 1½ times salary, travel accident insurance, medical expense coverage for the employee and dependents, and disability income insurance. Employees also are provided with "flexible credits" equal to from 3 to 6 percent of salary, depending on length of service. Each year, an employee is permitted to use his or her flexible credits to purchase benefits from among several options, including additional life insurance equal to one times salary, term life insurance on dependents, dental insurance for the employee and dependents, an annual physical examination for the employee, up to two weeks of additional vacation time, and cash. If an employee's flexible credits are insufficient to purchase the desired benefits, additional amounts can be contributed on a payroll-deduction basis.

A variation of this approach is to have the core plan be an "average" plan for which the employee makes no contribution. The employee then may receive credits if certain benefits are reduced. These credits can be used either to increase other benefits or, if the plan allows, to increase cash compensation.

Modular Plans

Another type of plan allows an employee a choice among several predesigned benefit packages. Typically, at least one of the packages involves no employee cost, and if an employee selects a more expensive package, the employee contributes to the cost of the package. Some employers may also include a bare-bones benefit package which results in cash being paid to an employee who selects it.

Under some plans using this "modular" approach, the predesigned packages may have significant differences, some being superior to others in certain respects, and inferior in others. Other plans using this approach have virtually identical packages, with the major difference being in the options offered for medical expense coverage. For example, the plan of one large bank offers three traditional insured plans, two HMOs, and a preferred provider organization.

Flexible Spending Accounts

Section 125 also allows employees to purchase certain benefits on a before-tax basis through the use of a flexible spending (reimbursement) account. FSAs, which technically are cafeteria plans, can be used by themselves or incorporated into a more comprehensive cafeteria plan. They are most commonly used alone by small employers who, primarily for cost reasons, are unwilling or unable to establish a broader plan. The cafeteria plans of most large employers contain FSAs as an integral part of the plan.

An FSA allows an employee to fund certain benefits on a before-tax basis through a salary reduction, which then is used to fund the cost of any qualified benefits that are included in the plan. However, they most commonly are used for employee contributions to the employer's medical expense plan, medical expenses not covered by the employer's plan, and dependent care expenses.

The amount of any salary reduction is credited to an employee's reimbursement account, and benefits are paid from this account when an employee properly files for such reimbursement. The amount of the salary reduction must be specified on a benefit-by-benefit basis prior to the beginning of the plan year during an enrollment period. Once made, changes are allowed only under certain circumstances discussed later in this chapter.

One issue faced by employers had been whether to limit benefit payments to the amount of a current account balance or allow an employee at any time during the year to receive benefits equal to the amount of his or her total annual salary reduction. For example, if an employee contributed $50 a month to an FSA to cover the cost of unreimbursed medical expenses, during the first month of the plan there would be only $50 of the $600 annual contribution in the account. If the employee incurred $400 of unreimbursed medical expenses during the month, should he or she be allowed a reimbursement of $50 or the full $400? The objection to allowing a $400 reimbursement is that the employer would lose $350 if the employee terminated employment before making any further contributions. Consequently most plans limited aggregate benefits to the total contributions made at the time benefits are received. However, a recent IRS regulation changed the rules, and medical and dental expense FSAs now must allow an amount equal to the full annual contribution for these benefits to be taken as benefits anytime during the year. Therefore the employee in the previous example would be entitled to a benefit payment of $400 after the first month. However, this regulation does not apply to other types of benefits such as dependent care under an FSA, and employers still have a choice of reimbursement policies for these.

If the monies in an FSA are not used during the plan year, they are forfeited and belong to the employer. Some employers keep the forfeited money and use it to offset the cost of administering the FSA program. However, almost anything can be done with the money, except giving it back individually to the persons who have forfeited it. Some employers give it to charity. Others credit it on a pro rata basis to the accounts of *all* participants in the FSA program for the following year or use it to reduce future benefit costs for all employees.

An election to participate in an FSA not only reduces salary for federal income tax purposes, it also lowers the wages on which Social

Security taxes are levied. Therefore, those employees who are below the wage-base limit after the reduction will pay less in Social Security taxes, and their future income benefits under Social Security will also be smaller. However, the reduction in benefits will be very small in most cases unless the salary reduction is very large. It should be noted that the employer's share of Social Security tax payments also will decrease, and in some cases the employer's savings actually may be large enough to fully offset the cost of administering the FSA program.

REASONS FOR EMPLOYER INTEREST

The growing employer interest in cafeteria plans can be traced to a number of factors. Many employers are concerned that employees may not fully appreciate the value of the benefits provided under conventional plans and hope that by giving an employee a specified total number of dollars for purchasing benefits and a list of available benefits and their costs, the employee will better perceive the total value of the benefits and the nature and relative costs of the individual benefits themselves.

The inflexible benefit structure of conventional employee benefit plans does not adequately meet the varying benefit needs of different employees and often leads to employee dissatisfaction. For example, single employees or older employees whose children are grown may see little value in substantial life insurance benefits. Also, the combined benefits of working couples may provide excessive coverage, the cost of which could be used for other purposes. Employers view the cafeteria approach to benefit planning as not only a means of more effectively meeting the benefit needs of different employees at a particular time, but also as a way of enabling an individual employee to better meet his or her needs as they change over time. Closely related is the feeling among employers that cafeteria plans are viewed as being less paternalistic than conventional employee benefit programs.

Employers also see the cafeteria approach to benefit planning as providing opportunities to control escalating benefit levels and costs associated with inflation and with the need to comply with federal and state legislation. Since a cafeteria plan essentially is a defined-contribution plan, rather than a defined-benefit plan, it provides a number of opportunities for controlling increases in benefit levels and costs. For example, it may encourage employees to choose medical expense options with larger deductibles to more efficiently use the fixed number of dollars allotted to them under the plan. It also may enable the employer to pass on to employees any increased benefit costs arising out of compliance with legislation prohibiting age and sex discrimination or mandating additional benefits. In addition, since increases in employer contributions for benefits are not tied directly to increases in benefit costs, the employer has the opportunity either to maintain its contributions at a fixed level or to grant percentage increases for benefits that are below the actual overall increase in employee benefit costs.

POTENTIAL BARRIERS

While the majority of employers have shown interest in the flexible approach to benefit planning, the failure of many of these employers to actually establish a cafeteria plan stems from the variety of obstacles that must be overcome before a plan can be successfully implemented. These potential barriers have included, among other things, (1) the tax environment; (2) the satisfaction of nondiscrimination rules; (3) potential problems associated with unwise benefit selection by employees; (4) negative attitudes on the part of employees, insurers, and unions; (5) adverse selection; and (6) increased implementation and administration costs. However, many of these barriers have been largely overcome or are less of an obstacle than in the past.

Taxation

Prior to the passage of the Revenue Act of 1978, a federal income tax picture clouded by the issue of constructive receipt probably was the principal barrier to the establishment of cafeteria plans. As previously mentioned, this is no longer an issue. However, each tax bill enacted by Congress seems to change the rules for cafeteria plans. This has led many employers to delay the implementation of cafeteria plans until the tax situation is more stable.

Nondiscrimination Rules

Section 125 imposes complex nondiscrimination tests on cafeteria plans, causing many employees to view the establishment of a cafeteria plan unfavorably. If these tests—an eligibility test, a concentration test, and a contributions and benefits test—are not met, highly compensated employees and/or key employees must include in gross income the value of the taxable benefits that could have been chosen under the plan. However, other employees suffer no adverse tax consequences.

The nondiscrimination tests are usually met by a full-fledged cafeteria plan that applies to all employees. However, particular care must be exercised in designing a plan that either covers only a segment of the employees or has only a small percentage of employees participating. The latter situation often occurs with flexible spending accounts.

The Eligibility Test

Cafeteria plans are subject to a two-part eligibility test, both parts of which must be satisfied. The first part of the test stipulates that no employee be required to complete more than 3 years of employment as a condition for participation and that the employment requirement for each employee be the same. In addition, any employee who satisfies the employment requirement and is otherwise entitled to participate must do so no later than the first day of the plan year following completion of the employment requirement unless the employee has separated from service in the interim.

The second part of the test requires that eligibility for participation must not be discriminatory in favor of highly compensated employees, who are defined as any of the following: officers, shareholders who own more than 5 percent of the voting power or value of all classes of the firm's stock, employees who are highly compensated based on all facts and circumstances, or spouses or dependents of any of the above.

The eligibility test uses Table 29–1, which is contained in IRS regulations and can best be explained with an example:

An employer has 1,000 employees, 800 nonhighly compensated and 200 highly compensated. The percentage of nonhighly compensated employees is 80 percent (800/1,000), for which the table shows a "safe harbor" percentage of 35. This means that if the percentage of nonhighly compensated employees eligible for the plan is equal to at least 35 percent of the percentage of highly compensated employees eligible, the plan satisfies the eligibility test. Assume that 160 people, or 80 percent of the highly compensated employees, are eligible. Then at least 28 percent, or 224, of the nonhighly compensated employees must be eligible ($.80 \times .35 = .28$ and $.28 \times 800 = 224$). The table also shows an unsafe harbor percentage of 25 percent. Using this figure instead of 35 percent yields

TABLE 29–1
IRC Section 125 Eligibility Test Safe and Unsafe Harbor Percentages

Nonhighly Compensated Employee Concentration Percentage	*Safe-Harbor Percentage*	*Unsafe-Harbor Percentage*
0–60	50	40
61	49.25	39.25
62	48.50	38.50
63	47.75	37.75
64	47	37
65	46.25	36.25
66	45.50	35.50
67	44.75	34.75
68	44	34
69	43.25	33.25
70	42.50	32.50
71	41.75	31.75
72	41	31
73	40.25	30.25
74	39.50	29.50
75	38.75	28.75
76	38	28
77	37.25	27.25
78	36.50	26.50
79	35.75	25.75
80	35	25
81	34.25	24.25
82	33.50	23.50
83	32.75	22.75
84	32	22
85	31.25	21.25
86	30.50	20.50
87	29.75	20
88	29	20
89	28.25	20
90	27.50	20
91	26.75	20
92	26	20
93	25.25	20
94	24.50	20
95	23.75	20
96	23	20
97	22.25	20
98	21.50	20
99	20.75	20

160 employees. If fewer than this number of nonhighly compensated employees are eligible, the eligibility test is failed.

If the number of eligible nonhighly compensated employees falls between the numbers determined by the two percentages (from 160 to 223 employees in this example), IRS regulations impose a facts-and-circumstances test to determine whether the eligibility test is passed or failed. According to the regulations, the following factors will be considered: (1) the underlying business reason for the eligibility classification, (2) the percentage of employees eligible, (3) the percentage of eligible employees in each salary range, and (4) the extent to which the eligibility classification is close to satisfying the safe-harbor rule. However, the regulations also state that none of these factors alone is determinative, and other facts and circumstances may be relevant.

The Concentration Test

Under the concentration test no more than 25 percent of the tax-favored benefits provided under the plan can be provided to *key employees*. A key employee of a firm is defined as any person who at any time during the current plan year or the preceding 4 plan years is any of the following:

- An officer of the firm who earns from the firm more than 50 percent of the IRC limit on the amount of benefits payable by a defined-benefit plan. This amount is indexed annually. For purposes of this rule the number of employees treated as officers is the greater of 3 or 10 percent of the firm's employees, subject to a maximum of 50. In applying the rule the following employees can be excluded: persons who are part-time, persons who are under 21, and persons with less than 6 months of service with the firm.
- One of the 10 employees owning the largest interests in the firm and having an annual compensation from the firm of more than $30,000.
- A more-than-5-percent owner of the firm.
- A more-than-1-percent owner of the firm who earns over $150,000 per year.
- A retired employee who was a key employee when he or she retired or terminated service.

This test is a particular problem if an employer has a large percentage of key employees and if key employees, being higher paid, contribute large amounts to flexible spending accounts.

Contributions and Benefits Test

Cafeteria plans cannot discriminate in favor of highly compensated participants with respect to contributions or benefits. Section 125 states that a cafeteria plan is *not* discriminatory if the plan's nontaxable benefits and total benefits (or the employer contributions allocable to each) do not discriminate in favor of highly compensated employees. In addition, a cafeteria plan providing health benefits is *not* discriminatory if contributions under the plan for each participant include an amount equal to 100 percent of the health benefit cost for the majority of similarly situated (that is, family- or single-coverage) highly compensated employees or to at least 75 percent of the health benefit cost for the similarly situated participant with the best health benefit coverage.

Contributions exceeding either of these amounts are nondiscriminatory if they bear a uniform relationship to an employee's compensation.

Unwise Employee Benefit Selection

Often employers are concerned that many employees may not have the expertise to select the proper benefits from among the alternatives offered under a cafeteria plan. Among other things, unwise employee benefit selection may result in inadequate employee protection following a catastrophic loss, in employee dissatisfaction with the plan, and in an increased potential for liability suits against the employer. To avoid, or at least minimize, these problems, employers establishing cafeteria plans must establish effective ongoing communication programs aimed at educating (and perhaps even counseling) employees about the full implications of various benefit choices available to them. However, despite the employer's best efforts, there remains a risk that the communication of incomplete or incorrect information may give rise to increased corporate liability. Moreover, in some cases, a strong conviction on the part of an employer that the organization has a moral obligation to prevent employees from financial injury through faulty decisions may itself be a major barrier to the establishment of a cafeteria plan.

Negative Attitudes

Negative attitudes on the part of employees, insurers, and unions also may serve as obstacles to the institution of a cafeteria plan.

Employees

Negative reactions on the part of employees to an announced proposal to convert from a conventional fixed benefit plan to a cafeteria plan can arise from a variety of sources: for example, suspicion concerning the employer's motivation in making the change, a fear that some important long-standing benefits may be lost, and an apprehension about now having to make choices among benefits of which the individual employee has little knowledge. Since employee support is critical if a cafeteria plan is to be truly successful, the employer must be willing to commit the time and resources necessary to combat these negative attitudes through adequately informing the employees about the reasons for the proposed program, its advantages and disadvantages, and its future implications for them. Moreover, by soliciting the opinions of employees on their perceived benefit needs and incorporating those findings into the decision-making process, the employer will not only help to allay initial employee concerns, but also minimize negative employee attitudes once the cafeteria plan has been instituted.

Insurers

The growth of the cafeteria approach to benefit planning also has been inhibited by the reluctance or inability of some insurance companies to underwrite the optional benefits an employer may wish to include in a cafeteria plan, or to provide meaningful assistance in connection with the implementation and administration of such a plan. While few insurers seem unwilling to experiment with almost any new concept, most have been concerned with the problem of adverse selection because of employee choice. Although the potential for adverse selection is a real problem that must be faced in underwriting a cafeteria plan, insurers are finding it is possible to control the problem at an acceptable level by incorporating certain safeguards in plan design. As a result, the number of insurers willing to underwrite cafeteria plans and provide administrative services for them has grown.

Unions

Unions generally have had a negative attitude toward employee benefit plans that contain optional benefits. Union management often feels that bargaining over optional benefits is contrary to the practice of bargaining for the best benefit program for all employees. As a result, most cafeteria plans do not apply to union employees.

Adverse Selection

When employees are allowed choice in selecting benefits, the problem of adverse selection arises because those employees who are likely to have claims will choose the benefits that will minimize their out-of-pocket costs. For example, an employee who previously selected a medical expense option with a high deductible might switch to a plan with a lower deductible if medical expenses are ongoing. An employee who previously rejected dental insurance or legal expense benefits is likely to elect these benefits if dental care or legal advice is anticipated in the near future.

It should be noted that adverse selection is a problem whether a plan is insured or self-funded. It also exists outside of cafeteria plans if choice is allowed. However, the degree of choice within a cafeteria plan tends to make the potential costs more severe unless actions are taken to combat the problem.

Several techniques are used to control adverse selection in cafeteria plans. Benefit limitations and restrictions on coverage can be included if a person wishes to add or change coverage at a date later than initial eligibility. This technique has been common in contributory benefit plans for many years. Another technique is to price the options accordingly. If an option is likely to encourage adverse selection, the cost to the employee for that option should be increased above the level that would have been charged if the option had been the only one available. Such pricing has been difficult in the past but is becoming easier and more accurate as more experience with cafeteria plans develops. The control of adverse selection is also one reason for the use of modular plans. If, for example, the medical expense plan in one option is likely to encourage adverse selection, the option may not include other options for which adverse selection is also a concern (such as dental or legal expense benefits). To further counter increased costs from the medical expense plan, the option may also offer minimal coverage for other types of benefits.

Administrative Costs

Cafeteria plans involve a number of additional developmental, administrative, and benefit costs over and above those associated with conventional employee benefit programs. Because of the greater complexity associated with employee choice, employers establishing cafeteria plans encounter higher initial and continuing administrative costs associated with, among other things, the need for additional employees to administer the program, additional computer time to process employee choices, and a more comprehensive communication program. However, as cafeteria plans have grown in popularity, numerous vendors have developed products that enable employers to carry out these administrative functions in a more cost-effective manner.

In addition to adverse selection, other factors are associated with cafeteria plans that might lead to increased benefit costs. For example, if an employee elected to divert a portion of the employer's contribution from a deferred compensation benefit (such as a profit-sharing plan) to an option involving current benefit payments (such as health insurance), the employer would lose the opportunity to recapture that contribution if the employee were to leave the company before becoming fully vested. Also, the establishment of a cafeteria plan may involve what one benefit consulting firm terms "buy-in" costs for the employer. While conventional employee benefit plans generally require employees to contribute at a uniform rate for group life insurance, cafeteria plans usually charge employees at rates that vary according to age. Since a shift from a conventional benefit plan to a cafeteria plan would increase substantially the cost of group life insurance for older employees, the employer may be required to subsidize that group.

CONSIDERATIONS IN PLAN DESIGN AND ADMINISTRATION

Before committing itself to the establishment of a cafeteria program, an employer must be sure a valid reason exists for converting the company's traditional benefit program to a flexible benefit approach. For example, if there is strong employee dissatisfaction with the current benefit program in general, the solution may lie in clearly identifying the sources of dissatisfaction and making appropriate adjustments in the existing benefit program rather than shifting to a cafeteria plan. However, if employee dissatisfaction arises from widely differing benefit needs on the part of the employees, conversion to a cafeteria plan may be appropriate. Beyond having a clearly defined purpose for converting from a traditional benefit program to a cafeteria program and being willing to bear the additional administrative costs associated with a flexible benefit approach, the employer faces a number of considerations in designing the plan and the system for its administration.

Plan Design

Numerous questions must be answered before a cafeteria plan can be designed properly. What benefits should be included in the plan? How should benefits be distributed between the basic and optional portions of the plan? How should an employee's flexible credits be calculated? To what extent should employees be allowed to change their benefit selections?

Benefits to Be Included

Probably the most fundamental decision in designing a cafeteria plan is determining what benefits to include. If an employer wants the plan to be viewed as meeting the differing needs of employees, it is important to receive employee input concerning the types of benefits perceived as being most desirable. An open dialogue with employees undoubtedly will lead to suggestions that every possible employee benefit be made available. The enthusiasm of many employees for a cafeteria plan will then be dampened when the employer rejects some, and possibly many, of these suggestions for cost, administrative, or psychological reasons. Consequently, it is important that certain ground rules be established regarding the benefits that are acceptable to the employer.

The employer must decide whether the plan should be limited to the types of benefits provided through traditional group insurance arrangements or be expanded to include other welfare benefits, retirement benefits, and, possibly, cash. At a minimum, it is important to ensure that an overall employee benefit program provide employees with protection against all major areas of personal risks. This suggests that a benefit program make at least some provision for life insurance, disability income protection, medical expense protection, and retirement benefits. However, it is not necessary that all these benefits be included in the cafeteria plan. For example, most employers have retirement plans separate from their cafeteria plans because of Section 125 requirements. Other employers make a 401(k) plan one of the available cafeteria options.

One controversial issue among employers who have adopted cafeteria plans is the extent to which cash should be an available option. Arguments in favor of a cash option often are based on the rationale that employees should not be forced to purchase optional benefits if they have no need or desire for them. In addition, cash may better fulfill the needs of many employees. For example, a young employee's greatest need may be the down payment for a home, and an older worker's greatest need may be the resources to pay college tuition for children. Some employers may believe the primary purpose of a cafeteria plan is to provide employee benefits only and not current income. If more than a modest amount of cash is available, employees will view the plan as a source of increasing their wages or salary rather than as an employee benefit. Therefore, the amount of cash that may be withdrawn often is limited. Also, experience has shown that the majority of employees will elect nontaxable benefits in lieu of cash.

In some respects, a cafeteria plan may be an ideal vehicle for providing less traditional types of benefits. Two examples are extra vacation time and child care. Some plans allow an employee to use flexible credits to purchase additional days of vacation. When available, this has proven a popular benefit, particularly among single employees. A problem may arise, however, if the work of vacationing employees must be assumed by nonvacationing employees in addition to their own regularly assigned work. Those not electing extra vacation time may feel resentful of doing the work of someone else who is away longer than the normal vacation period.

In recent years, there has been increasing pressure on employers to provide care for the children of employees. This represents an additional cost if added to a traditional existing benefit program. By including child care benefits in a cafeteria plan, those employees using them can pay for their cost, possibly with dollars from an FSA. However, lower-paid employees may be better off financially by paying for child care with out-of-pocket dollars and electing the income tax credit that is available for dependent care expenses. This issue is discussed more fully in Chapter 22 of the *Handbook.*

Another important consideration is the number of benefits to include in the plan. The greater the number of benefits, particularly optional benefits, the greater the administrative costs. A wide array of options also may be confusing to many employees and require the need for extra personnel to counsel employees or answer their questions.

A final concern is the problem of adverse selection. As previously mentioned, this problem can be controlled by proper plan design.

Basic versus Optional Benefits

As mentioned earlier, many cafeteria plans consist of two portions—a core of basic benefits received by all employees, and a second layer of optional benefits that may be purchased by each employee with flexible credits provided by the employer. Once a list of benefits has been determined, it is necessary to decide which benefits should be basic core benefits and which should be optional. At a minimum, the basic benefits should provide a reasonable level of protection against the major sources of personal risk and probably should include at least some life insurance, disability income, medical expense, and retirement benefits (unless these are included under a separate retirement plan). Some employers have included additional but less-critical benefits such as travel accident insurance or dependent life insurance in the basic portions of their plans.

The optional layer of the plan may include additional benefits not included in the basic plan and additional amounts of coverage for some of the basic plan's benefits, such as additional amounts of life insurance on the employee. In addition, the employee may have the option of electing alternative benefits to some or all of the benefits provided in the basic plan. For example, for an additional cost an employee may elect a medical expense plan with a smaller deductible. The plan will be more meaningful to employees if all or most employees can purchase at least some of the optional benefits.

Because of the current provisions of Section 125, cafeteria plans that include both taxable and nontaxable benefits should not include deferred compensation arrangements other than those involving 401(k) plans in the optional benefit layer if the issue of constructive receipt is to be avoided.

Level of Employer Contributions

An employer has considerable latitude in determining the amount of flexible credits made available to employees to purchase benefits under a cafeteria plan. These credits may be a function of one or more of the following factors: salary, age, family status, and length of service.

The major difficulty arises when the installation of a cafeteria plan is not accompanied by an overall increase in the amount of the employer's contributions to the employee benefit plan. It generally is felt that each employee should be provided with enough flexible credits so that he or she can purchase some optional benefits, which, together with basic benefits, are at least equivalent to the benefits provided by the old plan. This probably will lead an employer to determine the amount of flexible credits so that each employee receives an amount of flexible credits comparable to the difference in value between the benefits under the old plan for that employee and the basic benefits under the new cafeteria plan.

Including an FSA Option

An FSA option under a cafeteria plan enables employees to lower their taxes and therefore increase their spendable income. Ignoring any administrative costs, there probably is no reason not to offer this option to employees for benefits such as dependent care. However, salary deductions for medical expenses pose a dilemma. While they save taxes for the employees, they also may result in an employee obtaining nearly 100 percent reimbursement for medical expenses. This may have the effect of negating many of the cost-containment features contained in the employer's medical expense plan. In addition, employers now are faced with the risk of having employees terminate employment and filing claims that exceed their contributions up to the time of termination.

Employees' Ability to Change Benefits

Because the needs of employees change over time, a provision regarding employees' ability to change their benefit options must be incorporated into a cafeteria plan. This typically occurs on an annual basis because Section 125 requires that benefit elections under a cafeteria plan be made prior to the beginning of a plan year. These elections cannot be changed during the plan year except under certain specified circumstances if the plan allows such changes. While there is no requirement that a plan allow these changes, some or all of them are included in most plans. Changes in benefit elections are permissible under the following circumstances:

- Changes in family status. However, a change in benefit elections must be consistent with the change in family status. IRS regulations do not specifically define what is meant by changes in family status. However, the regulations include examples of the following:
  - An employee's marriage or divorce.
  - The death of an employee's spouse or a dependent.
  - The birth or adoption of a child.
  - The commencement or termination of employment by the employee's spouse.
  - A change from part-time to full-time employment status or vice versa by the employee or the employee's spouse.
  - An unpaid leave of absence taken by either the employee or the employee's spouse.
  - A significant change in an employee's or spouse's health coverage that is attributable to the spouse's employment.

- Separation from service. An employee who separates from service during a period of coverage may revoke existing benefit elections and terminate the receipt of benefits. However, the plan must prohibit the employee from making new benefit elections for the remainder of the plan year if he or she returns to service for the employer.
- Cessation of required contributions. A cafeteria plan can terminate coverage if an employee fails to make the required premium payments for the benefits elected. The employee is then prohibited from making new elections for the remainder of the plan year.
- Plan cost changes. A cafeteria plan can allow for an adjustment of employee contributions if the cost of a health plan is increased or decreased by an insurance company or other independent third-party provider of benefits. Such an adjustment is not allowed because of changes in self-insured health plans. Regulations also allow the revocation of previous elections and the selection of another health plan with *similar* coverage if costs are increased *significantly.* IRS regulations do not define either of the italicized terms.
- Plan coverage changes. An employee may also change to a *similar* health plan if a third-party provider of health benefits *significantly* curtails or ceases to provide health coverage during a plan year. This provision is particularly helpful in situations involving the insolvency of a provider of health benefits.

Two situations may arise to complicate the issue of benefit changes. First, the charges to employees for optional benefits must be adjusted periodically to reflect experience under the plan. If the charges for benefits rise between dates on which employees may change benefit selections, the employer must either absorb these charges or pass them to the employees, probably through increased after-tax payroll deductions. Consequently, most cafeteria plans have annual dates on which benefit changes may be made that are the same as the dates when charges for benefits are recalculated. This also usually relates to the date on which any insurance contracts providing benefits under the plan are renewed.

The second situation arises when the amount of the employees' flexible credits are based on their compensation. If an employee receives a pay increase between selection periods, can the employee be granted additional flexible credits to purchase additional benefits at that time? (Is this a change in family status that will allow additional benefits to be elected?) Under most cafeteria plans, the flexible credits available to all employees are calculated only once a year, usually at a date prior to the date by which any annual benefit changes must be made. Any changes in the employee's status during the year will have no effect on an employee's flexible credits until the following year on the date a recalculation is made.

Communication

The complexity of a cafeteria plan, compared with a traditional employee benefit plan, requires additional communication between the employer and the employees. Since the concept is new, employees will have many questions. It is doubtful if all these questions can be answered through written information, and group and individual meetings between employees and representatives of the employer probably will be required to explain the operation of the plan. Obviously, the need for these meetings will be greatest when a cafeteria plan is first installed and for newly hired employees.

Many employees unaccustomed to making choices about benefits also will seek advice concerning their benefit selections, and an employer must decide whether to require employees to make their selections with little guidance or to provide counseling services. Either alternative may have legal as well as moral implications. When counseling is provided, it is imperative that it be provided by a qualified and competent staff.

Updating the Plan

Any employee benefit plan will need periodic updating. However, some unique situations exist for cafeteria plans. Since such plans are advertised as better meeting the needs of individual employees, the employer must continually monitor the changing needs and desires of employees. As employee interest increases for benefits not included in the plan, they should be considered for inclusion. If little interest is shown in certain available benefits, a decision must be made regarding their continued availability, and, if certain optional benefits are selected by most employees, perhaps they should be incorporated as basic benefits.

The employer is faced with a dilemma if employee benefit costs rise more rapidly than the increases in flexible credits made available to the employees. For example, if the amount of flexible credits are a function of an employee's salary, which is usually the case, an increase of 10 percent in salary results in an increase of 10 percent in flexible credits. However, at the same time, the employee may be faced with an increased cost of 20 percent to retain the optional benefits currently selected under the plan. The employee must either reduce benefits or pay for a portion of the increased cost through additional payroll deductions. Obviously, neither situation is appealing to the employee. In deciding whether to increase flexible credits further, so the employee can choose the same benefits as previously selected, the employer is faced with the difficult task of balancing employee satisfaction with benefit cost control.

CONCLUSION

This chapter has discussed the concept of cafeteria approaches to benefit planning, the attractiveness of cafeteria plans to employers and employees, obstacles to their establishment, and basic issues in their design. Chapter 30 continues the discussion of flexible benefits from an operational viewpoint.

CHAPTER 30

CAFETERIA PLANS IN OPERATION

Melvin W. Borleis

The number of cafeteria plans in the United States has been growing steadily since the mid-1970s. As soon as the preferential tax treatment of these plans was codified by the addition of Section 125 to the Internal Revenue Code (IRC or Code) in 1978, a number of employers adopted them, at least to permit employees to make what were previously taxable medical plan contributions on a tax-deductible basis and/or to establish flexible spending accounts (FSAs). While these basic arrangements were communicated to employees as being flexible benefit plans designed to meet diverse employee needs and help increase spendable income by reducing federal tax, it is most likely that the tax savings were, in many instances, the prime motivation for their existence. Later, as the plans became more commonplace and they began to offer many more choices than before, they were used to achieve additional objectives including: permitting the employee some true discretion over how his or her compensation is received, giving the employer an advantage over competitors in recruiting new employees, and creating a more favorable impression of the employer to promote productivity and help decrease turnover.

Today, as employers have become more familiar with such plans, attention has turned to using them to help control spiraling employer costs in the health care area. As this purpose has materialized, plans have become more complex, including a selection among a number of indemnity type plans, health maintenance organizations (HMOs), and preferred providers. One object of increased choice may now be to encourage the employee, through skillful pricing techniques, to select the most efficient medical and/or dental arrangement. This chapter describes how these plans operate to achieve all these objectives, from the rudimentary objective of the delivery of tax-efficient compensation, to cost-transfer and control techniques, to meeting employee needs. Emphasis is on the "nuts and bolts" issues involved in operating these somewhat complex plans.

HOW CAFETERIA PLANS OPERATE

A "cafeteria" plan is defined by the IRC as a plan that permits the participant to choose between two or more benefits consisting of cash and qualified benefits. This definition has been changed back and forth in the tax law several times to include or exclude the term "cash." At the time of this writing (summer 1991), "cash" *is* included in the definition. By including the cash requirement, the formal definition of a cafeteria plan then would require the participant to execute a choice between taxable cash and a qualified (or specified nontaxable) benefit. Thus, for example, a choice between two otherwise nontaxable benefits, such as an HMO or a medical indemnity plan, would not meet the definition of a cafeteria plan for purposes of the law. However, the concept of salary reduction (reducing one's taxable income by some amount and directing that amount be used to purchase nontaxable benefits) is a choice between taxable cash and a qualified benefit. This choice, assuming that the benefit plan in question is not solely a 401(k) plan, would require the existence of a cafeteria plan. Thus, the choice between cash and an otherwise nontaxable benefit is a necessary, as well as a sufficient, condition to have a cafeteria plan.

A cafeteria plan is an intriguing device, in that by itself it does not have to provide any benefits in a traditional sense. Most traditional benefit plans provide specified benefits to participants in certain events, such as disability and death. The cafeteria plan simply permits the participant to choose between other benefit plans or cash. If such cash would already have been paid to the employee, say in the form of salary, the plan itself may not necessarily be providing a direct benefit other than the benefit of immediate tax avoidance. Certainly, if the employer makes independent contributions to the cafeteria plan, those contributions constitute a benefit.

In essence though, what a cafeteria plan does is direct contributions to and participation in other benefit plans. As such, the cafeteria plan is relatively simple in concept but more involved in operation.

To some extent employers offered benefit choices to employees long before there were flexible benefit plans. Many contributory plans permitted employees to elect the level at which they would participate. An example might be to offer group term life insurance to employees on an after-tax contributory basis and to permit the employee to elect one, two, or three times pay as coverage, with contributions varying based on the election. Such an arrangement does not require or meet the definition of a cafeteria plan but nonetheless offers the employee a choice in the level of coverage he or she desires. However, permitting the employee to reduce salary by $100 per month and have $1,200 placed in a medical spending account annually is a choice between a *taxable cash amount* and a *nontaxable medical benefit* and, therefore, requires the existence of a formal cafeteria plan. These types of choices can be integrated into one program for any given employer. In this case, the employer may communicate all choices to the employee as part of a flexible benefit plan, but only one of the choices would truly require the existence of a formal "cafeteria plan" as defined in the IRC. From the employee's standpoint, the flexible benefit plan would include all the choices, but from a legal standpoint, only certain choices would be considered under the cafeteria plan. Thus, there is a distinction between the *appearance* of the plan (the way the plan is presented to participants) and the provisions in the actual cafeteria plan document itself. For purposes of this chapter, the term *cafeteria plan* is used to mean a legally defined plan that meets all the criteria of Section 125 of the IRC, while *flexible benefit plan* is used to represent the plan communicated to employees, since this latter plan may contain more choices and elements than the former.

It is possible to have a cafeteria plan that includes after-tax contributions from the employee, but there seems to be little or no advantage in this structure, since such contributory benefit plans are permitted without the use of the cafeteria plan. Today, most employers offering flexible benefit plans that include after-tax employee contributions may communicate those benefits as part of the flexible benefit plan but do not include them in the formal cafeteria plan document. Again, there is a distinction between the presentation of the plan and the plan itself.

The Role of a Cafeteria Plan

The role of the cafeteria plan can best be seen by examining the flow of contributions to other plans controlled by the cafeteria plan. In a traditional (noncafeteria) benefit structure, as shown in Figure 30–1, three kinds of benefits are provided. "Benefit A" represents benefits paid for solely by the employee. These might include such optional benefit plans as long-term disability coverage or a contributory group life insurance plan. "Benefit B" represents those plans funded or provided solely by employer contributions. Included here may be the pension plan, any employer-provided welfare coverage, and paid time off. Lastly, the structure includes a medical plan to which both the employee and the employer contribute. The arrows in Figure 30–1 represent the contributions to these various benefit plans.

Figure 30–2 illustrates this same set of benefits using a cafeteria plan. In this case, the cafeteria plan serves solely to permit the employee to make what were previously taxable contributions on a now pretax basis. All other benefits and contributions in the program have remained as they were in the traditional structure.

FIGURE 30–1
Traditional Benefit Plan Structure

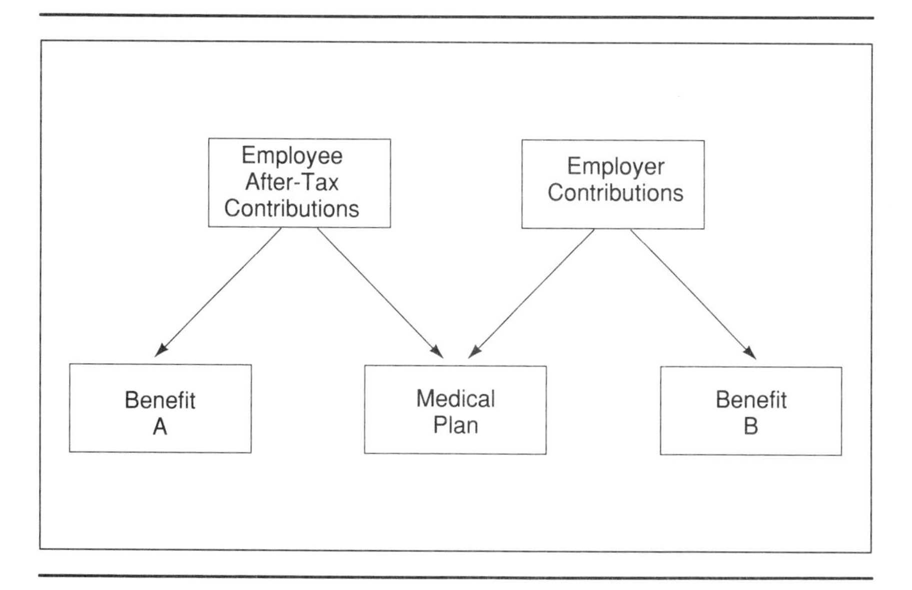

FIGURE 30–2
Basic Cafeteria Plan

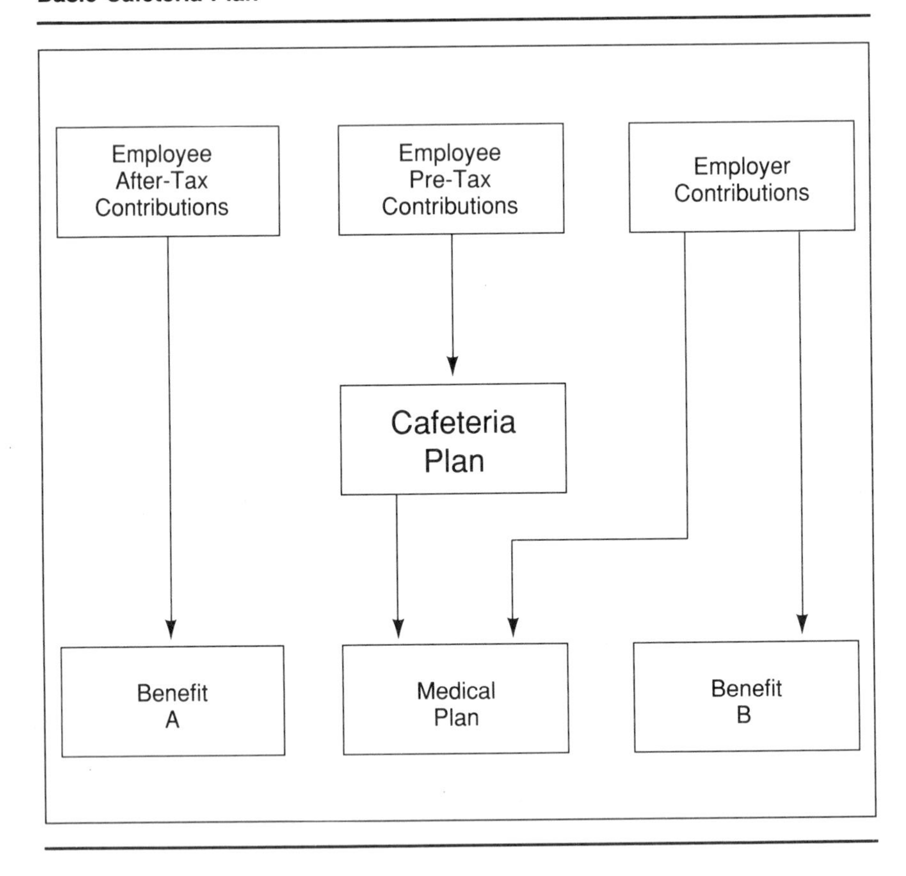

In Figure 30–3, the cafeteria plan has been expanded to include flexible spending accounts (FSAs), the choice of three different medical plans, and an option to receive cash if there are any unused employer contributions. Employer contributions are directed to the cafeteria plan and dispersed from there based on employee election. This does not mean *all* employer contributions are funneled through the cafeteria plan—only those over which the employee has some choice. The employer could—and this is the most common case—continue to pay part of the medical plan cost directly. This is simply a function of deciding how much control the employer wishes to give to the employee. For example, if the annual cost of Medical Plans 1, 2, and 3

FIGURE 30–3
Expanded Cafeteria Plan

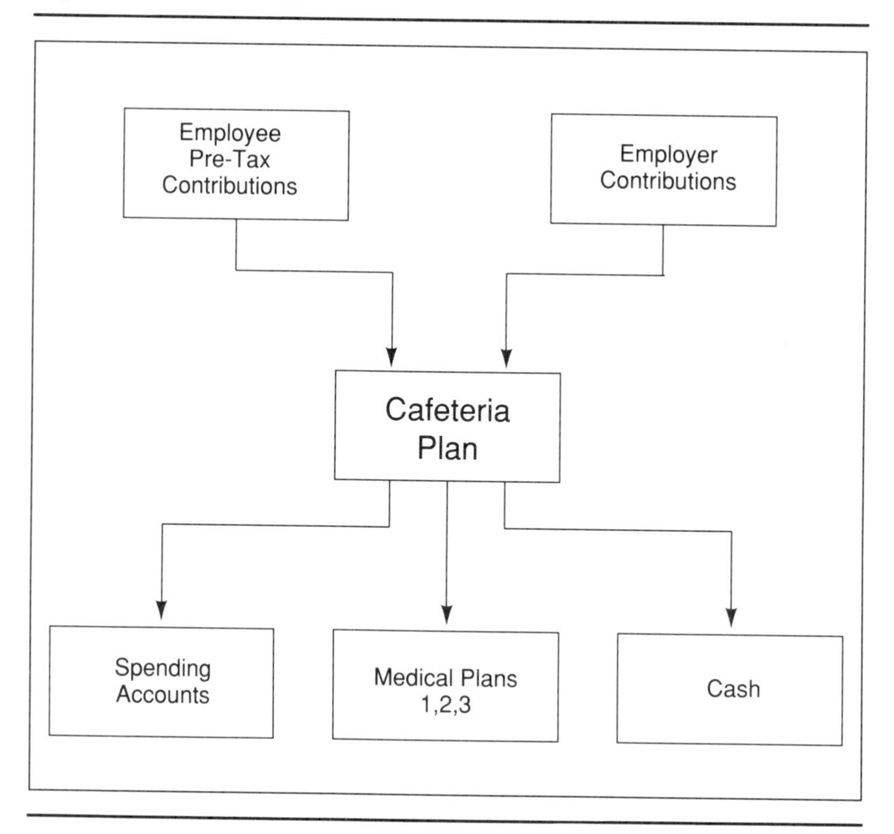

Note: Those benefits provided solely by employee after-tax contributions and those paid for solely by the employer (Benefits A and B, respectively, in Figure 30–2) have been removed from this figure since they are assumed to be outside the cafeteria plan.

were $2,500, $2,000, and $1,800, respectively, the employer contribution to the cafeteria plan could be any amount desired. Assume Plan 2 for $2,000 provides coverage under the traditional medical indemnity plan in place prior to creating the cafeteria plan and the employer wants to ensure that employees have enough ''flexible dollars'' to buy coverage under that plan without making any additional contributions. In this case, the employer can contribute $2,000 to the cafeteria plan, and if an employee elects medical coverage under Plan 2, the full employer contribution is consumed by that choice. If the employee elects Plan 1, costing $2,500 for, say, a higher level of coverage, he or she must contribute the additional $500 through salary reduction. Also, if this employee wants a medical FSA, the amount placed in the FSA would have to come from salary reduction. There could be no cash election in either of these situations since there are no remaining unused flexible dollars. However, if the employee were to elect Medical Plan 3, say an HMO, with a cost of $1,800, there would be $200 remaining that could be taken as cash or placed in the spending account.

If the employer did not wish the full cost of the coverage to be directed by the employee, it might contribute $1,800 to the medical plan directly and only $200 to the cafeteria plan. In this case, the cost of Plan 2, as far as the cafeteria plan is concerned, would be $200, Plan 1 would be $700, and Plan 3 would be $0. The cost to the employee (paid by salary reduction) for Plan 2 still is $0; it is $500 for Plan 1, and Plan 3 yields $200 of available cash. The same result is achieved, only the contribution and the cost of the options as communicated to the participants are different.

If the employer wished to transfer some of the cost of Plans 1 and 2 to the employee, the employer contribution to the medical plan might still be $1,800 directly, but the contribution to the cafeteria plan would be perhaps only $100 as opposed to the $200 in the example. In this situation, it would now cost the employee (through salary reduction) $100 to purchase coverage under Plan 2 and $600 to purchase coverages under Plan 1. This can also be used as an incentive to attract people to Plan 3, which may be a plan designed to control medical costs more efficiently than the other plans.

Naturally, any combination of contributions and option pricing is possible to achieve plan objectives. However, employers have quickly determined that it pays to provide a sufficient number of flexible dollars as an employer contribution so that employees can purchase the same coverage they had prior to the creation of the cafeteria plan without additional cost. At least this may be the case in the first year of the cafeteria plan, and it is particularly true if no employee contributions were ever taken for medical coverage before implementation of the cafeteria plan. However, some employers may include some cost transfer immediately upon implementation of a flexible benefit plan.

In Figure 30–4, the cafeteria plan has been expanded to include a number of other benefit choices and a new source of flexible dollars has been added, those that result from trading other benefits. The most

FIGURE 30–4
Comprehensive Cafeteria Plan

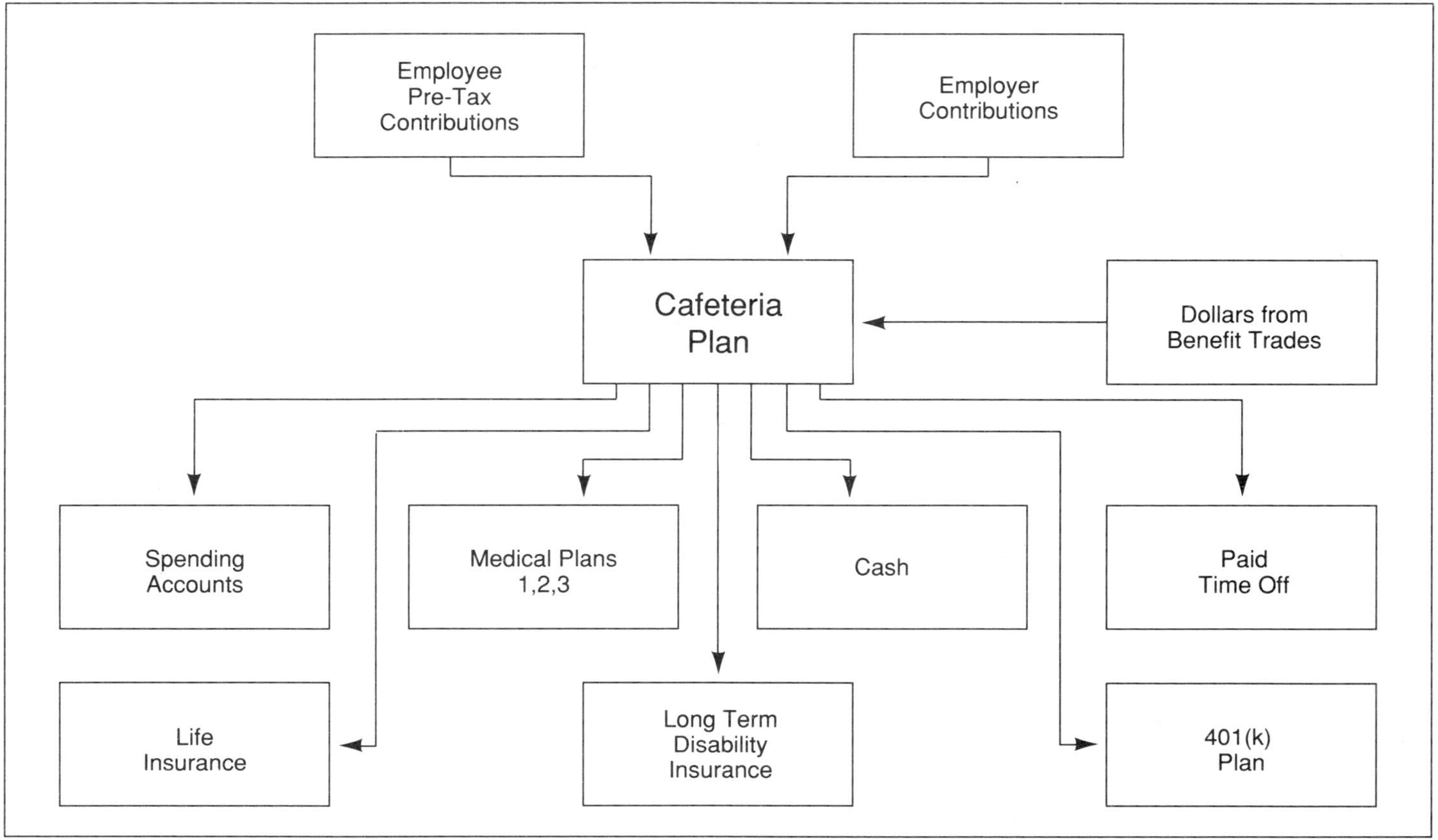

common benefit traded is paid time off, so that an employee might elect to trade a few days of vacation time for additional flexible dollars to be spent on other benefits. The concept of vacation trading is discussed later in this chapter. The figure encompasses cafeteria plans in varying degrees of complexity. However, the role of the cafeteria plan in all cases is to direct the contributions to and therefore the participation in the other plans. Plans maintained outside the cafeteria plan to which employees make contributions on an after-tax basis can continue to be so provided and can even be included on the employee election form and communicated as part of the flexible benefit plan provided by the employer. They do not have to be part of the cafeteria plan.

Salary Reduction Concepts

The cornerstone of many cafeteria plans is the concept of salary reduction. Through salary reduction, the employer uses a cafeteria plan to permit employees to make otherwise taxable contributions to existing traditional plans on a pretax basis. The most common example of this is using a cafeteria plan to permit employees to make monthly contributions to a medical plan and to have those contributions be extracted from salary before the application of federal or Social Security tax. This arrangement has come to be known as "salary reduction."

It is important to note that while the employee views this arrangement as a reduction and redirection of the amount in question to purchase benefits, what really is happening is that the amount has become an employer contribution. For example, consider an employee earning $25,000 annually as taxable income and contributing $83.33 a month after taxes toward the cost of providing family coverage under a medical indemnity plan. The employee sees the $83.33 as a salary deduction and considers it a direct cost to himself or herself. Under a cafeteria arrangement, the $83.33 deduction becomes a salary *reduction* and is taken from salary *before* the application of tax. In this case, the employee is still likely to consider the salary reduction as his or her own contribution. However, the reason that the $83.33 now escapes taxation is because it is now considered as an employer contribution to a medical plan. Thus, for tax purposes, this employee is assumed to have an annual wage of $24,000 and the employer is making a $1,000 ($83.33 x 12 [rounded]) nontaxable contribution to the medical plan on his or her behalf.

The concept of salary reduction is important to the operation of many cafeteria plans, since it serves as a means of creating contributions to the plan. However, while such salary reductions result in nontaxable employer contributions to these plans, the employee will view the contribution as his or her own. This is particularly true in the case of flexible spending accounts being funded wholly from salary reduction amounts.

Salary reduction has implications beyond simply providing a method for making contributions to a cafeteria plan that are free from federal income tax. For example:

- To the extent the salary reduction reduces an employee's annual compensation below the Social Security wage base ($55,500 in 1992 for Social Security, $130,200 for Medicare), or if the salary prior to any reductions does not exceed these amounts, the employee will pay less Social Security and/or Medicare tax. Likewise, the tax paid by the employer on behalf of this employee will also be less, representing a cost savings for the employer. It should be noted that if a 401(k) plan is a part of the cafeteria plan, contributions to that plan from salary reductions to the cafeteria plan do not escape consideration for Social Security and Medicare.
- Social Security benefits will be computed based on the new, reduced salary. While this has minimal impact (the reduction in ultimate benefit is small compared with the FICA tax saving), it is nonetheless a result of salary reduction.
- Since most states and other municipal taxing entities base their income tax on the amount taxable for federal purposes (at least as far as wages are concerned), the use of salary reduction also can serve to reduce these taxes. In 1991, only two states (New Jersey and Pennsylvania) consider salary reduction contributions to cafeteria plans as part of earnings for purposes of state income tax. However, each state and local government has its own laws in this regard and they should be reviewed before establishing a cafeteria plan. Also, a number of states include salary reduction amounts in compensation for purposes of determining the tax for unemployment insurance and workers' compensation.
- Other benefit plans may be affected. Group life insurance, long-term disability, and sick leave plans may base benefits on actual salary. Pension and profit-sharing plans also may need to be revised to reflect the desired level of compensation on which benefits are based.

• The new pay could affect those eligible for overtime or similar base-pay-related payments. Bonus policies also should be reexamined.

• The new salary amount is used for personal financial purposes such as eligibility for a mortgage and other credit applications.

• The employer also may need to recognize a difference between a salary reduction and a salary deduction. If an employer were providing medical coverage at no cost to an employee and the employee is on an authorized leave of absence, the employer might continue coverage during such leave. (The employer does not have to do this, but many do.) If the employer, however, required a monthly contribution from the employee for the coverage while the employee was working, chances are the employer would want that contribution to continue during periods of unpaid leave. The argument can be made that the employee who is now earning $24,000 a year (as opposed to the $25,000 before the cafeteria plan), truly has a salary of $24,000 and is now covered by an employer-provided (free from contribution by the employee) medical plan.

It is interesting to note that the above issues appear only because of salary reduction. Had the employee in the example above been hired at a salary of $24,000 and had the employer been providing the medical coverage at no cost to the employee (a structure yielding the same financial result as the salary-reduction approach), none of these issues would be likely to arise. Of course, other considerations, such as the competitiveness of starting salaries, the involvement of the employee in the medical plan, and the way employees view their direct compensation and benefits would have to be addressed. All these issues should be evaluated when considering any significant amounts of salary reduction.

Creating and Spending Flexible Dollars

While flexible benefit plans come in different sizes and shapes and may be presented to employees as having significantly differing structures, all such plans have as their core element the creation and spending of flexible credits or dollars. Since these plans serve to direct contributions to other benefit plans as participants choose to participate in them, the flexible benefit plan must have a source of credits or dollars that can be so directed. The remainder of this chapter refers to this medium of exchange as *flexible dollars*. Regardless of whether a flexible benefit plan is a simple salary-reduction type, a reduction-to-core type, a modular or a prepackaged plan, or a plan offering a broad array of choices and exchanges, it will, at its innermost level, look and operate the same as any other flexible benefit plan. This is true because the primary purpose of the plan is to provide a mechanism for the participant to create flexible dollars and a means for those dollars to be spent. The only differences are the number of sources of flexible dollars and the number of ways they can be expended. This can be seen by further analysis of the possible types of flexible benefit plans.

- *Simple Salary-Reduction Arrangements.* Employees elect to reduce salary, using the approach discussed earlier in this chapter, and direct that portion of their income to buy other benefits. In the simplest case, this may involve reducing salary to pay for medical plan contributions and possibly to fund a medical spending account and/or a dependent care account. Even in this rudimentary structure, the flexible plan is facilitating the creation and spending of flexible dollars. In this case, there is only one means by which the employee can create flexible dollars, that of salary reduction. There are three ways these dollars can be spent: to pay premiums to a medical plan, to fund a medical care spending account, to fund a dependent care spending account, or any combination thereof.
- *Core-Plus Options.* The employer provides the traditional benefit programs as a core program with lower levels of coverage than in the original plans. The employer is saving money (since plans providing lesser coverage are assumed to have less cost associated with them) and the employer passes along some portion of that savings to the employee in the form of an employer contribution to the flexible benefit plan. The employee can then use this contribution to purchase additional benefits to bring his or her coverage back up to the level originally provided under the traditional program, to purchase other offered benefits, or (if the plan permits) to take all or part of the difference in cash. Should the employee desire to purchase more benefits than can be bought with the flexible dollars provided by the employer, additional dollars may be created through salary reduction. This popular flexible benefits plan design still exhibits the same characteristics of creating flexible dollars and spending them. In this case, there are two sources of flexible dollars: employer contributions that result from reducing the level of coverages in the traditional benefit plans, and salary reduction. The employee may have more places to spend those dollars including a cash election and spending accounts.

• *Modular or Prepackaged Plans.* The only difference between this type of flexible benefit plan and the plan described above is that the employee may not select individual benefit coverages independently from another. Rather, the benefit plans are prepackaged in modules or groups that must be selected in their entirety. For example, if the employee wants the better medical coverage, he or she may have to select a higher amount of life insurance, since this latter benefit is packaged with the former. These arrangements had, until recently, been thought to be easier to administer and were designed further to eliminate some elements of adverse selection. However, the plans are not exceptionally popular with employees because they do not permit the employee the full range of possible choices, and their use to control adverse selection has been shown to be unnecessary. Nonetheless, these structures still involve the creation and spending of flexible dollars.
• *Full-Choice Plans.* In these arrangements, employees are permitted to choose among a wide variety of benefits and may have a greater number of flexible dollars to spend. Here the employer provides the employee with a set amount of flexible dollars, may permit salary reduction, and may also permit the employee to trade existing benefits (such as excess vacation time) for yet more flexible dollars. These dollars then could be spent on a wide array of benefits including cash elections, deposits to 401(k) plans, and FSAs. However, the internal structure of this flexible benefit arrangement still involves the creation of flexible dollars and spending of these dollars to purchase desired coverages.

Thus, one could conclude that all flexible benefit plans operate in essentially the same manner. They revolve around the creation and spending of flexible dollars or credits. It is possible in any of the structures discussed above to incorporate after-tax contributions. Thus, an employee could pay for a long-term disability plan or group term life insurance in excess of $50,000 with traditional after-tax contributions while paying for group life insurance up to $50,000 and other benefits with pretax flexible dollars that have been created from any number of sources.

Sources of Flexible Dollars

There are a variety of ways to create flexible dollars. First, existing employer contributions to some or all of the benefits to be provided can be made to the flexible benefits plan and redirected by the employee.

Additionally, new employer contributions can be used. Employees can create flexible dollars through the use of salary reduction or by selling off vacation time that would otherwise be taken in the next year. Prior vacation that has already been carried forward might be frozen by the employer and sold off to create flexible dollars as well. Using carry-forward vacation for this purpose can result in a cost saving, since the number of dollars given for an hour or day of vacation can be frozen until all such time is consumed. Further, carry-forward vacation can be eliminated.

Additional sources of flexible dollars can come from reducing the benefit program to a lesser level or by the employee's election of lesser coverage or nonelection of unneeded coverage.

Spending Flexible Dollars

The flexible dollars created in the flexible benefit plan can be used to provide coverage under any of the following:

- Medical indemnity plans, including those with preferred provider organizations (PPOs).
- Health maintenance organizations.
- Dental plans.
- Vision care plans.
- Flexible spending accounts.
- Group term life insurance, including accidental death and dismemberment insurance.
- Short-term disability insurance.
- Long-term disability insurance.
- 401(k) plans.
- Cash.
- Vacation or other time-off plans.

Flexible (tax-free) dollars cannot be used for scholarships or fellowships, certain transportation benefits such as van-pooling, educational benefits, certain *de minimis* benefits such as those described in Section 132 of the IRC (including dependent term life insurance), or meals and lodging. Under current tax law there is no provision to explicitly permit their use to pay premiums to a long-term care plan. With the number of sources of flexible dollars available and the number of ways they can be spent, a wide variety of combinations is possible in the plan design.

USING CAFETERIA PLANS TO CONTROL COSTS

As the costs of benefit plans, driven almost totally by spiraling medical costs, have continued to rise rapidly, employers have turned to cafeteria plans to help harness a seemingly otherwise uncontrollable expense. Basically, there are only two ways that medical cost control can be achieved through a cafeteria plan. The first is to transfer a portion of the cost to the employee or the government and the second is to use the mechanism to provide an incentive for employees to participate in plans that encourage more efficient delivery of health care. The former results in an immediate savings to the employer, while the latter has a longer-term payoff for both the employer and the employee. To illustrate the use of a cafeteria plan to effect cost transfer, consider an employer who is providing an indemnity-type medical plan with a cost per employee unit of $2,000 per year. Assume also that the employee is making a contribution toward that cost of $60 per month, or $720 a year on an after-tax basis. This represents a traditional benefit structure and is shown in column I of the chart in Figure 30–5.

Under the traditional approach to funding this medical plan, the employee's contribution is $720 a year after-tax and the employer's is $1,280 per year. The true cost to the employee on an after-tax basis is

FIGURE 30–5
Medical Plan Contributions—Cost Transfer

	I *Before Flex*	*II* *After Flex A*	*III* *After Flex B*
Employee	$ 720	$ 720	$ 840
Employer	$1,280	$1,280	$1,160
After-tax Cost to Employee*	$ 720	$ 504	$ 588

*Assumes a 30% rate for the combination of federal taxes and FICA.

$720 per year. As shown in column II, if a cafeteria plan is introduced into the structure and is used to permit the employee contribution on a pretax basis, the employee still contributes $720 per year and the employer $1,280 per year, but the employee's real cost would be reduced to $504 per year, resulting in a savings of $216 for the employee. However, if, as shown in column III, concurrent with the introduction of the cafeteria plan the employer were to raise the employee premium $120 from $720 per year to $840 per year, the employer cost of the plan would decrease by $120 to $1,160 per year, and the new $840 per-year contribution on the part of the employee would have a net cost of $588. Thus, the employer cost is decreased and the real (after-tax) cost to the employee also is decreased. In essence, the employer has transferred part of the cost to the employee by raising the annual employee contribution and part of the cost to the government by consuming some of the tax savings that would otherwise have passed to the employee. Taken to its extreme, the employer could have increased the employee cost to well over $1,000 per year and, at the assumed tax rate of 30 percent, still not altered the after-tax cost to the employee. However, since employees still view the pretax salary reduction amount as their own contribution, such a plan design would not likely have been popular when first implemented. (For purposes of determining the figures above, a 30 percent rate has been used to represent the combination of federal taxes as well as Social Security taxes.) The numbers will, of course, vary depending on the tax rate assumed, but 30 percent seems reasonably conservative since for a single taxpayer in 1990, the 28 percent marginal federal rate begins with a taxable income of slightly under $20,000.

Another method of transferring cost through a cafeteria plan involves the use of multiple medical plans. Assume that an employer had provided a fairly lucrative medical plan to employees at no cost to them and this plan had a cost of $2,500 per year per employee unit. This plan is called "medical plan 1" as shown in Figure 30–6. Assume further that two additional medical plans are created: Plan 2 is not quite as lucrative as Plan 1 and is estimated to cost $2,000 per employee unit per year, and Plan 3 is yet a lesser benefit plan and is estimated to cost $1,800 per employee unit per year.

To encourage employees to participate in Plan 2, the employer might contribute $300 per year, which could be directed to a spending account or possibly taken in cash. If the employee wanted to participate in Plan

FIGURE 30–6
Cost Control Using Multiple Medical Plans

	I *Real Cost*	*II* *Spending Account*
Medical Plan 1	$2,500	0
Medical Plan 2	$2,000	$300
Medical Plan 3	$1,800	$400

3, the employer would contribute $400 to a spending account or permit the employee to take this amount in cash. The advantage of this arrangement to the employee is that he or she can use the money in the spending account to cover expenses, such as eyeglasses, that would typically not be covered under even the most generous comprehensive medical plan. Of course the money in the spending account can also be used to pay deductibles and coinsurance amounts.

The advantage to the employer is clear, in that if all employees switched from Plan 1 to Plan 2, the employer would save $200 per employee. This savings comes from the fact that Plan 2 provides lesser benefits and therefore has a lesser cost. To the extent that benefits are less and claims remain the same, the cost has been transferred to the employee. It should be noted here that the employer will never realize the full amount of savings because of adverse selection. In the worst possible case of adverse selection, the employer could lose a substantial amount. This results if all employees who do not have medical claims elect to participate in Plan 3 thus receiving $400 each from the employer, and all those who typically had claims remain in medical Plan 1 and claims are the same as they were in the previous year. In this case, the employer has simply given away $400 to each employee who did not incur any medical claims. In that first year, adverse selection has created a loss for the employer.

The remedy for this situation is to adjust the prices for Plan 1 in the following year. Perhaps in the next year, that plan may require an employee contribution and the amount given to encourage people to move to Plan 3 might remain the same. Additionally, changes may be made in Plan 1 to increase deductibles or copayment amounts to compensate for the adverse selection. This, in turn, may necessitate changes in Plans 2 and 3.

Thus, the design and pricing of medical plan options in a cafeteria plan is an ongoing process. Each year, prices and incentives can be adjusted to achieve the desired result. Five additional points regarding cost transfer through the use of a cafeteria plan remain to be made.

- There is an absolute limit to the amount of cost that can be transferred to employees in any situation. This will be a function of the compensation levels of the employees involved. Once that limit is reached, additional cost transfer is counterproductive.
- The real purpose in using multiple medical plans as shown in Figure 30–6 is not to create employer savings by using an incentive that is less than the real differential between the plans but to encourage employees into plans that may provide slightly lesser benefits or that may promote more efficient delivery of health care services. To the extent this is achieved, some measure of cost control is possible.
- The difference between most medical plan options (other than a choice between an indemnity plan and an HMO or PPO) usually is the level of deductible, copayment, and the maximum out-of-pocket expense that can be borne by the employee. Care must be taken in setting these values, since in achieving the objective of cost transfer, one may begin to cause the plan to fail to meet its primary objective of providing benefits to those truly in need. Raising the deductible for an employee who is seriously ill, incurring significant medical expenses, and in dire financial need may not be in the best interest of all concerned.
- As the differences between these plans become more complex, it becomes more and more difficult for employees to make informed choices about them.
- Lastly, it is not the cafeteria plan that has saved any cost; it is the fact that cost has been transferred to the employee and that lesser benefits have been provided. The cafeteria plan is simply the mechanism used to facilitate this and the mechanism has a cost. The maximum savings occurs by simply changing from Plan 1 to Plan 3 as the employer provided plan with no contribution to a cafeteria plan; however, this is not likely to be as popular with employees.

Controlling Total Benefit Costs

The previous examples deal solely with costs for medical plans. This is appropriate because the medical plan offers the largest potential savings in any cafeteria plan arrangement. Many of the other plans require only minimal contributions and therefore present limited cost savings opportunities. However, to the extent that any employee contributions to any plan that previously were being made on an after-tax basis are transferred to a pretax basis, the employer will have some cost savings. For all those employees who are earning below the Social Security wage base, the employer's contribution to Social Security on any salary reduction amounts represents reduced cost. This also is true, but to a lesser extent, for those employees earning below the wage to which the Medicare portion of the Social Security tax is applied.

Also, the concept of employer contributions that can be directed to purchase benefits applies equally across all benefit plans. Thus, an employer could limit cost increases in the benefit package as a whole by opting for what is referred to as a "defined contribution approach." In this case, the employer fixes the amount of contribution it will make to the benefit plan as a whole, contributes that amount to the cafeteria plan and the employee directs that amount to be spent as he or she wishes. If additional amounts are needed to purchase the same benefits in future years, as will most certainly be the case, those amounts will come from the employee, unless the employer decides to increase its contribution. The employer, though, exercises this control.

ADMINISTRATION OF A CAFETERIA PLAN

Administration of a cafeteria benefit plan is quite different from that of a traditional program where the employee enrolls once and remains until employment terminates. All employees have essentially the same coverage, so the administration generally is the same. In the case of a flexible benefit plan, the employee enrolls and re-enrolls each year and makes choices on how and where to apply his or her flexible dollars. Each employee will spend those dollars differently, and because of this heavy employee involvement and the differences between individuals, the task of administration becomes doubly important. The plan administrator must be able to quickly answer questions concerning the program and determine the benefits that each participant has.

When flexible benefit plans were first being designed and implemented, the administration was thought to be onerous, and concern over burdensome administrative tasks was the single biggest obstacle to their adoption. In some instances it remains so today. However, while a flexible benefit plan involves more administrative tasks than a traditional approach, it need not result in overly difficult or extremely expensive administration. Today, most payroll systems easily accommodate salary reduction amounts for cafeteria and 401(k) plans or a combination of the two. Also, human-resource systems, including micro-computer based systems for smaller employers, have sufficient capacity to store election data, provide data for enrollment forms, permit inquiries on coverages and facilitate management and administrative reporting. Software to perform many of these tasks is available commercially and can easily be customized to fit most plan designs.

Five administrative tasks are of critical importance: development of administrative rules, the annual enrollment process, payroll and accounting issues, administering the spending account, and communicating the plan to participants.

Development of Administrative Rules

Once the program has been designed, there is a need for a very specific and detailed set of administrative procedures and practices. Throughout each year, administrative situations will arise that generally are not contemplated in the design of the plan and to ensure uniform administration, proper administrative procedures and rules should be developed in advance. Examples of issues to be addressed in the administrative document may include the following:

- How are flexible dollars computed? What happens in the case of different pay periods such as hourly, weekly, biweekly?
- How are the prices for the various options determined for each payroll type?
- What happens in the case of unpaid leaves of absence? Will contributions to the various plans be continued and, if so, how? Will the employee make after-tax contributions during such period and, if so, to which plans? What happens if only a portion of such contributions is received?
- How are newly hired employees enrolled in the plan, and which choices are they given? How are credits calculated for such employees?
- What changes are permitted during the course of the year, and exactly how will they be administered?

- All administrative forms used in the operation of the plan should be contained in the manual along with instructions on how to complete the forms and what to do with them after completion.
- The administrative procedure should set forth how conversions and trades of salary and vacation time into flexible dollars take place and what result is obtained.
- Exactly what types of expenses will be covered by any flexible spending accounts? What degree of claims adjudication is required, and how will it be accomplished?
- What reports will employees receive throughout the year, and who will prepare them? What management reports will be produced, who will prepare them, and to whom will they be sent?
- How will changes in salary during the course of the year affect the various benefits selected?
- What impact will the various choices have on other benefit plans and personnel policies, and what changes are being made in them to accommodate the flexible benefits program?
- If there are default values that result from employees not returning enrollment forms, what are they and how will they be implemented? Are they different in the first year of enrollment than in subsequent years?

The size and complexity of the administrative procedures and rules are, of course, a function of the complexity of the flexible benefit plan involved. The administrative document may be small in the case of a plan offering only a few choices or more sizeable in the case of more comprehensive programs. In any event, the document should be maintained from year to year as situations arise and decisions made regarding them.

Annual Enrollment Process

The most important administrative task in any flexible benefit program is the annual enrollment process. It is at this time that the employee must have all the information necessary to make the choices he or she desires. Most likely, this also is the single largest administrative effort in operating the plan. The annual enrollment process involves the following tasks: obtaining the basic employee data; performing the calculations for enrollment and preparing the individual enrollment form; distributing the form to employees; obtaining the completed form back from employees, editing and correcting data, recording the information and issuing a confirmation report; and preparing all administrative reports necessary for the orderly operation of the program.

Obtaining the basic data may be as simple as extracting information from the payroll system. Additional information may be required, depending on the complexity of the plan. For example, if the plan involves the use of previously carried-forward vacation amounts, that information may have to be gathered from a separate source. Typically, the basic employee data required includes such elements as employee name, address, identification number or Social Security number or both, work location, employment status (exempt, non-exempt), birth date, date service began (for either computing the number of flexible dollars the employee has or for determining vacation eligibility or sick leave eligibility), salary amount, frequency of pay, accrued carryover vacation, current medical coverage (single, family), marital status, and the like. These data allow the plan administrator to calculate the number of flexible dollars the employee will have or be able to create and the prices of the benefits on which those dollars may be spent. The amount of data required clearly is a function of the complexity of the plan and the amount of computation to be performed. This task usually is more involved in the first year of the enrollment process, and in future years the validity of the data tends to increase.

Creation and distribution of the enrollment form consists of performing the calculations mentioned above and posting them on an individual enrollment form for each employee. For very simple plans involving only a few choices, where prices of the benefits are not dependent on any individual data, and where a number of flexible dollars is easily determined or they come solely from salary reduction, the amount of computation in the preparation of the enrollment form is small. However, in the case of plans involving vacation trades, employer contributions based on service and pay or other factors, and where prices are a function of family status or other demographic information, more elaborate computations are required. Experience with the enrollment process has shown that enrollment errors can be significantly reduced if employees are not required to perform computations. Thus, everything that can be calculated beforehand and placed on the enrollment form serves to reduce future error. Enrollment forms can be mailed to employee homes, sent to office or work locations, or distributed at meetings. A two-part form offers an advantage in that the employee may keep one part of the completed enrollment form.

Obtaining the completed form is the next step. Usually, completed forms are returned to the plan administrator to check and edit for completeness. In the case of large employers, the checking and editing may be performed on an automated basis. At a minimum, editing involves seeing that the number of flexible dollars each employee has spent is, in fact, equal to the number of dollars available. In this case, a cash election is assumed to be dollars spent. Invalid elections must be identified. The administrator must keep track of all returned election forms so that employees who have not returned them can be contacted in advance of the final date on which enrollment forms will be accepted. Those employees whose enrollment forms contain invalid elections or are illegible or incomplete, must be contacted directly so that elections can be corrected. Alternatively, default conditions can be invoked. Once any employee's enrollment form is complete and correctly recorded, a confirmation report can be produced. This report serves to confirm to the employee that the elections he or she has made have been recorded by the plan administrator.

Management reports and administrative reports can be produced once the enrollment process is concluded. Part of this process also involves computing salary reduction amounts and other deductions that need to be passed to the payroll system. Also, coverage and eligibility reports to the various insurance carriers and claims administrators should be produced.

Using technology to reduce the amount of paper involved in the enrollment process is an approach that appeals to large employers, and some employers have established automated voice response systems to provide information to participants and to permit enrollment over the telephone. This methodology is quite effective, particularly where there are only a few choices that employees have to make. Touch-screen interactive computer systems, installed in kiosks at various work sites, also can help increase the efficiency of the enrollment process.

Payroll and Accounting Issues

Payroll and accounting issues are mentioned here briefly since the establishment of a flexible benefit plan impacts the interaction between payroll and accounting. Decisions need to be made on how the various salary-reduction amounts will be shown on the paycheck stub. If amounts are shown individually by benefit choice, these must be computed and a new pay-stub design may be required in order to accommodate them. Alternatively, if only one amount is shown, an insert in the paycheck may be required to explain that amount. If there is automatic reporting between the payroll and general ledger systems, some modification may be required as items (as a result of salary reduction or vacation trade) may now appear on different lines in the general ledger. Also, additional liability accounts will need to be created in the general ledger to reflect the difference between flexible dollars created through salary reduction (or possibly other means) and those actually spent in the same time period. This is particularly true in the case of spending accounts funded by salary reduction. The dollars removed from salary in each pay period must accumulate in a liability account until such time as they are spent. On the other hand, in the case of a medical reimbursement account, the employee may file a claim for more than the number of dollars yet extracted from pay. In this case, appropriate accounting entries must be made.

Flexible dollars created from different sources may accrue at different rates. For example, dollars created as a result of salary reduction normally accrue each pay period, while those created from vacation trade may accrue monthly or over whatever time period vacation is computed. Dollars created from the sale of carryover vacation may accrue at the beginning of the year. Flexible dollars spent for various plans also accrue at different rates. Contributions to medical plans accrue periodically in concert with payroll periods. However, the use of vacation days may occur at any time during the course of the year. Appropriate procedures and methods should be developed in advance to deal with these issues.

Administering a Flexible Spending Account

As indicated earlier in this chapter, most flexible benefit programs involve the establishment of spending accounts for employees. Typically, two accounts are possible, one for medical and the other for dependent care expenses—both funded by flexible dollars. Employees file claims for reimbursement from the accounts—a process that involves the completion, examination, and adjudication of the claim form; the recording of the appropriate accounting entries; and the preparation of a check and explanation of benefit report for the employees and miscellaneous management and accounting reports. Periodic statements may be provided to employees advising them how much they have used to date and how much remains in their spending accounts.

The operation of a spending account is treated in a manner similar to a medical claim, and most insurance companies or third-party administrators who provide medical claim services provide claims processing for a flexible spending account. There are distinct advantages to this approach, since it can reduce the number of forms the employee has to file and the amount of time between filing and payment. For example, one typical expense claimed against a medical spending account is for medical expenses claimed under the medical plan but not reimbursed therefrom. In this situation, the employee files a claim for the medical expense against the medical plan, receives an explanation of benefits, and then files a claim (for the difference between the original claim and the payment) against the flexible spending account. If the same entity is receiving both claims, the second claims process can be made a part of the first process so that when the medical claim is filed, the employee simply indicates on that claim form that any unreimbursed amounts should be paid from his or her spending account.

Alternatively, the plan sponsor may choose to administer the spending account directly. In the case of a small number of participants, this can be a manual process. However, with a large number of participants (500 or more), some mechanized process probably is warranted. Again, software is commercially available for this purpose.

Communicating the Plan

Many traditional benefit plans work well with little or no communication; a flexible benefit plan does not. The success of the plan hinges in great part on how well employees understand what the program is designed to do and how to utilize it. It is important to recognize that, although a flexible benefit plan can become complex in design and administration, the concept behind it is relatively straightforward. The employees simply need to understand what the plan is intended to do and how they can make it work for them. This involves understanding how many flexible dollars can be created, how they are created, where they can be spent and the advantages and disadvantages of creating or spending them in a particular way. The ability of employees to understand even very complex programs should not be underestimated. Once the concept is clear, employees will find ways of using the program to their advantage, and this level of involvement is necessary for a successful program.

Communication programs involve four phases:

1. *Announcement phase.* During this time the intention to implement a flexible benefit program is communicated to the employees. This is the time to communicate general concepts and plan objectives to employees through any of the communication vehicles available such as letters, pamphlets, and payroll stuffers. The use of group meetings and audiovisual techniques is ideal.

2. *Educational phase.* Employees must be educated about the plan. Once the objectives and concepts are known, detailed information about how the plan will operate and what the employee needs to do in order to use the plan for best results must be provided. There is no such thing as too much communication material, and employees should be provided with newsletters, bulletins, brochures and pamphlets—as much detailed information as possible. Again, group meetings and audiovisual presentations are helpful.

3. *Enrollment phase.* This is the most important phase in the communication program. Here, the employer's objectives are at least threefold: reduce the amount of administrative effort and errors in the enrollment process, reduce the amount of time the enrollment process consumes, and ensure that employees have a positive feeling about the plan and their enrollment in it. In more complex plans, employees may have difficulty making choices and develop a negative view of the plan for that reason. Individually prepared enrollment forms and kits are helpful. Group meetings using audiovisual presentations are strongly encouraged at this point. Some employers have prepared videotapes detailing the process for completing the enrollment form that can be made available to employees on an individual basis. They also could be taken home so that employees could view them with their families as they are going through the enrollment process. Several innovative communications techniques, including voice-response systems and interactive video systems have been used in this phase not only to communicate but also to facilitate the enrollment process.

It is important that the enrollment process be completed in a reasonably short period of time. Even though this may involve the physical distribution of a multi-part form to the employee and follow-up to receive the form back, the shorter the time frame during which this is accomplished, the better the result will be. As soon as forms are received and the enrollment data entered into the administrative system, a confirmation report should be distributed to the employee.

Since most flexible benefit plans operate on a calendar-year basis, the enrollment phase will be completed during the late fall of the year before the year in which it becomes effective. Confirmation reports should be issued to employees before the start of the year. In fact, if a confirmation report was issued in October or November, it may be appropriate to have an additional report effective January 1 to advise employees that the program has commenced and reaffirm their participation in it.

4. *Continuation phase.* Throughout the year, miscellaneous reports to employees advising them of such things as amounts remaining in spending accounts are appropriate. Occasional communication on how the plan is operating and how many tax dollars have been saved, are helpful. A continuing newsletter is ideal. During this phase it is appropriate to communicate how the plan is performing with respect to the objectives set for it. This is so even if the objective is cost control; it simply requires an honest and credible approach.

The communication program associated with a flexible benefit plan is broader in scope than that used with traditional plan design and represents, at least in the year of implementation, an additional administrative task. However, it is one where commensurate return is possible.

SPECIAL RULES FOR CAFETERIA PLANS

Section 125 of the IRC is a relatively brief section of the Code, and to date there are only three IRS regulations with respect to it. Proposed regulation 1.125-1, issued in 1984, deals primarily with elections, constructive receipt, and selected nondiscrimination issues. This regulation was designed in part to put an end to certain practices regarding spending accounts. Regulation 1.125-2T appeared in 1986. This temporary regulation deals only with the types of benefits that can be provided by a cafeteria plan and is assumed to have been replaced by proposed regulation 1.125-2, issued in 1989, which addresses the same issues as 1.125-2T but in more detail. Also, this regulation provides more guidance into the operation of spending accounts and vacation trades. It is well beyond the scope of this chapter to provide a detailed discussion of all the rules set forth by these regulations, and the reader who is designing and/or implementing a cafeteria plan is encouraged to review them thoroughly. However, the following is a brief summary of several of the more important rules to be followed.

Nondiscrimination Rules For Cafeteria Plans

Since the cafeteria plan serves to direct contributions to and participation in other (presumably nontaxable) benefit plans, those plans must each meet their own nondiscrimination tests as prescribed by tax law and regulation. For example, medical plans have their own nondiscrimination rules as set forth in Section 105 of the IRC. Therefore, if an election to participate in a nontaxable medical plan is allowed as part of the cafeteria plan, each medical plan in question must meet the nondiscrimination requirements applicable to it. This also is true for dependent care plans, 401(k) plans, life insurance plans, and the like.

Beyond the above rules, the cafeteria plan itself will probably provide some nontaxable benefits to employees. No definition of these exists in tax regulation at the time of this writing, but they are assumed to at least include such benefits as salary-reduction amounts and employer contributions. A cafeteria plan must meet three nondiscrimination tests: the eligibility test, the benefits test, and the concentration test.

- *Eligibility Test.* This test simply requires that the benefits be available to a classification (a group) of employees which itself does not discriminate in favor of highly compensated employees. For this purpose, a highly compensated employee is defined as any officer, a shareholder owning more than 5 percent of the voting power or value of employer stock, or a highly paid person (determined by facts and circumstances) or the employed spouse or dependent of an employee who meets any of the previously mentioned criteria.
- *Contribution and Benefits Test.* Under this test, the benefits under the plan and/or the contributions to the plan cannot favor highly compensated participants. The definition of a highly compensated participant is the same as that for a highly compensated individual, but refers only to those who are participants in the plan.
- *Concentration Test.* This test requires that no more than 25 percent of the total nontaxable benefits under the plan can be for the benefit of "key" employees. A "key" employee is defined in Section 416 of the Internal Revenue Code and is generally: any officer earning more than $54,482 annually (in 1991—amount is adjusted each year), or any of the 10 largest employee shareholders earning in excess of $30,000 annually (1991 amount), or any 5 percent owner of the employer, or any 1 percent owner earning more than $150,000.

No regulations as to how to specifically apply the three tests above have as yet been issued by the IRS. Employers who sponsor cafeteria plans should make a good–faith effort to comply.

Making and Changing Elections

In a cafeteria plan, employees make elections as to the various benefits they want to receive. These elections must be made prior to the point where the period of coverage under those benefits begins. In most cases, a cafeteria plan will operate on a calendar-year basis. Thus, employee elections for one year must be made before the end of the prior year. Once elections have been made and the plan year commences, those elections are immutable under cafeteria plan regulations except "on account of and consistent with" a change in family status. A change in family status can include any of the following:

- The marriage or divorce of the employee.
- The death of the employee's spouse or other dependent.
- The birth or adoption of a child of the employee.
- The commencement or cessation of employment by the employee's spouse or the change in the spouse's (or other employee's) employment from full-time to part-time or vice versa.
- The commencement of an unpaid leave of absence by either the employee or the spouse, or a major change in the health care coverage of the employee or the spouse as provided through the spouse's employer medical plan.

Beyond these, the plan can permit employees to elect coverage under a different health plan if the coverage under the plan in which they are currently participating has been significantly curtailed by an independent third-party provider or if such coverage ceases. Further, if the cost of such a plan provided by an independent third-party provider increases or decreases, the plan is permitted to increase or decrease the contributions made by the participants. If the cost increase is significant, the plan can permit employees to elect coverage, on a prospective basis, under a different medical plan that may be provided.

While the regulations regarding elections deal reasonably adequately with changes in family status, they do not address all the situations that could arise and that might seem to justify a change in election. For example, if an employee who elected coverage under a health maintenance organization is relocated to a work location where such coverage is not available or totally impracticable, a change in medical coverage would be appropriate and probably acceptable. Likewise, should a dependent reach an age at which that dependent is no longer covered by the medical plan or should he or she cease to be a full-time student, some revisions in coverage may be appropriate. It should be noted that the regulations define when changes in elections are *permitted*. They do not, however, *require* that any cafeteria plan allow for such changes. In other words, the plan itself could limit the ability of participants to change elections more severely than the regulations provide. They could not, however, be more liberal. It also is important to note that these elections apply to the cafeteria plan as a whole, as well as to flexible spending accounts. Thus, employers could apply more strict conditions to the flexible spending account to reduce their risk of loss. Careful consideration should be given to these issues during plan design.

Operating the Spending Account

Two types of spending accounts are common in most cafeteria plans—one for health care expenses and one for dependent care expenses. In the past, spending accounts were also used for certain legal expenses permitted under a group legal services plan under Section 120 of the IRC. However, because of the fact that Section 120 has had a tendency to expire and be revised on a frequent basis, the use of a spending account to pay expenses under this type of a plan is virtually nonexistent. Also, nonhighly compensated employees have a tendency not to participate in such legal expense plans. Even dependent care plans, while they do form a part of a number of cafeteria plans, tend to have limited participation. Recent surveys have found that of all the dollars paid out of spending accounts, it is reasonable to assume that over 90 percent come from health care spending accounts.

A wide variety of expenses can be covered by a health care spending account. Generally, such a plan can reimburse for any expenses covered by Section 213 of the IRC including expenses for services in a hospital or any care by physicians, dentists, or registered nurses; prescription drugs; dental services; vision care including eyeglasses, contact lenses, or prescription sunglasses; psychiatric and/or psychological care; therapy including special education for the handicapped; travel expenses to receive medical treatment, including ambulance service; and a host of miscellaneous expenses including hearing aids, prosthetics, and guide dogs. A full description of covered expenses can be found in IRS Publication 502. Certain expenses cannot be reimbursed including undocumented services (such as automobile mileage on a private car), premiums for health coverage of any type, or expenses for cosmetic surgery or cosmetic procedures intended to improve appearance as opposed to promoting proper functioning of the body for the prevention or treatment of an illness. (Procedures to correct birth defects or to correct disfigurement resulting from an accident or a disease can be reimbursed.) There is no prescribed maximum for reimbursements from a health care spending account, but, to not discriminate in favor of highly compensated employees, a fixed dollar amount is required. Most employers use a $1,000–$3,000 maximum.

In general, the expenses that can be paid from a dependent care account are those that would otherwise be payable from a dependent care assistance plan as provided for in Section 129 of the IRC. The maximum amount of reimbursable expense is $5,000 for a single taxpayer or a married couple filing jointly (the maximum includes the amounts in the spending accounts of both spouses, if applicable); it is $2,500 for a married person filing separately. Dependent care expenses must be for a "qualifying individual" and the expense must be "employment related." A "qualifying individual" is a dependent of the employee, for federal income tax purposes, who is under age 13. Alternatively, a qualifying individual can be a dependent of the employee (or can be the employee's spouse) who is physically or mentally incapable of self-support if the individual spends at least eight hours each day in the employee's home. To be employment-related, the expenses must have been incurred so as to permit the employee to work. Expenses for services rendered outside the home are covered as well. If the facility providing the care does so for more than six individuals, the facility must be a licensed dependent care facility and/or comply with all state laws. A number of additional rules and definitions apply to dependent care expenses, each of which is described in IRS Publication 503.

The basic rules for operating a health care or dependent care spending account are similar. Key procedures to follow include the following:

- The coverage period for benefits under a flexible spending account must be one year. This can be violated if there is a short plan year when a plan is established or if the plan year is changed. This requirement is relatively easy to follow, since most cafeteria plans operate on a calendar-year basis anyway.

• Flexible spending accounts are permitted to reimburse only those claims incurred during the period of coverage. A claim is assumed to be incurred when the service is actually rendered. Thus, if a medical service is provided in 1990, the expense is incurred at that point. This expense, if claimed, must be paid from the 1990 flexible spending account, even though the invoice for the expense may not be received until 1991. From an administrative standpoint, this means that the ability to file claims against a flexible spending account applicable for a given year will most likely stand for several months into the following year. A two-month to three-month grace period is generally followed by most employers operating such accounts.

• Money deposited into a flexible spending account must be consumed by qualifying expenses claimed against that account during the year or be forfeited. The forfeiture remains an asset of the employer; it does not revert to the government. The employer may do anything with the forfeiture it likes, including redistributing it to the participants in the plan in the following year. The general rule is that the amount given to any employee cannot in any way be linked to the amount forfeited by that employee.

• For a health care flexible spending account, the plan must operate under the "uniform coverage" rule. This means that the amount of coverage applicable to the full year must be available throughout each day in the plan year. Thus, expenses are reimbursed as they are submitted, no matter how many flexible dollars have actually accrued (from an accounting standpoint) in the individual's account at that point. For example, if an employee elects to have coverage under a health care flexible spending account of $1,200, the salary reduction for such coverage is $100 per month and the total amount of coverage available *at any time during* the year is $1,200. So, if the employee submitted a qualified expense of $1,200 in the second month of coverage, this expense would be paid from the flexible spending account even though only $200 of the funding for the account existed at that point.

While this may seem to pose a financial risk to the plan sponsor, when contributions are taken in the aggregate (considering the amount of salary reduction taken from all participants versus the total number of claims settled at any point in time), this does not pose a true risk. There is the risk that upon receiving payment for an expense in excess of the funded amount, the employee may terminate service and cease making payments into the spending account. This risk is borne by the plan sponsor. Offsetting this, however, is the ability of the plan sponsor to recapture forfeitures and the fact that no interest need be paid on accumulated funds. Therefore, the uniform coverage rule has not been a major obstacle to the use of flexible spending accounts. It should be noted that the uniform coverage rule does not apply to flexible spending accounts established to pay dependent care expenses.

The above discussion is conceptual in nature, and there are many rules and nuances involved in operating spending accounts. Again, the reader is encouraged to review the regulations thoroughly.

Dealing with Vacation Trades

Only a few regulations exist governing the use of vacation time in a cafeteria plan, but thoughtful administrative procedures are required to deal with them. Basically, all that is involved in trading time off for dollars is to permit the employee to either agree to take less vacation time in a given year than that to which he or she is entitled and to receive flexible dollars in return, or to permit the employee to purchase additional time off with flexible dollars that have been created through other means.

If any of these elections are incorporated into the flexible benefits plan, the days of vacation over which the employee has control are referred to as "elective days" and all other days as "nonelective days". The regulations prescribe that nonelective days be used first and elective days last in any year. Elective days cannot be carried over into future years as that would cause the flexible benefits plan to create a mechanism whereby the employee could defer compensation into another year. However, if elective days are not used in the year in question, they can be cashed out (that is, the employee can receive taxable dollars for them) at the end of that year.

For example, if an employee has 10 days of vacation to be taken in calendar year 1991, and if he or she elects (assuming the plan so permits) to buy 3 additional days in that year, by consuming the appropriate number of flexible dollars, then the employee has 13 days of vacation for that year. Those three purchased days are the elective days and are assumed to be used last. Thus, if this employee uses only eight vacation days in the year, he or she would have two nonelective days and three elective days unused. If the normal policy of the employer were to permit unused vacation time to be carried over into the next year, only the two unused nonelective days would qualify. The remaining three elective days would have to be either forfeited or cashed out before the year ends.

Carrying this example one step further, assume the flexible benefits plan permitted the employee to purchase up to a maximum of three days, but that it also permitted the employee to trade up to five days of time off to create additional flexible dollars. In this case, the employee who does not purchase any additional time off would still have five elective days, since that is the number of days that could have been traded. If this employee took only five days of vacation in the year, the remaining five days (because they are elective days) cannot be carried over. They can, of course, be cashed out. The employee who purchases three extra days in this case would have eight elective days and five nonelective days, or thirteen days of vacation in total. If this employee uses eight of those days, none of the remaining five days can be carried over since they were all elective days.

When vacation trades are used, three key administrative issues must be addressed:

- A decision must be made as to how much vacation time will be subject to trade, and at what rate. Since the election to trade or not must be made before the start of the year, the base salary on some fixed date prior to the start of the year may be the appropriate exchange rate. In this case salary increases in the next year are ignored for this purpose. Adequate communication of this fact is required.
- It is also important to determine the unit of trade. Trading in days is easier to administer than trading in hours, unless the employer is accustomed to operating the vacation plan on an hourly basis.
- Since it is likely that those with longer service will have more discretionary vacation time available to trade, and since it is probable that these longer service employees are being paid more than those with much less service, care must be taken to ensure that the plan is not discriminating in favor of highly compensated individuals. This same issue must be examined in the situation where existing carried-over vacation days are being traded for flexible dollars.

The use of vacation trades can serve to permit employees to create more flexible dollars without salary reduction. However, these dollars actually come from the employer and thus represent a true additional cost. This may be offset by the fact that the employee will be working during the time that would otherwise be spent on vacation. Also, the business needs of the employer should play a major role in deciding whether or not to include vacation trading in the flexible benefit plan. For example, if the employer would like to encourage employees to take unpaid leave because of declining business conditions, then a plan where employees can purchase additional time off by using salary reduction can help accomplish this objective. Alternatively, if there is a large backlog of work, a plan that permits employees to sell time off may be beneficial.

IMPACT OF A CAFETERIA PLAN ON OTHER PLANS AND POLICIES

While one of the primary points made in this chapter is that the cafeteria plan serves to direct contributions to and participation in other plans, one cannot conclude that it has absolutely no affect on those plans. Indeed, the existence of choice among many plans will result in design changes within those plans. Also, the cafeteria plan can affect other plans, policies, and administrative procedures even though they may not be a part of it.

For example, if the flexible benefit plan provides a choice between two or more medical indemnity plans, there must be a discernible difference between those plans. This applies to the benefits provided from those plans as well as the price tag placed on them. Thus, small differences ($100 for example) in deductibles are relatively meaningless. This may not be totally true if the employer is moving from a medical plan with a very low deductible such as $50. In this instance, the next best plan in the set of choices may well have a $100 or $150 deductible. However, if there is a third plan, it should probably have a $300 or $500 deductible. While small differences in plan design may not be significant, the same is not necessarily the case with regard to price. Here, a difference of $100 per year for coverage can cause employees to select a plan providing lesser benefits. Naturally, these amounts will vary depending on the employee group and the price for all options. The pricing of the various options, particularly with respect to the medical plans should be reviewed each year to ensure that the plan is operating as desired.

The existence of flexible spending accounts also may affect other plans. For example:

- The existence of a health care flexible spending account can mean there is not much need for a vision care plan, since such expenses can be paid from the flexible spending account. Also, vision care plans tend to have relatively small benefits as compared with the cost of vision care services.
- There may not be as much need for a very lucrative dental plan, as these expenses also can be paid from the flexible spending account. This is particularly true for such coverage as orthodontia and prosthetic devices. However, this result may only be fully achieved if the employer also makes some type of contribution to the spending account on behalf of employees.
- The use of a dependent care flexible spending account can reduce some pressure to have other types of dependent care benefits. However, if the account is funded solely through salary reduction, it does not have the same intensity and it competes, specifically in the case of lower-paid employees, with the child care tax credit. However, if the employer makes a contribution to the cafeteria plan and if those flexible dollars can be directed to the dependent care account (as well as other benefits) then the flexible spending account will be perceived as providing better coverage for those who need it. This approach also will seem more fair to those employees who do not have a need for dependent care, as they can use the employer contribution for other benefits.

Using vacation trading in the cafeteria plan can have an impact on the vacation policies themselves. First, the issue of carrying forward vacation time should be reevaluated when using the cafeteria approach. The introduction of the cafeteria plan may serve as an ideal time to eliminate this practice if the employer so desires. Also, if the cafeteria plan permits the employee to purchase time off, personnel and business policies must be examined to ensure that the process can work. In these cases, employees may come to the end of the year with some unused time which they will want to take before the year is ended. This can result in more vacation time being used in the last month of the year, a time when vacation and holiday time normally is high anyway, than expected. Also, for those who must work during that time, procedures must be established so that unused elective days can be cashed out as needed.

The general administration of the vacation plan also must accommodate the cafeteria plan. For example:

- A policy of requiring six months of full-time employment before vacation can be taken may conflict with the ability to trade days for flexible dollars for newly hired employees.
- If supervisors typically grant time off without involvement of the benefit department, or if such time is not recorded, the cafeteria plan can be defeated.
- Lastly, the vacation tracking system may have to be modified.

One additional plan that is worthy of discussion is the long-term disability (LTD) plan. If an LTD plan exists and if it is wholly paid for by employee after-tax contributions, then the benefits from that plan are (under current tax law) not subject to federal tax when received. In this case a benefit level of two thirds of normal earnings would result in the employee having essentially the same level of spendable income in the event of disability as he or she had while actively employed, at least in the first few years. A benefit level of 50 percent of normal earnings may be deemed as acceptable since work-related expenses disappear in the case of disability. (The actual level of benefit will have been set by the employer and will be commensurate with its philosophy regarding the spendable income needs of a person who is disabled.) However, if this plan is incorporated into the cafeteria plan and is paid for with flexible (pretax) dollars, then the benefits, when received are subject to federal income tax. In this case, a benefit level of 50 percent will not achieve the same result as it did before.

It is possible to permit the employee to choose whether or not to let the benefit or the premium be taxable, and it is also possible to have an election between LTD plans with different levels of benefits. This structure should probably be avoided since it is very difficult for all but the most astute employees (or those that know they are going to be eligible for LTD) to determine what is best for them.

In essence then, one must carefully evaluate the plans to be included in the cafeteria plan, looking for the possible impact of the cafeteria plan on them. General personnel policies and administrative procedures and systems also should be reexamined for possible impact.

SUMMARY

The cafeteria plan is clearly a plan whose time has come. Through the use of such plans, employers can construct programs that permit employees to have more command over their own compensation; employer costs, within some reason can be controlled; and compensation can become more tax efficient. The workings of such programs are, as shown in this chapter, relatively straightforward, but care must be taken in the design phase to be sure of the impact on other plans and policies.

The administration of these types of programs is not to be feared and can be accommodated given the state of sophistication of today's payroll and human-resource systems, the availability of software packages to perform such functions as the enrollment process, and the willingness of third-party administrators to perform services in all areas, including the administration of flexible spending accounts. The tax environment currently, and for the foreseeable future, favors these arrangements.

PART 8

RETIREMENT AND CAPITAL ACCUMULATION PLANS

This part begins in Chapter 31 with an overview of the important issues involved in the design of retirement plans in general—both defined benefit and defined contribution plans.

Chapter 32 deals with profit-sharing plans, and this is followed by a discussion of thrift and savings plans in Chapter 33. The increasingly important 401(k) cash or deferred arrangement is covered in Chapter 34.

Chapter 35 provides an in-depth look at the various types of employee stock ownership plans, and Chapter 36 reviews the currently hot topic of cash balance pension plans.

Chapter 37 deals with retirement plans for the self-employed, concentrating on Keogh (HR-10) plans, individual retirement accounts (IRAs), and simplified employee pension plans (SEPs).

Chapter 38 covers executive retirement benefit plans and how they complement qualified retirement programs. Chapter 39, Retirement Plans for Not-for-Profit Groups and Chapter 40, Section 457 Deferred Compensation Plans cover retirement arrangements for employees in certain not-for-profit and government sectors of the economy.

This part concludes with Chapter 41 on Retirement Preparation Programs which are becoming increasingly important as both employers and employees recognize the significance of appropriate planning for retirement.

CHAPTER 31

RETIREMENT PLAN DESIGN*

Everett T. Allen, Jr.

Although pension plans vary in terms of specific provisions, they generally fall into one of two categories—they are either *defined benefit* or *defined contribution* in nature. Today, most employees are covered by defined benefit plans; this reflects the fact that large employers and unions historically have favored the defined benefit approach. Since the mid 1970s, however, a significant percentage of all new plans established have utilized the defined contribution approach.

A defined benefit plan provides a fixed amount of pension benefit. The amount of each employee's benefit usually depends on length of service and pay level; for example, a pension of 1 percent of pay for each year of service. In collectively bargained plans, however, pay often is not taken into account; the monthly pension might be a fixed dollar amount (such as $15) for each year of service. In any event, a defined benefit plan promises a fixed level of benefit, and the employer contributes whatever is necessary to provide this amount.

By contrast, the defined contribution approach focuses on contribution levels. The employer's contribution may be fixed as a percent of pay or as a flat dollar amount, or it may be based on a variable such as a percent of profits. In some cases, the employer contribution is totally variable and is established each year on a discretionary basis. However it is determined, the contribution (along with any amount contributed by the employee) is accumulated and invested on the employee's behalf. The

---

*This chapter originally appeared in *Employee Benefits Today; Concepts and Methods* (Brookfield, Wisc.: International Foundation of Employee Benefit Plans, 1987).

amount of pension an employee receives will thus vary depending on such factors as length of plan participation, the level and frequency of contributions, and investment gains and losses.

There are several different types of defined contribution plans. The two most commonly used for pension purposes are the deferred profit-sharing plan and the money purchase pension plan. In a profit-sharing plan, the employer contribution is related to profits or made on a discretionary basis. The money purchase pension plan requires a fixed employer contribution, regardless of profits. Other defined contribution plans (such as savings or Section 401(k) plans) can be used as primary pension vehicles but are usually adopted to supplement basic defined benefit pension plans. Because the focus in this chapter is on pension arrangements, only deferred profit-sharing and money purchase plans are discussed; other defined contribution programs are covered in subsequent chapters.

It should also be noted that there is growing interest in hybrid arrangements—plans that involve features of both defined benefit and defined contribution plans. Target benefit, cash balance, and floor offset plans are examples of these hybrid approaches and are discussed later in this chapter.

Regardless of the approach chosen, a pension plan should be designed so that it supports overall employer objectives. This chapter begins with a discussion of these objectives and how they are influenced by the employer's environment and attitudes. Specific design features are then described, with differences between the defined benefit and defined contribution approaches noted, as appropriate. Finally, these two approaches are evaluated from the viewpoint of both employers and employees.

EMPLOYER OBJECTIVES

Business organizations do not exist in a vacuum. They possess individual characteristics and operate in environments that influence what they can and want to accomplish in providing employee benefits. Factors that can affect employee benefit planning and, in particular, the choice between defined benefit and defined contribution programs, include the following:

- *Employer characteristics*. Is the organization incorporated or unincorporated, or is it tax-exempt? Is it mature, or young and growing? Are profits stable or volatile? What growth patterns are anticipated? What are the firm's short- and long-term capital needs? What are its personnel needs, now and in the future?

• *Industry characteristics.* Is the employer part of a clearly defined industry group? Is this industry highly competitive? Does it have a distinct employee benefit pattern? Is it important, from the standpoint of attracting and retaining employees or for cost considerations, to provide benefits or maintain cost levels that are consistent with those of other companies in the same industry?

• *Employee characteristics.* What is the composition of the employee group? How are employees distributed in terms of age, sex, service, and pay? Is this distribution likely to change in the future? How many employees are in the highly compensated group?

• *Diversity of operations.* Does the employer operate its business on a diversified basis? If so, should the same or different benefits be provided for employees at each location or in each line of business? How will such factors as profit margins, competitive needs, costs, employee transfer policies, and administrative capabilities affect this decision?

• *Collective bargaining.* Are any employees represented by a collective bargaining unit? Are benefits bargained for on a local basis or is a national pattern followed? Is a multiemployer plan available for some employees and is it an acceptable alternative? How will benefits gained through collective bargaining affect benefits for nonrepresented employees?

• *Community.* Is the employer (or any of its major operating units) located in a large, urban area or is it a dominant employer in a discrete geographic location? What is the role of the employer in the community? What social and civic responsibilities does the employer want to assume? How important is its image in the community? What other employers compete for labor in the local marketplace?

Answers to these questions (and the list is only illustrative) need to be taken into account in setting specific employee benefit plan objectives. The employer's basic compensation philosophy is also important in the objective-setting process, as is its attitude on:

- The role of employee benefits in protecting income in the event of economic insecurity.
- The extent to which employee benefits are considered a form of indirect or deferred compensation.

- Whether employee cost sharing is necessary or desirable.
- Whether employees can or should bear the risks of inflation and investment performance.
- The use of employee benefits in meeting personnel planning needs.
- The amount of choice to be given employees in structuring their own benefits.
- The importance of cost levels, cost controls, and funding flexibility.
- The desirability of integrating plan and statutory benefits.
- The treatment of highly compensated employees.

Each employer will have specific and sometimes unique objectives in establishing or modifying an employee benefit plan. And, as noted, these objectives will be influenced by the employer's environment and its attitudes on matters such as those listed above.

Most employers want to attract and retain desirable employees. An adequate benefit program will certainly be of value in achieving this objective. It also seems reasonably clear that the absence of an adequate benefit program will have a negative effect on recruiting and retention efforts. What is not clear, however, is whether a generous benefit program will have an increasingly positive effect in this regard. In the opinion of many employers, money otherwise spent on extra benefits would be more useful in meeting recruitment and retention objectives if it were directed to other elements of compensation.

A competitive benefit program is another common employer objective. This objective must be clarified before it can be implemented. For example, will competitiveness be measured by industry or local standards, or by both? Industry standards might be more relevant for highly skilled employees and executives. For employees whose skills are readily transferable to other industries, however, local practice could be much more important. Once the competitive standard is established, the employer must decide where it wants to rank—as average, above or below average, or among the leaders. It is also important to establish the means by which competitiveness will be measured. The most common technique compares benefits payable at certain times (e.g., at normal retirement) for employees with different pay and service combinations. This approach must be used with caution because it tends to focus on single events and does not consider the value of other plan provisions. More sophisticated techniques, which measure the relative value of plans by provision, in total, and with reference to both employer- and employee-provided benefits, can be used for this purpose.

Cost objectives can have a major impact on plan design. Employers should set specific objectives for liabilities that will be assumed as well as for annual cost accruals. They must also consider the need for contribution flexibility and the control of future costs that are sensitive to inflation and investment risk.

Employer objectives for income-replacement levels are critical to the design of pension plans. Most employers seek to provide a pension benefit that, together with primary Social Security benefits, replaces a percentage of the employee's preretirement gross income. In establishing income-replacement levels, these factors should be taken into account:

- Employers rarely contemplate full replacement of gross income, primarily because of tax considerations. Most employers also feel that employees should meet some of their own retirement needs through personal savings (many maintain supplemental plans to help employees in this regard). Further, they expect that most employees will have lower living expenses after they retire.
- Income-replacement objectives are often set with reference to the employee's pay level during the final year of employment or average pay during the three- or five-year period just prior to retirement.
- The percentage of income replaced is generally higher for lower-paid employees than for higher-paid employees.
- Income-replacement objectives are usually set so that they can be achieved in full only by employees who have completed what the employer considers to be a "career" of employment (usually 25 or 30 years); objectives are proportionately reduced for individuals who have shorter service.

Obviously, income-replacement objectives that are set with reference to an employee's final pay and length of service can best be met through a defined benefit plan that bases benefits on final average pay. Achieving such objectives with a career pay defined benefit plan is more difficult, but not impossible. Accrued benefits under a career pay plan can be updated periodically to keep benefits reasonably close to final pay objectives. Although it is almost impossible to establish and meet final pay income-replacement objectives with a defined contribution plan, contribution levels can be set so that, under reasonable expectations for pay growth and investment return, final pay objectives might be approximated. As a practical matter, though, actual experience is not likely to coincide with the assumptions used. Thus, actual benefits will probably be larger or smaller than anticipated, depending on experience. Table 31–1 sets forth a typical set of income-replacement objectives.

Many other objectives—for example, the desire to provide employee incentives or to foster employee identification with overall corporate goals through stock ownership—can affect plan design. In any event, once objectives have been established, they should be ranked in order of priority. In some situations, certain objectives can be achieved only at the expense of others. If this is the case, the relative importance of all objectives should be clearly understood.

PLAN PROVISIONS

A pension plan must contain provisions governing which employees are covered, what benefits they will receive, and how and under what conditions these benefits will be paid. Federal tax law plays an important role in this regard because a plan, to be tax-qualified, must meet the requirements of the Internal Revenue Code (IRC) and supporting regulations and interpretations issued by the Internal Revenue Service (IRS) through various public and private rulings.[1]

Employers have no choice with respect to certain mandatory plan provisions (e.g., if an employer wants to change the plan's vesting schedule, employees with at least three years of service must be given the right to elect vesting under the prior provision). Other mandatory provisions give the employer some latitude (e.g., a plan must provide for vesting, but the employer can choose between two permissible schedules). Some provisions are not mandatory but must meet certain requirements if they are included in a plan (e.g., a plan need not require employee contributions,

---

[1]A detailed discussion of the IRC requirements for qualified retirement plans is beyond the scope of this chapter. They are referred to here only in general terms and are described in the following nine chapters of the *Handbook* in the context of the individual plans to which they apply. Also, the reader is referred to the discussion of the qualification requirements for retirement plans in Chapter 55 of the *Handbook* which is presented there for small business plans but is applicable to retirement plans in general regardless of their size.

TABLE 31–1
Illustrative Income-Replacement Objectives (Employee with 30 Years of Service)

Final Pay	*Retirement Income as a Percentage of Final Pay**
Under $25,000	80–70%
$25,000 to $50,000	75–65%
$50,000 to $100,000	70–60%
$100,000 to $200,000	65–55%
Over $200,000	60–50%

*Including primary Social Security benefits.

but if it does, contributions made by highly compensated employees cannot exceed those made by lower-paid employees by more than a percentage established under the tax law. By and large, the requirements of federal tax law revolve around the central concept that a plan cannot discriminate as to coverage, contributions, and benefits—as well as in operation—in favor of highly compensated employees.

The discussion that follows covers the major plan features an employer must consider and the approaches most commonly used in establishing actual plan provisions. The emphasis is on the practical aspects of design, rather than on legal requirements.

Service Counting

With rare exceptions, an employee's service will be relevant to his or her benefits under the plan. Specifically, service can be used to determine eligibility for (1) participation in the plan, (2) vested benefits, (3) benefit accruals, (4) early retirement, and (5) ancillary benefits (e.g., spouse or disability benefits). In most plans, service will also be a factor in determining the amount of an employee's benefit.

The law imposes explicit requirements on how service is to be determined for the first three purposes listed above. Generally, service must be measured over a 12-month period (a computation period) that may be a plan, calendar, or employment year. Any such period in which an employee is credited with 1,000 hours of service will be considered a full year of service. The employee's hours of service can be established by counting actual hours worked or by using one of several ''equivalency'' methods permitted by regulations. Alternatively, an ''elapsed time'' method can be used to measure service. The law also requires the inclusion of provisions dealing with breaks in service and the conditions under which service before and after such breaks must be aggregated.

For purposes of early retirement and ancillary benefits, service can be determined on any reasonable basis the employer establishes, provided the method does not discriminate in favor of highly compensated employees. As a practical matter, however, most employers adopt a uniform method of calculating service for all plan purposes.

Administrative considerations are important in choosing a service-counting method. Actual hours-counting, for example, may prove impractical for a plan covering exempt employees who do not maintain detailed records of hours worked. One of the most popular of the available equivalency methods is ''monthly'' equivalency, which credits an employee with 190 hours for any month in which at least one hour of service is credited. The elapsed time method, which—with the exception of break-in-service aspects—measures service from date of employment to date of termination, is also popular. However, these methods give part-time employees the equivalent of full-time service. In situations where this could be a problem, different methods of counting service can be used; for example, service for part-time employees could be determined by actual hours-counting, and the elapsed time method could be used for full-time employees. The use of different methods is permissible only if it does not result in discrimination.

Eligibility for Participation

A plan may require that an employee complete a minimum period of service and attain a minimum age to be eligible to participate. In general, the maximum permissible service requirement is one year, although up to two years may be used in pension plans (without CODAs) that provide for full and immediate vesting. The highest minimum age that can be used is 21.

These minimum age and service requirements can be useful in plans that necessitate maintenance of individual records for participants—defined contribution plans, contributory plans, or plans funded with individual life insurance or annuity contracts. Some administrative cost and effort is avoided by excluding young or short-service employees from such plans until they are beyond what is considered the high-turnover stage of their employment. By contrast, there is very little (if any) administrative work associated with early terminations under a noncontributory defined benefit plan funded with an arrangement that does not require individual employee allocations—for example, a trusteed plan—and plans of this type often provide for eligibility immediately upon employment. However, if the plan bases benefits on years of *participation* (rather than years of service), the use of minimum age and service requirements will reduce the period of participation and, as a result, will reduce benefit costs to some extent. Also, Pension Benefit Guaranty Corporation (PBGC) premiums can be avoided (in plans which are insured) for those employees who have not met the plan's eligibility requirements. Thus, these requirements are sometimes used in noncontributory defined benefit plans.

In the past, maximum-age provisions—typically excluding employees hired after age 60—were common in defined benefit plans. (Such provisions cannot be included in defined contribution plans). However, 1986 legislation now prohibits the use of a maximum-age provision in any type of qualified plan. Instead, defined benefit plans may provide that the normal retirement age for individuals hired after age 60 will coincide with the completion of five years of participation.

Another type of eligibility requirement relates to employment classifications. A plan may be limited to hourly or to salaried employees, to represented or nonrepresented employees, or to individuals employed at certain locations or in specific lines of business. An employee will have to fall within the designated classification to be eligible to participate. Employers must take care that such plans meet the coverage requirements of the IRC.

Plans that limit eligibility to employees who earn more than a stipulated amount are no longer permitted because of changes made by the Tax Reform Act of 1986.

Employee Contributions

Some employers prefer that employees contribute toward the cost of their pension benefits. This preference may be philosophical or it may be founded on more pragmatic considerations of cost and benefit levels. Arguments in favor of noncontributory plans seem to have been more persuasive, however. Employee contributions involve additional administrative effort and cost. Further, if a plan is contributory, an employer may face problems with nonparticipating employees who reach retirement age and cannot afford to retire. Another practical consideration is that almost all collectively bargained plans are noncontributory. An employer that has such a plan will find it difficult to require contributions under plans for nonrepresented employees.

The most compelling factor favoring noncontributory plans is federal tax law. Employer contributions to a pension plan are tax deductible; employee contributions are not.[2] Thus, on an after-tax basis, it is more cost-efficient to fund benefits with employer contributions. (This relative efficiency was diminished somewhat by the lower individual and corporate tax rates effective in 1987, but it still exists.)

Most defined benefit plans do not, in fact, require employee contributions, nor do deferred profit-sharing plans. Both types of plans may permit voluntary employee contributions—that is, contributions that are not required as a condition of participation. Although many pension plans have such an option, very few employees have taken advantage of the opportunity to make these additional contributions.

Employee contributions are more often required as a condition of participation in money purchase pension plans. In theory, the arguments for and against employee contributions are the same for these plans as they are for other arrangements. However, employers often choose the money purchase approach because of cost constraints; where this is the case, employee contributions may be necessary to bring total contributions to a level that will produce adequate benefits. Further, these plans are often viewed—and communicated to employees—as being similar to savings plans where employee contributions are matched by employer contributions.[3]

If employee contributions are required, they are usually set as a percentage of compensation—typically, from 2 to 6 percent. If the plan benefit formula is integrated with Social Security by providing a higher accrual rate for pay over a stipulated level, the same pattern is followed with the contribution rate. If the benefit formula is 1 percent of pay up to $10,000 and 1.5 percent on pay over this amount, for example, the contribution rate might be 2 percent of pay up to $10,000 and 3 percent over this amount.

---

[2]Employee contributions can, of course, be made on a before-tax basis under a deferred profit-sharing plan that has a cash or deferred option meeting the requirements of Section 401(k).

[3]Matching employer contributions under a defined contribution plan as well as after-tax employee contributions have to satisfy an "actual contribution percentage" (ACP) test. This test is similar to the "actual deferral percentage" (ADP) test used for elective contributions under a Section 401(k) plan.

Retirement Ages

Normal Retirement Age

Almost all pension plans specify 65 as normal retirement age. Those plans that have permitted employees to enter after age 60 have usually set the normal retirement age as 65 or, if later, after the completion of five years of participation. Because the law now prohibits the use of a maximum age for participation, this latter definition of normal retirement age will be used in almost all plans.

It is possible—but relatively uncommon—to specify an age under 65 as the plan's normal retirement age. For one thing, providing full benefits before age 65 can be expensive. For another, provisions of this type can result in a violation of age-discrimination laws unless they are carefully designed and operated.

At one time, the concept of a normal retirement age was very significant for defined benefit plans. It was the age at which employees could retire with full, unreduced benefits and without employer consent. Moreover, it was the age at which most employees were expected to retire and the age at which full, unreduced Social Security benefits became available. In most plans, it also marked the point at which pension accruals stopped; continued employment beyond normal retirement usually did not result in increased benefits.

This concept has become diffuse in recent years. Many employers now provide for the payment of full accrued benefits, without reduction, on early retirement after the completion of certain age and service requirements. And, in fact, most employees do retire before age 65. Because of changes in age discrimination laws, benefits must accrue for service beyond normal retirement; also, for individuals born after 1937, the Social Security normal retirement age has been raised. For all practical purposes, a plan's normal retirement age remains significant primarily for determining the value of accrued benefits at any point in time and for determining the amount of any reduction for benefits payable in the event of early retirement. The normal retirement age concept has even less significance in defined contribution plans: once an employee is vested, the value of plan benefits is the same regardless of the reason for the employee's termination (although a retiring employee might have more options as to how the benefit is to be paid).

The distinction between retirement and termination of employment can be important for other employee benefit programs. Some employers, for example, continue employer-supported life insurance and medical expense benefits for retired employees but not for those who terminate employment before qualifying for early retirement. Further, distributions on account of retirement according to plan provisions (and after age 55) will not be subject to the 10 percent additional tax levied on early distributions from a qualified plan.

Early Retirement

Most pension plans permit an employee to retire and receive benefits prior to the plan's normal retirement age. It is customary to require that the employee have attained some minimum age and completed some minimum period of service to qualify for this privilege. The minimum age most frequently used is 55. Minimum service is often set at 10 years, although both shorter and longer periods are used.

The benefit amount payable at early retirement is less than that payable at normal retirement because, in most plans, the employee will not have accrued his or her full benefit. This will not be the case if a defined benefit plan limits service that can be counted in calculating benefits and the employee has already completed the full service period. Even in this situation, however, the benefit could be smaller if it is based on final average pay and the employee loses the advantage of the higher pay base he or she would have achieved if employed until normal retirement age.

Early retirement benefits can be reduced for another reason as well. When benefit payments start before the employee's normal retirement age, they will be paid over a longer period of time; a reduction factor may be applied to recognize these additional payments. This could be a true actuarial factor or, as is more often the case, a simple factor such as one half of 1 percent for each month by which early retirement precedes normal retirement. This type of reduction takes place automatically in a defined contribution plan because the annuity value (in the marketplace) of the employee's account balance will reflect the employee's age and life expectancy.

Many defined benefit plans do not fully reduce the retirement benefit to reflect the early commencement of benefit payments. For example, some plans use a factor of one quarter of 1 percent instead of the one half of 1 percent factor mentioned above. Another common approach is to apply no reduction factor at all if the employee has attained some minimum age (e.g., 60 or 62) and has completed some minimum period of service (e.g., 25 or 30 years) or if the sum of the employee's age and service equals or exceeds a specified number such as 85 or 90.

It is important to understand that there will be additional plan costs when less than a full actuarial reduction (or its equivalent) is used. It is also important to recognize that this type of provision will encourage early retirement and must be considered in the context of the employer's personnel planning needs and objectives.

Deferred Retirement

Prior to the advent of age discrimination laws, it was uncommon for plans to permit deferred retirement solely at the employee's option. If deferred retirement was permitted, it was customary to provide that the benefit payable at actual retirement would be the same as that available at normal retirement—that is, there would be no increase in benefits due to continued employment.

Age discrimination laws, particularly the amendments enacted in 1986, have changed all this. An employee can no longer be discharged for reasons of age; this protection has also been extended to employees over age 70.[4] Further, benefits must continue to accrue under the plan formula for pay and service after the plan's normal retirement age. Thus, as a practical matter, deferred retirement will be permitted under all plans and it will be common for benefits to accrue until the time of actual retirement. However, many plans have or will add a provision that limits the total period of service that can be taken into account for calculating plan benefits; service after this maximum has been reached, whether before or after normal retirement age, will not be taken into account but pay will be considered up until actual retirement.

Retirement Benefits

Because the defined contribution and defined benefit approaches are totally different in terms of plan provisions for determining retirement benefits, they will be discussed separately in this section. A description of the basic concepts of each of these approaches is followed by brief discussions on hybrid plans, Social Security integration, federal tax law limits on contributions and benefits, and the restrictions applicable to "top-heavy" plans.

---

[4]A limited exception allows the use of a mandatory retirement age of 65 for "bona fide" executives whose annual employer-provided retirement benefit (from all sources) is at least $44,000.

Defined Contribution Plans

An employee's retirement benefit under a defined contribution plan—at normal, early, or deferred retirement—is his or her account balance at the time of retirement. This account balance depends on the amounts credited to the employee's account by way of (1) direct contributions, (2) reallocated forfeitures, and (3) investment gains or losses. The annuity value of this account balance—that is, the amount of pension it will generate—depends on then current interest rates and the employee's age at the time the balance is applied to provide a benefit. If the employee purchases an annuity from an insurance company, the annuity value may also reflect the employee's sex. (Even though laws prevent an employer from discriminating on the basis of sex, insurers are not yet required to use unisex factors in pricing their annuity products.)

The contributions made on an employee's behalf under a money purchase pension plan can be made by the employer or by the employee from after-tax income. These contribution rates are fixed and are stipulated in the plan. Although they can be stated in dollar amounts, they are usually expressed as a percentage of pay. For example, the employer contribution to a noncontributory plan might be set as 6 percent of pay. A contributory plan might require an employee contribution of perhaps 3 percent of pay with a matching employer contribution.[5] Contribution rates are usually established on the basis of projections, using reasonable assumptions for growth in pay and investment results, as to the level of replacement income the contributions will generate for employees retiring after completing a career of employment with the employer. Actual experience is likely to differ from the assumptions employed, with the result that actual benefits will be more or less than those projected.

Contributions under a profit-sharing plan typically are made by the employer only—that is, after-tax employee contributions are not mandatory. These contributions are allocated to employees in proportion to pay. Although allocations can be weighted for service, they rarely are; it is almost universal practice to allocate on the basis of pay only. If the plan has a cash or deferred arrangement, an employee electing to defer is, in a sense, making a contribution; however, the deferred amount is considered to be an employer contribution. In any event, the employer

---

[5]As noted earlier, matching employer and after-tax employee contributions under a money purchase plan must satisfy an ACP test.

contribution may be determined by formula or, as is often the case, on a discretionary basis from year to year. The contribution amount may be established with a view toward ultimate benefit levels. However, unlike the money purchase pension plan, the profit-sharing plan does not require an employer commitment as to contribution levels and thus provides flexibility as to cost levels and funding.[6]

Both money purchase pension plans and profit-sharing plans may permit employees to augment their account balances by making voluntary or supplemental contributions. These can be made on an after-tax basis or, in the case of a profit-sharing plan (and within permissible limits), through a reduction in pay. Changes in the taxation of distributions and restrictions on in-service withdrawals from profit-sharing plans may reduce the popularity of this plan feature.[7]

Forfeitures, the second source of credits for an employee's account, arise when employees terminate employment without being fully vested in their account balances. These nonvested amounts can be used to reduce employer contributions or they can be reallocated to employees in the same manner that employer contributions are allocated. Profit-sharing plans often reallocate forfeited amounts. In the past, money purchase plans were required to use forfeitures to reduce employer contributions. Whether this practice will change now that these plans can also reallocate forfeitures remains to be seen.

A third and very important source of credits to an employee's account consists of investment results. Contributions and forfeitures allocated to an employee are invested and the employee's account balance is credited with any investment gains or losses. Some plans invest only in a single fund and all employees share in the aggregate gains and losses. It is more common, however, for employers to offer two or more investment funds and allow employees to choose how their account balances are invested. Available choices might include a fixed-income fund (or a guaranteed interest contract with an insurance company) and an equity fund. In the case of a profit-sharing plan, the employee might also be given the choice of investing in an employer stock fund. (In some

---

[6]Although this contribution flexibility exists, the tax law does require that there be "substantial and recurring" contributions. To date, this requirement has not been clearly defined by the IRS.

[7]Voluntary (unmatched) after-tax employee contributions are also subject to the ACP test. This, too, could have an adverse effect on the use of this feature.

profit-sharing plans—and many savings plans—a minimum amount must be invested in employer stock.)

Defined Benefit Plans

A defined benefit plan is structured to provide a fixed amount of pension benefit at the employee's normal retirement age. The benefit can be a flat dollar amount or flat percentage of pay. It is more common, however, for employees to accrue a unit of benefit for each year of service or participation in the plan. This unit can be a percentage of pay (e.g., 1 percent) or, in the case of some negotiated or hourly employee plans, a dollar amount (e.g., $15).

If a plan provides for a pay-related benefit, the benefit can be determined with reference to the employee's pay each year (a career pay plan) or it can be determined with reference to the employee's pay averaged over a period (such as three or five years) just prior to retirement (a final pay plan). The final pay plan has the advantage of establishing an employee's pension amount on a basis that reflects preretirement inflation, but the employer assumes the cost associated with such inflation. The career pay plan does not protect employees to the same extent, but employers who adopt such plans generally update accrued benefits from time to time to bring actual benefits in line with current compensation. An employer who does this retains some control over the cost of inflation. (A defined contribution plan is, in effect, a career pay plan, but there is no equivalent practice of updating accrued benefits; however, employees might have some degree of inflation protection if the investment return credited to their account balances is higher because of such inflation.) The value of benefits under a nonpay-related plan can also be eroded by inflation. Most of these plans are negotiated, however, and benefits are periodically updated through the collective bargaining process.

The actual formula used in a plan may provide for a full unit of benefit for each year of service or participation, or there may be a maximum period (e.g., 30 years) for which benefits are credited. Some plans provide for a full credit for a specified number of years and a partial credit for years in excess of this number. In any event, the actual design of the formula (including the choice of a career or final pay approach) should reflect the employer's objectives as to income replacement levels.

Hybrid Plans

Some employers have adopted hybrid pension arrangements—plans that incorporate some of the features of both the defined contribution and defined benefit approaches.

One such arrangement is the "target benefit" plan. In this type of plan, a defined benefit formula is used to determine each employee's targeted retirement benefit. An acceptable actuarial cost method, along with acceptable assumptions, is used (although not necessarily by an actuary) to determine a contribution for each employee assumed to be sufficient to provide the targeted benefit. At this point, the plan becomes defined contribution in operation. Individual accounts are established for employees, and all investment gains and losses are credited to their accounts; ultimate retirement benefits will be determined by actual account balances. For most tax law purposes, including Section 415 limits, a target benefit plan is treated as a defined contribution plan. Also, it is not subject to the plan termination insurance provisions of ERISA.

Another hybrid arrangement is the "floor-offset" plan. Here, a defined contribution plan (typically a deferred profit-sharing plan) is used as the primary vehicle for providing retirement benefits. Recognizing that many factors (e.g., investment performance and inflation) might result in the defined contribution plan providing less than adequate benefits in some situations, the employer also maintains a defined benefit floor plan. This floor plan uses a defined benefit formula to establish a minimum benefit. If the defined contribution plan provides a benefit that equals or exceeds this minimum, no benefit is payable from the floor plan; if the defined contribution benefit is less than this minimum, the floor plan makes up the difference. Thus, the total benefit from both plans is equal to the minimum described in the floor plan.

A third hybrid arrangement that has attracted much interest is the "cash balance" plan. This type of plan is, in fact, a defined benefit plan that provides a definitely determinable benefit, requires an annual actuarial valuation, and is subject to all of the tax law requirements that apply to defined benefit plans. Thus, for example, the defined benefit Section 415 limits apply to cash balance plans. Further, these plans are subject to the plan termination insurance provisions of ERISA. In operation, however, the cash balance plan appears to have defined contribution characteristics. Typically, an employee's retirement benefit is based on career average pay, and each year's benefit accrual is indexed to increase at some stipulated rate. This same rate is used to discount the present value of the employee's accrued benefit. The overall actuarial structure of the plan is such that the employee's accrued benefit may be expressed as an "account balance," and the annual "addition" to this account may be expressed as a percent of the employee's current pay. The effect of this is that the plan may be communicated to employees as though it were a defined contribution plan. It should be noted, however, that actual employer contributions and actual investment return on plan assets may not be the same as the annual additions and rate of increase credited to employee accounts. Chapter 36 covers cash balance plans in more detail.

Integrated Formulas

Most pay-related plans are integrated in some fashion with Social Security benefits. The concept of integration recognizes that Social Security benefits are of relatively greater value to lower-paid employees than they are to the highly compensated—particularly on an after-tax basis. Thus, integrated formulas are weighted to compensate for this difference. This approach is sanctioned by federal tax law, but stringent rules must be followed to prevent the plan from discriminating in favor of highly compensated employees.

There are, in general, two ways for integrating plan and Social Security benefits. The first approach—the "excess" method—provides a contribution or benefit for pay over a stipulated level (the integration level) that is higher than that provided for pay below this level. The second approach—the "offset" method—is used only in defined benefit plans and provides that the employee's gross plan benefit is reduced by some amount representing the employer-provided portion of the employee's Social Security benefit.

For defined contribution plans, the contribution rate for pay above the plan's integration level is limited to two times the rate for pay below the integration level. (The integration level for a defined contribution plan may be any amount up to the Social Security taxable wage base at the beginning of the plan year.) Also, the spread between the two contribution rates cannot exceed the greater of (1) 5.7 percent, or (2) the Social Security tax for old-age benefits. This percentage gap is further reduced if the plan's integration level is set at a level which is more than 20 percent but less than 100 percent of the current Social Security taxable wage base. If set between 20 percent and 80 percent of this base, the gap becomes 4.3 percent; if set between 80 percent and 100 percent, it becomes 5.4 percent.

For defined benefit excess plans, the accrual rate for pay above the plan's integration level cannot be more than two times the accrual rate for pay below this level. In addition, the spread between these accrual rates cannot exceed a "permitted disparity"—three quarters of 1 percent for each year of participation up to a maximum of 35 years, or a maximum spread of 26¼ percent. The integration level for these plans may be any amount up to the Social Security taxable wage base at the beginning of the plan year. The permitted disparity will be reduced, however, if the plan's integration level exceeds the Social Security covered compensation level—the average of Social Security taxable wage bases for the preceding 35 years. The permitted disparity will also be reduced for plans with a subsidized early retirement benefit.

For defined benefit offset plans, the benefit otherwise accrued cannot be reduced, by the offset, by more than 50 percent. Also, the offset cannot exceed three quarters of 1 percent of final average pay up to the Social Security covered compensation level, multiplied by years of service up to a maximum of 35 years. The three quarters of 1 percent factor will be reduced if the offset is based on pay in excess of the Social Security covered compensation level, and for early retirement benefits.

A plan that does not meet these integration requirements may still be able to achieve a tax-qualified status by demonstrating that contributions and/or benefits do not discriminate in favor of highly compensated employees under the provisions of Section 401(a)(4) of the IRC.

Limitations

The IRC imposes several limitations on contributions and benefits for highly compensated employees. One, which was added by the Tax Reform Act of 1986 limits the amount of pay that can be taken into account for most qualified plan purposes; initially this limit was set at $200,000. Another change affects profit-sharing plans with a cash or deferred arrangement: the maximum amount that can be deferred each year by an employee on an optional basis is limited to a dollar amount that was initially set at $7,000.

Under Section 415 of the IRC, a defined benefit plan cannot provide a benefit that exceeds $90,000, or 100 percent of pay, if less, per year. This $90,000 limit is actuarially reduced for retirements before the Social Security retirement age. The annual addition under a defined contribution plan for any employee cannot exceed $30,000 or 25 percent of pay, if less. An overall limit applies to individuals covered under both a defined benefit and a defined contribution plan. In effect, the combined plan dollar limit is 125 percent of the limits considered individually. The combined plan percentage limit is 140 percent. Most employers maintain ''excess benefit'' plans to restore benefits lost by reason of these limits.

All of the dollar amounts referred to above are indexed to increase with changes in the Consumer Price Index (CPI), generally beginning in 1988. The $30,000 limit for defined contribution plans, however, will not be increased until changes in the CPI have caused the defined benefit plan limit to increase to $120,000.

Top-Heavy Plans

Special rules apply to any plan that is considered top-heavy. In general, this occurs when the value of accrued benefits for key employees is more than 60 percent of the value of all accrued benefits. If this happens:

- The benefit accrual for non-key employees under a defined benefit plan must be at least 2 percent of pay for up to 10 years.
- The contributions made for non-key employees under a defined contribution plan must be at least 3 percent of pay.
- The Section 415 limits can be further reduced unless special conditions are met.
- Special and more rapid vesting requirements will apply.

Vesting

A tax-qualified pension or profit-sharing plan must provide that the value of any employee contribution is vested at all times. In addition, an employee must be vested in the accrued benefit attributable to employer contributions at normal retirement and, in any event, after a reasonable length of service. An employer may satisfy this requirement with either of two vesting schedules. The first, and simplest, is five-year ''cliff'' vesting—all accrued benefits fully vest after five years of service. The second schedule permits graded vesting; 20 percent of accrued benefits vest after three years of service and that percentage increases in 20 percent multiples each year until 100 percent vesting is achieved after seven years. There are two exceptions to these new standards: (1) negotiated multi-employer plans may continue to use 10-year cliff vesting, and (2) top-heavy plans must provide for 100 percent vesting after three years of service or provide for graded vesting with a 100 percent interest achieved in six years.

It should be noted that vesting refers to the right to receive accrued benefits in the form of a retirement benefit. The law does not require an employer-provided death benefit if an employee dies after meeting the plan's vesting requirements; however, the law does require automatic joint and survivor protection if a vested employee dies.

Defined benefit plans usually provide that if an employee terminates employment, his or her vested benefit will be payable at retirement. Defined contribution plans usually pay the employee's vested account balance at termination, although the employee must be given the opportunity to leave the balance in the plan to be paid at a later time. Most plans, including defined benefit plans, have a provision permitting the payment of small benefit amounts (worth less than $3,500) at termination.

Death Benefits

Qualified plans must comply with the joint and survivor requirements of the IRC—whether the vested employee dies before or after retirement. These benefits, however, need not be provided at any cost to the employer.

Even though the inclusion of employer-provided death benefits is fully optional, if they are included the IRS requires that they be incidental to the primary purpose of the plan, which is to provide retirement benefits. This requirement limits the amount of preretirement lump-sum death benefits to 100 times the employee's expected monthly pension or the reserve for this amount, if greater. (An employee's full account balance, of course, can be paid under a defined contribution plan.) Postretirement death benefits provided under an optional form of payment are generally limited so that no more than 50 percent of the value of the employee's pension can be used to continue death benefits to individuals other than the employee's spouse.

Although death benefits are optional, most defined contribution plans provide for a death benefit of the employee's remaining account balance at time of death—whether before or after retirement.

The practice for defined benefit plans varies. If plan benefits are funded with individual life insurance policies, there is likely to be a preretirement death benefit up to 100 times the employee's expected monthly pension. Except for this type of insurance, however, it is unusual for defined benefit plans to pay lump-sum benefits from employer contributions. (If employees have made contributions, these are almost always payable as a death benefit, usually with interest but less any pension payments made to the employee prior to death.) The most common form of employer-provided death benefit under defined benefit plans is a spouse or survivor benefit, under which some part of the employee's accrued benefit is payable, in periodic installments, to the employee's spouse or some other survivor. This benefit is usually payable for life in the case of a spouse or another adult such as a dependent parent; in the case of surviving children, the benefit is usually payable until the child reaches a stipulated age. Although such a benefit could be paid for deaths occurring both before and after retirement, postretirement survivor benefits are provided less frequently because of their higher cost. For the most part, survivor benefits are limited to surviving spouses. As noted, however, some plans will pay benefits to dependent parents or children if there is no surviving spouse.

An employer can provide a survivor benefit indirectly by subsidizing the rates used for joint and survivor protection; that is, by not charging the employee the full actuarial cost of the protection. The customary practice of employers who want to pay for this benefit, however, is simply to do so on a basis that involves no cost to employees.

Disability Benefits

A pension or profit-sharing plan need not provide a disability benefit as such. Of course, if an employee is otherwise vested and terminates employment because of disability, regular benefits payable on termination of employment must be available.

Most employers provide disability income benefits under separate plans. When this is the case, the employer's pension arrangement usually operates to complement the disability income plan by providing for continued benefit accruals or contributions during the period of disability.

Some employers, however, make their pension arrangement the major source of benefits for employees who incur a long-term disability (usually one that lasts for more than six months). Under a defined contribution plan, for example, the employee might be fully vested in his or her account balance, regardless of service, and this amount could be made available in the case of disability—either in a lump sum or in the form of installment payments. A defined benefit plan could treat the disability as an early retirement even though the employee had not satisfied the regular requirements, and might even waive the reduction in benefit that would otherwise occur at early retirement. A defined benefit plan might also provide for a separately stated benefit in the case of disability, possibly with more liberal age and service requirements than those that apply for early retirement. Disability income benefits from defined benefit plans are found more often in negotiated plans than they are in plans covering nonrepresented employees.

From the standpoint of benefit adequacy, employees are usually better off with separate, pay-related disability benefits. Those benefits payable from qualified plans (whether defined contribution or defined benefit) reach reasonable levels only for those employees who have long periods of service or participation.

Other Plan Provisions

Provisions dealing with the following matters must also be included in any pension arrangement:

- The employer's right to amend and terminate the plan.
- Protection of employee rights in the event of plan mergers or the transfer or acquisition of plan assets.
- Treatment of employees on leave of absence (including military leave).
- Rehiring of retirees who are receiving benefits.
- The ability to make benefit payments to a payee who is a minor or otherwise incompetent.
- A prohibition against employees making assignments (except for qualified domestic relations orders (QDROs).
- The rights and obligations of plan fiduciaries, including the right to delegate or allocate responsibilities.

DEFINED CONTRIBUTION VERSUS DEFINED BENEFIT PLANS

A critical decision for any employer who is about to adopt a pension plan is whether to use the defined contribution or defined benefit approach or a combination of the two. As noted at the outset of this chapter, most employees are now covered by defined benefit plans, but the defined contribution approach has grown in popularity since the passage of the Employment Retirement Income Security Act (ERISA). Some of this popularity is attributable to the positive treatment afforded these plans by legislation over the past 10 years; for example, the laws dealing with individual retirement accounts (IRAs), simplified employee pensions (SEPs), 401(k) plans, employee stock ownership plans (ESOPs), and flexible compensation arrangements. Some is also due to legislation that has made it increasingly difficult to design and administer defined benefit plans—changes in the Social Security normal retirement age, joint and survivor requirements, age and sex discrimination laws, provisions relating to qualified domestic relations orders, and the like.

Whatever the reason, more and more employers, including those who maintain defined benefit plans, are examining the defined contribution approach to providing retirement benefits. Thus, it is important to understand and evaluate the basic characteristics of both approaches. The following factors should be considered in deciding which approach is appropriate in a given situation:

1. Most employers have specific income-replacement objectives in mind when they establish a retirement plan. A defined benefit plan can be structured to achieve these objectives. The defined contribution approach will probably produce benefits that either fall short of or exceed these objectives for individual employees.
2. By the same token, most employers want to take Social Security benefits into account so that the combined level of benefits from both sources will produce the desired results. Defined contribution plans can be integrated with Social Security benefits to some extent by adjusting contribution levels, but integration can be accomplished more efficiently under defined benefit plans.
3. The defined benefit plan requires an employer commitment to pay the cost of the promised benefits. Thus, the employer must assume any additional costs associated with inflation and adverse investment results. The defined contribution plan transfers these risks to employees and allows the employer to fix its cost.
4. A deferred profit-sharing plan offers an employer the ultimate in contribution and funding flexibility. The money purchase pension plan, however, offers little flexibility because contributions are fixed and must be made each year. Although the defined benefit

plan involves an employer commitment as to ultimate cost, there can be significant funding flexibility on a year-to-year basis through the use of various actuarial methods and assumptions, the amortization of liabilities, and the operation of the minimum-funding standard account. (There is less flexibility with respect to establishing the annual charge to earnings for defined benefit plans, however, as a result of new accounting standards.)

5. The other side of the cost issue concerns benefits for employees. A defined benefit plan can protect the employee against the risk of preretirement inflation. In a defined contribution plan, this risk is assumed by the employee, who must rely primarily on investment results to increase the value of benefits during inflationary periods.
6. Employees also assume the risk of investment loss under a defined contribution plan. Many observers feel it is inappropriate for the average employee to assume such a risk with respect to a major component of his or her retirement security.
7. The typical defined contribution plan provides that the employee's account balance is payable in the event of death and, frequently, in case of disability. This, of course, produces additional plan costs or, alternatively, lower retirement benefits if overall costs are held constant. An employer who is interested primarily in providing retirement benefits can use available funds more efficiently for this purpose under a defined benefit plan.
8. Many observers believe that a more equitable allocation of employer contributions occurs under a defined benefit plan because the employee's age, past service, and pay can all be taken into account; the typical defined contribution plan allocates contributions only on the basis of pay. On the other hand, the very nature of a final pay defined benefit plan is that the value of total benefits accrued becomes progressively greater each year as the employee approaches retirement; under a defined contribution plan, a greater value will accrue during the early years of participation. As a result of the greater values accrued in earlier years, defined contribution plans produce higher benefits and costs for terminating employees than do defined benefit plans.
9. Profit-sharing and savings plans offer two potential advantages that are not available under defined benefit and money purchase

pension plans. Profit sharing can create employee incentives. These plans can also invest in employer securities, giving employees, as shareholders, the opportunity to identify with overall corporate interests.

10. Younger employees are apt to perceive a defined contribution plan, with its accumulating account values, to be of more value than a defined benefit plan. The reverse is probably true for older employees. Thus, the average age of the group to be covered can be critical.
11. Defined benefit plans are subject to the plan-termination provisions of ERISA, thus requiring the employer to pay annual Pension Benefit Guaranty Corporation (PBGC) premiums and exposing the employer's net worth to liability if the plan is terminated with insured but unfunded benefit promises. Defined contribution plans do not have this exposure.

These factors will have different significance for different employers, and a choice that is appropriate for one organization may be inappropriate for another. Many employers will find that a combination of the two approaches is the right answer—a defined benefit plan that provides a basic layer of benefits, along with a defined contribution arrangement that is a source of supplemental benefits.

CHAPTER 32

PROFIT-SHARING PLANS

Bruce A. Palmer

Programs providing retirement income have received great attention in recent years. The reasons for this attention are many and varied but most relate fundamentally to inflation, other economic problems, and the inability of individuals to provide for their own retirement security without assistance from some formal group savings or social program. With the growth in concern over the future viability of the Social Security program and its ability to provide meaningful benefits to most retirees, substantial additional attention has been focused on employer-sponsored retirement programs.

This chapter continues the discussion of retirement plans that began in Chapter 31 and extends throughout Part Eight of the *Handbook*. Specifically, the chapter focuses on profit-sharing plans as defined in Section 401(a) of the Internal Revenue Code (IRC). Collectively, these plans constitute a major component of the overall retirement benefit structure existing in the private sector.

DEFINITION OF PROFIT SHARING

A profit-sharing plan is a plan or program for sharing company profits with the firm's employees. The contributions to a qualified, deferred profit-sharing plan are accumulated in a tax-sheltered account to provide income to employees during their retirement years. Historically, deferred profit-sharing plans also have provided for the distribution of moneys on other prescribed occasions to employees or their beneficiaries.

According to federal income tax regulations:

> A profit-sharing plan is a plan established and maintained by an employer to provide for the participation in his profits by his employees or their beneficiaries. The plan must provide a definite predetermined formula for allocating the contributions made to the plan among the participants and for distributing the funds accumulated under the plan after a fixed number of years, the attainment of a stated age, or upon the prior occurrence of some event such as layoff, illness, disability, retirement, death, or severance of employment.[1]

Under the Employee Retirement Income Security Act of 1974 (ERISA) and the IRC, profit-sharing plans are treated as defined contribution or individual account plans. As such, an employer is under no financial obligation to provide a specific dollar amount of benefit at retirement in these plans.

Periodic (for example, annual) employer contributions to profit-sharing plans are allocated to individual accounts set up for each plan participant.[2] These contributions are augmented by each employee's share of investment earnings and possibly further by forfeitures of account balances created when nonvested (or partially vested) participants terminate their employment with the sponsoring firm. The amount of benefit available to the participant will be solely a function of the amount in the individual account at the time of retirement and the level of monthly income which that accumulated amount will purchase.

The concept of profit sharing, in its broadest sense, encompasses any program under which the firm's profits are shared with its employees. Thus, it includes both cash plans and deferred–distribution plans. Under cash plans, profit-sharing amounts are distributed to employees currently as a bonus or a wage/salary supplement. Consequently, these distributions are includable in the employees' income in the year of distribution and taxed on top of their wages, salaries, and other income.[3] Deferred-distribution profit-sharing plans are programs in which the profit-sharing

---

[1]Reg. 1.401-1(b)(1)(ii).

[2]Federal regulations require that an individual account be maintained for each plan participant in defined contribution plans.

[3]Payments under cash profit-sharing plans may be made as soon as the respective participants' allocations are determined. Thus, the structure of these plans is simplified since there is no trust fund, no assets to be invested, and so on. Of course, the major disadvantage of these plans is that the payments are currently taxed to the participants.

amounts are credited to employee accounts (held under trust) and accumulated for later distribution (for example, upon retirement, or some other specified event, such as death, disability, or severance of employment, or according to the terms of any plan withdrawal provisions).

In actuality, there is a third approach to profit sharing since it is possible for a firm to have a combination cash and deferred profit-sharing plan covering essentially the same group(s) of employees. Under this arrangement, a portion of the profit-sharing allocation is distributed currently to the participant with the remainder deferred. A combination plan can be designed in one of two ways: (1) two separate plans may be established—one cash and the other deferred, or (2) only one plan is created, and it possesses both current and deferred features. This latter type of combination plan sometimes is referred to as a *cash or deferred* profit-sharing plan (CODA). Most frequently these arrangements are referred to as 401(k) plans.

In this chapter, the term *profit-sharing plan* shall refer to the deferred-distribution form and will not include cash profit-sharing or 401(k) plans unless otherwise noted. Cash profit-sharing plans are *not* qualified plans within the meaning of IRC Section 401(a), and 401(k) plans are discussed in detail in Chapter 34 of the *Handbook*.

On rare occasions, profit-sharing plans provide for the payment of supplementary contributions (usually voluntary) by the covered employees. However, this chapter does not address any distinctive features that might be attributed to contributory profit-sharing plans nor does it cover thrift or savings plans,[4] which are described in Chapter 33 of the *Handbook*. Also, a substantial majority of thrift plans today have 401(k) arrangements. Plans of this type are included in the discussion of 401(k) plans in Chapter 34.

---

[4]The IRS does not have a separation or division of requirements addressing only thrift plans. Thus, many thrift and savings plans qualify with the IRS under the profit-sharing rules and hence would be deemed to be profit-sharing plans. However, the purist would argue that there still exists a fundamental difference between a contributory profit-sharing plan and a thrift or savings plan. In the latter case, employer contributions to the plan are usually fixed at some predetermined percentage "match" (e.g., 25, 50, or 100 percent) of the employee contributions for the purpose of encouraging thrift on the part of the employee. Thus, employer contributions to a thrift plan are dependent primarily on the "level of employee thrift." In contrast, employer contributions to a contributory profit-sharing plan are primarily a function of the "level of profits." Further, in contributory profit-sharing plans where the employee contributions are voluntary, employer contributions to a participant's account usually are not made contingent on the payment of contributions by the participant.

IMPORTANCE OF PROFIT-SHARING PLANS

While several notable profit-sharing plans had been in existence prior to 1939, that year seems to signal the beginning of the major growth experienced in profit-sharing plans. In 1939 the U.S. Senate's endorsement of the profit-sharing concept, together with subsequent favorable tax legislation, provided the stimulus for the establishment of profit-sharing plans. In the 25 years preceding the enactment of ERISA, the number of deferred profit-sharing plans doubled approximately every 5 years. However, the reforms and uncertainties created by ERISA's enactment had a major deterrent effect on the establishment of all types of qualified plans, initially even including profit-sharing plans. Today, profit-sharing plans are extremely important in terms of the number of annual new plan approvals. This prominence is largely due to the strong interest in 401(k) plans.

The importance of profit-sharing plans is further underscored by the dual purpose that they serve in the overall structure of retirement-income planning. Profit-sharing plans often exist as the sole retirement-income plan in many firms, particularly in firms of small-to-medium size in which employers may feel unable to assume the financial commitment associated with a money purchase or defined benefit pension plan. In larger firms, profit-sharing plans often are established as a supplement to a defined benefit pension plan. There are several advantages to this combination approach. In addition to enhancing the possibility of greater total benefits, the pension plan can provide employees with protection against the down-side risk that corporate profits will be low, leading to minimal contributions to the profit-sharing plan and, ultimately, to the payment of inadequate profit-sharing plan benefits.

EMPLOYER OBJECTIVES IN ESTABLISHING A DEFERRED PROFIT-SHARING PLAN

An employer normally has a number of specific objectives in electing to establish a qualified deferred profit-sharing plan. A major objective, of course, is to provide a vehicle, on behalf of covered employees, for the accumulation of tax-favored assets that, in turn, will constitute a primary source of income at retirement. As part of the overall objectives in establishing a qualified plan of any type, employers seek the various tax advantages associated with such a plan. These include the deductibility (within limits) of employer contributions, the tax-free accumulation of moneys held in trust under the plan, the current nontaxability to employees of employer contributions and investment earnings on plan assets, and special income tax treatment accorded qualifying lump-sum distributions.[5] In addition, employers typically have one or more other important objectives in establishing a qualified profit-sharing plan.

As part of a firm's overall compensation scheme, profit-sharing plans play a significant role in compensating employees and achieving various employee benefit objectives. In addition, many firms establish profit-sharing plans in the hope of improving their productivity and efficiency. Finding ways to increase productivity is a major concern in the United States today. For many firms, costs have increased more rapidly than revenues leading to declining profitability. Establishment of a profit-sharing plan may lead to improved employee morale and provide a source of motivation to employees to perform in a more productive and efficient manner. Since employer contributions to the plan are tied to the firm's profits, a profit-sharing plan provides employees with a direct incentive to become more efficient and more productive, resulting in lower costs and higher profits to the firm.[6] To the extent that these anticipated results are realized, employees, management, and stockholders alike should all benefit from the establishment of a profit-sharing plan.

Although both profit-sharing and pension plans create asset accumulation and financial security for covered employees and their depen-

---

[5]Under prior law, qualifying lump-sum distributions were eligible for the so-called 10-year forward averaging treatment. Capital gains treatment could also be elected for any pre-1974 portion of the distribution. The Tax Reform Act of 1986 repealed the 10-year averaging rules and applied a 6-year phaseout of the capital gains treatment accorded pre-1974 amounts. The new tax treatment provides for 5-year forward averaging on a one-time basis, but only for qualifying distributions made after attainment of age 59½. A special election, or transition rule, is available for individuals who attained age 50 before January 1, 1986. This special transition rule permits the "grandfathered" group to continue to have the entire pre-1974 portion of a qualifying lump-sum distribution taxed as a long-term capital gain, at a maximum rate of 20 percent. Further, members of the grandfathered group can elect to apply either 5-year or 10-year (at 1986 tax rates) averaging to all or the remaining portion of the lump-sum distribution. This special treatment is even available to qualifying lump-sum distributions made prior to age 59½.

[6]Arguments also can be presented against this line of reasoning. For example, it is argued that profit-sharing plans reward poor performance equally as well as good performance, thereby questioning whether profit-sharing plans are truly motivational. Further, there is an issue as to how many employees in a firm can really influence profitability. In summary, the relationships among motivation, increased productivity, and the establishment of deferred profit-sharing plans are still strongly debated issues.

dents, these two approaches provide the employer with substantially different levels of funding flexibility. Under a money purchase or a defined benefit pension plan, the employer has a fixed commitment (not contingent on profit levels) to contribute amounts that meet certain ERISA-prescribed minimum requirements.[7] In most instances, these requirements will result in the employer having to make contributions to the plan during each and every year. Under a profit-sharing plan, it is possible for the firm to not make any contributions to the plan for a given year (or several years). This offers greater relative contribution flexibility to the employer under the profit-sharing approach. The lack of a fixed yearly contribution obligation under profit-sharing plans is especially advantageous for small businesses and for new firms that may be unable to assume the fixed costs required of pension plans. In years of no profits, or when profits fall below a predetermined level, no employer contributions need to be made. In contrast, in years of high profits, larger-than-average contributions can be made to the profit-sharing plan. For these reasons, profit-sharing plans possess maximum flexibility with regard to employer contributions.

In establishing any new retirement-income plan, most employers will want to take employee desires into account. Younger and middle-aged employees may prefer the individual account approach inherent in a profit-sharing arrangement. The individual account approach often provides an opportunity to accumulate large sums on behalf of younger employees. Conversely, older employees generally tend to prefer a defined benefit plan (with its predetermined level of promised benefits) to either a profit-sharing or a money purchase pension plan. A profit-sharing or money purchase plan generally will not provide an accumulation of moneys sufficient to provide adequate retirement benefits for those employees near retirement at the time the plan is established. In choosing between the two approaches, profit sharing (or money purchase) and defined benefit, the employer should consider the age distribution of the employee group to be covered by the plan. In the decision-making process, the employer should also take into consideration the firm's hiring objectives. A defined contribution plan may be preferred if the firm is

[7] For money purchase plans, this entails the payment of a fixed rate of contribution; for defined benefit plans, it requires the payment of contributions at a level necessary to fund the promised benefits. In both cases, it means a specific contribution commitment without regard to the profit levels of the firm.

interested primarily in hiring less-experienced, younger employees. In contrast, a defined benefit plan is likely to be more attractive to older executives hired from other firms. Based on these factors, the employer may decide to have a combination profit-sharing and defined benefit plan to appeal to both young and older workers.

An employer may be influenced by other objectives in deciding to adopt a profit-sharing plan. For example, the individual account feature provides employees with the opportunity to share in favorable investment results, which potentially could lead to much higher levels of monthly benefits at retirement.[8] In contrast, favorable investment earnings reduce employer costs under defined benefit plans. In addition, defined contribution plans including profit-sharing permit the reallocation of forfeitures of nonvested (and partially vested) terminated participants among the remaining participants, thus providing the possibility of even greater benefits to those employees who remain with the firm for long periods.[9] To the extent an employer wants the firm's long-service employees to share in both forfeitures and favorable investment earnings, the profit-sharing approach may be preferred.

An employer also may prefer certain other features that can be incorporated into the design of a profit-sharing plan whose inclusion in pension plans is either prohibited or substantially restricted. Specifically, the employer may want to provide covered employees with the option to make withdrawals from their individual accounts while still actively employed, or the employer may desire that the funds held in the profit-sharing trust be invested in employer stock or other employer securities to a greater extent than permitted under a pension plan. When profit-sharing plan assets are invested in employer securities, employees have the opportunity to participate to an even greater extent in the success of the company.

Finally, the employer may want to avoid certain regulatory requirements imposed on defined benefit pension plans. These include satisfying

---

[8]However, the employee also is exposed to the down-side risk of low or otherwise unfavorable investment results. This may be a potential source of employee (and possibly employer) dissatisfaction with the plan and, in addition, requires a greater sensitivity on the part of the employer to fiduciary obligations associated with the investment of plan assets. The exposure to potentially increased fiduciary liability constitutes an important disadvantage associated with the adoption of defined contribution plans.

[9]In the future, the issue of forfeitures and their reallocation may become less important because of the faster vesting requirements imposed by the Tax Reform Act of 1986.

minimum funding standards, payment of plan termination insurance premiums to the Pension Benefit Guaranty Corporation (PBGC), and the exposure to contingent employer liability and the attendent impact on the firm's accounting and financial reports. In addition to their many advantages, profit-sharing plans possess several important disadvantages. One relative disadvantage of profit-sharing plans relates to the difficulty of providing employees with adequate credit for any period of past service (i.e., service prior to plan inception). Past service credits can be incorporated with relative ease in most defined benefit pension plans. Second, the ultimate benefits payable at retirement under a profit-sharing plan (or any other defined contribution plan) may be inadequate for those employees near retirement at the time of plan inception. Third, profit-sharing amounts contributed to the plan in any year usually are allocated among the individual employee accounts on the basis of each employee's annual compensation. Thus, age and years of service generally are ignored in the profit-sharing allocation formula. Fourth, the allocation patterns under profit-sharing plans are such that relatively larger amounts are provided to short-service employees who terminate with vested rights compared with what occurs under defined benefit plans. Additional disadvantages of profit-sharing plans relate to the employee's assumption of the inflation and investment risks (see footnote 8) and the risk of little or no profits to the firm, which, collectively, could result in inadequate benefits at retirement.

QUALIFICATION REQUIREMENTS APPLICABLE TO DEFERRED PROFIT-SHARING PLANS

For the most part, the same or similar qualification requirements apply equally to both pension plans and deferred profit-sharing plans. These requirements relate to (1) the plan provisions being contained in a written document (ensuring a formal, enforceable plan), (2) plan permanency, (3) communication of plan provisions to the employees, (4) the plan being established and operated for the exclusive benefit of plan participants or their beneficiaries, (5) minimum participation (eligibility) standards, (6) nondiscrimination in coverage and contributions/benefits, (7) minimum vesting standards, and so forth. Because of the similarity of regulatory treatment between pension plans and profit-sharing plans, the discussion of the general legal requirements for plan qualification are minimized here.

There are, however, a few ways in which profit-sharing plans are treated differently from pension plans for qualification purposes. Additionally, although pension and profit-sharing plans alike are subject to the same eligibility and vesting rules, the eligibility and vesting provisions included in many profit-sharing plans contain more liberal requirements.

A significant regulatory difference between plans relates to the investment of plan assets in employer securities. Pension plans (including both defined benefit and money purchase plans) are restricted in terms of their ability to invest plan assets in employer stock. These plans are subject to the ERISA Section 404 requirement that no more than 10 percent of the fair market value of plan assets can be invested in qualifying employer securities and employer real property.[10] This limitation does not apply to profit-sharing plans. As a result, profit-sharing plans may invest their assets in qualifying employer securities and employer real property without restriction as to percentage limitation.[11]

Many employers believe that the investment of a portion of profit-sharing plan assets in employer stock provides employees with an additional incentive to improve their performance in job-related activities. The extent to which profit-sharing plans invest a portion of the plan assets in employer stock is likely to be related to several factors, including company size, overall profitability of the firm (including future prospects as regards profitability), marketability of the stock, and others. Historically, the investment of profit-sharing plan assets in employer stock has been widespread among very large companies and also among companies whose ownership is closely held. Because both advantages and disadvantages are present, great care should be exercised in making decisions concerning the investment of plan assets in employer stock.

As mentioned earlier, profit-sharing plans are not subject to certain provisions of ERISA affecting qualified defined benefit pension plans. These primarily relate to the minimum funding standards and the various plan-termination insurance requirements. Further, in defined benefit plans, forfeitures must be used to reduce future employer contributions to

---

[10]From the covered employee's standpoint, this limitation may not be as important under a defined benefit plan as it is under a money purchase plan. Any appreciation in the employer's stock under a defined benefit plan serves to reduce future employer contributions, thus resulting in no direct benefit to the employee.

[11]Of course, investment of profit-sharing plan assets in employer stock (along with other investment media) must meet the prudent expert standard of ERISA.

the plan. In contrast, under profit-sharing plans, forfeitures may be used either to reduce future employer contributions or reallocated among the remaining participants (the usual case), thereby increasing the amounts in the participants' individual accounts.[12]

In addition to those qualification requirements that are distinctive of profit-sharing plans, as described above, other requirements imposed on all qualified plans frequently are satisfied differently under profit-sharing plans. The following discussion focuses on two areas: (1) eligibility (participation) requirements, and (2) vesting requirements.

Permissible eligibility requirements include *(a)* a minimum age requirement of 21 and *(b)* a minimum period of service of one year. (A two-year service requirement is permitted, together with age 21, if the plan provides for full and immediate vesting upon satisfying the plan's eligibility requirements.) These eligibility requirements apply to both profit-sharing and pension plans alike. Under the Tax Reform Act of 1986, effective for plan years beginning after December 31, 1988, qualified plans must also satisfy a complex set of coverage and benefit nondiscrimination rules. For many deferred profit-sharing plans in existence today, the eligibility and coverage provisions tend to be more liberal than what are required as minimum standards for qualification purposes, and they also tend to be more liberal than those commonly employed in pension plans.

Most profit-sharing plans provide broad coverage of employees, although they often exclude seasonal and part-time employees (e.g., those who work fewer than 1,000 hours per year). (*Note:* Once employees meet the "one-year-at-1,000-hours requirement," the plan cannot thereafter exclude them as seasonal or part-time.) Some plans make employees eligible on the date of hire, and many others use a minimum service requirement of less than one year. In addition, most profit-sharing plans do not use a minimum age requirement, and these plans, historically, rarely have been integrated with benefits payable under Social Security.

Regarding vesting, the Tax Reform Act of 1986 specifies that profit-sharing plans must meet one of two alternative minimum vesting standards: (1) five-year cliff vesting, or (2) seven-year graded vesting. Under the five-year rule, plan participants are not required to have any

---

[12]From the standpoint of remaining plan participants, the advantage inherent in profit-sharing plans that accrues from reallocation of forfeitures is somewhat mitigated by the presence of more rapid vesting typically found in profit-sharing plans. See *infra*.

vested rights in employer-provided benefits until after the completion of five years of service, at which point the participants must be 100 percent vested. Under the seven-year graded vesting rule, participants must be at least 20 percent vested after the completion of three years of service, with the required vesting percentage increasing by 20 percent each year until 100 percent vesting is reached at the end of seven years.[13]

A substantial majority of profit-sharing plans provide more liberal vesting than prescribed under the IRC Section 411(a) alternative minimum vesting standards. In fact, a significant percentage of profit-sharing plans provide full and immediate vesting upon plan participation. Other plans provide full vesting if a participant's employment is terminated "through no fault of the employee;" this might occur, for example, at the closing of a plant, department, or smaller organizational unit. Finally, while the law requires that full vesting occur at retirement and upon plan termination, nearly all deferred profit-sharing plans also provide full vesting in the event of the participant's death or total and permanent disability.

The liberal coverage and eligibility and vesting provisions typically found in most profit-sharing plans are consistent with an overall employer objective of providing employees with an incentive to work more efficiently, which, it is hoped, will lead to increased profits for the firm.[14]

---

[13]These rules became effective for plan years beginning after December 31, 1988. They replaced the original "10-Year Rule," the "5-to-15 Year Rule," and the "Rule of 45" created by ERISA. Collectively bargained multiemployer plans are permitted to continue to comply with the 10-Year Rule. Plans that are classified as "top-heavy" must still comply with additional vesting requirements imposed under the Tax Equity and Fiscal Responsibility Act of 1982 (TEFRA). Specifically, if a plan is "top-heavy," its vesting schedule must comply with one of two rules: *(a)* "three-year cliff vesting," or *(b)* "six-year graded vesting."

[14]It also should be noted that the employer's contributions (costs) to a profit-sharing plan are not increased or otherwise affected either by a larger number of participants (through more liberal eligibility requirements) or through more rapid vesting; assuming, of course, that nonvested forfeitures are reallocated among the remaining participants (the typical case) rather than used to reduce future employer contributions. (While this statement is generally true, it is not applicable to those profit-sharing plans that base their contribution on a percentage of compensation subject to a maximum contribution based on profit.) This is in direct contrast to the situation that occurs in either a money purchase or a defined benefit pension plan. Pension plans that are designed with more liberal eligibility and vesting rules result in higher costs to the employer. Thus, to reduce total plan costs, pension plans generally impose more restrictive eligibility rules and less liberal vesting requirements than those used in deferred profit-sharing plans. It is important to note, however, that under profit-sharing plans the *allocation* of both contributions (profits) and forfeitures among plan participants would be affected by a plan's eligibility and vesting requirements.

This objective can be maximized in a deferred profit-sharing plan only through broad participation, through the imposition of few eligibility restrictions, and through the providing of liberal vesting.

In conclusion, the employer's reason(s) for establishing a deferred profit-sharing plan should have a direct bearing on the specific eligibility and vesting requirements adopted by the plan. That is, an objective of creating employee incentives would indicate short periods for vesting and minimum or no eligibility requirements. Other objectives, such as maximizing the retirement income that may be provided to long-service employees from a specified amount of employer contribution, might indicate longer vesting periods and more stringent eligibility requirements subject to the minimum qualification standards.

CONTRIBUTIONS TO DEFERRED PROFIT-SHARING PLANS

The subject matter pertaining to profit-sharing contributions constitutes a most important topic in regard to the overall design of deferred profit-sharing plans. It is these contribution amounts, together with investment earnings and forfeiture reallocations, that ultimately determine the amount of funds available for distribution to plan participants at retirement or upon other prescribed occasions.

The discussion of profit-sharing contributions is divided into three major subsections. These subsections describe, respectively, the various methods of ascertaining contribution amounts to deferred profit-sharing plans, alternative formulas for allocating the profit-sharing contributions among plan participants, and the maximum limits imposed under federal tax law on contributions and allocations.

Methods of Determining Profit-Sharing Contributions

A most important concern of profit-sharing plans centers on the question, "How much of the profits should be shared with the employees?" In regard to a specific employer, the portion or percentage of profits that should be contributed is likely to depend on several factors, including the (1) amount and stability of the firm's annual profits; (2) capital requirements of the firm (e.g., needs for working capital, reserves, and expansion); (3) level of return to be provided stockholders on their investment in the firm; (4) presence (or absence) of other capital accumulation or retirement income programs sponsored by the firm; (5) portion of profits that is to be used in upgrading the (cash) payroll levels of the employees; (6) federal tax law, which places limitations on annual contributions, deductions, and allocations to participants' accounts; and, of course, (7) objectives of the plan, particularly the extent to which management believes that the profit-sharing plan serves as a motivator to covered employees and the extent to which employee behavior can affect, in a significant way, the profit levels of the particular firm in question.[15]

A second area of interest relating to profit-sharing contributions concerns how profits are to be defined in the plan. Employers have considerable flexibility in making this determination since "profits" are not defined in great detail under federal tax law. Traditionally, "profits" have related to current-year profits, although it has been legally permissible for deferred profit-sharing plans to base their profit-sharing contributions on both current profits and profits accumulated from prior years. With the passage of the Tax Reform Act of 1986, profits are no longer required for contributions, and employers are permitted to make contributions even when there are no current or accumulated profits. Further, profits can be defined either in terms of "before-tax profits" or "after-tax profits," with the majority of companies basing their profit-sharing contributions on before-tax profits.[16] Additionally, a significant number of plans provide that only profits in excess of some stipulated minimum dollar amount (e.g., $100,000) or in excess of a minimum return to stockholders (e.g., 30 cents per share) are available for profit sharing.[17]

---

[15]One fairly basic concept in this regard is to split profits equally into three shares: *(a)* one third to employees in the form of profit-sharing contributions, *(b)* one third to stockholders in the form of dividends, and *(c)* one third to customers, either through price reductions or expenditures for product improvement. In some instances, element *(c)* is eliminated, with that share going into company surplus and being available for reinvestment in the company's operations. It is important to note that when companies provide as much as a one-third share of profits to employees, it may be that not all of these moneys will flow into a deferred profit-sharing arrangement because of limitations on tax deductions and allocations (and possibly for other reasons). Rather, a substantial portion of these profit-sharing moneys might be distributed immediately to the employees.

[16]It should be noted that employers are permitted to determine "profits" in accordance with generally accepted accounting principles, even when this may differ from the calculation of profits under federal income tax law.

[17]Even when a specific provision for a minimum return on capital is not included in a profit-sharing formula, the concept generally is taken into consideration in the profit-sharing deliberations in an indirect way.

Conditions such as these are commonly referred to as "prior reservations for capital," or simply, "prior reservations." Their purpose is to protect the financial interests of the company's shareholders. Employers who incorporate a prior reservation in determining their profit-sharing contributions commonly share a greater percentage of profits, once the reservation has been satisfied, than plans that do not include a prior reservation. The rationale for smaller profit-sharing percentages (often between 5 percent and 10 percent of before-tax profits) in companies not stipulating a prior reservation is that these percentages are applied to all profits, not just those amounts in excess of some stipulated level, as is the case with employers that specify a prior reservation.

Most important, profit-sharing contribution methods differ according to whether profits are shared on the basis of a fixed formula, with its terms and conditions communicated in advance to plan participants, or whether the company's board of directors in a discretionary manner determines the annual percentage of profits to be shared. Although the use of a predetermined, fixed-contribution formula is not required under the law (and, consequently, no specific minimum level or rate of contribution is required),[18] profit-sharing contributions must meet two other legal requirements. Specifically, the contributions must be "substantial and recurring,"[19] to lend support to the qualification requirement pertaining to plan permanency, and these contributions cannot be applied in any manner (either in amount or time) that would result in discrimination in favor of highly compensated employees. So long as these general restrictions are complied with, an employer may establish any method or formula for determining the profit-sharing amounts that are to be contributed to the plan.

The major advantage of the discretionary approach is its tremendous flexibility in the annual determination of contributions. Under this approach, the board of directors has the opportunity of viewing past experience along with the firm's current financial position and capital requirements before making the decision as to the portion of profits to be shared in the current year. Contribution rates may be adjusted upward or downward from previous years' rates based on any number of factors, including the current financial picture of the firm. Under the predetermined formula approach, the plan itself would have to be amended to

[18]Reg. 1.401-1(b)(2).

[19]Reg. 1.401-1(b)(2).

accommodate an employer's desire to adjust the profit-sharing contribution rate. Use of the discretionary method also ensures that the firm will not have to make contributions to the deferred profit-sharing plan in amounts that exceed the maximums that may be deducted currently for federal income tax purposes.[20]

When the discretionary approach is used, the plan often stipulates minimum and maximum percentages of profits to be distributed (for example, 10 percent to 30 percent of profits). These limitations restrict the range within which the board of directors may exercise discretionary authority in regard to contributions to the profit-sharing plan. Other illustrations of discretionary arrangements include "discretionary, but not to be less than 10 percent of before-tax profits," and "discretionary, but approximately 20 percent of before-tax profits." The purpose of such arrangements is to provide some guidelines or constraints to the board of directors as it exercises its discretionary authority. Any of these guidelines could include some form of a prior reservation for capital.

At one time, the Internal Revenue Service required that deferred profit-sharing plans include a fixed-contribution formula. However, as a result of several court decisions to the contrary, the IRS rules were liberalized to permit employers to determine profit-sharing amounts without a predetermined formula. Although approved by the Internal Revenue Service, the discretionary method is not without its disadvantages. For example, a discretionary approach may lead to lower employee morale and a weakened sense of financial security. Without a fixed formula, employees may feel uncertain about whether they can count on sharing in the profits that they have helped produce. In this context, the argument for using a fixed formula is that the "ground rules" are established in advance. At the beginning of each year, employees have the knowledge that their share of the profits will be determined in accordance with the terms contained in the formula.

Second, some type of formula method takes many of the burdens and pressures off the board of directors in making decisions on profit-sharing amounts during periods of economic instability (for example, when the firm has experienced high profits during the current year, but a

---

[20]While this is a legitimate concern when fixed-contribution formulas are used, satisfactory results may be obtained through the inclusion of a condition in the plan specifying that contributions not be in excess of the maximum deductible amount. Thus, this concern should not be viewed as a deterrent to the use of predetermined, or fixed-contribution, formulas.

severe economic downturn is forecast for next year; or, conversely, there are low profits in the current year with much brighter prospects for next year). Previously established guidelines are helpful to the board of directors when these circumstances arise.

A third potential disadvantage is that the Wage-Hour Division of the Department of Labor requires that a company use a definite formula if the firm desires to exclude the profit-sharing contributions from regular pay rates in calculating overtime pay. However, if the profit-sharing contributions are allocated to participants on a basis that includes overtime pay or if the plan provides for full and immediate vesting, contributions determined on a discretionary basis do not have to be included in pay when computing overtime rates.

Finally, the discretionary method exposes the contributions to the potential risk that they will come under any wage (and price) guidelines in effect at the time the contributions are made to the plan. For example, in 1979 the President's Council on Wage and Price Stability released its decision on the treatment of profit-sharing plans. Profit-sharing contributions determined under a discretionary approach were treated as incentive pay and, therefore, fell within the wage guidelines. In contrast, qualified deferred profit-sharing plans that used a fixed formula did not come under the wage guideline calculations to the extent that the formula was not changed.

Despite the discretionary approach's tremendous flexibility, its disadvantages are major reasons why many large employers use a fixed formula method. Smaller companies (up to 1,000 plan participants) have a greater tendency to determine profit-sharing contributions on a discretionary basis, since they appear to be more concerned with contribution and financing flexibility.

An unlimited variety of fixed profit-sharing formulas exist from which an employer may choose. These formulas can specify a fixed percentage or sliding scale of percentages (either ascending or descending) based on before-tax or after-tax profits, with or without a prior reservation. Examples using a fixed percentage are "10 percent of before-tax profits" and "25 percent of before-tax profits but no more than the amount that is available as a current tax deduction." An illustration of a formula involving a sliding scale (ascending) used by one large company is "3.5 percent on the first $100 million of before-tax profits, 5.0 percent on the next $50 million, and 6.0 percent on before-tax profits in excess of $150 million." (Because of obvious concerns about employee motivation, a formula providing for a scale of decreasing percentages rarely is used.) An example of a fixed formula with a prior reservation is "20 percent of before-tax profits in excess of 5 percent of net worth." Certainly, many other examples of predetermined formulas exist.

In addition to its relative inflexibility, a predetermined formula poses difficulties, from an employee relations perspective, in changing the formula when the amended formula clearly produces a lesser share of profits for the employees. Thus, careful consideration must be given to the initial decision as to the profit-sharing percentage(s) that will be included in the formula. To take advantage of the desirable features of both discretionary and fixed formulas, some employers (especially smaller firms) choose a combination method that provides a minimum fixed-contribution rate with additional profit-sharing amounts determined by the board of directors on a discretionary basis. The specific approach adopted, whether discretionary, predetermined formula, or some combination, and the precise details of the method chosen should be reflective of the employer's goals and objectives for the plan and the perceived impact of the plan and its profit-sharing method upon the employee group.

Methods of Allocating Employer Contributions among Plan Participants

Once the amount of profit-sharing contributions has been determined for the year, these moneys must then be allocated to the individual participants' accounts. Although not requiring a fixed (or predetermined) formula for calculating the level of contributions, the law does require that a predetermined formula for allocating profit-sharing contributions among employee accounts be specified in the plan. This is to ensure that the contribution allocation does not discriminate in favor of the firm's highly compensated employees. In judging whether a plan meets the qualification requirements, the IRS must be able to examine the allocation formula to determine that allocations will be made in a nondiscriminatory manner.

A wide range of alternative methods exist for allocating profit-sharing contributions among individual employee accounts, depending on the nature of the plan and employer objectives. The most commonly used approach is based on compensation (with age and years of service ignored), whereby amounts are allocated according to the ratio of each individual employee's compensation to the total compensation of all covered participants for the year. To illustrate, assume employee A has compensation of $20,000 during the year. If total covered compensation for all plan participants is $400,000 for the year, employee A would be entitled to 5 percent ($20,000 divided by $400,000) of the total profit-sharing allocation. If aggregate profit-sharing contributions are $50,000 for the year, employee A's share would be $2,500 (5 percent of $50,000). In using this allocation formula, the plan sponsor must specify the amounts to be included in determining compensation. For example, compensation for an individual participant may include all compensation paid during the plan year, even though this individual was a plan participant for only part of the year. Instead, compensation may be defined to include only amounts earned during the portion of the year that the employee also was a participant in the plan. Compensation also must be defined in terms of whether it consists of base (or regular) pay only, or if it includes bonuses, overtime, commissions, or other forms of cash compensation as well.[21] An allocation method based on compensation usually presents no discrimination problems so long as compensation is determined in a nondiscriminatory manner.

Another type of contribution allocation formula bases the allocation on both compensation and length (years) of service. Formulas incorporating both compensation and service typically allocate profit-sharing contributions on the basis of each participant's number of "points" awarded for the current year in proportion to total credited points of all plan participants for the year. Commonly, one point might be awarded for each $100 of compensation. An additional point, for example, might be given for each year of service.[22] To illustrate, an employee earning $25,000 with 15 years of service would be credited with 265 points [($25,000/$100 = 250) + 15]. The contribution allocation to this employee's account is determined first by dividing 265 by the total number of points credited to all plan participants during the year. This

---

[21]If the profit-sharing plan does not contain a fixed predetermined contribution formula (i.e., the plan uses a discretionary method), the plan is required under federal labor law (1) to provide for full and immediate vesting, or (2) to include overtime earnings in any definition of compensation on which the allocation of contributions is based; otherwise, the profit-sharing allocations themselves must be added to base pay rates in computing overtime pay. See *supra*.

[22]It is possible that more than one point would be credited to each year of service. Further, units other than $100 might be used in determining the number of points to be awarded for a specific amount of compensation. Considerable flexibility exists in specifying the exact way in which the points are to be awarded, conditioned on the point system not being found by the IRS to be discriminatory.

ratio is then applied to the total profit-sharing contribution to derive the employee's share.

Relatively few deferred profit-sharing plans allocate contributions according to length of service only. Previous rulings indicate that the IRS will closely scrutinize any contribution allocation formula based on length of service (either service-only formulas or compensation-and-service formulas) for the purpose of ascertaining whether the "prohibited discrimination" exists. Discrimination may occur when highly compensated employees have longer periods of service than do other employees.

In summary, a contribution allocation formula determines participant shares for accounting and record-keeping purposes. These moneys are allocated to individual employee accounts. However, contribution dollars are not necessarily segregated for investment purposes. While the profit-sharing trust may permit each participant's account to be invested in "earmarked" assets (an insurance contract, for example), profit-sharing contributions often are received, administered, and invested by the trustee as commingled assets. In the latter case, the balance in each participant's account at a specific time simply represents his or her current share of the total trust assets.

Maximum Limits

A number of maximum dollar limits apply to deferred profit-sharing plans. Several relate to maximums placed on the amount of profit-sharing contributions that may be deducted, for federal income tax purposes, by an employer in any one tax year. Other limits, such as the "annual additions limit" and the "1.0 Rule," relate to maximums imposed on employer-provided contributions/benefits under qualified plans. Collectively, these limits place important constraints on what employers can do for their covered employees through deferred profit-sharing arrangements.

An overriding consideration here is that profit-sharing contributions, when added to all other compensation paid an employee for the year, must be "reasonable" for the services performed by the employee and, in addition, be shown to be an "ordinary and necessary expense" of doing business.[23] If this is not the case, the IRS may deny the employer a tax

---

[23]This statement is not restricted to profit-sharing contributions but is equally true for all forms of compensation.

deduction for any part or all of the profit-sharing contributions (and, possibly, other compensation amounts as well) made on behalf of the employee.[24]

In the context of specific maximums, probably the single most important constraint is the IRS limit on deductible contributions. This limit is set forth in IRC Section 404. For deferred profit-sharing plans, the basic limit is that annual deductible contributions may not exceed "15 percent of compensation otherwise paid or accrued during the taxable year to all employees under the plan."[25] The 15 percent limitation applies regardless of the manner in which employer contributions are determined (i.e., discretionary versus fixed formula, or type of formula). However, this limit applies only to employer contributions to a deferred profit-sharing arrangement. Employers who provide for both cash and deferred profit sharing, either through an IRC Section 401(k) cash or deferred plan or through separate cash and deferred plans, are subject to the 15 percent deduction limit only on contributions to the deferred portion of the profit-sharing arrangement. Thus, if an employer's profit-sharing arrangement calls for the sharing of 30 percent of before-tax profits, and if 40 percent of this amount is to be distributed in cash (with the balance deferred), then the limit of IRC Section 404(a)(3) applies only to the 18 percent [30% − (30%) × (40%)] of before-tax profits that is contributed to the deferred plan. Furthermore, the 18 percent of before-tax profits (or a portion thereof) will be deductible as a contribution to the deferred profit-sharing plan to the extent that this amount does not exceed 15 percent of the total compensation of plan participants.

Prior to the passage of the Tax Reform Act of 1986, employers were permitted to create "credit carryovers" and "contribution carryovers." A "credit carryover" occurred whenever the employer's contribution for the year was less than the maximum allowable deduction of 15 percent of covered compensation. This credit was carried forward to be available for employer use in any subsequent tax year in which contributions exceeded the 15 percent limit. This enabled employers to take larger tax deductions in later years of higher profits (and larger profit-sharing contributions). A

---

[24]In most large publicly held firms the question of "unreasonable compensation" arises only on an infrequent basis. When this question is raised, it tends to be in those businesses whose ownership is closely held by a small number of individuals.

[25]IRC Section 404(a)(3).

''contribution carryover'' was created whenever the employer's contributions for a given year exceeded the maximum allowable deduction for that year. This amount could be carried forward and deducted in a subsequent year in which the employer's contribution that year was less than the otherwise allowable deduction (e.g., 15 percent of covered compensation). This permitted employers to make large contributions in earlier, high-profit years that exceeded the deductible amount with the excess carried forward and available for deduction in later years of lower profit-sharing contributions.

Unfortunately, the 1986 tax law repealed the ''credit carryover'' provisions and applies a 10 percent excise tax penalty to employer contributions exceeding the current allowable deduction. (''Credit carryovers'' created and accumulated prior to 1987 can still be used to increase the otherwise available deduction limitations for tax years beginning after December 31, 1986.) Since these carryover provisions enhanced employer contribution flexibility, their restriction may lead to an eventual decrease in the popularity of profit-sharing plans.

Additional deduction limits apply when an employer sponsors both a pension plan and a profit-sharing plan that cover a common group of employees. A 25 percent (of covered compensation) aggregate limit applies when both a profit-sharing plan and a money purchase pension plan exist.

In the case of a combination profit-sharing plan and defined benefit pension plan, the maximum annual deductible contribution to the combined plans is limited to 25 percent of covered compensation, or, if larger, the amount necessary to meet the minimum funding requirements of the defined benefit plan alone.[26] If circumstances are such that the minimum funding rules require the employer to contribute amounts to the defined benefit plan during a year that are in excess of 25 percent of covered compensation, the employer, in effect, is precluded from making a deductible contribution to the profit-sharing plan that year. The separate 15 percent deduction limit on employer contributions to the profit-sharing plan still applies in combination pension and profit-sharing plans.

Contributions, together with forfeiture reallocations, in deferred profit-sharing plans are subject to the ''annual additions limit'' of IRC Section 415(c). This section of the code prescribes limitations on the

---

[26]See IRC Section 404(a)(7).

amounts of moneys that can be added, on an annual basis, to individual participants' accounts under defined contribution plans. Specifically, a qualified defined contribution plan may not provide an annual addition, in any year, to any participant's account which exceeds the lesser of *(a)* 25 percent of compensation (for that year) or *(b)* a stipulated dollar amount ($30,000 for 1991). A separate qualification requirement, apart from IRC Section 415, specifies that in determining *(a),* only the first $200,000 (indexed) of compensation can be considered.[27] Contributions in excess of the IRC Section 415 limits will result in disqualification of the plan. Thus, employers must be certain that these limits are satisfied. Conceivably, the annual additions limit could reduce the contribution that an employer might otherwise make to the account of an individual participant in a given year.

The term *annual additions* includes *(a)* employer contributions, *(b)* forfeiture reallocations, and *(c)* any employee contributions. For purposes of the annual additions limit, investment earnings allocated to employee's account balances, rollover contributions, and loan repayments are not part of annual additions. Since this chapter is concerned primarily with deferred profit-sharing plans funded exclusively with employer contributions, component *(c)* of the annual additions limit is of little importance here and therefore will be ignored.

Many employers have combination pension and profit-sharing arrangements designed to provide significant amounts of retirement income from the pension plan and to provide for asset accumulation through the establishment of the required individual accounts under the profit-sharing plan. In essence, there are two basic ways of having a combination plan that includes a deferred profit-sharing arrangement: (1) a money purchase pension plan together with a profit-sharing plan; and (2) a defined benefit pension plan plus a profit-sharing plan. In the first arrangement, since both are defined contribution plans (and assuming the plans cover the same group of employees), the combined plans must comply with the annual additions limit of the lesser of 25 percent of pay or a stated dollar maximum ($30,000 in 1991). In addition, the 15 percent annual maximum on deductible employer contributions, in effect, would act as an "internal" limit with regard to the portion of the 25 percent that might be accounted for by employer contributions to the deferred profit-sharing

[27]The 1992 limit is $228,860.

program. Further, any forfeiture reallocations (under either the profit-sharing or money purchase plan) may cause a reduction in the amounts that otherwise could be contributed to the profit-sharing plan in order to comply with the annual additions limit.

When a defined benefit pension plan is combined with a deferred profit-sharing plan covering the same employees, the 1.0 Rule of IRC Section 415(e) applies.[28] In essence, this rule requires the calculation of defined benefit and defined contribution plan fractions and provides for an aggregate limit equal to the lesser of 1.25 (as applied to the Section 415 dollar limits) or 1.4 (as applied to the Section 415 percentage-of-pay limits).

ALLOCATION OF INVESTMENT EARNINGS AND FORFEITURES

In addition to specifying a contribution allocation formula, deferred profit-sharing plans also must prescribe methods for allocating investment earnings and forfeitures among the participants' accounts. These allocation methods, depending upon the circumstances, may differ from the method applied in allocating employer contributions.

Allocation of Investment Earnings

Unless profit-sharing allocations are ''earmarked'' for investment purposes (for example, when life insurance contracts are purchased), these moneys will be pooled and invested on an aggregated basis. The investment earnings generated from these commingled funds, in turn, must then be allocated to each participant's account. The most equitable approach is to base the allocation on the respective sizes of the individual account balances. Presumably, the funds assigned to each participant's account contribute in a pro rata fashion to the total investment earnings of the plan. As such, each account should share on a pro rata basis in these earnings. Thus, if a participant's account balance comprises 10 percent of

[28]It is assumed here that the reader is familiar with the mechanics of this rule and the IRC Section 415 defined benefit limitations (the lesser of 100 percent of compensation averaged over the highest three consecutive years or a stated dollar amount—1992 limit of $112,221).

the total of all account balances, that participant's account should be credited with 10 percent of the total investment earnings. Because investment earnings invariably are allocated on the basis of individual account balances, the plan will be applying procedures that will differ between the allocation of investment earnings and the allocation of employer contributions.

Investment earnings on assets held under the profit-sharing trust are measured on a "total return" basis. That is, investment earnings for a given year are defined to include interest and dividends, as well as adjustments in the market value of the underlying assets during the year of measurement. The net result is that the assets of the profit-sharing plan must be valued periodically to determine their market value.[29] In fact, the IRS requires that the accounts of all plan participants be valued in a uniform and consistent manner at least once each year.[30] It is common for large plans to conduct valuations monthly. Frequent asset valuations accommodate more rapid benefit payouts after employment separation and, in addition, enhance the plan's ability to permit participants to change, periodically, their investment selections. Another argument favoring frequent market valuation of plan assets is that the plan participants are treated more equitably. This is particularly important in the general overall treatment of plan transactions (primarily withdrawals) that occur between valuation dates. The issue facing the plan on the occasion of withdrawals (whether partial or total) relates to the appropriate values to be placed on the account balances and, consequently, the dollar amounts available for distribution. More frequent asset valuations will assist in achieving equitable results *(a)* between individuals making withdrawals and those who do not, and *(b)* among individuals making withdrawals at different points in time. This issue also includes the policy question of whether investment earnings are to be credited to individual account balances for the period between the last valuation date and the date the funds are withdrawn. If

---

[29]This does not apply when the entire assets of the plan are invested with a life insurance company through its "general asset account." Rather, in this event transactions with plan participants (e.g., withdrawals) occur on a book-value basis, and interest earnings are credited to participants' account balances according to the life insurance company's own accounting procedures. See Dan M. McGill and Donald S. Grubbs, Jr., *Fundamentals of Private Pensions,* 6th ed. (Homewood, Ill.: Richard D. Irwin, 1989), p. 658, footnote 17.

[30]Certain exceptions exist. For example, an annual valuation is not required when all of the plan assets are invested, immediately, in individual annuity or retirement contracts meeting certain requirements. See Revenue Ruling 73-435, 1973-2 C.B. 126.

interest is not credited for this period, the amounts (interest) lost to the participants making withdrawals could be substantial unless relatively frequent valuations (e.g., monthly or every two months) are made.

Allocation of Forfeitures

Forfeitures arise when participants terminate employment and the funds credited to their accounts are less than fully vested. As described earlier, the qualification requirements applicable to deferred profit-sharing plans permit the periodic reallocation of forfeitures among the remaining plan participants. While profit-sharing plans are also permitted to use forfeitures to reduce future employer contributions, seldom is this the case. The advantage of being able to reallocate forfeitures is somewhat lessened by the rapid vesting typically provided in profit-sharing plans which, in turn, reduces the amount of forfeitures available for reallocation. Further, forfeiture reallocations, together with employer contributions, must comply with the "annual additions limit" contained in IRC Section 415.[31]

All methods of forfeiture reallocation are subject to the principal requirement that they not discriminate in favor of the firm's highly compensated employees. Potential discrimination is of particular concern when forfeitures are reallocated on the basis of account balances. This concern centers on the premise that highly compensated employees are more likely to have longer periods of service, and that they therefore will have much larger account balances than other plan participants. Thus, if account balances constitute the basis for reallocating forfeitures, highly compensated employees may be entitled to substantially larger shares of forfeitures than other employees. The IRS may find this practice to be discriminatory, but the IRS does not hold that it is inherently discriminatory, or that the plan will automatically fail to qualify, simply because the plan reallocates forfeitures on the basis of account balances.[32] The IRS requires that this basis of reallocation be tested annually to determine whether the plan, in fact, is discriminatory. This is accomplished through

---

[31]See *Supra.*

[32]See Revenue Ruling 71–4 and Revenue Ruling 81–10. Revenue Ruling 81–10 basically restates the position of the IRS contained in Revenue Ruling 71–4, but it also provides a permissive formula that can be applied in determining whether forfeiture reallocations based on account balances produce the prohibited discrimination. See also the discussion of this topic in Carmine V. Scudere, "Is It too Risky to Allocate Forfeitures under a P/S Plan on the Basis of Account Balances?" *Journal of Pension Planning and Compliance,* July 1981, pp. 288–93.

submission of all pertinent plan data to the IRS for its determination. Because of concern over a potential charge of discrimination (and possible loss of the plan's qualified status), "account balances" is a seldom-used method in reallocating forfeitures. Instead, forfeitures generally are reallocated on the basis of each participant's compensation—the same method typically used in allocating employer contributions. Under normal circumstances, a compensation-based method will result in an equitable reallocation of forfeitures among plan participants and thus will not likely be viewed as discriminatory by the IRS.

LOAN AND WITHDRAWAL PROVISIONS

A large number of deferred profit-sharing plans provide participants with access to funds on prescribed occasions earlier than actual retirement. This is accomplished through inclusion of loan or withdrawal provisions in the plan.

Loan Provisions

Many profit-sharing plans contain loan provisions. These provisions allow participants to borrow up to a specified percentage (e.g., 50 percent) of the vested amounts in their individual accounts. While profit-sharing plans are not legally obligated to contain a loan provision, certain regulatory requirements will apply when such a provision is included. One requirement is that loans must be made available to all plan participants on a reasonably equivalent basis. Further, loans cannot be made available to highly compensated employees on a basis that is more favorable than that available to other employees. In addition, loans must be repaid in level payments (made at least quarterly) and must bear a reasonable rate of interest. Regarding any loans not repaid, the Internal Revenue Service may view them as withdrawals, in which case they must meet the conditions described below. So long as the specified terms are properly drawn and prudent, the loans will be exempted from the prohibited transaction provisions and also should comply with the fiduciary standards under ERISA.

It is possible that certain loans will be treated as plan distributions and, therefore, subject to current income taxation. Generally, loans will be treated as plan distributions (and subject to taxation) unless two conditions are met:

(1) The participant's total outstanding loan amount does not exceed the *lesser* of *(a)* one half of the present value of the participant's nonforfeitable benefit or *(b)* $50,000. Further, the $50,000 limit is reduced by the participant's highest outstanding loan balance during the preceding 12-month period.
(2) The loan (according to its terms and conditions) must be repaid within five years; however, the five-year repayment rule is waived for loans whose proceeds are applied to purchase a dwelling used as a principal residence of the participant.

Withdrawal Provisions

In the past, some deferred profit-sharing plans have provided for the automatic distribution of plan assets to employees (during active employment) after the completion of a stated period of participation or after the lapse of a fixed period of years.[33] Other plans provided employees with the option to withdraw portions of the moneys in their individual accounts on ''the attainment of a stated age, or upon the prior occurrence of some event such as layoff, illness, disability, retirement, death, or severance of employment.'' Distributions to participants on these prescribed occasions are permitted under Reg. 1.401–1(b)(1)(ii). Distributions of profit-sharing funds made sooner than the happening of any one of the aforementioned events may lead to the disqualification of the plan.

An employee's right to withdraw funds from a deferred profit-sharing plan is dependent on the actual plan provisions, because the plan is under no legal obligation to permit such distributions. In fact, some plans do not permit withdrawals prior to a participant's termination of employment. In any event, only vested amounts are available to be withdrawn.

When a profit-sharing plan provides for automatic distributions (or permits voluntary withdrawals) after a fixed number of years, IRS regulations require that only funds that have been deposited for at least

---

[33]The inclusion of such provisions is prohibited in IRC Section 401(k) cash or deferred profit-sharing plans. In general, withdrawal provisions applicable to 401(k) plans are much more restrictive than the rules that apply to traditional deferred profit-sharing plans as described here. The reader is referred to Chapter 34 of the *Handbook* for a discussion of these more restrictive provisions.

two years may be distributed. Thus, if employer contributions have been credited to a participant's account for three years, only contributions made in the first year plus investment income credited that year, are eligible to be withdrawn.[34] Of course, distributions of funds held less than two years may be made in the event of ". . . disability, retirement, death . . ." without affecting qualification. Further, distributions of moneys held less than two years may be made upon the showing of "hardship" if this term is sufficiently defined and consistently applied under the plan. In any event, the actual amounts withdrawn are taxable to the participant in the year in which the distribution is received. In addition, a 10 percent penalty tax is now applicable to many types of "premature" distributions from qualified plans. (See *infra*). Thus, the future attractiveness of automatic and other early distributions from profit-sharing plans is likely to be severely diminished.

Relative Advantages and Disadvantages of Loans and Withdrawals

Plan provisions permitting loans or withdrawals prior to termination of employment provide participants with much added flexibility. Employees may use these funds for down payments on homes, for children's college education expenses, or for other financial needs. A potential disadvantage is that these provisions (particularly withdrawal provisions) may prevent the plan from accumulating sufficient funds at retirement.

Loan provisions have certain inherent advantages over withdrawal provisions. Specifically, funds made available through a loan do not create taxable income to the borrowing employee. In addition, since loans are likely to be repaid, the retirement income objective of the profit-sharing plan is protected. Some potential disadvantages of loan provisions are

1. The administrative expense associated with processing loans.
2. An employee objection to being charged interest on his or her "own money."

---

[34]After completion of five years of participation in the plan, an employee is legally permitted to withdraw all employer contributions credited to his or her account, including moneys contributed during the two years preceding the date of withdrawal. The completion of five years of participation is an "event" within the meaning of Reg. 1.401–1(b)(1)(ii), making the two-year rule inapplicable.

3. The overall investment earnings on the total asset portfolio when the loan interest rate is below the earnings rate at which the trustee could otherwise invest the borrowed funds.[35]

Previously, profit-sharing plans containing withdrawal provisions had to be concerned with the "constructive receipt doctrine." The question arose whether the right to withdraw *any* moneys from a participant's individual account, whether or not exercised, constituted constructive receipt of *all* (withdrawable) moneys allocated to the account. If the constructive receipt doctrine applied, all such amounts available to be withdrawn would be taxable currently to the participant, even though the moneys are not actually withdrawn. To avoid application of the constructive receipt doctrine to amounts not withdrawn, plans usually assessed a substantial penalty (e.g., denying participation rights for six months) on employees who made withdrawals. Today, however, the constructive receipt doctrine no longer presents a problem in deferred profit-sharing plans. The Economic Recovery Tax Act of 1981 (ERTA) amended IRC Section 402(a)(1) of the Internal Revenue Code, which deals with the taxation of benefits from qualified retirement plans. Under the amended provision, distributions from qualified plans are taxed only when actually received by the participant; they are not taxed simply because they are made available to the participant. Thus, the basis for the constructive receipt doctrine has been removed from IRC Section 402(a)(1). This affects the tax treatment of all qualified plans, including profit-sharing plans, and it applies both to distributions at termination of employment and to withdrawals made by active employees. The amended provision became effective for taxable years beginning after December 31, 1981. Today, profit-sharing plans need not contain withdrawal penalties or restrictions simply to avoid constructive receipt issues. However, plan sponsors should determine whether, and to what extent, these penalties and restrictions are desirable in order to meet plan objectives and to control administrative costs.

Since the passage of the Tax Reform Act of 1986, the biggest drawback to including withdrawal provisions is the 10 percent penalty tax. This additional tax is applied to early distributions from all qualified retirement

---

[35]This last disadvantage exists only to the extent that the plan treats participant loans as loans from the entire assets of the trust, rather than treating them as loans from the participants' own individual accounts.

plans, including profit sharing. An early distribution is one made prior to age 59½, death, or disability. Exemptions are permitted for (1) periodic annuity benefits, after separation from service, paid over the life (or life expectancy) of the employee or the joint lives (or joint life expectancies) of the employee and beneficiary; (2) distributions to an employee that are used to pay deductible medical expenses; (3) distributions to a participant, after age 55, who has separated from service and (4) payments to a former spouse or dependent under a qualified domestic relations order (QDRO).

ADDITIONAL FEATURES OF DEFERRED PROFIT-SHARING PLANS

Two additional features pertaining to deferred profit-sharing plans are worthy of mention. These features relate to the inclusion of life insurance benefits and integration of the plan with Social Security benefits.

Life Insurance Benefits

Life insurance benefits may be incorporated into the design of qualified deferred profit-sharing plans.[36] First, life insurance coverage on key personnel may be purchased by the trust as an investment. It can be argued that the profit-sharing trust has an insurable interest in the lives of certain employees who are "key" to the successful operation of the firm. These key employees may include officers, stockholder-employees, and certain other employees of the company. Contributions to the profit-sharing trust are dependent on the continued success and profitability of the firm. If future profitability is contingent on the performance of these key employees, then the profit-sharing trust is likely to suffer a substantial reduction in future contribution levels upon the death of one or more of these individuals. Under these circumstances, if permitted by the trust agreement, the trustee may protect the profit-sharing trust against potential adverse consequences by purchasing insurance on the lives of the key employees. In such cases, the life insurance contracts are

[36]Only a limited treatment of life insurance in qualified profit-sharing plans is provided. For more information, see Allen, Melone, Rosenbloom, and VanDerhei, *Pension Planning*, 6th ed. (Homewood, Ill.: Richard D. Irwin, 1988), pp. 269–73; and McGill, and Grubbs, *Fundamentals of Private Pensions*, pp. 669–73.

purchased and owned by the trust, with the necessary premiums paid out of trust assets. The trust is designated as the beneficiary under such contracts and at the key employee's death the insurance proceeds are allocated among the individual participant accounts generally according to the size of the respective account balances.[37]

Second, most deferred profit-sharing plans provide a benefit payable at the death of a participant. At a minimum, a death benefit equal to the participant's individual account balance is generally paid. Reg. 1.401–1(b)(1)(ii), however, permits amounts allocated to participants' accounts to be used to purchase incidental amounts of life insurance coverage. There are several reasons for which a participant might want explicit life insurance benefits provided under the profit-sharing plan, including (1) the relatively small accumulation (and, consequently, available death benefits) in the participant's account during the early years of participation, and (2) inadequate amounts of coverage provided under the employer's group life insurance program.

To the extent that profit-sharing contributions are used to purchase life insurance on plan participants, these contributions must meet certain limitations. However, the limitations are sufficiently liberal that, in many cases, it is possible for plan participants to acquire substantial amounts of life insurance coverage. Specifically, if the funds used to pay life insurance premiums have been accumulated in the participant's account for at least two years, or if the funds are used to purchase either an endowment or a retirement-income contract, there are no IRS limits on the amount of life insurance that can be purchased (or the portion of the account balance that may be used to pay premiums). If neither of these requirements is met, the aggregate amount of funds used to pay life insurance premiums must be less than one half of the total contributions and forfeitures allocated to the participant's account. Additional restrictions pertaining to the inclusion of life insurance (on plan participants) in profit-sharing plans are (1) that the plan must require the trustee to

---

[37]In contrast to the purchase of life insurance on plan participants (see *infra*), the purchase of life insurance on key employees, for the collective benefit of the trust, does not create any current income tax liability for the participants. Furthermore, the tests requiring that life insurance be incidental in amount do not apply to the types of life insurance purchases described above. However, as a practical matter, the trust is not likely to invest a substantial portion of its assets in such life insurance coverage. Also, under ERISA's fiduciary provisions, the trustee is under the obligation to show that the purchase of life insurance on key personnel is a prudent investment and in the best interests, collectively, of the plan participants.

convert the entire value of the life insurance contract at or prior to retirement either to cash or to provide periodic income (in order that no portion of such value is available to continue life insurance protection into the retirement years), or to distribute the insurance contract to the participant; and (2) that the participant must treat the value (P.S. 58 cost) of the pure life insurance protection as taxable income each year.[38]

To maintain its qualified status, a plan must meet the requirements of Reg. 1.401–1(b)(1)(ii). However, life insurance need not be purchased on *all* plan participants to achieve qualification. Rather, the purchase of life insurance can be the decision of individual participants (with some electing coverage and others not) so long as all participants are offered the same opportunity. To accomplish this, the trust agreement should expressly allow each participant, individually, to direct the trustee to purchase specific investments (e.g., insurance contracts) and ''earmark'' them for the participant's account. Normally, the trustee is the applicant and owner of any life insurance contracts purchased on the lives of the plan participants. In addition, the trustee pays the premiums on the policies, although these amounts are then charged directly to the individual accounts of those participants electing insurance coverage. Typically, the insured participants designate their own personal beneficiaries. In this case, death proceeds are paid by the insurer directly to the named personal beneficiary. If the trustee is designated as beneficiary, the death proceeds are paid to the trustee, who, in turn, credits the proceeds to the deceased participant's account.

Integration with Social Security

Deferred profit-sharing plans are seldom integrated with the benefits payable under Social Security (OASDI). A major reason is that any employee incentive objective sought by the employer would tend to be diminished by a plan design that calls for contributions at a lower rate on behalf of employees earning less than a specified minimum.

---

[38]The reason for a current tax liability is that the premium for the pure insurance protection is deemed by the IRS to be a distribution from the trust and therefore currently taxable to the plan participant. The amount that must be included in the participant's gross income each year is determined as follows: [(face amount minus cash value) × (the *lower* of the Table P.S. 58 attained age rate or the insurer's own premium rate for individual one-year term insurance)]. With each succeeding year, the first factor in this formula decreases (provided the face amount is held constant) while the second factor increases. The portion of the premium applied to the buildup of the cash value is considered to be an investment of the trust and, consequently, is not treated as a current distribution or subject to any current tax liability.

If a profit-sharing plan is to be integrated, it must be done on a step-rate excess-earnings basis. This requires that an integration level be established. The integration level is a chosen dollar amount such that the employer contribution rate differs between earnings above and below this amount. Specifically, the employer contribution rate is greater on compensation in excess of the integration level. While lesser dollar amounts is permitted, the integration level often is defined as the current Social Security maximum taxable wage base (e.g., $55,500 in 1992).

Current law requires that the *difference* between the employer contribution rate applied to compensation in excess of the integration level and the contribution rate applied to compensation below the integration level not exceed the *lesser* of (1) 5.7 percent (or the tax rate for the old age insurance portion of OASDI, if greater) or (2) the contribution rate applied to compensation below the integration level.[39] To illustrate, if a 3 percent contribution rate is applied to earnings below the integration level, then a maximum of 6 percent can be contributed on excess compensation above the integration level. Similarly, if the employer contributes 7 percent on earnings below the integration level, then no more than 12.7 percent can be applied to excess compensation.[40]

Frequently, an employer sponsors both a pension plan and a deferred profit-sharing plan covering the same overlapping group of employees. If both plans are integrated, the regulations prohibit the combined integration under both plans from exceeding 100 percent of the integration capability of a single plan. If maximum integration is desired, the simplest approach is to integrate one plan fully and not integrate the other plan at all. Other combinations are permissible, however.

DISTRIBUTIONS

Earlier sections described specific events leading to distributions under profit-sharing plans. The discussion here is limited to the form and taxation of distributions from qualified deferred profit-sharing plans.

---

[39]The 5.7 percent must be reduced if the integration level utilized is less than the Social Security taxable wage base. In addition, IRC Section 401(a)(4) can permit a plan to qualify even if it violates (1) and (2) above.

[40]For a general rule, let x denote the employer contribution rate applied to compensation below the integration level. Then the maximum contribution rate that can be applied to compensation in excess of the integration level is (a) $2x$, when $x \leq 5.7$ percent or (b) $x + 5.7$, when $x > 5.7$ percent.

Form

Distributions from profit-sharing plans may take several forms, including lump-sum, installment payments, or a paid-up annuity. Withdrawals during active employment or distributions to employees who have terminated employment (for reasons other than death, disability, or retirement) generally are made in the form of a lump-sum payment.[41] At death or disability of the plan participant, distributions usually consist of lump-sum or installment payments. Distributions at retirement typically are payable either as a lump sum, in installments, or as a life annuity provided through an insurance company. To the extent that the plan permits an annuity payout form, it must satisfy ERISA's rules relating to qualified joint-and-survivor annuities.

Taxation

In general, the tax treatment of distributions from qualified profit-sharing plans is identical to the tax treatment accorded distributions from qualified pension plans. However, the tax treatment accorded distributions consisting of employer securities holds particular importance to profit-sharing plans. Profit-sharing plans are not subject to ERISA's 10 percent limitation on the investment of plan assets in employer securities and tend to invest more heavily in employer securities as a result. When employer securities are distributed as part of a lump-sum distribution under such conditions that otherwise qualify the distribution for favorable tax treatment, IRC Section 402(e)(4)(J) permits the entire net unrealized appreciation on the securities (excess of fair market value over cost basis of the securities to the trust) to escape taxation at the time of the distribution. In effect, the participant can elect, at the time of distribution, to be taxed only on the amount of the original employer contributions (i.e., the trust's cost basis) and defer the tax on any unrealized appreciation until the securities are sold at a later date. Alternatively, the participant can choose to be taxed on the entire value of the employer securities at the date of distribution.

---

[41] As indicated earlier, the applicability of a 10 percent penalty tax on premature distributions may cause employers to limit the availability of in-service withdrawals from profit-sharing plans. Further, when terminating employment prior to age 59½, participants may choose to roll the funds into an individual retirement account (IRA) to avoid imposition of the penalty tax.

CHAPTER 33

THRIFT AND SAVINGS PLANS

Henry Bright
Harry McBrierty

Thrift plan is the trade name given to an employee benefit plan that promotes savings and thrift among employees by requiring each participant to make periodic contributions to the plan in order to be credited with an employer contribution on his or her behalf. The amount of the employer contribution usually relates, in whole or in part, to the amount the participant contributes. These plans also are referred to as *savings plans, thrift incentive plans, savings and investment plans,* and by a variety of other names that generally denote an employee savings feature.

With a few exceptions, all thrift plans have been established since the late 1950s. Their prevalence among employers of all sizes has grown continuously. However, their growth in the 1980s was phenomenal. This, no doubt, is due in large part to the fact that thrift plans are ideally suited for a cash or deferred arrangement whereby the participants' contributions to the thrift plan are on a tax-deferred, salary reduction basis under Section 401(k) of the Internal Revenue Code (IRC). In fact, in recent years, thrift plans are often referred to as *401(k) plans*. It should be noted, however, that not all 401(k) plans are thrift plans and not all thrift plans are 401(k) plans.

The popularity of thrift plans is also due to their relatively low cost to the employer and to their enthusiastic acceptance by most employees. From the employer's viewpoint, a thrift plan is a retirement program that can provide significant benefits, which are financed to a great extent by the contributions of its employees (depending on the ratio of the employees' contributions to its own). From the employees' viewpoint, a thrift plan provides an incentive to save and gives them the opportunity to realize an immediate and substantial return on their own contributions, with the added opportunity of accumulating investment earnings on a deferred tax basis and receiving benefits on a favorable tax basis upon retirement or termination. In addition, under 401(k) thrift plans, the employees may make their contributions on a salary-reduction basis and thereby reduce the amount of taxes they pay in the year during which they make the contributions.

The impact that the Tax Reform Act of 1986 (TRA '86) is having on thrift plans is not yet conclusive. Many of the revenue-producing provisions of that Act make some of the features of thrift plans less attractive. For example, the 10 percent penalty tax on withdrawals before age 59½ makes thrift plans less attractive as a means of accumulating savings for use prior to retirement. Also, the $7,000 indexed cap on elective deferrals and the smaller permissible disparity between the contributions of highly and nonhighly compensated employees lessen the attractiveness of these plans to higher-paid employees. On the other hand, the elimination of or reduction in the amount of IRA deductions makes 401(k) thrift plans more attractive to many employees as a means of savings on a tax-deferred basis. Early signs indicate that TRA '86 is not having a significant impact on the popularity of thrift plans, especially those that use a 401(k) cash or deferred arrangement.

This chapter discusses thrift plans in general and does not attempt to describe in detail the specific provisions that apply to plans that utilize the cash or deferred arrangement afforded under IRC Section 401(k). The provisions that apply to 401(k) thrift plans are discussed more thoroughly in Chapter 34 of the *Handbook*.

QUALIFIED STATUS UNDER INTERNAL REVENUE CODE

The Internal Revenue Code includes no specific provisions relating to thrift plans as such. *Thrift plan* is simply a term used in the industry to describe a contributory defined contribution plan that provides an individual account for each participant with benefits based solely on:

- The amounts contributed to the participant's account;
- Any income, expenses, gains, and losses; and
- Any forfeitures of accounts of others that may be allocated to the participant's account.

This description is the same as that of a profit-sharing plan and of a money purchase pension plan, because thrift plans are qualified under Section 401(a) of the Internal Revenue Code as either profit-sharing plans or money purchase pension plans. The plan instrument must specify if the plan is intended to be qualified as a profit-sharing plan or a money purchase pension plan. Technically, a thrift plan could alternatively be qualified as a stock bonus plan if it has all of the attributes of a stock bonus plan.

The provisions of the IRC that govern profit-sharing plans are different in certain respects from those that govern money purchase pension plans. Accordingly, differences exist in the provisions and in the operations of a thrift plan, according to whether it is qualified as a profit-sharing plan or as a money purchase pension plan. Table 33–1 lists some of the principal differences between the two types of thrift plans.

Features common to both types of thrift plan are that (1) the plan must provide a definite, predetermined formula for allocating contributions among the participants in the plan, and (2) the plan must provide for valuation of plan assets at least once a year.

PLAN PROVISIONS

Most provisions of thrift plans are similar to those of other employee benefit plans qualified under Section 401(a) of the IRC. The plan must be so structured that, in addition to satisfying the objectives of the employer, it conforms to the requirements of the Internal Revenue Code, the Employee Retirement Income Security Act (ERISA), and other applicable governmental rules and regulations.

Eligibility Requirements

Employees must be eligible to participate on reaching age 21 or on completing one year of service, whichever is later. However, if the plan is not a 401(k) plan and provides immediate 100 percent vesting, the plan may require as much as two years of service before the employee is eligible. (Prior to 1989, any thrift plan that provided immediate 100 percent vesting could impose a three-year service requirement.) An employee cannot be excluded from participation under a thrift plan because of attainment of a specified maximum age. In practice, most thrift plans permit participation after a year or less.

TABLE 33–1
Principal Differences between Two Types of Thrift Plans

Feature	*Plan Qualified as a Profit-Sharing Plan*	*Plan Qualified as a Money Purchase Pension Plan*
1. Amount of employer contributions	No definite formula required. Usually expressed as a percentage of employee's contributions.	There must be a fixed formula for determining the amount of employer contributions.
2. Source of employer contributions	May provide that they will only be made out of current or accumulated profits.	Are required to be made even if there are no current or accumulated profits.
3. Employer contributions in excess of normal formula	Plan may provide for such excess contributions to be made at the employer's option.	No excess contributions may be made.
4. Withdrawal of employer contributions prior to severance of employment	May be permitted (contributions must have accumulated for at least two years or employee must have at least five years of plan participation).	No withdrawal of employer contributions is permitted except on severance (or attainment of normal retirement age).
5. Qualified joint and survivor annuity	Must be offered only if the purchase of an annuity is an available method of distribution.	Must be offered as the primary method of distribution.
6. Limit on tax deductions for employer contributions to thrift plan		
a. No other plan maintained	15 percent of covered compensation.	None, but note that Section 415 of the IRC effectively imposes a maximum on contributions of 25 percent of covered compensation.
b. Separate profit-sharing plan maintained	Combined limit of 15 percent of covered compensation.	Combined limit of 25 percent of covered compensation.
c. Separate defined benefit pension plan maintained	Combined limit of 25 percent of covered compensation.	Combined limit of 25 percent of covered compensation or, if greater, the required minimum defined benefit plan contribution.
7. Favorable tax treatment for lump-sum distributions on termination or retirement	Available, provided there is no other profit-sharing plan benefit, or, if there is, provided a lump sum also is received thereunder.	Available, provided there is no other pension plan benefit, or if there is, provided a lump sum also is received thereunder.

As with other qualified plans, a thrift plan must cover a sufficient number of employees (after certain permitted exclusions) to satisfy the "percentage test," the "ratio test," or the "average benefits test" of Section 410(b) of the Internal Revenue Code.

The percentage test is satisfied if the plan benefits at least 70 percent of all nonhighly compensated employees. The ratio test is satisfied if the percentage of nonhighly compensated employees that benefit under the plan is at least 70 percent of the percentage of highly compensated employees that benefit. The average benefits test is satisfied if the plan benefits a nondiscriminatory classification of employees and if the average benefit percentage of the nonhighly compensated employees is at least 70 percent of the average benefit percentage of the highly compensated employees.

Employee Contributions

The requirement for employee contributions is a distinguishing characteristic of all thrift plans. This is because the amount of the employer's contributions and the predetermined formula for allocating those contributions among the participants are almost always based on the amount that each participant contributes.

Many thrift plans permit the employee contributions to be made on a tax-deferred basis. Under these arrangements, the employee contributions are deducted from the employee's pay and no federal income taxes are due on them until they are paid to the employee or his or her beneficiary. Plans that use this type of arrangement are referred to as *401(k) thrift plans* and are subject to special nondiscrimination, withdrawal, and other provisions that do not apply to other thrift plans. Again, these and other special 401(k) provisions are discussed very briefly in this chapter and are covered in more detail in Chapter 34.

All thrift plans require one type of employee contribution, and some thrift plans permit a second type. The first type is that which determines the employee's share of the employer's contribution. The second type is an employee contribution in excess of the maximum employee contribution of the first type. Employee contributions of the second type have no effect whatsoever on the amount of the employer's contribution or on the employee's allocated share of the employer's contribution. For convenience, these types of employee contributions are referred to in this chapter as *basic employee contributions* and *voluntary employee contributions*, respectively.

Basic Employee Contributions

It is not necessary for a thrift plan to require or permit all participants to contribute at the same rate. Most plans permit employees to choose the amount to be contributed, up to the maximum permissible, and some plans have different maximums for different classifications of employees. For example, a plan may permit employees with fewer than a certain number of years of service or participation to contribute within a specified range, while this range may be greater for employees with more years of service or participation. In addition, many plans specify that a minimum contribution, expressed either as a dollar amount or as a percentage of pay, is required. The minimum requirement usually is included for administrative purposes; but in the past, this minimum was believed to affect the amount of voluntary employee contributions that a plan might permit.

Basic employee contribution requirements must not result in discrimination in favor of highly compensated employees. Such discrimination could arise because of inadequate plan coverage for lower-paid employees or because the rates of contribution and benefits are less for lower-paid employees under a plan that provides for optional rates of contribution.

Voluntary Employee Contributions

A provision for voluntary employee contributions is an optional feature included in some thrift plans. This provision enables participants to take advantage of the favorable tax treatment afforded the earnings on such contributions. Voluntary employee contributions normally are accounted for separately.

Employer Contributions

The employer's contribution in a thrift plan generally is defined as a fixed percentage of basic employee contributions, although this is not a requirement for a plan qualified as a profit-sharing plan. That percentage also may vary for different classifications of employees as long as the classifications are nondiscriminatory. Some thrift plans qualified as profit-sharing plans provide that the employer, at its discretion, may make contributions in excess of the defined amount of contribution. Thrift plans qualified as money purchase pension plans cannot provide for such additional contributions, since the benefits would no longer be definitely determinable.

The employer's contribution is most often allocated among the participants in direct proportion to the basic employee contribution of each participant. However, other methods of allocation (such as a varying percentage based on years of service or participation) may be used, provided they are not discriminatory.

TRA '86 Employee and Employer Matching Contributions Nondiscrimination Test

TRA '86 added a special nondiscrimination test that applies to determine if employee and employer matching contributions under any thrift plan are discriminatory. The purpose of this test is to ensure that the benefits of the highly compensated employees are not significantly higher than those of other employees. The test is satisfied if the "average contribution percentage" for eligible highly compensated employees does not exceed the greater of (1) 2 times the average contribution percentage for all other eligible employees, subject to a maximum equal to the average contribution percentage for all other eligible employees plus two percentage points, or (2) 1.25 times the average contribution percentage for all other eligible employees. The schedule in Table 33–2 illustrates the permissible percentages.

The average contribution percentage for each group of employees is the average of the contribution percentages of all employees in that group. The contribution percentage of each individual is determined by dividing

TABLE 33–2
Permissible Employer Contributions for Highly Compensated Employees

Average Contribution Percentage of Nonhighly Compensated Group of Employees	*Maximum Average Contribution Percentage of Highly Compensated Group of Employees*
1%	2%
2	4
3	5
4	6
5	7
6	8
7	9
8	10
9	11.25
10	12.50
11	13.75
12	15.00

the sum of the employee's own contributions (both basic and voluntary) and the employer's matching contributions made on his or her behalf during the year by the amount of compensation that he or she received during the year.

If the employee contributions to the thrift plan can be made on either a before-tax or after-tax basis, the before-tax contributions must be separated from the after-tax contributions, and a separate nondiscrimination test must be satisfied with respect to each type of contribution. In making such tests, the percentages specified in Table 33–2 apply with respect to each test. In addition, if one or more highly compensated employees are eligible to make both types of contributions, a second test must also be satisfied *unless* the average contribution percentage of the highly compensated group of employees under either the test that applies to the before-tax contributions or the test that applies to the after-tax contributions is equal to or less than 1.25 times the average contribution percentage of the nonhighly compensated group of employees under that test.

To satisfy the second test, the sum of the average contribution percentage of the highly compensated group of employees under the before-tax contributions test plus the corresponding percentage under the after-tax contributions test cannot exceed the greater of:

- The sum of:
  - *(a)* (1.25 times the average contribution percentage of the nonhighly compensated group of employees under the before-tax contributions test or under the after-tax contributions test, whichever test has the *greater* percentage)

    plus
  - *(b)* (2 times the average contribution percentage of the nonhighly compensated group of employees under the before-tax contributions test or under the after-tax contributions test, whichever test has the *lesser* percentage, subject to a maximum equal to such lesser percentage plus two percentage points)

- Or the sum of:
  - *(a)* (1.25 times the average contribution percentage of the nonhighly compensated group of employees under the before-tax contributions test or under the after-tax contributions test, whichever test has the *lesser* percentage)

    plus

(b) (2 times the average contribution percentage of the nonhighly compensated group of employees under the before-tax contributions test or under the after-tax contributions test, whichever test has the *greater* percentage, subject to a maximum equal to such greater percentage plus two percentage points)

Forfeitures

When a plan participant incurs a break in service, his or her nonvested benefits may be forfeited and, thereby, become available for other uses. Forfeitures under a thrift plan either may be included as part of the employer's contribution (or, stated in another way, used to reduce the amount of the employer's contribution), or may be allocated among the participants in addition to the employer's contribution.

When forfeitures are included as part of the employer's contribution, they are allocated, of course, to the accounts of the participants in the same manner as the rest of the employer's contribution. If the forfeitures are allocated in addition to the employer's regular contribution, they generally are allocated among the participants in the same manner as the employer's contribution, but they may be allocated under other methods. However, if some other method is used, it may be necessary to demonstrate to the IRS that such other method does not discriminate in favor of highly compensated employees. After forfeitures have been allocated to the accounts of the participants, they generally are treated as though they were employer contributions.

Limits on Contributions to Employees' Accounts Each Year

Section 415 of the Internal Revenue Code places a limit on the total amount of employer contributions, forfeitures, and employee contributions that can be credited to the accounts of any participant during a specified year.

This limit, which applies to the aggregate of all defined contribution plans of the employer, requires that the sum of the employer's contributions and forfeitures allocated to an employee's account plus the total of his or her employee contributions (both basic and voluntary) cannot be greater in any year than the *smaller* of *(a)* 25 percent of his or her pay, or *(b)* a specified dollar amount that is subject to increase to take into account cost-of-living adjustments. This dollar amount was originally

$25,000 in 1974; had increased to $45,475 on January 1, 1982; and was reduced by the Tax Equity and Fiscal Responsibility Act (TEFRA) to $30,000 on January 1, 1983. It is to remain at $30,000 until the IRC 415 dollar limit for defined benefit plans reaches $120,000, at which time it will increase in tandem with the defined benefit plan limit, with the defined contribution limit being equal to one fourth of the defined benefit limit.

If the employee is also a participant in a defined benefit plan of the employer, an overall limitation exists on the amount of his or her benefits under both types of plans. Consequently, the above limit on the defined contribution-plan benefit may have to be reduced if the required reduction is not made under the defined benefit plan, so that the total benefit from both the defined contribution and defined benefit plans does not exceed the overall limitation.

The overall limitation is tested by adding the percentage of the maximum limitation computed separately for each type of plan that is being provided for an employee. The resulting sum must not exceed 125 percent for the dollar limitations or, if less, 140 percent for the percentage limitations.

The overall limitation could be met by reducing benefits under either plan. It usually is preferable to make the reduction in the defined benefit plan, because the precise amount of reduction required cannot be determined until the employee retires, and because the reduction in a defined benefit plan does not become effective until retirement. However, other considerations may make it preferable to reduce the defined contribution plan. A choice should be made and incorporated in the plan document.

Investment of Contributions

Most thrift plans provide for more than one investment fund or type of investment. The participant may specify the percentage of his or her own contributions to be invested each year in each fund. A similar choice may or may not be available to the participant concerning the investment of employer contributions allocated on his or her behalf. Plans that permit the participant to choose investment funds typically provide that the participant may change the specified percentages and may transfer funds credited to his or her account from one investment fund to another on a periodic basis.

Other thrift plans, primarily because of the accounting complexities caused by a multitude of investment options, restrict the options available to employees. Some of those plans, nevertheless, permit participants nearing retirement age to make a one-time election to transfer funds from an equity-type investment fund to either a fixed-income or a guaranteed-income fund, so that fluctuations in value may be minimized as participants near retirement.

Under proposed regulations issued by the Department of Labor, limited protection from fiduciary liability will be given to individual account plans that offer at least three diversified categories of investments that have materially different risk and return characteristics and with respect to which the participants are given the opportunity to exercise control. If and when the regulations are finalized, many employers will no doubt choose to offer at least three such investment options and to comply with the Department of Labor regulations in order to take advantage of this protection.

Among the more common investment funds are employer stock, fixed-income funds invested in government bonds or notes, guaranteed-return contracts offered by insurance companies, common stock funds, and money market funds, not necessarily in that order. The relative popularity of different investment funds can vary widely at different times; a tendency exists for one or the other type of investment to become extremely popular at certain times, often for very good reasons.

In any case, because both the financial markets and the plan's needs and objectives change over the course of time, it is sound policy to review the available choice of investment funds at regular intervals and to make changes when necessary or appropriate. The plan's wording should be designed to facilitate the making of such changes.

Vesting

Because of their nature and purpose, and as an incentive to encourage broad participation, thrift plans commonly provide for fairly rapid vesting, usually on a graded basis. However, the minimum vesting requirements for thrift plans are the same as for all other qualified pension and profit-sharing plans. In brief, since 1989 all employer contributions and funds attributable thereto have been required to vest at least as rapidly as under one of these alternatives:

1. After 5 years of service, 100 percent vesting.
2. After 3 years of service, 20 percent vesting, plus an additional 20 percent for each of the next 4 years (100 percent after 7 years of service).

Of course, an employee must always be 100 percent vested in funds attributable to his or her own contributions and be 100 percent vested in the total account on reaching normal retirement age.

Many thrift plans in the past used what is called *class-year vesting*. Under these plans, each year's employer contributions ("class") and the earnings thereon were accounted for separately until they were fully vested, which would be from two to five years after they were made. At that time they would typically be distributed to the employee unless he or she elected to defer receipt until retirement. Under these plans it was possible that an employee would never be 100 percent vested prior to his or her normal retirement age in all of the employer contributions credited to his or her account. Class-year vesting was repealed by TRA '86 and has not been allowed after 1988.

Withdrawals While in Service

The in-service withdrawal provisions included in a thrift plan generally are dependent on the objective of the employer in establishing the plan. For the great majority, when the objective of the plan is to provide a means by which the participants can accumulate funds that may be used to meet their financial needs before (as well as after) retirement, the withdrawal provisions are very liberal. However, if the objective of the plan is solely or primarily to provide a source of income after retirement, the withdrawal provisions, if any, are not as liberal. The 10 percent additional income tax imposed by TRA '86 on taxable withdrawals prior to age 59½ has undoubtedly made in-service withdrawal provisions less attractive.

Withdrawal of Employee Contributions

The in-service withdrawal of all or a portion of an employee's own contributions and interest earned thereon is permitted under many thrift plans. Such a provision must not be such that it can be reasonably expected to result in manipulation of the employer's contribution. Prior to the passage of the Economic Recovery Tax Act of 1981 (ERTA), plans that permitted withdrawal of interest on employees' contributions often provided for restrictions or penalties designed to avoid constructive receipt. While no longer needed for that purpose, many such restrictions may be retained to further discourage manipulation and to encourage savings for retirement.

The potential for the manipulation of employer's contributions arises if the employee is permitted to withdraw all or a portion of basic employee contributions (the employee contributions to which the employer's contribution is geared) without penalty so that he or she could effectively use the same contributions year after year and thereby manipulate the formula allocating the employer's contribution under the plan. The IRS has ruled that plans permitting such manipulations without penalty will not be qualified under Section 401(a) of the Internal Revenue Code. This problem is avoided by providing an appropriate penalty, which is typically the suspension of participation for a specified period such as six months.

The withdrawal of voluntary employee contributions does not present any problems concerning the manipulation of the employer's contributions.

Withdrawal of Employer Contributions

The in-service withdrawal of all or a portion of the employer's contributions in which the participant has a vested interest is permitted in many thrift plans qualified as profit-sharing plans. Such withdrawals are not permissible prior to a participant's normal retirement age under thrift plans that are qualified as money purchase pension plans. The amounts withdrawn normally must have been accumulated in the trust fund for at least two years, although amounts that have not been accumulated for at least two years may be withdrawn by employees with at least five years of participation.

401(k) Thrift Plan Withdrawals

In-service withdrawals under 401(k) thrift plans are more restrictive. An employee's salary reduction contributions ("elective deferrals") cannot be withdrawn prior to age 59½ unless it can be demonstrated that the withdrawal is due to hardship. If the employer's contributions are used to satisfy the nondiscrimination tests that apply to cash or deferred arrangements, then these contributions are subject to the same withdrawal restrictions as apply to the employee's own elective deferrals. However, starting in 1989 any such employer contributions, investment earnings on such contributions, and investment earnings on the employee's own elective deferrals may not be withdrawn prior to age 59½ even for hardship reasons.

Loans

Loans to plan participants are permissible under thrift plans if such loans are expressly allowed by the plan on a nondiscriminatory basis; are adequately secured; bear a reasonable rate of interest; and provide for repayment in substantially equal installments, payable not less frequently than quarterly, spread out over a specified period not greater than five years. The amount of a loan cannot exceed the *lesser* of:

1. $50,000 minus the highest outstanding loan balance of the participant during the preceding 12 months.
2. An amount (inclusive of any existing loans) equal to 50 percent of the participant's vested interest, but this 50 percent limit changes to 100 percent if the loan is for $10,000 or less. However, only 50% of the participant's vested interest may be used as security for a loan, and because of this, many plans that use only the participant's vested interest as security for a loan are also applying the 50% limit to loans of $10,000 or less.

The loan may be for a period longer than five years, if the purpose of the loan is to acquire the principal residence of the participant.

To ensure that loans will not affect the investment performance that could be expected if loans were not permitted, many plans provide that loans will be treated as a directed investment by the participant of the proportion of the account represented by the loan. The investment yield credited to such directed investment then is based solely on the interest payments made in the repayment of the loan.

Distributions on Retirement or Termination

Benefits on the retirement or termination of service of a participant under a thrift plan normally are distributed in a lump-sum payment, by a series of installment payments, or through the purchase of an annuity contract from an insurance company. Lump-sum payments are the most common form of distribution.

Thrift plans that are qualified as money purchase pension plans must offer a qualified joint and survivor annuity as a method of payment. Thrift plans that are qualified as profit-sharing plans must offer this method of payment only if the purchase of annuities is a permitted method of distribution under the plan. Many plans that are qualified as a profit-sharing plan have eliminated the purchase of an annuity as a method of distribution to avoid the complications associated with qualified joint and survivor annuities. Participants who wish to have a life annuity purchased on their behalf may roll over that portion of the distribution exclusive of their own after-tax contributions to an individual retirement account (IRA) sponsored by an insurance company within 60 days after the date they receive their distribution from the thrift plan and use such amount to purchase an annuity. However, the employee's own after-tax contributions cannot be transferred to an individual retirement account. The plan itself could pay the proceeds, including employee contributions, in installments over a fixed period that is not longer than the joint and last survivor life expectancy of the participant and his or her designated joint pensioner.

A thrift plan is required to commence the payment of benefits to a participant not later than the 60th day after the close of the plan year in which the *latest* of the following events occurs: (1) attainment of age 65 or an earlier normal retirement age specified under the plan; (2) passage of 10 years from the time participation in the plan commenced; or (3) termination of service with the employer.

The payment of benefits to the participant may be deferred to a date later than the dates specified above if (1) the plan permits such a deferral and the participant submits to the plan administrator a signed written statement that describes his or her benefit and the date on which the participant elects to have it commence, and (2) the deferral of such payment will not cause the benefits payable on death to be more than "incidental" (which means, essentially, that the participant should be expected under normal life expectancies to receive most of the benefit. See proposed IRS Regulation 1.401(a)(9)-2 for a precise calculation). For example, a participant who retires at age 65 might elect to defer receipt of any benefits until age 70 and then take a percentage of the fund (such as 10 percent) each year thereafter.

Benefit payments to the participant (or to his or her surviving spouse in the event of the participant's death prior to the benefit commencement date) may not be required to commence prior to the participant's normal retirement age without the consent of the recipient. An exception to this rule is that benefits with a total value of $3,500 or less may be cashed out involuntarily if the plan so provides.

In practice, benefit payments under a thrift plan typically begin shortly after the date of termination of the participant's service, although some plans provide that payments will not begin until the participant has been gone long enough to incur a forfeiture that is not required to be restored in the event of his or her reemployment.

Since 1990, benefit payments to employees born on or after July 1, 1917, have had to begin not later than April 1 of the year following the year in which the employee attains age 70½, even if he or she is still in the service of the employer at that time.

Top-Heavy Provisions of TEFRA

TEFRA imposes restrictions on plans that are "top-heavy." A plan is said to be *top-heavy* if 60 percent or more of the total of all account balances are for key employees (officers and significant owners).

The principal requirements for top-heavy plans are: (1) vesting at 20 percent after two years service, grading up to 100 percent after six years, or 100 percent vesting after three years' service; (2) an employer contribution for each nonkey participant of at least 3 percent of compensation (or, if smaller, the highest percentage received by any key employee); and (3) if the participant is also covered by a defined benefit plan, the overall dollar limitation is based on 100 percent, rather than 125 percent, of the separate dollar limitations, unless additional conditions are met.

TAX ASPECTS

Contributions

Contributions to qualified thrift plans are afforded the same tax treatment and considerations afforded contributions to other qualified pension, profit-sharing, and stock bonus plans. These are discussed briefly here.

1. The employer can take a current deduction for its contributions to the plan (provided the contributions are not in excess of the prescribed deductible limits), and such contributions are not taxable to the employee or his or her beneficiary until actually distributed.
2. Employee elective deferral contributions under a 401(k) thrift plan, up to a certain limit ($8,728 in 1992), are not included in an employee's taxable wages for federal income taxes. (They are, however, subject to FICA tax withholding.) All other employee contributions are included in an employee's taxable wages and may not be claimed as a tax deduction.

3. The contributions of both the employer and employees are allowed to earn and compound income on a tax-free basis (to the extent that such income is not deemed to be unrelated business income of the trust), and such earnings are not taxable to the employee or his or her beneficiary until they are actually received.

Distributions

The taxation of distributions from thrift plans varies, of course, in different circumstances. Distributions and withdrawals from qualified thrift plans are taxed in the same manner as distributions and withdrawals from other qualified pension, profit-sharing, and stock bonus plans. It is not the purpose of this chapter to discuss in detail the taxability of distributions from qualified plans, but some general tax features are mentioned here.

1. Employee contributions that have been made from after-tax dollars are not subject to federal income tax when distributed or withdrawn. However, any withdrawal in respect of employee after-tax contributions is treated as including a pro rata portion of investment earnings on those contributions, and that portion is taxable. This pro rata rule does not apply to a withdrawal of after-tax contributions contributed prior to January 1, 1987, if the plan—as in effect on May 5, 1986—permitted such a withdrawal.
2. Employee elective deferral contributions under a 401(k) thrift plan, and employer contributions and investment earnings on both the employer and employee contributions are taxable as ordinary income when distributed or withdrawn. In addition, a 10 percent penalty is imposed if the distribution or withdrawal is made before age 59½, unless the distribution is due to a separation of service after attaining age 55, is in the form of a level life annuity, or meets certain other specified exceptions. If the distribution is a qualified lump-sum distribution, alternative taxation is available as described in (3) and (4) below.
3. Special five-year-averaging tax treatment is available on a one-time basis for qualified lump-sum distributions received after age 59½ by employees who have participated in the plan for at least five years. A transitional rule applies to participants who attained age 50 before January 1, 1986, that allows them to use pre-1987 lump-sum tax rules on a one-time basis.

4. Alternatively, a qualified lump-sum distribution may be rolled over into an IRA on a tax-free basis. Such a rollover is available if the qualified lump-sum distribution is received before age 59½, as well as after that age.
5. If stock of the employer is distributed as part of a qualified lump-sum distribution or if such stock is attributable to the employee's own contributions, the unrealized appreciation in the value of such stock during the period that it is held in the trust fund is not taxable at the time of distribution unless the employee elects in accordance with IRS rules to include such unrealized appreciation in his taxable income.
6. The first $5,000 of any otherwise taxable distribution from the trust fund due to the employee's death is excluded from federal income tax if such death benefit is paid in a lump sum, or if it is forfeitable and paid in installments. All plans of the employer must be combined in applying this exclusion.

In general, the options on form and timing of payments that can be made available under thrift plans are valuable, because they allow for flexibility in an employee's overall tax planning.

ADMINISTRATIVE CONSIDERATIONS

A primary consideration in the design and operation of any thrift plan is the administrative and recordkeeping capabilities available to the employer. A thrift plan is required to allocate the contributions to the plan each year among the participants and must provide for an annual valuation of the trust investments (on a specified date each year) to allocate the investment gains or losses (realized and unrealized) among the accounts of the participants. While such allocations are required to be performed only once a year, many employers (primarily those with sophisticated recordkeeping capabilities) choose to perform either or both allocations more frequently, often on a monthly or quarterly basis.

It is necessary under a thrift plan to be able to determine the benefits to which a participant is entitled. To make such a determination, it is necessary to be able to ascertain *(a)* the amount of the employee's own contributions (both basic and voluntary) and the funds attributable thereto and *(b)* the amount of the employer contributions and forfeitures that have been credited to the participant's account and the funds attributable thereto. In addition, if employer stock is distributed to the participant, it is necessary, for tax purposes, to ascertain the time of acquisition and the cost to the trust fund of each share of stock distributed to the employee.

It is also necessary to be able to ascertain that the plan satisfies the nondiscrimination rules that apply to employee and employer matching contributions and, if a cash or deferred arrangement is involved, to be able to ascertain that the elective deferral contributions of the highly paid employees, as compared to those of the other employees, satisfy the special nondiscrimination tests that apply to 401(k) plans.

Other tasks involved in the administration of a thrift plan include: communicating to each participant the amount of his or her accrued benefits (normally done at least once a year); enrolling the eligible employees as participants in the plan; and obtaining their authorizations for the deduction of the desired employee contributions, their investment fund designations, and their beneficiary designations (and subsequent changes in such authorizations and designations).

While the general operation of a thrift plan is fairly simple and easy to understand, the accounting methods and recordkeeping system required to maintain the accounts and to determine the benefits of the participants can be quite complex, depending on the variety of options available to the participants.

CHAPTER 34

SECTION 401(k) PLANS: CASH OR DEFERRED ARRANGEMENTS

*Jack L. VanDerhei**

Conventional deferred profit-sharing plans, thrift and savings plans, and employee stock ownership plans are discussed in Chapters 32, 33 and 35 of the *Handbook,* respectively. This chapter deals with Section 401(k) cash or deferred arrangements (CODAs), which enhance these and certain other plans. Under a CODA, an employee can receive what normally would be the automatically deferred *(nonelective)* employer's contribution to one of a number of qualified retirement plans. This is no different from the way conventional deferred plans operate. With a CODA, however, the employee also has the option of receiving the amount of the employer's contribution in cash as currently taxable income. Additionally, under a CODA an employee is entitled to make *elective* contributions of amounts that could otherwise be received in cash to an employer's qualified plan on a before-tax basis, thereby increasing the employee's spendable income and avoiding any federal income tax on the amount until it is received as a plan distribution.

CODAs are not a new concept; they have existed since the 1950s. They were beset by legislative and regulatory doubt during the mid-

---

*Parts of this chapter are based on material that appears in Everett T. Allen, Jr., Joseph J. Melone, Jerry S. Rosenbloom, and Jack L. VanDerhei, *Pension Planning*, 6th ed. (Homewood, Ill.: Richard D. Irwin, 1988).

1970s, but the Revenue Act of 1978 and the Internal Revenue Service (IRS) proposed regulations of 1981 opened the way for these plans, and their growth since 1981 has been significant.

This chapter reviews the legislative history of these plans, the technical requirements they must meet, some special considerations that must be taken into account, and their relative advantages and disadvantages to employers and employees.

LEGISLATIVE HISTORY OF CODAs

Before 1972, the IRS provided guidelines for qualifying cash-option CODAs in a series of revenue rulings. In essence, more than half the total participation in the plan had to be from the lowest-paid two-thirds of all eligible employees. If this requirement was met, employees who elected to defer compensation were not considered to be in constructive receipt of the amounts involved even though they had the option to take such amounts in cash. Salary-reduction plans satisfying these requirements also were eligible for the same favorable tax treatment.

In December 1972, the IRS issued proposed regulations that stated that any compensation an employee could receive as cash would be subject to current taxation even if deferred as a contribution to the employer's qualified plan. Although directed primarily at salary-reduction plans, the proposed regulations also applied to cash-option profit-sharing plans.

As the gestation period for the Employee Retirement Income Security Act (ERISA) was coming to an end, Congress became increasingly aware of the need to devote additional time to the study of the CODA concept. As a result, ERISA included a section that provided that the existing tax status for CODAs was to be frozen until the end of 1976. Plans in existence on June 27, 1974, were permitted to retain their tax-favored status; however, contributions to CODAs established after that date were to be treated as employee contributions and, as a result, were currently taxable. Unable to meet its self-imposed deadline, Congress extended the moratorium on CODAs twice, the second time until the end of 1979.

The Revenue Act of 1978 enacted permanent provisions governing CODAs by adding Section 401(k) to the Internal Revenue Code (IRC or

Code), effective for plan years beginning after December 31, 1979. In essence, CODAs are now permitted, as long as certain requirements are met.

This legislation, in itself, did not result in any significant activity in the adoption of new CODAs, and it was not until 1982, after the IRS issued proposed regulations in late 1981, that employers began to respond to the benefit-planning opportunities created by this new legislation. By providing some interpretive guidelines for Section 401(k), and specifically sanctioning "salary-reduction" plans, the IRS opened the way for the adoption of new plans and for the conversion of existing, conventional plans. For example, many employers converted existing aftertax thrift plans to CODAs to take advantage of the Section 401(k) tax shelter on employee contributions.

The Tax Reform Act of 1984 provided some subtle modifications to Section 401(k). The original specification of the nondiscrimination standards for cash or deferred plans appeared to permit integration with Social Security. This ambiguity was resolved by applying both the general coverage tests and a special actual-deferral-percentage (ADP) test (both described later in this chapter) to all CODAs. The 1984 legislation also extended cash or deferred treatment to pre-ERISA money purchase plans, although contributions were limited to the levels existing on June 27, 1974.

The changes imposed by the Tax Reform Act of 1986 (TRA '86) were much more substantive. In addition to reducing the limit on elective deferrals, this legislation provided a new definition of highly compensated employees, restricted the ADP test, modified the list of contingencies on which distributions from CODAs are permitted, and reduced the employer's flexibility in designing eligibility requirements for these arrangements.

In 1988 the IRS released final regulations reflecting changes made by the Revenue Act of 1978 and simultaneously issued newly proposed regulations for CODAs as affected by the Tax Reform Act of 1986. The proposed regulations were modified in May 1990, and additional guidance was contained in proposed regulations under Section 401(a)(4) in September 1990. At the time of this writing, the IRS had just released final regulations replacing all the 1988 proposed and final regulations on these subjects and the amendments to regulations under Section 401(k) issued in May 1990.

TECHNICAL REQUIREMENTS

Section 401(k) states that a qualified CODA is any arrangement that:[1]

1. Is part of a profit-sharing or stock-bonus plan, a pre-ERISA money purchase plan, or a rural electric cooperative plan[2] that meets the requirements of Section 401(a) of the Code.
2. Allows covered employees to elect to have the employer make contributions to a trust under the plan on behalf of the employees or directly to the employees in cash.
3. Subjects amounts held by the trust that are attributable to employer contributions made pursuant to an employee's election to certain specified withdrawal limitations.
4. Provides that accrued benefits derived from such contributions are nonforfeitable.
5. Does not require, as a condition of participation in the arrangement, that an employee complete a period of service with the employer maintaining the plan in excess of one year.

As a tax-qualified plan, a CODA must meet all the general nondiscriminatory requirements applicable to such plans. The special requirements for CODAs are covered in the following material. Before discussing these requirements, however, it is important to understand the difference between *elective* and *nonelective* contributions. Elective contributions are amounts that an employee could have received in cash but elected to defer. Nonelective contributions are employer contributions that are automatically deferred under the plan.

Type of Plan

As noted, a CODA may be part of a profit-sharing or stock-bonus plan. This, of course, includes thrift and savings plans. The only qualified

---

[1]The regulations generally provide that a partnership arrangement that permits partners to vary the amount of contributions made to a plan on their behalf on a year-to-year basis will be deemed to constitute a CODA.

[2]For purposes of IRS Sec. 401(k), the term *rural electric cooperative plan* means any pension plan that is a defined contribution plan and is established and maintained by a rural electric cooperative or a national association of such cooperatives. For further details see IRC Sec. 457(d)(9)(B).

defined contribution plan that cannot be established as a CODA is a post-ERISA money purchase or defined contribution pension plan.[3]

In practice, most CODAs fall into one of two categories—either cash or deferred profit-sharing plans, or thrift and savings plans. CODAs also can be subdivided into plans that involve employer contributions only, both employer and employee contributions, and employee contributions only. Plans involving only employee contributions are not expected to be used to a great extent, largely because of the difficulty these plans will experience in satisfying the special tests that are described later.

Individual Limitations

TRA '86 imposed a $7,000 annual limitation on the exclusion of elective deferrals. This limit is indexed annually for changes in the cost of living and reached $8,475 in 1991. Any excess amounts (and the earnings on them) are included in the employee's gross income. This limitation applies to the aggregate elective deferral made in a taxable year to all CODAs and simplified employee pensions (SEPs; described in Chapter 37). The limit is reduced by any employer contributions to a tax-deferred annuity (described in Chapter 39) under a salary-reduction agreement; however, the limitation is increased (but not to an amount in excess of $9,500) by the amount of these employer contributions.

Elective deferrals in excess of the annual limit (plus the earnings on such amounts[4]) may be allocated among the plans under which the deferrals were made by March 1st following the close of the taxable year, and the plan may distribute the allocated amount back to the employee by April 15th.[5] Although such a distribution will be includable in the employee's taxable income for the year to which the excess deferral relates, it will not be subject to the 10 percent excise tax that may otherwise apply to distributions prior to age 59½. Any income on the excess deferral will be treated as earned and received in the taxable year in which the excess deferral is distributable.

---

[3]CODAs are not available to tax-exempt organizations unless adopted before July 2, 1986, or to state or local governments unless adopted before May 6, 1986.

[4]Plans do not need to include income for the period between the end of a plan year and the date excess amounts are distributed.

[5]Excess deferrals are taken into account in applying special nondiscrimination tests (described later in this chapter) if not distributed during the taxable year of deferral.

Any excess contribution not distributed by this date will remain in the plan, subject to all regular withdrawal restrictions and to the penalty for early withdrawals if distributed later. The amount will be taken into account in applying the special nondiscrimination tests. Moreover, the amount will again be treated as taxable income when it is later distributed.

A second limit caps the amount of pay that can be taken into account for most qualified plan purposes, including the determination of contributions and benefits, at $200,000. This limit also is indexed to changes in the cost of living.

Nondiscrimination in Coverage

To be qualified, a CODA must satisfy the general coverage provisions for all qualified plans. A plan must satisfy any one of the minimum coverage tests described in Chapter 33.

In addition to meeting one of the basic coverage tests, plans (other than negotiated multiemployer plans) must meet a *minimum number of participants test.*

In applying these requirements, it is permissible to exclude from consideration any employees covered by a collective bargaining agreement if there is evidence that retirement benefits were the subject of good-faith bargaining. It also is possible to exclude nonresident aliens who receive no income from the employer from sources within the United States, certain airline pilots, and employees not meeting minimum age and service requirements.

Nondiscrimination in Contributions

For a CODA to be qualified, the contributions under the plan must be nondiscriminatory. To satisfy this requirement, the plan must meet an actual-deferral-percentage (ADP) test by the close of each plan year.

The first step in applying this test is to determine the actual deferral percentage for each eligible employee; that is, the percentage of each eligible employee's salary that is deferred into the plan. This is done by dividing the amount of an employee's elective deferrals (contributions) by the amount of the employee's compensation. In addition, the employer may include in the numerator any matching or nonelective contributions that satisfy the CODA nonforfeitability and distribution requirements (described later in this chapter). Excess deferrals must be taken into account in this testing even if they later are distributed to comply with the annual cap on elective deferrals.

For purposes of a 401(k) plan, *compensation* refers to compensation as defined by IRC Section 414(s). An employer may limit the period taken into account to that portion of the plan year or calendar year in which the employee was an eligible employee, provided that this limit is applied uniformly to all eligible employees under the plan.

It should be noted that this percentage is determined individually for all eligible employees, whether or not they actually participate. Thus, the ADP for an eligible but nonparticipating employee is zero.

The next step is to divide the eligible employees into two groups—the highly compensated employees[6] and all other eligible employees (the nonhighly compensated employees). For each of these groups, the individual actual deferral percentage for each employee is computed and the group average is found. If the average ADP for the highly compensated employees does not exceed the average ADP for the nonhighly compensated employees by more than the allowable percentage, the test is satisfied for the year. Formulas for the allowable percentages are set forth in Table 34–1.

It should be noted that the ADP test determines a maximum *average* actual deferral percentage for the highly compensated employees and

---

[6]A highly compensated employee is defined as one who meets at least one of the following conditions:

1. A 5 percent owner.
2. A person earning over $75,000 a year in either the current or preceding year.
3. A person earning over $50,000 a year in either the current or preceding year who is or was in the top 20 percent of all active employees for such year.
4. An officer earning over 50 percent of the dollar limit for annual additions to a defined benefit plan in either the current or preceding year.

In determining who is an officer, no more than 50 individuals (or 10 percent of the employee group, if smaller) need be taken into account. If an employee is a family member (lineal ascendant or descendant and spouse) of a 5 percent owner or one of the top 10 highly paid employees, both will be treated as one person for purposes of the nondiscrimination tests. The $50,000 and $75,000 amounts are indexed to reflect increases in the Consumer Price Index (CPI). If an employee (other than a 5 percent owner) earned less than the test amount in the year before the year he or she entered the prohibited group and was not an officer in that prior year, the employee will not be a member of the prohibited group for the entrance year unless he or she is among the top-paid 100 employees for that year.

TABLE 34–1
Maximum Allowable Average ADPs for Highly Compensated Employees

If Average ADP for Nonhighly Compensated Employees (ADP_{NHC}) Is:	*Then Average ADP for Highly Compensated Employees (ADP_{HC}) May Not Exceed:*
Less than 2 percent	2 times ADP_{NHC}
At least 2 percent but less than 8 percent	ADP_{NHC} plus 2 percent
8 percent or more	1.25 times ADP_{NHC}

Examples

1. If the ADP for the nonhighly compensated employees is determined to be 1 percent, then the ADP for the highly compensated employees can be as much as 2 percent (2 × 1%).
2. If the ADP for the nonhighly compensated employees is determined to be 4 percent, then the ADP for the highly compensated employees can be as much as 6 percent (4% + 2%).
3. If the ADP for the nonhighly compensated employees is 10 percent, the ADP for the highly compensated employees can be as much as 12.5 percent (1.25 × 10%).

does not indicate the maximum deferral percentage for any individual in this group. As long as the average deferral percentage for the highly compensated employees as a group is less than or equal to the maximum allowed, it is permissible for an *individual* in this group to defer an amount in excess of that limitation.

If any highly compensated employee is a participant under two or more CODAs of the employer, all such CODAs will be treated as one CODA for purposes of determining the employee's ADP.

Where a plan combines salary deferral with employer contributions and/or employee after-tax contributions, it is necessary to satisfy multiple-use test based on both the ADP and the actual contrib[illegible]ed percentage (ACP) tests.[7] Both the ACP and multiple-use tests are [illegible] in Chapter 33 of the *Handbook*.

---

[7]It is important to note that the regulations do not allow the full [illegible] 34–1 for both ADP and ACP tests simultaneously. Specific[illegible] represented by the first two rows in the right-hand column of [illegible] of the two tests.

-rent in Table
-atical formula
be used for one

Aggregation Rules

Employee Stock Ownership Plans (ESOPs). ESOPs are required to be tested for nondiscrimination separately from other plans. This means that the ADP (and ACP) tests are performed for the ESOP plan taking into account only ESOP contributions. Likewise, the non-ESOP portion of the plan will be tested only on contributions under the non-ESOP portion of the plan. The multiple-use test illustrated in Chapter 33 applies separately to the two portions of the plan.

Collectively Bargained Plans. Collectively bargained plans are exempt from ADP testing until the 1993 plan year. At that time, a collectively bargained 401(k) plan must satisfy the ADP test in order for the CODA to be qualified. If a 401(k) plan covers both union and nonunion employees, the regulations clarify that separate tests apply.

Nondiscrimination Rules for Combined Plans

If a CODA consists of both elective contributions and nonelective contributions, the nonelective portion of the plan must satisfy the general coverage tests for all qualified plans and the general nondiscrimination requirements with regard to contributions. Elective deferrals under a CODA may not be taken into account for purposes of determining whether a plan has met these requirements.

Combined plans can satisfy the nondiscrimination requirements by one of two methods. In both cases, the nonelective portion must satisfy the general rules mentioned above; however, the special CODA qualification rules may be met either by the elective portion of the plan alone or [illegible]e combined elective and nonelective portions of the plan.

[illegible]The following example, adapted from Proposed Regulation Section [illegible]k)-1, illustrates the application of these rules. An employer with foll[illegible]oyees maintains and contributes to a profit-sharing plan the [illegible]ounts:

no[illegible] [illegible]f each employee's compensation, where such amounts *do* req[illegible] [illegible]he Section 401(k) nonforfeitability and distribution

2 percent of each employee's compensation, where such amounts *do* satisfy the Section 401(k) nonforfeitability and distribution requirements; and

Up to 2 percent of each employee's compensation, which the employee may elect to receive as a direct cash payment or to contribute to the plan.

In 1987, employees 1 through 9 received compensation and deferred contributions as indicated below.

Assuming that none of the employees is a 5 percent owner or officer, only employees 1, 2, and 3 are highly compensated employees. The ADP test will not be satisfied if only the elective contributions are measured, since the average ADP for the nonhighly compensated employees is zero, and as can be seen from Table 34–1, the maximum allowable average ADP for the highly compensated employees would also be zero (2 × 0 percent). As a result of the fact that the highly compensated employees generated an average ADP of 2 percent in this example, the combined plan would not satisfy the nondiscrimination tests.

However, the nondiscrimination test may be satisfied if the elective contributions meet the Section 401(k) nonforfeitability and distribution requirements. In that case, the average ADP for the nonhighly compensated employees will be 2 percent (0 percent elective + 2 percent nonelective) and, as can be seen from the table, this would allow a maximum average ADP for the highly compensated employees of 4 percent (2 percent + 2 percent). The actual average ADP for the highly compensated employees is 4 percent (2 percent elective + 2 percent nonelective). Therefore, the ADP test is not violated.

Note that the plan must also satisfy the coverage requirements described earlier. However, there will be no difficulty satisfying such a test in this example, because all employees were eligible to benefit under the arrangement.

Increasing the Probability that the ADP Test Is Met

There are several ways in which an employer can minimize or eliminate the possibility that a plan will not meet the ADP test. Some of the techniques that might be used for this purpose are listed here.

Employee	Compensation	Six Percent Nonelective Contribution	Two Percent Nonelective Contribution	Elective Contribution Elected to be Deferred
1	$100,000	$6,000	$2,000	$2,000
2	80,000	4,800	1,600	1,600
3	75,000	4,500	1,500	1,500
4	40,000	2,400	800	0
5	30,000	1,800	600	0
6	20,000	1,200	400	0
7	20,000	1,200	400	0
8	10,000	600	200	0
9	5,000	300	100	0

1. The plan can be designed so that it is in compliance. For example, the employer can make an across-the-board nonelective 5 percent contribution for all employees that satisfies the CODA nonforfeitability and distribution requirements. Employees can then be given the option of contributing up to 1.5 percent of pay by way of salary reduction, and the plan will always satisfy the ADP test since the maximum allowable average ADP for the highly compensated employees could be as much as 7 percent (5 percent + 2 percent) but, in fact, does not exceed 6.5 percent (5 percent nonelective + 1.5 percent elective).
2. The plan can be designed to encourage maximum participation from the nonhighly compensated employees. This can be done under a savings plan, for example, by providing for higher levels of employer contributions with respect to lower pay levels.
3. Limits can be placed on the maximum amounts allowed to be deferred.
4. The plan can include a provision allowing the employer to adjust deferrals (either upward or downward) if the plan is in danger of failing to meet the ADP test.
5. The employer can make additional nonelective contributions at the end of the plan year to the extent necessary to satisfy the test. (Such contributions, of course, would have to satisfy the CODA nonforfeitability and distribution requirements.)
6. Contributions for a plan year can be determined in advance of the plan year and, once established on a basis that satisfies the ADP

test, fixed on an irrevocable basis (except, possibly, that non-highly compensated employees could be given the option of increasing their contributions).

Eliminating Excess Contributions

If the ADP tests are not satisfied, the plan must eliminate excess contributions to keep the plan qualified. Excess contributions are defined as the *difference* between (1) the aggregate amount of employer contributions actually paid over to the trust on behalf of highly compensated employees for such plan year and (2) the maximum allowable contributions for highly compensated employees, based on the average ADP for nonhighly compensated employees as shown in Table 34–1.

A CODA will not be treated as failing to meet the ADP requirements for any plan year if one of two conditions is met before the close of the *following* plan year:

1. The amount of the excess contributions for such plan year (and any income allocable to such contributions[8]) is distributed.
2. To the extent provided in regulations, the employee elects to treat the amount of the excess contributions as an amount distributed to the employee and then contributed by the employee on an after-tax basis to the plan. (This procedure is known as *recharacterization.*)

Excess contributions are distributed by returning contributions made on behalf of highly compensated employees in order of the actual deferral percentages beginning with the highest of such percentages. In other words, the highly compensated employee with the largest ADP would have contributions returned until one of the following occurs:

1. The ADP test is satisfied (that is, the relationship between ADP_{NHC} and the adjusted ADP_{HC} satisfies the requirements expressed in Table 34–1).
2. The ADP for the highly compensated employee with the largest ADP is reduced to the level of the highly compensated employee with the second-largest ADP.

---

[8]Plans do not need to include income for the period between the end of a plan year and the date excess amounts are distributed to participants.

Successive iterations of this procedure are continued until the ADP test is satisfied.

Distributions of excess contributions (and income) may be made without regard to any other provision of law (for example, qualified domestic relations orders will not be violated). Moreover, although the returned amounts are treated as taxable income to the employee, the 10 percent penalty tax on early distributions from qualified retirement plans does not apply to any amount required to be distributed under this provision.

Although the plan has until the close of the following plan year to distribute or recharacterize excess contributions to avoid disqualification, an excess contribution may result in a 10 percent penalty tax *for the employer* unless it is distributed (together with any income allocable thereto) before the close of the first 2½ months of the following plan year. Any amount distributed or recharacterized will be treated as received and earned by the recipient in his or her taxable year for which the contribution was made.

For nondiscrimination purposes, recharacterized amounts are treated as employee contributions for the year in which the elective contribution would have been received (but for the deferral election). Thus they must be tested under the Section 401(m) tests described in Chapter 33. In addition, recharacterized amounts are subject to the CODA withdrawal restrictions, they must be nonforfeitable, and they will count against the employer's maximum deductible limit.

Nonforfeitability Requirements

The value of all elective contributions to a CODA must be fully vested at all times. The value of nonelective contributions must vest in accordance with one of ERISA's prescribed vesting standards.[9] It should be noted, however, that the vested amount of elective contributions cannot be considered for this purpose. Thus, the vesting of nonelective contributions must be accomplished independently.

---

[9] Two vesting standards are available (unless the plan is top-heavy). The first standard requires that all accrued benefits must be 100 percent vested after five years of service. The second standard permits graded vesting, with 20 percent of accrued benefits vesting after three years of service and that percentage increasing in 20 percent multiples each year until 100 percent vesting is achieved after seven years.

Distribution Requirements

Limitations on Withdrawals

A common provision in many profit-sharing and savings plans permits an actively employed participant to make a withdrawal of some part of his or her vested account balance. Sometimes this withdrawal right is limited to hardship situations, but more often a withdrawal can be made for any reason subject to some period of suspension from plan participation.

In the case of a CODA, in-service withdrawals are severely limited. The value of elective contributions (and nonelective contributions that are aggregated with elective contributions to meet the special CODA nondiscrimination rules) are distributable only on one of the following conditions:

1. Death.
2. Disability.
3. Separation from service.
4. The termination of the plan, provided no successor defined-contribution plan (other than an ESOP or SEP) is established.[10]
5. The sale of substantially all of the assets used by the corporation in a trade or business if the employee continues employment with the corporation acquiring the assets.
6. The sale of a corporation's interest in a subsidiary if the employee continues employment with the subsidiary.

Distributions on account of a plan termination or because of a sale of a subsidiary or assets must be a distribution of the participant's entire interest in the plan. The Technical and Miscellaneous Revenue Act of 1988 (TAMRA) expands these exceptions to cover other transactions that have the effect of sales of assets or subsidiaries.[11]

---

[10]A successor plan does not include a plan that does not overlap the 401(k) plan (that is, a plan under which fewer than 2 percent of employees eligible for the 401(k) plan are eligible).

[11]To qualify for the exception, the Technical and Miscellaneous Revenue Act of 1988 (TAMRA) reconfirms that distributions upon termination of a plan without the establishment or maintenance of another defined contribution plan (other than an ESOP), or upon disposition of assets or disposition of a subsidiary, must be lump-sum distributions without regard to the age-59½ requirement, as well as other required events for income-averaging eligibility, the election of the lump-sum-distribution treatment requirement, and the five-year minimum plan participation requirement.

Hardship Withdrawals. In the case of profit-sharing or stock-bonus plans, distributions of elective contributions are permitted at age 59½, or before 59½ for hardships. However, hardship withdrawals are limited to the amount of an employee's elective deferrals, without investment income.

Limiting the withdrawal of elective contributions to hardship cases can be of significance to many employers, since it can have a negative effect on the participation of lower-paid employees, thus creating problems in meeting the ADP test. The regulations define hardship in a very narrow way. The hardship must be caused by immediate and heavy financial needs of the employee for which other resources are not reasonably available.[12] Plans may use a "safe harbor" under which certain expenses are deemed to be heavy and immediate needs. These expenses include: medical expenses (and amounts needed in advance to obtain medical care) for the employee, spouse, and dependents; the purchase (excluding mortgage payments) of a principal residence for the employee; the payment of tuition (and related medical fees) for the next twelve months of postsecondary education for the employee, spouse, children, and dependents; and a payment to prevent eviction from or foreclosure on the employee's principal residence.

The plan may reasonably rely on the employee's representation that a heavy and immediate financial need cannot be met by insurance; reasonable liquidation of assets of the employee, spouse, or children (unless protected by the Uniform Rights to Minors Act); cessation of the employee's 401(k) or after-tax contributions to the plan; other distributions or loans from any plans maintained by the participant's current employer or any previous employer or by a loan from any commercial source on reasonable terms.

A plan may provide that a distribution will be deemed necessary to satisfy a financial need if all of the following requirements are met: the distribution is not in excess of the amount necessary to meet the need, the employee has taken all distributions available and all loans permissible under all plans maintained by the employer, the employee is precluded from taking any 401(k) or after-tax contributions to any plan maintained

---

[12]Plans may ignore the fact that the expense was foreseeable or voluntarily incurred by the employee. Employers are permitted to make changes in the hardship distribution rules (even for existing account balances) without causing a prohibited cutback in accrued benefits.

by the employer for a period of 12 months, and the employee's 401(k) contributions of the following taxable year are limited to the $7,000 (adjusted) annual limit reduced by the amount of 401(k) contributions made in the taxable year when the hardship withdrawal was made. Hardship distributions may be grossed up for federal, state, and local taxes and penalties, including the 10 percent additional income tax on early distributions.

Nonhardship In-Service Withdrawals. It should be noted that some amounts might still be available for nonhardship, in-service withdrawals. As already noted, nonelective contributions may be withdrawn (unless they are designated to be part of the ADP test). Finally, even elective contributions may be withdrawn from a profit-sharing or stock-bonus plan on a nonhardship basis after the employee attains age 59½.

OTHER CONSIDERATIONS

The preceding has dealt with the requirements of federal tax law for the qualification of CODAs. There are, however, other issues that must be addressed. The following section discusses the federal income taxation of CODA distributions, the status of elective contributions for purposes of Social Security, other employer-sponsored plans, and state and local taxes. It also discusses the express limits on 401(k) contributions, the treatment of excess deferrals, the effect of such contributions on deduction limits, and the Section 415 limitations on contributions and benefits.

Federal Income Taxation of CODA Distributions

CODA distributions arising out of employer contributions (including before-tax employee contributions) or investment income are subject to the same federal income tax treatment as any other qualified plan distribution when the employee has no cost basis. (A detailed discussion of these provisions is provided in Chapter 49.) If after-tax employee contributions were made to the CODA, a portion of the withdrawal will be excluded from federal income tax; otherwise, the entire withdrawal will be taxable. Moreover, with certain limited exceptions, a 10 percent penalty tax will apply to distributions (other than those that are not subject to the regular federal income tax because they are returns of employee contributions) made before the participant's death, disability, or attainment of age 59½.[13]

Social Security

Originally, elective contributions to a CODA were not considered to be wages for purposes of Social Security. Thus, they were not subject to Social Security (FICA) tax, nor were they taken into account when calculating Social Security benefits.

This was changed by the 1983 Social Security amendments. As of 1984, elective contributions are considered as wages for Social Security (and federal unemployment insurance) purposes. Thus, FICA taxes are paid on such amounts (if they are under the taxable wage base) and are taken into account when calculating an employee's Social Security benefits.

Other Employer-Sponsored Plans

A matter of some concern to employers was the question of whether an employee's elective contributions could be considered as part of the compensation base for purposes of other tax-qualified plans. This uncertainty was resolved in 1983 when the IRS ruled that the inclusion (or exclusion) of elective contributions under a CODA as compensation in a defined benefit pension plan does not cause the pension plan to be discriminatory. The IRS also noted that the inclusion of nonelective contributions will still be subject to the discrimination standards.

Employers also maintain other pay-related employee benefit plans. These include short- and long-term disability income plans, group term life insurance, survivor income benefits, and, in some cases, medical

---

[13]Specifically, exceptions are granted if the distributions are:

1. Part of a series of substantially equal periodic payments made for the life (or life expectancy) of the employee or the joint lives (or joint life expectancies) of the employee and his or her beneficiary.
2. Used to pay medical expenses to the extent the expenses exceed 7½ percent of adjusted gross income.
3. Payments to alternate payees pursuant to a qualified domestic relations order (QDRO).

expense benefit plans. There appear to be no legal reasons why pay, for the purpose of these plans, cannot be defined to include elective contributions made under a CODA. If such contributions are to be included, care should be taken to make sure that necessary plan and/or insurance contract amendments are made so that compensation is properly defined.

To be qualified, a CODA must not condition any other benefit provided by the employer, either directly or indirectly, on the employee electing to have the employer make or not make contributions under the arrangement in lieu of receiving cash. This does not apply to any matching contribution made by reason of such an election.

State and Local Taxes

Unfortunately, the treatment of elective contributions under state and local tax laws is less than clear. For years, many states followed principles of federal tax law in the treatment of employee benefits. This practice was also followed by many local governments that impose some form of income tax.

With the increased use of IRAs in the 1980s, and with the publicity that CODAs have received, there has been growing concern among state and local tax authorities over the potential loss of tax revenue. As a result, the question of state and local taxation of elective contributions has become an important issue.

At this time, the tax treatment of these amounts is uncertain in many jurisdictions. Some state and local authorities have indicated that they will follow federal tax law. However, a few already have announced that elective contributions will be taxable and subject to employer withholding. It seems reasonable to expect that many more state and local authorities will adopt this latter position.

Deduction Limits

Section 404 of the IRC imposes limits on the amount an employer can deduct for contributions made to qualified plans. For profit-sharing plans, this limit is expressed as 15 percent of the payroll of the employees covered. If the employer has both a defined benefit plan and a defined contribution plan, the combined limit is 25 percent of the covered payroll.

Elective contributions affect the maximum deduction in two ways. First, they reduce the amount of the covered payroll to which the percentage limitations apply, thus reducing the dollar amount available as a maximum deduction. Second, they are considered to be employer contributions and thus reduce the amount otherwise available for the employer to contribute and deduct.

As a practical matter, the effect of CODAs on these limits should not be of great concern to most employers. For those who maintain liberal plans, however, the level of elective contributions permitted might have to be limited in order to preserve deductions for regular employer contributions.

Section 415 Limits

Section 415 of the IRC imposes limits on the contributions and benefits that might be provided for an employee under qualified plans. These limits are expressed both as a percentage of pay and as a dollar amount. A combined limit applies when an employee participates in both a defined-benefit and a defined-contribution plan. These limitations should affect only a few, if any, employees in most situations. Nevertheless, it is important that they be observed. A plan will be disqualified if it violates these limitations.

ADVANTAGES AND DISADVANTAGES OF CODAs

Advantages

The advantages of CODAs are significant, although most of them accrue to employees, rather than to employers. Nevertheless, the advantages to employers are important.

From an employer's viewpoint, CODAs have all the advantages normally associated with any employee benefit plan. Thus, they should be of material value in attracting and retaining employees, improving employee morale, achieving a better sense of corporate identification (when employer securities are involved), and so forth. In addition, they can serve specific corporate objectives such as increasing the level of participation in an existing plan that has had conventional after-tax employee contributions. For some employers, converting a conventional savings plan to a CODA, and thus increasing take-home pay for participating employees, could alleviate pressures for additional cash compensation.

Under a CODA, employees have the flexibility of determining on a year-to-year basis whether to take amounts in cash or defer these amounts under the plan. Since employee needs and goals change from time to time, this element of flexibility could be important.

If a conventional savings plan is converted to a CODA, the participating employees not only realize an immediate increase in take-home pay, but their contributions are accumulating under a tax shelter. This means that an employee can receive investment income on amounts that otherwise would have been paid in taxes. Over a period of years, the cumulative effect of this can be substantial. Finally, when amounts are distributed and subject to tax, the actual amount of tax paid might be considerably less than would otherwise have been the case. Installment distributions could be taxed at a lower effective tax rate (because of lower levels of taxable income and indexed tax brackets). Furthermore, lump-sum distributions also may qualify for favorable five-year-averaging tax treatment.

Disadvantages

The disadvantages of CODAs also should be recognized. From the employer's viewpoint, these plans involve complex and costly administration. Also, the employer must be prepared to deal with employee relations and other problems that can occur in any year that the plan fails to satisfy the ADP test. These plans also involve more communications efforts than are associated with conventional employee benefit plans.

From the viewpoint of employees, the disadvantages of CODAs are not as great. In fact, the only significant disadvantage is that elective contributions are subject to the previously mentioned withdrawal limitations and the possible application of the early distribution tax. This could be of major importance to some employees, particularly those at lower pay levels, and could be a barrier to their participation in the plan.

CHAPTER 35

EMPLOYEE STOCK OWNERSHIP PLANS (ESOPs)

Robert W. Smiley, Jr.
Gregory K. Brown

INTRODUCTION AND OVERVIEW

Employee Stock Ownership Plans (ESOPs)

Employee stock ownership plans have evolved from a novel academic concept into a sophisticated tool of corporate succession and finance that is well integrated into the mainstream of the American business community. During the period of this evolution, a fairly well-developed body of law has emerged at a legislative and regulatory level as well as through judicial interpretation. ESOPs have been used not only for business succession and capital formation by owners of closely held companies, but also have been used as an employee benefits tool and defensive measure by many publicly held corporations or as a means of taking a publicly held company private. This chapter will provide the reader with a road map to the development of ESOPs as well as the legal, financial, and accounting considerations that must be dealt with in order to implement an ESOP. As this chapter will evidence, great care in planning is necessary in order for a corporation (and its shareholders) to decide whether or not an ESOP is feasible and will serve its (and their) goals and objectives and, if so, to implement the ESOP to serve those ends.

Kelsoism, Two-Factor Economics, and the Results

Louis Kelso started a movement almost 30 years ago that has, through his own efforts and the efforts of many other capable people, resulted in millions of Americans owning part or all of the companies they work for—"a piece of the action." His concept is "universal capitalism," and its thrust is to spread the benefits of capital ownership to all Americans, not just to a few. Simply put, Kelso divides the economic sphere into two factors: labor (the human factor) and capital (the nonhuman factor). Hence the name *two-factor economics*. He originally proposed that the ownership of productive assets would be represented by shares of stock in corporations that make capital expenditures. These shares would be owned by new capitalists, the employees of the companies making these capital expenditures. This shift to new capitalists was to be accomplished through the use of corporate credit and reinvestment into the capital necessary to repay any indebtedness arising from the use of such credit. What Kelso proposed was to have every company set up a tax-qualified employee stock ownership plan and its attendant trust. The trustee would then go to the financial community and borrow money to buy stock in the company the employees work for. The loan would be repaid out of the profits produced by the new plant and equipment that would be purchased with the proceeds of the stock sale. Ultimately, the employees (or their beneficiaries at death) on disability, retirement, or other termination of service would receive their shares, and "would live happily ever after" on the dividends. There are now well in excess of 11,000 such plans across the country and more being adopted every day.

Background and Description

The first stock bonus plans were granted tax-exempt status under the Revenue Act of 1921. In 1953, the Internal Revenue Service (IRS) first recognized the use of a qualified employees' plan for debt financing the purchase of employer stock when it published Revenue Ruling 46. In recent years, Congress has encouraged the use of the ESOP financing technique in at least 21 different pieces of legislation.

Employee stock ownership plans generally can be described as defined contribution, individual account plans similar to stock bonus plans and profit-sharing plans. By relating ESOPs to these familiar employee benefit plans, a base can be established from which these plans can be analyzed and reviewed. As a form of stock bonus plan, ESOPs differ from profit-sharing plans in that an ESOP must make distributions in employer stock, although cash can be distributed—provided the employee is given the option to demand his or her distribution in employer securities or the other special requirements discussed later in this chapter are met. It is the ESOP's ability to borrow based on the credit of the company that allows the ESOP to be used as a technique of corporate finance. An ESOP is essentially a stock bonus plan that uses borrowed funds to finance the purchase of a company's stock for the firm's employees. The ESOP is a tax-sheltered employee benefit plan on the one hand, and a bona fide technique of corporate finance on the other.

The statutory definition of an ESOP is a defined contribution plan:

1. Which is a stock bonus plan that is qualified, or a stock bonus and a money purchase plan both of which are qualified under IRC Section 401(a), and that are designed to invest in qualifying employer securities; and
2. Which is otherwise defined in IRS regulations.

An ESOP must also meet special distribution, put option nonallocation, and voting requirements discussed later in this chapter.

The following example will illustrate the simplest and most basic use of an ESOP.

An Example. Assume that a company in a 40 percent combined federal and state income tax bracket has pretax earnings of $150,000, a covered payroll of $600,000, and makes a $90,000 (15 percent of $600,000) contribution to the plan, which then buys stock from the company.

Compare this situation with a profit-sharing plan to which the company contributes the same amount. Table 35–1 shows the effect of different plans.

Leveraged ESOPs

An ESOP also may leverage its investments to acquire employer stock, something that a normal pension or profit-sharing plan (except under very limited circumstances) is not permitted to do. This feature makes an ESOP very useful in debt financing. For example, assume the ESOP borrows $500,000 for seven years at a below-market annual interest rate of 6.14 percent. (The lender relies on the solvency of the company.) The

TABLE 35–1
Comparing Plans

	No Qualified Plan	*Profit-Sharing Plan*	*ESOP*
Pretax income	$150,000	$150,000	$150,000
Less contribution	0	90,000	90,000
Net taxable income	150,000	60,000	60,000
Income tax (federal and state)	60,000	24,000	24,000
Net after-tax income	$ 90,000	$ 36,000	$ 36,000
Company cash flow	$ 90,000	$ 36,000	$126,000*

*The $90,000 contribution goes to work inside the corporation, as additional equity capital.

ESOP then buys $500,000 worth of stock from the company, and the company can use this money as additional working capital in any way it wishes. The company then contributes to the ESOP approximately $90,000 each year, which is used to pay the principal and interest on the $500,000 loan. The company gets a tax deduction for the entire $90,000, even though part of it is used to pay the principal. Assuming a 40 percent corporate tax rate, the company has reduced its ultimate tax bill by $200,000, and the cash flow of the company has been increased by $200,000, the amount of the tax reduction. At the same time, the employees have become beneficial stockholders of the company and, presumably, now have a greater interest in making the company more profitable and in generating the profits necessary to repay the loan.

The Economic Recovery Tax Act of 1981 (ERTA) altered the funding limits applicable to leveraged ESOPs. Whereas prior to ERTA the combination of limits on deductible contributions and maximum allowable annual additions created a practical limit to the size of an ESOP loan, ERTA greatly expanded that limit. After ERTA a plan sponsor may contribute on a deductible basis an amount up to 25 percent of covered payroll to be used solely for principal reduction on an ESOP loan. In addition, the sponsor may contribute on a deductible basis an unlimited amount to service interest on the loan. Relevant adjustments were made to Internal Revenue Code (IRC or Code) Section 415 to allow for the allocation of all released shares (that is, forfeited and reallocated loan shares need not be considered "annual additions" for purposes of the limitations). Obviously, this allows a much larger block of stock to be purchased than could have been under pre-ERTA law.

For purposes of this chapter, an ESOP is defined as a qualified stock bonus plan, or a combination stock bonus and money purchase pension plan, that meets certain requirements under the Employee Retirement Income Security Act of 1974 (ERISA), as amended, and under the Internal Revenue Code of 1986, as amended, that allows the plan to borrow from, or on the credit of, the company or its shareholders, for the purpose of investing in the company's securities. The trust gives the lender its note for the money borrowed, which may or may not be secured by a pledge of the stock. Alternatively, the company borrows the money and makes a back-to-back loan to the ESOP on similar terms. The company, shareholders, or both, guarantee the loan. Usually there is an agreement with the lender that the company will make contributions to the trust in sufficient amounts to repay the loan, including interest. As the plan contributions are used to repay the loan, a number of shares are released to be allocated to the employees' individual accounts. As with other qualified plans, benefits usually are paid after employees die, retire, or otherwise leave the corporation.

Alternatives to an ESOP

Plans other than an ESOP can aid employers in their financing and also provide employees with the benefits of stock ownership. Compliance with the requirements of the definition of an ESOP is necessary only if the trust forming part of the plan is to be a borrower for the purpose of acquiring stock. If stock is to be acquired without this debt financing, any plan of the eligible individual account variety can be used to accomplish essentially the same purpose. Such plans include profit-sharing plans, stock bonus plans, savings plans, and thrift plans as well as ESOPs. However, the other benefits of an ESOP are available only through an ESOP, including the tax-free rollover and the dividend deduction explained later in this chapter. One of the more attractive stock ownership alternatives was the payroll-based TRASOP (PAYSOP) whereby benefits were funded entirely with what would otherwise be tax dollars. *The PAYSOP was repealed when the ESOP tax credit under Code Section 41 was repealed by the Tax Reform Act of 1986 (TRA '86).* Even though benefits under a PAYSOP were very small, on an individual participant basis, the fact that they resulted in a tax credit (as contrasted with a deduction) to the company effectively doubled their value from a corporate point of view.

Plans other than an ESOP can aid the company in its financing and also provide employees with the benefits of stock ownership. The most common alternative is a profit-sharing plan (including a 401(k) profit-sharing plan). While trust borrowing with corporate or shareholder guarantees is prohibited, most if not all of the benefits of an ESOP are available to the company and to the employees through a well-designed profit-sharing plan. Distributions may be made to participants in either cash or stock. Contributions may be made in cash or stock; and cash, once contributed, may be used to purchase company stock from the company or the shareholders, as long as certain rules are followed.

The next-most common alternative is a stock bonus plan, which is similar to a profit-sharing plan except that benefits are normally distributable in stock of the employer. IRC Section 401(a)(23) now permits a stock bonus plan to distribute cash in lieu of stock, provided the employee has the right to have his or her distribution in employer securities, unless the special cash-only distribution provisions of IRC Section 409(h)(2) apply. The primary purpose of a stock bonus plan is ''to give employee-participants an interest in the ownership and growth of the employer's business.''[1] This distinction in purpose from pension plans and profit-sharing plans is important in interpreting the fiduciary responsibility provisions of ERISA.

Thrift plans and savings plans[2] were not previously defined in federal income tax law but would encompass the whole gamut of very successful plans that match employee contributions on some basis. Under many thrift and savings plans, especially the larger plans, a very high percentage of the investments is in company stock.

As for these non-ESOP plans being able to repay company debt, the same amount that an ESOP would have borrowed can usually be borrowed by the company directly, and then contributions to the non-ESOP plan can be made in company stock having a value equal to the amount of the amortization payments on the debt. If the stock goes up in value, from the point of view of company costs, it will be less costly for the company than for the trust to incur the debt. The reason is that less

---

[1]Rev. Rul. 69-65, 1969-1 C.B. 114.

[2]ERISA Sec. 407(d)(3).

stock will be contributed by the company if the shares increase in value as the future contributions are made, thereby reducing the repurchase liability for closely held companies because fewer shares of stock have to be redeemed.[3] Additional stock will not have to be contributed to the ESOP to pay the interest, because the interest already is deductible as an expense by the company.

A money purchase pension plan may be structured as part of an ESOP. As discussed earlier, after ERTA a leveraged ESOP can be structured to provide contributions in excess of 15% of covered payroll. If a contribution of more than 15% of payroll is desired without using a leveraged ESOP, a money purchase pension plan, combined with a stock bonus plan, may be in order. The pension plan could be a savings plan, and since savings plans generally require the employee to contribute, some assurance of employee contributions can be made by establishing an attractive matching rate. The two plans combined then would permit a deductible contribution of up to 25% of covered payroll.

A money purchase pension plan alone is not an ESOP, but can be if combined with a stock bonus plan as part of an ESOP. The money purchase plan that forms a part of an ESOP will generally be subject to some of the requirements applicable to money purchase plans (except, for example, the 10% limit on investments in employer stock under ERISA Section 407(a) and the joint and survivor annuity requirements of IRC Sections 401(a)(11) and 417 and ERISA Section 205), as well as the special requirements that apply to an ESOP under IRC Section 4975(e)(7) and the regulations thereunder.

The primary purpose for including a money purchase plan as part of an ESOP is to increase the tax-deductible limits on employer contributions from the normal 15% of compensation limit applicable to stock bonus plans to 25% of compensation, when "credit carryovers" attributable to years prior to 1987 are not available under IRC Section 404(a)(3)(A). After the enactment of ERTA, however, such use of a money purchase pension plan will generally no longer be necessary if leveraging is used, because ERTA increased the deduction limits appli-

---

[3]Robert W. Smiley, Jr., "How to Plan for an ESOP's Repurchase Liability," Prentice-Hall's *Pension and Profit-Sharing Service* (Englewood Cliffs, N.J.: Prentice-Hall, April 3, 1980), pp. 1,431–40; and Smiley, "How to Plan for an ESOP's Repurchase Liability," Prentice-Hall's *Pension and Profit-Sharing Service* (Englewood Cliffs, N.J.: Prentice-Hall, February 27, 1987), pp. 1,215–29.

cable under IRC Section 404(a)(9) with respect to employer contributions used to repay an ESOP loan. In the case of a nonleveraged ESOP, the use of a money purchase plan may still be attractive to increase tax-deductible contributions, provided the employer is willing to make the definite contributions required each year under the money purchase plan.

ESOP as a Financing Vehicle

This subject is covered in greater detail under "Corporate Objectives in Establishing ESOPs" later in the chapter.

Generally, employee stock ownership plans serve a variety of corporate objectives above and beyond the primary objective of providing an employee benefit. ESOPs also serve as a technique of corporate finance. In this hybrid role, ESOPs also can be used for:

- Capital formation.
- Low-cost borrowing.
- Solving succession of ownership issues.
- Refinancing existing debt.
- Estate planning.
- Financing an acquisition or divestiture.

Considerable care is required in structuring the ESOP for these various uses.

CORPORATE OBJECTIVES IN ESTABLISHING ESOPs

ESOP as an Employee/Employer Benefit Plan

Advantages to the Employer

The principal reasons for the continuing rise in interest in ESOPs are the number of potential advantages of their use by the employer (and shareholder[s]). From an employer's standpoint, their primary objectives are to:

Increase employee motivation and productivity through ownership participation.

Increase cash flow by creating tax deductions with stock contributions.

Transfer business to key employees on a tax-favored basis.

Refinance existing debt at more favorable rates with pretax dollars.

Create a market for shares of stock held by current shareholders.

Aid in estate planning (both before and after death) for one or more shareholders.

Create an alternative to sale of the company to outsiders or to a public offering.

Divest a subsidiary, acquire an existing subsidiary or division, or finance the acquisition of a company or business.

Convert existing pension/profit-sharing plan(s) from pure expense items to tax-saving or corporate finance vehicles.

Serve as a means of charitable giving.

ESOPs are recognized as being able to solve corporate financial needs in the following ways:

1. Financing future growth with pretax dollars.
2. Financing future growth at below-market interest rates.
3. Refinancing existing debt, repaying both principal and interest with pretax dollars.
4. Increasing cash flow without increasing sales or revenue.
5. Motivating employees to regard the company through the eyes of an owner by letting them share in a "piece of the action" and possibly receive tax-deductible dividends.
6. Creating a friendly base of stockholders (employees) as opposed to disinterested speculators in the public marketplace.
7. Creating a tool to help attract and retain high-quality management and supervisory personnel while cutting down on employee turnover.
8. Encouraging employee ownership of closely held company stock (without relinquishing voting control).
9. Improving employee relations.
10. Ensuring the future growth of the company through increased employee productivity and increased company profitability.
11. Converting present employee benefit plans from pure expense items and liabilities to vehicles that increase working capital and net worth.

12. Providing an in-house, liquid market for stock while remaining private.
13. Enabling private shareholder(s) to sell all or part of their holdings at fair market value without the expense and uncertainty of a public securities offering.
14. Enabling private shareholder(s) to defer paying federal capital-gains taxes, perhaps indefinitely.
15. Creating a financial tool for estate planning that can provide liquidity for payment of federal estate taxes.
16. Divesting an incompatible subsidiary without the publicity, expense, and uncertainty of finding an outside buyer.
17. Acquiring a company with pretax dollars, and amortizing acquisition financing with pretax dollars.
18. Providing for the potential recapture of the prior three years' federal income taxes.
19. Using in conjunction with takeover defense strategy, retiring stock, or "going private."
20. Increasing the yields to stockholders.

Disadvantages to the Employer

As with almost all things, ESOPs have some disadvantages. The value of the company's stock may be independent of company performance. If the company's stock experiences a market decline or a decline based on appraised values, a substantial risk of employee dissatisfaction may occur. This dissatisfaction may be accentuated if there is leveraging in the ESOP. In most cases, however, the direct link between company performance and trust fund performance will only be a disadvantage if the company stock performs poorly.

Further, since an ESOP may have to make distributions in stock, and since the employee may owe taxes, the company must be certain that the employee has sufficient cash to pay taxes. Otherwise, the stock must be sold to pay taxes, possibly creating a morale problem. The put option provision (described later in this chapter) usually alleviates this problem.

Dilution is a key disadvantage. When new stock is contributed to the trust, or purchased from the company, the earnings per share on each remaining share may be reduced. A careful analysis must be made to determine whether this potential disadvantage is offset by the increase in working capital and the increased cash flow from the tax savings.

The emerging repurchase liability is another problem that must be dealt with. Again, a careful analysis and the series of solutions available here must be worked through, scheduled, and acted on.[4]

Voting control may become an issue, unless the ESOP is monitored with considerable forethought. Sometimes, this change of voting control is what is desired; if it is not, the safeguards that are available should be established in order to avoid a loss of control.

The degree of risk is another factor. The ESOP invests primarily in employer securities and may subject the trust funds to capital risks. The value of the benefit to both the employer and the employee depends on the performance of company stock and the timing of the financing.

Advantages to Employees

The advantages of an ESOP to employees are obvious: they receive stock in the company that employs them without any cash outlay or financial liability, and without any income tax liability until they receive the stock.

If employees receive company stock in a lump-sum distribution, they can escape current taxation of the unrealized appreciation in the company stock until they sell the stock. They are required to pay tax only on the trust's basis (or fair market value, whichever is lower) in the year a lump-sum distribution is made. This can be quite a benefit if the stock has done well and the employees hold the stock until the tax year in which a sale appears most advantageous to them. In smaller companies, the stock usually is sold immediately, either to the trust or to the company.

Other advantages to employees include:

1. The participant may claim favorable tax treatment on a lump-sum distribution under Code Section 402(e)(4) or may roll over such distribution on a tax-deferred basis under Code Section 402(a)(5).
2. If a lump-sum distribution is made, the participant is not immediately taxed on the unrealized appreciation on the employer's securities distributed; however, an election to be taxed on the unrealized appreciation may be made.

---

[4]Smiley, "How to Plan for an ESOP's Repurchase Liability," pp. 1,215–29.

3. Dividends paid on ESOP stock are taxable to the recipient and deductible by the employer when paid or distributed to participants (or their beneficiaries). If the dividends are used to repay ESOP loans, the dividends are not taxable to the recipients, but allocations may be accelerated to participants.

Disadvantages to Employees

The major potential drawback is the ''all eggs in one basket'' problem, the lack of diversification. If the employer company has financial difficulties, the employee can suffer a double loss; he or she can lose both the ESOP benefits and the job.

Having to sell a block of stock in a closely held corporation can be very difficult. With the put option requirements the problem is easier, but an employee could let his or her put option expire and be faced with this problem well into retirement.

Because most distributions are in company stock, ESOPs will place the employees in the position of having to sell the stock they receive, because they usually will not have the cash to pay the taxes due on the amount of the distribution. An individual retirement account rollover, or a rollover to another qualified plan, may eliminate this need for cash to pay taxes at the time of the distribution.

Employees also must face the problem of a liquidity crisis if the employer (or ESOP) does not have sufficient cash on hand to purchase distributed shares. Proper planning by the employer can generally eliminate this problem; however, it must be considered.

Leverage to purchase employer securities is rarely a disadvantage to the employees if the employer is assuming the risk of the loan.

Corporate Finance Applications

More Effective Capital Formation

The primary advantage resulting from the use of ESOP financing techniques is greater cash flow. The basic ESOP model provides for financing new capital formation and corporate growth, with pretax dollars being used to repay debt. While conventional loans require repayment of principal with after-tax dollars, ESOP financing enhances the ability of the employer company to meet debt-service requirements with pretax dollars. (See Table 35–1.)

Reduced Borrowing Costs

An independent bank, insurance company, mutual fund, or other qualified commercial corporate lender may exclude from its income 50 percent of the interest received on loans that are directly made to an ESOP, or that are made to an employer that in turn lends the proceeds to its ESOP, provided a number of technical rules are met, which are described below. The loans must be used to purchase employer securities of the employer corporation. The 50 percent interest exclusion is also available for companies with nonleveraged ESOPs. A loan to an employer will qualify if the employer contributes stock to an ESOP equal in value to the amount of the loan within 30 days of the loan, such stock is allocated to participants within one year, and the term of the loan does not exceed seven years. Financing institutions with a "tax appetite" will pass on part of this tax savings, thereby reducing borrowing costs. The after-tax yields to tax-paying financial institutions on ESOP loans, even after significant rate reductions to borrowers, is still greater than on a conventional loan.

Omnibus Budget Reconciliation Act of 1989 (OBRA). The Omnibus Budget Reconciliation Act of 1989 (OBRA '89) has placed the following substantial new restrictions on the availability of the IRC Section 133 partial interest exclusion, which are likely to curtail its use:

1. The exclusion is available only if, immediately after the ESOP's acquisition of stock with the loan proceeds, the ESOP owns either more than 50% of each class of outstanding stock of the issuing corporation or more than 50% of the total value of all stock of the issuing corporation (in each case, exclusive of certain nonvoting, nonconvertible preferred stock).

   (a) A penalty tax is imposed on the employer under IRC Section 4978B if the securities acquired with the loan proceeds are disposed of by the plan within three years after their acquisition (or transfer). The tax will equal 10% of the amount realized on the disposed securities. Exceptions for distributions in the normal course, exchanges of employer securities in tax-free reorganizations, diversification options, etc., are provided in the same manner as under IRC Section 4978, relating to the penalty tax for disposing of securities acquired in an IRC Section 1042 nonrecognition transaction.

The excise tax is also imposed on a disposition of employer securities prior to allocation to the accounts of participants or their beneficiaries where the full proceeds of such disposition are not allocated to their accounts, regardless of whether such disposition occurs within three years of the ESOP acquisition (or transfer).

The excise tax provisions of IRC Section 4978B do not apply to securities purchased by an employee stock ownership plan for which the selling shareholder has elected special tax treatment under the provisions of either IRC Section 1042 or IRC Section 2057 (as in effect for estates of decedents dying before December 20, 1989). The excise tax provisions of IRC Sections 4978 and 4978A (as in effect for estates of decedents dying before December 20, 1989), respectively, apply to those securities.

A disposition of employer securities will be treated as having been made in the following order for purposes of the excise tax:

(i) From employer securities acquired during the three-year period ending on the date of such disposition, beginning with the securities first so acquired;
(ii) From employer securities acquired before such three-year period unless such securities (or the proceeds from such disposition) have been allocated to accounts of participants or their beneficiaries;
(iii) From securities otherwise qualified for the partial interest exclusion acquired during the three-year period ending on the date of such disposition beginning with the securities first so acquired; and
(iv) From any other employer securities.

If a disposition occurs as a result of certain reorganizations, operation of law, death, retirement, disability, or separation from service, the disposition shall be treated as made from employer securities in the opposite order of the priorities listed above.

(b) The exclusion is unavailable during any period in which the ESOP's ownership proportion fails to meet the more-than-50% rule, regardless of the reason. Thus, for example, if an ESOP acquires 51% of the company's stock and distributes shares to participants which are then either held by the participants or redeemed by the company, thus causing the ESOP's ownership percentage to fail to meet the more-than-50% rule, the exclusion will be unavailable until the ESOP in some manner exceeds the 50% level again. However, the IRS is authorized to issue regulations that would allow for after-the-fact compliance if the ESOP acquires sufficient stock to meet the more-than-50% rule within 90 days of the failure (or a longer period not exceeding 180 days).

The more-than-50% rule may be satisfied by counting all stock in any ESOP maintained by the employer (or other member of the employer's controlled group). The IRS is also authorized to issue regulations that would treat warrants, options, contracts to acquire stock, convertible debt interest, and other similar rights as stock for purposes of the more-than-50% rule. However, options held by an ESOP are not to be counted toward the more-than-50% rule when determining the amount of stock of the corporation held by the ESOP.

2. The exclusion is only available for loans with a term not in excess of 15 years.
3. The ESOP must provide for full pass-through of voting rights on allocated stock to participants, not merely pass-through on "major" issues, as is normally required for closely held companies. In addition, if the plan acquires convertible preferred stock, that stock must carry voting rights equivalent to the stock into which it may be converted. There is no requirement for pass-through of voting rights on unallocated stock. Full voting pass-through is required only if the lender utilizes the interest exclusion under IRC Section 133; if not, then only limited voting pass-through will continue to be required for closely held company ESOPs for stock acquired after the relevant effective date discussed below.
4. The new requirements are generally effective for loans made after July 10, 1989. In addition, special transition rules provide that OBRA amendments *do not* apply to a loan made after July 10, 1989:

   (a) If the loan is made pursuant to a written, binding commitment in effect on July 10, 1989, and, to the extent the proceeds of such loan are used to acquire employer securities, pursuant to a written, binding contract (or tender offer) in effect on July 10, 1989;

(b) If the loan is an immediate allocation securities acquisition loan made on or before July 10, 1992, pursuant to a written agreement entered into on or before July 10, 1989, and such agreement evidences the intent of the borrower to enter into securities acquisition loans on a periodic basis;

(c) If the loan is made pursuant to a written binding commitment in effect on June 6, 1989, or to the extent that the proceeds of the loan are used to acquire employer securities pursuant to a written binding contract (or tender offer) in effect on June 6, 1989;

(d) To the extent the loan is used to acquire employer securities pursuant to a collective bargaining agreement setting forth the material terms of the ESOP (or referencing an existing ESOP), which was agreed to on or before June 6, 1989, by one or more employers and employee representatives (and ratified on or before such date or within a reasonable period thereafter); and

(e) With respect to which governmental filings were made on or before June 6, 1989, specifying a loan to be a securities acquisition loan or required for the ESOP to acquire more than the threshold percentage of the employer's stock.

The grandfather element with respect to governmental filings relates only to governmental filings required for the ESOP debt to be issued or for the necessary percentage of the corporation's stock to be acquired by the ESOP. Thus, this rule is not satisfied by applying for or obtaining an IRS determination letter relating to the ESOP's tax-qualified status.

A further special effective date applies to loans not otherwise grandfathered under the rules governing plans not satisfying the more-than-50% requirement. Under this special rule, the more-than-50% requirement does not apply in the case of a loan made after July 10, 1989, if:

- The requirements of the 50% provision are otherwise satisfied by substituting ''at least 30%'' for ''more-than-50%; and
- Either the loan is made on or before November 17, 1989, the loan is made after November 17, 1989, pursuant to a written binding

commitment in effect on November 17, 1989, or to the extent that the proceeds of the loan are used to acquire employer securities pursuant to a written binding contract (or tender offer) in effect on November 17, 1989.

In addition, the general effective date provisions do not apply to a loan made after July 10, 1989, to refinance securities acquisition loans (determined without regard to the otherwise disqualifying rules governing loans between related parties) made on or before such date or to refinance loans grandfathered under the general provision if:

- Such refinancing loan otherwise meets the partial interest exclusion rule (as in effect before the OBRA '89 amendment);
- The outstanding principal amount of the loan is not increased; and
- The term of such loan does not extend beyond the later of the last day of the term of the original securities acquisition loan or the last day of the seven-year period beginning on the date the original securities acquisition loan was made.

The refinancing rules also apply to mirror loans, in which the original securities acquisition loan consists of a loan to the employer with a corresponding loan to the ESOP, and the loan is restructured so that the loan is directly from the financial institution to the ESOP with a guarantee from the employer, rather than a loan from the employer. The refinancing rules also apply to a series of refinancings. The original lender need not have been a "qualified lender" for purposes of qualifying for the special refinancing provisions. (See IRS Notice 90-6 for guidance on the written commitment requirement for the grandfather rules.)

5. OBRA '89 also added a reporting requirement for ESOPs. IRC Section 6047(e) now provides that Treasury may require the filing of information returns respecting the plan or any IRC Section 133 loan by:

   (a) Any employer maintaining, or the plan administrator of, an ESOP that acquires employer securities in a Section 133 transaction or holds stock with respect to which the Section 404(k) dividends-paid deduction applies,
   (b) Any ESOP lender, or
   (c) Both.

Transfers of Ownership

If stock of a closely held corporation is sold to an ESOP under circumstances where the sale would otherwise qualify as a long-term capital gain, no tax must be paid at the time of the sale, on all or part of the realized gain, provided the following requirements are satisfied. In order to qualify for this very favorable Code Section 1042 treatment, the ESOP must own either (1) at least 30 percent of the value of the outstanding equity of the company after the sale, on a fully diluted basis (other than certain nonvoting, nonconvertible preferred stock), or (2) at least 30 percent of each class of outstanding stock of the company on a fully diluted basis (other than certain nonvoting, nonconvertible preferred stock), after the sale, and the sales proceeds must be reinvested in replacement securities (''qualified replacement property'') within a 15-month period that begins three months before and ends 12 months after the sale. The replacement securities must be securities of a domestic (that is, United States) operating company and may be public or private securities, giving the seller a virtually unlimited choice. In practice there are very few restrictions although care must be taken to avoid certain passive-income company pitfalls for the unwary. Tax is then deferred until the qualified replacement property is sold; or if the replacement securities become a part of the seller's estate, the capital gains tax is never paid because the replacement securities enjoy the advantage of a step-up-in basis at the holder's death.

If the stock in a closely held corporation is sold to an ESOP on or after July 10, 1989, the seller must have held such stock for at least three years before the time of the sale (one year for sales before July 10, 1989).

An excise tax is imposed on the employer for certain dispositions of the stock acquired by the ESOP in the transaction within three years after sale. (Also, see above OBRA '89 changes.) The stock that is purchased by the ESOP may not be allocated to the seller, members of his or her family (brothers, sisters, spouse, ancestors, and lineal descendants and to anyone related to the seller within the meaning of Code Section 267(b) [Code Section 409(n)(1)(A)] or any shareholder who owns more than 25 percent in value or number of any class of outstanding employer stock (or a controlled group member). In determining whether a person owns more than such 25 percent in value or number, the constructive ownership rules of Code Section 318(a) apply, taking into account stock held by a qualified plan.

However, individuals who would be ineligible to receive an allocation of qualified securities just because they are lineal descendants of other ineligible individuals may receive an allocation of Code Section 1042 securities as long as the total amount of the securities allocated to the lineal descendants is not more than 5 percent of all Code Section 1042 securities. In computing this percent amount, all employer securities sold to the ESOP by the seller that are eligible for nonrecognition treatment (including outstanding stock options) are taken into account, according to the TRA '86 Conference Report.[5] Existing shareholders may dispose of all or a portion of their shares without the potential dividend treatment that may apply to a corporate redemption under Code Section 302. ESOP financing permits the acquisition of stock from existing shareholders using pretax dollars, and the existing shareholders are selling capital assets that can be taxed as long-term capital gains. While TRA '86 repealed the long-term capital-gains deduction, the treatment of a sale of securities as a capital gain or loss is still material to the calculation of a taxpayer's tax liability. Normally, for closely held companies, corporate stock redemptions are fraught with potential dividend treatment problems, and require the use of after-tax dollars.

Refinancing Existing Debt

An ESOP may be used to refinance existing corporate debt and to repay it with pretax dollars, thereby lowering the borrowing costs. Besides cash contributions, the company could issue new shares of stock to the ESOP equal in value to the amount of debt assumed by the ESOP thus helping cash flow. This will effectively make the repayment of debt tax-deductible (within the limits of Code Section 404(a)(9)), and the interest paid thereon will qualify for the partial interest exclusion of Code Section 133 (and probably a lower interest rate). Sophisticated lenders generally understand that they have greater security with an ESOP, since their payment is made out of pretax earnings, and the lender gets paid even before the tax collector. Dividends are now deductible by the employer if

---

[5]*At* p. II–852. IRC Sec. 409(n) appears to exclude lineal descendants of a 25% owner; in other words, the lineal descendants' exception would not apply to a 25% owner, including shares deemed owned by such owner through attribution. If so, this would severely limit application of this exception. However, this interpretation seems contrary to the use of the words "any other person" in IRC Sec. 409(n)(1)(B).

used to repay ESOP debt. In addition, ESOP loans may be refinanced, provided certain requirements are met.

Alternative to Going Public

The costs of a public stock offering, SEC registration, and the high expense of operating as a publicly owned company can be avoided through ESOP financing. The shares may be acquired by the ESOP from the company, existing shareholders, or both. Since employee shareholders are usually more loyal as shareholders than outsiders, and because an in-house market is usually more stable, the value of the stock may not be subject to the sometimes wild fluctuations found in the public market. In some situations, the ESOP shares will have a higher value than a comparable public company because the ESOP shares may not be subject to a ''minority-interest discount.'' A minority interest is usually worth somewhat less than a proportionate share of the total value of the company when the company is valued on an ''enterprise (or control) basis.'' This is because minority shareholders cannot control company policy in many important areas that affect them, such as compensation, dividends, selection of officers, sale or purchase of assets, and other crucial corporate decisions.

Financing an Acquisition or Divestiture

ESOP financing provides a way for a company to spin off a division or subsidiary to a new company owned by the employees in whole or in part through an ESOP. The new company earnings then would be available to pay off the purchase price, which may have been financed by an installment purchase from the divesting company—or through loans and equity provided from outside lenders, venture capitalists, investor/operators expert in leveraged buyouts or a specialized ESOP leveraged buyout (LBO) fund. The success of any leveraged buyout turns on the capacity of the ongoing business to amortize the acquisition debt. The increased after-tax cash flow available through ESOP financing can enhance materially the probability of a successful transaction, because repayment of the acquisition indebtedness may be accelerated. In an ESOP leveraged buyout transaction, the employer may effectively amortize both principal and interest payments from pretax income. In contrast, only interest is deductible in a conventional leveraged buyout. As a result, ESOP leveraged buyouts are able to support acquisition debt more easily, and the viability of the transaction may not be affected as adversely by fluctuations in interest rates or economic cycles.

The same technique in reverse may be used to finance the acquisition of other companies. The often increased pretax earnings of the acquired company and the generally increased employee payroll (because of the added payroll of the acquired company), are variables that may permit accelerated repayment of the debt incurred for financing an acquisition.

Estate Planning

An ESOP may provide a ready market for the shares of a deceased shareholder. Acquisitions of employer stock from the estate can be debt-financed and then repaid with pretax dollars. Note, however, that the ESOP purchase of those shares, which cannot be at a price in excess of appraised fair market value, will then set a price for estate tax valuation purposes and for the shares held by any remaining shareholders.

Prior to the enactment of OBRA '89, the Internal Revenue Code included two incentives for estates of deceased shareholders to sell shares to ESOPs. These provisions included an assumption of estate-tax liability by an ESOP and a deduction of 50% of the proceeds from an estate sale of employer stock to an ESOP for purposes of determining the amount of a decedent's gross estate under federal estate-tax laws. Both of these provisions, however, have been repealed and will be of interest only to estates that are still open with respect to decedents who died prior to July 13, 1990 (in the case of the estate-tax assumption), and prior to December 20, 1990 (in the case of the estate-tax deduction). Now that these incentives are gone, the estate of a deceased shareholder can look at an ESOP primarily for liquidity purposes.

Problem Areas in ESOP Financing

Acquisition of Stock

ESOPs may acquire stock from parties in interest if no more than "adequate consideration" is paid. If the purchase price exceeds fair market value, the acquisition from a "party in interest" or "disqualified person" would constitute a prohibited transaction subject to penalty taxes and corrective action under Code Section 4975 and ERISA Section 406, would probably violate the fiduciary duty of prudence, and the fiduciaries would have liability for any resulting losses.

Care must be taken, if the stock is not publicly traded, to determine the value of the company stock. Use of an outside appraisal is now mandatory with the addition of the independent-appraiser requirement of IRC Section 401(a)(28) and the issuance of proposed regulations under ERISA Section 3(18). The Internal Revenue Service and the Department of Labor are currently closely scrutinizing ESOP acquisitions of employer stock, especially with respect to fair market value and equity allocation issues.

OBRA '89 added new Section 502(1) to ERISA requiring that the Department of Labor assess a penalty equal to 20% of the "applicable recovery amount" involved in any judgment or settlement involving a breach or violation of fiduciary liability or against a nonfiduciary who knowingly participates in such breach or violation. The Department does retain, in its sole and nonreviewable discretion, the right to waive or reduce the penalty where it determines in writing that either (i) the fiduciary or other person acted reasonably or in good faith, or (ii) it is reasonable to expect that the fiduciary or other person will not be able to restore all losses to the plan without severe financial hardship unless such waiver or reduction is granted. The penalty is also reduced by the amount of any excise tax on prohibited transactions paid to the IRS.

Debt Financing

ERISA Section 408(b)(3) and IRC Section 4975(d)(3) provide for a prohibited-transaction exemption for an ESOP loan primarily for the benefit of participants. The collateral given for a party-in-interest loan by the ESOP must be limited to employer stock, and the loan must bear no more than a reasonable rate of interest. However, if these conditions are not met, the entire loan may be subject to prohibited transaction penalty taxes, corrective action, and, of course, fiduciary liability.

Usually a loan will be primarily for the benefit of participants if the proceeds are used to acquire company stock on fair terms for the benefit of employees in connection with the financing of corporate capital requirements. Primary security for the loan should be corporate credit, and the company will generally be required to either guarantee the loan, or make a commitment to pay sufficient dividends on the company stock, and/or make sufficient contributions to pay off the debt, or both. Liability of the ESOP for repayment of the loan must be limited to payments received from the company, including dividends, and to any stock remaining in the ESOP that is still used as collateral. The loan, by its nature, must be *nonrecourse* on other ESOP assets. In other words, no person entitled to payment from the ESOP will have any right to any asset of the ESOP other than the payments received from the company, including dividends, and the pledged stock not yet received from the suspense account.

The employer contributions required to service debt principal and interest must not exceed the allocation limitations under IRC Section 415. However, since forfeitures of loan shares and dividends used to repay ESOP debt on such shares are effectively allocated at cost (not current fair market value), and forfeitures of leveraged shares and dividends are not considered annual additions, the value of actual allocations may exceed 25 percent of pay or the then-in-effect dollar limit. However, when more than one third of the contribution for the plan year is allocated to highly compensated employees, forfeitures of leveraged shares are considered as annual additions, as are ESOP interest payments, for the plan year.

Determination Letter

The usual Internal Revenue Service determination letter issued under Code Section 401(a) offers little protection for the more difficult compliance issues in ESOP financing. While the letter applies to the formal requirements for the tax exemption of the ESOP, it does not apply to issues of operational compliance with the prohibited transaction exemptions under ERISA Section 408(b)(3) and (e) and under Code Section 4975(d)(3) and (13). It is possible to request and to receive a determination letter that the ESOP is qualified under IRC Section 4975(e)(7) by completing and filing IRS form 5309 in addition to the regular application materials. The ERISA Conference Report and the leveraged ESOP regulations direct the Internal Revenue Service and Department of Labor to give *all* aspects of ESOP financing special scrutiny—ostensibly to protect the interests of participants and to prevent abuses of the ESOP technique.

Existing Plan Conversions

If the prudence requirement (discussed later in this chapter) of ERISA is satisfied, the assets of an existing plan may be used to acquire company stock either directly from the company or from existing shareholders by converting the existing plan into an ESOP. The conversion of an existing plan into an ESOP is accomplished by means of an amendment to the plan. This subject is covered in more detail later in the chapter.

Which Type of ESOP Provides What Benefits?

Even though ESOPs are a technique of corporate finance, they are also compensation programs. The company contributions to these plans involve real economic costs incurred in exchange for employee services. As a form of compensation, they have the advantage of making the employees owners of a company. This may, in fact, be their main advantage.

Not all ESOPs, however, are the same. Selecting the proper form depends on the characteristics and goals of the sponsoring company and how the plan is to be used. Careful consideration must be given to how the plans differ. Often, the use of an ESOP and its many tax and other benefits is not desired, and another type of plan may be in order. It should be remembered that there is a wide range of options available, which allows employers great flexibility in tailoring a plan to their needs.

Simplicity is a virtue in the benefit field. Stock bonus plans have this major attribute. They are not subject to Code Section 4975(e)(7) regulations. They can use any equity security, including nonvoting and/or nonconvertible stock, which may be an important consideration when voting control is a key issue. Stock bonus plans, which do not meet the ESOP requirements, cannot be leveraged if the loan is guaranteed by the company, nor can the stock bonus plan acquire company stock from a shareholder using the popular tax-deferred rollover provisions of Code Section 1042. Nor may the stock bonus plan facilitate the use of the many other tax benefits discussed in this chapter that are available only to ESOPs. Stock bonus plans may distribute cash in lieu of employer securities, but the employee still has the option to require that his or her distribution be made in employer securities. A profit-sharing plan that invests primarily in company stock is not subject to this demand from employees to distribute company stock.

Leveraged ESOPs enhance immediate transfers of the ownership of companies, subsidiaries, and divisions from the existing owners to the employees. They are, however, subject to the ESOP regulations, including the put option requirements and the "special scrutiny" mandates. The leveraged ESOP is required to invest primarily in common stock or noncallable, convertible preferred stock of the employer.

ESOPs and Corporate Performance

Increased employee productivity often is cited as one advantage of ESOPs. *Productivity* is a term with a decidedly nonspecific meaning. It can be expressed in terms of dollar output per hour of labor, but little, if any, agreement exists among experts on how to increase it—and how to break down the relative contributions of capital and labor. It is almost impossible to prove that giving millions of workers a piece of the action will motivate them to increase productivity. Each company has a group of diverse employees with diverse temperaments, interests, goals, and objectives, and each group may react differently. Some employees are "long-term oriented"; they think and talk years ahead. Other employees are much more "short-term oriented." Obviously, there are millions of employees in between. Each company has to analyze its own employee base, make careful and well-thought-out value judgments, and decide which kind of employees it has and wishes to attract.

It is the most fundamental tenet of capitalist theory that economic efficiency is based on individual incentive. The idea that employee-ownership companies would be more efficient than conventionally owned companies follows this common-sense conclusion. If an employee's reward is fixed, what reason is there to work harder, smarter, faster, or more creatively? When the rewards are tied directly to productive effort, as they can be in an ESOP company, most employees should be more motivated and productive. Employee attitudes *should* be consistent with their work ethic. Since the late 1970s, researchers have put this reasoning to measurement in several studies.

One study found that employee-ownership companies were 1.5 times more profitable than their comparison companies.[6]

Another study found that employee-ownership companies had an average annual productivity rate 1.5 percent higher than the national average in their industries during the period 1975 to 1979.[7]

One survey of 43 majority-employee-owned companies found that they had an average annual increase in productive employment of almost three times their respective industries.[8]

Another study reviewed the performance of publicly traded companies in which employees own at least 10 percent of the outstanding

---

[6]Michael Conte and Arnold Tannebaum, *Employee Ownership,* (Ann Arbor: University of Michigan Survey Research Center, 1980), p. 3.

[7]Thomas R. Marsh and Dale McAllister, "ESOPs Tables," *Journal of Corporation Law* 6, no. 3 (Spring 1981), pp. 614–17.

[8]Corey Rosen and Katherine Klein, "Job-Generating Performance of Employee-Owned Companies," *Monthly Labor Review,* August 1983, pp. 15–19.

shares, compared them to their competitors, and found the employee-owned firms outperformed their competitors on measures of sales growth, average operating margins, average return on equity, and the ratio of book value to share growth.[9]

A study sponsored by the National Venture Capital Association found that companies that shared ownership with employees grew one-third faster in terms of sales, but no faster in terms of employment, than companies that did not share ownership. Further, companies that offer ownership to more than 51 percent of their employees had employment growth rates along with increases in net margins two to four times higher than nonemployee-ownership companies, while companies that offer ownership only to key employees had employment growth rates 50 percent lower than companies with no employee-ownership plan at all.[10]

A 1985 study found that ESOP companies did perform better than the overall U.S. economy in the study period 1972 to 1981.[11]

All of these studies share an underlying assumption that employees work harder and smarter because they are owners. None of them is conclusive that employee ownership is the cause; each study suggests that employee ownership is, in some way, positively related to superior corporate performance.

The most significant study to date, "Employee Ownership and Corporate Performance," by Michael Quarrey, The National Center for Employee Ownership, October 1986, found that ESOP companies in the large sample used were much better performers than their matched comparison companies and their industries in the post-plan period and, unlike the prior studies, did conclude that employee ownership was the reason. Compared to their competitors, ESOP firms grew 3.5 to 3.8 percentage points faster per year after they set up their plans than they had before. Over a 10-year period these figures would represent a 40 percent increase in jobs at ESOP companies and a 40 percent increase in sales.

---

[9]Ira Wagner and Corey Rosen, "Employee Ownership: Its Effect on Corporate Performance," *Employment Relations Today,* Spring 1985, pp. 77–82.

[10]Mathew Trachman, "Employee Ownership and Corporate Growth in High-Technology Companies," Report to the National Venture Capital Association, (Arlington, Va.: National Center for Employee Ownership (NCEO), 1985).

[11]Craig Lawrence Boyan, "Employee Stock Ownership Plans: How the Characteristics of an ESOP Affect Its Performance." Undergraduate thesis, Harvard University, 1985.

Further, companies that in some positive way changed the roles of employees and managers generally performed better.[12]

There appears to be, at least in manufacturing companies, some correlation between the existence of ESOPs and increases in productivity.[13] The U.S. Senate Finance Committee did a survey of companies using ESOPs. More than 80 companies responded, and statistical results were gained from 72 that included complete information. The results provided Senator Russell B. Long, then chairman of the Senate Finance Committee, with vital information to help him show Congress and the regulatory agencies that the pronounced success of ESOP and TRASOP companies is contributing to the economic welfare of the country. The following averages emerged from this important study: at the time of the ESOP installation, which took place three years prior to the study, the typical company had been in business 24 years. Over the prior three years, an average of 7 percent of the ownership of the company was transferred each year—until the employee stock ownership plan had 20.6 percent of the company stock. During those three years, from pre-ESOP to post-ESOP, annual sales increased from $19,596,000 to $33,780,000, a 72 percent rise. The number of employees increased from 438 to 602, representing an employment jump of 37 percent. The incentive provided by employee stock ownership may have had an effect in significantly raising the productivity from $44,700 sales per employee to $56,000—an increase of 25 percent. The annual profit generated before the ESOP was $794,000, and it soared (post-ESOP) to $2,039,000, an increase of 157 percent. In this profile, the company paid taxes prior to the ESOP that averaged $312,000 per year. Post-ESOP, that typical ESOP company paid an average of $780,000, an increase in revenue to the government of 150 percent. While the sample was fairly small, other ESOP companies can report similar results.

A nationwide survey indicates that most American adults (more than 80%) believe that workers at employee-owned companies work harder and pay more attention to quality and the firm's financial performance than do workers at nonemployee-owned companies. More than half the

---

[12]Corey Rosen and Michael Quarrey, "How Well Is Employee Ownership Working?" *Harvard Business Review* 5, September–October 1987, pp. 126–130.

[13]Randy G. Swad, "ESOPs and Tax Policy: An Empirical Investigation of the Impact of ESOPs on Company Operating Performance." Ph.D. dissertation, Louisiana State University, 1979.

workers surveyed said they would be willing to trade their next wage increase for a shared ownership in their firms. People almost unanimously would choose an otherwise similar product from an employee-owned company than one from a nonemployee-owned company. This was the most comprehensive public opinion poll ever conducted on employee ownership.[14]

The authors' own experience, consisting of observations of several hundred ESOP companies, would tend to confirm these results, as does the Rosen, Klein, and Young book, *Employee Ownership in America: The Equity Solution,* cited earlier in this chapter. Several new studies have been completed and are explained and referenced in *Employee Stock Ownership Plans: Business Planning, Implementation, Law, and Taxation* by Robert W. Smiley, Jr., and Ronald J. Gilbert; Maxwell Macmillan/Rosenfeld Launer, 1990. (See especially Chapter 3 and the 1991 Yearbook.)

SPECIAL FIDUCIARY LIABILITY RULES UNDER ERISA FOR ESOPs

There are special fiduciary liability rules under ERISA for ESOPs. The primary purpose of a stock bonus plan (the ancestor and major building block of an employee stock ownership plan) is "to give employee-participants an interest in the ownership and growth of the employer's business" (Revenue Ruling 69–65). This distinction is critical to interpreting the fiduciary responsibility provisions of ERISA. ERISA Section 404(a)(1) requires that fiduciaries act for the "exclusive purpose of providing benefits to participants," and serving as a "prudent man acting in a like capacity . . . would . . . in the conduct of an enterprise of a *like character* and with *like aims.*"

The purpose of ESOP financing is twofold:

1. To use corporate credit to acquire ownership of employer stock for participants; and
2. To finance the capital requirements of the employer corporation.

---

[14]The Bureau of National Affairs, "Employee Ownership Plans: How 8,000 Companies and 8,000,000 Employees Invest in Their Futures," A BNA Special Report, 1987.

No other qualified plans may incur debt to be used to finance corporate capital requirements or may be used as vehicles for debt financing transactions involving parties-in-interest. Revenue Ruling 79–122 properly recognizes the ESOP "as a technique of corporate finance." The *prudent man* and *exclusive purpose* requirements of ERISA Section 404(a)(1) and the *exclusive benefit* rule of IRC Section 401(a) must be analyzed and interpreted with the understanding that the ESOP is a technique of corporate finance.

As long as an ESOP prudently acquires and holds company stock as the benefit to be provided to employees, ERISA's Sections 404(a)(2) and 407(b)(1) (which specifically permit an ESOP to be wholly invested in employer stock) are satisfied. Also under Revenue Ruling 69–494, the exclusive benefit rule generally is satisfied if:

1. The purchase price does not exceed fair market value; and
2. The prudent man standard also is complied with.

Section 803(h) of the Tax Reform Act of 1976 makes it clear that Congress intended for ESOPs to be used under ERISA as a technique of corporate finance. IRC Section 4975(d)(3) and ERISA Section 408(b)(3) provide for prohibited-transaction exemptions, which are available only to an ESOP and are not applicable to conventional stock bonus or profit sharing plans.

The legislative history of the Tax Reform Act of 1986, including statements by a number of senators on the floor of the Senate, indicate Congress's clear intention that ESOPs are a technique of corporate finance.[15]

Internal Revenue Code

The Exclusive Benefit Rule

Generally, the Internal Revenue Code requires that a qualified retirement plan be maintained for the exclusive benefit of employees. However, with respect to ESOPs, this standard is modified to require that the investment in stock of the employer maintaining the plan be for the "primary purpose" of benefitting its employees. This "primary purpose" rule is

---

[15]Congressional Record, June 19, 1986, pp. S7901–S7912 and S. Rep. No. 313, 99th Cong., 2nd Sess. p. 677 (1986).

liberally construed to mean that the investment in company stock could benefit the employer maintaining the plan and its shareholders as long as the *primary purpose* of such investment is to benefit employees. Generally, a fiduciary who meets the prudent man rule contained in ERISA Section 404(a)(1) will be deemed to have satisfied the exclusive-benefit rule (''primary purpose'' rule in the case of ESOPs) contained in IRC Section 401(a).

The Prudent Man Rule

The prudent man rule, as indicated above, must be interpreted in light of the nature and purpose of the plan and, in particular, the characteristics of the plan as communicated to participating employees. However, satisfaction of the conditions contained in Revenue Ruling 69-494 does *not* mean that the prudent man rule has been satisfied. The prudent man rule would appear to be controlling. It will be some time before the courts have resolved exactly what the prudent man rule means. The IRS and DOL appear to prefer to leave the resolution on a case-by-case basis.

The Department of Labor's final regulation pertaining to the investment of plan assets under ERISA's ''prudence'' requirement does not specifically address the issue of an ESOP's investments in company stock under the prudence rule. Further, since the ESOP regulations do not provide a mechanical test for determining compliance with this definitional requirement of an ESOP, the IRS and DOL have apparently determined that ''designed to invest primarily'' is a subjective standard relating to the purpose of an ESOP as an employee benefit plan and means just that. (For reference see DOL Opinion Letter 83-6.)

Fiduciary Rules

The general fiduciary rules of ERISA are applicable to ESOPs. These rules are discussed in the next subsection. However, neither ERISA nor its legislative history gives any indication about how the general fiduciary rules are to be applied to ESOPs. Although ESOPs are exempt from the diversification requirements, and specific transactions involving ESOPs are exempt from the prohibited transaction rules, the general fiduciary responsibility provisions of ERISA for trustees and other fiduciaries are to act prudently, in the sole interests of participants and beneficiaries, and for the exclusive purpose of providing them benefits and defraying reasonable administrative expenses. The ESOP may meet these standards even though other persons, such as the employer and its shareholders, may derive benefits from the ESOP.

Employee Pension Benefit Plan

ERISA Section 3(2) defines the key aspects of all employee pension benefit plans, including ESOPs. ESOPs are recognized as different from other types of pension plans and are permitted to purchase and hold employer securities, whereas other plans may not. However, it is important to note that ESOP administration and management are subject to both the provisions containing the fiduciary standards and the prohibited transaction restrictions. Each and every aspect of an ESOP transaction must be analyzed in terms of ERISA Section 404 and Sections 406 through 408. While a fiduciary must abide by the plan and the trust documents, these documents must be otherwise consistent with the duties of fiduciaries, and these duties override plan documents. The primary purpose of an ESOP as an employee benefit plan is to provide participants with an equity interest in the employer, with retirement benefits being provided through employer stock. The primary responsibility of the fiduciaries would not be to maximize retirement benefits through investments in assets other than employer stock, but rather to maximize the benefits attributable to investing "primarily" in employer securities.[16]

ERISA Fiduciary Rules

Exclusive Purpose Rule

This rule has been discussed earlier in this section. It is contained in ERISA Section 404(a)(1)(A), and is directed at making sure the plan is operated for the benefit of employees. It has a direct impact on ESOP loans and purchases and sales of employer securities. Such self-dealing is subject to special scrutiny by the regulatory agencies. ESOP fiduciaries are urged to "scrupulously exercise their discretion" in approving the nature, purpose, and the like, of transactions with the ESOP.

---

[16]ERISA Sec. 407(d)(6)(A); *Congressional Record,* June 19, 1986, pp. S7904 and 7905; and DOL Advisory Opinion Letter 83-006A (January 24, 1983).

Prudent Man Rule

ERISA Section 404(a)(1)(B) states the prudent man rule. It is a comparative rule and is to be viewed with reference to the "special nature and purpose of employee benefit plans."[17] The relative riskiness of a specific investment does not make such investment, per se, prudent or imprudent. Accordingly, it would appear that a prudent ESOP fiduciary, subject to fiduciary duties under ERISA Section 404(a)(1), is one who prudently acquires, holds, and distributes employer stock for the benefit of participants (and their beneficiaries) and who prudently uses debt financing where appropriate in a manner consistent with the plan documents and the provisions of Title I of ERISA.

Diversification Rule

ERISA Section 404(a)(1)(C) states the diversification rule, and ERISA Section 404(a)(2) specifically provides that an eligible individual account plan is not subject to the general diversification requirements of 404(a)(1)(C), but only to the extent the plan invests in "qualifying" employer securities or employer real property.

One other important exception to this diversification rule: The diversification rule and related aspects of the prudent man rule are not violated by the acquisition or retention of the employer's stock—provided the acquisition and retention is consistent with ERISA Section 407. ERISA Section 407 contains an exception from the normal 10 percent limitation with respect to employer securities, so long as the ESOP explicitly provides for such acquisition and holding. ERISA Section 404(a)(2) does not seem to permit the holding of employer securities if such holding would *otherwise* be considered not for the exclusive benefit of the employees. We thus have a "facts and circumstances" test, and the agencies retain for themselves the advantage of the "hindsight rule"—being able to look at a transaction or series of events with the clear piety of absolute knowledge and history. To the extent the ESOP does diversify its investment in assets to hold assets other than employer stock, it is subject to the investment-diversification requirement of ERISA Sections 404(a)(1)(C).

Document Rule

ERISA Section 404(a)(1)(D) states the "document rule." ERISA controls the conduct of ESOP fiduciaries, and the plan document(s) now can only

---

[17]See H. R. Rep. No. 93-1280, 93d Cong., 2d Sess., 302 (1974).

authorize conduct that is consistent with ERISA. An ESOP fiduciary may be required to disregard the plan and trust agreement if compliance with those documents would be inconsistent with ERISA.

Prohibited Transactions and Special Exemptions and Exceptions

Fortunately for employers and shareholders, ERISA contains statutory exemptions from many of the restrictions that would otherwise prohibit ESOP transactions. ERISA's Sections 406 through 408 contain the prohibited-transaction restrictions and the related exemptions. These restrictions apply independently of the fiduciary standards. Violation of any of the fiduciary standards or of the prohibited transaction restrictions by a fiduciary may result in civil penalties and personal liability. ERISA Section 409 provides that a fiduciary in breach will be personally responsible for any losses to the ESOP as a result of his or her breach, and that profits must be restored.

Several exemptions from ERISA's general fiduciary provisions apply to ESOPs. An ESOP is not subject to the prohibition on acquiring and retaining an investment in qualifying employer securities that exceeds 10 percent of the fair market value of its assets. ESOPs are also exempt, with limitations, from the diversification requirement.

An ESOP also may purchase stock from (or sell stock to) the employer, a major shareholder, or any other party in interest without violating the prohibited transaction rules, provided the transaction is for adequate consideration and no commission is charged to the plan. See, for example, Prop. DOL Reg. Section 2510.3-18.

An ESOP may leverage its stock purchases, if the interest rate is reasonable, if the loan is primarily for the benefit of plan participants and their beneficiaries, and if certain other stringent requirements are met.[18] The only collateral acceptable for certain exempt loans is the stock purchased with the loan proceeds. The employer, however, may give any collateral it may have available.

The ESOP loan documents for an exempt loan must specifically provide that all the foregoing relating conditions be met, and that:

1. The loan will be repaid only from employer contributions made to enable the trustee to repay debt, earnings attributable to

[18]Sec. 408(b)(3) of ERISA and Sec. 4975(d)(3) of the IRC Code.

contributions, earnings on unallocated shares, and dividends on stock acquired with the loan proceeds or the proceeds of another exempt loan.

2. The lender's recourse on the note against the trust must be limited to the stock used as collateral and to the contributions and other amounts described in (1) above.
3. Each year, as the loan is repaid, the stock is allocated to the accounts of active participants as payments are made under the loan, according to the prescribed formulas.
4. The loan must be for a fixed term and satisfy certain requirements in the event of default, including that a party-in-interest lender may not accelerate payments in the event of default and that the loan must not be payable on demand of the lender except in the case of default.[19]

Special Fiduciary Problems

Securities Exchange Act of 1934

As mentioned in Chapter 3 of this *Handbook,* the 1934 Securities Exchange Act relates to the rules regarding transactions in securities normally conducted on national securities exchanges and in the over-the-counter markets. It contains both registration and antifraud provisions. The act's registration and antifraud provisions are beyond the scope of this chapter. Since the rules in regard to all qualified plans (including ESOPs) are in a state of change, the current securities aspects should be carefully checked prior to engaging in transactions with the ESOP. For example, on February 19, 1981, the Securities and Exchange Commission (SEC) eliminated Rule 10b-6 for all employee benefit plans. Previously this rule on trading by persons interested in a distribution of securities required that ESOPs (and other employee benefit plans) stick to a strict set of criteria. In another example, the SEC exempted a qualified plan from the SEC requirement of the 5 percent beneficial owner disclosure rule in company proxy statements. The SEC reasoned that the true beneficial owners of the stock are the plan participants when there is full voting pass-through, and when the plan documents and participants control the disposition of the stock.

---

[19]Labor Regs. Sec. 2550.408 b-3(m); Treas. Reg. Sec. 54.4975-7(b)(13).

National Bank Act

The Glass-Steagall Act relates to nationally or federally chartered banks and the activities engaged in by these entities. This act permits banks to act as trustees and places the responsibility for this exercise of fiduciary responsibility squarely on the bank's board of directors.

Blue-Sky Laws

Various states have laws and rules relating to transactions of employer securities. These laws generally require disclosure of the transactions and can be extremely complicated. Normally, there are exemptions for transactions with an ESOP, but there are exceptions, and care should be exercised that the applicable state laws are complied with.

Tender Offers

In recent years corporations subject to tender offers have established an ESOP after the tender offer is made, or used a previously established ESOP to secure loans to purchase additional employer securities in an effort to defeat the tender offer. This allows for more employer securities to be in "friendly" hands. The tender offer area is complicated and fraught with potential problems for an ESOP that borrows and/or purchases stock in an effort to defeat the tender offer, particularly if the trustees purchase employer securities at a premium price. If the tender offer is successful, the ESOP will generally be a minority shareholder in a debt-ridden corporation, and if the tender offer is unsuccessful, the ESOP will own stock for which the trustees paid too much. If these transactions violate the exclusive-benefit rule:

- The trust could lose its tax-exempt status,
- Any contributions to the ESOP could be nondeductible,
- The earnings of the trust could become taxable, and
- Any partial interest exclusion under IRC Section 133 could be lost.
- Any borrowing by the ESOP that is not primarily for the benefit of the participants is a prohibited transaction that subjects disqualified persons to excise taxes.

Even the decision on how shares are to be tendered became subject to special consideration. For a more detailed analysis, see the most recent "BNA Tax Management Portfolio on ESOPs" (354–4th) by Jared Kaplan, Gregory K. Brown, and Ronald L. Ludwig (p. 28).

Procedural Prudence and Leveraged Buyouts

Procedural prudence requires that independent ESOP fiduciaries be represented by one or more independent fiduciaries or that the ESOP fiduciaries be represented by independent financial and legal counsel, and that the interests of the ESOP and the participants and beneficiaries be fairly represented in meaningful negotiations. The ultimate responsibility for the decisions made by an ESOP fiduciary rests with the fiduciary. Procedural prudence must be strictly observed. The DOL advisory letters in the Blue Bell, Inc., ESOP transaction provide meaningful guidance.[20]

Summary

Each of the laws discussed here has some relevance to ESOPs. These laws highlight the importance of carefully considering the structure of an ESOP in terms of the relationships created and contemplated among the employer (and its officers and directors), the trustee, the shareholders, the public, and the participants. Responsibilities should be carefully discussed and allocated—at the outset. Once determined, careful monitoring and documentation of the ESOP's administration is mandatory for a smooth-running and trouble-free plan.

PLAN DESIGN CONSIDERATIONS

Application of Issues Inherent in All Qualified Plans to ESOPs[21]

Coverage

The requirements of IRC Section 410, which impose the age and service conditions for eligibility to participate, are applicable to ESOPs. In

---

[20]*See* letter dated September 12, 1983, from Mr. Charles M. Williamson, Assistant Administrator for Enforcement, Pension and Welfare Benefit Programs, to Gareth W. Cook, Esq., Vinson & Elkins, Houston, Texas, regarding Raymond International, Inc., and letter dated November 23, 1984, from Mr. Norman P. Goldberg, Counsel for Fiduciary Litigation, Plan Benefits Security Division, to Charles R. Smith, Esq., Kirkpatrick, Lockhart, Johnson & Hutchison, Pittsburgh, Pennsylvania, regarding Blue Bell, Inc.

[21]See, generally, Ronald S. Rizzo, *Specific Drafting and Other Problems of ESOPs* (New York: Practising Law Institute, 1979); Kaplan, Brown, and Curtis, "BNA Tax Management Portfolio on ESOPs" (354–5th), 1991; and Smiley and Gilbert, *Employee Stock Ownership Plans: Business Planning, Implementation, Law, and Taxation* (New York: Maxwell Macmillan/Rosenfeld Launer, 1991).

practice, however, most ESOPs are more liberal. This is partially because employers adopting ESOPs have expressed a desire to permit employees to participate in a "piece of the action," and also to provide the maximum compensation base for purposes of assuring that contributions to the ESOP are sufficiently large to make the loan payments and are deductible under Section 404 of the Code. Many ESOPs do not have minimum age requirements. They may provide for a single, retroactive entry date. However, certain individual limitations on these generally liberal plan provisions may be important.

The rules that apply to all qualified plans for the inclusion or exclusion of particular groups or classes of employees are applicable to ESOPs and are covered elsewhere in the *Handbook*. Two different ESOPs may be established for purposes of satisfying the nondiscrimination and coverage tests if the proportion of employer securities to the total plan assets is substantially the same in each ESOP, and if either the securities held by each ESOP are the same class or the *ratio* of each class of employer securities to all classes of employer securities in each ESOP is substantially the same.[22]

The regulations on ESOPs[23] specifically prohibit a plan designated as an ESOP after November 1, 1977, from being integrated, directly or indirectly, with contributions or benefits under Social Security. These regulations are *excise* tax regulations. Therefore, integrating the plan would not disqualify it. However, a prohibited transaction would exist if the plan engaged in a loan or another extension of credit to a disqualified person, and therefore an excise tax would be due.

The proposed regulations issued under both IRC Sections 401(a)(26) and 410(b)(1) both indicate that the ESOP features of a 401(k) plan and the non-ESOP features thereof are to be considered separately in determining compliance with the minimum coverage and minimum participation rules. Moreover, the proposed and final regulations issued under the nondiscrimination rules of IRC Sections 401(k) and 401(m) provide that these features are to be treated separately in determining compliance with those rules. However, these regulations are questionable in light of relevant statutory language and legislative history.

---

[22]Treasury Reg. Sec. 54.4975–11(e)(2).

[23]Treasury Reg. Sec. 54.4975–11(a)(7)(ii).

Break-in-Service Rules

The two groups of break-in-service rules that are important for solving ESOP design and drafting problems are the eligibility break-in-service rules and the vesting break-in-service rules. Under these rules, an employee may have a one-year break in service if he or she fails to complete more than 500 hours of service in the relevant computation period. These rules are identical for ESOPs and other qualified plans. These rules are covered in detail in other chapters of this book and apply to ESOPs the same as to other qualified plans.

Under the regulations, if any portion of a participant's account is forfeited, employer securities that have been acquired with the proceeds of an exempt loan may be forfeited only after other assets have been forfeited. For example, if a participant's account reflects both company stock acquired with the proceeds of an exempt loan and other investments, the participant's forfeiture(s) first must come from the other investments—if the amount forfeited is greater than the other investments available, then some of the company stock may be forfeited. If the distribution is to be deferred, say, until some specified age and/or actual retirement, the ESOP must generally provide for separate accounts for prebreak and postbreak service.

Most ESOPs do not have a "repayment" provision under the cash-out and buy-back rules of ERISA. Any such repayment may be a problem under the Securities Act of 1933 and relevant state securities laws. The repaid amount is voluntary on the part of the employee, and, therefore, none of the exemptions discussed later would be available, since employee "contributions" are being used to acquire employer securities. If state securities laws permit, an alternative is to establish a separate account-vesting schedule or to provide that any repayments will not be used to purchase employer stock.[24]

Reemployment Problems

It is possible for a plan to require that a former participant who is reemployed after a one-year break in service meet the eligibility requirements of the plan again. However, once the eligibility requirements are again satisfied, participation is retroactive at least to the reemployment

---

[24]Treasury Reg. Sec. 1.411(a)-7(d)(5)(iii).

date; if overlapping plan years are involved, allocations and distributions already may have been made, making reallocation impossible.

Additionally, some care should be taken in utilizing the complex set of rules that relate to crediting and disregarding service for eligibility purposes.[25] When designing this section of the plan, and when designing the vesting computation period, several well-thought-out and well-presented examples can go a long way in educating the plan sponsor on just what the provisions mean. ESOPs traditionally have been used by larger companies, and larger companies generally rehire employees on a more regular basis than smaller companies.

Section 415 Considerations

As a condition of tax qualification, a defined contribution plan must provide that the annual addition to the account(s) of a participant for a limitation year may not exceed the lesser of a stated dollar amount or 25 percent of the participant's compensation. This annual addition includes contributions to all defined contribution plans of the sponsor in which the employee is a participant, forfeitures allocated to his or her account, and, if participant contributions are permitted (or required), the participant's own contributions. Dividends paid on employer securities that are used to repay ESOP debt are not counted as annual additions.[26]

Section 415(c)(6) of the Code excludes employer contributions used to pay loan interest and also excludes forfeitures of leveraged employer securities from the annual-additions limitations in the case of ESOPs that are established under 4975(e)(7) of the Code. However, these exclusions apply only if no more than one third of the employer contributions to the ESOP for a limitation year are allocated to the accounts of participants who are highly compensated employees within the meaning of IRC Section 414(q). When securities are released from the suspense account provided for the holding of the "unpaid-for securities," the contributions (but not dividends) used by the ESOP to pay the loan are treated as annual additions to participants' accounts, not the value of the securities released from the suspense account, which could conceivably be much greater (or much less).

---

[25] Labor Reg. Sec. 2530.202-2(b)(2).

[26] U.S. Senate, Committee on Finance, *Report to Accompany H.R. 3838,* 99th Cong., 2nd sess., May 29, 1986, Rept. 99–313, p. 682.

If the special one-third rule is violated, then the forfeitures of leveraged employer securities are included in the computation of the annual addition at fair market value; that is, the share forfeitures are normally valued at fair market value. Several potential problems arise because of this treatment of the forfeitures. First, accurate and timely valuations are critical so as to permit a proper and timely allocation. Second, in the event of an audit, if the employer securities that were forfeited and reallocated to participants' accounts in a plan year were undervalued, the plan could be disqualified if the additional value, as determined by the IRS, increased any participant's annual addition beyond the permissible maximum amount. Third, since most loans require fixed payment dates, timely valuations are necessary to know whether the plan is qualified by the time the employer's contribution is due, because of forfeitures being revalued. The forfeiture suspense accounts, which are permitted by the final Code Section 415 regulations, require limiting employer contributions first—so, with forfeitures high enough, an ESOP may end up in default on the loan, since large enough contributions cannot be made on a timely enough basis to amortize the loan repayment on schedule. To solve this problem, an employer may vary the plan year for which contributions (made after the end of the year but before the tax-year due date, including extensions) are attributed. The employer may also set up individual Section 415 suspense accounts, which defer annual additions to a later plan year, or alternatively (or concurrently), not permit forfeitures to arise until a terminated participant incurs five consecutive one-year breaks in service.

The resolution to this problem comes to a certain extent from amendments to both Section 415 (the allocation limits) and Section 404 (the deductibility limits). After ERTA, an employer contributing to a leveraged ESOP may contribute and deduct an amount up to 25 percent of covered participants' compensation for purposes of principal reduction. Additional contributions used to service interest due on the ESOP loan are deductible in any amount. The Tax Reform Act of 1986 (TRA '86), as amended by the Technical and Miscellaneous Reform Act of 1988 [TAMRA] and OBRA '89), also permits a corporate deduction for dividends on leveraged shares (whether or not allocated) if used to repay principal and/or interest on any loan used to acquire those shares, provided the dividends are reasonable (and do not make the participants' total compensation unreasonable). These dividends are not considered annual additions. Dividends on allocated shares may, however, be used to make loan payments only if the account to which dividend(s) would have been allocated is allocated shares having a fair market value not less than the amount of such dividend(s). Furthermore, the allocation must be made in the year the dividend(s) otherwise would have been allocated.

The allocation limits in Section 415 eliminate from consideration as annual additions employer contributions used to make interest payments on an ESOP loan and reallocated forfeitures of ESOP stock originally purchased with an exempt loan.

These amendments partially resolved the obvious difficulty arising when three equally inflexible requirements (debt service, deduction limits, and allocation limits) are applied on different, sometimes unrelated, bases to the same transaction. For a particular company, therefore, the deductible and allocable contribution will set the practical limit for the amount of an ESOP loan after giving consideration to deductible dividends.

When designing the ESOP, the other plans of the employer have to be taken into account. The other plan(s) might be drafted to provide for a reduction in benefits under the other plans before reducing benefits under the ESOP. This would help to minimize the Code Section 415 problems and, at the same time, maximize the allocations to the ESOP participants. The typical order of priority appears to be to first refund participants' contributions under all plans; second, if more of a reduction is required, then place the excess forfeitures in a forfeiture suspense account or reduce or reallocate them in the *other* defined contribution plans; and, thirdly, defer the creation of forfeitures until a terminated participant has incurred five consecutive one-year breaks in service. Furthermore, under the combined benefit limits of IRC Section 415(e), a related defined benefit plan (whether or not frozen or terminated) might provide for first reducing the accrued benefits under the defined benefit plan.

Reversion of Employer's Contributions

As a qualified plan, an ESOP must provide that no part of the plan's assets are to be used for or diverted to purposes other than the primary benefit of participants. In an ESOP, there are *unallocated* shares and *allocated* shares (disregarding the forfeiture suspense account). The nonreversion provision applies to both the allocated and unallocated securities.

Employer contributions may be returned if made under a good-faith mistake of fact (but not a mistake of law) or if deductions are disallowed and those contributions were conditioned on deductibility, if that condition is specifically stated in the plan document.

Employer contributions may also be conditioned on initial qualification, but not on continued plan qualification, according to Revenue Ruling 91-4 and the Revenue Act of 1987. That ruling also made clear that a permissible reversion will not be treated as a forfeiture in violation of Section 411(a) of the Code, even if an adjustment is made to participants' accounts that are partially or wholly nonforfeitable. If this is done, participants' accounts should be adjusted by first withdrawing assets other than employer securities. Note, however, the nondeductible excise provisions of IRC Section 4972 for nondeductible contributions.

Compensation Used for Deductions

In Revenue Ruling 80-145, the IRS addressed the definition of *compensation* for computing the deduction limitation under Code Section 404(a)(3) and 404(a)(7). The IRS held that the deduction limits are based on total compensation, even in a situation where the plan defines compensation (for allocation purposes) as excluding certain items (such as limiting compensation to basic pay). Some ESOP companies may increase their deductible ESOP contributions by properly applying these guidelines. Note also the definition of *compensation* in Code Section 401(a)(17) and the final nondiscrimination regulations issued under Code Section 401(a)(4). However, no deductions are permitted for the amount of contributions that cause the Section 415 limits to be exceeded.

Potential Difficulties to Anticipate

Leveraging

While leveraging has its positive aspects, some potential negatives exist that should be considered. Further, there will be an immediate dilution of existing shareholders' interests if the company issues new shares, or shares not previously outstanding, to the ESOP; this may, however, be offset by the other benefits, and a careful analysis should be done.

The loan documents for leveraged ESOP transactions may also expressly require the employer to make contributions at least sufficient to amortize securities-acquisition debt. This "commitment" of cash flow is offset in many cases by increased employee morale and the use of many ESOP tax benefits.

Contributions and dividends used to pay for a large block of stock purchased all at once can be a substantial cash drain over a long time. Further, a contraction in business conditions resulting in fewer employees could be construed as a termination or a partial termination of the plan, triggering full vesting for affected participants. If the shares that are then distributed are subject to the put-option requirements (to be discussed in subsequent sections of this chapter), they may have to be purchased with nondeductible dollars, causing an additional and often untimely cash drain.

If the covered compensation for deduction (and/or allocation) purposes drops below the threshold amount for making required payments on ESOP debt, or if the one-third rule is violated, then the ESOP may not be able to make its required payments on the ESOP note unless the employer makes an additional loan, the proceeds of which are used to repay the preexisting loan. If this could be a problem, careful negotiation with the lender is important at the outset.

Allocations to Employees' Accounts

Suspense Account. An ESOP is required to contain specific provisions governing annual accounting for employer securities purchased with the proceeds of an exempt loan. The ESOP must provide for a suspense account to which the securities acquired with the proceeds of an exempt loan must first be credited, even if the securities are not pledged as collateral for the loan. Also, all ESOPs must provide for the release of the securities and their allocation to participants' accounts as payments of principal or payments of principal and interest are made with respect to the loan. Further, if the income from the securities is to be used to repay the loan, both the ESOP and the loan agreement must provide for that. The provisions relating to the release of the shares from the suspense account for allocation to employees' accounts should be contained in the loan documents.[27] The regulations require that the securities be released from the suspense account of the ESOP in the same manner that the loan agreement provides. If there is no pledge of shares relating to the loan agreement, then the plan administrator, plan committee, or other relevant plan fiduciary must select a method of release.

---

[27]Treas. Reg. Secs. 54.4975–11(c), 54.4975–7(b)(8); Labor Reg. Sec. 2550.408b-3(h).

Shares can be released from the suspense account in two ways. Under the first method permitted by the regulations, the number of securities released each year is equal to the number of securities held in the suspense account immediately before release—multiplied by a fraction, the *numerator* of which is the amount of principal and interest payments for the year, and the *denominator* of which is the sum of the numerator plus the amount of future principal and interest payments to be made during the remaining term of the loan, including the current year. The number of future years must be definite and cannot take into account any possible extensions or renewal periods. If the interest rate is variable, the interest is computed, for purposes of the fraction, by using the interest rate applicable at the end of the plan year in which the fraction is applied.

The second method entails releasing securities based on the payment of principal alone. When a loan is amortized over a period of years, the interest portion of the payment is higher in the early years than in the late years. Many lenders would prefer that the shares be released based *only* on principal payments, so that they stay secured. This second method permits more collateral coverage for lenders, because the shares are not usually being released as quickly under this method. The only other restrictions on this second method provide that the release based solely on principal payments must be part of a term loan that provides for annual payments of principal and interest that are not cumulatively less rapid than level annual payments of principal and interest over ten years. In computing amounts of principal under this method, interest is disregarded only to the extent it would be disregarded under standard loan amortization tables.[28] Apparently the agencies are concerned that the terms of the loan might provide greater interest payments during each year of the loan than would be permitted under standard loan-amortization tables.

The unrealized appreciation or depreciation on the suspense-account securities is not allocated to the participants' accounts. Shares are allocated at cost, then the value is extended to show a dollar amount reflected at fair market value on the participant's periodic account statement. Employees who become participants in an ESOP after securities have been purchased and credited to the suspense account, but prior to these securities being released, will share in the unrealized appreciation or depreciation that occurred prior to their participation and will realize that appreciation or

---

[28]Treas. Reg. Sec. 54.4975–7(b)(1)(ii); Labor Reg. Sec. 2550.408b-3(h)(2).

depreciation on distribution from the plan in the form of cash or, if the distribution is made in the form of stock, upon exercise of their put option or a subsequent sale. The reverse is also true, in that employees who were participants when the shares were credited to the suspense account will not share in the unrealized gains or losses if they are not participants when the securities are released.

The forfeiture provisions must be so drafted as to require that a participant forfeit other plan assets before a forfeiture of employer securities may occur. When more than one class of employer securities has been allocated to the participant's account, forfeitures must reduce each class of security proportionately.[29]

Dividends. Dividends paid on securities allocated to participants' ESOP accounts, to the extent not utilized to repay ESOP debt, may be allocated to participants' accounts with respect to which the dividends were paid and either reinvested in company stock or invested in other assets. Alternatively, these dividends may be distributed to participants and their beneficiaries. If dividends on allocated shares are used to repay the loan, the shares allocated to each participant's account by reason of such use must have a fair market value at least equal to the amount of dividends used, as further discussed later in this chapter, in order for such dividends to be deductible.

Dividends from the securities purchased with the proceeds of an exempt loan but not yet allocated, to the extent not utilized to repay the loan, would be allocated entirely to participants' accounts either:

1. Based on prior account balances; or
2. Based on current compensation.

Alternatively, the dividends paid on unallocated shares may be currently distributed to participants or be used to repay debt (both principal and interest) on the same basis as such dividends would be allocated to participants' accounts.

The OBRA '89 amendments to IRC Section 404(k) restrict the deductibility of dividends used to repay a securities acquisition loan to those dividends paid on the securities acquired with the loan proceeds, and not to dividends on other stock that may be in the plan. This change expressly

---

[29]Treas. Reg. Sec. 54.4975–11(d)(4).

applies to employer securities acquired by an ESOP after August 4, 1989. While the legislative history and informal remarks by IRS representatives indicate that no inferences should be made with respect to the scope of dividend deduction on employer securities acquired by an ESOP before August 5, 1989, at least one private letter ruling (8921101, March 3, 1989) indicates that such dividends are deductible. (This ruling, of course, cannot be cited as precedent or be relied upon by other taxpayers, and IRS's position on the issue is subject to change.)

A special transitional rule applies to securities acquired with the proceeds of the loan made pursuant to a written binding commitment in effect on August 4, 1989, to the extent the proceeds of such loan are used to acquire employer securities pursuant to a written binding contract (or tender offer) in effect on August 4, 1989. Employer securities are not considered to have been acquired by an ESOP on or before August 4, 1989, for example, if the securities were acquired by a qualified plan on or before August 4, 1989, but the plan was not an ESOP until after August 4, 1989.

Finally, no inferences should be made with respect to the permissible sources of payment on exempt loans under Title I of ERISA. That is, it is theoretically possible under ERISA that dividends paid on allocated shares may not be used to repay ESOP acquisition debt.

Allocation of Cost Basis of Shares

Most ESOP allocation sections specify two accounts for each participant. This practice occurs because of the suspense-account requirement, Code Section 415, and the requirement that employer securities acquired with the proceeds of an exempt loan be allocated to participants' accounts in terms of share units rather than in monetary terms.[30] The first account is the "company stock account," which contains employer securities. The other account is the "other investments account," which is maintained to account for the participant's share of plan assets other than employer securities.

Amounts contributed to an ESOP must be allocated as provided under Sections 1.401-1(b)(1)(ii) and 1.401-1(b)(1)(iii) of the regulations. These sections relate to the requirement for a definite, predetermined formula for allocating contributions among participants. Cost-basis accounting is

[30]Treas. Reg. Sec. 54.4975–11(d)(2).

used primarily to determine the net unrealized appreciation in employer securities upon distribution. Therefore, acquisition of employer stock must be accounted for, as provided under 1.402(a)-1(b)(2)(ii) of the regulations. This section refers to the determination of the cost basis of the securities of the employer and sets forth four methods to treat cost basis. Cost basis is used primarily to determine the net unrealized appreciation in employer securities on distribution. The plan document need not specify which cost basis rule is adopted, although the chosen rule should be reflected in the trustee's or plan administrator's permanent plan records.

The reasons to track the cost basis of shares for the participants include some valuable options for participants' tax planning such as enjoying a lower overall tax for participants' distributions, especially when long-term capital-gains-tax rates are lower than ordinary income tax rates (which they have been historically). At the participant's election, a participant who receives stock in a single-sum distribution that qualifies for lump-sum-distribution treatment may pay tax on his or her distribution based solely on the cost basis of the shares. The taxability of the gain is deferred until the participant sells the stock received in the distribution. This means if a participant holds onto the shares, no tax is due on the amount of the gain over the ESOP trust's basis in those shares until the shares are considered sold for tax purposes.

Public Policy Problems

With all the recent excitement and interest surrounding ESOPs in public companies, it is hardly surprising that Congress has decided to take a long, hard look at ESOP tax advantages. Congress granted the tax incentives to ESOPs to promote the wider ownership of capital. The basic question that now interests Congress is whether or not the benefits of ESOPs outweigh the potential revenue losses. Corollary questions include the following:

- Are employees better off with or without ESOPs?
- Do ESOPs link employee income to the performance of the company and thereby align more closely employee, management, and shareholder interests?
- How are public companies actually structuring their ESOPs? Do they have good intentions? Are they simply replacing other benefits in order to get a more favorable tax treatment?
- Are ESOPs in the best interests of other shareholders?

The ESOP is clearly a long-range plan. This requires, of course, a healthy legislative environment. While plans that permit and encourage employee ownership have been around for decades, the tax benefits are fairly recent, and a rather important consideration is their ongoing effectiveness. Some practitioners are of the opinion that the ESOP tax advantages are "tax expenditures," (which they simplistically define as any of the taxpayers' money not going to the government and that taxpayers therefore get to "keep" [since the government doesn't take it]). Such definition implies that any money the government can take but doesn't, is being spent indirectly by the government. The authors are not of that school of thought. However, it is important to realize that many policymakers have this view, and they ask questions like, "Who will pay the taxes saved or deferred by the establishment of ESOPs?" and "How is this claim on the federal treasury made by ESOPs to be reconciled with other claims?" After many hearings and careful deliberations over 15 years, it is stated congressional policy to support ESOPs. Over 21 pieces of legislation since 1974 indicate this support in an unmistakable way.

Other questions, however, are more pertinent and deserve thoughtful consideration. For example, "Do ESOPs result in employees having too many eggs in one basket?" "When employees' retirement income and their salaries are both dependent on the financial position of their employer, what will result over the long run?" Care should be taken to examine when and if other plans should be implemented to help spread the retirement risk.

Voting Rights

Since the block of securities held in the ESOP may constitute a controlling interest, how voting rights are handled is very important, now and in the future. All ESOPs must satisfy the requirements of Code Section 409(e) with respect to voting rights on employer securities acquired after 1979. A stock bonus plan that is not an ESOP is subject to these requirements for shares acquired after December 31, 1979, only if *no* class of the employer's securities is publicly traded. A stock bonus plan of a closely held company must provide that each participant is entitled to exercise any and all voting rights in the employer's securities allocated to his or her account with respect to corporate matters that involve the voting of shares for or against corporate mergers, consolidations, sales of all or substantially all of the corporation's assets, recapitalization, reclassifications, liquidations, and dissolutions, or such similar matters as the Secretary of the Treasury may prescribe by regulation, if (1) the plan is maintained by an employer whose stock is not publicly traded, and (2) if, after acquiring securities of the employer, more than 10 percent of the plan's assets are invested in securities of the employer as required by Code Section 401(a)(22). Voting requirements for ESOPs other than stock bonus are treated elsewhere in this chapter.

After December 31, 1986, Code Section 401(a)(22) eliminated the pass-through voting requirement for ESOPs maintained by certain newspapers, and Code Section 409(1)(4) also permitted such newspapers to acquire nonvoting common stock in certain instances after December 31, 1986. This passing-through of voting-rights requirements for closely held companies extends not only to ESOPs but to any eligible individual-account plan, other than a profit-sharing plan, that invests more than 10 percent of its assets in the plan sponsor's stock.

The voting requirements of Code Section 409(e) apply only to shares of employer stock allocated to participants' accounts. To the extent that shares are not allocated or have been acquired with the proceeds of an exempt loan and not yet released from the suspense account, voting rights usually are exercised by designated fiduciaries at their own discretion. However, this is not the case when the little-used "one-person, one-vote" rule of Code Section 409(e)(5) is used.

An ESOP of a publicly traded employer whose securities are of a type generally required to be registered under the Securities Exchange Act of 1934 must pass through voting rights on all matters for all allocated shares, even nonvested shares. Code Section 409(e)(2) requires that participants and beneficiaries be entitled to direct the manner in which securities of the employer (not just "employer securities" as described in Code Section 409(l)) allocated to their accounts are to be voted on all matters. These provisions would appear to apply only to shares of employer securities acquired after December 31, 1979.

On or after October 22, 1986, an ESOP maintained by an employer that has no registration-type class of securities may permit each participant to have one vote with respect to each issue he or she is entitled to direct the trustee to vote, without regard to the actual number of shares allocated to his or her account. The trustee may vote the shares held in the plan in the proportions so directed by the participants.[31] An ESOP can be

[31]Code Sec. 409(e)(5).

restructured with respect to its pass-through voting requirements whether or not the company has registration-type securities or where the ESOP document provides that unallocated shares will be voted in the same proportion as participants direct the voting of allocated shares, or where the ESOP plan document provides another voting method (i.e., where the shares are voted on a majority-rule basis) so that the ESOP may provide each participant with one vote as long as the trustee votes the shares held by the ESOP in proportion to the votes of all participants. Therefore, the trustee must give up all voting discretion on unallocated shares in order to use this voting method. Under prior law, voting pass-through on a one-person, one-vote basis was only permitted with respect to issues for which the law did not require voting pass-through.

However, note that some practitioners point to a provision in the tax-credit ESOP regulations, which state that allocated shares for which no direction is received may not be voted. No such rule is reflected in the statutory language of IRC Section 409(e), and it is the authors' experience that few, if any, IRS District Directors require such a provision.

When voting pass-through (the right of participants to direct the voting of their allocated shares) is required by law but not all of the shares held by the ESOP have been allocated to participants, the unallocated shares are voted in the manner prescribed by the ESOP document. The ESOP document may provide that the unallocated shares will be voted in the same proportion as participants vote allocated shares. In most cases, however, any unallocated shares are voted by the ESOP administrative committee or ESOP trustees and must be voted in the best interests of participants and beneficiaries. If the ESOP trustee is a bank or other institution, the trustee usually votes unallocated shares as directed by a committee appointed by the company. Only in extreme and unusual circumstances—when the trustee knows (or should know) that the voting instructions given to it are clearly improper (perhaps because of coercion or misinformation) and violate ERISA—may the trustee exercise its own judgment regarding the voting of such shares. Because there are no voting pass-through provisions contained in ERISA, the DOL takes the position that the trustees are ultimately responsible for the voting of all shares, both allocated and unallocated. This may be the case, according to the DOL, despite explicit plan provisions that, as required by IRC Section 409(e), vest voting direction authority in plan participants (and their beneficiaries) with respect to allocated shares and prescribe procedures for the voting of unallocated shares. No regulatory or legislative clarification of this point is in sight.

When voting pass-through is not required by law, the shares usually are voted by the fiduciary. However, voting rights may be provided to participants in excess of what is required by law, from full pass-through on all allocated shares on all issues requiring a shareholder vote, to limiting the vote to certain specific issues (such as the election of one or more corporate directors or limiting the vote to vested shares only). The procedures to be followed to solicit voting instructions should be established so as to permit participants to vote without any improper interference. Generally, participants will be sent the same shareholder meeting notice and any proxy solicitation materials that are sent to all other shareholders. The disclosure requirements for shareholder meetings are generally done in accordance with applicable state corporate laws and corporate bylaws (and SEC rules when a company is publicly traded). The proxy solicitation card or form instructs the ESOP trustee how to vote the shares and will generally be tabulated by the company on instructions given to or by the ESOP trustee. All participant voting must be kept confidential and free of duress or coercion.

OBRA '89 added an additional voting requirement. In order to obtain the partial interest exclusion under IRC Section 133 on securities-acquisition loans made after July 10, 1989 (with certain exceptions), the ESOP must provide for full pass-through voting rights on allocated stock to participants, not merely pass-through on "major" issues. In addition, if the plan acquires convertible preferred stock, that stock must carry voting rights equivalent to the stock into which it may be converted. There is no requirement for pass-through of voting rights on unallocated stock. Full voting pass-through is required only if the lender utilizes the interest exclusion under IRC Section 133; if not, then only limited voting pass-through will continue to be required for closely held company stock.

Rights and Restrictions on Employer Securities

General Rule

Historically, employer securities held by a qualified plan must have "unrestricted" marketability.[32] This rule was further modified by T.I.R. 1413's prohibition on a mandatory "call" option exercisable by the employer within a specified time. The regulations provide that employer

[32] Rev. Rul. 57–372 1957–2, C.B. 256, modified by Rev. Rul. 69–65 1969–1 C.B. 114.

securities acquired with the proceeds of an exempt loan may not be subject to a ''put, call, or other option, or buyout, or similar arrangement,'' except that restrictions required under federal and state laws are permitted.[33] Since this applies only to securities purchased with the proceeds of an exempt loan, a violation of this provision will result in a prohibited transaction and the loss of tax benefits that depend upon the plan being an ESOP. However, since Revenue Ruling 57-372 continues to apply, a violation of this provision would also result in plan disqualification if the violation takes the form of a buy-sell, call option, or other market-restricting arrangement and could result in a loss of all of the tax benefits dependent upon qualified ESOP status.

Right of First Refusal

The regulations permit a customary right of first refusal to attach to certain securities. First, the securities must not be publicly traded at the time the right may be exercised. Second, the right of first refusal may be only in favor of the employer, the ESOP, or both, in any order. Third, the right must not be in favor of shareholders *other* than the ESOP. Last, the right of first refusal must lapse no later than 14 days after written notice of the offer to purchase has been given to the party holding the right.

Further, the payment terms and purchase price must not be less favorable to the seller than the *greater* of (1) the purchase price and other terms offered by the buyer (other than the sponsor or the ESOP, who has in good faith made an offer to purchase), or (2) the value of the security determined on the most recent valuation date under the ESOP.[34]

If the seller of employer securities is a disqualified person and the ESOP is buying, a special valuation date applies. The purchase price is determined on the date of the proposed transaction. A disqualified person is a person described in 4975(e)(2) of the Code. The key difference between a *party in interest* and a *disqualified person* is that, whereas ERISA says only that all employees are parties in interest, under the Code only employees earning 10 percent or more of the yearly wages of an employer are disqualified persons. Thus, most employees receiving in-service distributions will not be disqualified persons even though they are parties in interest.

---

[33]Treas. Reg. Sec. 54.4975–7(b)(4); Labor Reg. Sec. 2550.408(b)-3(d).

[34]Treas. Reg. Secs. 54.4975–7(b)9, 54.4975–11(d)(5); Labor Reg. Sec. 2550.408b-3(1).

Buy–Sell Agreements

An ESOP is not permitted to enter into agreements obligating it to acquire securities from a shareholder at an indefinite time in the future that is determined by the occurrence of an event—including certain events like the death of a shareholder.[35]

An ESOP also is not permitted to be obligated to put-option arrangements.[36] Ostensibly the purpose of these prohibitions is to eliminate the possibility that plan fiduciaries may be required to act imprudently in the future, at the time of purchase.

Even agreements spelling out that the transaction will take place at fair market value and for adequate consideration at the time the obligation becomes due will not be acceptable, since the purchase (for all of the reasons outlined in this chapter) may not be an acceptable transaction.

Option arrangements, however, are permissible. An ESOP may enter into an agreement that would provide the ESOP with an option to purchase employer securities from a shareholder at some definite or indefinite date in the future. This type of arrangement clearly is in the interest of both the ESOP and the participants, since it provides a place to purchase employer securities and gives the fiduciaries a chance to determine the prudence of the exercise of the option. Careful drafting would require that the ESOP trust provisions specifically permit such agreements, but not require that they be entered into.

Put Options

One key question that has always troubled nearly everyone concerned with ESOPs is "What good is stock without a market?" Part of the answer has been set forth in regulations[37] and modified by statute.[38]

Code Sections 401(a)(23) and 409(h) provide that participants or beneficiaries receiving a distribution of employer stock from an ESOP (or TRASOP or stock bonus plan) generally must be given a put option for the stock if the employer securities are not readily tradable on an established market. This means that a participant who receives a distribution

---

[35]Treas. Reg. Sec. 54.4975–11(a)(4)(ii).

[36]Treas. Reg. Sec. 54.4975–7(b)(10); Labor Reg. Sec. 2550.408b-3(j).

[37]Treas. Reg. Sec. 54.4975–7(b)(10); Labor Reg. Sec. 2550.408b-3(j).

[38]Revenue Act of 1978, Sec. 17(n).

of stock from the plan has a right to require that the employer repurchase employer securities under a fair valuation formula.

As finally codified by The Revenue Act of 1978 and its legislative history and by TRA '86, the put option must give these benefits:

1. The trustee of the participant's individual retirement account must be able to exercise the same option.
2. The participant must have at least 60 days after receipt of the stock to require that the employer repurchase the stock at its fair market value[39] and make payment within 30 days if the shares were distributed as part of an installment distribution.
3. The ESOP *may* be permitted to take the employer's role and repurchase the stock in lieu of the employer.
4. The participant must have an additional 60-day period in which to exercise the put option in the following plan year.[40]
5. If the shares were distributed as part of a lump-sum distribution, payment for the shares must begin within 30 days after the exercise of the put option on a schedule at least as rapid as substantially equal annual payments over a period not exceeding five years, at the option of the party buying back the stock. Under Code Section 409(h)(5), the seller must be given a promissory note that will accelerate (all become due at once) if the buyer defaults on any installment payment. The installment note must have adequate security and carry a reasonable interest rate.

The legal obligation to grant a put option is applicable under a leveraged ESOP where the employer's securities are not readily tradable on an established market, if the shares were acquired by an ESOP in a leveraged transaction. This put-option requirement also applies to employer securities acquired after December 31, 1979, by unleveraged ESOPs qualified under Code Section 4975(e)(7), whether leveraged or not. Under an ordinary stock-bonus plan sponsored by an employer without a readily tradable class of securities, the employer is legally obligated to grant a put option for its securities distributed to participants by the plan, but only if such securities were acquired after December 31,

---

[39]IRC Sec. 409(h)(3).

[40]IRC 409(h)(4).

1986, and to any shares acquired after December 31, 1976, if the plan included a cash distribution option.

A put option is always required on distributed stock that was acquired with the proceeds of an exempt loan and that is not publicly traded, even if the plan is subsequently changed from an ESOP. After ERTA, this does not apply in the case of a bank that is prohibited from purchasing its own stock if participants are given the right to receive benefits in cash thereby eliminating the need for the put option. Also, if it is known at the time the exempt loan is made that honoring the put option would cause the employer to violate federal or state law, the put option must permit the securities to be put to a third party having substantial net worth at the time the loan is made and whose net worth is reasonably expected to remain substantial. Very few individuals would, or could, accept the obligations of a perpetual putee. Also, the substituted putee rule was clearly not intended to cover situations in which the employer may be temporarily prevented from honoring the option, such as in the situation when the employer sponsor has no retained earnings from which to purchase securities (a requirement of many states). Not even companies whose shares are readily tradable on an established market can afford to ignore the put-option requirements. For example, if the shares held by the ESOP are not readily tradable on an established market, then the put-option rules apply. Sometimes public companies are acquired and are no longer public. Sometimes trading is suspended in certain securities, or perhaps the company goes "private" or fails to meet the continuing rules of the exchange(s) on which it is traded (that is, no longer readily tradable on an established market). Sometimes a publicly traded company's ESOP distributes shares that are not freely tradable (e.g., subject to SEC Rule 144). In any case in which the employer securities are no longer readily tradable on an established market, the put-option rule becomes effective.

Payments under put options also may not be restricted by loan agreements, other arrangements, or the terms of the employer's bylaws or articles of incorporation, except to the extent necessary to comply with state laws.[41]

The ESOP will very likely lose its attractiveness as an employee benefit plan if terminating employees and their beneficiaries are liable for

[41]Treas. Reg. Sec. 54.4975–7(b)(12)(v); Labor Reg. Sec. 2550.408b-3(1)(5).

taxes on shares for which there is no market. Also, this lack of marketability is a factor in determining the value of the shares and, without a put option, there will likely be a lower valuation of the securities. The company may offer to repurchase shares voluntarily, under even more favorable terms and conditions than the law requires, even when not required to do so by law and may do so under conditions that do not have to conform in any respect to the rules applicable to mandatory put options.[42] However gratuitous this desire may be, if these discretionary put options are granted in a manner that is not uniform and nondiscriminatory, prohibited plan discrimination may result. The problem can be eliminated if, for example, the discretionary put options are for a fixed number of securities for each and every party receiving a distribution.

Under the requirements of IRC Section 401(a)(28)(B), the ESOP must provide "qualified employees"—those who are at least 55 years old and who have at least 10 years of *participation* in the plan—an opportunity to diversify their plan holdings. This applies only to shares acquired after December 31, 1986. Section 401(a)(28)(B) imposes this as a qualification requirement that plans must permit qualified participants to diversify the investment of at least 25% of their ESOP account during the qualified election period. The qualified election period is the six-year period commencing with or after the plan year in which the participant attains age 55 (or, if later, with the plan year in which the participant has completed 10 years of participation). Further, in the final year of the qualified election period, the plan must afford the participant the opportunity to diversify the investment of at least 50% of the balance of his plan account (less any prior portion diversified). Participants are apparently entitled to one election each year during the election period. For companies whose ESOP shares are not readily tradable on an established market, this provision will have the practical effect of accelerating the repurchase liability created by the plan's distributions. However, under IRS Notice 88-56, I.R.B., 1988-19, no diversification need be provided if the fair market value of the employer stock allocated to a participant's account is less than $500.

An ESOP may satisfy this diversification requirement in two ways:

1. The plan may distribute, in stock or in cash, the portion of a participant's account subject to the diversification requirement to

---

[42]Treas. Reg. Sec. 54.4975-11(a)(7)(i); Labor Reg. Sec. 2550.407d-6(a)(6).

him within 90 days of the period in which the diversification election may be made. If the plan distributes stock (even though it is not required to do so), the put-option requirements apply and the stock may be rolled over into an IRA. The IRA retains the put right only if the stock is not readily tradable on an established market at the time of the distribution; if it distributes cash, the participant may roll the cash over into an IRA.

2. A plan may offer at least three investment options (other than employer stock) to qualified employees. Alternatively, an option to transfer assets to a plan that permits at least three investment options (other than employer stock). Because of its similarity to distribution options of cash or stock, the authors believe that the mere offering of the option to liquidate ESOP shares should not be considered as a ''sale'' and ''purchase'' under federal and state securities laws.

Valuation

For nonpublicly traded employer stock acquired after December 31, 1986, all determinations of fair market value in connection with an ESOP must be based on an independent appraisal.[43] IRS regulations issued under Code Section 170(a) may establish standards for determining what constitutes an independent appraiser; otherwise, the proposed Department of Labor regulations on adequate consideration now deal with this issue. The final regulations under Code Section 4975 and proposed DOL regulations require that a valuation be made in good faith on the basis of *all* relevant factors affecting the value of securities.[44]

Conversions and Mergers involving ESOPs

Conversion to an ESOP

Under the proper circumstances, existing pension and profit-sharing plans may be converted (by amendment) into ESOPs. If the requirements of prudence and the exclusive-benefit rule under ERISA can be satisfied, existing assets of such converted plans may be used to acquire employer

---

[43]IRC Sec. 401(a)(28).

[44]Treas. Reg. Sec. 54.4975–11(d)(5). See also *Donovan v. Cunningham* 716 F2d 1455 (5th Circuit, 1983), Cert. denied, June 18, 1984.

securities. However, **the conversion into an ESOP of an existing plan's investments in general assets that have been accumulated for the purpose of providing retirement benefits should be undertaken with extreme caution.** Fiduciaries should carefully document why the conversion was prudent and consistent with the exclusive benefit requirement. Normally, it is only when the fortunes of the company and the value of the stock decline following a conversion that the fiduciaries are called upon to explain.

Almost all the rules discussed earlier in this chapter come into play with a conversion, and accelerated vesting may be required, along with the preservation of distribution options. The shares may be purchased from existing shareholders, the employer corporation, and/or the public market.

Conversion of a defined benefit plan into an ESOP involves both the amendment of the character of the plan from a defined benefit plan to a defined contribution plan and the use of all or part of the plan assets to buy employer stock. Such a conversion is treated as a termination of the plan for purposes of Title IV of ERISA. Therefore, Code Section 411(d) will require 100 percent vesting of participants' actuarially determined benefits. Annuity distributions must be offered to participants in addition to the plan's other distribution requirements. If the employees are given a choice between receiving their accrued benefits in the form of an annuity and having the present value of such benefits invested in employer stock, care must be taken to comply with all applicable federal and state securities law requirements. Other types of plans, such as thrift and savings plans, also may be converted.

Conversion of a money purchase pension plan into an ESOP may result in 100% vesting if the new ESOP does not constitute a comparable plan.

For taxable years beginning after December 31, 1986, the ability to deduct up to 25% of participants' compensation (instead of the normal 15% of compensation) for contributions to a stock bonus or profit-sharing plan is eliminated except to the extent that the increased deduction results from prior years' contributions being below 15% of compensation. The unused deduction carryforwards that accumulated for taxable years beginning prior to January 1, 1987, are preserved and may be used after 1986 to increase the deduction limit to 25% of participants' compensation. Finally, pre-1987 contribution credit carryovers attributable to the existing plan under IRC Section 404(a)(3)(A) are available for use under a converted ESOP, provided the preexisting plan was a stock bonus or a profit-sharing plan. No credit carryover is permissible if the converted ESOP is derived from a money purchase pension plan or defined benefit plan.[45]

For any conversion, the provisions of such plans with respect to permissible investments are indeed critical. Since vested employee accounts are being used to purchase qualifying employer securities, the plan provisions almost universally require substantial amendments.

Potential fiduciary liability for plan conversions may exist. Further information is available by reading the following decisions: (1) *Usery* v. *Penn,* 426 F.Supp. 830 (W.D. Okla. 1976), *aff'd d sub nom. Eaves* v. *Penn,* 587 F.2d 453 (10th Cir. 1978); (2) *Marshall* v. *Whatley,* No. 77 Civ. 04-A (E.D. Va. Apr. 18, 1977); and (3) *Baker* v. *Smith,* No. 80 Civ. 3067 (E.D. Penn. Aug. 6, 1980).

A number of labor issues may have to be considered, including the existence of any collective bargaining agreements.

Pension-Reversion Excise-Tax Exemption

For terminations of defined benefit plans occurring before January 1, 1989, the Code permitted the direct transfer of all or a portion of the excess assets to an ESOP if certain conditions were met. If these conditions were met, the portion of the reversion so transferred was not subject to excise taxes thereon, and the amount of the transferred reversion was not includible in the income of the sponsoring employer. With the expiration of this provision, such a transfer would involve income and excise taxes and a number of Code qualification issues, all of which are discussed in General Counsel Memorandum 39744 (July 14, 1988).

Mergers into an ESOP

Each qualified plan, as a condition of qualification, must provide that, in the case of merger or consolidation with or transfer of assets or liabilities to any other plan after September 2, 1974, each participant must receive a benefit immediately after the merger, consolidation, or transfer, determined as if the plan being transferred were then terminated. This means

---

[45]This is because pension plans had no pre-1987 contribution carryovers. *See* T.I.R. 1413, Q&A T–9 (1975).

that any participant must receive no less than the benefit the participant would have been entitled to receive before the merger, consolidation, or transfer, determined as if the plan into which the transfer occurs had then terminated.[46] These conditions will be referred to as *the transfer rules*. The rules are extremely complicated and generally beyond the scope of this chapter. However, a few of the more essential rules are presented here.

If two or more defined contribution plans are merged or consolidated, the transfer rules will be met if all of the following conditions are met:

1. The sum of the account balances in the plans equals the fair market value of the assets of the surviving plan on the date of the merger or consolidation,
2. The assets of each plan are combined to form the assets of the plan as merged, and
3. The participants' balances in the plans that survive right after the merger are equal to the sum of the participants' account balances (individually determined) in the plans just before the merger.

A defined benefit plan being merged into an existing ESOP is considered as being, first, converted to a defined contribution plan, and then, once converted, it is considered as merged.[47] The Pension Benefit Guaranty Corporation (PBGC) requires the plan administrator to allow each participant to elect in writing either to receive the value of the participant's accrued benefits in the form provided under the plan or to have plan assets equal in value payable as an annuity transferred to an individual account under the ESOP.[48] This election probably constitutes a sale within the meaning of Section 2(3) of the Securities Act of 1933 and would require compliance unless some exception from registration is available. In addition, care must be taken to preserve distribution options to the extent required under Code Section 411(d)(6).

Conversion from an ESOP

If the conversion out of an ESOP is accomplished by plan merger, consolidation, or transfer of assets, the transfer rules would apply. There

---

[46]IRC Secs. 401(a)(12), 414(l).

[47]Treas. Reg. Sec. 1.414(l)-1(i).

[48]P.B.G.C. Opinion 76–30 (March 8, 1976); P.B.G.C. Opinion 76–12 (January 27, 1976).

may be significant problems under the anti-cutback rules of Code Section 411(d)(6), because the participant's right to demand stock may be considered a ''protected right'' for purposes of the anti-cutback rules. If the plan merger, consolidation, or transfer of assets out of an ESOP is into another type of defined contribution plan, it will not necessarily trigger a termination within the meaning of the vesting requirements of Code Section 411(d)(3). The key issue is the fiduciary decision as to what extent employer stock will be sold in light of the conversion.

To the extent employer stock continues to be held under the plan, the conversion out of an ESOP also will not in itself relieve the employer from the put-option requirements. The put-option rule applies only when employer securities are distributed and enough securities of the employer could be converted to other assets to permit distributions in other assets or future contributions may supply enough cash for many years. Outstanding loans are a problem on the conversion out of an ESOP. To the extent unallocated shares held as collateral are sold, the proceeds should be used to retire ESOP debt, absent an extremely favorable ESOP interest rate. If indebtedness would still remain thereafter, however, the ESOP fiduciaries have three options: (1) defer the conversion until the loan is paid off, (2) seek a specific exemption from the prohibited transaction rules of ERISA Section 408(a) and Code Section 4975(c)(2), or (3) proceed with the conversion risk and incur the penalties imposed with respect to prohibited transactions. There is a further risk that plan fiduciaries may be held liable for any losses incurred by the plan as a result of their violation of the prohibited transaction provisions of ERISA Section 409(a), and they may be removed by a court. The same fiduciary considerations applicable to converting *to* an ESOP are applicable in converting *from* one.

Last, converting to any other kind of plan but an eligible individual-account plan gives rise to an absolute 10 percent limitation of ERISA Section 407 on the holding of employer securities.

Types of Employer Securities

With the changes brought about by the Technical Corrections Act of 1979, the definition of *qualifying employer securities* in Code Section 4975(e)(8) incorporates by reference the definition of *employer securities* set forth in Code Section 409(1) (which was added by the Revenue Act of 1978). This definition includes stock of the employer and certain controlled group members, which meets *one* of the following requirements:

1. Common stock readily tradable on an established securities market.
2. If there is no readily tradable common stock, common stock having a combination of voting power and dividend rights at least equal to the classes of common stock having the greatest voting power and the greatest dividend rights.
3. Preferred stock convertible (at any time at a reasonable conversion price determined at the date of acquisition) into common stock meeting one of the above definitions.

This definition of employer securities is applicable to stock acquired by a statutory ESOP after December 31, 1979. Note that any kind of capital stock may be contributed or purchased on a nonleveraged basis, if the plan is a stock bonus plan that is not an ESOP or an ESOP that is otherwise primarily invested in qualifying employer securities. However, to the extent that an ESOP acquires stock that is not a qualifying employer security, the special ESOP tax benefits (tax-free rollover, partial interest exclusion, special deduction limitations, and so on) do not apply.

Cash versus Stock Distributions

Until the changes brought about by the Revenue Act of 1978, the Technical Corrections Act of 1979, and the Miscellaneous Revenue Act of 1980, the regulations for ESOPs required that the portion of an ESOP consisting of a stock bonus plan must provide for benefits to be distributable only in stock of the employer.[49] This provision restated the requirements applicable to stock bonus plans set forth in Treasury Regulation Sections 1.401-1(a)(2)(iii) and 1.401-1(b)(1)(iii).

The Revenue Act of 1978 provided that a leveraged ESOP could distribute cash in lieu of employer securities so long as the participant could demand that his or her distribution be made in employer securities.

The Technical Corrections Act of 1979 provided that the cash-distribution option available to an ESOP under Code Section 4975(e)(7) and 409A(h), which is now 409(h), be made effective with respect to distributions of benefits after December 31, 1978.

---

[49]Treas. Reg. Sec. 54.4975–11(f)(1).

The Miscellaneous Revenue Act of 1980 added Code Section 401(a)(23), which permits any qualified stock bonus plan, not just an ESOP or TRASOP, to make distributions of benefits in either cash or stock after December 31, 1980, so long as the participant or beneficiary has the right to demand distributions in the form of employer stock. ERTA further modified this to provide that mandatory cash distributions could occur if the articles or bylaws of the corporation restrict ownership of substantially all the company's stock to current employees and an employees' trust.

Finally, TAMRA provides that a participant does not have the right to demand that benefits be paid in the form of stock with respect to the portion of the participant's stock that the participant elected to diversify.

Special Distribution Requirements

TRA '86 imposes new requirements on the timing of distributions from an ESOP. These requirements apply to distributions attributable to employer stock acquired by the ESOP after December 31, 1986.

Unless a participant otherwise elects, or resumes employment following a resignation or dismissal but before the distribution date, Code Section 409(o) requires the distribution of his or her ESOP benefits to begin no later than the last day of the plan year following the plan year of normal retirement age, disability, or death, or of the fifth plan year following the plan year in which his or her employment terminates for other reasons. An exception to this general rule exists under IRC Section 409(a)(1)(B) for leveraged shares until the corresponding ESOP debt is repaid; however, IRC Sections 401(a)(9) and 401(a)(14) require that distribution begin by the earlier to occur of (i) the April 1 next following the calendar year in which the participant attains age 70½, or (ii) the sixtieth day following the plan year during which the participant has attained the plan's normal retirement age, reached the tenth anniversary of the date he commenced participation in the plan, and separated from service.

Generally, unless a participant otherwise elects, distribution of ESOP benefits must be made at least as rapidly as substantially equal, annual installments over a period not exceeding five years. However, for participants whose benefits exceed $500,000 in value, the distribution period may be extended (up to an additional five years) by one year for each $100,000 ($124,690 in 1992) (or fraction thereof) by which the value of benefits exceeds $500,000 ($623,450 in 1992).

Subject to these and other qualified plan nondiscrimination requirements, an ESOP may retain discretion in determining the timing and form of distributions without regard to the restrictions on discretionary distribution options generally applicable to qualified plans under the Retirement Equity Act of 1984 (REA).

Early Distribution Excise-Tax Exception

TRA '86 imposes a 10 percent excise tax on taxable distributions (after 1986) from a qualified plan to a participant prior to age 59½, unless the distribution occurs as the result of the participant's death, disability, or terminated employment after age 55 under the plan, or is rolled over into an IRA. This excise tax generally did not apply to any ESOP distributions prior to 1990. In addition, cash dividends on employer stock that are passed through to ESOP participants are not subject to this excise tax even after 1990.

Which Distribution is Best?

A nearly universal participant question is "Which distribution type is best—cash or stock?" The answer depends on the tax picture of the employee, the interplay of the lump-sum distribution rules under the Code, and the net-unrealized-appreciation provisions of Code Section 402(e)(4)(D) and (J) and regulations issued thereunder, which provide that the taxable amount of a lump-sum distribution does not include net unrealized appreciation on the employer's securities distributed to a participant. *Net unrealized appreciation* is the excess of the fair market value of the employer securities at the time of distribution from a plan over the trust's adjusted basis in the securities. The net unrealized appreciation on the date of distribution is taxed as a long-term capital gain when the securities are subsequently disposed of. Any additional appreciation is either short- or long-term capital gain, depending on how long the stock is held by the distributee.[50] The participant may, however, not have a choice as to whether he or she receives a lump-sum distribution or installments; this decision may be reserved for the fiduciary, committee, or plan administrator who must consider plan and employer liquidity in making a choice as to the form of distribution.

---

[50]Rev. Rul. 81–122 1981–1 C.B.

To determine which distribution is most advantageous, calculate the total tax from lump-sum treatment with each of the various possibilities. Surprisingly, in many large distributions, taking stock may result in a lower tax, both currently and subsequently. TRA '86 eliminates the preferential tax treatment for capital gains after December 31, 1986. However, it permits an ESOP distributee to elect to include any appreciation in value of employer stock while in the ESOP (net unrealized appreciation) as part of the taxable amount eligible for special income-tax averaging available for certain lump-sum distributions. Considerations should also be given to the excess-distribution tax provisions of Code Section 4981 and the possible advantageous use of an individual retirement account (IRA) rollover.

Rollovers

Rollovers are very flexible for lump-sum distributions (and certain "partial distributions") from ESOPs. The stock may be distributed, then sold, and the proceeds contributed to an IRA, provided the proceeds are contributed within the statutory 60-day period. Alternatively, partial rollovers are permitted, and of course, if the stock is acceptable to an IRA custodian or trustee, the stock can go right into the IRA. No tax is due by participants or beneficiaries if these special IRA rules are followed. The disadvantage of an IRA, however, is that the various options available by carefully calculating the tax effect of stock and cash in a lump-sum distribution are not available if the distribution stays in an IRA until distributions start. If a distribution is rolled over into an IRA, the benefit of the lump-sum and capital-gains provisions of the Code are not available. The subsequent distributions from the IRA are taxed at ordinary earned-income tax rates, and the special averaging and capital-gains rates are lost forever. The only exception is when the amount rolled over is subsequently rolled over into another qualified plan.

Deduction of Employer Dividend Payments

The last sentence of Section 803(h) of the Tax Reform Act of 1976 reflects the intent of Congress to permit the employer to structure an ESOP "to distribute income on employer securities currently." The regulations provide that an ESOP will not fail to meet[51] the qualification

[51]Treas. Reg. Sec. 54.4975-11(a)(8)(iii) and 54.4975-11(f)(3).

requirements of Code Section 401(a) merely because the ESOP provides for the current payment of income with respect to employer securities.

OBRA '89, DEFRA, and TRA '86 made substantial and meaningful changes to the tax treatment of dividends on employer stock.

1. *Cash dividends paid to participants and beneficiaries.* Code Section 404(k) permits a deduction to a corporation for the amount of dividends paid in cash by such corporation with respect to employer securities if:

1. Such employer securities are held on the record date of the dividend by a tax-credit ESOP or an ESOP that meets the requirements of Section 4975(e)(7) of the Code and regulations issued thereunder and is maintained by such corporation or a controlled group member thereof; and
2. In accordance with the ESOP provisions, one of the following occurs:
   a. The dividend is paid in cash directly to the participants and beneficiaries in the plan, or
   b. The dividend is paid in cash to the ESOP and is distributed to the participants and beneficiaries in the ESOP not later than 90 days after the close of the plan year in which paid.

The Temporary Regulations issued under Section 404(k) expressly provide that the dividend deduction is available with respect to qualifying employer securities within the meaning of Subsection 409(1) of such corporation held by an ESOP and also is available with respect to other employer stock of the corporation (not just qualifying employer securities) but only if such dividends may, if the plan specifically authorizes, be immediately distributed under the terms of the plan and all of the applicable qualification and distribution rules.

It should be noted, however, that the Temporary Regulations indicate that the deduction is allowed for the taxable year of the corporation during which the dividends are *received* by the participants. However, after the Temporary Regulations were issued, the statute was amended by TRA '86 and OBRA '89 to provide that dividends paid to participants will be allowed as a deduction in the taxable year of the corporation in which the dividend is "paid or distributed to the participants" without expressly requiring "receipt" by the participants. Thus, it is unclear whether the "receipt" requirement of the Temporary Regulations continues to apply—a conservative course would be to assume that it applies. The deduction for dividends actually paid out is allowed even if plan participants may elect to receive or not to receive payment of dividends. Furthermore, the OBRA '89 amendments appear to limit the deductibility of dividends paid on stock acquired after August 4, 1989, to dividends paid on employer securities within the meaning of Code Section 409(l).

2. *Dividends applied to loan payments.* The Tax Reform Act of 1986 and TAMRA expands the deduction for dividends by permitting a corporation to deduct the amount of cash dividends paid on employer stock held by an ESOP (both allocated and unallocated shares) to the extent that the dividends are used by the ESOP to make payments (of principal and interest) on the ESOP loan used to acquire those shares. Code Section 404(k)(2) significantly enhances the ability to finance ESOP transactions on a pre-tax basis. Note that dividends on allocated shares may be used to make payments on such a loan only if the account to which the dividends would have been allocated is allocated shares with a fair-market value not less than the amount of the dividend that would have been allocated. Such allocation must be made in the plan year the dividend would otherwise have been allocated. The deduction, which applies for taxable years commencing after October 22, 1986, is allowed for the taxable year of the corporation in which the dividends are so applied.[52]

It appears that cash dividends paid on both allocated and unallocated ESOP shares should be able to be used to make deductible ESOP loan payments on shares leveraged with that loan without violating the requirements of Section 4975.

Finally, dividends used to repay an ESOP loan will not be considered an annual addition for Section 415 purposes. In certain extreme and egregious situations the IRS might attempt to recharacterize such dividends as employer contributions and therefore attempt to treat such dividends as annual additions. Such dividends will be disregarded for purposes of determining the limitations on an employer's deduction under Section 404.[53] The OBRA '89 amendments restrict the deductibility of dividends used to repay a securities-acquisition loan to those dividends paid on securities acquired with the loan proceeds and not to dividends on other stock that may be in the plan. (See "Dividends" earlier in this chapter).

---

[52]Tax Reform Act of 1986, Section 1173(c)(1).

[53]U.S. Senate Committee on Finance, 99th Congress, 2nd Session, *Report to Accompany H.R. 3838,* Rept. 99–313, p. 682.

3. *Miscellaneous matters.* Section 404(k) dividends are treated as taxable income rather than as a nontaxable return of basis in the case of a contributory ESOP. No partial-dividend exclusion on dividends paid in cash to participants and beneficiaries is permitted to the participants, and all such dividends will constitute ordinary income to the participants or recipients. Withholding is *not* required with respect to such dividend payment, nor are FICA or FUTA taxes withheld on these amounts.

Under IRC Section 411(a)(11)(C), the distribution of dividends in excess of $3,500 is not subject to the general rule requiring participant consent. Finally, deductible dividends that are distributed to participants and their beneficiaries are exempt from the 10% early distribution tax of IRC Section 72(t).

Furthermore, in the case of a leveraged ESOP, the deduction appears to apply to cash dividends paid to participants and beneficiaries with respect to unallocated shares held in a suspense account, not just shares allocated to participants' accounts, although the statute does not expressly address the issue. However, the authors perceive that the Senate Finance Committee Report takes a contrary position.[54]

In drafting an ESOP plan document, consideration should be given to whether the distribution of cash dividends will be automatic or subject to the periodic choice of the ESOP fiduciaries, the ESOP participants, or even the board of directors of the employer corporation. In either case, the dividend payout could be restricted to vested shares. If the board of directors makes the choice, rather than the trustees, such choice may be justified on the grounds that it generates a corporate deduction that concurrently benefits the ESOP participants and beneficiaries.

Finally, Code Section 404(k) provides that the deduction for ESOP dividends may be disallowed if the IRS determines that such dividend constitutes in substance an evasion of taxation. Although the statute says "avoidance," the legislative history suggests that "evasion" was the intended standard.

One question not answered in the statutes or in the legislative history is the following: Can an employee make a voluntary contribution of cash or employer stock to the ESOP and thereby create the deduction for the employer on dividends paid on such stock?

---

[54]U.S. Senate Committee on Finance, *Report to Accompany H.R. 3838*, Rept. 99-313, (May 29, 1986) p. 1,033.

An employee may make aftertax voluntary contributions to a tax-qualified retirement plan such as an ESOP. While nothing in the statute or the legislative history would preclude this, it is not inconceivable that the IRS might take the position that such a voluntary contribution by an employee is outside the purposes of IRC Section 404(k) and, therefore, creates a windfall deduction to an employer with respect to the stock contributed by the employee. Since the statute contains no restrictions concerning the source of the stock contribution, such a position by the IRS would be of highly questionable validity, unless it can prove a tax-evasion scheme.

Other problems that should be addressed include: the voluntary contributions in kind may be prohibited transactions, for which there may be no exemption if the in-kind contribution of stock is not valued accurately; the voluntary contributions may reduce the allocation of employer contributions because of the reduction in the IRC Section 415 annual additions; and the nondiscrimination test of IRC Section 401(m) will be violated if the voluntary contributions are skewed in favor of highly compensated employees.

Stock Purchase by an ESOP

When a taxpayer sells shares of stock, he or she recognizes gain to the extent of the excess over the taxpayer's adjusted basis in the stock. When the stock is redeemed by the issuing corporation, the transaction is considered a distribution by the corporation, with respect to its stock, and will be taxable as a capital gain (or loss) only if the requirements of Code Section 302(b) are satisfied. Otherwise, it is a dividend to the shareholder and taxed twice—once at the corporate level and then again at the shareholder level.

The ESOP is clearly a separate legal entity, and so under normal circumstances the sale by a shareholder to an ESOP would be taxed as a sale or exchange at capital-gains rates, too, although no preferential rates exist at the time of this writing for long-term capital gains. Basis in the stock will not be taxed, only the proceeds in excess of the basis. However, the IRS may view certain transactions as a redemption by the sponsoring employer and hence subject to dividend treatment.

Revenue Procedure 87-22 sets forth operating rules with respect to the issuance of an advance ruling of the IRS: that the proposed sale of the employer's stock by a shareholder to a related employee plan is a sale or exchange, rather than a corporate distribution taxable under Code Section 301. The revenue procedure only provides a safe harbor, and failure to meet its tests will not be an automatic application of Code Section 301 to the sale of stock to a qualified plan. These guidelines do not, as a matter of law, precisely define the only situations in which the sale of stock to a plan will avoid treatment as a corporate distribution of property under Code Section 301. In the absence of such a ruling, the tax ramifications of such a sale will be subject to examination on audit.

A favorable ruling under Revenue Procedure 87-22 will be issued if three conditions are met:

1. The combined beneficial interests of the selling shareholder and all related persons in the plan on the date of the sale cannot exceed 20 percent of the total plan beneficial interests. This requirement will *not* be satisfied if *any one* of the following occurs:
   a. The combined covered compensation of the selling shareholder and related persons on the date of the sale exceeds 20 percent of the total compensation of all participants under the plan.
   b. The total account balances (vested and nonvested) of the selling shareholder and related persons under the plan on the date of the sale exceeds 20 percent of the account balances of all plan participants.
   c. The total interest (vested and nonvested) of the selling shareholder in any separately managed fund or account within the plan on the date of the sale exceeds 20 percent of the total net assets in that fund or account.

   In determining whether the interest of the selling shareholder and related persons in any fund exceeds 20 percent of the net assets of that fund, there may be excluded from consideration any separately managed fund or account of a plan that at no time may be invested in the employer's securities.[55] For purposes of these tests, "related person(s)" includes the spouse, parents, grandparents, children, and grandchildren of the selling shareholder.
2. The second requirement for a private letter ruling is that the restrictions on the disposition of the employer's stock held and distributed

[55]Rev. Proc. 87–22, I.R.B. 1987–20,11.

by the employee plan can be no more onerous than the disposition restrictions on at least a majority of the shares of the employer's securities held by other shareholders. Certain rights of first refusal that comply with the provisions of the ESOP regulations are acceptable restrictions that can apply to employer securities held or distributed by an ESOP.

3. The third requirement is that there be no intention, plan, or understanding on the part of the employer to redeem from the plan any of the stock being purchased by the plan from the selling shareholder.

Tax-Deferred Sale of Stock to an ESOP

For taxable years beginning after July 18, 1984, DEFRA added Code Section 1042, which permits a shareholder of a closely held corporation to sell employer stock that has been held for more than three years to an ESOP and defer the taxation of gain to the extent that he or she purchases securities of other corporations. The sale must otherwise qualify for long-term capital-gains treatment and the shares must not have been received by the seller from a qualified employee plan (such as an ESOP) or pursuant to an employee incentive program (such as by exercising a stock option. The replacement securities must be purchased within the 15-month period that begins 3 months before and ends 12 months after the sale of employer stock to the ESOP. The replacement securities must be securities of corporations whose passive investment income in the taxable year preceding the taxable year of purchase did not exceed 25 percent of gross receipts, and which satisfies other technical rules, including the rule that more than 50 percent of the assets of the corporation are, at the time the security is purchased or before the close of the replacement period, used in the active conduct of the trade or business. After the sale the ESOP must own either: (1) at least 30 percent of value at the fully diluted equity of the employer (other than certain nonvesting, nonconvertible preferred stock); or (2) at least 30 percent of each class of stock of the company, on a fully diluted basis (other than certain nonvoting, nonconvertible preferred stock). An excise tax is imposed on the employer for certain dispositions of the stock by the ESOP within three years after the sale. The stock that is purchased by the ESOP generally may not be allocated to the seller, members of his or her family, or any shareholder who owns more than 25 percent of any class of employer stock. (See "Transfers of Ownership" earlier in this chapter).

Other ESOP Considerations

Characteristics of the Employer. An ESOP must be established by a corporate employer. However, an S Corporation that establishes an ESOP would lose its S Corporation status, and it may be difficult (or impossible) for a professional corporation to establish an ESOP.

S Corporations. Except in limited circumstances, a trust may not hold shares of an S Corporation. Since a trust established under an ESOP generally must hold shares of the employer corporation, an S Corporation may lose its S Corporation status upon funding of an ESOP.[56]

Professional Corporations. There are no provisions in ERISA or the IRC that prevent a professional corporation from establishing an ESOP. However, most state statutes proscribe the ownership of shares by anyone who is not a member of the respective profession. Thus, in some states, shares could not be held by a trust or distributed to a participant who was not a member of the respective profession.

These state statutes conflict with the IRC requirement that a plan not discriminate in favor of highly paid employees. The IRC would require an ESOP of a professional corporation to include any nonprofessional employees of the corporation. Ultimately, shares of the corporation would have to be distributed to these employees, yet such a distribution would violate most states' statutes.

A solution allowing adherence to both the nondiscrimination requirement and the state statutes might be to establish a qualified plan other than an ESOP to cover the nonprofessional employees of the corporation.[57] The use of two plans to avoid the nondiscrimination requirement is questionable, however, because Treasury Regulation Section 54.4975-(11)(e) states that an ESOP shall not be designated as one of two or more plans for purposes of Section 410(b)(1). A House Report indicates that an ESOP and another plan should not be considered a single plan for purposes of determining whether the plan meets the nondiscrimination requirements.[58] The additional participation requirements of Section 401(a)(26) also make such a scheme questionable. However, note that ESOP may be aggregated

---

[56]IRC Sec. 1361.

[57]*See* IRC Sec. 401(a)(26) and 410(b).

[58]H.R. Rep. No. 1515, 94th Cong., 2d Sess. 541 (1976).

with other plans for purposes of the average benefits percentage test of Code Section 410(b)(2).

Past rulings might provide some guidance on the issue of ESOPs in professional corporations. In 1975, the Attorney General of Georgia issued an opinion concerning an ESOP whose assets were held by a trustee who was not a member of the requisite profession. The opinion states that the fact that the trustee holds the legal title of the shares does not result in a violation of the state's professional corporation law. The Attorney General of Michigan has issued an opinion that an ESOP may own stock of a professional corporation where the trustees and all participants are duly licensed professional employees of the employer.[59]

Written Instrument

All employee benefit plans must be established pursuant to a written instrument, which must:

1. Name one or more fiduciaries or delineate a procedure by which the fiduciary is named by the employer or an employee organization;
2. Provide a procedure for establishing and carrying out a funding policy consistent with the plan;
3. Describe any procedure for allocating responsibility under the plan for the operation and administration of the plan;
4. Provide a procedure for amending the plan; and
5. Specify the basis on which payments are made to and from the plan.[60]

Trust Requirement: Management of the Trust

All assets of the plan must be held in a trust and be managed by a trustee named in the plan or appointed by a named fiduciary. The trustee has exclusive authority to manage and control the assets of the plan.[61] However, the plan may provide that the trustee is subject to the direction and authority of the named fiduciary.[62] The plan may provide that the

[59]Michigan Attorney General Opinion No. 5285 (March 20, 1978).

[60]ERISA Sec. 402.

[61]ERISA Sec. 403(a).

[62]ERISA Sec. 403(a)(1).

named fiduciary may appoint an investment manager to manage the assets of the plan.[63]

Situs of the Trust

Section 401(a) requires that the assets of the trust generally be maintained in the United States.[64] However, Section 404(a)(4) provides that the mere fact that a trust has a foreign situs will not prevent the employer from deducting contributions to it. Similarly, beneficiaries of a trust having a foreign situs but meeting all other requirements of the IRC will receive the same tax benefits as beneficiaries of a domestic trust.[65] ERISA Section 404(b) requires that the indicia of ownership of the trust be kept within the jurisdiction of the United States District Courts.[66]

Valuation of Employer Securities

Proper valuation of employer securities contributed or sold to the plan is an important and difficult aspect of plan administration. Improper valuation of employer securities contributed to the plan may result in the loss of some deductions if the valuation is overstated. If the value is understated, potential deductions will also have been foregone. If the ESOP purchases the securities for more than their fair market value, an excise tax could be imposed (together with required corrections and liability to the responsible fiduciaries), and in egregious circumstances, disqualification of the ESOP might result.[67] For nonpublicly traded employer stock acquired after December 31, 1986, all determinations of fair market value in connection with an ESOP must be based upon a valuation by an independent appraiser. Treasury regulations will establish standards for determining what constitutes an independent appraiser along the lines of regulations issued under the charitable-contribution provisions of IRC Section 170(a)(1).[68]

---

[63]ERISA Sec. 402(c)(3).

[64]Treas. Reg. Sec. 1.41–1(a)(3)(i) (1956).

[65]IRC Sec. 402(c).

[66]DOL Regs. Sec. 2550.404b-1 (1977).

[67]IRC Sec. 4975, 401(a); ERISA Sec. 502(l).

[68]IRC Sec 401(a)(28)(C).

ADDITIONAL ESOP CONSIDERATIONS

SEC Aspects

1933 Securities Act

On February 1, 1980, the Securities and Exchange Commission issued Release No. 33-6188 on the application of the 1933 Securities Act to employee plans. The purposes of the release were to provide guidance to the public and to assist employers and plan participants in complying with the '33 act. The release

Discusses circumstances under which interests in plans and related entities may be subject to the requirements of the '33 act,

Provides an analysis of the criteria to be used to determine when an offer or sale of security will occur,

Discusses the various exemptions from the act's registration provisions,

Discusses the act's application to the various types of securities transactions in which plans may engage, as well as resales of securities participants acquire through the operation of the plan, and

Describes the methods of registration of securities under the act.

The interests of employees in a plan are securities only when the employees voluntarily participate in and contribute to the plan. Employee interests in plans that are not both voluntary and contributory are not securities and are not subject to the act, according to the release. While the release is lengthy and is intended to provide guidance, it does point out that it should not be viewed as an all-inclusive treatment of the subject and that the SEC staff will continue to provide interpretive advice and assistance on request, as will the courts.

Another release (Release No. 33-6281), issued January 22, 1981, further clarifies the SEC's position on the application of the 1933 Securities Act to employee benefit plans, as well as describes developments under the act after the 1980 release was issued. Both releases are invaluable to an understanding of the issues involved.

Whether the ESOP has an independent bank trustee is another factor affecting the impact of the securities laws on the ESOP. Employer securities purchased by an independent trustee may be sold by an ESOP or distributed to and resold by participants who are not deemed affiliates of the employer without registration under the '33 Act. Shares purchased on the open market by an employer-controlled ESOP must be registered prior to resale by plan participants, and such securities are subject to very limited resale privileges until they are registered.

Securities Exchange Act of 1934

The Securities Exchange Act of 1934 is designed to regulate the trading markets for publicly held securities. The compliance requirements are beyond the scope of this chapter. However, the 1934 act raises at least three significant issues with respect to the operation of an ESOP:

1. Under what circumstances is an ESOP required to comply with the shareholder-reporting provisions of Sections 13(d) and 16(a) of the 1934 act?
2. Are purchases and sales of employer stock subject to the short-swing profit-recovery provisions of Section 16(b) of the 1934 act?
3. Are borrowings by the ESOP to acquire employer stock subject to the margin requirements adopted by the Federal Reserve Board under the 1934 act?

These questions should be answered for each ESOP that is established by a publicly traded company.

Other Reporting and Disclosure Rules

Additional reporting and disclosure rules that should be looked at include:

1. Section 15(d) provides that if a registration statement pursuant to the 1933 act must be filed with respect to certain stock-related qualified plans, then the registrant must file "such supplementary and periodic information documents and reports as may be required pursuant to Section 13 of this title."

2. Section 16(a) Reporting-Rule 16a-8(a)(2) provides that the "vested beneficial interests in a trust" must be reported by officers and directors and beneficial owners of more than 10 percent of any class of equity security, and they must report periodically on changes of ownership. The rules are exceedingly complex, and several exemptions may be available.

3. The 1934 act's antifraud rules apply to both initial sales as well as to subsequent sales. Section 10 of the 1934 act prohibits the use of manipulative and deceptive devices in the trading of securities. Certain fraudulent and deceptive practices are crimes. Various other rules require an issuer and its affiliate(s) to follow certain procedures in the repurchase of its stock, which might apply to the ESOP's trustee.

Accounting Considerations[69]

ESOPs must address some difficult accounting issues, both from the employer's point of view in preparing the financial statements, and in the trust accounting and participant accounting areas.

Employer Accounting Considerations

In 1976 the American Institute of Certified Public Accountants (AICPA) issued a statement of position on accounting issues relating to ESOPs (SOP 76-3). The accounting guidance outlined in that statement of position is considered preferable by the Financial Accounting Standards Board as well as the SEC, according to a footnote to SFAS No. 32.[70]

The statement of position recommended the following accounting treatment:

- The debt of the ESOP should be recorded as a liability in the employer's financial statements when the debt is guaranteed by the employer, or when the employer commits itself to make future contributions to the ESOP that are sufficient to service the debt.
- The offsetting debit to the liability recorded by the employer should be accounted for as a reduction of shareholders' equity. Because no real expansion of equity has occurred, the increase in capital stock resulting from the issuance of shares to the ESOP is offset by the debit to equity (the equity contra account), set up when the loan is recorded. If new shares are not issued by the company, and the ESOP purchases shares

---

[69]This section has been reviewed and substantially updated by Rebecca J. Miller, a partner in the Rochester, Minnesota, office of the accounting firm of McGladrey & Pullen. A portion of this material, which originally appeared in Richard Reichler, ed., *Employee Stock Ownership Plans: Problems & Potentials,* was written by Norman N. Strauss. Copyright 1977, 1978, Law Journal Seminars–Press. Reprinted by permission of the publisher.

[70]American Institute of Certified Public Accountants, Accounting Standards Division, "Statement of Position on Accounting Practices for Certain Employee Stock Ownership Plans," issued December 20, 1976.

from existing shareholders, the accounting treatment with respect to establishing the equity contra account is the same.

- Each year the amount contributed to the plan to reduce the loan balance should be charged to compensation expense. The portion of the contribution representing interest on the borrowing should be separately identified and charged to interest expense. Both the liability and the equity contra account should be reduced symmetrically as the loan is amortized.
- All common shares held by an ESOP should be treated as outstanding shares in the earnings-per-share computation.

During 1989, substantial interpretive revisions were made in the application of SOP 76-3. These were made by the Emerging Issues Task Force (EITF) of the Financial Accounting Standards Board (FASB). Briefly, these interpretations provide for the following:

1. The debt of the ESOP is to be recorded by the plan sponsor without regard to any commitment or guarantee. The simple fact that the cash to service the debt will originate with the employer, either in the form of dividends or contributions, is sufficient to require the employer to record the obligation.[71]

2. The measurement of compensation cost is no longer based solely upon the principal paid for the year. Instead, there is a new minimum expense recognition technique based upon the equation:

$$\left[\frac{\text{Shares allocated for the period}}{\text{Total shares purchased}} \times \text{Original principal}\right] + \text{Interest expense} - \text{Dividends}$$

For plans that release shares using the principal-only method, this will always equal the principal paid. Plans that use the principal-and-interest method of collateral release will experience a different pattern of cost recognition than under the former interpretation of the SOP.

Note that, because this was a fairly dramatic change, the EITF did authorize a degree of cushion. Employers whose ESOPs predated the release of the consensus opinion use the prior method of cost recognition, as long as it results in a cost figure that is at least 80 percent of this

---

[71]EITF Consensus 80–10.

method. If the 80 percent standard is not achieved, they must increase their compensation cost to the 80 percent standard.[72]

3. Further, the classification of the equity was addressed during 1989. The SEC has long held that the classification of stock subject to a put is not fully under the control of the issuer. This is ASR 268. The EITF issued a conclusion that ESOPs whose stock is subject to the put option of IRC Section 409(l) will be subject to this standard. In that event, those shares would be taken out of permanent equity and recorded as temporary capital at the "mezzanine" level. Any related "contra equity" account also would be reclassified. This seems to be a very controversial area, and apparently, the SEC has been willing to modify the strict interpretation of this standard in some cases.[73]

4. Further, at the end of 1989, the EITF issued an opinion regarding the earnings per share consequences of convertible preferred stock held by an ESOP. Detail of that position is beyond the scope of this chapter. Suffice it to say that the convertible shares would not generally be considered outstanding in determining the primary earnings per share, but would be in determining fully diluted earnings per share.[74]

When the ESOP acquires shares already outstanding on a leveraged basis, the existing shareholders' equity section of the employers' balance sheet will be reduced, and increases in equity will be recorded as the debt is satisfied. A separate line-item deduction in the stockholders' equity section is made. In the event the ESOP acquires newly issued shares of stock on a leveraged basis, the existing shareholders' equity section of the employer's balance sheet will not decline, as the effect of establishing the equity section contra account will be offset by the increase in equity resulting from the issuance of additional shares. More detailed information on the accounting treatment ESOPs require may be found in Chapter 12 of *Employee Stock Ownership Plans: Business Planning, Implementation, Law, and Taxation* by Robert W. Smiley, Jr., and Ronald J. Gilbert and listed in the bibliography at the end of this chapter.

As the ESOP makes its payments, the corresponding liability on the balance sheet should be reduced, and the stockholders' equity section

---

[72]EITF Consensus 89–8.

[73]EITF Consensus 89–11.

[74]EITF Consensus 89–12.

also adjusted. The accounts will move symmetrically[75] if the principal-only method of collateral release is used. In the event that the principal-and-interest method of collateral release is applied, the contra account and the remaining balance on the acquisition note will no longer move symetrically.

When reporting dividends per share, the dividends should be charged to retained earnings, just as dividends paid to any other shareholder. Dividends are *not* compensation expense, even if they are passed through to participants, and are instead merely a charge against retained earnings. Dividends paid on common stock of the employer may be invested in additional stock of the employer. Such dividends do not give rise to income and should increase treasury stock and/or paid-in capital in jurisdictions where this is permitted, rather than reduce retained earnings. Furthermore, pursuant to the Tax Reform Act of 1986, a tax deduction for the ESOP's sponsoring corporation can be obtained for dividends (on allocated and unallocated shares) paid in cash within 90 days to participants, or dividends can be used to repay an ESOP loan (leveraged ESOP). For financial reporting purposes these dividends are not generally classified as compensation expense. They remain dividends chargeable to retained earnings. However, any tax benefit realized can be credited to the current tax provision.[76]

The earnings per-share issues are diverse. Under the SOP, common shares held by a leveraged ESOP are considered outstanding whether or not they are released from collateral.[77] Convertible preferred stock is considered outstanding as described earlier. This area generated a great deal of controversy at the time the SOP was issued and is still controversial today. Although the current generally accepted accounting principle (GAAP), SOP 76-3, is clear, many practitioners wish to differentiate their case and apply a different accounting standard that could result in fewer shares outstanding.[78] This conflict, as well as other issues, has resulted in the accounting community bringing the issue back to the table. The Accounting Standards Executive Committee of the American Institute of Certified Public Accountants, one of the entities involved in establishing accounting principles, initiated a project in 1989 to examine the state of

---

[75]AICPA Statement of Position, para. 8.

[76]Footnote to *SFAS No. 96*, para. 75, 141.

[77]AICPA Statement of Position, para. 11.

[78]*APB Opinion No. 25*.

accounting for ESOPs and to draft any necessary revisions. The exposure draft of this new standard was expected early in 1991. Implementation would occur after the final version is issued.

When an ESOP receives a contribution in excess of the allowable deduction limitation, such excess is usually treated as a timing difference by the employer in determining the provision for income tax, since excess contributions made in one year can generally be carried over to ensuing years.

In addition to the general issues of leveraged ESOPs, special ESOP applications have resulted in some specific accounting patterns. For example, under prior law an employer could terminate a defined benefit plan and transfer any excess directly to an ESOP, thus avoiding the related income taxes and penalties on the reversion. This transaction created some unique accounting issues. These were resolved by FASB's Emerging Issues Task Force.[79] This position varies somewhat from the traditional reporting of leveraged ESOPs in two significant ways. First, only allocated shares are considered outstanding for calculating earnings per share. Second, the compensation cost for a period is measured by the fair market value of the shares released, not their cost.

Another special application of ESOPs relates to their use in leveraged buy outs. This is an area for which the accounting has yet to be resolved. In the interim, the traditional SOP 76-3 standard is generally being applied.

The footnotes should be as complete and descriptive as possible, and must at the barest minimum, include a description of the plan, including the purpose, any formula for contributions, how the trust assets are held, its effective date, and how employer stock has been (or will be) purchased. The current qualified status of the plan, dates of determination letters from the IRS, and a complete description of the loan also should be listed.

ESOP Accounting Considerations

The primary objective of a defined contribution plan's financial statements is to provide information about *(a)* plan resources and how the stewardship responsibility for those resources has been discharged, *(b)*

---

[79] *EITF Opinion 86–27.*

the results of transactions and events that affect the information about those resources, and *(c)* other factors necessary for users to understand the information provided.

The financial statements of a defined contribution plan should include:

- A statement that includes information regarding net assets available for benefits of the plan as of the financial statement date.
- A statement that includes information regarding the changes during the period in net assets available for benefits of the plan.

The accrual basis of accounting should be used in preparing information regarding net assets available for plan benefits and related changes. The accrual basis requires that purchases and sales of securities be recorded on a trade-date basis. If the settlement date is after the financial state date, however, and *(a)* the fair market value of the securities purchased or sold just before the financial statement date does not change significantly from the trade date to the financial statement date and *(b)* the purchases or sales do not significantly affect the composition of the plan's assets available for benefits, accounting on a settlement-date basis for such sales and purchases is acceptable.[80] The information should be presented in such reasonable detail as necessary to identify the plan's net assets available for benefits and related changes. The trust must also account for the cost basis of the shares of stock held by the trust for purposes of calculating net unrealized appreciation in the accounts of participants receiving employer securities on distribution.[81]

The cost-basis accounting for shares is actually done by the participant recordkeeping system. Each year the trustee is informed about the cost basis of the shares distributed to participants and beneficiaries during the year, so the trust's cost basis can be adjusted in the shares yet held by the trustee.

For another current and detailed explanation see Rebecca J. Miller, "Accounting for ESOP Transactions," *Journal of Employee Ownership Law, and Finance,* National Center for Employee Ownership, vol. II, no. 3 (Summer 1990).

---

[80]ERISA Sec. 103(b)(3)(A).

[81]Treas. Reg. Sec. 1.402(a)(1)-(b)(2).

ESOP Administration and Manuals for Recordkeeping Rules

It is strongly suggested that written manuals be adopted to provide continuity in administration in the event of personnel turnover and, perhaps more important, to document the many discretionary decisions of the sponsoring company to ensure "uniform and nondiscriminatory" application. This latter function conceivably would forestall potential litigation in the event of a participant's dissatisfaction with a particular policy.

The need for quality administrative materials is particularly necessary in light of recent court activity. In the past, administrators operated under a standard that only required them to prove that they were not "capricious or arbitrary" in evaluating a participant's options under the plan. The new standard may be the "de novo" standard of review. This is literally a review of any participant claim as if it were entirely new; that is, no prior similar request was ever received to set any precedent. Although the "de novo" standard can be limited by good plan drafting, it still hangs over the head of an administrator and requires him or her to focus attention on the details of plan administration.

Manuals that would be advisable include: a brief plan interpretation, with examples covering the salient provisions; an accounting procedures manual, which specifies the various choices about methods discussed in this section; a distribution procedures manual, which reflects the company's policies on timing and method of distributions; and a general administration manual designed to include all of the documentation required to be available to and for participants. Other manuals may be useful and should be designed for individual cases.

One disadvantage of these types of manuals is that once a policy is formally documented, it becomes potentially enforceable. Briefly, whatever a manual documents must be what is done.

Repurchase Liability

The ESOP repurchase liability[82] has not been given much attention. Basically, it arises because the employer contributes cash or stock and the stock has to be bought back, usually at an increased price. And, the

---

[82]Robert W. Smiley, Jr., "How to Plan for an ESOP's Repurchase Liability," Prentice-Hall's *Pension and Profit-Sharing Service*, (Englewood Cliffs, N.J.: Prentice-Hall, 1987), pp. 1,215–29; and Robert R. Bumgarner and R. Alan Prosswimmer, "ESOP Repurchase Liability," *Journal of Employee Ownership, Law, and Finance*, National Center for Employee Ownership, vol. II, no. 4 (Fall 1990).

employer must buy it back—for cash. Since ESOPs are relatively new, the cash needed to repurchase company stock from departed employees and their beneficiaries has not yet created a problem for many companies. But there is a clear risk it will, unless companies properly plan for it. It is the authors' opinion that, potentially, this is the most serious difficulty the ESOP will experience. Since the repurchase liability affects the value of company stock, the balance sheet and income statement, the number of shareholders, and employee morale, it must be forecasted and planned for.

The first step in facing this potential problem is to develop a projection of future cash requirements. A computer model specifically suited for this purpose is particularly advantageous, since without one it is almost impossible to see how the plan operates under different assumptions, and how the company's income, cash flow, and balance sheet are affected. The final step is to analyze the various funding methods to determine which would work best in a particular situation. It is conceivable that the repurchase liability could consume more cash than the company could contribute in a given year, since the entire contribution may be used to make repurchases. All the more reason to plan!

The repurchase liability is partially alleviated by varying distributions over time, varying the size of the contribution, varying the stock and cash contributions mix, properly timing stock repurchases, and carefully planning for the proper use of dividends on employer securities and of income on other assets. Other solutions include going public, private placements, being acquired, or the creative use of corporate-owned life insurance.

The employee's diversification right is a new concept added by TRA '86. It allows employees an elective diversification of their ESOP account balances as to securities acquired after December 31, 1986. This election is extended to any employee who is age 55 or older and has 10 years of plan participation in the ESOP. Elections for the first five years may cover up to 25 percent of an employee's account balance (less the portion diversified). The election in the final year may cover up to 50 percent of his or her account balance (less any prior portion diversified).

Companies should not be discouraged from adopting or continuing an ESOP because of the "unknown" repurchase liability, nor should a company adopt an ESOP without ample consideration of the potential repurchase liability. Instead, careful advance planning, ongoing review, good communications, increased productivity, and increased company profits, as well as continued flexibility and encouragement from Congress and the government agencies, should solve almost every problem created by the repurchase liability—but not without planning for it today. The repurchase liability plan must be implemented properly, carefully maintained, and revised as often as necessary to reflect the real world.

ESOPs and Plan Disqualification

If an employee stock ownership plan is ruled not to meet the requirements of either Code Section 401(a) or Code Section 4975(e)(7), a variety of problems result. First, any sales to such a plan will not qualify for the tax-free rollover treatment provided under Code Section 1042, since that section requires that the sales be made to a plan within the meaning of Code Section 4975(e)(7).

Moreover, any loan by a lender to an ESOP will not qualify for the partial interest exclusion provided in Code Section 133 because that section requires that the plan be an employee stock ownership plan within the meaning of Code Section 4975(e)(7). While the lender will lose the ability to get the partial interest exclusion, properly drafted yield-protection language in the loan documentation will ultimately shift that burden to the employer.

Disqualification will also have a negative effect on both the employer and its employees. Plan contributions will no longer be deductible under Code Section 404 (with its special limitations for ESOPs) but may be deductible under the ordinary and necessary provisions of Code Section 162. For the employees, disqualification will mean that the value of their vested account balances will be immediately taxable to them as ordinary income, and all earnings of the ESOP will be subject to tax, thereby diminishing the account balances of the employees.

401(k) Plans and ESOPs

Most 401(k) plans maintained by employers are profit-sharing plans. However, a 401(k) plan may also be a stock bonus plan. Thus, the salary-reduction contributions made by participants and employer matching contributions may be invested in employer stock. In that case, all of the requirements relating to stock bonus plans would apply to the 401(k) stock bonus plan. Particular care and attention should be given to applicable federal and state securities law provisions since, if the participant's salary-reduction contributions are allowed to be invested in employer stock, plan registration and related disclosure may be required.

A further variation are 401(k)-leveraged ESOPs known as *KSOPs* (under which participant elective deferrals and stock dividends are used to repay stock acquisition debt) and *MSOPs* (under which employer contributions and dividends on the stock are used to repay stock acquisition debt). Both take careful planning and scrutiny of *all* ERISA and Code issues: KSOPs, because of their use of participant elective deferrals to repay ESOP debt, are currently under IRS scrutiny.

Wage-Concession ESOPs

Several notable ESOPs—including those established by Eastern Airlines, Continental Airlines, Pan American World Airways, Inc., Republic Airlines, Inc., Western Airlines, Inc., Pacific Southwest Airlines, Inc., CF&I Steel Corporation, and PIE Nationwide, Inc.—have involved wage concessions in exchange for shared equity provided by an ESOP as a quid pro quo for stock ownership. These were companies in which productivity improvements and reduced labor costs were necessary to ensure corporate survival. Such ESOPs are the exception rather than the rule. In fact, according to surveys conducted by the National Center for Employee Ownership, less than 5 percent of the ESOPs established in the United States to date have involved wage concessions or contributions by employees.

In other ESOPs—such as those of Weirton Steel, Northwestern Steel & Wire Co., Rosauers Supermarkets, Inc., and Omak Wood Products, Inc.—employees accepted wage reductions to assist in the financing by which they acquired the company. The number of ESOPs in this category is small but it is growing geometrically as more employees find that they can compete with Wall Street buyers to buy and own a majority of the companies that employ them.

COMPARISON OF ESOPs WITH OTHER EMPLOYEE STOCK OWNERSHIP ARRANGEMENTS

Stock ownership arrangements have been around for a long time. Sears Roebuck & Co. has had a profit-sharing plan invested primarily in employer securities since July 1916. The Proctor & Gamble Co. had a plan prior to 1900 where employees shared ownership. When the Revenue Act of 1921 was enacted, certain types of stock bonus trusts and profit-sharing trusts were granted tax exemptions. Many of the qualified deferred-compensation plans are currently permitted to invest and hold employer securities. This *Handbook* discusses many alternatives to an

ESOP as well as many compensation arrangements that can supplement an ESOP. See Chapters 32, 33, 34, 38, 55, 56, and others.

Other Defined Contribution Plans

Defined contribution plans generally can give the feeling of meaningful employee ownership. The account balances of the participants, like a mutual fund, reflect how much gain or loss there is for the year. The ESOP is unique among employee stock ownership arrangements. First, it generally involves a broad base of employees and is operated within the purview of qualified deferred-compensation plans, giving it considerable flexibility. Second, it permits financing acquisitions of employer securities through borrowing, by using the credit of the employer. Third, the initial purchase of stock on a leveraged basis generally means the employer is permanently committed to an ESOP-type plan, at least for the period of the loan repayment. From the employee's point of view, it's very hard for an employer to ''back out'' of a plan once the stock has been acquired by the trust. Other qualified plans cannot leverage to acquire the employer's stock by using the credit of the employer.

However, sometimes a non-ESOP eligible individual-account plan may serve many of the same purposes as an ESOP without some of the obvious disadvantages such as put options, specific allocation of shares, required distributions in employer securities, and the like. The eligible individual-account plan, however, can help an employer add to its capital by means of contributions in employer securities or by cash contributions that purchase newly issued (or treasury) stock. Employees also share in the economic benefits of corporate success in a visible way. All of these plans must face the repurchase liability problem eventually, however.

Other Stock Plans

Stock ownerships opportunities are granted to executives and other selected employees in many other ways. These include incentive stock plans under Code Section 422A, nonqualified stock-option plans, stock-appreciation-rights plans, performance share plans, phantom stock plans, restricted stock plans, key-employee stock plans, employee stock-purchase plans under Code Section 423, stock *gifts* by the employer, stock sales to employees by the employer or by shareholders, and so on. Most of these are aimed at a limited group of employees, and since the con-

FIGURE 35–1
ESOP Tax Shield

	Without ESOP	*With ESOP*
Operating pretax income	1000	1000
Less: ESOP contribution	-0-	500
Pretax income	1000	500
Less: Income taxes	400	200
Net income	600	300
Equity		
Start of year	5000	5000
Add: Ret'd earnings	600	300
Add: ESOP stock purchase	-0-	500
	5600	5800

Source: Benefit Capital, Inc., Los Angeles, California.

text is so different, it is difficult to make comparisons. The qualified stock-purchase plan under Code Section 423, while directed to a broad-based group, is substantially different from an ESOP, in that the contribution required of the employee is a major part of the acquisition cost. An ESOP's stock acquisition costs are, in most instances, borne solely by the employer! Compare this to the ESOP tax benefits shown in Figures 35–1 and 35–2.

FIGURE 35–2
Benefit of Tax Savings

	Company			
	A	*B*	*C*	*D*
Value of transaction	20.0	8.0	4.0	2.0
Payroll	2.0	2.0	2.0	2.0
Ratio (%)	1000	400	200	100
ESOP contribution	.5	.5	.5	.5
Tax savings on ESOP contribution (40%)	.2	.2	.2	.2
ESOP tax savings for 5 years' pay this percent of value	5%	12.5%	25%	50%

Source: Benefit Capital, Inc., Los Angeles, California.

CONCLUSION

Several million Americans are covered by ESOPs, with millions more being included in ESOPs every year. Employee stock ownership plans involve a complex array of business, legal, tax, accounting, and investment-banking questions that are best handled by those with experience in employee ownership. These questions include the basic ones any employer asks, such as "Do we want it?" "What will it do for us?" "How do we get out of it if something happens?" and "What do our employees get and when?" There are also many additional questions that require expertise in the ESOP area to answer fully. The legal questions include all the qualification questions under Code Section 401; the distribution, eligibility, and vesting sections; the fiduciary and prohibited-transaction questions under ERISA; the accounting and financial questions; securities and corporate-law questions; alternative financing question; and myriad more. Congress has continually sought to encourage employers to share the fruits of capital and labor through profit participation and a "piece of the action." The ESOP is the latest, most popular, by far the most practical, and in many ways, the least expensive approach to providing employees with a piece of the company in which they work on a tax-favored, creditor-proof basis. More than 11,000 companies are enjoying the many benefits of employee ownership. ESOPs continue to be the most popular benefit plan available today.

BIBLIOGRAPHY

"Assessing Employee Stock Ownership Plans (ESOPs)." Research Institute of America, Inc., Staff Recommendations, December 3, 1979.

Bell, Daniel. *Bringing Your Employees into the Business: An Employee Ownership Handbook for Small Business.* Kent, Ohio: Kent Popular Press, 1987.

Blasi, Joseph. *Employee Ownership: Ripoff or Revolution?* Cambridge, Mass.: Ballinger Books, 1988.

Blasi, Joseph Raphael. *Employee Ownership through ESOPs: Implications for the Public Corporation.* New York: Pergamon Press, 1987.

Bonaccorso, Matthew J.; Sheridan M. Cranmer; David G. Greenhut; Daphne T. Hoffman; and Neil Isbrandtsen. "Survey of Employee Stock Ownership Plans: Analysis and Evaluation of Current Experience." Master's thesis, University of California at Los Angeles, 1977.

''Broadening the Ownership of New Capital: ESOPs and Other Alternatives.'' A Staff Study prepared for the use of the Joint Economic Committee, 94th Congress, 2nd Session, June 17, 1976.

Bumgarner, Robert R., and R. Alan Prosswimmer. ''ESOP Repurchase Liability.'' *Journal of Employee Ownership, Law, and Finance* II, 4, (Fall, 1990), The National Center for Employee Ownership (NCEO).

Bureau of National Affairs. *Employee Ownership Plans: How 8,000 Companies and 8,000,000 Employees Invest in Their Futures*. Washington, D.C.: BNA Books, 1987.

Chow, Andrew; Thomas Cunningham; Michael Horstein; and Jerrald Zweibel. ''Repurchase Liability for ESOPs and Other Employee Stock Ownership Plans.'' Master's thesis, University of California at Los Angeles, 1979.

Conte, Michael. ''Employee Stock Ownership Plans in Public Companies.'' *Journal of Employee Ownership, Law, and Finance,* I, 1 (Fall 1989), NCEO.

Conte, Michael, and Arnold S. Tannenbaum. *Employee Ownership*. Report to the Economic Development Administration, U.S. Department of Commerce. University of Michigan, Institute for Social Research, June 15, 1977.

Conte, Michael, and Arnold Tannenbaum. *Employee Ownership*. Ann Arbor: Survey Research Center, University of Michigan, 1980.

Curtis, Jack. ''ESOPs as a Takeover Defense Strategy.'' *Journal of Employee Ownership, Law, and Finance* I, 1 (Fall 1989), NCEO.

Curtis, John E., Jr., and Anna Jeans. ''ESOPs: A Decade of Congressional Encouragement.'' *Tax Management Compensation Planning* 12, 377 (December 1984).

Drucker, Peter F. *The Unseen Revolution*. New York: Harper & Row, 1976.

Durso, Gianna. ''Usage of ESOPs in Public Companies.'' *Journal of Employee Ownership, Law, and Finance* I, 1 (Fall 1989), NCEO.

Ellerman, David. ''What Is a Workers' Cooperative?'' Somerville, Mass.: Industrial Cooperative Association.

Epstein, Stanley A. ''Employee Relations Considerations in Establishing ESOPs.'' *Employee Relations Law Journal* 3 (Autumn 1977), pp. 266–80.

ESOP Association. *ESOP Survey 1990*. Washington, D.C.

ESOP Association. *How the ESOP Really Works*. Washington, D.C.: The ESOP Association, March 1988.

———. *Proceedings* of the National Employee Stock Ownership Conferences (Washington, D.C., 1980–1991). Washington, D.C.: ESOP Association of America, 1980–1991.

———. *Structuring Leveraged ESOP Transactions*. Washington, D.C.: The ESOP Association, 1988.

Ewing, David W. and Pamela M. Banks. ''When Employees Run the Company: An Interview with Leamon J. Bennet.'' *Harvard Business Review,* January–February 1979, pp. 75–90.

Frisch, Robert A. *ESOP: The Ultimate Instrument of Corporate Finance.* Massapequa, N.Y.: Norwood Associates, 1989.

______ . *The Magic of ESOPs and LBOs.* Rockville Centre, N.Y.: Farnsworth Publishing Company, 1985.

Gordon, Lilli, and John Pound. ''ESOPs and Corporate Control.'' *Journal of Employee Ownership, Law, and Finance* I, 1 (Fall 1989), NCEO.

Gougis, Chester A. ''The Role of Convertible Preferred Stock in Public Company ESOP Transactions.'' *Journal of Employee Ownership, Law, and Finance* I, 1 (Fall 1989), NCEO.

Hoerr, John. ''ESOPs: Revolution or Ripoff?'' *Business Week,* April 15, 1985.

Hoffmire, John. ''Practitioner Conduct: The Need for Open Debate.'' *Journal of Employee Ownership, Law, and Finance* II, 1 (Winter 1990), NCEO.

Hourihan, Jennifer. ''The Public Market for ESOP Notes.'' *Journal of Employee Ownership, Law, and Finance* I, 1 (Fall 1989), NCEO.

Hyde, Alan, and Craig Livingston. ''Employee Takeovers.'' *Rutgers Law Review* 41 (Summer 1989), pp. 1131–95.

Kalish, Gerald, ed. *ESOPs: The Handbook of Employee Stock Ownership Plans.* Chicago, Ill.: Probus Publishing Company, 1989.

Kaplan, Jared. ''Legal Considerations for ESOP Loans.'' *Commercial Lending Review* 2 (Winter 1986–1987), pp. 20–24.

Kaplan, Jared, and Mark Bogart. ''TRA Favors ESOPs.'' *The Tax Times,* Oct. 1986, p. 1.

Kaplan, Jared, and Gregory K. Brown. ''Uses of Leveraged ESOPs in Corporate Transactions.'' *New York Law Journal,* Sept. 16, 1985.

Kaplan, Jared, Gregory K. Brown, and John E. Curtis, Jr. *BNA Tax Management Portfolio on ESOPs.* Washington, D.C.: Tax Management, Inc., 1987.

Keeling, J. Michael. ''ESOPs and TRA '86: The Political Record in the *Congressional Record.*'' *Compensation and Benefits Management* 4 (1991), p. 43.

Kelso, Louis O., and Mortimer J. Adler. *The Capitalist Manifesto.* New York: Random House, 1958; reprint ed., Westport, Conn.: Greenwood Press, 1975.

______ . *The New Capitalists.* New York: Random House, 1961; reprint ed., Westport, Conn.: Greenwood Press, 1975.

Kelso, Louis O., and Patricia Hetter. *Two-Factor Theory: The Economics of Reality.* New York: Random House, 1967.

Kelso, Louis O., and Patricia Hetter Kelso. *Democracy and Economic Power: Extending the ESOP Revolution.* Cambridge, Mass.: Ballinger Publishing Company, 1986.

Kurland, Norman G. ''Beyond ESOP, Steps toward Tax Justice, Part 1.'' *Tax Executive,* April 1977.

———. ''Beyond ESOP: Steps toward Tax Justice, Part II.'' *Tax Executive,* July 1977.

Latta, Geoffrey W. *Profit Sharing, Employee Stock Ownership, Savings, and Asset Formation Plans in the Western World.* Philadelphia: University of Pennsylvania, 1979.

Law Journal Seminars–Press. *ESOPs in Financial Transactions.* New York: Law Journal Seminars–Press, 1987.

Lee, M. Mark. *ESOPs in the 1980s.* New York: American Management Association, 1985.

Lewis, Stuart. ''ESOP Provisions in the 1984 TRA.'' *Tax Management Compensation Planning Journal* 13, 17 (Jan. 1985).

Lindberg, Kenneth W. ''Combining ESOPs and 401(k) Plans.'' *Journal of Employee Ownership, Law, and Finance* I, 1 (Fall 1989), NCEO.

Ludwig, Ronald L. ''Employee Stock Ownership Plans after ERISA.'' *Employee Relations Law Journal* 1 (Winter 1976).

Ludwig, Ronald L., and Jeffrey R. Gates. ''The Final ESOP Regulations—A Return to Certainty.'' *Prentice-Halls' Pension and Profit-Sharing Service,* Englewood Cliffs, N.J.: Prentice-Hall, March 23, 1978, pp. 1,237–54.

Lurie, Alvin D. *ESOPs Made Easy.* Jacksonville, Fla.: Corbel, 1985.

Marsh, Thomas, and Dale McAllister. ''ESOPs Tables: A Survey of Companies with Employee Stock Ownership Plans.'' *Journal of Corporation Law* 6, 3 (Spring 1981).

Mattingly, William, and Zarina O'Hagin. ''Into the Future—ESOPs after 1986.'' *Taxes* 64, 699, (Nov. 1986).

———. ''Planning for ESOPs under the Tax Reform Act of 1986.'' *Taxes* 63, 323 (May 1985).

Maldonado, Kirk F. ''Employee Stock Ownership Plans,'' in *Employee Benefits Handbook,* edited by Jeffrey D. Mamorsky. Boston: Warren, Gorham & Lamont, 1987.

———. ''Employee Stock Ownership Plans under the Tax Reform Act of 1987.'' *Tax Management Memorandum* 28 (1987), pp. 15–26.

———. ''Why Banks Are Turning to ESOPs.'' *Journal of Bank Taxation* 1 (1987), pp. 43–45 and 63.

May, Richard C., Robert MacDonald, and Bradley Van Horn, ''Valuation Issues in Leveraged ESOPs.'' *Journal of Employee Ownership, Law, and Finance* II, 1 (Winter 1990), NCEO.

Midkiff, Robert R., and Luis Granados. ''Choosing an ESOP Trustee.'' *Journal of American Society of CLU and ChFC,* November 1987.

Miller, Marilyn V. "The Ins and Outs of ESOP Administration." *Financial Planner* 10 (January 1981), pp. 28–32.

Miller, Rebecca J. "Accounting for ESOP Transactions." *Journal of Employee Ownership Law, and Finance* II, 3 (Summer 1990), NCEO.

______ . *ESOPs—Practical Applications.* New York: American Institute of Certified Public Accountants, 1988.

National Center for Employee Ownership. *Beyond Taxes: Managing an Employee Ownership Company.* Oakland, Calif.: NCEO, 1987.

______ . *An Employee Buyout Handbook.* Oakland, Calif.: NCEO.

______ . *The Employee Ownership Casebook.* Oakland, Calif.: NCEO, 1988.

______ . *An Employee Ownership Reader.* Oakland, Calif.: NCEO, 1983, updated 1987.

______ . *The Employee Ownership Research Review.* Oakland, Calif.: NCEO, 1985, updated 1987.

______ . *Employee Ownership: A Union Handbook.* Oakland, Calif.: NCEO.

______ . *How ESOP Companies Are Handling Repurchase Liability, 1988.* Oakland, Calif.: NCEO.

______ . *International Developments in Employee Ownership, 1990.* Oakland, Calif.: NCEO.

______ . *Peter's Principled Pies, 1989.* Oakland, Calif.: NCEO.

______ . *The Record of ESOP Leveraged Buyouts, 1990.* Oakland, Calif.: NCEO.

______ . *Structure and Implementation of ESOPs in Public Companies.* Oakland, Calif.: NCEO, 1989.

Neece, Roger, Jr. "The Role of the Financial Advisor in Multi-Investor Leveraged ESOP Transactions." *Journal of Employee Ownership, Law, and Finance* II, no. 1, The National Center for Employee Ownership (Winter 1990).

Northeast Ohio Employee Ownership Center. *"Employee Stock Ownership Plans in Ohio."* Kent, Ohio: NOEOC, Kent State University, 1989.

Olson, Deborah Groban. "Some Union Experiences with Issues Raised by Worker Ownership in the U.S.: ESOPs, TRASOPs, Co-ops, Stock Plans, and Board Representation." *Wisconsin Law Review,* December 1982.

Park, Chong. "The Record of ESOP Leveraged Buyouts." *Journal of Employee Ownership, Law, and Finance* II, 1 (Winter 1990), NCEO.

Practising Law Institute. *ESOPs and ESOP Transactions.* New York: Practising Law Institute, 1990.

______ . *ESOPs 1990: New Strategies in ESOPs, Leveraged ESOPs, and Other Benefit Plans which Invest in Employer Securities.* New York: Practising Law Institute, 1990.

______ . *ESOPs 1989: New Strategies in ESOPs, Leveraged ESOPs, and Other Benefit Plans which Invest in Employer Securities*. New York: Practising Law Institute, 1989.

______ . *Tax Strategies for Leveraged Buyouts and Other Corporate Acquisitions and Restructurings*. New York: Practising Law Institute, 1987 (Course Handbook #261).

Pratt, Shannon P. *Valuing a Business: The Analysis and Appraisal of Closely Held Companies*, 2nd ed. Homewood, Ill.: Dow Jones–Irwin, 1989.

Prentice-Hall Law and Business. *Employee Stock Ownership Plans . . . New Techniques, Special Features, and Enhanced Incentives under the Tax Reform Act of 1986*. Clifton, N.J.: Prentice-Hall, 1987.

______ . *Update 1990: Employee Stock Ownership Plans*. Englewood Cliffs, N.J.: Prentice-Hall Law & Business, 1990.

Presidential Task Force on Project Economic Justice. *High Road to Economic Justice*. Arlington, Va.: Center for Economic and Social Justice, 1986.

Quarrey, Michael. *Employee Ownership and Corporate Performance*. Oakland, Calif.: NCEO, 1986.

Quarrey, Michael; Joseph Blasi; and Corey Rosen. *Taking Stock: Employee Ownership at Work*. Cambridge, Mass.: Ballinger Publishing Company, 1986.

Reichler, Richard. ''Deficit Reduction Act Makes Significant Changes to Rules Governing ESOPs.'' *Journal of Tax* 62, 70 (February 1985).

______ . *Employee Stock Ownership Plans: Problems and Potentials*. New York: Law Journal Press, 1978.

Reilly, Robert. ''Owners of Closely Held Corporations Can Reap Special Benefits from ESOPs.'' *Tax. for Accts.* 36, 362 (June 1986).

''The Role of the Federal Government and Employee Ownership of Business.'' Committee Print, Select Committee on Small Business, United States Senate, 96th Congress, 1st Session, March 20, 1979.

Rosen, Corey. ''A Primer on Leveraged ESOPs.'' *Journal of Employee Ownership, Law, and Finance* II, 1 (Winter 1990), NCEO.

Rosen, Corey M.; Katherine J. Klein; and Karen M. Young. *Employee Ownership in America: The Equity Solution*. Lexington Mass.: Lexington Books, 1986.

Rosen, Corey, and Michael Quarrey. ''How Well Is Employee Ownership Working?'' *Harvard Business Review,* September–October 1987, pp. 126–32.

Simmons, John, and William Mares. *Working Together*. New York: Alfred J. Knopf, 1983.

Smiley, Robert W., Jr. ''ESOP Financing.'' *Journal of Employee Ownership, Law, and Finance* II, 1 (Winter 1990), NCEO.

______ . "How to Plan for an ESOPs Repurchase Liability." *Prentice-Hall's Pension and Profit-Sharing Service.* Englewood Cliffs, N.J.: Prentice-Hall, February 27, 1987, pp. 1,215–29.

Smiley, Robert W., Jr., and Edward M. Bixler. "The ESOP." *Advanced Markets Digest* 3, 1 (Winter 1989), First Capital Life Insurance Company.

______ . "ESOP's Eleven Commandments." *Advanced Markets Digest* 3, 3 (Summer–Fall 1989), First Capital Life Insurance Company.

______ . "The Seven Myths of ESOPs." *Advanced Markets Digest* 3, 2 (Spring 1989), First Capital Life Insurance Company.

Smiley, Robert W., Jr., and Ronald J. Gilbert. *"Employee Stock Ownership Plans: Business Planning, Implementation, Law, and Taxation.* Larchmont, New York: Prentice-Hall/Rosenfeld Launer, 1989, Maxwell Macmillan/Rosenfeld Launer, 1990 and *Yearbook* published 1991.

Speiser, Stuart M., ed. *Main Street Capitalism: Essays on Broadening Share Ownership in America and Britain.* New York: New Horizons Press, 1989.

Speiser, Stuart M. *A Piece of the Action.* New York: Van Nostrand Reinhold, 1977.

U.S. Congress Joint Economic Committee. *Employee Stock Ownership Plans (ESOPs).* Hearings before the Joint Economic Committee, 94th Cong., 1st Session, Part 1, December 11, 1975; Part 2, December 12, 1975. Washington, D.C.: U.S. Government Printing Office, 1976.

U.S. General Accounting Office. *Employee Stock Ownership Plans: Benefits and Costs of ESOP Tax Incentives for Broadening Stock Ownership.* (GAO/PEMD97-8) Washington, D.C., February 1986.

______ . *Employee Stock Ownership Plans: Interim Report.* Washington, D.C.: United States GAO, February 1986.

______ . *Employee Stock Ownership Plans: Little Evidence of Effects on Corporate Performance.* Washington, D.C.: United States GAO, October 1987.

U.S. General Accounting Office, Comptroller General. *Employee Stock Ownership Plans: Who Benefits Most in Closely Held Companies?* (HRD-80-88), Washington, D.C., June 20, 1980.

Wagner, Ira. *Report to the New York Stock Exchange on the Performance of Publicly Held Companies with Employee Ownership Plans.* Arlington, Va.: NCEO, 1984.

Wassner, Neil A. "ESOPs, Can They Work for Your Corporation?" *Pension World,* June 1977.

Welch, John. "Fiduciary Aspects of Employee Stock Ownership Plan Investments in Employer Securities." *Real Property and Probate Trust Journal* 23, 4 (Winter 1988), pp. 575–631.

Wells, Colin A. ''The Role of Key-Man Life Insurance in an ESOP.'' *Financial Planner* 10 (January 1981), pp. 34–36.

Wessinger, Samuel Y. *A Brief History of The ESOP Association*. Washington, D.C.: The ESOP Association, 1986.

Winter, Linda. *Employee Buyouts: An Alternative to Plant Closings*. New York: The Conference Board, 1983.

Wuebel, Peter A. ''ESOPs—Alive and Well: A Legislative Update. *The Corporate Growth Report* 8, 2 (April 1990).

CHAPTER 36

CASH BALANCE PENSION PLANS

Lawrence T. Brennan
Dennis R. Coleman

ONE EMPLOYER'S STORY

The origins of the cash balance pension plan lend credence to the maxim "Necessity is the mother of invention." The cash balance plan concept was "invented" in the mid-1980s in response to a perceived need that could not be adequately met by more traditional retirement vehicles. The seeds were sown when Bank of America attempted to redress some of the shortcomings of its traditional retirement plan.

A Retirement Plan Dilemma

The Bank's final-average-pay, Social Security offset, defined benefit pension plan was like those of many other U.S. companies. It provided ample and secure benefits for its long-service employees and retirees but very little in the way of benefits to its younger, shorter-service workers, many of whom were unaware that the plan even existed. Those who were aware of it were indifferent to its promise of a future income equal to some percentage of future pay, starting at some time in the distant future. In fact, in one attitude survey 30 percent of the Bank's employees responded that they had so little understanding of the plan's complicated formula that they were incapable of expressing an opinion as to whether or not they were satisfied with the plan. That statistic alone spoke volumes for the plan's ineffectiveness as a people motivator, and clearly it did little to facilitate the Bank's efforts to attract and retain its mostly young, mobile work force. Equally troubling were certain other aspects of the Bank's traditional plan that had not kept pace with the Bank's changing objectives:

- The "blank check" design inherent in the plan's final-average-pay benefit formula resulted in fluctuating costs and liabilities that were escalating unpredictably.
- Generous incentives for early retirement and retiree cost-of-living increases were becoming too costly.
- The Social Security offset—subtracted directly from the gross benefit amount—was seen as a double-edged sword. Participants perceived it as a direct "takeaway," whereas the Bank recognized that a portion of any future reductions in Social Security benefits (or slowdown in their rate of growth) would have to be picked up by the plan.
- Employee misunderstanding and confusion were exacerbated by the fact that two key elements of the plan's benefit formula—the determination of final average pay and the amount of the Social Security offset—are unknown until actual retirement and are very difficult to predict.

Anticipated Improvements

After an exhaustive study, the Bank tentatively concluded that a defined contribution approach might, in principle, better address its needs because:

- The "age neutral" benefit accrual pattern of defined contribution plans, under which the amount of company contributions allocated to accounts each year is unrelated to age, would fit with the Bank's philosophical compensation objective of providing "equal pay for equal work, regardless of age." Such an accrual pattern would be far more appealing to younger employees, since plan benefits accrue at a more rapid pace in the earlier years of plan participation as compared to the more "backloaded" accrual patterns typically found in defined benefit plans.
- In contrast to the complex benefit formula contained in its traditional plan, a defined contribution formula would be straightforward and easy for employees to comprehend.
- Employees' appreciation of a defined contribution plan would be reinforced at regular intervals through periodic statements reflecting

contributions and earnings credited to their individual accounts since the last valuation date and their new balances at the end of the current valuation period.

- Defined contribution plans provide distributions upon termination of employment in the form of lump-sum cash distributions—a feature not usually seen in traditional defined benefit plans and one that holds great appeal to employees.

Reservations about the Change

In spite of these considerations, the Bank was nevertheless reluctant to abandon the defined benefit approach and switch to a defined contribution approach for the following reasons:

- Switching would result in older employees accruing less benefits as they approached retirement than if they had they continued participating in the defined benefit plan.
- No effective mechanism exists within a defined contribution framework to provide past service benefits, updated accrued benefits, or directly provide lifetime annuities—features of its existing plan the Bank considered vital.
- A defined contribution format transfers the investment risk to the employee. If the employee makes unwise investment elections or retires or terminates in a down market, or if the fund's managers achieve unsatisfactory results, the adequacy of the employee's retirement income could be jeopardized. The Bank was concerned that employees, having limited resources and a shorter "time horizon" than the Bank, might be ill-equipped to accept or handle this level of risk. (A 401(k) savings plan was already in place, which earmarked the Bank's match for investment in Bank stock.)
- Retirement benefit adequacy can also be undermined by preretirement withdrawals and, in contributory plans, by inadequate employee participation.
- Defined contribution plans lack funding flexibility. The Bank's existing defined benefit plan, on the other hand, allowed it to anticipate turnover, amortize gains and losses, and provide a range of contribution levels, thereby facilitating its ability to manage the incidence of cash costs.

A Decision Is Made

The Bank concluded that the ideal vehicle to satisfy its disparate needs would be an entirely new kind of plan that melded the best features of both a defined benefit plan and a defined contribution plan into a single plan. Thus the cash balance concept was born—the invention necessitated by the call for a more comprehensible retirement plan that would not sacrifice essential employee benefit security.

WHAT IS A CASH BALANCE PLAN?

How does a cash balance plan blend, within a single vehicle, the seemingly inconsistent characteristics of defined benefit and defined contribution plans? A cash balance plan is a defined benefit plan that, like all defined benefit plans, embodies a firm promise to pay a formula-determined benefit at retirement. However, it is designed to operate—and to be perceived by employees—like a defined contribution plan. So, instead of expressing the retirement benefit promise as a monthly pension that is a function of final or career-average pay or a flat dollar amount per year of service, it is expressed in terms of an individual account to which benefit dollars and interest are credited at predetermined rates. At any point in time, in effect, the account represents the present value of the underlying earned pension benefit. The plan typically works this way:

1. A "cash balance" account is established for each employee when he or she becomes a member of the plan. These accounts are not directly related to plan assets; they are merely a record-keeping device to keep track of and communicate the current lump-sum value of each participant's accrued pension benefit. If the plan is replacing an existing pension plan, an existing employee's initial account would consist of an "opening" balance, typically equal to the actuarial present value of his or her accrued prior plan benefits.

2. Typically, the employee's account balance would be updated each month thereafter to reflect additional employer-provided benefit credits. These are likely to be computed as a flat percentage, such as 4 percent or 5 percent, of the employee's pay; alternatively, such pay-based credits may be weighted to take into account age or years of service in order to skew the benefit in favor of older or longer-service employees. (Some hourly plans provide benefits that are independent of pay, such as $50 or $100 per month.) In addition, Social Security integration can be achieved by crediting a higher contribution rate on a portion of the employee's pay above a specified level. (Note that although such cash balance benefit credits are perceived as "employer contributions," they are unrelated to the amount the employer actually contributes to the plan.)

3. Employees' account balances are also credited with interest at a rate specified in the plan. However, the rate is not tied to the actual investment performance of the plan's assets and, in most cases, is related to some recognized outside index, such as the Consumer Price Index (CPI) or the yield on one-year Treasury bills. Since this rate usually varies from year to year, it generally is communicated to employees well before the start of the year.

4. Because it is qualified as a pension plan, withdrawals may not be made during employment.

5. The vesting schedule is in line with those of most individual account plans. In other words, vesting is at least as rapid as in a traditional pension plan. Vested employees who terminate usually may choose to receive an immediate distribution of their accounts in a lump sum, perhaps to be rolled over into an individual retirement account (IRA), or in the form of an annuity commencing immediately. Alternatively, terminating employees may elect to leave their balances in the plan, accruing interest credits, until retirement age.

6. Most cash balance plans provide a preretirement death benefit equal to the full account balance. Where the beneficiary is the spouse, the spouse typically has the choice between a lump-sum distribution equal in value to the account and a benefit in the form of an annuity that is the actuarial equivalent of the account.

7. At retirement, the accumulated balance is available as a lump sum or is convertible into any of a number of optional forms of annuity the plan makes available. Of course, the normal form of benefit for a married employee must be a "qualified joint and survivor annuity" unless spousal consent to an alternate benefit form is obtained.

An Example

Let's look at an example of how an employee's cash balance account grows over time. Table 36–1 exemplifies a typical pattern for a new employee earning $30,000. The plan provides 5 percent pay-based credits

TABLE 36–1
Cash Balance Example

Year	*Account Value (Beginning of Year)*	*Pay-Based Credit*	*Interest Credits**	*Account Value (End of Year)*
1	$ 0.00	$1,500.00	$ 52.50	$1,552.50
2	1,552.50	1,500.00	161.17	3,213.67
3	3,213.67	1,500.00	277.46	4,991.13
4	4,991.13	1,500.00	401.87	6,893.00
5	6,893.00	1,500.00	535.01	8,928.01

*Assuming credit based on midyear value of account.

and 7 percent interest credits. Note that after one year this employee has a $1,552 account balance. Further, after five years the account represents about 30 percent of pay, and the employee is probably fully vested at that point. Notice too the ''magic'' of the compound interest growth. In the first year the interest credit is only 3.5 percent of the pay-based credit, whereas by the fifth year it represents about 35 percent.

COMPARISON WITH TRADITIONAL PLANS

Let's examine a little more how cash balance plans combine within a single vehicle significant aspects of both defined contribution and defined benefit plans. From the defined contribution side, they incorporate a number of features with broad employee appeal:

- An easy-to-understand benefit formula.
- Individual accounts, the current value of which is communicated through periodic statements as a lump-sum cash amount.
- Payouts available in the form of lump-sum cash distributions or lifetime annuities.
- Rapid vesting.
- Benefit accruals that are ''age neutral.''

However, unlike defined contribution plans, cash balance plans retain certain inherent defined benefit advantages that are beneficial to both employers and employees:

- The ability to eliminate "takeaways" by continuing, as a grandfathered minimum, a preexisting plan's final-average-pay formula for employees near retirement.
- Dependable and secure income. (Accounts can never go down; they always increase at a specified rate.)
- The ability to provide past service benefits and benefit updates if necessary and affordable.
- Funding flexibility. The plan is funded on an actuarial basis, which allows the employer to contribute any cash amount within the usual Internal Revenue Service (IRS) minimum and maximum deductible contribution limits. (Expensing under Financial Accounting Standards Board [FASB] rules is equally flexible. In fact, many traditional plans enjoy a cash contribution holiday after conversion, and pension income often will be generated.)
- Benefits are guaranteed—implicitly by the minimum funding requirements of the Employee Retirement Income Security Act (ERISA) and explicitly by the Pension Benefit Guaranty Corporation (PBGC).
- Attractive annuity options, such that if an employee wants a life annuity there is no need to take the account outside the plan to an insurer, where selling expenses and profit margins would make the same annuity benefit more costly.
- The shielding of participants from investment risk.
- The employer bears the investment risk but retains the ability to formulate a risk/reward investment policy for plan assets consistent with its own objectives.

Since its inception six years ago, the cash balance concept has grown by leaps and bounds. Today, the concept is embraced by well over one hundred plan sponsors, many of them "Fortune 500" companies. Close to one million employees already participate in such plans. This rapid growth in only six years is probably due to the fact that they offer tangible "rewards" to both employers and employees.

The Employee's Perspective

From the employee's perspective, a typical cash balance plan looks like a money purchase pension plan under which the employer contributes a fixed percentage of payroll and the interest rate appears roughly comparable to what might be obtained in a fixed-income investment such as a guaranteed investment contract (GIC). (A key difference is that unlike a GIC, the plan's specified interest rate is a guarantee that extends, not just for one, three, or five years, but for as long as the employee remains a plan participant.) Thus, the employee perceives his or her benefit to be an individual account the current value of which is expressed understandably as an ever-increasing lump-sum cash amount. And since the annual credits to the employee's account typically are stated in terms of a fixed percentage of compensation, growth of account values mimics the age-neutral accrual pattern characteristic of defined contribution plans.

Contrast this pattern with traditional final-average-pay pension plans, which target relatively more financial firepower on older employees and those who stay until retirement. Under such plans, employees of different ages with equal pay typically appear to accrue the same benefit; that is, the same amount of normal retirement annuity income for a given year of service. Actually, however, because the money set aside on behalf of a younger employee will earn interest far longer than it will for an older employee, less is actually required to be set aside on his or her behalf to provide this same pension benefit at normal retirement age. In addition, the prior service benefits already earned under a final-average-pay plan automatically increase each year in line with increases in the average salary upon which pension benefits are based. For these reasons, younger employees have less dollar value "put away" for them under traditional plans than do their older co-workers. For example, in a typical final-average-pay plan, the value of the identical incremental pension benefit earned by an employee aged 60 could be expected to be more than 10 times that of an employee aged 35!

Thus, compared to the traditional pension plan, the cash balance approach is relatively more generous to younger employees and employees who terminate earlier in their careers. (This is a fairness issue with which the employer must be comfortable, and many have concluded that the pluses of cash balance are well worth this investment. In truth, most have already crossed this bridge philosophically by providing level accruals under their savings plans.) The graph in Figure 36–1 illustrates these differences by comparing the annual cost at various ages, as a percentage of current pay, of providing an equivalent pension benefit commencing at age 65 under a typical cash balance plan and a typical final-average-pay plan.

Like a money purchase plan, a cash balance plan typically would offer a choice of distribution in the form of a lump sum or an annuity. (The latter

FIGURE 36–1

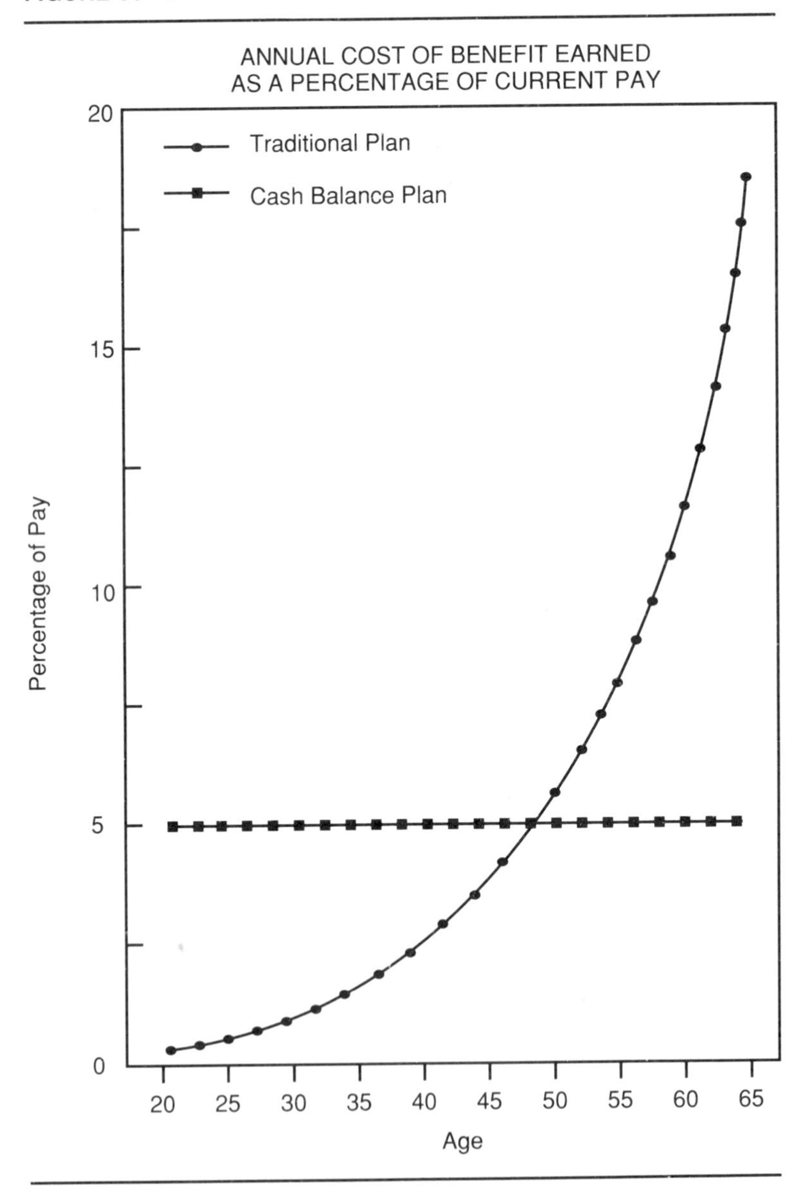

choice is, of course, a legal requirement.) If the employee is 100% vested upon termination, the lump-sum amount is equal to the current value of his or her cash balance account, whereas if the participant chooses an annuity form of distribution, the annuity amount is the actuarial equivalent of the account balance.

The Employer's Perspective

As noted, from the employee's perspective the cash balance plan looks more like a defined contribution plan than it does like a traditional defined benefit pension plan. From the employer's perspective, on the other hand, things look quite different. Since the plan is in actuality a defined benefit plan that is actuarially funded on an aggregate basis, participant "accounts" are merely a record-keeping device and not directly related to the underlying assets of the plan. Similarly, the investment earnings of the trust are unrelated to the predetermined rate of interest credited to the accounts as specified in the plan. Thus, the employer bears the investment risk (and reward) and may experience fluctuating costs as a result, although such fluctuation usually will be significantly less than in a traditional plan.

Over the long run, however, since most cash balance plans credit an interest rate roughly equivalent to a one-year Treasury bill rate, in those situations the actual earnings of the trust can be expected to exceed the predetermined rate specified in the plan to be credited to participant accounts. Thus, the employer's cost, though more volatile, typically will be lower than the corresponding cost under a money purchase plan with an investment return equivalent to the cash balance plan's predetermined interest rate. (The converse would argue that employee account balances could be greater under a money purchase plan for the same employer cost, but the trade-off is the employer's assumption of the investment and mortality risks under a cash balance plan.) In the unlikely event that poor investment experience by the employer would result in the actual earnings of the trust failing to keep up with the predetermined interest rate specified in the plan, employees' accounts would nevertheless grow by the predetermined interest rate. The employer will gradually absorb such loss, typically on an amortized basis.

In practice, the fact that there is no direct connection between the interest rate credited to employee accounts and the actual return on the plan's underlying assets can work to the employer's advantage. It can enable the employer to invest for the long run, thereby increasing the plan's potential to earn a rate of return on plan assets in excess of the plan's predetermined interest rate. The amount of this anticipated excess, known as the *investment differential,* permits an employer to fund the plan on a discounted basis—the discount reflecting anticipated differences between the plan's actual long-term investment experience and the plan's specified interest rate. This can have the effect of significantly reducing plan costs. For example, a "5 percent of pay plan" might require a contribution of perhaps only 4 percent of pay, after a realistic investment differential reflecting anticipated investment policy is taken into account. Discounting for anticipated turnover prior to vesting would further reduce the cost, perhaps to 3.5 percent of pay. Of course, if the anticipated investment differential fails to materialize, the employer's cost as a percentage of pay gradually will rise (which is also what happens in a traditional pension plan when the actuarial assumptions are not realized).

Employees as well as their employer can benefit from this arrangement—employees by receiving the guaranteed return specified in the plan document; the employer by retaining the investment potential to earn a greater actual return. (As noted, most plans so far have guaranteed a one-year Treasury bill rate, which historically has exceeded the inflation rate by .5 percent to 1 percent.) This arrangement usually is considered as an appropriate trade-off, given employees' natural aversion to risk where their retirement income is concerned and the plan's relatively long-term horizon. In addition, to the extent that investment returns are favorable and employer costs decrease, employers can opt to share the savings with employees in the form of account adjustments or other plan enhancements.

PLAN FUNDING

Because cash balance plans are qualified as defined benefit plans, they are subject to the generally applicable defined benefit plan funding rules. Accordingly, contributions are actuarially determined, thereby providing flexibility as to both the timing and amount of contributions. For example:

- A range of funding methods is available. Turnover and other expected experience under the plan (including the investment differential discussion, above) can be anticipated and discounted for in advance, and gains or losses that arise can be amortized.
- Subject to legal limitations as to minimum and maximum contributions, employers can vary the amount of funding from year to year.

- If a plan is overfunded, no cash outlay may be required (or even allowed) until the overfunding is eliminated.
- Employers in temporary difficulty can use a ''funding waiver'' to defer a contribution without immediate consequences to employees who can continue to accrue benefits under the plan.

CONVERSION OF AN EXISTING PLAN

Conversion of a traditional pension plan to a cash balance plan is accomplished by amendment; no plan termination is required. However, because the plan amendment cannot by law result in a decrease in any employee's previously accrued benefit, the first step in the transition process typically involves the conversion of the pension benefits already accrued as of the date of transition into a lump-sum equivalent amount, which becomes the initial ''opening'' account balance. (If the opening balance is not so determined, the anti-accrued-benefit-cut-back rule must be tested when the employee subsequently terminates employment.)

One problem that invariably must be addressed in the conversion process is that of keeping ''whole'' certain employees who might otherwise be adversely affected by the changeover. In other words, unless special provision is made for such employees, a cash balance conversion might mean lower benefits at retirement than would have been provided by the preexisting plan had it remained in effect. One group generally needing such protection is older employees who will be retiring in the next several years. They will henceforth be receiving the *same* annual incremental benefit values as younger employees (instead of 10–20 times greater values as under the prior plan) but will not benefit from the longer duration of compounding of interest that will inure to the younger employees under the new cash balance plan.

Similarly, potential benefit shortfalls incident to the transition are also often felt by midcareer employees (ages 45–54), who have neither the benefit of higher cash balance accruals in the past nor the expectation of receiving the higher accruals at the older ages that they would have received had the old plan remained in place. An employer looking at the younger part of this age spectrum generally will face the difficult philosophical question of how much (if any) of the projected pension ''promise'' under the old plan should be preserved for employees who have many years of future service remaining.

Probably the most common means of dealing with these issues, particularly in the case of older employees, is through the mechanism of ''grandfathering''; that is, providing that their benefits will in no event be less than if the preexisting plan had remained unchanged. This involves the administrative headache of running two plans—the old and the new—for several years, but many employers have concluded that such an ironclad guarantee is worth the added administrative work involved.

Other common approaches to dealing with potential benefit shortfalls include:

- Subsidizing the opening balance. This might involve computing the initial balance using a somewhat lower interest discount rate, a mortality table that reflects a longer life expectancy, or in plans that subsidized early retirement, an average retirement age (such as age 62) rather than normal retirement age (age 65). Alternative approaches along the same lines would be to provide a minimum opening balance equal to (1) what the balance would have been had the cash balance plan been in effect in the past (that is, an enhanced ''retrospective'' transition opening balance) or (2) an enhanced ''prospective'' opening balance equal to the present value of any difference between old-plan and new-plan benefits projected to retirement date. In either case, appropriate measures should be taken to prevent windfalls for employees who terminate before reaching retirement. One approach often used to address this concern is to attach an ''earn out'' provision to these enhanced benefits.
- Use of so-called transitional credits; that is, supplementary additional future-service credits, in addition to the regular pay-based credits, for older, longer-service employees. For example, if the regular annual cash balance credits are 5 percent of pay, affected employees might receive an extra 5 percent, or 10 percent in total. Along the same lines, the amount of the supplementary credits could vary based on a ''point criterion'' (age plus service) at date of conversion, or some other sliding scale, so as to more accurately target anticipated benefit shortfalls. In such a case the formula for determining the varying amount of the supplementation typically would be calculated by reference to a comparison of the old- and new-plan benefits projected to retirement and designing a supplemental credit stream such that it will bridge any undesirable shortfalls. Employers utilizing this approach have run the gamut from a simple, ''smoothed'' table of supplemental credits appli-

cable to all, to individually computed supplemental credits (different for each employee).

• Enhancing the savings plan's company-matching contribution. This offers all employees, including those who might otherwise experience a retirement shortfall, the opportunity to add to their retirement income.

LEGAL CONSIDERATIONS

Since cash balance plans are qualified under the Internal Revenue Code as defined benefit pension plans, they are subject to the same qualification requirements as other such plans, including:

- Minimum participation rules that limit the age and service requirements an employer can impose as a condition of participation in the plan.
- Coverage and nondiscrimination rules designed to prevent the plan from discriminating in favor of highly compensated employees.
- Vesting rules, which limit the period of required service before an employee earns or becomes entitled to a nonforfeitable benefit under the plan.
- Accrual rules, which limit the extent to which a plan may "backload" benefit accruals.
- Rules limiting the amount of contributions and benefits that may be provided through qualified plans on behalf of plan participants.
- Minimum funding rules designed to ensure the solvency of defined benefit pension plans.
- Minimum distribution rules that govern the timing, duration, and form of benefit payments.

In addition, in common with other defined benefit plans, cash balance plans are subject to ERISA, including the reporting and disclosure requirements of Part 1 of Title I of ERISA, the fiduciary-responsibility provisions of Part 4 of Title I of ERISA, and the plan termination insurance provisions of Title IV of ERISA.

Note, however, that applicable law has evolved over the years with traditional defined benefit plans, not cash balance plans, in mind. Despite this, the IRS apparently is predisposed to looking favorably on the cash balance concept as evidenced by the fact that many cash balance plans have received favorable determination letters with respect to their compliance with the pre–Tax Reform Act of 1986 (TRA '86) law (the law as in effect before plan years beginning in 1989).

Without a doubt, the most sweeping changes brought about by tax reform in the qualified-plan area are the new, greatly expanded nondiscrimination rules incorporated in the regulations under IRC Section 401(a)(4). As a general rule, plans may meet these new requirements in one of two ways. The first is by satisfying a design-based safe harbor. Although the final regulations include a cash balance safe harbor, it applies only to "plain vanilla" cash balance plans; that is, plans that are not integrated and under which current accruals are not affected by age, service, or transitional or grandfather provisions.

The alternative path to compliance, the so-called general test, involves the calculation of benefit accrual rates for each participant and a comparison of relative coverage at each rate by the highly compensated and nonhighly compensated employees. Cash balance plans typically provide relatively greater benefits during an employee's early years than do traditional defined benefit plans, and since younger employees usually earn less than older employees, in most cases cash balance plans can be expected to demonstrate compliance under the general test with greater ease than more traditional plans.

CONCLUSION

Does the proliferation of the cash balance concept in the few short years since its inception signal a turning point in the evolution of pension plan design? Or is cash balance nothing more than a passing fad? Although the evidence is not yet conclusive, one thing is known for sure. The cash balance plans adopted so far have been received with enthusiasm both by plan sponsors adopting them and employees participating in them, and more and more employers are looking closely at the concept.

CHAPTER 37

INDIVIDUAL RETIREMENT ARRANGEMENTS (IRAs), SIMPLIFIED EMPLOYEE PENSIONS (SEPs) AND HR-10 (KEOGH) PLANS

Ernest L. Martin
*William H. Rabel**

By the end of 1989, American workers had a total of $493.7 billion invested in individual retirement arrangements (IRAs), simplified employee pensions (SEPs), and HR-10 (Keogh) plans. The combined assets of these retirement vehicles for individuals and the self-employed had more than doubled since 1985 ($230.4 billion).[1] The sheer magnitude of this investment is indicative of the scope of the plans. While the Tax Reform Act of 1986 (TRA '86) has, as many had predicted, slowed the rate of growth in both total assets of and individual participation in these plans, the fact remains that IRAs, SEPs, and Keogh plans remain the primary vehicles by which individuals not covered by corporate pension plans and the unincorporated self-employed can take advantage of tax-favored status to provide for retirement income.

---

*The authors wish to acknowledge the assistance of Dan J. Fitzgerrell, Director, Pension Operations, the Principal Financial Group, while retaining sole responsibility for any errors or omissions.

[1] *Employee Benefit Notes*, Employee Benefit Research Institute, Washington, D.C., vol. 11, no. 7 (July 1990), pp. 3–4.

This chapter will trace briefly the backgrounds and discuss the features of IRAs, SEPs, and Keogh plans. It also will provide, at its conclusion, information regarding the distribution of assets of these plans by financial institutions and discuss participation patterns and the legislative environment of the plans.

INDIVIDUAL RETIREMENT ACCOUNTS

At the beginning of the 1970s, substantial numbers of American workers were covered by private pension plans. One important sector of the labor force, however, still was not receiving the benefits of a federal income tax policy that had fostered the growth of qualified plans. This sector, comprising employees of companies without pension plans was forced to rely on accumulated after-tax savings to provide for future retirement income. Furthermore, unlike those covered by qualified plans, individuals in this sector were required to pay income taxes on the annual earnings of their after-tax retirement savings.[2] Thus, such individuals found it doubly difficult to accumulate funds for their future retirement.

In 1974, Congress enacted the Employee Retirement Income Security Act (ERISA), which profoundly affected the pension field. This act, as modified by subsequent legislation, provided in part that an individual could make an annual tax-deductible contribution of 100 percent of personal service compensation up to $2,000 to an individual retirement arrangement. Contributions for spouses to a spousal IRA and the availability of benefits to spouses also were made possible, as described later in this chapter. The funds in the account accumulate on a tax-free basis until the individual retires and begins to receive distributions. Provided distributions begin within the authorized age period, withdrawals are taxed as ordinary income in the year that they are received. Since 1979, employers have been allowed to set up simplified employee pension plans for their employees. These plans use IRAs as a funding instrument and are subject to certain special requirements.

---

[2]Tax-exempt investments, of course, would be an exception to this rule.

Eligibility

Initially, IRAs were created for the employee aged 70½ years or less who was not an active participant in a qualified employer-sponsored pension plan. Today, workers in this age range who are covered by a qualified plan can still make tax-deductible contributions to an IRA, but only if earnings fall below certain amounts, as described later in this chapter.

From 1981 through 1986, the eligibility requirements were broader and included anyone under age 70½ receiving personal service compensation, without regard to participation in a qualified plan and without regard to the amount of received compensation. During this period, which also coincided with a relatively high level of interest rates and inflation, many Americans set up IRAs.

Deductible Contributions

The portion of the population that could make tax-deductible contributions to an IRA was narrowed by income limitations built into TRA '86. Congress felt that the Act's lower tax rates fostered a reasonable level of after-tax savings.

Individuals under age 70½ who are not covered by a qualified employer plan (defined below) may make annual deductible contributions up to $2,000 or 100 percent of compensation, whichever is less. For the purpose of determining the maximum annual contribution an eligible individual can make to an IRA, compensation is held to include any payment received for rendering personal service, such as salaries, wages, commissions, tips, fees, and bonuses. Since 1984, it also has included all taxable alimony and separate maintenance payments received under a decree of divorce. Investment income and capital gains cannot be included in the calculation of compensation for IRA contribution purposes. Moreover, although a community-property state regards one half of a spouse's income as belonging to the other spouse, the non-working spouse cannot count this amount for purposes of determining compensation.

The deductibility of contributions for individuals who are active participants in a retirement plan maintained by their employers, or for married couples filing jointly where either spouse is covered by a qualified plan, is summarized in Table 37–1.

TABLE 37–1
Deductibility of IRA Contributions for Taxpayers Covered by a Qualified Plan

Taxpayer Status	*Maximum Adjusted Gross Income for Fully Deductible Contribution*	*Phaseout Range*
Single	$25,000	$25,001–$35,000
Married/joint	40,000	40,001–$50,000
Married/separate	0	1–$10,000

Workers covered by an employer plan who have an adjusted gross income of $25,000 or less ($40,000 if married and filing jointly) receive the full deduction for contributions up to $2,000.

For individuals earning $25,000–$35,000 ($40,000–$50,000 for couples filing jointly), deductions will be reduced proportionately as income increases within the $10,000 spread that is shown. Thus, if an unmarried individual earns $26,000, his or her deductible contributions will decrease by $200 to $1,800 ($26,000 − $25,000 = $1,000; $1,000 = 10 percent of $10,000; 10 percent of $2,000 = $200). Workers covered by a qualified plan and whose adjusted gross income exceeds $35,000 ($50,000 for married couples filing jointly) do not receive a tax deduction for contributions.

Married people filing separately will have proportionate reductions in their IRA deductions between zero and $10,000 of income. Such a person earning $4,000 would be able to deduct up to $1,200 (40 percent of $2,000 = $800; $2,000 − $800 = $1,200).

Contributions may be attributed to a calendar year if they are made by the April 15 deadline for filing a tax return in the following year. This provision prevents the taxpayer from having to guess what his or her earnings will be before the end of the tax year.

An *employer-maintained retirement plan* is defined as: one that receives favorable tax treatment under Internal Revenue Code Section 401(a); an annuity qualified under 403(a); a simplified employee pension; a plan of the United States Government (or any political subdivision or government agency or instrumentality); a plan qualified under 501(c)(18); or a tax-sheltered annuity under 403(b). An *active participant* in a *defined contribution qualified plan* generally is one for whom any contribution is made or forfeiture reallocated during the year, or for whom any contribution is required to be made, whether actually made or not. In a *defined benefit plan,* an active participant is one who is not excluded under the plan's eligibility requirements at any time during the plan year ending with or within the individual's taxable year.

A working spouse with an IRA can set up a separate IRA (called a spousal IRA) for a spouse who is not working or who earns little and elects to be treated as not earning compensation for the year. The maximum combined contribution to the two accounts is limited to the lesser of $2,250 or 100 percent of personal service compensation. To receive a deduction for the spousal contribution, the husband and wife must file a joint tax return. Contributions may be split in any way as long as no more than $2,000 is paid into either account. If a nonworking spouse begins to work, the spousal account then becomes a regular account and the spouse may contribute to it 100 percent of compensation up to $2,000 for that year. Contributions to spousal accounts must cease by the year the elder spouse reaches age 70½. However, if the younger spouse continues to be eligible otherwise, he or she may establish a new IRA and contribute to it until the year in which he or she reaches age 70½.

A divorced spouse with a spousal IRA (or one separated under a decree of separate maintenance) can continue to make deductible contributions to the spousal IRA. The contributions are limited to the lesser of $1,125 or the sum of the spouse's compensation and taxable alimony. Also, the spousal IRA must have been established for at least five years prior to the calendar year of the divorce, and the ex-spouse must have made contributions in at least three of the previous five years.

The tax penalty for contributions in excess of the allowable amount for a year is 6 percent of the excess. The tax penalty continues to apply year after year to excess contributions and earnings on those excess contributions until they are removed from the account. The tax penalty is not deductible.

The penalty for excess contributions may be avoided under any one of three conditions. First, the amount of excess contributions and any earnings on them may be withdrawn before the individual's federal income tax return is filed for the year when the excess contribution is made. Earnings on the excess contributions must be treated as taxable income for the year the contribution was made. Second, excess contributions made in a preceding year subsequently may be applied to years when an employee's contributions are less than the maximum permitted. Third, if the excess contribution is made based on erroneous information supplied by a financial institution and accepted in good faith, the excess may be withdrawn at any time.

As discussed in greater detail below, IRAs may be funded through trust or custodial agreements, or through annuity contracts sold by life insurance companies.[3] For a contract to qualify under the tax code, it must meet several stipulations. First, the contract must not be transferable. Second, premiums must not be fixed and must have a ceiling of $2,000. Third, policy dividends must be applied to the next year's premium or used to purchase additional benefits. Fourth, IRA assets may not be invested in life insurance contracts. And, finally, the entire interest of the owner must be nonforfeitable.

Nondeductible Contributions

Individuals may make nondeductible contributions to an IRA, irrespective of their income. The annual limit on the combination of deductible and nondeductible contributions is 100 percent of personal service income, up to $2,000 (or $2,250 where contributions are made to a spousal IRA) per year. Earnings accumulate tax-free until they are withdrawn, at which time they are treated as normal IRA retirement benefits. That portion of withdrawals representing nondeductible contributions is, of course, not taxed on withdrawal.

It may be in the taxpayer's interest to treat otherwise-deductible IRA contributions as nondeductible under certain circumstances; such treatment is permissible under the law. For example, a tax deduction would not be of value in a year when the individual had no taxable income, even though he or she received personal service compensation.

The taxpayer must report nondeductible contributions for the year when they are made. In addition, the following information must also be reported: (1) any distributions from an IRA; (2) the amount by which (*a*) total nondeductible contributions for all preceding years exceeds (*b*) the total distributions from IRAs that were excludable from gross income for such years; (3) the total balance of all IRAs owned by an individual as of the close of the calendar year in which the tax year ends; and (4) such other information as required by the Secretary of the Treasury.

---

[3]Prior to November 6, 1978, endowment contracts could be purchased to fund IRAs. However, this no longer is permitted. Although some IRAs funded by endowments undoubtedly remain in force, they will not be discussed in this chapter except to note that the cost of insurance is not deductible.

Excess contributions are subject to a 6 percent excise tax. If the amount of the contribution is overstated, the taxpayer is subject to a $100 penalty.

Because nondeductible contributions trigger burdensome reporting requirements, some experts recommend that such savings be funneled into an annuity rather than an IRA. Annuities share the advantage of tax deferral on earnings until the payment period, and there are no limitations on contributions. However, an individual also needs to consider differences in investment return or risk in weighing the alternatives.

Rollovers

The law permits a tax-free transfer of assets from one IRA to another. These so-called rollovers also are permitted from the following types of plans into an IRA: (1) pension and profit-sharing plans qualifying under Section 401(a) of the Internal Revenue Code (IRC), (2) tax-deferred annuities meeting the requirements of Section 403(b), and (3) bond-purchase plans that are no longer offered but may still be in effect after having been started under now-repealed Section 405 of the Internal Revenue Code. Also, proceeds received as a distribution from a qualified plan because of the death of a spouse can be rolled over tax-free into an IRA. Rollovers provide an element of flexibility that fosters investment, administrative, and other benefits arising from consolidation.

Every IRA-to-IRA rollover must meet two major requirements in addition to several other less important ones. First, an individual is limited to only one tax-free rollover per IRA in any one year. However, it is worth noting that it is possible to make a direct transfer of funds from one funding agency to another without being considered to have made a rollover subject to the one-year restriction. Second, the rollover must take place within 60 days after the distribution is made. Any funds withdrawn but not rolled over are treated as a premature distribution, as described below. However, TRA '86 extends the period for deposits that are frozen in a financially distressed financial institution until 10 days after funds become available. Either whole or partial rollovers may be made, and the owner must notify the funding agency that a rollover is being effected. Funds from a regular IRA may not be rolled over into a qualified plan, although the reverse is not true.

Three tests must be met when an individual is rolling over money or other property from a plan qualified under Section 401(a) into an IRA. First, only employer contributions or deductible qualified voluntary employee contributions (discontinued under TRA '86) may be rolled over. If nondeductible employee contributions are rolled over, they shall be treated as excess contributions and subjected to the penalties discussed above. Second, the rollover must be completed within 60 days. Third, the distribution must be made because the employee is separated from service, has reached age 59½, or has died or become disabled, or because the plan has been terminated. Unlike IRA-to-IRA rollovers, there is no limit of one transfer per year.

Under certain circumstances partial rollovers are permitted from employer plans. The amount rolled over must consist of at least 50 percent of the balance and must be due to separation from service, disability, or a person's being the beneficiary of a death benefit when a spouse dies. However, unlike other distributions, death benefits rolled over into an IRA may not subsequently be rolled over into a qualified plan.

Whether a partial or a total rollover of assets has been made from a qualified corporate or Keogh plan into an IRA, assets may then be rolled over again into the qualified plan of a subsequent employer; however, such a "rerollover" is allowable only if it is permitted by the subsequent employer's plan and if the assets of the IRA consist solely of the assets from the first qualified plan and earnings on those assets. The individual should not contribute to an IRA that is set up as a conduit between two qualified plans. Rather, to keep from losing favorable tax treatment, he or she should set up a second IRA for his or her contributions.

Rollover amounts may not be deposited in a spouse's IRA except when resulting from the taxpayer's death.

Assets rolled over into an IRA from a tax-sheltered annuity can be rerolled over into another tax-sheltered annuity.

Funding Agencies and Investments

Individuals have a large degree of freedom in the way they allocate their contributions in any particular year among the various financial institutions that offer IRAs. In addition, the amount allocated to any given institution need not remain fixed—the entire contribution may go to one plan in one year, and then be shifted to another plan the next year.

Among the financial institutions offering IRAs are commercial banks, savings and loan institutions, brokerage firms, mutual fund management companies, credit unions, life insurance companies, and companies that offer a broad variety of financial services. Accounts may be so arranged that the owner may make all investment decisions, or such decisions may be turned over completely to a financial institution.

Self-Directed Accounts

Where the individual decides to make all investment decisions, a self-directed retirement trust is set up. A corporate trustee is selected to take charge of all assets and to ensure that the activities of the account conform to the rules of the law. In some cases, the corporate trustee is directly connected with the financial institution through which the IRA is marketed. Alternatively, the services of a single independent trustee may be marketed by one or more brokerage or other financial services firms or both. These firms link up with a trustee in the belief they can serve their clientele more effectively by staying in their particular field, and by recommending another organization to provide services that clients need. Such an arrangement is not devoid of benefits for the firm recommending the trustee. Investments of the trust may bring to it brokerage or underwriting fees, or both. The trust also engenders a certain amount of goodwill, which may enhance other business relationships between the trustee and the firm that markets its services.

Normally, the trustee charges the grantor (contributor to the IRA) three types of fees. The first is an acceptance fee, a flat charge to cover the expense of setting up the trust. For example, such a fee might be $35 for the grantor and $5 for a spousal account. The second fee is an annual charge expressed as a percentage of the assets in the trust, subject to a minimum amount. For example, a fee might be 0.0015 of the first $100,000 and 0.0010 of any amount over that, subject to a minimum charge of $35 for the grantor's account and $5 for the spousal account. Finally, charges may be levied for services, such as certain processing activities, statements, returned checks, disbursements, terminations, and the like.

Self-directed trusts have provided great investment latitude since IRAs first were introduced, and, as a matter of practice, grantors have invested in all types of assets, including securities, commodities, debt instruments, real property, and personal property. However, after 1981, grantors have had less flexibility. Assets in an IRA may no longer be invested in collectibles, including works of art, rugs, antiques, metals, gems, stamps, alcoholic beverages, or other items of tangible personal property specified by the IRS. TRA '86 provided some relief to "gold bugs" and "hard money" advocates by permitting investments in legal tender gold and silver coins minted by the U.S. Treasury.

Single-Institution Trust or Custodial Accounts

Many persons setting up an IRA do not want to actively manage the assets in the account. Instead, they prefer to invest them with a particular financial institution such as a bank, a broker, or a savings and loan institution. The customer chooses from among the investment options offered by the institution—for example, various types of accounts, certificates of deposit, and investment funds—according to his or her belief as to what will offer the greatest rate of return or least risk in the long run.

In response to the desire of customers for a single-institution approach, financial institutions of all types have developed trust or custodial accounts. Although some technical distinctions exist between the trust and custodial approaches, from the purchaser's standpoint these differences are inconsequential in terms of cost or service.[4] For purposes of simplicity, and to help distinguish them from self-directed trusts, all such accounts will be called "custodial accounts." The institution with which funds are invested will be called the "custodian." However, this simplification of terms should not be construed as implying that all institutions are equally attractive—the customer should shop as carefully for an IRA as for any other product.

Just as there is a wide variety of financial institutions offering single-institution accounts, there is a wide variety of charges. Many deposit institutions, such as banks and savings and loan institutions, do not assess a direct charge for setting up an IRA. They operate under the philosophy that this is a way to attract funds and that costs will be covered by the margin between the rate of interest earned by the institution and what is credited to the IRA. Other institutions levy charges that are similar to those employed with self-directed trusts. Also, some investments, such as mutual funds and annuities, may contain a specific sales load in addition to certain ongoing charges for managing the assets in the portfolio.

Insured Plans

Traditionally, premiums for annuity contracts were commingled with other funds accumulated over various periods. They were invested in the general account of the life insurance company, which guarantees a

---

[4]Institutions providing these accounts may adopt model forms provided by the Treasury Department (No. 5305 for trusts and No. 5305A for custodial accounts), or request a letter of opinion concerning the acceptability of their own prototype master form. Many institutions have chosen the latter approach.

minimum rate of return and assumes the full investment risk. Because interest rates were comparatively stable for most of the 20th century, consumer savings were not considered "hot money," which moved rapidly among investment alternatives seeking the highest rate of return. Insurers made long-term investments and remained competitive in the market for savings as well as for protection.

The traditional practice of commingling funds received in different periods works very well in a stable financial environment. However, in periods of rising inflation, policies designed as savings vehicles find it difficult to compete favorably because rates of return on new investments rise more rapidly than the rates of return on the entire portfolio. The reverse holds true in the case of deflation, of course, but savers throughout the world have grown cynical about the possibility that prices will stabilize, much less decline, in the foreseeable future. Therefore, instead of settling for a long-run rate of return, they have demanded products reflecting current market rates of return, and financial institutions, including life insurance companies, have responded.

Life insurance company annuity products that were developed for the IRA market offer a wide range of investment options and guarantees. Most still offer a minimum rate of return over the life of the contract, in which case the insurer must balance maturities in the portfolio to be able to meet guarantees and, at the same time, stay competitive with other financial institutions offering current market rates. Some contracts (e.g., some of those invested in equities) offer no investment guarantees at all, thus shifting the investment risk to the policy owner. Premiums from such contracts are invested to gain a rate of return that is competitive in the market the insurer wishes to penetrate, and the policy owners may be offered a variety of investment portfolios from which to choose. Often the policy provides that new premiums and existing funds may be shifted from one portfolio to another. In effect, an annuity policy that does not guarantee a rate of return can be compared to a mutual fund that offers a guaranteed annuity option at a given date.

Typically, three types of charges are associated with insured IRAs.[5] First are those that vary as a percentage of the premium. The most prominent of these is the sales charge, designed to cover the agent's commis-

[5]Those IRAs still extant that are funded by policies containing an element of life insurance protection (e.g., endowment contracts) also contain a charge for the mortality risk.

sion. It is worth noting that many companies now market annuities having no sales load. A second charge, a fixed amount per annum, is designed to cover the expenses of putting the policy on the company's books and maintaining the policy. The final type of charge is designed to cover the cost of investing funds. It is expressed as a percentage of the assets, subject to a minimum amount.

DISTRIBUTIONS

Distributions from an IRA are subject to penalties if they begin before the owner attains age 59½ (with the exception of death or disability), or later than April 1 of the calendar year following the year in which the owner attains age 70½ (hereinafter referred to as age 70½). Distributions must begin after the latter date whether the owner has actually retired or not. All distributions, except those representing nondeductible contributions, are taxable as ordinary income in the year they are received. The form the distributions take varies somewhat with the type of financial institution through which they are funded.

The individual's interest in an IRA may be distributed in a lump sum or, alternatively, may be paid over (*a*) the individual's remaining lifetime; (*b*) the lives of the individual and designated beneficiary; (*c*) a period not extending beyond the life expectancy of the individual; or (*d*) a period not extending beyond the joint life expectancy of the individual and designated beneficiary.

If the individual's designated beneficiary is other than the spouse, then the amount of the periodic distribution must meet the following test: The present value of the distributions projected to be made to the participant, while living, must be more than 50 percent of the present value of the amounts projected to be made to the participant and the designated beneficiary. The purpose of this rule is to ensure that the plan exists to benefit the worker, rather than the worker's beneficiary.

Trust or Custodial Accounts

The distribution options are identical for both self-directed and single-institution IRAs. The first approach is the single-sum distribution, whereby the account owner receives all contributions and the interest earned on them in one payment. However, a single-sum distribution may have unfavorable consequences for the individual's tax liability and postretirement financial security. Because of the progressive nature of income tax rates, a single distribution of any size could subject the depositor to a much higher tax bill than would result from a series of smaller distributions.

In most cases, it is advisable for the individual to at least begin with the second approach, the period certain option, which allows the distribution of benefits to be made in a series of payments. These disbursements may be spread out over a period that may not exceed the distribution timing described above. If the depositor chooses, the payments may be received over a shorter time. The limitation on the distribution period, when coupled with the requirement that the depositor begin to receive distributions not later than age 70½, in effect prevents a depositor from using an IRA as a mere tax shelter for investments, rather than as a means of providing for retirement income.

If the depositor dies *after* distribution from the account has begun, the balance of the account must be distributed to the beneficiary at least as rapidly as the rate that the depositor had selected. With three exceptions, if the depositor dies *before* distribution has started, the balance must be distributed within five years of the depositor's death. The first exception is that a beneficiary may elect to take payments in substantially equal installments for a period of up to his or her life expectancy. In this case, payments must begin within one year after the depositor's death. The second and third exceptions relate to surviving spouses who are beneficiaries. In such a case, the spouse may elect not to receive the distribution until the date when the depositor would have reached age 70½. (If the surviving spouse dies in the meantime, payments to a subsequent beneficiary are treated as though the spouse were the depositor.) Or under the third exception, the surviving spouse can treat the balance as his or her own IRA, subject to the regular IRA distribution requirements.

Typically, custodians make several payment intervals available for election by depositors—including monthly, quarterly, semiannually, or annually—thus accommodating the budgetary needs of most retired persons.

Usually, one associates retirement benefits with the concept of a lifelong pension. However, only a life insurance company can offer payments for a lifetime, through the mechanism of a life annuity contract. Such lifetime payments cannot be offered by a bank, a savings and loan institution, or any other thrift institution. Indeed, under the life-expectancy distribution option of a custodial account, it would not be at all unusual for an individual to outlive the life expectancy established for an IRA account and thus to exhaust the funds. After all, life expectancy is only an average figure. To provide life income annuity options to their depositors, some custodians have established arrangements with one or more life insurance companies, under which immediate life annuities may be purchased by depositors at retirement, using custodial account funds. This arrangement allows a depositor to avoid tax complications by utilizing the rollover provisions previously described. Although such an annuity purchase does not provide the depositor with a guarantee of annuity rates during the period when contributions to an IRA are being made, as an insured plan would have, this limitation may possibly be offset by the increased investment flexibility provided during the accumulation period by the noninsured IRA.

Insured Plans

The individual annuity contracts issued by insurers to fund IRAs provide that at retirement (normally between ages 59½ and 70½) a policy owner can select one of the settlement options guaranteed in the contract. No option need be selected prior to that time. Because of established minimum distribution requirements under the Internal Revenue Code, described above, policy owners cannot select an interest-only option. However, both the period certain and the life income annuity options are made available.

The maximum length of time over which a distribution under an insured IRA can be stretched was described at the beginning of this section, and is the same as it is for custodial IRAs. When a policy owner selects a period certain distribution, it is permissible to make early withdrawals. It is advisable for the depositor who selects a period certain guarantee to designate a beneficiary.

A life income annuity may be designed so that all payments cease at the death of one or more annuitants, or it may pay until death but guarantee a minimum number of payments. In practice, most persons who choose a life income option also elect at least a minimum period certain. The prospect of giving up the full purchase price of an annuity when death occurs immediately after payments begin is a risk that most annuitants are unwilling to take. Of course, the longer the minimum guarantee period of a life income annuity, the more expensive the annuity.

Any assets remaining after the death of the depositor or the death of the second annuitant in the event of a joint and last survivor annuity, either before or after distributions have started, are subject to the same rules that apply to custodial IRAs.

No trustee or custodian is required for insured plans because the policy is endorsed to conform with IRS requirements.

U.S. Retirement Bonds

In the past, some individuals preferred to have their IRA funds invested in United States government securities over any other investment. To facilitate IRA investments in government obligations, the Treasury created a special series of bonds issued in denominations of $50, $100, and $500. Although the bonds are no longer sold, some are still outstanding. They may be kept until retirement age or redeemed early and rolled over into an IRA.

The interest on these bonds is compounded semiannually, and the rate is determined by the Treasury. The bonds were designed to conform with the requirements and restrictions applicable to IRAs. The payment of interest stops when the holder reaches age 70½, and at this time the bond is considered to be redeemed for tax purposes even if redemption has not taken place.

Taxation of IRA Retirement Benefits

Provided that the amount of the retirement benefit meets minimum requirements, it is taxed as ordinary income in the year received (subject to penalties on excess distributions described later in this chapter), irrespective of the funding mechanism. This taxation policy applies to sums received under life income options as well as under periods certain. One rationale underlying the tax policy is that because contributions are tax deductible when made, they are regarded as a deferred wage that therefore should be subject to taxation at some point. Of course, there is no tax on nondeductible contributions.

Five- or ten-year forward averaging provisions on lump-sum distributions are not available for IRA distributions.

Disability Benefits

A worker who becomes disabled before age 59½ may withdraw all or part of the funds in an IRA without incurring a penalty in the form of an excise tax. Under Regulation 172-17(f), a person is considered to be disabled if he or she is "unable to engage in any substantial gainful activity by reason of any medically determinable physical or mental impairment which can be expected to result in death or to be of long or continued duration."

Distributions of contributions and investment income to a disabled person under 59½ years of age are taxed as they would be at normal retirement age under an IRA. It should be noted, however, that some funding agencies charge a "back-end load" for premature withdrawals, even if the individual is disabled.

Penalties for Premature Distribution or Borrowing

Under TRA '86, any withdrawal of funds from a tax-favored retirement plan prior to age 59½ may result in a penalty tax of 10 percent of the amount withdrawn over and above the ordinary income tax on the distribution.

This general rule has exceptions when applied to IRAs, however. Distributions may be made (1) where the taxpayer is disabled or (2) to the beneficiary or estate of a deceased taxpayer. Furthermore, if nondeductible contributions are made to an IRA, a certain proportion of any distributions will be attributed to those contributions, and therefore that portion will not be subject to taxation. The amount excluded is the proportion that the nondeductible contribution bears to the total value of the amount at the year's end plus any distributions made during the year.

An example will clarify the rule. Assume that an individual aged 45 withdraws $4,000 from an IRA, and that he or she had never made nondeductible contributions to an IRA. The taxpayer will have to pay income tax on the $4,000 plus an excise tax of $400.

Assume further that the individual had made nondeductible contributions of $6,000 over several years and at the end of the taxable year the value of the IRA was $20,000 after the $4,000 withdrawal. Taxes would be payable on only $3,000 of the $4,000 distribution, because $1,000 would be attributable to nondeductible contributions:

$$\$4{,}000 \times \frac{\$6{,}000}{\$20{,}000 + \$4{,}000} = \$1{,}000 \text{ excluded}$$

Note that there are some special rules that apply to IRAs: (1) all IRAs are treated as a single contract; (2) all distributions within a single year are treated as one distribution; and (3) the value of the IRA is calculated as of the end of the calendar year with or within which the tax year ends.

Although the IRA owner may transfer the account to a spouse pursuant to a divorce decree and not trigger a tax penalty, any other assignment is treated as a constructive distribution of the assigned amount. Thus, if any portion of an IRA is pledged as collateral for a loan, that portion is treated as a distribution and is subject to both ordinary income tax and the tax penalty for the year in which the pledge was made.

A depositor who borrows from an IRA is considered to have received the entire interest in the account. Thus, the fair market value of the entire account is taxed as ordinary income and the account loses its tax-exempt status.

Penalty for Insufficient Distribution

The owner of an IRA incurs a nondeductible penalty if distributions are not begun by April 1 of the year following attainment of age 70½, or if individual distributions are less than the amounts described earlier under the section on distributions. The penalty is a tax of 50 percent on the difference between the amount that should have been distributed and the amount that was distributed. Thus, if the distribution for a year should have been \$600 and was actually only \$400, the penalty would be \$100 (50 percent of \$600 − \$400).

Penalty for Excess Distribution

Excess distributions made from qualified retirement plans, tax-sheltered annuities, and IRAs are subject to a 15 percent excise tax. The person receiving the distributions must pay the tax, which may be reduced by any payment of the 10 percent excise tax on early withdrawal (if any take place).

A distribution of the greater of \$112,500 (as adjusted for price increases after TRA '86 went into effect—\$140,276 in 1992) or \$150,000 is regarded as being excessive. Certain distributions are exempt, however, namely: (1) distributions made on the death of the account owner; (2) distributions made under a qualified domestic relations order (e.g., to a former spouse) if the distribution is includable in the recipient's income; (3) distributions attributable to nondeductible contributions; and (4) rollover distributions.

If an individual receives a lump-sum distribution, the \$112,500 (as indexed) amount is increased by a multiple of five (e.g., \$112,500 × 5

= $562,500), and the test for an excess distribution becomes the greater of $750,000 or the indexed amount increased by the multiple of five.

Postdeath distributions from retirement plans are subject to an additional estate tax of 15 percent of the retiree's "excess retirement accumulation" in lieu of the 15 percent tax on excess distribution. This amount is computed by subtracting (1) the present value of $112,500 (as indexed) over the period of the deceased retiree's life expectancy immediately prior to death, from (2) the value of the decedent's interest in all qualified employer plans. The estate tax on the excess retirement accumulation may not be offset by any credits (such as the unified credit). A reasonable rate of interest, in accordance with rules prescribed by the Secretary of the Treasury, must be used in computing present value.

The 15 percent penalty tax on excess distribution does not apply to amounts accrued before August 1, 1986, provided grandfathering protection afforded by TRA '86 was elected.

SIMPLIFIED EMPLOYEE PENSIONS

A simplified employee pension (SEP) plan is an arrangement under which an employer contributes to an IRA that is set up for each covered employee. First authorized in 1979, SEPs simplify the administration and reduce the paperwork associated with many other types of pension plans; for this reason, they are especially attractive to smaller employers. In particular, SEPs reduce the paperwork normally required for HR-10 or corporate plans covering common-law employees.

Nonelective SEP

There are two types of SEPs. One is compulsory, or nonelective, in that all eligible employees are included. The other is elective, in that employees may choose to participate through a salary reduction plan (sometimes called a SARSEP, for salary reduction SEP), or may choose not to participate and receive their full salaries. The elective plan is a form of "cash or deferred compensation arrangement" (CODA), like the familiar 401(k) plan. Throughout this section it will be assumed that a SEP is nonelective unless specified otherwise.

For a SEP to qualify for favorable tax treatment, an employer must make contributions for all eligible employees. An employee must be eligible if he or she is at least 21 years of age, received at least $300 (indexed for inflation—$363 in 1992) of compensation for service during the calendar year, and worked for the employer during three of the preceding five years. These rules also may extend to employee groups controlled by the employer, even though such groups technically are employed by a separate firm (such as a wholly owned subsidiary) if exclusion of such group would result in discrimination in favor of the prohibited group. Two exceptions to these general rules are (1) members of a collective bargaining unit that engaged in good-faith bargaining of retirement benefits and (2) certain nonresident aliens.

Contributions on behalf of employees are excludable from their income as follows: 15 percent of total employee compensation up to $200,000, or $30,000 of the contribution, whichever is less. Both the $200,000 base and the $30,000 limit were to be indexed for inflation. In 1992, the compensation base was $228,860, although the contribution limit remained at $30,000. In addition, an employee covered by a SEP may treat the SEP as an IRA and make deductible or nondeductible contributions under IRA rules, but only to the extent the employer contributes less than $2,000.

Employer contributions to a SEP must be made for all eligible employees in a manner that does not discriminate in favor of any "highly compensated" employees—sometimes called "prohibited classes," as defined by IRC Section 414(q). Among the highly compensated are those earning more than $75,000 per year in general (as indexed), or $50,000 (as indexed) if within the top-paid group of employees. Discrimination is automatically deemed to exist if contributions do not represent a uniform percentage of each eligible employee's total compensation and favor the-prohibited group, although integration with Social Security is permissible. Unionized employees and aliens usually are excluded from the process of determining whether a plan is discriminatory.

The integration of pension plans with Social Security is an important benefit distribution technique for the employer. Rules generally applicable to qualified defined contribution plans permit a limited difference between the contribution percentage that is applied to salary below and above the Social Security wage base or some other integration level.

Some of the requirements typically associated with pension plans also apply to SEPs. For example, the plan must be in writing, it must set forth the eligibility requirements, and it must specify the ways in which contributions are computed. However, SEPs are somewhat unusual in that

(1) all rights to contributions are 100 percent vested in the employee immediately, and (2) an employee may freely withdraw funds, subject to the penalties described above for withdrawing funds from an IRA. Most employers would consider these vesting provisions to be a disadvantage.

Elective SEP

Under an elective SARSEP, the employee has the option of receiving his or her full salary, or deferring receipt of as much as $7,000 (indexed for inflation) per annum under a CODA. In 1991, the index amount was $8,475. Elective deferrals under a SARSEP are treated as wages for employment tax purposes, just as under a 401(k) or a tax-sheltered annuity plan.

A SARSEP may be installed only if at least 50 percent of employees contribute, and only if the employer had 25 or fewer employees during the previous year. A nondiscrimination test limits the average amount deferred as a percentage of compensation for highly compensated employees. The percentage they may defer individually can be no more than 125 percent of the average deferral percentage of all other eligible employees.

HR-10 (KEOGH) PLANS

The Self-Employed Individuals Tax Retirement Act of 1962 established the framework by which unincorporated small business owners and partners could set up and participate in tax-qualified pension plans popularly referred to as HR-10 (for an early version of the bill) or Keogh plans (for U.S. Rep. Eugene Keogh, sponsor of the bill).

Prior to the passage of this act, owners and partners of unincorporated businesses were ineligible to participate in a tax-qualified pension plan. Whereas the owner and sole employee of an incorporated business could enjoy the tax benefits of participation in a qualified pension plan, his unincorporated counterpart could not. Moreover, while employees of an unincorporated owner or partner were eligible to participate in such a plan, their employer could not. The 1962 act eliminated much of the inequity.

The 1962 act imposed considerably stricter limitations for Keogh plans than existed for corporate pension plans. Subsequent legislation, however, in the form of ERISA, the Economic Recovery Tax Act of 1981 (ERTA), the Tax Equity and Fiscal Responsibility Act of 1982 (TEFRA), and TRA '86 has so liberalized the provisions of Keogh plans that today there are few differences between them and corporate plans. Of all this legislation, TEFRA had the greatest impact on Keogh plans, rendering changes in eligibility rules, vesting, plan administration, discrimination rules, and many other aspects.

Eligilibity

In order to be eligible to establish a Keogh plan, an unincorporated sole proprietorship or partnership must be engaged in a business with a profit motive. Both owners/partners and their self-employed common-law employees are eligible to participate. For Keogh plan purposes, a common-law employee is one for whom an employer has the right to control and direct the results of the work and how it is done. Ministers, members of religious orders, full-time insurance salespeople, and U.S. citizens employed in the United States by foreign governments are not generally considered self-employed common-law employees for Keogh plan purposes, although distinctions to determine whether income is from self-employment can be subtle. A lawyer, for example, who is employed by a corporation would not be considered a self-employed person; however, if that same lawyer established a sole proprietorship by practicing law during the evenings, the earnings from that practice would establish eligibility for that lawyer to participate in a Keogh plan. Similarly, a pastor of a church would not be regarded as self-employed with respect to income derived from those services, but if the pastor also performed wedding ceremonies independent of his church duties, the income derived would qualify as self-employment income. In all cases, the law provides that earned income for Keogh plan purposes must be derived from self-employment in which the individual's services materially helped to produce the income.

Capital gains from disposal of property are not considered self-employment income, although net earnings (e.g., commissions) from the sale of property are.

Eligibility for participation in Keogh plans is the same as for corporate plans discussed elsewhere in this book. Full-time employees who are below age 21 or have less than one year of service may be excluded from coverage.

Establishing a Keogh Plan

A Keogh plan must be in writing. It can be drafted in the form of an individualized trust instrument, or it can be described in either a master plan or a prototype plan, either of which uses a standardized plan form. In the case of a master plan, a sponsoring organization—a trade or professional association, a bank, an insurance company, or a mutual fund—both funds the benefits and acts as plan administrator. If a prototype plan is utilized, the sponsoring organization funds the benefits, but the employer administers the plan. Whether an employer chooses to draft an individualized trust instrument or to adopt a master plan or a prototype plan, the plan should be submitted for approval by the IRS. Since the passage of TEFRA, the owner-employee is no longer required to seek out an institutional trustee, and in fact can now serve as the plan trustee.

In addition to providing a written instrument describing the plan, the owner-employee must make a contribution to the plan in order to bring the plan into legal existence.

The plan must cover at least 50 employees or, if there are fewer than 125 total employees, at least 40 percent of all eligible employees. For purposes of determining eligibility, an owner-employee may disregard employees covered by collective bargaining agreements regarding retirement benefits and employees below age 21 or those with less than two years of service.

Keogh plans are subject to the same nondiscrimination and vesting rules as apply to corporate pension plans.

An owner-employee setting up a Keogh plan may establish a defined contribution plan, including a profit-sharing plan, a money purchase pension plan or a defined benefit plan.

A Keogh plan administrator must file annual reports to the IRS. IRS Publication 560 lists the forms and reports that must be filed.

Contributions

For a defined contribution Keogh plan, an employer may make annual tax-deductible contributions of the lesser of $30,000 or 25 percent of net earned income on behalf of each participant in the plan. Contributions to a profit-sharing plan are limited to a maximum of 15 percent of all participating employees' compensation for a year.

In the case of a defined benefit Keogh plan, the maximum annual benefit may not exceed the lesser of $90,000 (as indexed) or 100 percent of average compensation for the three consecutive highest-earning years. In 1992, the indexed annual benefit maximum was $112,221.

If an employer exceeds these limits, any excess contribution is subject to a penalty tax of 10 percent of the nondeductible contributions if such contributions are not withdrawn by the end of the tax year. Such excess contributions, however, may be carried forward to apply to the next year after payment of the penalty tax for the current year.

An employer should consult an actuary to determine the maximum allowable contribution to fund a defined benefit plan.

For money purchase plans, the maximum contribution is 25 percent of participating employees' compensation.

If an employer establishes both a defined contribution plan and a defined benefit plan for itself and its common-law employees, the maximum combined deductible contribution is the greater of 25 percent of the participating employees' compensation for the year or the contribution necessary to meet the minimum funding standard for the year.

If, as a result of overstating pension liabilities for a defined benefit plan, an employer underpays income tax by $1,000 or more, there is a tax penalty on the underpayment of 10 to 30 percent, depending upon the percentage relationship of the deduction claimed to the correct deduction.

Contributions to a Keogh plan generally are applied to the current tax year. However, they can be applied to a previous tax year if (1) they are made by the due date of the tax return for the previous year, including extensions; (2) the plan was established by the end of the previous year; (3) the plan treats the contributions as though it had received them on the last day of the previous year; and (4) the employer (*a*) specifies in writing to the plan administrator or trustee that the contributions apply to the previous year, or (*b*) deducts the contributions on the tax return for the previous year.

A promissory note is not considered a contribution to a Keogh plan for tax-deductibility purposes.

For purposes of determining the maximum deductible contribution to a Keogh plan, all defined contribution plans must be treated as a single plan, and all defined benefit plans must be treated as a single plan.

Voluntary Nondeductible Contributions and Elective Deferrals

Participants may be permitted to make nondeductible voluntary contributions to a Keogh plan in addition to the employer contributions.

Such voluntary nondeductible contributions are limited to a maximum of 10 percent of the participant's compensation received for all years under all plans, subject to the overall limits for defined contribution or defined benefit plans.

While such voluntary contributions are currently taxable, the interest build-up on them is not taxed until such time as distributions begin, a major advantage in building the value of the account.

Employees who participate in a profit-sharing Keogh plan can also elect to defer a portion of compensation by making elective distributions to a 401(k) plan, a Section 501(c)(18) plan, a SEP, or a tax-sheltered annuity.

Rollovers

The amount in a participant's Keogh plan account can be rolled over into another qualified plan or an IRA. However, nondeductible contributions cannot be rolled over. The rollover must be completed within 60 days of receipt of the distribution from the Keogh plan. A plan participant cannot roll over distributions into a spousal IRA. A surviving spouse can roll over a Keogh plan distribution as though he or she were the plan participant, but only into an IRA. Rollovers for partial distributions must be made to an IRA only. The decision to roll over a distribution from a Keogh plan into an IRA must be in writing and is irrevocable.

Distributions

Penalty-free distributions from a Keogh plan may begin as early as attainment of age 59½ and must begin no later than the participant's attaining age 70½.

There is a penalty tax of 10 percent on premature distributions, subject to exceptions for death of the participant, total and permanent disability of the participant, early retirement, decreed divorce settlements, and other events. Keogh plans also are subject to the imposition of an excise tax on a participant who fails to take the minimum distribution, as discussed earlier in this chapter in the section on IRAs.

A Keogh plan must provide that, unless the participant otherwise chooses, the payment of benefits must begin within 60 days of the latest of (1) the plan year in which the participant reaches the earlier of age 65 or the normal retirement age, (2) the plan year in which occurs the 10th anniversary of the year in which the participant came under the plan, or

(3) the plan year in which the participant separated from service. These requirements do not waive the minimum distribution rule that distributions must begin by age 70½.

The proceeds from a Keogh plan account can be paid in the same manner as proceeds from other plans. The options include the lump-sum distribution and periodic distributions from the accumulated reserves of an annuity offered by a life insurance company.

A plan may provide for early retirement based on a service requirement or for actuarially reduced benefits as a result of separation from service before a participant reaches the age requirement for an early retirement benefit.

Keogh plans are subject to minimum distribution requirements. Each participant must begin to receive his or her entire interest in the plan by the required beginning date, or else begin receiving regular periodic distributions by the required beginning date; the periodic distributions must be in annual amounts calculated to distribute the entire account interest over the participant's life expectancy, or the joint life expectancy of the participant and designated beneficiary. Defined benefit plans and certain money purchase plans must provide automatic survivor benefits.

Five percent owners of the employer are subject to special restrictions regarding distributions.

TRENDS AND THE LEGISLATIVE ENVIRONMENT

As many had predicted following the passage of the Tax Reform Act of 1986, the limitations on deductibility imposed by that legislation and such factors as confusion regarding the new rules have had a significant impact on participation in IRAs. The extent of this impact can be gauged from several indicators.

In 1983, when the deductibility of contributions to IRAs was less restricted, a survey of workers by the Employee Benefit Research Institute (EBRI) revealed that 16.7 million workers had made contributions to IRA accounts in the most recent tax year. A similar EBRI survey in 1987, following the passage of TRA '86, revealed that 14.3 million had made IRA contributions, a considerable decline.[6]

---

[6]The authors are grateful for the research efforts of Ms. Jennifer Davis, of the Employee Benefit Research Institute, in providing this information.

Another indicator of the negative impact of TRA '86 is the slowing of the growth of IRA/Keogh assets. In 1984, total assets of IRA and Keogh accounts had a growth rate of 41 percent, and in 1985, 32 percent. In 1987, this growth rate began slowing at a more rapid pace, so that by 1989, the growth rate was only 15.7 percent.[7]

In tax year 1982, following legislation that expanded eligibility for making deductible contributions to IRAs, 13.2 percent of all federal tax returns claimed a deduction for IRA contributions. A sample of returns for tax year 1988 indicates that only 5.9 percent of returns claimed such a deduction.[8]

In 1986, 40 percent of all deductible IRA contributions were made by taxpayers with $50,000 or more in adjusted gross income. In 1987, when the restrictions of TRA '86 went into effect, this proportion decreased to 19 percent.[9]

As a percentage of real annual personal savings, new IRA/Keogh assets fell from over 60 percent in prereform 1985 to a low of 26 percent in 1988.[10]

A study conducted by EBRI concludes that factors other than deductibility of contributions to IRAs have had some impact on the decline in IRA participation. Cited as additional factors in the decline are consumer confusion over the new rules, less advertising by financial institutions, and the smaller tax advantage afforded by the new and lower tax rates. The fact that the study revealed that the decline in participation cut across all income and age categories indicates that more factors than deductibility were at work.

The same study points out that the decline in IRA participation was accompanied by a greater movement toward participation in tax-deferred 401(k) plans. In fact, EBRI states, "Recent trends in the use of tax-deferred 401(k) retirement plans and individual retirement accounts (IRAs) suggest that even if Congress broadens IRA eligibility, more workers are likely to rely on 401(k)s."[11]

---

[7] *Employee Benefit Notes,* vol. 11, no. 7 (July 1990), pp. 4–5. See also vol. 10, no. 7 (July 1989), pp. 4–5.

[8] *Employee Benefit Notes,* vol. 11, no. 7 (July 1990), p. 4.

[9] *Employee Benefit Notes,* vol. 11, no. 7 (July 1990), p. 5.

[10] See "Individual Saving for Retirement—The 401(k) and IRA Experiences," EBRI *Issue Brief,* no. 95 (October 1989).

[11] *EBRI News,* Employee Benefit Research Institute, Washington, D.C., October 31, 1989.

There is no question that while the impact of TRA '86 on IRA participation has not been as great as the pessimists feared, and in fact there is evidence that nondeductible contributions are more popular than first thought, it has been very significant indeed.

Keogh plans have never reached the level of popularity of IRAs, and the growth rate of the former has been relatively static for several years. As of the end of 1987, only 5.6 percent of an estimated 10 million self-employed individuals participated in a Keogh plan.[12]

The share of total IRA/Keogh assets held by mutual funds and stock brokerage self-directed accounts has steadily increased to the point that those two types of financial institutions accounted for 41.9 percent of such assets by the end of 1989. Other types of financial institutions and their share of the assets were commercial banks (22.0 percent), savings and loans (17.3 percent), mutual savings banks (4.7 percent), credit unions (5.3 percent), and life insurance companies (8.9 percent).[13]

Congressional initiatives to liberalize existing provisions regarding IRAs exist in several forms. Bills to restore partial deductibility for IRA contributions regardless of income level, or to permit penalty-free withdrawals before age 59½ for certain purposes, are under consideration on both the Senate and the House floors. Given the existence of the federal budget deficit, the chances of passage of any bill involving further tax expenditures for IRAs are at best uncertain.

---

[12]EBRI *Issue Brief,* no. 89 (April 1989).

[13]*Employee Benefit Notes,* vol. 11, no. 7 (July 1990), pp. 3–4.

CHAPTER 38

EXECUTIVE RETIREMENT BENEFIT PLANS

Garry N. Teesdale
Bernard E. Schaeffer

Special executive retirement benefits often are needed in addition to an organization's broadly based employee retirement plan. Many reasons exist for such arrangements. One is that executives themselves may have special needs. Another is that qualified plans must be nondiscriminatory, and a purpose of executive plans is to discriminate in favor of an executive or group of executives on a practical and economical basis. Also, basic company plans often have built-in limits that prevent giving equal recognition to the highest pay levels.

This chapter discusses the following executive retirement benefits:

Why executive retirement benefits?
Total planning context.
Supplemental executive retirement plans (SERPs).
Deferred compensation agreements.
Legal, accounting, and related background considerations.
Summary.

WHY EXECUTIVE RETIREMENT BENEFITS?

Special Needs of Executives

Executives, particularly top executives, differ from the remaining work force of a company. They often have unique abilities and have an impact so great that extraordinary efforts are made to attract them and recognize their achievements. For an officer who joins the company in middle or later career, this may necessitate the promise of full career-equivalent retirement benefits. It also may necessitate the promise of benefits to replace those given up when leaving the prior employer.

For an executive being recruited, or one who is otherwise in a ''high risk'' situation, it is often appropriate to provide pension guarantees in case he or she is terminated prematurely. Changes in corporate direction often result in the unscheduled change of the top executive team. Further, many executive jobs involve such pressure that ''burnout'' can be a problem, and it may be mutually advantageous to the company and the individual to make available unreduced retirement benefits at a younger age than can be offered to the entire work force.

The compensation of top executives is high enough so that they may seek to postpone the receipt and taxation of a part of current earnings. At the same time, the company may wish to postpone a part of their compensation and make it depend on their meeting stated conditions such as continued employment, availability to consult after retirement, or noncompetition after retirement. Also, a significant part of an executive's compensation may be geared to the operating success of the company and be payable in addition to salary.

Limits of Basic Plans

The limits on recognizing the earnings of top executives in basic retirement plans include restrictions on the *types of pay counted* (perhaps base pay only, excluding bonuses or incentives); the *amounts of pay* counted (limited by the Tax Reform Act of 1986)[1], and the level of contributions or benefits that may be provided (including the Employee Retirement Income Security Act (ERISA) limits).[2]

Social Security reflects income only up to the maximum taxable wage base, and its benefit formula is weighted in favor of lower-paid

---

[1]IRC Section 401(a)17 limits the amount of compensation includable for purposes of determining benefits or contributions to $200,000, indexed for inflation.

[2]IRC Section 415 states the ERISA limits on benefits or contributions for individuals under qualified plans. The benefit limit is $90,000 annually, and the contribution limit is $30,000 annually. Under IRC Section 415(d) the defined benefit limit is indexed for inflation beginning in 1988; the contribution limit is indexed when the benefit limit reaches $120,000.

employees. As a result, it can provide only a small fraction of an executive's retirement income. Companywide plans usually are integrated with Social Security to make up part of this difference. However, Social Security benefits are fully indexed for inflation, while plan benefits are only partly adjusted for inflation, if at all, and usually on an occasional ad hoc basis. This means the combined pension from a plan and Social Security has better inflation-proofing for the lower-paid worker than for the top executive, because Social Security represents a higher percentage of the lower-paid worker's total retirement income.

TOTAL PLANNING CONTEXT

Executive retirement planning is part of a total picture that also includes salary, short-term and long-term incentives, and other qualified and nonqualified benefits. These interact, and all should be planned on an integrated basis to achieve an optimum result.

Therefore, several steps are appropriate in designing the executive retirement plan. First, consider the effects of any existing or contemplated long-term incentive arrangements or capital accumulation arrangements that may also provide for the executive's retirement needs. These include, for example, stock options, stock appreciation rights, phantom stock, stock bonuses, performance units or shares, and restricted stock and cash accumulation plans.

Second, take whatever reasonable steps are available to provide for the needs of the executive within the qualified plan. The tax and funding advantages of a qualified plan should be enjoyed to the maximum extent, within the framework of company policy for employees generally. Such measures include:

1. Recognizing the executive's service and earnings as fully as possible in computing plan benefits—for example, by removing nonstatutory upper limits on credited earnings and counting some or all of current bonus or incentive payments. The extent to which this meets other objectives of the organization, of course, must be considered. Some organizations may prefer to base retirement income only on salary, and to regard bonuses and incentive payments as extras, on the basis of which executives should make their own provision for added retirement income. This typically will not be the case, however, where companies have carefully established the mix of compensation tied to strategic design objectives. This also must coordinate with the organization's policies on the plan's recognition of bonuses, overtime, and the like for employees below the select executive level, as compensation must be defined in a nondiscriminatory manner in qualified plans.

2. Integrating the qualified plan with Social Security to the fullest extent. This permits the plan to focus on the part of pay in excess of the Social Security wage base—to slant its formula in favor of the higher paid worker—within allowable limits.

3. Introducing other design features into the qualified plan that can provide for executive needs. Depending on the company, its population distribution of executives and other employees, and its objectives, such features might include: *(a)* an unreduced benefit for early retirees with long service[3]; *(b)* a benefit formula that gives more than proportional credit for persons hired within, say, 20 years of the normal retirement age; or *(c)* provisions that permit optimum coordination of executive plan benefits with the qualified plan.

4. Adding a cash or deferred arrangement (CODA) and advising the executive to make maximum use of salary reduction contributions up to the limit of $7,000 (indexed for inflation beginning in 1988).[4] Since such amounts are excluded from gross income when contributed, and the investment earnings are also tax-exempt until drawn out as benefits, they can accumulate to much higher levels than if taxed at the outset and during each year of their income accumulation. The percent of compensation that highly compensated employees may defer is limited by a rule that relates it to the percent that nonhighly compensated employees actually defer.[5]

SUPPLEMENTAL EXECUTIVE RETIREMENT PLANS

Supplemental executive retirement plans usually are adopted for one of the following reasons:

---

[3]IRC Section 415(b) reduces the $90,000 defined benefit limit in the same manner as Social Security benefits are reduced for retirement at or after age 62 and by the full actuarial reduction for retirement before age 62.

[4]IRC Section 402(g).

[5]IRC Section 401(k)(3).

1. To restore to the executive any benefits lost under qualified plans because of maximum provisions.
2. To provide full benefits for short-service executives.
3. To provide more generous benefits for executives than for the rest of the work force.
4. To provide unreduced benefits at an earlier age.

They can cover either select groups of executives—all above a stated level—or specifically designated individuals. Supplemental plans, like qualified plans, take either the defined benefit or the defined contribution form.

Defined Benefit

If the benefit is defined, it may be a flat-dollar amount, an indexed-dollar amount, or a percent of some part of earnings with or without service weighting and with or without indexing. It may be offset by the basic pension plan, by the value of specified incentives, by the value of deferred compensation contracts, by Social Security, or by benefits paid by a previous employer. Payment may be for life or for a specified period.

A typical formula might provide 2 percent of final average earnings per year of service, including credit for predecessor-company service, usually to a combined maximum of 25 or 30 years, less basic plan benefits from both the current and former company and primary Social Security. A variation might provide 4 percent per year, to a maximum of 15 years, less company plans. Other companies simply guarantee a stipulated percentage—usually 50 percent to 75 percent—less current and predecessor-company benefits. The formula usually applies to total annual compensation (base salary and annual incentives).

In addition, such guarantees could either reproduce the company's basic survivorship benefit formula or increase it.[6] The ancillary benefits are either similar to those of the company's basic plans or more generous. The plan also may include options to convert from one form of annuity (such as single-life) to another form (such as joint-life) or to earlier or

---

[6]IRC Sections 401(a)(11) and 417 require that the benefit provided under the basic plan to a surviving spouse be at least 50 percent of the employee's benefit, making a supplemental survivor's benefit desirable in many cases.

later retirement. The basis of converting from one form of benefit to another may be actuarially equivalent or may be subsidized or penalized by the employer. The plan's obligations following retirement may be unconditional or be conditioned on the executive's meeting requirements for length of service, noncompetition after retirement, or availability to consult after retirement. Conversely, the obligation may be limited specifically to those cases where the executive is terminated without cause or becomes disabled. In other words, within the limits of reasonableness, the plan may be designed to meet whatever simple or complex objectives the parties seek.

When the purpose is to provide unreduced benefits at an age lower than the qualified plan's normal retirement age, the employer has the choice of (1) paying a lifetime supplement, which restores the qualified plan's early retirement reduction, or (2) paying a temporary full benefit up to normal retirement age and deferring the commencement of the executive's qualified plan benefit until the normal age.

Defined Contribution

If contributions are to be defined, the first step is to spell out how. They may be related to the individual's earnings, to his or her performance, to the company performance, and so on. They even can be stated-dollar amounts. The so-called contribution cannot be transfered to an entity insulated from the employer's creditors. In fact, it usually is represented only by a bookkeeping entry. There is no typical pattern for such defined contributions: each plan is designed to meet its own set of objectives. Frequently, a dollar amount or percent of pay is stipulated.

The second step is to determine a basis of ''investment'' growth. One approach is to hold specified assets earmarked for the purpose of defining such growth and meeting the benefit obligation when due. Another approach is to make hypothetical investments to determine the growth. Alternatives include defining the growth by reference to the employer's earnings, a specified fixed or variable interest rate, or a specified index of investment yield or asset fluctuation, or of wage or living-cost fluctuation. Many companies use the prime rate or the rate available to them for short-term borrowing.

As with defined benefit–type plans, other decisions include the commencement, timing, and duration of payments, the options to be offered, and the conditions for continuing payment. Lifetime payments to the executive or to specified dependents can be arranged by purchase of a life insurance contract (with the employer as beneficial owner).[7] Unlike a qualified defined contribution plan, lifetime payments also can be offered with the employer directly assuming the longevity risk.

A defined contribution arrangement can slide over into the defined benefit area, depending on what added promises are made, and how closely benefits are limited to the specific growth of the agreed-upon "contributions."

Comparative Merits of Defined Benefit and Defined Contribution Approaches

The relative merits of defined benefits versus defined contributions are not the same for a single executive, a group of executives, or a qualified plan. For a single executive, or several executives with similar age and service characteristics, defined benefits and defined contributions are simply different approaches. The defined benefit may be a more direct way of achieving the goal of retirement security. The defined contribution may be a more appropriate way of gearing the level of retirement security to the events that determine the amount of contribution and the rate of accumulation. The main differences between the two approaches parallel those between qualified pension and profit-sharing plans—that is, the risk or reward of investment performance lies with the employer in defined benefit plans, and with the executive in defined contribution plans; and vesting tends to be more rapid under defined contribution plans.

For a group of executives with varied age and service characteristics, there is a further consideration. If the goal is to provide a given level of retirement security, the defined benefit approach may be the more convenient way of achieving it. If the goal is to reward group performance, the defined contribution approach, with contribution levels based on results, may be best. Note, however, the level of contribution needed to produce the same deferred benefits increases dramatically with the age at which it is set aside. Therefore, if the goal is both retirement security and reward for group performance, a more suitable approach may be a defined contribution plan under which the total contribution reflects the business

[7]IRC Section 72(u) makes annuities unattractive by annually taxing the increase in the value of the annuity to the employer-owner.

performance of the organization, but the allocation to each individual is actuarially weighted for current age and, perhaps, also adjusted for length of past service.[8]

DEFERRED COMPENSATION AGREEMENTS

A deferred compensation agreement focuses primarily on the aspect of earnings deferral and secondarily on the aspect of retirement income. The emphasis is more on the idea of an individual arrangement than of a plan perhaps covering more than one executive (although deferral for individuals may be done under the umbrella of a master agreement). While supplemental retirement plans (discussed in the preceding section) provide clear added benefits, a deferred compensation agreement delays receipt of specific income and places it in some peril.

Tax Purposes of Deferral

Traditionally, the idea behind deferred compensation agreements was to postpone income and thereby achieve a lower tax bracket. Marginal income tax rates were steeply graduated in the 1940s through the 1960s relative to compensation levels, and interest earnings and inflation had not reached the high rates prevailing in the late 1970s. It often was desirable for the executive to defer the receipt and taxation of a part of pay until retirement, when his or her total income would be lower, as this would frequently result in significantly lower tax rates.

However, events in the late 1970s and the 1980s changed this relationship. High inflation and interest rates in the late 1970s required the crediting of substantial earnings to amounts deferred to keep the executive "whole." Although inflation and interest rates significantly declined in the 1980s, the need to credit earnings on deferred amounts continues. Beginning in 1982 the maximum federal income tax rate was reduced to 50 percent; as a result many executives' taxes would not decrease after

---

[8]Note that such a combined approach is not permitted under a qualified profit-sharing plan (except in the unlikely circumstance that the allocations as a percent of individual earnings will be as favorable to the low-paid as to the high-paid employee—Revenue Ruling 57-77).

retirement.[9] The impact of taxes on compensation planning was further lowered beginning in 1987 with the maximum tax rate reduced to 38.5 percent and in 1988 through 1990 to 28 percent.[10] Beginning in 1991 a third tax bracket was added, increasing the maximum tax rate to 31 percent.[11]

Nontax Purposes of Deferral

While tax planning continues to be a prominent consideration, the other objectives for deferral have grown in relative importance. The principal purpose of deferred compensation since 1981 has been to provide executives with a pretax growth of amounts deferred. However, given the low marginal federal income tax rates in effect beginning in 1989, an executive may find it advantageous not to defer compensation and to invest the after-tax amount in a tax-sheltered investment, such as a universal life insurance policy or a variable-rate annuity.[12] Additional goals are to postpone or spread out the receipt of income beyond the executive's prime working life; to even out the effect of bonuses; to bind the executive to the organization for an extended period, by making receipt of the agreed amounts conditional on loyalty, availability, and the like; or simply to provide additional retirement income.

Substance of Agreement

Much of the earlier discussion of defined contribution supplemental retirement plans applies equally to deferred compensation agreements. This includes, first, the definition of what compensation will be deferred;

---

[9]IRC Section 1, amended by the Economic Recovery Tax Act of 1981.

[10]IRC Section 1, amended by the Tax Reform Act of 1986. In 1988 through 1990 the maximum marginal rate of tax may be 33 percent, due to the 5 percent surtax imposed to phase out the 15 percent tax bracket and personal exemptions.

[11]IRC Section 1, amended by the Revenue Reconciliation Act of 1990. The maximum marginal rate of tax may be higher than 31 percent due to the phase-out of personal exemptions and itemized deductions.

[12]For example, $10,000 deferred and invested at 7.5 percent per year for 10 years yields an after-tax amount of $14,221, applying a 31 percent marginal federal tax rate. If the executive receives the $10,000 and the same tax rate applies in the year of receipt, the executive has $6,900 to invest. If this sum is invested in a tax-sheltered investment the executive must earn a 9.76 percent annual rate of return to produce the same $14,221.

and second, the rules determining appreciation and earnings on such sums. Usually, particularly if the deferral is voluntary, there will be a defined formula for earnings growth. Occasionally, there may be circumstances where no provision is made for growth—where the obligation is simply to pay the stated amounts at a specified future time. Also applicable are the comments on earmarked assets, and on the choices as to benefit options under supplemental retirement plans.

The degree to which the contract limits the executive's rights to the deferred benefits (making them conditional on his or her availability to consult, or on refraining from competition with the company), and the degree to which the employer adds to the executive's rights (through inflation guarantees, commitments to provide added payments to dependents, and so on) are matters of mutual agreement between the parties.

Drafting the Agreement

A deferred compensation agreement should be embodied in a written contract, specifically authorized or ratified by the corporation's directors. Drawing it up is a work of infinite care. The document must be drafted to accomplish the various nontax objectives that are being sought, and also to anticipate other pertinent circumstances that may arise—death, sickness, business changes, and so on. At the same time, it should protect the executive from incurring any tax liability until the deferred amounts actually are received. Finally, the agreement should be so structured that the employer is entitled to a tax deduction when the payments are made.

If the deferral is elected by the employee in lieu of income that could be taken currently, the IRS has indicated the following measures will protect the employee from constructive receipt in advance of actual payment: (1) the election to defer must be irrevocable, (2) the election should be made before the services for which the income is payable are performed, and (3) the period of deferral should be specific.[13] Measures short of these standards may suffice but leave the taxpayer vulnerable to challenge by the IRS.

---

[13]Revenue Ruling 60-31.

LEGAL, ACCOUNTING, AND RELATED BACKGROUND CONSIDERATIONS

The application of federal law to executive retirement plans, as contrasted to qualified plans, has an important impact on their design. These considerations are discussed below.

Prohibitive Conditions for Funding

If an executive retirement plan is formally funded, it must satisfy ERISA's benefit and fiduciary requirements—including those concerning reporting, disclosure, vesting, accrual, joint and survivor annuity, other intricate benefit standards, merger and transfer rules, funding standards, fiduciary rules, prohibited transaction rules, and bonding.[14] But the plan still is not tax-qualified unless it is broadened to provide nondiscriminatory benefits for rank-and-file employees, in which case it is no longer an executive plan. The formal funding of executive retirement benefits has rarely been a worthwhile option because of the twin burdens of ERISA requirements and nonqualified tax status. Formal funding means placing plan assets beyond the reach of the employer and its creditors, usually by means of a trust. (See the discussion below of the income tax problems of nonqualified, funded benefits.)

Because executive benefits usually are unfunded, they depend on the future solvency of the company. This is a disadvantage to the executive; at the same time, the availability of the assets for corporate uses can be an advantage to the company.

Other ERISA and Tax Law Distinctions

To be exempt from ERISA's benefit and fiduciary rules, an executive retirement plan must be maintained ''primarily for . . . a select group of management or highly compensated employees''—as well as be un-

[14]ERISA Title I, ''Protection of Employee Benefit Rights,'' covers all retirement plans except as specifically exempted by Sections 4, 201, 301(a), and 401(a). The exemptions for executive plans are contingent on their unfunded status.

funded.[15] It can then discriminate in benefits and coverage to whatever extent is needed to meet its specific objectives.

ERISA, along with its benefit and contribution limits on qualified plans,[16] also defines a class of nonqualified "excess benefit plans," whose purpose is to pay benefits or contributions above those limits.[17] Excess benefit plans are particular examples of the executive retirement plans discussed in this chapter.

ERISA requires only minimal reporting and disclosure of unfunded executive retirement programs,[18] and none for those that are excess benefit plans.[19] Further, it omits such plans from its termination insurance program and from its federally imposed employer liability on plan termination.[20]

Normal Taxation and Deductibility of Benefits

Unfunded deferred executive benefits are deducted as business costs by the employer when they are paid to the executive (or assets representing their value are transferred to his or her unrestricted ownership).[21] The executive also reports the benefits as income at that time, with the following exception: If he or she is considered to have current access to the benefits, because the deferral is subject to cancellation by him or her without substantial penalty, the benefits can be deemed "constructively received" and taxable at the time he or she first has such access.[22] (This differs from qualified plans, where the availability of unpaid benefits is not a taxable event.)

A principal goal of executive retirement planning is to give some assurance that benefits will be paid—often including informal earmarking of assets—but not so much assurance that the executive currently is taxed

---

[15]ERISA Sections 201(2), 301(a)(3), and 401(a)(1).

[16]See footnote 2, this chapter.

[17]ERISA Section 3(36).

[18]Department of Labor Regulations 2520.104-23.

[19]ERISA Section 4(b)(5).

[20]ERISA Section 4021(b)(6).

[21]Federal Tax Regulations 1.404(a)-12(b)(2).

[22]Federal Tax Regulations 1.451-2; Revenue Ruling 60-31.

for the value of the amounts being deferred. (See the discussion below regarding informal funding and security devices.)

Reasonableness

Executive retirement benefits must represent reasonable rewards for service to be deductible by the employer as business expenses. (This also is true of qualified plans.)[23]

Taxation of Survivor Benefits

The value of survivor benefits under a nonqualified executive retirement plan, like that provided by a qualified plan, generally is included in the executive's gross estate for federal tax purposes.[24] If the beneficiary is the executive's spouse, an unlimited marital deduction is available regardless of whether the plan is qualified or nonqualified.[25] Also, the sum of gifts and bequests to beneficiaries other than spouses is tax-free up to $600,000.[26] Such amounts are subject to income tax (except to the extent they qualify for any part of the allowable exclusion—up to $5,000 in total—of employer-provided death benefits).[27] The estate tax attributed to survivor benefits is deductible in computing the income tax thereon.[28]

Taxation and Deductibility on Nonqualified Funded Benefits

The income tax problems of a nonqualified, formally funded executive retirement plan have existed for many years. The executive is taxed on the plan's assets as soon as they become either nonforfeitable or transferable, even though *benefits* are deferred. The executive thus can be required to pay taxes on moneys to which he or she does not yet have access.[29] The employer deducts its contributions when they become nonforfeitable to

---

[23]Federal Tax Regulations 1.162-7.

[24]IRC Section 2039.

[25]IRC Section 2056.

[26]IRC Sections 2001 and 2010.

[27]IRC Section 101(b).

[28]IRC Section 691(c).

[29]IRC Sections 402(b) and 83.

the executive, provided a separate account is maintained for each participant.[30] Executive plans are seldom formally funded because of these problems combined with the ERISA requirements.

The investment earnings of nonqualified trusts are taxable, subject to most of the same rules as those applying to individuals.

Informal Funding and Security Devices

In recent years, the portion of a top executive's retirement benefit provided through unfunded, nonqualified arrangements has become significant. Accordingly, a significant portion of an executive's retirement income is dependent on the future solvency of the company and its ability and willingness to pay accrued benefits.

The risks that supplemental retirement benefits will not be paid when due tend to flow from one of three circumstances: (1) that current management or future management (such as after a corporate takeover) will not honor the agreements; (2) that the company will have insufficient liquidity to pay obligations; or (3) that the company may become bankrupt. The importance of these circumstances will vary.

In order to better secure the payment of benefits, companies have experimented with a wide range of internal and external quasi-funding and security devices. While none of these provides the assurances that formal funding provides, each can satisfy specific objectives and provide some degree of protection under particular circumstances. As is generally the case, if assets are held and informally earmarked to provide the source of future benefits, the company receives no deduction for the "contribution." Furthermore, it must pay tax on any investment earnings (unless the investment is tax-exempt). However, if the earmarked assets consist of stock in other companies, 80 percent of the dividend income is exempt from tax.[31]

Two commonly used techniques include the use of "rabbi trusts" and corporate-owned life insurance. A rabbi trust can be useful to prevent corporate management from dishonoring agreements to pay retirement benefits. Under the arrangement, a company creates an irrevocable trust for the benefit of participating executives. Since the trust is irrevocable,

---

[30] IRC Section 404(a)(5).

[31] IRC Section 243.

it places the assets beyond the reach of current or future management, but specifically within the reach of the company's creditors in the event of bankruptcy or insolvency.

Corporate-owned life insurance, on the other hand, is a common method of informally setting aside or earmarking assets to provide liquid funds that can be used to pay executive retirement benefits, but provides no security value since the company is both the policy owner and beneficiary, to avoid constructive receipt issues.

If an insurance contract is purchased on the life of the executive to back up the supplemental retirement plan, it must be carried as an asset of the corporation and be payable to the corporation. Premiums may not be deducted from the corporation's taxable income. However, the investment earnings of the contract are not currently taxable to the corporation (although the insurer may have to pay tax on them, and this may be reflected in the dividends or premiums); nor are policy dividends or death benefits taxable when received by the employer.[32] However, if the policy matures other than by death, is cashed in, or produces annuity payments, the value in excess of the net premiums paid is taxed to the employer as ordinary income.[33]

Generally, if insurance has a place as an earmarked asset, it is for small companies with substantial survivorship promises or other needs for liquidity on the executive's death. The use of insurance also has been attractive to other companies due to favorable tax leveraging, although the advantages have been greatly reduced by the Tax Reform Act of 1986.[34]

The use of corporate-owned life insurance to fund executive retirement benefits should be viewed as a corporate investment. There is significant downside risk to this investment, and alternative investment mechanisms should be evaluated as part of the decision to purchase insurance. The evaluation must include consideration of all pertinent factors, including opportunities or the need to utilize assets within the company's own operations, other available investment returns, time horizons, and risk factors.

---

[32]IRC Sections 264 and 101.

[33]IRC Section 72.

[34]IRC Section 264(a)(4) makes life insurance less attractive to small companies. Interest on loans in excess of $50,000 from company-owned policies purchased after June 20, 1986, is not deductible, making borrowing to pay premiums unattractive.

Federal Insurance Contributions Act (FICA) Tax

Benefits under executive plans are subject to FICA tax at the later of the time when (1) the services are performed, or (2) there is no longer a substantial risk of forfeiture.[35] Under prior law, nonqualified benefits often escaped taxation entirely, under one of several loosely defined exemptions for payments made on account of retirement.

For deferred compensation payments that become nonforfeitable during active employment, this change will have little practical effect, since most executives earn more than the Social Security wage base. However, if nonqualified benefits become nonforfeitable at retirement, the consequences will vary. If the retired executive has no other income subject to FICA tax, his or her nonqualified plan payments will be taxed. On the other hand, if there is earned income during retirement that is greater than the taxable wage base, the nonqualified plan payments will not produce any additional FICA liability.

FICA Self-Employment Tax

If the deferred benefits are tied to the performance of future services—for example, a substantial consulting requirement—the executive may run the risk of being declared self-employed, and therefore be liable for the FICA self-employment tax at the time the payments are received.[36]

Earnings Test

The Social Security earnings test for receipt of benefits does not apply to amounts earned by an employee before retirement, even though paid on a deferred basis after retirement.[37] However, if the deferred benefits are tied to the performance of postretirement services, some portion of the

---

[35] IRC Section 3121(v)(2).

[36] FICA tax on self-employment income is levied under IRC Section 1401. To determine whether an individual is retired, or whether he or she has performed substantial services in self-employment, the Social Security Administration considers several factors, which are outlined in Social Security Regulation 404.446.

[37] A special rule applies to corporate directors. Social Security Act Section 211 treats compensation deferred by corporate directors as received in the year earned for purposes of the Social Security earnings test.

payments may count toward the earnings test. The result would be to cancel $1 of Social Security benefits for each $3 of earnings in excess of specified amounts paid before age 70.[38] The $1-for-$2 trade-off will remain in effect for anyone under 65. Starting in the year 2000, the foregoing references to age 65 will gradually rise, reaching 67 in the year 2027.[39]

Accounting and SEC Disclosure

Accounting principles require that the cost of deferred benefits, net of estimated deferred tax deductions, be recognized as a current expense over the executive's active employment. The value of benefits accrued or amounts contributed as well as the value of accumulated benefits to date must be disclosed. The same standards apply whether the benefits are funded or unfunded.[40] The fact that such costs must be recognized as current expenses during the executive's service, even though payment will not be made until a future time, must be considered at the outset, as it can influence the initial decision to adopt a plan.

The Securities and Exchange Commission (SEC) requires the clear disclosure of executive compensation and retirement arrangements.[41] Aside from the disclosure requirements, there are no significant securities law issues in connection with the usual forms of unfunded executive retirement benefits. However, if employee contributions are permitted and are treated as invested in securities of the employer, deferred compensation could turn into a security requiring registration.

Shareholder-Employees in Closely Held Corporations

When the executives of a corporation also are its directors and principal shareholders, a deferred compensation agreement with them may lose some of its credibility. If the corporation has the financial ability to pay

---

[38]In 1991, for individuals between the ages of 65 and 70 the earnings limit is $6,720 and for individuals between 62 and 65 the limit is $7,080.

[39]Social Security Act Sections 203(f) and 216.

[40]*Financial Accounting Standards Board Statement No. 87*, Employers' Accounting for Pensions (December 1985).

[41]Standard Instructions for Filing Forms under Securities Act of 1933; Securities Exchange Act of 1934 and Energy Policy and Conservation Act of 1975—Regulation S-K, 17 CFR Section 229.10 et seq.

the deferred amounts currently, the IRS might assert that the doctrine of constructive receipt applies. Where deferred compensation arrangements are provided, in addition to basic pay, for the shareholder-employees of a closely held corporation, the question of reasonableness is certain to receive closer IRS scrutiny.[42]

However, situations exist when such a company would be justified in deferring a part of compensation and making it conditional on the long-term performance of any corporation. If the corporation then performed exceedingly well over a period of years, the ultimate payment of the deferred amounts might be justified as a reasonable reward for good management, even if payment of the same amounts on a current basis might have been found to be unreasonable.

Even then, however, the corporation might have interim problems in satisfying the IRS that any reserves being booked for payment of the deferred amounts should not be taxed as accumulated earnings.[43]

Therefore, in a closely held corporation, the deferrals for a major shareholder may better be handled through share accruals or expansion of ownership (with buy-back agreements if necessary).

Employees of Tax-Exempt Organizations

Special rules apply to executive plans of tax-exempt organizations such as hospitals, colleges and universities, and trade associations. Voluntary deferrals of compensation are limited to $7,500 per year and must be distributed in accordance with rules similar to those applying to qualified plans.[44] The $7,500 ceiling is reduced dollar for dollar by contributions to tax-sheltered annuities and cash or deferred arrangements.[45] Distribution must begin by April 1 of the year after attaining age 70½, whether or not the executive has retired.[46] If distribution begins before the executive's death, two thirds of the amount deferred must be distributed over his or her life expectancy. If distribution begins after the executive's death,

---

[42]Federal Tax Regulation 1.162-7.

[43]IRC Sections 531-537.

[44]IRC Section 457.

[45]IRC Section 457(c).

[46]IRC Section 401(a)(9)(c).

deferred amounts must be paid over no more than the life expectancy of the surviving spouse or other beneficiary.[47]

If compensation is deferred in a manner that does not comply with the foregoing rules, it will be taxed in the year earned unless subject to a substantial risk of forfeiture.[48] The IRS has interpreted this rule to apply not only to voluntary deferrals of compensation by the executive but to all forms of deferral, including nonqualified retirement benefits paid for solely by a tax-exempt employer.[49] As deferred compensation from tax-exempt entities is not usually forfeitable, the Internal Revenue Service's position precludes virtually all nonqualified deferred retirement benefits for their executives.[50] The IRS is expected to affirm this position in regulations, although business and professional groups have questioned the validity of its position on this matter. Retirement arrangements for nonprofit organizations are covered in Chapter 39 followed by a discussion of executive retirement plans for tax-exempt organizations under IRC Section 457 in Chapter 40.

SUMMARY

An executive retirement plan can add to an executive's benefits, bringing them up to or above those offered the general work force. It can provide unreduced early retirement, a full pension after short periods of service, extra protection for dependents, deferral of current earnings, and guarantees of income beyond working life. Since it is free of the requirements for qualified plans, it can be drawn up to meet the particular needs of the individual executive or of a select group of executives. Aside from providing added benefits for the executive, it also can impose added obligations. Plan design is concerned with avoiding the tax pitfalls of nonqualified plans, rather than enjoying the tax advantages of qualified plans.

---

[47]IRC Section 401(a)(9)(B).

[48]IRC Section 457(f). Under IRC Section 83 property is subject to a substantial risk of forfeiture if it cannot be sold or transferred and is forfeited on termination of employment.

[49]Notice 87-13, Q&A 27, (January 26, 1987).

[50]Deferral arrangements entered into before August 17, 1986, are exempt from the rule. Notice 87-13, Q&A 28, (January 26, 1987).

CHAPTER 39

RETIREMENT PLANS FOR NOT-FOR-PROFIT GROUPS

Dwight K. Bartlett III
Howard Lichtenstein

The retirement security needs of employees of not-for-profit corporations do not differ fundamentally from those of employees of for-profit corporations or governmental entities. In planning for their retirement, employees may accumulate retirement funds through the so-called three-legged stool of economic security, which consists of the Old-Age and Survivors benefits of the Social Security program, an employer-sponsored pension plan (primarily paid for by the sponsor), and private savings. Nevertheless, the history of the development of retirement plans for such organizations and the differing rules and regulations applying to such plans have led to substantial differences in plan design. These differences arise from the tax-exempt nature of not-for-profit organizations, the desire to provide a favorable employment climate in view of the socially desirable nature of the organization's activities and purposes, the historically unstable economic viability of some of these organizations, and perhaps some other reasons.

In brief, the organizations whose retirement plans are discussed in this chapter are private corporations existing for the purpose of promoting the public's health, education, and welfare and research related thereto. As such, these organizations are qualified as tax-exempt under Internal Revenue Code (IRC or Code) Section 501(c)3. This tax-exempt status led to the view that their employees could not be covered under the Social Security program when it was first enacted. Subsequently, the Social Security Act was amended to permit employees of such organizations to elect on a corporatewide basis whether they wished to be covered under Social Security, and, most recently, the Social Security Act was further amended to cover employees of not-for-profit organizations on a compulsory basis.

It also was assumed that many not-for-profit corporations could not afford to pay for retirement plans that would provide adequate, if any, retirement benefits and that tax regulations and nondiscrimination rules should be structured in ways to encourage employees of such organizations to contribute to supplemental retirement programs on a voluntary basis. These programs are a form of personal savings but have many of the features and tax benefits of pension plans. As shall be seen, the rules limiting discrimination in benefits and contributions in favor of higher-paid employees generally did not apply to these plans until quite recently.

Another concern that heavily influenced the design of retirement programs in this field is the high mobility of individual employees from one not-for-profit employer to another or in and out of the field, and it was felt that a high degree of so-called portability of accrued benefits was needed for these employees.

Still another circumstance of not-for-profit employees that has influenced plan design significantly has been the unavailability, particularly for senior executives, of other forms of noncash compensation such as stock options and cash bonuses that have been considered inappropriate in some not-for-profit organizations.

Many of the actual or perceived differences in circumstances of employees of not-for-profit organizations have substantially diminished over the years. Most employees in the field work for organizations that have prospered in recent years, both in financial terms and public appreciation of the value of their services. Nevertheless, differences do remain, and past differences continue to influence the design of plans for employees of not-for-profit corporations and their legislative and regulatory environment.

THE NOT-FOR-PROFIT SECTOR

While the not-for-profit sector is a vital, large, and fast-growing industry, it is poorly defined and measured. It is particularly important that this sector of the economy be properly defined so that it may take its proper place in public policy, academic research, and business considerations.

Contributing to the confusion in defining and measuring the size of the sector is the wide assortment of entities that qualify for either tax-exempt status or not-for-profit status under the IRC. The Code provides for more than 20 different types of not-for-profit tax-exempt organizations, ranging from churches to chambers of commerce, from nursery schools to colleges, from mutual insurance companies to health charities, and from foundations to community-based social-service organizations.

One can aggregate the more than 20 tax-exempt IRC sections into four or five broad categories of not-for-profit organizations:

1. *Fund-raising or Funding Agencies*—The familiar names in this category would include organizations such as United Way, Catholic Charities, Jewish federations; national health charities such as the American Heart or American Cancer Associations or March of Dimes; and various private foundations and endowment funds. These organizations raise their funds primarily by seeking charitable donations and then distribute the funds to their affiliated and other community-based agencies. The process of assessing needs and distributing funds is, thus, the second major function of these agencies.

2. *Educational*—This group consists of both private and parochial schools ranging from preschool classes through postgraduate education. The financing of these organizations emanates from fees for service and income from endowment funds as well as some income from other funding agencies.

3. *Social Welfare Organizations*—Included in this category are organizations that provide services to the community such as hospitals, day-care centers, homes for the aged, Boy Scouts, Girl Scouts, cancer support groups, Planned Parenthood, travelers aid groups, and thousands of other community-based agencies.

4. *Religious Organizations*—This category includes churches, synagogues, and social-service and health-related facilities run by various religious organizations.

5. *Membership Organizations*—These typically are organizations such as labor unions, trade groups, bar associations, burial societies, and so on. Typically they are financed by the collection of membership dues.

As the not-for-profit-sector reaches its rightful position of prominence in our society, better statistics are becoming available concerning its size and makeup. Many publications place the actual number of organizations at about 900,000, while others have used figures as high as two or three million. Generally, the higher estimates include local religious congregations and local chapters of national organizations, whereas the lower ones are based solely on those formally registered with the IRS. The not-for-profit sector employed 7.8 million persons in 1985 and 8.6 million in 1990, and it is projected to employ 9.3 million in 1995. This accounts for 7.3 percent of all employed individuals. The not-for-profit labor force is growing faster than total employment is growing, and, as we enter the 1990s, it is expected to continue to outpace the growth of other sectors of our economy. Various estimates of this market's purchasing power range from a minimum of 4 percent to as high as 15 percent of the gross national product. As the federal government shifts the role of the not-for-profit organization from service provider to that of spokesman for the view that local communities should care for their own, one would expect this growth in market size and financial strength to continue.

RETIREMENT PLAN DESIGN CONSIDERATIONS

Types of Plans

There are two basic types of pension plans—defined benefit plans and defined contribution plans. Defined benefit plans may be structured so that benefits are a function either of career average salary or final average salary. They may or may not be structured to provide some form of portability as described later in this chapter, and they may or may not require employee contributions. The two types of plans may provide for guaranteed postretirement inflation protection by indexing pensions to increases in the Consumer Price Index (CPI), usually with a maximum annual adjustment, such as 4 percent. They may recognize service with the employer prior to the effective date of the pension plan or choose not to do so. Historically, the defined benefit plan was either the only plan or the primary plan with a supplementary defined contribution plan. However, since the enactment of the Employee Retirement Income Security Act (ERISA), there has been a shift away from defined benefit and toward defined contribution plans. Contributing factors to this include demographic changes, changes in the levels of plan integration, and the changing burdens of federal pension regulation, including the mandatory plan termination insurance program of the Pension Benefit Guaranty

Corporation (PBGC). Such regulation has significantly increased the administrative cost of defined benefit plans in relation to that of defined contribution plans.

Defined contribution plans may take various forms including, but not limited to plans that provide for contributions as a straight percentage of compensation and plans that have a step-rate formula, that is, a certain percentage of compensation up to a specified limit and an additional percentage above that limit. They may provide for employee contributions. They also may fall within the family of thrift or profit-sharing plans, with or without matching employer contributions as an inducement for further personal savings and with or without a 401(k) arrangement. There also is a host of hybrid plan designs such as cash balance plans or target benefit plans.

There are various voluntary, supplementary plans, the most popular of which, today, is the Section 403(b) or tax-sheltered annuity plan. The purpose of a voluntary program is to provide the third leg (personal savings) of the "three legged stool." As noted below, under current law Section 403(b) annuities receive favorable tax treatment under the IRC, and, historically, this has been the retirement savings vehicle for those men and women working in the not-for-profit sector of the U.S. economy. It is interesting to note that the federal government decided recently to prohibit the adoption of 401(k) plans by employers in the not-for-profit sector, presumably because employees in this sector already have adequate, tax-favored opportunities through their 403(b) plans. Although not totally alike, the tax benefits provided under 401(k) and 403(b) plans are quite similar.

There also is a family of nonqualified pension vehicles that have been used from time to time to satisfy the special interests or needs of highly compensated executives of not-for-profit organizations. These Section 457 deferred compensation plans are similar to those used in the for-profit sector and are described in Chapter 40 of the *Handbook*. The nonqualified status and consequent lack of tax deductibility of employer contributions to such plans is of no consequence to tax-exempt not-for-profit organizations.

In view of the historically lower earnings levels in certain parts of the not-for-profit sector and the general lack of perquisites similar to those commonly found in private industry, the typical employee benefit package of not-for-profits attempts, to the extent possible, to be generous. Over the last 10 or so years, with the bold leadership of a relatively small handful of people, compensation in this industry, including employee benefits, has been raised to a level more closely commensurate with its contribution to society. It is recognized that in the absence of stock options and similar forms of compensation available in the for-profit sector, the employee benefit package often is the only source of asset accumulation for those in this sector.

Pension Portability

One plan feature of particular interest to the not-for-profit sector is "portability." With regard to pension plans, portability addresses problems caused by job mobility—that is, the movement of members of the work force from employer to employer. Portability generally involves some way of carrying one's pension to another employer in the form of an account balance in the case of a defined contribution plan or an annuity or service credit in the case of a defined benefit plan. Pension portability is important to all segments of our economy but has special significance to those working in the not-for-profit sector, where job advancement often requires moving from city to city. The sector could not survive without the willingness of people to make such relocations, and minimizing the loss of pension benefits resulting from job mobility is key.

Pension loss caused by lack of portability at the time of a job switch arises from three sources: the lack of vesting of accrued pensions, spending for current consumption the lump-sum payout of the value of accrued pensions, and the failure of accrued pension credits to be updated for subsequent salary increases. The remedies for the first two sources of loss are quite straightforward—that is, providing for full and immediate vesting of all accrued pension benefits and the elimination of lump-sum settlement of all accrued pensions at the time of a job switch. The third problem is relevant only to defined benefit plans with benefits based on final average salary and is more difficult to remedy. One possible approach is to treat the employee's entire working career, regardless of where it may have taken place, as if the employee had worked for his or her final employer throughout the entire career. Thus the retiring individual's pension with the final employer would be determined using all periods of service with all employers reduced only by the amount of vested pensions from previous employers. This approach is particularly workable with a multiemployer pension plan that covers many companies in the same or similar industries at different work locations. It is important to note that under this approach the final employer in effect bears the cost burden of updating the vested pension from prior employers' plans for subsequent salary progression. However, this is a price some employers are willing to pay to attract highly qualified and experienced executives. Very liberal vesting also is important for the success of this approach, which parallels, somewhat, that of the Social Security system—the classic example of a successful portability arrangement. There are costs attributable to the vesting of pensions. When ERISA established the various minimum vesting requirements, the cost of those requirements was significant because pension plans were being changed from providing minimal or no vesting, except at retirement, to providing relatively liberal vesting. The pension system in our country today has absorbed most of those costs so that further liberalization in vesting beyond legal requirements has little additional cost to the plan sponsor.

Another approach to portability advocated by some is to give terminating employees the right to deposit the value of their accrued pensions in some type of clearinghouse arrangement so that they, rather than their former employers, benefit from the future investment earnings on their pension credits. By so doing, the plan's sponsor would be losing the actuarial gains represented by any excess of the actual investment income over that assumed in the reserve for the vested pensions. Critics of this approach argue that in addition to adding to plan costs, there will be substantial costs arising from the bureaucracy needed to implement it.

REGULATORY ENVIRONMENT

The regulatory environment for retirement plans generally has witnessed rapid change, which is difficult for plan sponsors, professional practitioners, and regulators, themselves, as evidenced by the postponement of the effective compliance dates of various regulations because of the literal avalanche of comments and criticisms received.

IRC Section 403(b) Plans

The overall regulatory environment for retirement plans is covered elsewhere in the *Handbook*, and this chapter focuses on those aspects applicable to Section 403(b) plans that are unique to the not-for-profit sector. Section 403(b) of the IRC permits employees of Section 501(c)(3) not-for-profit organizations and public school systems to defer certain amounts of their compensation. Prior to the Tax Reform Act of 1986 (TRA '86), plans under this Code section were relatively unaffected by the outpouring of regulation.

Nondiscrimination Requirements

TRA '86 affected Section 403(b) plans in two important ways. First, if a 403(b) plan is not voluntary—that is, not paid for entirely by employee contributions—it is subject to the same coverage rules as other qualified plans. This means that the plan must cover the lesser of 50 employees or 40 percent of all employees and meet at least one of the following tests:

1. It must benefit at least 70 percent of all nonhighly compensated employees, or
2. It must benefit a percentage of nonhighly compensated employees, which is at least 70 percent of the percentage of highly compensated employees, or
3. The average percentage of compensation contributed on behalf of the nonhighly compensated employees must be at least 70 percent of that for highly compensated employees.

"Highly compensated" is a technical term in the IRC that generally refers to corporate officers, or employees earning over $60,535 in 1991, which increases annually as a result of being indexed to the CPI.

Limits on Deferrals

The second way TRA '86 impacted 403(b) plans was by imposing limits on the overall dollar amounts that employees covered under these plans can defer. A voluntary plan must be made available to all employees with respect to elective deferrals. Employees of tax-exempt charitable institutions have historically been allowed to voluntarily exclude up to 20 percent of includable compensation, under a salary-reduction agreement where such reduction was paid into a Section 403(b) annuity. These voluntary Section 403(b) annuities frequently are referred to as tax-sheltered annuities (TSAs) or tax-deferred annuities (TDAs). Section 403(b) voluntary plans have been affected by new dollar limits on deferrals. This limit presently is $9,500. In addition, TRA '86 introduced an aggregation rule whereby plans under Section 403(b) and other voluntary plans such as Section 401(k) and Section 457 plans are aggregated for purposes of testing whether or not the employee has reached the $9,500 limit. Consequently, in most instances, the maximum that an employee can voluntarily defer from his or her taxable income to all tax-advantaged plans is $9,500. Section 403(b) also contains a special "catch-up" provision for any employee who has completed 15 years of service with a not-for-profit organization. The "catch-up" is subject to various rules and formulas, but in general it permits those who are eligible to contribute a maximum of $12,500. The $12,500 is composed of the $9,500 maximum, plus a catch-up allowance of $3,000.

The overall limit on employer and employee contributions imposed by IRC Section 415 that is, a $30,000 aggregate contribution to an individual's account in any one year for all defined contribution plans combined, also is applicable.

Distributions, Withdrawals, and Loans

Prior to TRA '86, tax-deferred annuities were in many cases utilized as tax-deferred savings accounts. TRA '86 imposes penalties on lump-sum distributions from such accounts prior to age 59½ unless a case of hardship exists, there is a separation from service, or death or disability occurs. Distributions or withdrawals that do not meet any of these conditions are subject to an additional excise tax of 10 percent.

Prior to the introduction of restrictions on withdrawals, Section 403(b) plans permitted loans to participants who were secured by their plan account balances, but such features were not commonplace in most plans. However, with the restrictions on withdrawals came a greatly increased popularity of loan provisions. Generally, the maximum amount that can be borrowed is limited to the lesser of 50 percent of the account balance or $50,000. The required maximum repayment schedule normally is five years but may be extended to ten years if the loan is being used for the purchase of the participant's primary residence.

The new uniform commencement-date rules for receiving distributions from qualified retirement plans now apply to TSAs as well. As such, beginning in 1989, distributions must begin no later than the April 1 following the calendar year in which the employee becomes 70½.

It is interesting to note that, with all that has transpired from a regulatory point of view, Section 403(b) tax-deferred annuities have had the least burdensome changes imposed on them. Does this mean that there has been an ultimate shift toward voluntary accounts as the primary source of retirement funding? In the minds of many, this is now beginning to occur.

FUNDING APPROACHES

Insured Approach

To the extent that plans for not-for-profit corporations are similar to those of other corporations, they can be funded in similar ways. These include different types of insurance contracts, including individual policies, deposit administration contracts, immediate participation guarantee contracts, guaranteed income contracts, and the like. These contracts are described in Chapter 45 of the *Handbook*. Insurers also may offer a variety of services including assistance with document preparation, employee record-keeping, preparation of accounting data, benefit determination, and, in the case of defined benefit plans, periodic actuarial valuations. As might be expected, smaller organizations have shown a preference for contracts providing full service.

Trusteed Arrangements

Qualified retirement plans not entirely funded through insurance contracts must be handled through trusteed arrangements. The trustees, who sometimes are the principal officers of the corporation, have considerable latitude in the kind of investments that they may make with the pension fund, as long as they meet the fiduciary requirements, including the prudent expert rule. Investments can include insurance contracts; stocks and bonds, both governmental and nongovernmental; bank certificates of deposit; mutual funds of a variety of types; futures and options; and real estate.

INSURED FUNDING MECHANISMS

Many different products have been developed for use with Section 403(b) tax-sheltered annuity plans, including a variety of insurance company deferred annuity contracts.

Retirement Income Contracts

As defined in the IRC, an "annuity contract" can include contracts that provide incidental life insurance. Contracts of the so-called retirement income type fall into this category. These contracts typically provide a death benefit of the greater of the face amount of the policy or the cash value at the time of death. The face amount of the policy is 100 times the monthly annuity benefit that is guaranteed to be provided at the normal retirement age as specified in the policy if all premiums are paid as due. These contracts provide guaranteed benefits that include death benefits, cash values, and annuity benefits for a (guaranteed) level annual premium. They typically are participating in form, paying dividends that can be used to increase the values of the policy.

Life Insurance with Supplemental Annuity Rider

Life insurance contracts combined with a supplemental annuity rider also are acceptable as meeting the requirements of the Code as long as the cash values of the life insurance policy and the annuity rider combined are at least sufficient to provide a monthly annuity at retirement age not less than 1 percent of the face amount of the life insurance policy. These have not been very popular as funding mechanisms for tax-sheltered annuities, because employees holding these contracts are taxed on the annual term insurance value of the incidental life insurance protection according to tables in the IRS regulations. Known as "P.S. 58" costs, these are the same costs that are used to determine the taxable value of incidental life insurance protection provided under pension plans generally.

Flexible-Premium Contracts

Rather more popular has been a variety of pure retirement annuity contracts. Early in the history of tax-sheltered annuities the most popular was a fixed-premium, fixed-benefit contract similar to the retirement income contract previously described but with no life insurance benefit provided other than the amount of the cash value. As interest rates increased during the 1970s, these contracts were viewed as being less competitive and lacking in flexibility and mostly have been replaced by flexible-premium contracts that may offer a variety of investment options to the employer. Under these contracts the employee can pay, in any period of time, as much or as little as he or she wishes in premium payments, although the contract may specify a minimum size, such as $10, for any payment made, for obvious practical reasons. The maximum that the employee can pay may or may not be specified in the policy, but as a practical matter, it is limited by the maximum exclusion allowance provisions of the Code previously described. This flexibility in premium amount, for example, permits the employee to increase the premium payment when the amount of the employee's maximum exclusion allowance increases as a result of increases in the amount of salary. Or the employee may wish to make what is essentially a one-time premium payment to the policy to take advantage of the catch-up provision permitted in the maximum exclusion allowance. It also permits the employee to make no premium payment in a year without it constituting a lapse of the policy, although the policy may put limits on the duration of the suspension of payments, again for practical reasons.

In their original form, flexible-premium annuity contracts typically offered one investment option, the insurance company's general account. These contracts were typically "front-end" loaded, which means that the insurance company deducted from each gross premium payment a small part to cover its acquisition and administration costs, including agents' commissions, if any. Such front-end loadings might fall anywhere in the range of 3 to 9 percent. The remaining net premium would then be credited to a policy account and accumulated with interest until the policy was surrendered or converted to an annuity. The interest rate credited would be as declared by the insurance company from time to time and subject to some minimal guaranteed rate, typically 3 percent. The actual credited rate often is set on a "portfolio" basis; that is, the same rate is applicable to the entire fund balance of the policy and applies to all policies of the same type. Some companies, however, credit different rates on different "generations" of funds reflecting differing investment conditions over time.

The company attempts to set the credited rate at a level that allows it some margin between the rate and the earned rate on the associated portfolio of assets to cover items such as: (1) expenses not covered by the front-end loading, (2) risk charges for the mortality, interest, and expense guarantees of the policy, and (3) profits. However, in periods when market yields on new investments deviate substantially from asset portfolio rates, it may be desirable to reduce or increase the margin.

These policies also typically have a surrender charge, or back-end loading, which is deducted from the fund value in case the policy is surrendered for cash in the early policy years. A typical surrender charge formula would be 7 percent of the fund value on surrender in the first policy year, 6 percent in the second year, 5 percent in the third year, and so on until the surrender charge disappears after seven years. The rationale for the charge is twofold. One is to allow the insurance company to recover at least part of the policy's initial acquisition expense, which it may not have recovered from the other charges in the case of early surrender. The second is in recognition that to be competitive in terms of the credited interest rate on the fund balance, insurance companies typically have had to invest in fixed-income securities of mid-term or long-term maturities. This exposes the company to a risk of disintermediation in periods of rising interest rates and consequently falling values of fixed-income securities. The surrender charge serves both to discourage early policy termination and allows the company to recover at least in part the realized capital losses that may occur if it is forced to sell fixed-income securities in a rising interest-rate market.

Even with this protection insurers can experience painful losses on this type of policy when interest rates spike as they did in the late 1970s and early 1980s. Insurers found at that time that if they did not raise their credited interest rate to levels well beyond what they were earning on the associated assets, which were of older vintage and were yielding lower returns, they could experience substantial diminishment of new business and outflow of existing business. To address this problem several companies have experimented with variable surrender-charge formulas that parallel the changing relationship between market value and book value of the associated assets as interest rates change. At least in the case of policies issued in New York state, such surrender charges, whether fixed or variable, are subject to a maximum limit of 7 percent of the policy's current fund balance.

Guaranteed Income Contracts

In order to help cope with the problem of disintermediation, some insurers have introduced the concept of guaranteed income contracts (GICs). The GIC concept, first developed in the pension field, became a particularly attractive tool in the late 1970s and early 1980s, when interest rates were at historically high levels. However, because of the recent problems of several insurance companies concerning the make-up of their investment portfolios, GICs are being reviewed very carefully by plan sponsors. The GIC is conceptually just like a certificate of deposit issued by a bank. It has a fixed maturity date, which might typically be one year, three years, or five years from the commencement date. It provides a guaranteed interest rate if held to maturity, which is closely tied to new money rates available in the fixed-income security markets with comparable maturities. The premium deposit may be limited to a single sum at the commencement date, or the policy may provide an "open window" permitting variable deposits, subject to certain amount and time limits with the same guaranteed interest rate. As is the case with a bank certificate of deposit, early cash surrender carries with it a substantial penalty, which in effect protects the insurance company against disintermediation in periods of rising interest rates.

The policy might offer several different GIC options carrying different maturity dates. Upon maturity of the GIC, the policy normally provides that the maturity value of the GIC is rolled into a new GIC of the same duration with a new guaranteed interest rate reflecting market conditions that exist at that time.

Variable Annuities

Also widely used in this as well as other markets is the variable annuity. Frequently a policy will provide the employee an option of allocating his or her premiums between the guaranteed fund type of annuities just described and the variable annuity. The split may vary anywhere from 100 percent allocated to the guaranteed annuity, to 100 percent allocated to the variable annuity. Within the variable annuity, there typically are a number of investment options. The investment options are, in effect, mutual funds—that is, shares in an investment company that is a subsidiary of the life insurance company. The investments of the mutual funds may be managed by company personnel or have outside managers and may be of a variety of types, such as money market funds, bond funds, common-stock funds, or funds investing in a wide variety of types of assets. The funds must be used exclusively with the products of the life insurance company; that is, they cannot also be sold directly to the public as mutual funds. This has spawned the development of "clone" funds, which meet this requirement but, nevertheless, attempt to duplicate the investment style and holdings of publicly available mutual funds by using the same managers and investment objectives.

The variable annuity option may be restricted to the preretirement accumulation or may be available during the payout period, resulting in annuity payments that vary from month to month depending on the investment performance of the underlying assets.

The share values of the mutual fund reflect charges made by the investment company to cover its expenses, primarily its investment function. In addition, the insurance company may make further charges against the employees' fund balances consisting of shares in the mutual fund to cover, in part, its administration and acquisition expenses and risk associated with mortality guarantees, if any.

To the extent that employees elect the variable annuity option, they relieve the insurance company of the risks associated with disintermediation since the cash-surrender value of the variable annuity portion of the contract is based directly on the market value of the mutual shares held at the time of cash surrender. Therefore, typically there are not cash-surrender charges applicable to this portion of the contract, unlike the fixed annuity portion of the contract. There also has been a growing trend by insurers to do away with front-end loadings. This allows the insurance company to compete for new tax-sheltered annuity business on a more equal footing with other investment options available to employees under TSA plans, such as the direct purchase of no-load mutual funds. Typically, however, the asset charges of insurance products remain high compared with those of mutual funds themselves.

Policies that offer variable annuity options, as well as their issuers and agents, are subject to the various federal securities acts—the Securities Act of 1933, the Securities Exchange Act of 1934, and the Investment Company Act of 1940. The Securities Act of 1933 requires, for example, that products judged to be securities, such as variable annuities, must meet certain disclosure requirements, such as the preparation of a detailed prospectus intended to inform the present or intended holder of the securities of the policies and objectives of the investment fund and how they are to be carried out. They must be registered with the Securities and Exchange Commission (SEC) and are subject to certain rules that regulate the charges made by the issuer. It also means that insurance company sales and service personnel who handle variable annuities must be registered with the SEC. This usually involves passing one or more examinations administered by the National Association of Securities

Dealers. Some states also require individuals handling these products to meet qualifying standards.

Because of the complications arising both from the more difficult administration and more complex regulation of variable annuities, not all companies in the TSA field offer these products. Furthermore, it is the experience of at least one major insurer in this field that most employees shun the variable annuity option, presumably because their accumulations under the TSA plan represent a substantial part of their retirement savings and because they are unwilling to expose those savings to what they perceive as the additional risk associated with fluctuations in the market values of various securities.

Other Funding Mechanisms

In addition to annuity and life insurance contracts, IRC Section 403(b) provides other methods of funding a TSA plan. These include custodial accounts invested in mutual funds. The custodian must be a bank, credit union, or savings and loan association. Also, so-called face-amount certificates issued by a few mutual fund companies may be used for this purpose. These are not equity products.

While other funding vehicles have gained some popularity in the 403(b) market, life insurance company products have remained predominant in this area.

PRODUCT VENDORS

No discussion of retirement plans for not-for-profit groups would be complete without a description of the unique role of certain institutions identified with this market. Foremost among these is the Teachers Insurance and Annuity Association (TIAA) and its companion mutual fund, the College Retirement Equity Fund (CREF).

The famous industrialist and philanthropist Andrew Carnegie had a particular concern for education in the United States and particularly for the viability of institutions of higher education. Recognizing the need to improve the financial security of the faculty members of these institutions, he made of gift of $10 million in 1904 to establish free pensions for them. As large as this gift was, it soon became apparent that it was inadequate to meet the very great need, and, subsequently, the Carnegie

Foundation appointed a special commission on insurance and annuities, which ultimately led to the formation of TIAA in 1918.

Thirty colleges and universities joined the new retirement system created by TIAA in its first year, and since that time TIAA has dominated the retirement-plan field as insurer and service provider for private institutions of higher education as well as for public institutions of higher education whose employees are not covered under the regular state employee retirement systems. So thorough has this dominance been that even operating with a limited offering of investment options in a limited market, TIAA has become the fifth largest insurer in the United States, with $45 billion in assets, and at the end of 1989, CREF had $38 billion in assets. If considered as a single system, their combined assets of $83 billion make TIAA/CREF the largest private retirement system in the world.

From its inception, TIAA has stressed certain fundamental principles. All benefits accruing to participants should be fully funded and easily portable as faculty members move from one institution to another within the system. This led to a system of retirement benefits on a money purchase basis and later on a defined contribution basis as opposed to a defined benefit basis. It also led to the principle of full and immediate vesting of all accrued benefits regardless of length of service. In order to provide adequate benefits, the system is funded by contributions from both plan participants and their employers. To keep the cost of the system as low as possible, it operates without agents, and sales and service is performed exclusively by salaried personnel. With minor exceptions, TIAA has followed these principles for over 70 years.

Another factor in keeping the cost of the system down was the ability of TIAA to achieve and maintain tax-exempt status. It is qualified under IRC Section 501(c)(3) as an institution that exists for purposes of fostering education. Historically, the retirement plans insured by TIAA generally were not qualified under IRC Section 401(a) but were considered to meet the requirements of Section 403(b). Until recently this permitted institutions to structure the plans without concern for the qualified plan nondiscrimination requirements that were designed to prevent unreasonably high benefits from being paid to highly compensated individuals in relation to what is being provided to lower-paid individuals. This, for example, permitted institutions in the TIAA system to maintain separate plans for their clerical and labor forces and for their faculties even though in many cases the benefits for the former were smaller in relation to salary than for the latter. This advantage was lost as a result of TRA '86, and 403(b)–type plans now must also meet nondiscrimination tests. TRA '86 also ended TIAA's tax-exempt status with respect to income from products other than those used to fund pension funds, but these have historically been a minor part of TIAA's total business.

Over the years, TIAA has added other products, including ordinary life insurance, group life insurance, and health insurance. However, the single most significant development since its founding was the creation of CREF in 1952. CREF's creation came about as a result of increasing concern that the purchasing power of annuities established on a fixed-dollar basis would be severely eroded by the long-term effects of even a moderate rate of inflation. After considerable study it was concluded that a program of annuities whose benefits were indexed to the performance of an equity fund would provide not only substantial long-term protection against inflation but superior investment returns in comparison with fixed-dollar securities as well. Thus, TIAA became the first insurance company in the United States to provide its plan participants with the option of variable annuities. Generally, plan participants have flexibility in choosing what portions of their and their employer's contributions go to the variable and annuity options. This concept has become widely popular and has been adopted by many other retirement plans. Accumulations in CREF can be transferred to TIAA and converted to fixed-dollar annuities, but transfers in the reverse direction are not permitted.

During the decade of the 1980s TIAA came under increasing criticism with respect to what was regarded as the inflexible and paternalistic attitudes reflected in its principles of operation. Some of its participating institutions began to permit plan participants to elect alternatives to the traditional TIAA/CREF programs. Partly in response to those criticisms, TIAA/CREF has taken a number of steps. In 1984, an alternative group retirement annuity (GRA) plan was introduced. It provides a lump-sum cash option at retirement, although TIAA continued to recommend to its policy holders that retirement benefits should be provided only in the form of lifetime income. A number of market-valued investment options also have been added recently to complement the traditional stock equity fund of CREF. These include a money market fund in 1988 and a bond fund and social responsibility fund in 1990. The latter adds to the traditional objective of maximum investment performance consistent with risk, an objective of emphasizing investment in corporations whose business conduct meets certain social welfare criteria. How popular these new investment options will be remains to be seen.

The second institution that has specialized in providing retirement and related plans exclusively for not-for-profit institutions is Mutual of America Life Insurance Company. At the end of World War II, leaders in the United Way movement recognized that workers in their health and human services agencies needed coverage under the same kind of employee benefit programs that were available to employees of for-profit corporations. This was particularly true since, at the time, they were not covered by the Social Security system. Major insurance companies, including TIAA, declined to extend coverage to this group of employees, but offered to assist in the formation of a new, separate institution for this purpose. Thus, in 1945 the National Health and Welfare Retirement Association was founded and subsequently converted to a mutual life insurance company organization and renamed Mutual of America. While its charter has recently been changed to expand its market to include the entire range of not-for-profit institutions as well as governmental employee groups, its principal market continues to be in the health and human services field. The company has achieved rapid growth in recent years and now is the largest mutual life insurance company founded since the end of the second World War, with $6 billion in assets.

Mutual of America adopted some of the same principles as TIAA, including the sale and service of its products by salaried personnel rather than agents and the commitment to full and immediate vesting under its retirement plans. However, unlike TIAA, which has offered defined contribution type retirement plans exclusively, Mutual of America makes both defined contribution and defined benefit plans available and recommends the latter as superior since only a defined benefit plan can assure plan participants a predictable level of income in retirement. Recognizing the frequently low earnings of workers in the health and human services field, it recommends that employers pay the entire cost of the base plan while encouraging employees to contribute to a voluntary supplemental program such as a TSA, and it recommends that retiring employees should have the freedom to take retirement benefits in lump-sum form to achieve greater flexibility in tax and financial planning.

Mutual of America developed the unique portability program described previously that provides mobile participants with the same benefit that they would have received had they spent their entire careers in the social-service field with their final employers. It also recognizes the potential for erosion of fixed-dollar annuities by inflation and encourages its defined benefit policyholders to guarantee adjustment of retirement benefits in current payment status according to increases in the consumer price index, subject to a maximum annual adjustment such as 4 percent. The substantial cost of this indexing feature, however, has limited its adoption to a minority of its policyholders. Instead, many have adopted thrift plans funded by voluntary employee contributions and matching employer contributions in order to provide supplemental retirement benefits to maintain retirement income adequacy.

The substantial success of these two institutions in the not-for-profit field has encouraged life insurance companies and other financial institutions to enter the market, and some have done so with varying degrees of success. Nevertheless, TIAA and Mutual of America remain preeminent in their traditional target markets.

CONCLUSION

While the retirement security needs of employees of not-for-profit organizations are basically the same as those of employees in other sectors of the economy, there are differences in the way benefits are provided to meet those needs. The social and economic structures of the organizations themselves, the nature of the positions within the organizations, and their tax-exempt status all contribute to the way in which plans have been designed to provide retirement income to their participants. New methods have been developed over the years to deal with changing tax requirements, inflation, and other circumstances, and the field, no doubt, will adapt to additional changes and continue to grow in the future.

CHAPTER 40

SECTION 457 DEFERRED COMPENSATION PLANS

Daniel J. Ryterband

BACKGROUND

Deferred compensation plans allow employees to postpone receiving income for future service until some later date—most commonly, at retirement. Deferred amounts and income earned generally are not taxed until either paid or "made available" to plan participants. Deferred amounts generally are considered made available when participants acquire an immediate, nonforfeitable right to them.

Deferred compensation plans can be structured as pure deferred compensation plans, salary continuation arrangements, or a combination of both. In pure deferred compensation plans, employees enter into an agreement with their employer to reduce present compensation or to forgo a raise or bonus in return for the employer's promise to pay benefits at a future date. In salary continuation plans the employer pays an additional, supplemental benefit without reducing the employee's present compensation, raise, or bonus.

When properly structured, deferred compensation plans shield participants' deferred income from what are termed the tax "doctrines" of economic benefit and constructive receipt. The *doctrine of economic benefit* generally states that an economic benefit results when an economic or financial benefit, even though not in cash form, is provided to an employee as compensation, such as when an employee receives beneficial ownership of amounts placed with a third party, or when assets are unconditionally and irrevocably paid into a fund to be used for the employee's sole benefit. The *doctrine of constructive receipt* generally states that income, although not necessarily received in hand by an individual, is considered received and therefore currently taxable when it is credited to an account or set aside so that it may be drawn upon at any time and amounts receivable are not subject to substantial limitations or restrictions.[1] Generally, events triggering economic benefit or constructive receipt result in deferred amounts becoming made available to plan participants, and, thus, subject to current taxation. A mere unsecured promise to pay, however, does not constitute receipt of income.[2]

INTRODUCTION TO SECTION 457 PLANS

Section 457 plans are nonqualified deferred compensation plans available only to state and local government employers (including rural electrical cooperatives) and nongovernment organizations exempt from tax under Internal Revenue Code (IRC) Section 501. Examples of tax-exempt organizations under Section 501 include nongovernmental schools, private hospitals, labor unions, farmers' cooperatives, and certain trade associations, business leagues, private clubs, and fraternal orders. For the most part, they are nonprofit organizations serving their members or a public or charitable cause.

The Revenue Act of 1978 created IRC Section 457, allowing employees of state and local governments to defer up to $7,500 of compensation annually in plans meeting specified requirements. The Tax Reform Act of 1986 (TRA '86) extended Section 457's provisions to nonqualified deferred compensation plans of nongovernment tax-exempt employers. Section 457 severely limits deferral opportunities for employees of eligible employers.

Eligible employers generally use Section 457 plans in two ways:

1. As pure deferred compensation plans that allow participants to reduce their taxable salary in a manner similar to that of private-sector 401(k) plans.
2. As salary continuation plans that provide executives with supplemental retirement income.

---

[1]Reg. Sec. 1.451-2(a).

[2]Rev. Rul. 60-31, 1960-1 CB 174; Rev. Rul. 69-650, 1969-2 CB 106.

Plans meeting the complex requirements of Section 457 and of related laws and regulations receive favorable tax treatment (deferral of income tax), but deferred income is subject to Social Security and federal unemployment withholding at the time of deferral.[3] Section 457 classifies plans as either ''eligible'' or ''ineligible,'' each subject to the following specific requirements.

ELIGIBLE PLAN REQUIREMENTS

In eligible plans, deferred income and its earnings are tax-free until paid or made available to participants or beneficiaries.[4]

Eligibility for Plan Participation

Plan participation must be limited to employees and independent contractors performing service for the employer.[5] Before deferring compensation in any given month, participants must have previously entered into an agreement authorizing the deferrals.[6] Therefore, an active worker must wait until the beginning of the month after entering into an agreement before deferring any income. New employees can make deferrals in their first month of employment if they enter into an agreement on or before their first day of employment.[7] It is not necessary to execute a new agreement for each month.

Maximum Annual Deferral

The plan ceiling, or maximum annual deferral, is $7,500 or 33⅓ percent of includable compensation (generally the equivalent of 25 percent of gross compensation), whichever is less.[8] (The $7,500 limit, unlike limits applying to qualified plans, is not adjusted annually for changes in the

---

[3]IRC Sec. 3121(a)(5)(E), 3121(v)(3), 3306(b)(5), and 3306(r).

[4]IRC Sec. 457(a).

[5]IRC Sec. 457(b)(1), Reg. Sec. 1.457-2(d).

[6]IRC Sec. 457(b)(4).

[7]Reg. Sec. 1.457-2(g).

[8]IRC Sec. 457(b)(2).

cost of living.) Includable compensation is payment for service performed for the employer includable in current gross income and excludes amounts deferred.[9] Gross compensation generally equals gross income plus amounts deferred. For example, a participant with total compensation of $20,000 generally can defer a maximum of $5,000, which is the equivalent of 33⅓ percent of includable compensation or 25 percent of gross compensation. Deferred amounts exceeding this limit generally are treated as made available and subject to normal taxation in the taxable year deferred.[10]

For purposes of the plan ceiling, deferred income must be taken into account at its current value (in the plan year deferred, rather than the year received) unless subject to a substantial risk of forfeiture. Thus, if a participant agrees to perform services for current compensation plus income payable in the future, the present value of the amount payable must be determined to see if the plan ceiling has been exceeded. However, if the future compensation is conditioned on the participant's performance of substantial services for the employer, it is not valued until it is no longer subject to a risk of forfeiture.[11]

Catch-Up Provision

During any or all of the three taxable years ending before the year the participant reaches normal retirement age, participants may defer more than $7,500 or 33⅓ percent of includable compensation. This "catch-up" provision increases the annual deferral ceiling to $15,000 or, if less, the participant's normal ceiling plus aggregate unused annual ceiling amounts for deferrals in prior years.[12] For example, a 62-year-old participant, with gross compensation of $20,000 in an eligible plan with a normal retirement age of 65, who has underutilized deferrals in prior years by $10,000 could elect to defer a maximum of $15,000 in the present year. This amount is computed by adding the available catch-up limit of $10,000 to the normal limit of $5,000 (computed as 25 percent of $20,000).

---

[9]IRC Sec. 457(e)(5).

[10]Reg. Sec. 1.457-1(b)(2), Example 5.

[11]IRC Sec. 457(e)(6), Reg. Sec. 1.457-2(e)(3).

[12]IRC Sec. 457(b)(3).

Participants may not use the catch-up provision after the expiration of the three-year period even if it was not fully used in the three years preceding normal retirement age and whether or not the participant or former participant rejoins the plan or participates in another eligible plan after retirement.[13] Normal retirement age may be specified in the plan and defined as a single age or range of ages ending no later than 70½. In plans that do not specify normal retirement age, it is generally age 65 or the latest normal retirement age specified in the employer's pension plan, if later.[14]

Coordination With Other Plans

Maximum deferrals in 457 plans must be coordinated with amounts excluded from income under 401(k) plans, simplified employee pensions (SEPs), 403(b) plans, and amounts deductible under IRC Section 501(c)(18).[15] Amounts contributed to such plans reduce the amount participants can defer in an eligible 457 plan on a dollar-for-dollar basis. For example, if someone participates in both a 403(b) plan and a 457 plan and defers $4,000 to the 403(b), the 457 plan limit would be reduced to $3,500. Aggregate amounts in excess of eligible 457 plan limits generally are considered made available and taxable to the participant in the year deferred.[16]

Unfunded Nature of Plans

Deferred amounts and earnings must remain the sole property of the employer until made available to participants, subject only to the claims of the employer's general creditors.[17] This means eligible 457 plans must be "unfunded," and employers may not irrevocably set aside assets to make future benefit payments. (A "funded" plan is one in which plan assets are irrevocably set aside, giving participants and beneficiaries a secured interest.) This does not mean, however, that employers cannot do

---

[13]Reg. Sec. 1.457-2(f).

[14]Reg. Sec. 1.457-2(f)(4).

[15]IRC Sec. 457(c)(2).

[16]Reg. Sec. 1.457-1(b)(2), Example 6.

[17]IRC Sec. 457(b)(6).

anything to prefund future benefit obligations. Plans are considered unfunded as long as any assets set aside are available to meet the employer's obligations to general creditors, and participants have no greater security than that of any other general creditor. "Informal funding," or asset accumulation, is allowed, and most employers offer participants a choice among various plan investments. Participants, therefore, do exercise some ownership rights, and the ability to choose among various investments does not cause amounts deferred to be treated as made available.[18] Therefore, plan participants may choose among options available for investing amounts deferred, but they cannot have a secured interest in purchased assets and the assets cannot be segregated in any way that would put them outside the reach of the sponsoring employer's general creditors.

Because assets remain the sole property of the employer, participants are at risk of losing amounts deferred. This is a serious disadvantage of 457 plans; and a variety of solutions have been proposed to safeguard participant assets, including use of "rabbi trusts," surety bonds, and letters of credit. Use of such arrangements and instruments, however, could result in creation of insured funding (and thus prohibit general creditors access to deferrals), which results in loss of tax deferral under Section 457.[19] Clarifying guidance restricting the use of surety bonds and letters of credit in 457 plans is expected from the IRS. However, the IRS National Office has indicated informally that use of arrangements similar to rabbi trusts will be allowed in 457 plans. These arrangements will provide some protection for participants but will not shield amounts deferred from the claims of general creditors.[20]

Absence of Loan Provisions

Another result of assets remaining the sole property of the employer is that loans are not permitted in 457 plans. This is because participants have no secured, nonforfeitable benefit from which to secure the loan and because assets must remain subject to the employer's general creditors until made available.

---

[18]Reg. Sec. 1.457-1(b)(1).

[19]IRC Sec. 83(a).

[20]Conference of the American Law Institute, American Bar Association, September 6, 1990.

Availability of Benefits

Plan benefits cannot be made available until the participant separates from service or is faced with an "unforeseeable emergency," or until the calendar year when the participant attains age 70½, if later.[21] Separation from service generally occurs at the employee's termination, disability, death, or retirement.[22] Independent contractors are considered separated from service when their contracts expire, assuming the expiration constitutes a good-faith and complete termination of the contractual relationship. If the employer expects to renew the contract or hire the independent contractor as an employee, separation from service generally has not occurred.[23] An unforeseeable emergency is a severe financial hardship resulting from a sudden and unexpected illness, loss of property because of casualty, or other similar extraordinary and unforeseeable circumstance outside participant control. The need to send a child to college or to purchase a new home are not considered unforeseeable emergencies.[24] In addition, participants may not withdraw money if insurance, liquidation of the participant's assets, or discontinuing plan deferrals will relieve the hardship. Emergency withdrawals are permitted only in amounts necessary to satisfy the emergency need.[25]

Plan Distributions

Distributions from eligible plans must begin within 60 days after the later of the close of the plan year when a participant attains or would have attained the plan's normal retirement age or the day the participant separates from service.[26] Eligible 457 plans are subject to distribution beginning date requirements similar to those of qualified plans. Government 457 plan distributions must begin no later than April 1 of the calendar year following the year when an employee either retires or attains age 70½, whichever is later. The required beginning date for

[21]IRC Sec. 457(d)(1).

[22]Reg. Sec. 1.457-2(h)(2).

[23]Reg. Sec. 1.457-2(h)(3).

[24]Reg. Sec. 1.457-2(h)(4).

[25]Reg. Sec. 1.457-2(h)(5).

[26]Reg. Sec. 1.457-2(i).

tax-exempt employer 457 plans is April 1 of the year following the year the participant attains age 70½.[27]

Distributions beginning before a participant's death generally must satisfy the qualified plan incidental death benefit rules. The plan must pay beneficiaries amounts not distributed during the participant's lifetime using a method at least as rapid as the method used before death.[28] When distributions begin after a participant's death, the beneficiary must receive the entire amount within 15 years, or in the case of a spouse, within the beneficiary's life expectancy.[29]

Distributions paid over a period of one year or more must be made in substantially nonincreasing amounts.[30] Distributions do not qualify for special lump-sum five-year forward averaging treatment available to qualified plans.[31] Eligible 457 plan distributions (and amounts considered made available) are subject to regular income tax withholding as wages, and payments are reported on Form W-2.[32] However, amounts made available are not taxed if the participant or beneficiary irrevocably elects before distribution to defer payment until a later date.[33] For example, if someone separates from service at age 60 and elects to defer payment until age 65, the amount is not treated as made available (even though the person had the right to receive it) and remains tax-deferred until received.

Former participants may have any amount made payable to them transferred to another eligible plan without having amounts treated as made available.[34] However, a 457 plan distribution cannot be rolled over into an individual retirement account.[35] Distributions from 457 plans are exempt from the 10 percent penalty tax on withdrawals made before age 59½.[36] They also are exempt from the 15 percent tax assessed on excess aggregate annual distribution amounts.[37]

---

[27]IRC Sec. 457(d)(2) and 401(a)(9).

[28]IRC Sec. 457(d)(2)(B)(i).

[29]IRC Sec. 457(d)(2)(B)(ii).

[30]IRC Sec. 457(d)(2)(C).

[31]Let. Rul. 8119020, February 10, 1981.

[32]Rev. Rul. 82-46, 1982-1 CB 158.

[33]Reg. Sec. 1.457-1(b).

[34]IRC Sec. 457(e)(10).

[35]Rev. Rul. 86-103, 1986-2 CB 62.

[36]IRC Sec. 72(t).

[37]IRC Sec. 4980A.

Death Benefits

Death benefits received from 457 plans are not excludable from gross income as life insurance under IRC Section 101(a) or as an employee death benefit under IRC Section 101(b), regardless of whether the benefit is funded by life insurance on the participant.[38]

IRS Approval

Unlike qualified plans, eligible 457 plans need not apply to the IRS for approval but can and often apply for private letter rulings indicating the plan meets the requirements of Section 457. Plans not administered according to the law can lose the tax benefit of deferral. State and local government plans that do not comply with the statutory requirements of eligible 457 plans must be amended as of the first plan year beginning more than 180 days after IRS notification of any inconsistencies. A plan not amended within this grace period will be treated as an ineligible plan and becomes subject to the rules of Section 457(f). There is no grace period for plans of nongovernmental tax-exempt employers, who must maintain compliance at all times to maintain favorable tax treatment.[39]

INELIGIBLE PLAN REQUIREMENTS

Ineligible 457 plans are governed by separate rules under Section 457(f). To receive tax-preferred treatment in an ineligible plan, amounts deferred must be subject to a substantial risk of forfeiture. Unlike eligible plans, ineligible plans place no limits on the amount of deferrals made. Employers can therefore use ineligible plans to allow employees a contribution level above the eligible plan limit or to provide supplemental retirement benefits to selected executives. However, ineligible plans are better suited for employer contributions than for salary reduction due to the substantial risk of forfeiture provision. If an employer maintains both

---

[38]Reg. Sec. 1.457 1(c).

[39]IRC Sec. 457(b) last paragraph, Reg. Sec. 1.457-2(1).

an eligible and an ineligible plan, it is recommended they be maintained and administered separately for cost and compliance reasons.

Ineligible 457 plan deferred amounts are included in participant or beneficiary gross income in the first taxable year where there is no substantial risk of forfeiture, even if amounts are not received.[40] For a substantial risk of forfeiture to exist, a person's right to receive deferred amounts must be conditioned on future performance of substantial services.[41] Whether the risk of forfeiture is substantial depends on the facts and circumstances of each situation. For example, a substantial risk of forfeiture likely exists when rights to deferred payment are lost at termination of employment for any reason, but a requirement that rights are lost only at termination for cause or committing a crime generally would not create a substantial risk.

Taxation of distributions or amounts made available in ineligible plans is determined under IRC Section 72 annuity rules.[42]

PLAN AVAILABILITY AMONG EMPLOYEE GROUPS

Unlike most types of retirement plans, a 457 plan can be offered on a discriminatory basis with participation limited to only a few employees or even a single employee. The requirement that 457 plans be unfunded, however, can limit availability to certain employee groups, depending on whether the plan is maintained by a state and local government or nongovernment tax-exempt employer.

Title I of the Employee Retirement Income Security Act (ERISA) requires plans be funded, which conflicts with the Section 457 requirement that plans be unfunded with amounts deferred remaining the sole property of the employer. Tax-exempt employers' plans generally are subject to Title I requirements, and therefore must fall within one of the special Title I exceptions to meet both ERISA and IRC requirements. This conflict generally requires nongovernment tax-exempt employer 457 plans to restrict participation to a select group of management or highly compensated

---

[40]IRC Sec. 457(f)(1)(A).

[41]IRC Sec. 457(f)(3)(B).

[42]IRC Sec. 72 and 457(f)(1)(B), Reg. Sec. 1.457-3(a)(3).

employees (''top-hat'' plans) to avoid ERISA's funding requirements.[43] Clear guidelines have not yet been issued on the definition of management or highly paid employees for these purposes, but the requirements will likely be restrictive and based on income, management duties, and the ability to negotiate compensation with the employer.

Because state and local government employers are not subject to Title I of ERISA,[44] government employers can offer 457 plan participation to all employees (as well as independent contractors).

457 PLAN REPORTING AND DISCLOSURE

State and local government employer 457 plans are exempt from ERISA's reporting and disclosure requirements.[45] These employers do not have to comply with requirements for summary plan descriptions; summary annual reports and summary descriptions of material plan modifications; annual registration statements; and plan descriptions, annual reports, and other materials frequently requested by participants. Certain returns and reports (such as Forms W-2 and 1099-MISC), however, must be filed with the IRS, and participants and beneficiaries must receive information about their benefits when they terminate employment or receive benefit distributions.

Nongovernmental tax-exempt employer plans must meet ERISA's requirements for reporting and disclosure.[46] However, tax-exempt employer plans maintained for a select group of management or highly compensated employees can satisfy ERISA's reporting and disclosure requirements through an alternative compliance method under Department of Labor regulations. Under this method a statement must be filed with the Secretary of Labor declaring the plan is maintained primarily to provide deferred compensation for a select group of management or highly compensated employees. Plan documents must be provided upon request by the Department of Labor.[47]

---

[43]IRS Notice 87-13, 1987-1 CB 432.

[44]ERISA Sec. 4(b).

[45]ERISA Sec. 4(b)(1).

[46]ERISA Sec. 4(a), 201, 301, and 401.

[47]Labor Reg. Sec. 2520.104-23.

457 PLAN ACCOUNTING AND EXPENSING CONSIDERATIONS

As nontaxable entities, governments and other tax-exempt organizations maintaining 457 plans are not concerned with the tax deductibility of contributions. Many are subject to limited or fixed revenues and strict funding and expense allowances, however, and are therefore concerned with expense levels relevant to their budgeting considerations. Although amounts deferred in 457 plans are considered employer-paid, deferrals are not considered expenses until the taxable year when amounts are included in participant gross income. The reason is that 457 plans must be unfunded. The fact that an employer can and does informally fund the plan has no effect on this provision because the assets remain the property of the employer until made available to participants.[48]

The Government Accounting Standards Board (GASB) requires employers to disclose the value of assets held because 457 plan assets are subject to the employer's general creditors. Referred to as GASB Statement 2, this law requires employers with 457 plans to display the plan balance in an agency fund and to clearly disclose that assets are subject to creditors' claims until made available to participants according to plan terms.

INVESTMENT OF UNFUNDED 457 PLAN ASSETS

Most employers that informally fund 457 plans used for salary deferral purposes offer participants a variety of investment choices, including equity, bond, and money market funds; guaranteed interest contracts; bank deposit accounts; and fixed- and variable-annuity contracts. Fixed-annuity contracts are the most frequently offered investment vehicle, and investments offering a fixed rate of return attract the majority of deferrals.

Insurance companies are the predominant investment manager. Other managers include mutual funds, brokerage firms, banks, and invest-

[48] Reg. Sec. 1.404(a)-12, IRC Sec. 457(b).

ment advisers. In-house investment management is uncommon. Investment managers frequently are responsible for plan implementation, administration and record-keeping, and participant enrollment as well, but these functions can be contracted to service providers or performed in-house.

457 plan investments in life insurance, annuity contracts, and bank deposits present a number of issues. The cost of life insurance purchased with 457 plan deferral amounts is taxable to participants unless the employer retains all incidents of ownership of the contract, is sole beneficiary, and has no obligation to transfer the contract or pass through the proceeds to any participant or beneficiary.[49] The same reasoning applies to using annuities to accumulate assets in the plan. Although the employer may buy a separate annuity for each participant, employees are not taxed if they have no secured interest in the contract and the contract value remains subject to claims of the employer's general creditors.[50]

Federal Deposit Insurance Corporation (FDIC) "pass-through" insurance of 457 plan assets, providing insurance to individual participants rather than to the overall plan, is under debate. The FDIC insures 457 plan deposits in commercial banks up to $100,000 per employer. The now-defunct Federal Savings and Loan Insurance Corporation (FSLIC) insured assets up to $100,000 per participant in thrift institutions and thereby provided pass-through protection to 457 plan deposits. The FDIC assumed authority for insuring thrifts in 1989 and extended the $100,000 pass-through coverage protection previously provided by the FSLIC. However, the FDIC did not extend similar coverage to commercial-bank 457 plan deposits and has proposed eliminating it in thrifts. At issue is whether 457 plans should receive pass-through coverage as provided to 401(k) and other qualified plans, or whether pass-through coverage should be withheld as in other unfunded retirement arrangements. At the time of this writing, Congress was considering several proposals to protect the current pass-through status of thrift deposits and to extend it to commercial bank deposits.[51]

---

[49]Reg. Sec. 1.457-1(b)(2).

[50]Rev. Rul 72-25, 1972-1 CB 127; Let. Rul. 8329070, April 1, 1983.

[51]HR 5008, S 2694.

DEFERRED ARRANGEMENTS NOT CONSIDERED DEFERRED COMPENSATION PLANS

A 1987 IRS Notice interpreted Section 457 requirements as applying to all deferred arrangements. This was interpreted as meaning benefits like accrued sick time and vacation not used in the present year (as well as elective deferrals of compensation) would be subject to Section 457 restrictions.[52] The dollar value of these benefits that employees received would then directly reduce their allowable compensation deferral amount in eligible plans. Under this interpretation, state and local government and tax-exempt employers were severely restricted in providing deferred compensation and supplemental retirement benefits. Section 457 was later amended so that the following plans generally are excluded from Section 457 restrictions and are not considered as providing compensation deferral:[53]

1. Vacation and sick leave.
2. Compensatory time.
3. Severance pay.
4. Disability pay and death benefits.

To be exempt from Section 457, an arrangement must be legitimate and not an indirect method of deferring cash amounts. At the time of this writing, the IRS was examining exempt arrangements to differentiate between bona fide programs and those that may be subterfuges to defer compensation.

DEFERRED COMPENSATION PLANS NOT SUBJECT TO SECTION 457

Certain deferred compensation plans of state and local government and tax-exempt employers generally are not subject to Section 457 restrictions if certain conditions are met.

---

[52] IRS Notice 87-13, 1987-1 CB 432.

[53] IRC Sec. 457(e)(11).

Nonelective Deferred Compensation of Nonemployees

Plans providing nonelective deferred compensation for services not performed as an employee (e.g., independent contractors) are exempt from Section 457 restrictions for tax years beginning after December 31, 1987. To be considered nonelective, a plan must be uniform for all participants, offer no variations or options, and cover all persons with the same relationship to the employer.[54] For example, if a hospital gives a nonemployee doctor deferred compensation, the deferred compensation is considered nonelective only if all other nonemployee doctors are covered by the same plan.

Church and Judicial Deferred Compensation Plans

Deferred compensation plans of churches and church-controlled organizations for their employees generally are exempt from Section 457 requirements for tax years beginning after December 31, 1987.[55]

State judges' government deferred compensation plans use the tax rules for funded and unfunded nonqualified deferred compensation plans, rather than Section 457 rules, if certain requirements are met. In addition, participants are not subject to the substantial risk of forfeiture rule for ineligible plans.[56] Qualified state judicial plans must have existed continuously since December 31, 1978, and must require:

1. All eligible judges to participate and contribute the same fixed percentage of compensation.
2. The plan to provide no judge with an option that would affect the amount of includable compensation.
3. Retirement benefits to be a percentage of the compensation of judges holding similar positions in the state.
4. Benefits paid in any year not to exceed either 100 percent of a participant's average compensation for the highest three years, or if less, $90,000 adjusted for inflation ($112,221 in 1992).[57]

---

[54] IRC Sec. 457(e)(12).

[55] IRC Sec. 457(e)(13), 3121(w)(3)(A), 3121(w)(3)(B).

[56] Sec. 1107(c)(4) of P.L. 99-514 (TRA '86).

[57] Sec. 252 of P.L. 97-248 (TEFRA).

Nonqualified state judicial plans that do not meet these requirements are taxed as ordinary Section 457 deferred compensation plans.

Nongovernment Tax-Exempt Employer Deferred Compensation Plans

Grandfather provisions may apply to nongovernment tax-exempt employer plans in certain cases. Amounts deferred in tax-exempt employers' plans in taxable years beginning before January 1, 1987, generally are exempt from Section 457 restrictions. Amounts deferred after December 31, 1986, are exempt from Section 457 restrictions if deferrals are based on an agreement that on August 16, 1986, was in writing and stipulated deferrals of a fixed amount (or a fixed percentage of a fixed base amount) or an amount determined by a fixed formula. For example, participants who were deferring 5 percent of compensation according to a written plan on August 16, 1986, must make all subsequent deferrals at 5 percent for the amount to be considered fixed. An example of a fixed formula is a deferred compensation plan designed as a defined benefit plan in which deferrals to be paid in the future are in the form of an annual benefit equal to 1 percent per year of service times final average salary. Changes in the fixed amount or fixed formula result in loss of grandfathered status.[58]

Nonelective Government Employer Deferred Compensation Plans

A grandfather provision also is available to amounts deferred before July 14, 1988, in nonelective government plans by participants covered by a written agreement. To avoid Section 457 restrictions, the agreement must stipulate determining annual deferrals as a fixed amount or by a fixed formula. Amounts deferred on or after July 14, 1988, are exempt from Section 457 restrictions until the tax year ending after the effective date of an agreement modifying the fixed amount or fixed formula.[59]

---

[58]IRS Notice 87-13, 1987-1 CB 432.

[59]Sec. 6064(d)(3) of P.L. 100-647 (TAMRA).

Collectively Bargained Deferred Compensation Plans

Collectively bargained plans of both state and local government and nongovernment tax-exempt employers allowing nonelective income deferral may be excluded from Section 457 restrictions if certain conditions are met. To be grandfathered, a plan must cover a broad group of employees; have a definite, fixed, and uniform benefit structure; and have been in existence on December 31, 1987. A plan loses grandfathered status upon the first material plan modification after December 31, 1987. Modifications to nonelective plans are considered material only if they change the benefit formula or expand the class of participants. This grandfather rule generally applies only to union employees participating in a nonqualified, nonelective plan under a collective bargaining agreement. The rule also is available to nonunion employees if, as of December 31, 1987, participation was extended to a broad group of nonunion employees on the same terms as the union employees and union employees account for at least 25 percent of total participation.[60]

TAXATION OF NONELECTIVE DEFERRED COMPENSATION SUBJECT TO SECTION 457

The above discussion on deferred compensation plans not subject to Section 457 indicates that when specified requirements are met, nonelective deferred compensation is exempt from Section 457 rules and current taxation. However, many employees of state and local government and nongovernment tax-exempt employers are taxed on nonelective deferred compensation before they are entitled to receive it. For example:

> A nonprofit organization hires an employee under a five-year employment agreement to pay $50,000 annually. Assuming the employee works the entire five-year period, an additional $10,000 will be paid annually in years six through ten. Under current Section 457 rules (described previously), the employee would be taxed in year six on the entire present value of all five $10,000 payments. If we assume the discounted present value of

---

[60]IRS Notice 88-98, 1988-2 CB 421.

the $10,000 payments equals approximately $41,000[61] and the entire amount is subject to 28 percent tax, $11,480 would be paid in tax in year six even though only $10,000 is actually received.

This results in current taxation on amounts the taxpayer:

1. Has not yet received.
2. Has no current right to receive.
3. May not actually ever receive.

Since similar rules do not apply to private-sector employers, this practice places state and local government and nongovernmental tax-exempt employers at a distinct disadvantage in recruiting employees. Current Congressional efforts aim to correct this inequity by uniformly providing that nonelective deferred compensation is not taxable until actually received.[62]

CONCLUSION

Most 457 plans are maintained by state and local government employers for the purpose of salary reduction. However, in 457 plans maintained for salary-reduction purposes, the number of eligible persons that actually enroll generally is very low compared with similar private-sector plans such as 401(k) plans. This may be because of poor plan communication, absence of matching contributions (although 457 plans can be structured to provide an employer match), or a combination of both. The fact that participants are unsecured creditors of the employer and risk losing their deferrals if the employer goes bankrupt or becomes insolvent also may contribute to low participation.

457 plans used for purposes other than salary reduction are less common but are rapidly gaining in importance. Nongovernmental tax-exempt employers can use 457 plans to provide supplemental retirement benefits and salary continuation to certain high-paid executives. These plans function to:

---

[61]Calculated using a 7 percent discount rate, the present value of $10,000 received annually over five years equals $41,001.97.

[62]H.R. 3080, The Section 457 Reform and Simplification Act of 1989.

1. Provide benefits over IRC Section 415 limits on contributions to, or benefits from, qualified plans.
2. Offset the effect of the $200,000 maximum compensation cap of IRC Section 401(a)(17) when determining benefits or contributions to qualified plans.
3. Give valued employees additional death and disability benefits.
4. Impose "golden handcuffs" on valued employees or enhance early retirement benefits.
5. Increase benefits for executives recruited in mid-career who are unable to accrue maximum pension benefits in a qualified plan by normal retirement age.
6. Reward key employees for their contributions to the organization.

Employee eligibility in nongovernment tax-exempt employer plans is complicated, however, by conflicts between ERISA and IRC requirements and by lack of guidance in determining which employees constitute a select group of management or highly compensated employees.

Keen competition for talented employees forces employers to design plans attractive to an increasingly mobile work force. For state and local government and nongovernmental tax-exempt employers, 457 plans play an important part in meeting overall employee benefit plan objectives. A successful program, however, requires compliance with the complex requirements governing design, operation, and administration of Section 457 plans.

CHAPTER 41

RETIREMENT PREPARATION PROGRAMS

Edmund W. Fitzpatrick

After decades of slow growth, the number and scope of retirement preparation programs began to increase dramatically in the mid-1970s.[1] Some of the reasons for this phenomenon are:

The occurrence of double-digit inflation in the late 1970s and early 1980s, causing an increased concern over the effects of inflation on retirement purchasing power.

Federal legislation affecting private pensions and eliminating mandatory retirement.

Improved pension systems that enable more people to retire early.

Increasing complexity of the law taxing and otherwise affecting benefit plan distributions.

Recognition that the population and work force are aging and the political, economic, and employment implications of this.

Each of these factors represents a long-term trend that is likely to continue. Because this suggests continued growth of retirement preparation programs, a brief review of the trends seems warranted.

[1]Retirement preparation goes by many names, such as retirement education, retirement counseling, preretirement planning, and life planning.

FACTORS AFFECTING GROWTH OF RETIREMENT PREPARATION PROGRAMS

An Aging Population

In 1980, the population aged 55 and over was about 47 million and represented about 17 percent of the population (see Table 41–1). By the year 2025, this group is expected to number 98 million and, barring a new baby boom, constitute about 32 percent of the population. As these figures illustrate, the number of people who will be entering retirement will increase dramatically over the next 35 years.

The age-65-and-over population segment is also growing and has been for some time. While about one in eight persons is 65 or over today, in the year 2030 about one in five is expected to be 65 or over (see Table 41–2). Again, this ratio could change if the United States experiences another baby boom.

This great age shift of the general population has enormous implications for U.S. public policy, the economy, and business.

Increased Life Expectancy

Contributing to the aging of the population are significant increases in life expectancy. In fact, the fastest growing segment of population is the oldest one—the age-80-and-over segment. Longer life expectancies, of course, mean spending more years in retirement. If a man aged 62 and

TABLE 41–1
Projection of Population Aged 55 and Over

Year	*Persons Aged 55 and Over*
1980	47 millions
1990	53 millions
2000	58 millions
2010	73 millions
2020	92 millions
2025	98 millions

Source: U.S. Bureau of the Census

TABLE 41-2
Growth in the "Over 65" Population

Year	Persons Aged 65 and Over
1900	1 in 25
Today	1 in 8
2030	1 in 5

Source: U.S. Bureau of the Census

his wife aged 59 retire now, he will likely live another 17 years, until about age 78, and she will live another 23 years, until about age 82.

In reality, chances are that both will live even longer, since traditionally we have underestimated average life expectancies, and we continuously revise them upward. For example, in 1960 life expectancy at age 65 was 12.9 years for men and 15.9 years for women. By the year 2000, life expectancy at age 65 is expected to increase to 15.8 years for men and 20.7 years for women.

Early Retirement

The trend toward early retirement began decades ago and is continuing. In 1981, almost three of four employees (70 percent) were retiring early—that is, before age 65—and the great majority of this group retired at age 62 or before. Since this generally coincides with benefit eligibility under private and public pension systems (most notably, Social Security), it reinforces the notion that the great majority of employees will retire as soon as they think they can afford to. Indeed, studies show that most people retire when they believe they have the means in personal assets and public and private benefits to support themselves without working.[2]

The growth of benefit plans that continue coverage into the retirement years—such as health insurance and life insurance continuation plans—and the growth of 401(k) plans may permit more employees to

---

[2]*Issue Brief,* Employee Benefit Research Institute, June 1990, No. 103, p. 2.

retire early rather than stay on for economic reasons. Little information is available on the effect employer-provided postretirement health or life insurance coverage has on early-retirement decisions. Retirees are not eligible for Medicare benefits until age 65 unless they are disabled. A company considering changing the health coverage it offers its retirees needs to consider how the change might affect the early-retirement decisions of its employees.

Economic Trends

The inflation rate rises and falls with economic cycles, but the trend toward early retirement has continued virtually unaffected. Employees become more concerned with retirement finances when the inflation rate rises, as when it reached double-digit levels in the late 1970s and early '80s. Nevertheless, employees still retire early, in good times or bad, even though they may have doubts and fears about how well they are prepared financially.

Federal Legislation

The trend in private pension plans has been toward encouraging early retirement. This has caused concern at the federal level over the projected costs of financing Social Security benefits when people retire earlier and live longer. As a consequence, federal legislation over the past decade has sought to reduce the role of Social Security benefits as an incentive for early retirement. The 1983 amendments to the Social Security program gradually raise the normal retirement age (when full benefits are paid) from 65 to 67, beginning in 2003, reaching 67 in 2022. Moreover, further reductions are made in the level of benefits to those who retire earlier. The enactment of Social Security and Medicare legislation has now become almost an annual affair aimed at shoring up program financing and controlling rising costs.

Two reasons that Social Security is a favorite topic in retirement preparation programs are (1) the importance of Social Security income in retirement and (2) the fears many people have that something will prevent them from receiving the benefits they expect. One study found that among people aged 50 to 64 only one in four (25 percent) expresses a great deal of confidence in the system; another 43 percent have some confidence, and approximately one in four (26 percent) is not very confident.[3]

ONE RATIONALE FOR RETIREMENT PREPARATION PROGRAMS

The most important benefit of a retirement preparation program is that it can eliminate unfounded fears and help employees plan in a realistic, more effective way. Many if not most employees do not know how to make a fact-based estimate of the amount of income or assets they will need to finance their retirement. Many have never been exposed to inflation-adjusted projections, which often generate seemingly astronomical numbers, or to fundamental investment concepts such as compounding and the time value of money. They recognize, though, that the penalty for financial miscalculation can be severe. Retirement preparation programs can address these matters in a way that is understandable and useful for employee planning.

Retirement preparation programs can motivate employees to make their own decisions in their own interest and to act upon them. For example, they can show employees how to use savings and investment vehicles, including 401(k) plans, to accumulate assets for retirement. They can demonstrate the importance of continuing an investment management program during the retirement years to counter inflation and maintain retirement purchasing power. They can describe the most common mistakes retirees make and show how to avoid making them.

Not only do most employees want retirement information, they think their employers have a responsibility to provide it to them. A survey of persons 50 to 64 years of age conducted in late 1984 found that seven in ten believe that employers have some responsibility to counsel their employees on how to prepare for retirement. In the survey, men who were already retired felt the strongest about this, suggesting that their former employers may not have provided them with enough information.[4]

---

[3] *The Prime Life Generation,* A Report Describing the Characteristics and Attitudes of Americans 50 to 64 Years of Age. American Council of Life Insurance and Health Insurance Association of America, 1985, p. 22.

[4] Ibid., p. 29.

Most employees do not achieve the income they would like to have in retirement. A national survey found that 81 percent of employees and 84 percent of retirees feel their standard of living during retirement should be about the same as before retirement.[5] Yet, about three in four retirees in the 50-to-64 age group—presumably new retirees—are receiving less income after retirement (see Table 41–3).[6]

The reality is that the average income of persons over age 65 has been increasing relative to the rest of the population. However, the average income of this group is only about two thirds of the national average.[7] The growing account balances in 401(k) and other plans suggest that future retirees will cause the relative income of this 65-and-over group to continue to improve.

INDEPENDENT PLANNING BY EMPLOYEES

Employed persons in the 50-to-64 age group were asked if they planned to attend a retirement course as preparation for retirement. Only one in four said he or she planned to. About 44 percent said they had already consulted or planned to consult with a professional about retirement. In general, higher-income persons were much more likely to say they had consulted or planned to consult a professional than persons with lower incomes.[8]

A survey of employees over age 40 from seven large companies found the following:[9]

> Six in ten had made no plans for retirement and only one in ten had made any definite plans.
>
> 70 percent said they wanted to attend a retirement counseling program; 15 percent said they did not want to; and 15 percent refused to answer.

---

[5]Louis Harris and Associates, 1979 Study of American Attitudes Toward Pensions and Retirement, Commissioned by Johnson & Higgins (New York: Louis Harris and Associates, 1979), p. iv.

[6]*The Prime Life Generation,* p. 24.

[7]Yung-Ping Chen, "Economic Status of the Aging," Chapter of *Handbook of Aging and the Social Sciences,* Robert H. Binstock and Ethel Shanas, editors (New York: Van Nostrand Reinhold Company, 1986).

[8]"Special Report: Pre-Retirement Planning Grows," *National Life Underwriter,* June 25, 1990.

[9]Edmund W. Fitzpatrick, "An Industry Consortium Approach to Retirement Planning—A New Program," *Aging and Work,* Vol. 1, No. 3 (Summer 1978), pp. 184–88.

TABLE 41–3
Preretirement Income Compared with Retirement Income

Level of Income	*Total*
Now getting more	10%
About the same	15%
Somewhat less	25%
A lot less	45%
Don't know	5%

Source: *The Prime Life Generation,* American Council of Life Insurance and Health Insurance Association of America, 1985, p. 24.

Over two thirds expect to run into money problems in retirement, while only one in four expects to have a health problem.

Retirement preparation programs, they said, should be conducted in the early evening (56 percent), on weekends (13 percent), or in late evening (7 percent). Only one in four (24 percent) said they should be conducted during the day, which coincided with work hours.

EXTENT OF PROGRAM USAGE

A nationwide survey by Buck Consultants in July 1989 found that 38 percent of the 386 employers responding indicated that they offer preretirement planning programs on an ongoing basis. Eighteen percent of those not offering an ongoing program indicated that they plan to start one in the next two years. Another 32 percent said they expect to offer a program eventually.[10]

An organization may not have an in-house retirement preparation program but, instead, may make arrangements to send its employees to a program offered by an outside source, such as a community college. The extent to which small, medium, and large organizations are using such outside programs is not known. However, the proliferation of outside sources suggests that many companies and individuals are using them. For many companies, it may be the most cost-effective way of offering general retirement planning information.

---

[10] "Special Report: Pre-Retirement Planning Grows," *National Life Underwriter,* June 25, 1990, p. 9.

Generally, two factors must be present before a company is likely to have its own retirement preparation program: (1) an "adequate" pension plan, and (2) enough employees retiring each year to justify a program. Consequently, in-house retirement preparation programs tend to be concentrated among large companies with good retirement benefits.

CHARACTERISTICS OF PROGRAMS

Corporate Goals

Retirement preparation programs are more prevalent in organizations with early retirement incentives. In some cases, the programs are offered in conjunction with outplacement programs for terminated employees.[11]

An earlier study found that the main corporate goals of retirement preparation programs, in the view of personnel directors, are to improve employee relations, morale, and productivity (see Table 41–4).

Reflecting the strength of their commitment, a number of large corporations have created a position of "manager of retirement and retiree relations." This person, who may report to a vice president, has corporate-wide responsibility for retirement preparation programs and for retiree communications programs and the extent to which such programs are contributing to realizing corporate goals. His or her functions may include acquainting divisions with new developments and helping them to design, implement, and improve their retirement preparation and retiree communications programs.

Target Groups for Programs

Many companies face a backlog of employees when they begin to offer a retirement preparation program. Although an employer may invite all employees over age 50 or 55 to attend, the great majority of those accepted may be employees who have announced the date of their retirement or who are close to or past the average age of retirement in the company. When the backlog is reduced, all employees who have

[11]"Retirement Planning," *Employee Benefit Plan Review,* June 1990, p. 34.

TABLE 41–4
Corporate Goals for Retirement Preparation Programs, as Cited by Personnel Directors

	Frequency Selected by Personnel Directors (percent)
Improve relations with employees	91*
Reinforce morale/productivity	83
Fulfill social responsibilities	68
Enhance corporate image	53
Recruit and retain dependable employees	39
Induce early retirement among nonproductive employees	31
Protect funds in pension plans	29
Keep pace with competitors	22
Improve relations with unions	12
Comply with ERISA	8

*Many gave more than one goal.

Source: *Retirement Preparation: Growing Corporate Involvement* (New York: Research & Forecasts, 1980), p. 16.

reached the eligibility age will be given a more equal opportunity to attend.

Employees generally are encouraged to have their spouses attend the program with them. The extent of spouse participation will vary, depending on the efforts made by the employer to encourage their attendance, the convenience of the time and location of the program, and the nature of the program.

In one study, about 80 percent of the companies sponsoring retirement preparation programs reported they set a minimum age for attendance. About two in five of those companies set a minimum age between 50 and 54, and another two in five set the minimum between 55 and 59.[12]

A study by the International Foundation of Employee Benefit Plans found that many employers are planning to reduce the minimum age at which employees can attend a retirement preparation program. Age 44 is the anticipated average minimum age for participation.[13]

---

[12] "Special Report: Pre-Retirement Planning Grows," p. 48.

[13] "Retirement Planning," *Employee Benefit Plan Review,* June 1990, p. 34.

Content Coverage

Retirement preparation programs may be classified as narrow, medium, or comprehensive in terms of topic coverage. A *narrow* program may focus on only the employer's benefits (pension plans, savings and investment plans, health and life insurance coverage, postretirement benefits), Social Security, and the legal aspects of retirement.

A *medium* program in terms of comprehensiveness might have all the above topics plus two or three additional ones, such as projecting retirement income and expenses, income taxes, estate planning, and Medigap insurance.

A *comprehensive* program generally aims at all aspects of retirement living, including finances, health, living arrangements, psychological adjustments, new careers, use of leisure time, and community services.

The three topics that companies say employees find of greatest interest are:[14]

1. Understanding employer-provided benefits in retirement.
2. Social Security.
3. The financial planning process.

A list of the 14 most frequently included topics in retirement preparation programs, based on a 1989 nationwide survey, is shown in Table 41–5. In general, the higher a topic is on the list, the more important it is judged to be by the companies and, indirectly, by the employees attending the retirement preparation programs.

A recent survey found that coping with aging parents is an emerging concern for older employees and retirees. Forty percent of the survey respondents said eldercare issues are a component of their organization's retirement preparation program—with the great majority of them having added this topic within the past two years.[15]

Use of Computer-Generated Personal Financial Reports

A major concern of employees considering retirement is the long-term adequacy of their retirement income, since they realize they could live 20

---

[14] "Special Report: Pre-Retirement Planning Grows," p. 48.

[15] "Retirement Planning," *Employee Benefit Plan Review*, June 1990, p. 34.

TABLE 41–5
Subjects Covered in Preretirement Planning Programs Offered By 386 U.S. Employers, 1989

Subject	*Percentage of Programs*
Social Security	97
Benefits in Retirement	95
Savings and Investments	90
Financial Planning Process	85
Taxation of Benefits	84
Life Adjustments in Retirement	81
Health	75
Estate Planning	75
Income Taxes	65
Use of Time	61
Work In Retirement	60
IRAs	60
Where to Live	60
Using Professional Advisers	53

Source: Buck Consultants, 1989.

or 30 years after they retire. Some firms, as part of a retirement preparation program, are providing employees access to a variety of computer-generated personal financial reports. One type of report often provided is a projection of employee benefits. Another is a projection of Social Security benefits. Still another is a computer-generated personal financial report that is prepared by an outside source using personal data supplied by the employee combined with benefits information from the employer.

Financial planning reports can range from an analysis of pension plan distribution alternatives to a comprehensive personal financial plan that projects many years into the future and includes recommendations regarding investments, insurance coverages, taxes, wills and estate planning, and other important areas.

Often, these reports make a point of providing much explanatory material along with the financial data. For example, a report may provide a general introduction to the principles of personal finance as part of a discussion of the person's financial situation and recommendations for improving it. Since there is a limit to how much can be communicated effectively in a printed report, a seminar session or workshop session usually accompanies the reports so that employees and their spouses will have an opportunity to ask questions and clear up misunderstandings.

Personal financial reports can be very helpful to employees and can contribute much to their peace of mind as they consider retirement. Employers must be cautious about the sources of such reports that they recommend to their employees. If a source is included on the list, the employees will assume the employer endorses that source and possibly any recommendations the source makes. Therefore, before allowing a source to become associated with the company's retirement preparation program, the company needs to be satisfied with the source's objectivity, quality of work, suitability for its employees, and other aspects of the service to be provided.

There also is a trend for the computer-literate middle-aged or older employee to do his or her own computerized retirement financial planning on a home personal computer. Many well-designed personal financial-planning software programs can be purchased for $100 to $300. Much software also is available at even less cost in the form of "shareware." (Almost any neighborhood computer SIG—special interest group—can tell a person where to get shareware.) Large libraries often lend out financial planning software free or with only a small charge.

Who Conducts the Program

An organization's retirement preparation program may be conducted by (*a*) its own staff, (*b*) outside consultants, or (*c*) a combination of the two.

Large organizations generally prefer to use in-house staff to conduct their programs, though they may use outside experts in specific subject areas if they are not available within the organization. Retirement preparation material dealing with almost every retirement topic has been developed for seminar or workshop use without requiring subject-matter experts. A company may draw upon this material in planning and presenting its own program.

A not uncommon approach is for a firm to hire a consultant to serve as "program coordinator." This person generally has experience in organizing and presenting retirement preparation programs that rely on a speaker or resource person for each subject covered. The difficulty frequently encountered is finding knowledgeable, up-to-date experts who also are good communicators, will stick to the objectives of the program, and will be there as scheduled. Some firms hire a consultant to provide the materials and to conduct the complete program personally, except for the presentation and discussion of company benefits.

College- and university-based retirement preparation programs may draw upon experts from among their own faculties, which may include financial experts, gerontologists, psychologists, legal and medical specialists, and others. Additionally, they may draw upon experts from the local community, much as the "program coordinator" does.

Number and Length of Sessions

The time devoted to a retirement preparation topic in a group program may vary from one hour to three hours or more. Two hours per topic probably is typical, except for the financial topic(s), which may be allocated more time. In general, the total length of a program in terms of hours is related to the number of topics covered.

Scheduling Sessions

Several formats for scheduling program sessions are being used. Some of the most common are discussed below.

All-Day Programs

All-day programs of one, two, or three days may be used when employees are dispersed over a wide area and are brought in to attend a group program. Other companies simply prefer the full-day format, and it appears to be the most common.

In the case of dispersed employees, they and their spouses may be transported to a hotel or other meeting facility where the company conducts the program. A company without dispersed employees may run its program either entirely on work time or on part work time and part personal time, such as on a Friday and a Saturday, or from 3:00 in the afternoon until 9:00 in the evening on two weekdays.

One Session Per Week

One two-hour session per week for a number of weeks is also common. Typically, one topic is dealt with in each session, except that financial planning might be allotted two or even three sessions.

Half-Day Sessions

Having one two-hour session per week may be practical when there are large concentrations of employees at one site or within easy commuting distance of a central location. When employees are at a number of locations, some organizations use half-day sessions to reduce the number of meetings and associated travel time.

Size of Group

The size of the group attending generally will be determined by several factors, including the number of people who signed up to attend the program. The most common group size for retirement preparation group meetings, workshops, and seminars is 21 to 40. The second and third most common group sizes are 1 to 20 employees and their spouses and 41 to 55 employees and their spouses.[16]

Inviting Employees

It generally is agreed that all employees of a given age within a region, plant, or division should be invited at the same time. Even a hint of selective invitations will generate suspicion regarding management's purpose in offering the program. Attendance should not be made compulsory. If employees don't wish to attend, it is better to learn why and to correct the problem. Surveys show that up to 85 percent of employees over age 40 want to attend such programs.[17, 18]

In some cases, an initial reluctance exists among employees to attend, since they harbor concern that attendance could somehow jeopardize promotions and job assignments. One way to combat these concerns is by giving much publicity to the program and its pilot presentations. Notices on bulletin boards, articles in company publications, and supportive statements by top management are helpful.

Some organizations enlist the aid of employees who enjoy much trust among their peers. These employees are encouraged to attend the pilot program and to ask associates to join them. Also, publicizing the fact that specific supervisory and management personnel will attend the programs can help to dispel fears employees have about attending.

---

[16]"Special Report: Pre-Retirement Planning Grows," p. 48.

[17]"Retirement Planning," p. 34.

[18]Fitzpatrick, "An Industry Consortium's Approach to Retirement Planning," p. 187.

Employees are invited by notices on bulletin boards, articles in company publications, and by personal letters that go to the home. Letters to the home should be addressed to Mr. and Mrs. if the employee is married. In any case, the employee often is encouraged to bring any other person with whom he or she plans to retire. This is particularly important for single persons, who may retire (and share expenses) with a sister, brother, other relative, or friend. The chances are the single person will not bring another person, but much goodwill is generated by the sincere offer from the company. For the targeted employees (e.g., age 50 or 55 and over), a series of several invitational letters should be considered to ensure that a large percentage of these employees attend.

ESTABLISHING A PROGRAM

Basic Planning Questions

In establishing a retirement preparation program, a number of questions need to be answered:

1. What are the objectives of the program, and how will its success be measured?
2. Is top management committed to the program?
3. How much money can be devoted to the program? Over what period of time?
4. How many employees can be expected to attend the program? Who are they and where are they located? How many spouses probably will attend?
5. Are the company's retirement benefits adequate? Above average?
6. Are competitors offering retirement preparation programs? If so, what are the programs like?
7. What is the state of employee relations? Is there a problem that needs resolution before offering the program?
8. How concentrated or dispersed are the employees, and how will the program be made available to them?
9. Is the public relations value of the program important locally or nationally?

10. Is there a need to promote better understanding of company benefits, especially retirement benefits, among employees?

Program Design Considerations

The design of a retirement preparation program determines its effectiveness. There are four considerations.

1. In view of company characteristics, objectives, and the distribution of employees, what type of program or programs are feasible and will achieve the objectives? What trade-offs are necessary? What will be the measures of success?

2. Who should conduct the program? Central or division staffs? Consultants? Should there be a "traveling team" that conducts the program? Should employees be sent to programs conducted by community colleges or other organizations? Are subject-matter experts available (assuming they are needed) at proposed program locations?

3. Should the company purchase a commercially available package or develop its own? If purchased, should it be customized and by how much? (The development of professional-quality retirement counseling materials involves a commitment of time, money, and specialized expertise that most companies do not have, or which often is more profitably focused on the company's main business. Consequently, the tendency is for companies to purchase packaged programs and then to customize them.)

4. What should be the nature of program follow-up activities? Should there be periodic updates through written communications and through refresher meetings? Should there be encouragement for the formation of employee planning or investment clubs? What about postretirement communications? Should there be a formal postretirement program?

Selecting Program Materials

Materials employed in a retirement counseling program should be designed to maximize the probability of success. Here are some aspects to consider:

1. Are the materials compatible with company philosophy and with the basic values of the employees who will attend the program?

2. Do the materials support the specific objectives for the program in each area? The personal finances area? Health area? Other areas?

3. Is the content presented efficiently and at the appropriate level, given the target employees? Or is it shallow and vague with too much jargon, or too technical?

4. What is the visual impact of the materials? Impressive in appearance to imply importance? Easy to read and use? Is the print large enough?

5. With regard to audiovisual materials, are the visuals (photographs and artwork) pleasant, and (this is important) do the people look somewhat younger than the target employees? Is the narrator's style, tone, and pronunciation suitable for the employees? How easily can the audiovisual materials be used? What equipment is required? Who will set up and operate it?

6. Are skill-building exercises provided for employees? Checklists for planning? Games, simulations, small-group exercises, individual exercises, other aids? Are they merely entertaining or do they have a clearly identifiable objective?

7. How is the seminar or workshop designed? What will participants actually *do* in it—be active or passive? Is there a balance among lectures, audiovisual materials, small-group activities, group discussion, and individual work? What qualifications or training are required of the seminar/workshop leaders?

Conducting the Pilot Program

An important objective of a pilot program is to give other people in the organization an opportunity to make recommendations and take part in making the final decision on the program. A pilot program generally will become the final program because the organization already has tooled up to present it and has gained experience in doing so. If a manager skips the pilot and makes the final decision independently, those who did not have an opportunity to make recommendations could be a source of continuing criticism, which ultimately dooms the program.

Even though an organization may plan to have its own staff regularly conduct its retirement counseling programs, it may decide to involve an experienced outside consultant to co-conduct the pilot and thereby maximize the likelihood that the pilot will be successful.

The location of the pilot is important. It should be convenient to those expected to attend. Room size and shape must be appropriate for the number attending and for the desired seating arrangements; effective room temperature control is necessary; dimming the lights and covering the windows must be possible if audiovisual presentations are to be used; it should be free from outside noises; and it should have adequate electrical outlets. It may be important to have eating and sleeping accommodations close by.

Prior to conducting the pilot, there should be a detailed plan for its evaluation, complete with forms and procedures for how the data will be captured and analyzed and how the results will be used. Care must be exercised in how and when data are obtained from employees participating in the pilot program. Employees need to wear the "participant" hat and not the "evaluator" hat. In the program, they must concentrate on being a participant—and on their retirement concerns, needs, and objectives, or the evaluation will not have validity.

Postretirement Programs

Postretirement programs also are increasing in number and variety. Generally, they are aimed at updating former employees on benefits changes that may affect them, keeping them informed about company activities, and providing other information that may be of interest or help. A company may accomplish this through a special newsletter to retirees or by sending retirees the regular employee publication, which may include a section about and for retirees. Some companies hold annual affairs in large cities to which all retirees in the area are invited. Others send a person on tour from area to area to hold "update" meetings with groups of retirees. And some companies purchase subscriptions for all their retirees to a retirement-oriented newsletter or magazine.

BENEFITS OF RETIREMENT PREPARATION PROGRAMS

Benefits for the Employee

A well-designed retirement preparation program can have important benefits for employees and their spouses. Here are some of the major ones:[19]

---

[19]Edmund W. Fitzpatrick, "Retirement Counseling: A Necessity for the 1980's," *Textbook for Employee Benefit Plan Trustees, Administrators, and Advisors,* Proceedings of the 1979 Annual

1. Recognition that they have the responsibility for ensuring their own financial security and happiness in retirement (i.e., the company and union may help, but the ultimate responsibility is the employee's).
2. Better realization of the degree of control and options they have regarding future finances, health, personal relationships, and the like.
3. Knowing when retirement is financially possible for them—or what they must do to make it so.
4. An opportunity to articulate and discuss fears they and others may harbor about retirement.
5. An opportunity to specifically define one or more life-styles they would find enjoyable and affordable, so they can look forward to concrete and positive alternatives.
6. Identification of problems that could arise during their own retirement, which they have an opportunity to solve before retirement.

Benefits for the Employer

The employer that provides an effective retirement preparation program for employees also benefits. In fact, the employer may find the returns are considerably greater than the investment. Here are the major benefits the employer may enjoy:[20]

1. General performance levels of employees may improve; when employees believe their employer cares about them, they in return care more about the quality of their work.
2. The productivity of specific employees may improve, since they will be able to make an informed retirement decision, rather than be afflicted by indecision and perhaps hang on beyond the time when they wish to retire.
3. Employees gain a better appreciation of the value of the employee benefits provided.

Educational Conference, Vol. 21 (Brookfield, Wis.: International Foundation of Employee Benefit Plans, 1980), pp. 295–301.

[20]Ibid.

4. Employers can fulfill a social responsibility to loyal employees who helped the company prosper over the years.
5. It can help the employer maintain a leadership role in the employee benefits area.
6. It can result in positive feedback from retirees to present employees.
7. It can help to build and maintain a positive image in the community.

Postretirement Benefits

While the *pre*retirement benefits of retirement preparation programs seem clear, the benefits that result in the *post*retirement years are difficult to assess. It is probably true that narrow, one-session programs have less long-term effect than comprehensive, multi-session programs with periodic refreshers and updates. Longitudinal studies are needed that clearly demonstrate whether or not this is true and that identify cause-and-effect relationships. Study results are needed to identify the improvements that can maximize the return on the funds companies invest in such programs.

PROGRAM EVALUATION

In general, retirement preparation programs are not being subjected to formal evaluations based on measurable objectives. Most rely upon asking participants if they like the speakers, the content, the method of conducting, and so on. These findings are important—but they concern the process not the results. Employees typically are so grateful for retirement preparation programs that almost any program, regardless of quality, will be given a high rating by such an evaluation approach.

One hindrance to the use of more scientific evaluation procedures is the newness of the programs and the fact they are still evolving. It is not practical to invest in longitudinal studies, which may involve years, before an organization is satisfied that it has arrived at the "best" feasible program and has standardized the use of it.

Many existing longitudinal studies are seriously flawed, so caution must be exercised in considering their conclusions.[21] However, as more

---

[21]Francis D. Glamser, "The Impact of Preretirement Programs on the Retirement Experience," *Journal of Gerontology* 36, no. 2 (March 1981), pp. 244–50.

organizations get their programs in place and "fine-tune" them, there are likely to be a growing number of useful longitudinal studies based on experimental design methodology.

Another appropriate evaluation methodology is based on defining measurable human performance objectives.[22] This assumes that the basic rationale for a retirement preparation program is to cause people to plan their retirement and thereby prevent certain problems or unfulfilled expectations when they retire. If human-performance objectives are prepared for each topic or module in the program, effectiveness can be determined by measuring the degree to which participants achieve those objectives at the conclusion of the program. A human-performance objective, as used in this approach, needs to be both measurable and observable—as an example: "the participant will be able to identify his or her tax bracket and compute after-tax earnings from a given investment." "Pre–post" assessments may be used to determine not only achievement but also the "learning gain" produced by the program.

The measurable objectives evaluation approach makes possible evaluation/revision cycles capable of producing successively more powerful versions of a module or complete program. A program development activity employing this evaluation approach can produce a statistically validated program—one that can be expected to produce similar results each time it is used.

Figure 41–1 illustrates the use of this approach for evaluating a retirement financial planning workshop in which the human performance objectives took the form of 14 measurable and observable financial planning tasks. The effectiveness of the workshop was determined by (*a*) the percent of the participants who actually performed each of the tasks by the end of the workshop, and (*b*) the *gain* in the percent performing each task, based on a comparison of preworkshop achievement with post-workshop achievement.

A retirement preparation program is a vehicle for communicating information and influencing human behavior. Whether its objectives are achieved depends on the skill with which the vehicle is used. A person lacking musical talent and training may blow sour notes on a trumpet, but it is the fault of the player, not the horn. As with retirement preparation

---

[22]Edmund W. Fitzpatrick, "Evaluating a New Retirement Planning Program—Results with Hourly Workers," *Aging and Work,* Spring 1979, (Washington, D.C.: National Council on the Aging), pp. 87–94.

FIGURE 41–1

Short-Range Effect of Personal Financial Planning Module: Change in Percentage of White-Collar Clerical Employees Taking Specified Financial Planning Actions as a Result of Workshop

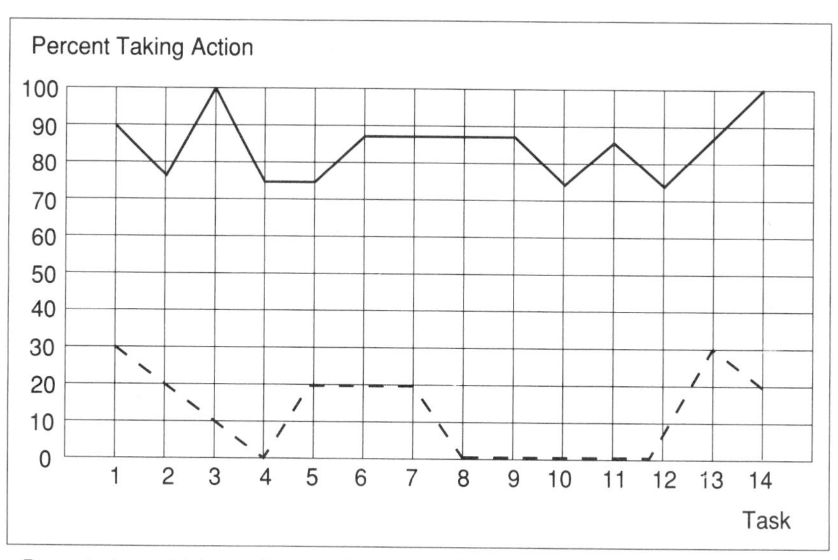

···Percent who had taken action prior to workshop.

—Percent who had taken action by end of workshop.

Financial Planning Tasks

1. Gathered and listed your important financial papers.
2. Discussed retirement finances in detail with your spouse or someone else.
3. Developed an estimate of your retirement expenses.
4. Developed a realistic, fact-based estimate of your future retirement income.
5. Determined what survivor's benefits you or your spouse (or other person) would get if either one of you died.
6. Figured the approximate amount of the nest egg you will have or will need at the time of your retirement.
7. Identified your own major financial assets and projected how they will grow in value between now and retirement.
8. Determined how much purchasing power your pension will lose in your retirement if inflation continues.
9. Figured how much money you would need in a fund to protect your pension from the effects of inflation.
10. Drawn your own Retirement Income Profile.
11. Obtained useful information for you to get more out of your savings and investments.
12. Used basic measures (e.g., growth versus income, risk versus return) in evaluating savings and investment alternatives.
13. Selected one or more investments four further investigation.
14. Made a plan to improve your own approach to saving and investing.

Source: Edmund W. Fitzpatrick, *Administrator's Guide: A Component of the Industry Consortium Retirement Planning Program* (Washington, D.C.: NCOA, 1980). p. 12.

programs, the quality of the output depends upon the quality of the input. The talent and monetary and physical resources being devoted to these programs are improving, compared with past years, and we can expect improved results.

CONCLUSION

Trends in our society suggest that retirement preparation programs will continue to grow. Recent and expected future federal legislation affecting Social Security and private plans may make retirement planning decisions increasingly more complex for employees who may wish to retire early. Retirement preparation programs can communicate valuable information to employees and identify fruitful savings and investment alternatives.

A realization exists that a satisfying retirement depends on more than financial security. "Free time" can be a blessing or a curse, depending on what is done with it. Retirement preparation programs, by helping individuals and couples explore aspects of life that may have been long ignored, can open new doors to life enrichment and happiness in the later years. Perhaps the greatest ultimate impact of these programs will be in these more personal areas. And this is important to a society with a large older-person population.

INDEX

Boldface numbers refer to pages in Volume I.

E

F

G

O

P

S

U

V

W

Also Available from Business One Irwin:

THE HANDBOOK OF 401k PLAN MANAGEMENT

Edited by Towers, Perrin, Forster, and Crosby

The first comprehensive guide to the fundamental issues and unique challenges of managing 401k plans. You'll discover how to maximize yield on maturing and growing assets, comply with new and changing regulations, as well as design and administer an efficient, flexible plan. (450 pages)

ISBN: 1-55623-620-4

GUARANTEED INVESTMENT CONTRACTS

Risk Analysis and Portfolio Strategies, Second Edition

Edited by Kenneth L. Walker

The only single, comprehensive guide that shows you how to administer and manage a portfolio of GICs. Includes detailed coverage of the evolution of the insurance industry in the pension marketplace so you can evaluate investment alternatives. (250 pages)

ISBN: 1-55623-573-9

REBUILDING AMERICA'S WORKFORCE

Business Strategies to Close the Competitive Gap

William H. Kolberg and Foster C. Smith

Discover how to overcome today's reported shortage of skilled employees by implementing new training techniques. Includes interviews and case studies that show you how to make maximum employee performance a reality. (250 pages)

ISBN: 1-55623-622-0

WORKFORCE AMERICA!

Managing Employee Diversity as a Vital Resource

Marilyn Loden and Judy B. Rosener, Ph.D.

Tap the talents of diverse employees within your organization for more productive working relationships! Shows you how to recognize and rectify problems that can inhibit the full participation of employees who are disabled or different from the predominately white male workforce. (250 pages)

ISBN: 1-55623-386-8